The
Nuclear Arms Race
Debated

The
Nuclear Arms Race
Debated

Herbert M. Levine

David Carlton

McGraw-Hill Book Company

New York   St. Louis   San Francisco   Auckland   Bogotá   Hamburg
Johannesburg   London   Madrid   Mexico   Montreal   New Delhi
Panama   Paris   São Paulo   Singapore   Sydney   Tokyo   Toronto

Library of Congress Cataloging-in-Publication Data

Levine, Herbert M.
    The nuclear arms race debated.

    Bibliography: p.
    1. Nuclear weapons—Addresses, essays, lectures.
2. Nuclear warfare—Addresses, essays, lectures.
3. Nuclear arms control—Addresses, essays, lectures.
4. Deterrence (Strategy)—Addresses, essays, lectures.
5. United States—Military policy—Addresses, essays,
lectures. 6. Arms race—History—20th century—Addresses,
essays, lectures. I. Carlton, David, date
II. Title.
U264.L48   1986   355'.0217   85-19750
ISBN 0-07-009862-X

This book was set in Times Roman by J. M. Post Graphics, Corp.
The editors were David V. Serbun and James D. Anker;
the production supervisor was Marietta Breitwieser;
the cover was designed by Rafael Hernandez.
Project supervision was done by The Total Book.
R. R. Donnelley & Sons Company was printer and binder.

THE NUCLEAR ARMS RACE DEBATED

1 2 3 4 5 6 7 8 9 0 DOCDOC 8 9 8 7 6 5

ISBN 0-07-009862-X

Contents

Editors

HERBERT M. LEVINE is a political scientist who taught at the University of Southwestern Louisiana for twenty years. He has written and edited several textbooks in political science, including most recently, *World Politics Debated: A Reader in Contemporary Issues* and *Challenge of Controversy: American Political Issues in Our Times*. He is currently a political writer.

DAVID CARLTON is Senior Lecturer in International History at the Open University in Great Britain on leave from a similar appointment at the Polytechnic of North London. He is the author of *Anthony Eden: A Biography* (1981) and co-editor of eight volumes produced under the auspices of the Rome-based International School on Disarmament and Research on Conflicts.

List of Contributors

ROBERT R. BARKER is Assistant Associate Director for Arms Control at the Lawrence Livermore National Laboratory.

LOUIS RENÉ BERES is Professor of Political Science at Purdue University. He is a specialist in foreign affairs and international law with particular reference to strategic and world-order studies. He is the author of *Mimicking Sisyphus: America's Countervailing Nuclear Strategy* and *Apocalypse: Nuclear Catastrophe in World Politics*.

HEDLEY BULL was Montague Burton Professor of International Relations, University of Oxford, and Fellow of Balliol College, Oxford. He served as Director, Arms Control and Disarmament Research Unit, London, from 1965 to 1967. He was the author of *The Control of the Arms Race* and *The Anarchical Society*. He died in 1985.

McGEORGE BUNDY was Special Assistant to the President for National Security Affairs from 1961 to 1966 and President of the Ford Foundation from 1966 to mid-1979. He is currently Professor of History at New York University.

ALBERT CARNESALE is Professor of Public Policy and Academic Dean of Harvard's John F. Kennedy School of Government. Dr. Carnesale served on the U.S. delegation to the Strategic Arms Limitation Talks, 1970–1972, and as the head of the U.S. delegation to the International Nuclear Fuel Cycle Evaluation, 1978–1980.

HUGH C. DeWITT, a theorist in the H division of Lawrence Livermore National Laboratory's Physics Department, works on the statistical mechanics of strongly coupled plasmas.

PAUL DOTY is the Director of the Center for Science and International Affairs and Mallinckrodt Professor of Biochemistry, Harvard University. Dr. Doty was involved in the Manhattan Project and was a member of the President's Science Advisory Committee in the Kennedy and Johnson administrations.

SIDNEY D. DRELL is Deputy Director of the Stanford Linear Accelerator Center. He is also a professor of theoretical physics and co-director of the Stanford Center for International Security and Arms Control. He has been an advisor to numerous government agencies, including the National Security Council, the U.S. Arms Control and Disarmament Agency, and the President's Science Advisory Committee. Drell received his Ph.D. from the University of Illinois in 1949.

LEWIS A. DUNN worked at the Hudson Institute and later accepted a position in the U.S. Department of State. He is the author of *Controlling the Bomb: Nuclear Proliferation in the 1980s,* a Twentieth Century Fund report.

ANNE H. EHRLICH is Senior Research Associate in Biology at Stanford University. She is author (with Paul R. Ehrlich) of *Extinction: The Causes and Consequences of the Disappearance of Species.* She was a consultant on the U.S. Government's *Global 2000* project and is on the Executive Committee of the Board of Directors of Friends of the Earth.

WYCHE FOWLER is a Democratic member of the House of Representatives from the State of Georgia. He is a member of the House Permanent Select Committee on Intelligence.

VICTOR GILINSKY served as a member of the U.S. Nuclear Regulatory Commission from 1975 to 1984. He received his Ph.D. in physics from the California Institute of Technology. He was a physicist at the Rand Corporation from 1961 to 1971.

LEON GOURE is the Director of the Center for Soviet Studies Science Applications, Inc. He was formerly Director of Soviet Studies and professor at the Center for Advanced International Studies at the University of Miami. He is the author of *Civil Defense in the Soviet Union, War Survival in Soviet Strategy,* and *Shelters in Soviet War Survival Strategy.*

COLIN S. GRAY is President of the National Institute for Public Policy in Fairfax, Virginia. He was formerly co-director of National Security Studies at the Hudson Institute and Assistant Director of the International Institute for Strategic Studies. He is the author of *The Soviet-American Arms Race; The Geopolitics of the Nuclear Era: Heartland, Rimlands and the Technological Revolution; Strategic Studies and Public Policy;* and *American Military Space Policy.*

TED GREENWOOD is Associate Professor of Political Science at the Massachusetts Institute of Technology. He is the author (with Harold A. Feiveson and Theodore B. Taylor) of *Nuclear Proliferation: Motivations, Capabilities, and Strategies for Control.*

General JAMES HARTINGER was Chief of the North American Aerospace Defense Command and the Air Force Space Command from 1980 to 1984. A graduate of the U.S. Military Academy, he has held numerous posts in the U.S. Air Force.

The HARVARD NUCLEAR STUDY GROUP consists of Albert Carnesale, Paul Doty, Stanley Hoffmann, Samuel P. Huntington, Joseph S. Nye, Jr., and Scott D. Sagan.

SIR JOHN HILL served as an Atomic Energy official with the U.K. Atomic Energy Authority from 1950 to 1981. He was chairman of the authority from 1967 to 1981.

STANLEY HOFFMANN is Professor of Government at Harvard University where he has taught since 1955. He is Douglas Dillon Professor of Civilization of France and Chairman of the Center for European Studies at Harvard. He is the author of many books, including *Gulliver's Troubles, Primacy or World Order,* and *Dead Ends.*

SAMUEL P. HUNTINGTON is Professor of Government at Harvard University. He was Thomson Professor of Government from 1967 to 1981, Clarence Dillon Professor of International Affairs from 1981 to 1982, and is currently Eaton Professor of the Science of Government. He served as coordinator of security planning for the National Security Council in 1977–1978 and is a consultant to numerous government agencies. He is the author of *The Common Defense, Political Order in Changing Societies,* and *American Politics: The Promise of Democracy.*

ROBERT JASTROW is a physicist who was the founder of the National Aeronautics and Space Agency's (NASA) Institute for Space Studies and served as its director until his retirement in 1981. He was head of the theoretical division of Goddard Space Flight Center of NASA from 1958 to 1961; and chairman of its lunar exploration committee from 1959 to 1960. He is now Professor of Earth Sciences at Dartmouth.

ROBERT JERVIS is a professor of political science at Columbia University. He has taught at Harvard, Yale, and UCLA. He is the author of *Perception and Misperception in International Politics, The Logic of Images in International Relations,* and *The Madness Beyond MAD.* He has been a Council of Foreign Relations fellow, 1970–1971, and a Guggenheim fellow, 1978–1979.

GEORGE F. KENNAN is Professor Emeritus of the Institute for Advanced Study, Princeton. He was minister-counselor in Moscow in 1945, Director of the Policy Planning Staff of the State Department in 1947, deputy counselor and chief long-range advisor to the Secretary of State, 1949–1950, U.S. Ambassador to the Soviet Union in 1952, and U.S. Ambassador to Yugoslavia from 1961 to 1963. He is the author of *American Diplomacy, 1900–1950; Russia, the Atom and the West;* and *The Nuclear Delusion,* among other works.

EDWARD KENNEDY has been United States Senator from Massachusetts since 1962. He served as Chairman of the Senate Judiciary Committee from 1979 to 1981 and has been ranking Democrat on the Labor and Human Resources Committee since 1981. He has been a major proponent of the nuclear freeze. He is the author (with Mark O. Hatfield) of *Freeze: How You Can Help Prevent Nuclear War.*

JENNIFER LEANING is a clinical instructor in medicine at Harvard Medical School. She received her M.D. from the University of Chicago Pritzger School of Medicine. Since 1979, she has been a member of the executive committee and board of directors of Physicians for Social Responsibility and has written and lectured extensively on issues of disaster management, civil defense, and survival after nuclear war. She is editor (with Langley Keyes) of *The Counterfeit Ark: Crisis Relocation for Nuclear War.*

ROBERT S. McNAMARA was Secretary of Defense from 1961 to 1967 and President of the World Bank from 1968 to mid-1981. He taught business administration at Harvard University between 1940 and 1943. He was an executive with the Ford Motor Corporation from 1946 to 1961, and served as its president in 1960–1961. He is the author of *The Essence of Security.*

HANS J. MORGENTHAU was a political scientist and lawyer who taught at the University of Chicago, City College of New York, Berkeley, Harvard, Northwestern, Columbia, and Yale. He held the Albert A. Michelson Distinguished Service Professorship at the University of Chicago and the Leonard Davis Distinguished Professorship at City College, City University of New York. He was the author of *Scientific Man vs. Power Politics, Politics Among Nations, In Defense of the National Interest,* and *A New Foreign Policy for the United States.*

JAMES E. MULLER teaches at the Harvard Medical School and is a founder of International Physicians for Prevention of Nuclear War.

NATIONAL CONFERENCE OF CATHOLIC BISHOPS is a canonical body through which the Catholic bishops of the United States exercise their pastoral office.

JOSEPH S. NYE, JR. is Professor of Government at Harvard University. He was Deputy to the Under Secretary of State for Security Assistance from 1977 to 1979 and is the author (with Robert Keohane) of *Power and Interdependence* and editor (with David Deese) of *Energy and Security.*

WOLFGANG K. H. PANOFSKY joined Stanford University as a physics professor in 1951 and has been Director of the Stanford Linear Accelerator Center since 1961. He received his Ph.D. from the California Institute of Technology in 1942. Panofsky has been a member of the President's Science Advisory Committee and the General Advisory Committee on Arms Control and Disarmament. He has also been an advisor to numerous government agencies, including the U.S. Arms Control and Disarmament Agency.

KEITH B. PAYNE is Executive Vice President and Director of National Security Studies at the National Institute for Public Policy in Fairfax, Virginia. He is a political scientist specializing in areas of U.S. and Soviet strategic and defense policy. He taught at the University of Southern California. He is the author of *Nuclear Deterrence in U.S.-Soviet Relations* and editor and contributor to *Laser Weapons in Space*.

DAVID H. PETRAEUS is a captain in the United States Army. He studied at the Woodrow Wilson School of Public and International Affairs at Princeton University. He received a B.S. from the U.S. Military Academy.

WILLIAM PROXMIRE has served as a U.S. Senator from Wisconsin since 1957. He is a Democratic member of the House-Senate Joint Economic Committee, the Ranking Minority Member of the Senate Banking Committee, and a member of the Senate Appropriations Committee. He is the author of *Report from Wasteland: America's Military-Industrial Complex*.

EDWARD L. ROWNY was a general when he retired from the U.S. Army in 1979. From 1973 to 1979, he was the representative of the Joint Chiefs of Staff to the United States strategic arms negotiation team in Switzerland. He was a vigorous opponent of the SALT II Treaty. President Reagan appointed him to the U.S. negotiating team in the Strategic Arms Reduction Talks (START).

SCOTT D. SAGAN is Staff Director of the Harvard Nuclear Study Group.

JONATHAN SCHELL is a staff writer for *New Yorker Magazine*. He is the author of *The Village of Ben Suc, The Military Half, The Time of Illusion,* and *The Fate of the Earth*.

JAMES R. SCHLESINGER is an economist who has held numerous government posts, including Chairman, Atomic Energy Commission, 1971–1973; Director, Central Intelligence Agency, February–July 1973; Secretary of Defense, 1973–1975; Assistant to the President, 1977; and Secretary of the Department of Energy, 1977–1979. He has been a senior advisor to the Center for Strategic and International Studies at Georgetown University since 1979.

HERBERT SCOVILLE, JR. served as Deputy Director for Science and Technology at the Central Intelligence Agency, 1955–1963; Assistant Director for Science and Technology at the Arms Control and Disarmament Agency, 1963–1969; and Director of the Arms Control Program at the Carnegie Endowment for International Peace, 1969–1971. He was also President of the Arms Control Association. He was the author of *MX: Prescription for Disaster*. He died in 1985.

BRENT SCOWCROFT is an air force officer. He has held numerous national security posts, including Special Assistant to the Director of the Joint Staff, Joint Chiefs of Staff, 1970–1971; military assistant to the President, 1972–1973; Deputy Assistant to the President for National Security Affairs, 1973–1975; Assistant to the President for National Security Affairs, 1975–1977; and member of the President's General Advisory Committee on Arms Control, 1977–1980.

GERARD SMITH was Chief of the United States Delegation to the Strategic Arms Limitation Talks from 1968 to 1972 and is the author of *Doubletalk: The Story of SALT I*. He also served as Special Assistant to the Secretary of State for Atomic Energy Affairs, 1954–1957; Director of the Policy Planning Staff of the Department of State, 1957–1961; a full-time consultant on the Multilateral Force, 1961–1964; and Ambassador at Large and Special Presidential Representative for nonproliferation matters, 1977–1980.

JAMES A. STEGENGA is a professor in the Department of Political Science at Purdue University. He is the author (with W. Andrew Axline) of *The Global Community*. His research interests include psychological explanations of warfare, and the psychological assumptions and ethical implications of nuclear deterrence doctrines.

K. SUBRAHMANYAM is the Director of the Institute for Defence Studies and Analyses in New Delhi. He is the author of *Indian Security Perspectives*.

PHILIP TOWLE is Deputy Director, Centre of International Studies, Faculty of History, University of Cambridge. He is the author of *Arms Control and East-West Relations* and the editor of *Estimating Foreign Military Power*.

PAUL C. WARNKE is an attorney who served as Director of the Arms Control and Disarmament Agency, 1977–1978; chief U.S. negotiator at SALT, 1977–1978; and special consultant to the Secretary of State, 1978–1981. He has been a partner in the law firm Clifford & Warnke since 1978.

CASPAR W. WEINBERGER has been the Secretary of Defense since 1981. He held numerous government posts, including Chairman, Federal Trade Commission, 1970; Deputy Director of the Office of Management and Budget (OMB), 1970–1972, and Director of OMB, 1972–1973; Counsellor to the President, 1973; and Secretary of the Department of Health, Education, and Welfare, 1973–1975. From 1975 to 1980, he held executive posts with the Bechtel Corporation.

GEORGE F. WILL is a syndicated columnist and a correspondent for ABC News. He was Washington editor of *National Review* in 1972 and is a political columnist for the *Washington Post* and *Newsweek*. He is the author of *The Pursuit of Happiness and Other Sobering Thoughts, The Pursuit of Virtue and Other Tory Notions,* and *Statecraft as Soulcraft: What Government Does.*

Preface

The advent of the nuclear age has brought with it an industry of commentators who make forecasts about the future of world politics and, above all, about the character of future wars. There is, however, nothing new about attempts to predict future war; but those who in the past have attempted to make accurate predictions faced formidable difficulties. Anyone doubting this assessment should obtain I. F. Clarke's fascinating book entitled *Voices Prophesying War, 1763–1984*.[1] In that work Clarke looks back over many decades and shows how rarely anyone—scholar or statesman—ever succeeded in forecasting the timing or circumstances of the outbreak of any particular major war let alone its course and outcome. And the advent of the nuclear age is unlikely to herald any increase in the accuracy of our ability to forecast the future.

Unfortunately, modesty and skepticism in this area have always been in short supply, and the invention of weapons of mass destruction has, if anything, increased the amount of dogmatism to be heard, whether among "hawks" or "doves." With the stakes so high, many commentators seem to be attracted more than ever towards either apocalyptic or ultra-complacent conclusions. Unconscious fascination with doomsday scenarios seems to lead many commentators to refuse to examine even the possibility that the next major armed conflict might actually terminate with fewer casualties than

[1] I. F. Clarke, *Voices Prophesying War, 1763–1984*. London: Oxford University Press, 1966.

in either World War I or World War II. Hence the undisguised relish with which some supporters of the Peace Movement have seized upon forecasts of a so-called "nuclear winter" which could bring climatic changes resulting in a serious risk of human extinction. On the other hand, some observers dogmatically insist, without evidence, that nuclear weapons will *never* be deliberately employed by any sane statesman because the consequences would be too horrendous to contemplate. Yet others opine that limited nuclear wars will indeed remain limited and even that a form of victory in such wars can be confidently expected. The editors of this volume, however, make only these assertions with absolute assurance: we are in no position to predict whether nuclear weapons will be used again in our lifetimes, nor can we say with any certainty what form each such use might take.

We urge our readers, therefore, to approach all the ensuing material with a great measure of skepticism. But even skepticism has its limits. Statesmen cannot avoid taking decisions on the basis of their best guesses as to the consequences for the future. In short, they can do no more than take calculated gambles, but they can also do no less. Our readers, as concerned citizens, should not be reluctant to offer *their* best guesses as to what the future holds and how best to attempt to shape it. All we ask is that they accept that definite foreknowledge is quite beyond attainment.

It is our hope that *The Nuclear Arms Race Debated* will contribute to an understanding about what the future may hold in an important area of public policy. This book seeks to provoke critical analysis of controversial issues about nuclear war; control of the production, deployment, and use of nuclear weapons; and the impact of nuclear weapons on international politics. It is directed primarily at undergraduate students interested in the central issues of the nuclear arms race.

The Nuclear Arms Race Debated is a text. Since the subject matter of the nuclear arms race draws upon so many disciplines—including political science, history, sociology, psychology, physics, military science, and biology—we have decided to direct our attention to some of the more contentious issues rather than to produce a comprehensive text. The headnotes to each chapter provide background information necessary to understand the articles. Our readers may feel, however, that they need more detailed information about the nature of nuclear weapons, the history of the nuclear arms race, the scale of nuclear arsenals, and some of the likely effects of the use of nuclear weapons. The list of Suggested Readings at the conclusion of this preface indicates sources that may be consulted for background information on particular aspects of the nuclear arms race.

In organizing this book we considered the areas of the nuclear arms race that have generated the most controversy. We have, consequently, structured the book into five chapters: (1) the nuclear arms race and world politics; (2) nuclear arms limitation: general principles; (3) superpower nuclear arms control: some prescriptions; (4) United States nuclear policy options; and (5) the wider proliferation of nuclear weapons.

Some of the debates within this structure deal with broad issues, such as the prospects of complete nuclear disarmament, the impact of horizontal proliferation, and the possibility of limited nuclear war. Other topics are about narrower subjects, such as the utility of the MX intercontinental ballistic missile and the need for a comprehensive test ban treaty. Many of the issues which have received wide public attention in the past decade are also considered here, including the value of the SALT (Strategic Arms Limitation Talks) II Treaty, the wisdom of a nuclear freeze, the declaration of a no-first-use policy in which the North Atlantic Treaty Organization agrees not to be the first to use nuclear weapons, the possibility of a nuclear winter, and the consequences of deploying weapons in space.

The selections in the debates are drawn from a variety of sources, including books, journals, magazines, and government documents. The authors of the debate articles include government policymakers, scholars, scientists, journalists, and political activists. They are, moreover, people of diverse philosophical backgrounds.

Since our purpose is to stimulate interest in the study of the nuclear arms race, we use a debate approach. We consider this method to be a useful way to study nuclear weapons and arms control. A question is asked, and an affirmative and a negative response is supplied. The chapter headnotes have already been mentioned. In addition, discussion questions appear at the end of each debate to encourage critical evaluation of each issue. A selected bibliography concludes each debate so that further study may be pursued.

The debate format may suggest that there is only a Yes and a No side to any issue. That is not our view. The answers to these questions must be hedged and qualified, particularly given the kind of subject matter treated in this book. Debating allows for major points of view to be expressed and understood, but the readers themselves must apply their own critical faculties to evaluate each issue.

Readers may use many methods to consider each debate. One useful way is to first understand the assumptions and views of each party. Are these assumptions and views similar or different in any way? Do the differences arise from differences about the facts? Do the authors agree about the consequences of certain actions? To what extent does the background of the authors influence their viewpoints? Do different ideological orientations determine the policy prescriptions of the authors? Finally, readers may ask whether there are ways of looking at the issues other than those represented in the selections.

We wish to express our thanks for the many useful comments and suggestions provided by editorial consultants who reviewed this text during the course of its development, especially to Martin Einhorn, University of Michigan; Lester R. Kurtz, University of Texas, Austin; Jerry Meisner, University of North Carolina; Mark Reader, Yale University; and Bruce M. Russett, Yale University. We also wish to thank our editors at McGraw-Hill, especially David Serbun and James D. Anker, the political science editors, and Annette Bodzin, the project supervisor.

Herbert M. Levine
David Carlton

Suggested Readings

Allison, Graham T., Albert Carnesale, and Joseph S. Nye, Jr. *Hawks, Doves, and Owls: An Agenda for Avoiding Nuclear War*. New York: Norton, 1985.

Calder, Nigel. *Nuclear Nightmares: An Investigation into Possible Wars*. New York: Viking Press, 1980.

Craig, Paul P., and John A. Jungerman. *Nuclear Arms Race: Technology and Society*. New York: McGraw-Hill, 1986.

Freedman, Lawrence. *The Evolution of Nuclear Strategy*. New York: St. Martin's Press, 1981.

Ground Zero. *Nuclear War: What's in It for You?* New York: Pocket Books, 1982.

Harvard Nuclear Study Group. *Living with Nuclear Weapons*. New York: Bantam, 1983.

Mandelbaum, Michael. *The Nuclear Future*. Ithaca, New York: Cornell University Press, 1983.

Nincic, Miroslav. *The Arms Race: The Political Economy of Military Growth*. New York: Praeger Special Studies, 1982.

Polmar, Norman. *Strategic Weapons: An Introduction*. 2nd ed. New York: Crane, Russak, 1982.

Russett, Bruce. *The Prisoners of Insecurity: Nuclear Deterrence, the Arms Race, and Arms Control*. San Francisco, California: W. H. Freeman, 1983.

Russett, Bruce M., and Bruce G. Blair (eds.). *Progress in Arms Control?: Readings from Scientific American*. San Francisco, California: W. H. Freeman, 1979.

Schroeer, Dietrich. *Science, Technology and the Nuclear Arms Race*. New York: Halsted Press, 1984.

Smoke, Richard. *National Security and the Nuclear Dilemma: An Introduction to the American Experience*. Reading, Massachusetts: Addison-Wesley Pub. Co., 1984.

Stanford Arms Control Group. *International Arms Control: Issues and Agreements,* 2nd ed. Eds. Coit D. Blacker and Gloria Duffy. Stanford, California: Stanford University Press, 1984.

Tsipis, Kosta. *Arsenal: Understanding Weapons in the Nuclear Age*. New York: Simon and Schuster, 1983.

Acronyms

ABM	Anti-ballistic missile
ACDA	Arms Control and Disarmament Agency
AD	Assured Destruction
ALCM	Air-launched cruise missile
ASW	Anti-submarine warfare
BMD	Ballistic missile defense
CND	Campaign for Nuclear Disarmament
CSB	Closely spaced basing
CTBT	Comprehensive Test Ban Treaty
C³I	Command, control, communications, and intelligence
DOD	Department of Defense
ERDA	Energy Research and Development Administration
FEMA	Federal Emergency Management Agency
FR	Flexible Response
GLCM	Ground-launched cruise missile
IAEA	International Atomic Energy Agency
ICBM	Intercontinental ballistic missile
INF	Intermediate range nuclear force
INFCE	International Nuclear Fuel Cycle Evaluation

LRTNF	Long-range theater nuclear forces
MAD	Mutual Assured Destruction
MBFR	Mutual and Balanced Force Reductions
MIRV	Multiple independently-targetable re-entry vehicle
NCA	National Command Authority
NWS	Nuclear weapon state
NNWS	Non-nuclear weapon state
NPT	Non-Proliferation Treaty
OTA	Office of Technology Assessment
PNET	Peaceful Nuclear Explosion Treaty
SALT	Strategic Arms Limitation Talks
SDI	Strategic Defense Initiative
SIOP	Single Integrated Operations Plan
SLBM	Submarine-launched ballistic missile
START	Strategic Arms Reduction Talks
TTBT	Threshold Test Ban Treaty

The
Nuclear Arms Race
Debated

Chapter One

The Nuclear Arms Race and World Politics

In this chapter, we shall consider the broad impact, both actual and potential, of nuclear weapons on the international system. We must first, however, frankly acknowledge that space constraints mean that some important underlying premises will have to remain largely unexamined. For example, there is no consensus among specialists and scholars about the nature of the international system either before or after the advent of the nuclear age. Here we shall largely confine ourselves to reviewing the judgments—varied enough by any standards—of those who belong to the so-called realist tradition which views international relations as a struggle for power between states whose objective is security in an anarchic world. Again, some of the disagreements about, say, the likely effects or capabilities of various types of nuclear weapons and delivery systems rest on detailed scientific evaluations which no nonspecialist can hope to follow, let alone challenge with confidence.

That the use of atomic bombs on Hiroshima and Nagasaki in 1945 profoundly modified the international system cannot be doubted. There is, however, much debate about the extent of the change. Additionally, it cannot be ignored that in the immediate aftermath of Hiroshima many commentators had expected consequences which have simply not materialized. For example, advocates of world federalism, who sought to create a union of the nations of the world comparable to that formed by the original thirteen states when they joined in the late eighteenth century to become the United

1

States, won a good deal of support for their contention that humankind faced imminent doom unless sovereign states ceased to exist and as such created instead a single world authority. Other luminaries, among them British cabinet minister Philip Noel-Baker, held that humanity could not wait for the creation of a world government and should therefore insist that sovereign states carry out complete disarmament forthwith; otherwise, catastrophe was unavoidable. There were those who believed that a few nuclear giants would consolidate power around two or three poles, effectively ending the independence of most of the small, nonnuclear states, as predicted in 1949 by George Orwell in his famous novel *1984*. On the other hand, some experts feared the opposite: a rapid spread of nuclear weapons to even more countries with, again, catastrophic implications, as when scientist C. P. Snow proclaimed in 1960, "Within, at most, six years China and six other states [will] have a stock of nuclear bombs. Within, at the most, ten years, some of these bombs are going to go off. . . . That is a certainty. . . ."

All these predictions have proven too apocalyptic. As a result, judgments are now rather complacent. This trend has led some alarmists to cite the story of the person who jumped off the Empire State Building and, when passing the fourteenth floor, remarked, "So far, so good." They remind us, as well, of Albert Einstein's dictum that the splitting of the atom had changed everything *except* our way of thinking. All the same, it would appear that in much of the day-to-day conduct of international life, nuclear weapons are of only marginal or even negligible importance. Contrary to Orwell's expectations, there are now more sovereign states—over 150—than ever before. Of these, no more than about 5 percent possess nuclear weapons. Even these nuclear-weapon states have been sparing in day-to-day diplomacy about reminding others of their nuclear muscle. Moreover, although actual use of nuclear weapons is by no means entirely unthinkable, most nonnuclear states seem less than overawed by their nuclear rivals. For example, Argentina—a nonnuclear-weapon state—decided to confront Great Britain—a nuclear-weapon state—in 1982 over control of the Falkland Islands in the south Atlantic. While Margaret Thatcher's government did make it clear that the Argentines would be resisted by military force, nuclear threats by London were, significantly, totally absent throughout the crisis, and the possibility that they might have been invoked was presumably discounted by the Argentine government. This episode suggests that some commentators may have at times overrated the extent to which nuclear-weapons nations view these weapons as a decisive card in their political and diplomatic negotiations, and that the international system has not, as some have predicted, been completely transformed by them.

That nuclear weapons have been of vital significance in the superpower relationship is, on the other hand, undeniable. Nobody can doubt that the possibility of their use decisively affected the outcome of the Cuban Missile Crisis of 1962. There have been other occasions—such as the Korean war and the Berlin crises—where their ominous shadow was recognized on both sides. But it may be thought that often too much is attributed to nuclear weapons, even in evaluations of the superpower relationship. For example, in the present conditions of approximate nuclear parity, would either the Soviets or the Americans expect to be believed if they threatened to initiate the use of nuclear weapons over some relatively marginal issue, such as, say, the fate of

Beirut? Probably not. Yet many authorities hold that some potential points of conflict between the two superpowers involve so much prestige that the possibility of a nuclear exchange cannot be excluded. If, for instance, the Persian Gulf, Eastern or Western Europe, Cuba, or Mexico seemed likely to switch from one camp to the other, would not the threatened superpower feel obliged to go to almost any lengths to preserve the essentials of the long-established status quo?

The problem for the superpowers is that clashes over such really vital interests cannot be ruled out, if only because their control over local actors is in some theaters often limited, or even negligible. Yet any such clash between Moscow and Washington surely cannot be resolved by the ancient test of which party has the greater military power. For the military power of each side is, for practical purposes, near to infinite. That two countries can now assuredly inflict truly unacceptable damage on each other is unique in history. It is this reality which has led some commentators to argue that military solutions to disputes between the superpowers are now unthinkable. But in some contingencies there may be no mutually acceptable alternative solutions available either. This may encourage the development of a unique premium on superpower leaders being able to demonstrate the possession not merely of military might, but also of the resolve to use it selectively—but ruthlessly—in defense of their vital interests.

This brings us to the questions which, perhaps more than any others, underlie practically all the debates in this section. First, can we be sure that the superpowers will never allow any quarrel between them to degenerate into an outright military encounter? Second, if not, could such a major military clash between them assuredly be limited to the nonnuclear level? Third, if that also proves impossible, could it be limited to a level of nuclear use which would be less than cataclysmic for one or both societies, or for humanity as a whole? Of course, nobody actually *knows* the answers to these questions. But serious commentators cannot avoid at least venturing their best guesses—no less than can political leaders—although they are inevitably unable to reach any consensus.

LIVING WITH NUCLEAR WEAPONS

In the first of our debates the late political science professor Hans Morgenthau argues that a nuclear encounter between the superpowers could only be of an irrational character. Although he had the reputation for being a hard-headed "realist," he believed that the advent of nuclear weaponry had rendered old-style warfare between the superpowers redundant. "The availability of nuclear power, more particularly in the form of nuclear weapons," he wrote, "has ushered in a new period of history which is at least as different from all of recorded history until 1945 than are, say, the Middle Ages from the ancient world or modern times from the Middle Ages." He did not deny that recourse to conventional warfare by either superpower could be "a perfectly legitimate instrument of national policy," provided nuclear weapons had not been invented. But he evidently did not believe, given the fact that both sides possess such weapons, that a major war could be limited to the conventional level or, indeed, be limited at all. For he noted that "the idea of the fire-break or the pause between either conventional war or limited nuclear war, on the one hand, and all-out nuclear war, on the other, is alien to the military doctrine of the Soviet Union." He was thus apparently convinced that any major armed conflict between the superpowers must end in total catastrophe. If he was correct about that, then the advent of the nuclear age does indeed constitute a revolutionary departure from all that went before. Small wonder, then, that Morgenthau concluded, "it is the almost inevitable danger of actual nuclear war, inherent in the dynamism of a generalized unlimited nuclear arms race, which makes nuclear arms control and in the end nuclear disarmament a question of life and death for us all."

The authors of the ensuing extract, all distinguished scholars at Harvard University, take a less apocalyptic view of the future and reject the all-or-nothing approach which Morgenthau's article exemplifies. In discussing writer Jonathan Schell's celebrated best-seller *The Fate of the Earth*,[1] they find Schell's "either/or vision appealing, but misleading." They continue: "It is appealing because it calls for action. And action is necessary. It is misleading because the future is not limited to a choice between nuclear holocaust and universal disarmament." The Harvard authors deny that catastrophe is necessarily imminent and even hold that premature disarmament in the absence of political preconditions may actually "enhance the risks of renewed nuclear arms races and wars." They point to the historical precedents, denying that war is "the inevitable result of a rivalry between two nations." In short, change in international relations does not have to be instantaneous; it may come over long periods of time. Hence, while they clearly do not expect any rapid transformation in the present competitive and essentially hostile Soviet-American relationship, they do not rule out that incremental change may, over many decades, greatly reduce mutual tension.

True, the Harvard authors share with Morgenthau the belief that nuclear weapons cannot be treated like other military arms in history. Yet they are more restrained in judging the extent to which such weaponry is different. They contend only that humanity "must live with them carefully, vigilantly, gingerly, always displaying the utmost caution." They also are less clear than Morgenthau about whether nuclear war could be kept limited, even speculating about whether defensive systems might or might not be desirable in that context. (Morgenthau, of course, flatly denied the possibility of creating such "desirable" defensive systems.) As well as entertaining the possibility of limited nuclear warfare, the Harvard authors admit to uncertainty about the extent of the potential impact of nuclear deterrence—the theory that a nuclear-weapon state can be prevented from attacking another nuclear-weapon state with nuclear weapons for fear that it will be destroyed in a nuclear counterstrike. They wonder, in particular, whether nuclear deterrence can be so effective as to create the kind of fire-break that might actually make conventional wars more likely, a premise which, in the superpower context, Morgenthau dismisses. Readers should ask themselves whether Morgenthau errs on the side of dogmatism, and whether the Harvard authors do so in the direction of complacency.

---

[1]Jonathan Schell, *The Fate of the Earth* (New York: Avon Books, 1982).

DETERRENCE

In our next debate, between U.S. Secretary of Defense Caspar W. Weinberger and political scientist James A. Stegenga, some of the same propensities for overstatement may be observed. In this case, however, the authors focus rather narrowly on the issue of mutual deterrence between the superpowers. Stegenga's approach is clearly that of the political scientist; Weinberger's, that of a day-to-day practitioner. Both writers acknowledge that deterrence is and has long been the "cornerstone" of United States security policy. Weinberger, for his part, does not question its merit, and is confident that President Ronald Reagan's strategic modernization program is all that is needed to ensure that deterrence successfully endures into the indefinite future. Stegenga, on the other hand, sees such confidence in deterrence as nothing more than an ideology or faith whose premises are never even questioned by the true believers who, he claims, dominate American political, military, and academic life. Interestingly, Weinberger's contribution serves somewhat to confirm this interpretation, for he at no point considers any alternative to deterrence. Stegenga offers us a large variety of possible alternatives ranging from pacifism through civilian resistance to accommodation with powerful neighbors. He concedes that *some* of these alternatives might be "impractical or otherwise objectionable." What he does not allow is that Weinberger and a majority of Americans might hold *all* the alternatives to be impracticable or objectionable, and that these people might thus be fully justified, from their point of view, in continuing to rely on deterrence. Readers will notice, however, that Stegenga, presumably writing in advance of Reagan's Strategic Defense Initiative (SDI) of March 1983, in which the president called for the development of space-age defense technologies, offers one alternative which, ironically, Weinberger would also now endorse: "development and deployment of some sort of technological defense against incoming Soviet missiles." But Weinberger would no doubt also insist that "deterrence" remains the cornerstone of United States defense policy for the foreseeable future, since nobody, not even Reagan, imagines that the SDI can give assured and total protection against incoming Soviet missiles for at least several decades, if indeed such protection can ever be achieved at all. Stegenga would presumably favor the adoption of one or more of his alternatives in the interim. Weinberger plainly would not.

An interesting point is raised by Stegenga when he writes, "For nuclear deterrence to be as dependable as its exponents suggest it is, the possibility for human error or communication breakdown or unauthorized action must be reduced to near zero." This he considers a difficult, if not impossible, task, "people, organizations and machines being what they are." This is a theme we shall take up again in the next debate. It is worth noting here that Weinberger does not even consider the likelihood of an accident when expressing such high confidence in the future of deterrence.

Another characteristic of Weinberger's approach is to stress the long pedigree of the United States' approach to nuclear deterrence. There is, he claims, "nothing new about it," and he evidently draws confidence for the future from the length of the period in which nuclear war has not occurred. To Stegenga, however, several decades do not constitute a particularly long time. In any case, he wonders whether the absence of war between the superpowers since 1945 has really been due to nuclear deterrence.

"Historians may well conclude," he writes, "that neither side's leaders ever had the intention the other side's leaders feared and thought they had discouraged with the threat of nuclear retaliation." Stegenga may or may not be correct on the substance of his judgment, but he surely cannot count on unanimity on the matter among historians. Soviet historians, for their part, seem unlikely ever to have the liberty to state, even if they should believe it, that the Soviet leaders have erred in constructing nuclear weaponry in anticipation of possible "imperialist aggression." As for historians in the West, there is rarely agreement among them about anything of substance, and they are unlikely to start seeing eye to eye on an issue as controversial as the merits of the cold war. But the serious point here is that Weinberger, like most leaders in both Washington and Moscow, appears to consider it a truism, right or wrong, that the other superpower is guided by real adversaries who actually have to be restrained by nuclear threats.

Finally, it is worth noting that Stegenga sees the United States' nuclear deterrent as intended to prevent "any substantial contemplated aggression against the West," that is, conventional as well as nuclear. Historically, this has certainly been the case. It still, of course, remains the official doctrine of the Western alliance, the North Atlantic Treaty Organization (NATO), despite the efforts of four distinguished Americans to promote a plan for a nuclear no-first-use declaration by both superpowers— a proposal to which detailed attention will be given in a later section. An interesting aspect of Weinberger's contribution, however, is that he is not nearly as forthright as one might have expected in supporting the so-called extended deterrent; that is, American willingness to risk a nuclear war with the Soviets to keep Western Europe from succumbing to conquest by superior conventional forces. Weinberger writes, "Our strategy is a defensive one designed to prevent attack—particularly nuclear attack— against us or our allies," and he wants the Soviets to recognize that "because of our retaliatory capability, there can be no circumstance where the initiation of a nuclear war at any level or of any duration would make sense." Yet official NATO policy is that NATO might indeed initiate nuclear war—admittedly at a relatively low level in the first instance—if faced with conventional defeat in Europe. Of course, Weinberger has never repudiated that doctrine. Nevertheless, his emphasis on deterring a *nuclear* encounter is a minor example of the kind of American proclamation (one pioneered substantially by former Secretary of State Henry Kissinger in a speech in Brussels in 1979) that has recently caused much alarm among West European political and military leaders, who increasingly wonder whether the days of the effectiveness of "extended deterrence" may be numbered. This problem, above all, underlies much of the debate about the appropriate direction of American security policy, as will be seen in a later section of this book.

ACCIDENTAL NUCLEAR WAR

We turn next to the question of whether a nuclear war is likely to be triggered by accident, an issue already touched upon by Stegenga. We are concerned here with an unintentional or unauthorized launch of nuclear weapons rather than with a war initiated on the basis of a miscalculation or the calling of a bluff. The history of major wars might indicate, on a superficial level, that purely accidental war is not to be expected. For as Michael Howard, the Regius Professor of History at the University of Oxford, has written: "If history shows any record of 'accidental' wars, I have yet to find them. Certainly statesmen have sometimes been surprised by the nature of the war they have unleashed, and it is reasonable to assume that in at least fifty percent of the cases they got a result they did not expect. But that is not the same as a war begun by mistake and continued with no political purpose."[2] Thus, the Crimean war of 1854, for example, was certainly the unintended result of mutual miscalculations among the British, the French, and the Russians, but the recourse to force among the powers was preceded by deliberate governmental decisions and even the issuing of ultimatums. This was also true in 1914, although one might perhaps argue that the fatal chain of events was initially triggered by an assassination in Sarajevo which no great power had authorized. History before 1945 may, in any case, provide little guidance today, for as James E. Muller, a founder of International Physicians for Prevention of Nuclear War, points out, we now live in a unique era when truly decisive blows may be struck against an adversary in less than thirty minutes, requiring a readiness on the part of the victim to make an equally rapid and maybe devastating response.

The dynamics of the arms competition between the superpowers are such that this warning time seems likely to shrink steadily, and if Reagan's SDI bears fruit we may eventually see attempted countermeasures being launched by computers rather than by human beings, and within minutes of a report of a supposed attack. This prospect is certainly alarming. The growth of technological sophistication is, however, not entirely negative in its implications. The superpowers are now much less vulnerable to unauthorized use of nuclear weapons than was the case in the 1950s, when appropriate safeguards were fewer and more primitive. Although Muller apparently sees dangers in the growth of the United States' "arsenal and the number of personnel involved," he appears to contradict himself somewhat when, a few sentences later, he argues that "the spread of nuclear weapons to less-developed countries with limited technical sophistication also increases the risk."

We shall later devote an entire section to the problems arising from the proliferation of nuclear weapons to countries which do not have the resources of the superpowers. But in the present context of our considering the risk of accidents, it seems fair to guess that if ever nuclear weapons are launched by unauthorized personnel, it is much more likely that a nonsuperpower will be involved. Moscow and Washington now have a good many years' experience in building safeguards into their nuclear systems, and even in identifying officers with the kinds of dangerous emotional problems to which Muller refers. On the other hand, the assurance given by General James Hartinger, former Chief, U.S. Air Force Space Command, presumably would not fully satisfy Muller, or indeed many of our readers. Furthermore, Hartinger entirely ignores the possibility that a political leader, rather than a subordinate, may become emotionally unbalanced. Yet, if, say Libya, which is often characterized as a "crazy state" because of its erratic foreign-policy behavior, obtained nuclear weapons, it seems improbable that assurances from a Libyan counterpart of Hartinger would seem even remotely as convincing as Hartinger's.

[2]Michael Howard, *The Causes of War and Other Essays* (London: Temple Smith, 1983), p. 12.

Another relevant point is whether the accidental or unauthorized launch of one or more nuclear missiles would necessarily be catastrophic for humanity. It is possible that a launch from a minor nuclear power preoccupied only with a regional adversary would turn out to be less dangerous for all humankind than would a launch by a superpower. Much of the outcome could depend on the target and whether, if the target should be a superpower, the means of delivery were so primitive as to permit effective interception. Clearly, the greatest danger would arise in the instance of, say, British or French weapons being launched accidently or without authorization against the Soviet Union, thereby leaving decision makers in Moscow in some doubt as to whether the United States itself was really responsible. This does not, however, seem the likeliest of scenarios.

Even in the case where an unauthorized launch (from whatever source) actually reached a superpower, we would not have any certainty about the consequences. Such an attack might indeed kill millions, as Muller rather dogmatically assumes. It also might not do so, depending on the target and on the number of missiles launched. We also cannot know, even in the worst case, in which millions are being killed, that the victim superpower would necessarily launch an immediate and massive counterattack on the other superpower. There is, however, a high risk that such an attack would be the result, and one having totally catastrophic implications. A number of leading civilian experts, including Paul Bracken of Yale University and Desmond Ball of the Australian National University, have recently stressed that once a nuclear conflict has begun, maintenance of an effective system of Command, Control, Communications, and Intelligence (C^3I) could be expected to break down almost immediately under the pressures which would arise from relevant decision times being extremely short and from the concomitant unavoidability of predelegation of authority to launch nuclear strikes.

The "hot line" between Moscow and Washington exists to permit speedy communication of the disavowal of an unauthorized attack, although there is no guarantee that the victim country would believe such a denial, nor that it would be received in time to prevent retaliatory actions beyond the control of political decision makers. And, following the shooting down of a South Korean airliner which intruded into Soviet airspace in 1983, few would have really high confidence that a similar incident involving nuclear missiles would not get out of hand. But is complete dogmatism on the point justified?

NUCLEAR WINTER

Whether a nuclear war came about by accident or by design, its likely consequences merit serious advance consideration. It is simply insufficient to assume without further analysis that humanity would be at the end of its relatively short existence on this planet, or even that modern civilization would assuredly end. The imponderables are too numerous to justify such hasty conclusions.

First, we do not know in advance which countries would take part in any particular nuclear war. Clearly a clash involving two third world countries possessing only primitive nuclear stocks, however grievous in its consequences, would not threaten the survival of humanity as a whole.

Second, even if a conflict between the two superpowers escalated to the nuclear level, it seems far from certain, as we have just argued above, that all-out nuclear war would necessarily result. In fact, a great variety of possibilities could be imagined. For example, Brian Martin, a physicist, has claimed that the number of immediate fatalities could be fewer than a thousand if a single Soviet nuclear weapon should be dropped on a particularly remote target, such as certain U.S. installations in the Australian outback.[3] The question then arises whether, after making every allowance for the fears of Ball and Bracken that were mentioned earlier, one could really be *certain* that in the eventuality of attack on a remote target uncontrolled nuclear escalation would automatically result. Readers may be able to construct for themselves several scenarios for a nuclear encounter between the superpowers that in their opinion could *conceivably* produce a total number of casualties smaller than that in World War I or II. (Assessments of actual *probabilities* in each case would be an entirely different and much more difficult exercise.)

The imponderables do not end there. Even if major nuclear war between the superpowers were to occur, whether humanity's survival would be put seriously at risk remains a matter for legitimate dispute, as our debate about nuclear winter illustrates.

The term "nuclear winter" gained currency in 1984, following the Conference on the World after Nuclear War held in October 1983, and the December 1983 publication of an article in *Science* on the climatic effects of nuclear war. The article is known as the TTAPS study, an acronym derived from the first letter of the names of the five authors.[4] Anne Ehrlich, an enthusiastic supporter of this study and attendee at the conference, summarizes the study's findings and seeks to convey the mood of the conference in the article we reproduce here. On balance, she believes that the climatic consequences of a serious nuclear conflict between the superpowers are likely to be dire for humanity. She argues, "Clearly, society can never again view the prospect of nuclear war as it did before. Any possibility of meaningful survival has been removed, and no place on Earth is safe from the nuclear winter." She also quotes without dissent the view of Paul Ehrlich that for the first time we "could not preclude the extinction of *Homo sapiens*."

Much less apocalyptic in his appraisal of the prospects of such a conflict is Caspar W. Weinberger, who in 1985 produced the "Report on the Potential Effects of Nuclear War on the Climate," reprinted here, in part. He, too, takes the TTAPS study seriously, but sees it as based on a one-dimensional model and hence not necessarily a reliable guide to what might actually happen. Weinberger is clearly more comfortable with a report of the National Academy of Sciences, published in 1984, which emphasizes the great uncertainties inherent in any calculations. Readers will no doubt reach their own conclusions as to which of the approaches seems the more valid.

In conclusion, we assume that there is at least wide agreement that whether humanity today is actually an endangered species holds deep significance for the entire debate

[3]Brian Martin, "Critique of Nuclear Extinction," *Journal of Peace Reseach* XIX, no. 4 (1982), pp. 287–300.

[4]Richard P. Turco, Owen B. Toon, Thomas P. Ackerman, James B. Pollack, and Carl Sagan, "Nuclear Winter: Global Consequences of Multiple Nuclear Explosions," *Science* 222 (December 23, 1983), pp. 1283–92.

about nuclear weapons and the future of the international system. For if Ehrlich is right, then would not the task of minimizing the risk of nuclear war justify almost limitless sacrifices of other values? If Weinberger is the sounder judge, would it not be more reasonable for citizens of Western nations to attempt to combine the quest for the avoidance of nuclear war, and indeed conventional war also, with the goal of preserving national independence and traditional democratic liberties?

1 Is It Improbable That We Shall Be Able to Live
Indefinitely with Nuclear Weapons?

YES

Hans J. Morgenthau

*The Fallacy of Thinking Conventionally about Nuclear
Weapons*

NO

Harvard Nuclear Study Group (Albert Carnesale, Paul
Doty, Stanley Hoffmann, Samuel P. Huntington, Joseph S.
Nye, Jr., and Scott D. Sagan)

Living with Nuclear Weapons: Is There a Choice?

The Fallacy of Thinking Conventionally about Nuclear Weapons
Hans J. Morgenthau

It is unsound to think in conventional terms about nuclear problems and, more particularly, about nuclear disarmament. But what is obvious to people reflecting theoretically about certain issues of the contemporary world is not necessarily obvious to the policy-makers. In other words, there exists a profound and wide gap between, on the one hand, our traditional modes of thought and action, and, on the other hand, the objective conditions under which we live.

The availability of nuclear power, more particularly in the form of nuclear weapons, has ushered in a new period of history which is at least as different from all of recorded history until 1945 than are, say, the Middle Ages from the ancient world or modern times from the Middle Ages. The very conceptions of nuclear 'weapon' and of nuclear 'war' are misnomers. For when we speak of weapons, we have in mind a rational relationship between a means, an instrument and an end. That is to say, we can use a gun to kill a man, we can use a cannon to breach a wall, and if we have set our mind upon killing a man or breaching a wall, then the use of a gun or of a cannon is a perfectly rational means to a rational end. The same is true of conventional violence in the collective sense, that is war. War, in the conventional sense, is a perfectly legitimate instrument of national policy in a society which is composed of sovereign nations, that is to say, of nations which have no secular superior above them, which cannot be forced to do something, which cannot be compelled to engage in certain behaviour, by legitimate superior authority. Violence, for better or for worse, its threat or actual application, is the inevitable result of the anarchic character of a society composed of sovereign nations. Thus it was from the beginning

of history to 1945 perfectly legitimate, perfectly rational to use the threat or the actuality of war for the purpose of defending or promoting the interests of individual nations. All this has been radically changed through the impact of the availability of nuclear weapons. For a nuclear weapon is not a weapon in the conventional semantic sense. It is not a rational means to a rational end. It is an instrument of unlimited, universal destruction, hence the threat or the actuality of a nuclear war is not a rational instrument of national policy because it is an instrument of suicide and genocide. It is exactly for this reason that for more than a quarter of a century the two major nuclear powers have been extremely careful not to come too close to the brink of nuclear war, both being fully aware, at least in a general philosophic sense, that nuclear war is a self-defeating absurdity.

However, from the beginning of history to 1945, when mankind thought naturally in pre-nuclear terms, it developed certain conceptions about weapons and war, which have not yielded in the minds of certain theoreticians, or even in the minds of practitioners, when they have time to think in theoretical terms, to the impact of an entirely novel phenomenon, the availability of nuclear weapons and of what we call euphemistically a nuclear war. So we have a disjunction between the conventional ways we think and act about nuclear weapons and the objective conditions, under which the availability of nuclear weapons forces us to live. Let me give a simple example of this disjunction from recent history. One of my former students, who has reached a kind of eminence, was for a considerable period of time one of the leading members of the Central Intelligence Agency (CIA). One of his tasks was to brief the Joint Chiefs of Staff about the

Hans J. Morgenthau, "The Fallacy of Thinking Conventionally about Nuclear Weapons," in David Carlton and Carlo Schaerf (eds.), *Arms Control and Technological Innovation* (London: Croom Helm, 1977), pp. 255–64.

basic issues which arose in the foreign and military policy of the United States. This official said to me that when he talked to General X about the difference between conventional and nuclear weapons, the latter said, of course, obviously, but when the former read this general's position papers, there was no trace of that recognition in them. There is a psychological and sociological problem here, which is of the most crucial importance for the future of humanity, that is our seeming inability thus far to adjust our conventional modes of thought and action to the objective conditions which the nuclear age imposes upon us. This is particularly true when consideration is given to the approaches to a nuclear strategy which have followed each other in the last 25 years in the United States. From the clean H-bomb through graduated deterrence, to the counter-force strategy of ex–Secretary of Defense, James Schlesinger, there is one impulse tying those different strategies together: to find a way by which a nuclear war can be fought in a conventional way, that is, to conventionalise nuclear war in order to be able to come out of it alive. In other words, there is what I would regard as an absurd attempt, not to adapt our modes of thought and action to the new objective conditions of the nuclear age but to transform those objective conditions in the light of the pre-nuclear modes of thought and action.

We have tried, then, instead of adapting our modes of thought and action to the objective conditions of the nuclear age, to conventionalise nuclear war in order to be able to fight and win it and to come out of it alive. And this is true not only with regard to military strategy but also with regard to disarmament and the attempts to develop a defence against nuclear war. For it is one of the characteristics of the nature of nuclear weapons that their destructiveness is so enormous that it has simply destroyed, disintegrated like an atomic bomb, the very conceptions from the beginning of history to the beginning of the nuclear age.

Let us very briefly consider the different attempts at a new strategy, which would allow us to use nuclear weapons without the universal, uncontrolled destructive effects, which, in theory, we correctly associate with nuclear weapons. Take the so-called clean H-bomb, which made its appearance at the beginning of the 1950s, that is an H-bomb that would not have the devastating indiscriminate effects which even the kiloton bombs dropped on Hiroshima and Nagasaki had. It was a bomb which would have very little if any fall-out and whose effects would be those of a gigantic conventional bomb. In the immortal words of a former Chief of Staff of the American Air Force, General Curtis LeMay, the nuclear bomb is just another bomb. The US Atomic Energy Commission in a book entitled *The Effects of Nuclear Weapons,* published in 1962, made short shrift of this idea when it said that there is no such thing as a clean H-bomb, and that all H-bombs are more or less unclean even though the distribution of blast, fire and radiation effects may be different in different designs of the bomb. But the idea that it is possible to devise an H-bomb which is not essentially different from a conventional bomb is utterly mistaken. Take the conception of graduated deterrence, that is a method of waging nuclear war, which does not escalate almost immediately into an all-out war, but in which in a rational, almost predetermined way, similar to a chess game, one side makes a move by, say, taking out one city, and the other side makes another move taking out a city of its opponent. Thus each side in a perfectly detached, rational way inflicts a certain degree of damage upon the other. It is this idea, which has gained wide acceptance in certain think-tanks where this kind of playing games with survival issues is highly developed. There is something to be said in favour of them in terms of the hypothetical possibilities that exist. However, in practical terms, it is inconceivable that living human beings, with the ideological conceptions and values which the policy-makers in the Soviet Union, the United States and China possess, would look at, say, the destruction of Chicago by the Soviet Union or at the destruction of Minsk by the United States with the same detachment with which chess-players would look at the exchange of pawns. They are bound to arrive very quickly at a point at which, aside from the aroused emotions, one side or the other or both sides will feel that in this rational simulation of a chess game, one or the other side will take advantage of the other, that is the equivalence, which is theoretically assumed between Minsk and Chicago, will not be self-evident to the players of the game. The Soviet Union will inevitably find that Minsk is more important than Chicago and the United States will find that Chicago is more important than Minsk. Thus they will find that this type of graduated deterrence is really not deterrence at all, because it leads inevitably by its own dynamism to escalation and to an all-out strategic war, which it was the first purpose of the enterprise to avoid. For once the United States has arrived at the conclusion that Chicago is more important than Minsk, it will take out two Soviet cities, which are regarded as the equivalent of another American city, whereupon the Soviet Union will take out two American cities, which are regarded as the equivalent of one Soviet city and before we know it, we shall be in the middle of the all-out nuclear war which we wanted to avoid in the first place. Furthermore, we have to reckon with the emotions, the passions of the people at large and of the policy-makers, for in such an undertaking started in the rational way I have indicated, enormous powers of passion are of course involved on both sides. The population of the United States will not look with equanimity at the successive, however rational, elimination or partial destruction of American cities and their inhabitants, nor will the people and the government of the Soviet Union, and hence again we have a force which almost inevitably will lead to escalation and to the various effects which the graduated deterrence was intended to avoid. Incidentally, those conceptions of limiting nuclear war, of making it possible to wage it without destroying oneself and one's enemy are peculiarly American and are the result of a humanitarian impulse within the framework of an utterly inhuman enterprise. Since we are confronted with the possibility of nuclear war, we want to make nuclear war as painless as possible, as limited as possible, one might even say, if so grotesque a juxtaposition is allowed, as hu-

mane as possible. On the other hand, the official military doctrine of the Soviet Union has never accepted those distinctions. That doctrine assumes that a war, especially a European war, which starts as a conventional or limited nuclear war and whose stakes the belligerents regard as being of prime importance, is bound to escalate into all-out nuclear war. Thus the idea of the fire-break or the pause between either conventional war or limited nuclear war, on the one hand, and all-out nuclear war, on the other, is alien to the military doctrine of the Soviet Union.

We shall next examine the counter-force strategy, whose philosophy the then Secretary of Defense, Robert S. McNamara, explained to an audience at the University of Michigan in 1962. It was an attempt to limit nuclear war, to make it acceptable as an instrument of national policy. The counter-force strategy is very simple; in fact, it assumes that a nuclear war can be waged and ought to be waged not against population and industrial centres, but against strictly military objectives. The revival of this doctrine in very recent times starts with the same assumption which has been fortified by the increase in the sophistication of nuclear weapons. . . . For in 1962 one could well make the case that it was impossible, in view of the character of nuclear weapons, to distinguish in practice strictly between military and civilian objectives, that the indiscriminate and widespread destructiveness of nuclear weapons was so enormous that a nuclear weapon aimed at a military objective was bound to destroy, by virtue of the mere proximity of civilian objectives, the latter as well. That argument is still valid, in my opinion. If the Soviet Union tries to take out the missile sites near Phoenix and Cheyenne, to give only two examples, the Soviet missiles are not likely to be so accurate as to be capable of destroying the missile sites without having any negative effect upon the adjacent population and industrial centres. But recent increases in accuracy may have improved the situation somewhat in this respect, and therefore there is a grain more merit in the recent revival of the counter-force strategy than in its original formulation. There is, however, a more profound argument against the counter-force strategy, namely its ultimate military purpose. In the case of the American version, which is the main version of the counter-force strategy, the United States will not initiate a nuclear war by a first strike. It will wait, in other words, until the other side has initiated a nuclear war by a first strike and then will attack the military targets, which the other side presents not merely in the form of missile sites, but of the missiles themselves. But the first strike has already emptied most or many of the missile sites. So it is necessary, then, to make a distinction—I have been assured that it is possible, even though I cannot see how it can be made—between missile sites which still contain their missiles and the other missile sites from which the missiles have already departed. Now let us suppose that this distinction can be made, and this exchange operates as intended. This of course depends on the enemy who started the war with the first strike not having destroyed all one's missile sites, and on one having a sufficient number of missiles left with which one can destroy the enemy missile sites which still contain missiles. Accept all of this and assume that the two belligerents knock out their land-based missiles reciprocally, what have they gained? They are in the same position that they were originally, except that now they have to rely exclusively upon the sea-borne deterrent and perhaps upon the airborne deterrent. So one would have the same distribution of destructive power with the same deterrent effect one had at the beginning of the war with only the difference that the mechanics of deterrent would have changed from land-based to sea-based missiles. Now there are people who say that land-based missiles are obsolete anyhow, and that they should be phased out through the arms control negotiations between the United States and the Soviet Union. If this position is correct, then in the projected counter-force encounter we would simply have engaged in a mutual disarmament enterprise by knocking each other's land-based missiles out and be in the same position as we were before, that is to say, there would be no victor and no vanquished.

This brings us to another point, that is the basic distinction between victory and defeat in war, which is again a distinction that is deeply ingrained in our consciousness, because it has been imposed upon us through millennia of historical experience. Thus the military, in particular, have found it unacceptable both in Korea and Vietnam that a conventional war should not end in the clear-cut victory of that side whose cause is regarded to be just, which is of course one's own side. The same reluctance to give up the distinction between victory and defeat can be noticed in our thinking on nuclear war. The idea that a nuclear war should necessarily end in a stalemate or in the mutual destruction of the belligerents is simply unacceptable to people who have made it their business to prepare for victorious wars. They are in the position of a banker or a businessman in general, whose purpose in life is to make a profit for his company, and all of a sudden he is faced with the contingency that the best he can hope for is to break even. He will never make a profit and pay a dividend on the stock of his company, which goes against his grain, against his nature. As far as nuclear war is concerned, this is the objective situation we face, a situation which again is utterly different from any situation which any nation has faced in the past: war itself becomes a completely senseless, irrational enterprise in that if it can be limited in terms of counter-force strategy, it will simply end in the same kind of equilibrium with which it started, only that the composition of the forces through which the equilibrium is presented will be different.

Take the concept of defence. It has been axiomatic throughout history that any new weapon will call forth sooner or later a counter-weapon, a defence against it. Let us assume that this axiom is borne out by historical experience. But it is still true that the destructiveness of nuclear weapons is so enormous, is so staggering to the imagination, that it is inconceivable in view of present technology to devise a defence against nuclear weapons. Thus, the abolition, for all practical purposes, of Anti-Ballistic Missiles (ABMs) by the two SALT negotiations, simply recognises an objective fact of nuclear life. But it should again be kept in mind how insistent the attempts were on both sides to find a defence against nuclear weapons, for once we have a defence against nuclear weapons, we have removed the main deterrent against nuclear war. If we can expect to come out of a nuclear war alive, then to wage or not to wage nuclear war becomes simply like the approach to conventional war, a matter of pragmatic, expedential calculation.

Let us now consider tactical nuclear war, which is another attempt to wage a nuclear war, which will not lead to the destruction of both sides, and which can lead to the victory or defeat of one or the other side. The conception of tactical nuclear war, that is to say, of the battlefield use of nuclear weapons, first of all is up against the impossibility of drawing an objective, generally recognised and recognisable line between tactics and strategy in general. The military schools in all countries have debated this question without ever arriving at a conclusion. For the distinction is not so much in the objective situation on the battlefield as in the minds of the military planner or director of military operations. Incidentally, the fact that the Hiroshima and Nagasaki bombs today are classified as tactical nuclear weapons, shows how far tactics can be stretched to cover what generally would be regarded as strategy. What might be intended by one side as a tactical manoeuvre may thus be interpreted by the other side as a strategic move, and the reply of the other side may either be interpreted in tactical or strategic terms by the first side. Since in such situations both sides are inclined to use a worst-case approach to the problems, that is to assume the worst in terms of the intentions of the enemy, the distinction is bound to break down very quickly. This is true not only of nuclear but of conventional war as well. But the problem is aggravated by the nature of nuclear war.

Assume for a moment as a hypothetical case that a conventional war breaks out in Central Europe, in which the United States and the Soviet Union are involved. The United States, which has about 7,000 so-called tactical nuclear warheads in Eu-

rope, uses some of them against the military objectives presented by the Soviet Union, such as bridges, military concentrations, ammunition dumps and logistic installations. But that may lead to the destruction of, say, certain cities in White Russia. The Soviet Union replies in the same tactical spirit by attacking the Channel ports, Brest, Cherbourg, Le Havre and so forth, in order to inflict upon the Western armies the same tactical disadvantages the Americans have tried to inflict upon the Soviet Union. But since the tactical targets are different in nature, asymmetric in the extreme on both sides, the Americans will ask themselves when they see Le Havre, Brest and Cherbourg going up in flames, what are the Soviets after? Is this tactical or is it strategic? Applying the worst-case interpretation, the Americans take out some of their cities as a reply to their move. The Soviets then reply in kind: if the Americans take out some of our cities, we take out some of theirs. And one morning we wake up, if we wake up at all, and we find that both sides are engaged in an all-out strategic war, not because either side wanted it, but because the objective dynamism of the initial act leaves neither side a choice.

Another rationalistic fallacy is causally connected with the attempt to make a distinction between all-out nuclear war and a civilised nice little nuclear war out of which both sides will come alive, namely the idea that the nature of war, as it appears to the historian in retrospect, is a result of conscious designs of the war-makers. This may sometimes have been the case, but it is by no means typically the case. It is much more likely that you take one step, to quote Goethe's Faust, which you are free to take, yet from the second on you are a slave of the first. That is to say, the consequent action is predetermined by the first step one has taken and one is not able to escape the inner logic, the inner dynamism of the first step. So it is a naïve, rationalistic illusion to think that the war-makers remain in control of the war. They are in control before they take the first step. Once they have taken the first step, the dynamism of that first step pushes them in the direction which that first step indicates. Abraham Lincoln said at the end of the American Civil War: 'It is sure that I have not controlled events, events have controlled me.' So here is a philosophic fallacy which attaches to the conception of the nature of man as a war-making animal, and that is another factor in the confusion and delusions to which the attempts at developing a rational strategy of nuclear war and nuclear disarmament are exposed.

Take, finally, the problem of nuclear disarmament which is, because of the nature of nuclear weapons and of nuclear war, fundamentally different from the problem of conventional disarmament. The conventional arms race is indeed an inescapable function of the balance of power. To simplify the situation by only speaking of two nations, we may say that both nations want to maintain an equilibrium between them. But they can never be sure whether they have calculated correctly their own military strength or that of the other side. So they need a certain insurance against miscalculation in their disfavour. In consequence, if the quantity of x would establish and maintain a balance between themselves and the prospective enemy, they must add to x a y, say 10 per cent more, in order to be sure that even if they have made a mistake in their disfavour, the balance is still maintained. The other side, seeing this addition of 10 per cent or y, must add z to its military power in order to make sure that it is not disadvantaged by the increase in the military power of the other side. The other side notes again that the enemy has added z to its power, so they add more and vice versa. So there is a cumulative inevitable increase in military power, which is another term for the conventional arms race.

To stop this arms race by disarmament agreements has proved to be possible only if the underlying political conflicts, which have given rise to the arms race in the first place, have been mitigated or eliminated. When one reviews the history of attempts to secure conventional disarmament from the end of the Napoleonic Wars to the present—

there have been scores of them—one realises that there have been only two successes, one temporary, the other permanent: the Washington Treaty for the limitation of naval armaments of 1922 and the disarmament of the American-Canadian frontier, both having been the result of the permanent or temporary elimination of political conflicts. So there is an element of hopelessness in the numerous attempts at conventional disarmament by means of an isolated technical approach.

The situation with regard to nuclear disarmament is, however, utterly different. For the dynamism which characterises the conventional military balance of power policies of nations does not apply to nuclear weapons. When it comes to machine-guns, one can never have enough of them, because there are always many more possible targets available than there are weapons to eliminate the targets. When it comes to nuclear weapons, there exists an optimum, which does not exist with regard to conventional weapons, beyond which to go is utterly irrational. If we are capable of destroying our enemy 10 times over, under the worst of conditions, it becomes utterly irrational to compete with him for the sake of being able to destroy him 15 times over, and our enemy, who is only capable of destroying us 6 times over, is by the same token not inferior at all. This simple and obvious syllogism has not escaped policy-makers in theory but it has escaped them in practice, because the impulse to get more and better nuclear weapons has proved to be irresistible. So the modes of thought and action which are perfectly appropriate for conventional weapons and for the conventional arms race have been transferred to the nuclear field, where they are bound to prove, and have already proved to be, to a certain extent, catastrophic. They have proved to be catastrophic in the economic sense, and they are bound to prove to be catastrophic in the very vital sense of the survival of Western civilisation, if not humanity, if the nuclear arms race is not stopped. In theory the Americans have recognised this, as have the Soviets. For this reason we have had the SALT talks. But when politicians get down to business and when they need the approval of their military establishments, they find themselves handicapped in transforming their theoretical insight into practical measures of nuclear arms control and later on disarmament.

We may thus conclude as we began: the issue of nuclear disarmament or at least of arms control is a literally vital issue, not only for the superpowers, not only for their allies, but for humanity. For with proliferation now having started in earnest, there is no doubt in my mind, and I think in the minds of most experts, that a nuclear arms race, not limited to two superpowers having responsible governments mortally afraid of each other, but

spreading over the whole globe is bound, sooner or later, to lead to an unspeakable catastrophe. For history shows, if history shows anything, that all nations have been governed at times by fools and knaves, and even a combination of both. That was bad enough before nuclear weapons existed. But imagine a fool or knave or a combination of both in the possession of nuclear weapons, and nuclear war will be unavoidable. So it is the almost inevitable danger of actual nuclear war, inherent in the dynamism of a generalised unlimited nuclear arms race, which makes nuclear arms control and in the end nuclear disarmament a question of life or death for all of us.

Living with Nuclear Weapons: Is There a Choice?
Harvard Nuclear Study Group (Albert Carnesale, Paul Doty, Stanley Hoffman, Samuel P. Huntington, Joseph S. Nye, Jr., and Scott D. Sagan)

. . . IS NUCLEAR WAR INEVITABLE?

An "absolute" vision of the nuclear future exists today. This vision is becoming more widespread and counsels that a nuclear holocaust is inevitable unless complete nuclear disarmament is achieved. This prediction is not of a world of enduring efforts to achieve security, but rather an either/or future: either complete success or complete failure; either global peace and disarmament or global nuclear holocaust.

Jonathan Schell, in *The Fate of the Earth*, has most eloquently preached that either/or philosophy:

> If we are honest with ourselves we have to admit that unless we rid ourselves of our nuclear arsenals a holocaust not only *might* occur but *will* occur—if not today, then tomorrow; if not this year, then the next. We have come to live on borrowed time: every year of continued human life on earth is a borrowed year, every day a borrowed day.[1]

This either/or vision is appealing, but misleading. It is appealing because it calls for action. And action is necessary. It is misleading because the future is not limited to a choice between nuclear holocaust and universal disarmament.

It is conceivable to defend predictions such as C. P. Snow's that nuclear war was certain within ten years, on the grounds that such warnings will be justified if war takes place in a hundred years.[2] But the difference between a decade and a century makes all the difference in the world when it comes to dealing with our nuclear predicament. Over a century, profound changes that reduce the risk of nuclear war are possible, partly as the result of deliberate, concerted actions. And iro.ically, . . . , some efforts to force profound changes within a decade could actually increase the prospect of nuclear use by encouraging miscalculations.

[1]Jonathan Schell, *The Fate of the Earth* (New York: Knopf, 1982), pp. 163–64.

[2]Thomas Powers *Thinking About the Next War* (New York: Knopf, 1982), p. 17.

From The Harvard Nuclear Study Group, "Living with Nuclear Weapons: Is There a Choice?" in *Living with Nuclear Weapons* (Cambridge, Mass.: Harvard University Press, 1983), pp. 233–55.

The either/or mentality can also lead to a false sense of despair, with very unfortunate consequences. Belief that nuclear war is inevitable can counsel a resignation or fatalism which would divert energy from practical political steps and thus make war more likely.

Modest steps matter. In the short run, we can take steps to reduce the probability of nuclear war, while gradually trying to improve international relations. And a future made up of short runs which improve by 1% a year would mean a dramatically different world within our children's lifetimes.

We do not belittle the central question raised by the either/or approach: Is nuclear war inevitable in a world of deterrence? The answer depends on two other questions: How long are we talking about? What else is going to happen?

Since humans are neither perfect nor perfectly rational, it would be foolish to deny that there is some chance of deterrence failing. . . . Even if that chance were low, it would eventually occur if the situation went on long enough. Eventually even the most skillful juggler is likely to drop a ball. But if there is enough time, the situation can be changed; the juggling game can be cautiously brought to an end. Or to alter the metaphor, if two people who strongly dislike each other are locked in a small room and armed only with hand grenades, it is not inevitable that they will blow each other up; they may eventually learn how to live together.

. . . [N]uclear disarmament may be an appropriate goal for the long term, but its successful achievement depends upon political preconditions and trust that can only be built slowly. Conventional weapons would still exist and the danger of conventional war might be increased if nuclear disarmament came too quickly. Moreover, premature disarmament in the absence of such political preconditions could enhance the risks of renewed nuclear arms races and wars. But if there is enough time—that is, if we continually take steps to reduce the risk of nuclear war—then the situation may change.

The nuclear dilemma is serious, the most serious danger mankind faces. But there is no reason to assume that absolute solutions—either holocaust or disarmament—are the only answers mankind is capable of developing. History shows that many important events have occurred in international relations over long periods of time. War is not the inevitable result of a rivalry between two nations. It has not been so in the past and need not be so in the future. It is especially misleading to focus on current dangers of war and to think that the technical and political environment of the future will remain unchanged while the future probability of war increases. Other factors that influence the likelihood of war can change too. Many future worlds are possible. . . .

TRENDS IN ARMS AND ARMS CONTROL

Two very important developments in nuclear weaponry could occur by 2020. The system of nuclear deterrence, which has since 1945 depended on the threat of retaliation, might in the future be based on defensive weaponry. Arms control, which has had limited, although still important, success thus far in the nuclear age might have more significant influence in the future.

The difficulties that have plagued efforts to build a defense against nuclear weapons in the past will continue to exist in the future. But unforeseen technological advances might possibly increase the prospects of what strategists call a "defense-dominated" nuclear system. There is little reason to expect such a technological switch from offense to defense, but it is not out of the question.

In such a world the consequences of a breakdown of deterrence might be less catastrophic than in the current world of near total mutual vulnerability. And, depending on the technology used, the incentives for increased arms racing might be diminished. That is the good news with respect to defensive systems. The bad news is that the degree to which such an evolution in nuclear deterrence would reduce the likelihood of war is not clear. . . .

WORRIES AND DILEMMAS

. . . The superpowers face two formidable dilemmas. On the one hand, if deterrence is entirely successful in averting any resort to nuclear weapons, won't nations feel more confident again about launching conventional wars? But if in order to deter these one tries to lower the nuclear threshold—to take measures that suggest a plausible early use of nuclear weapons—won't such measures be dangerous (and scare one's own population or allies)? On the other hand, once nuclear weapons have been used, what are the possibilities of control? A limited and selective use may appear controllable, but what if it fails to stop an opponent: does one then accept defeat rather than escalate? . . .

CONCLUSION: AVOIDING ATOMIC ESCAPISM

. . . Atomic escapism must be avoided. One form of escapism is to believe that nuclear weapons will go away. They will not. Because they will not, mankind must learn to live with them if we are to live at all. The other form of escapism is to think that nuclear weapons can be treated like other military weapons in history. They cannot. And because they are different, humanity must live with them carefully, vigilantly, gingerly, always displaying the utmost caution. . . .

QUESTIONS FOR DISCUSSION

1 Do fears about the prospects of nuclear war make wars with conventional weapons more likely to occur?
2 Are there any political or military conditions in which a conventional war between the United States and the Soviet Union would be likely to lead to a nuclear war?
3 Would the use of nuclear weapons in war ever be a rational instrument of national policy?
4 What is the difference between war with conventional weapons and war with nuclear weapons?
5 Is nuclear war likely to occur in this century? Why?

SUGGESTED READINGS

Baugh, William H. *The Politics of Nuclear Balance: Ambiguity and Continuity in Strategic Policies.* New York: Longman, 1984.

Brodie, Bernard (ed.). *The Absolute Weapon.* New York: Harcourt, Brace, 1946.

Carlton, David and Carlo Schaerf (eds.). *The Arms Race in the 1980s.* London: Macmillan, 1982.

Freedman, Lawrence. *The Evolution of Nuclear Strategy.* New York: St. Martin's Press, 1981.

Gompert, David C., Michael Mandelbaum, Richard L. Garwin, and John H. Barton. *Nuclear Weapons and World Politics.* New York: McGraw-Hill Book Company (for the Council on Foreign Relations/1980s Project), 1977.

The Harvard Nuclear Study Group. *Living with Nuclear Weapons.* New York: Bantam Books, 1983.

Kennan, George F. *The Nuclear Delusion: Soviet-American Relations in the Atomic Age.* New York: Pantheon Books, 1983.

Mandelbaum, Michael. *The Nuclear Revolution: International Politics Before and After Hiroshima.* New York: Cambridge University Press, 1981.

Powers, Thomas. *Thinking About the Next War.* New York: Knopf, 1982.

Russett, Bruce. *The Prisoners of Insecurity: Nuclear Deterrence, the Arms Race, and Arms Control.* San Francisco, California: W. H. Freeman & Co., 1983.

2 Is Nuclear Deterrence a Bankrupt Ideology?

YES

James A. Stegenga

Nuclear Deterrence: Bankrupt Ideology

NO

Caspar W. Weinberger

[*On Deterrence*]

Nuclear Deterrence: Bankrupt Ideology
James A. Stegenga

Faith is believin' what you know ain't true.

Mark Twain

The cornerstone of United States defense policy is nuclear deterrence: trying and confidently expecting to persuade the Soviet Union not to attack the United States, its allies, or its vital interests by threatening nuclear counterattack. For thirty-odd years now American national security managers have largely relied on this approach of deterring the Soviet Union by making threats of retaliatory damage they felt any sensible Soviet leader would find an unacceptable cost of any substantial contemplated aggression against the West.

The retaliatory damage would be inflicted by some or most of America's strategic nuclear warheads, numbering in the hundreds during the 1960s and numbering about 9000 in the early 1980s. They would be delivered to their targets by some or most of several hundred long-range bombers and several thousand ballistic missiles launched from North America and from submarines at sea. The targets of the promised devastation vary from one formulation to the next: Soviet society, Soviet cities, the Soviet population, Soviet military forces or troops or bases or equipment, war-supporting Soviet industry and infrastructure, the political apparatus that enables the Soviet elite to retain control, a complex mix of some or all of these targets. The retaliation might be rapid and "massive," with thousands of warheads delivered in a matter of a few hours onto their designated targets, resulting, according to one popular standard, in the immediate destruction of 50% of Soviet industry and the death of 50% of the urban population of the Soviet Union. Or the retaliation might be more graduated, controlled, and "limited," with a few dozen or a few hundred warheads delivered accurately to chiefly military targets and resulting in the death of "only" a few million Soviet citizens from "collateral" damage, radiation, and dislocations to an already-fragile Soviet economy. Common to all the formulations is the notion of dissuading Soviet aggression by threatening punishment.

Reliance upon and confidence in this approach to protecting the nation's safety and interests seems to have become almost an unquestioned article of faith among Americans. This article will argue, first, that nuclear deterrence has become an ideology or a quasi-ideological phenomenon, our embrace of it the embrace of the faithful. Second, the article offers a critical assessment of nuclear deterrence, recognizing the formidable obstacles to developing such an evaluation but nonetheless raising questions about both the reliability and the propriety of nuclear deterrence, suggesting that it may be a bankrupt ideology. When its intellectual properties are tested against social science knowledge and its moral implications are judged against moral principles, nuclear deterrence is found to be an alarmingly shaky cornerstone.[1]

I

An ideology is a set of interrelated sociopolitical beliefs or convictions.[2] But it is more than that. It is a particular *sort* of set, distinguishable from a

---

[1] The author gratefully acknowledges helpful comments from Peter de Leon, Carl Builder, and Bruce Bennett.

[2] The operational definition of ideology sketched in this section draws heavily on Giovanni Sartori (1969) and Edward Shils (1968).

From *Policy Sciences*, Vol. 16, No. 2 (1983). Elsevier Science Publishers, Amsterdam, The Netherlands.

mere sociopolitical program or outlook in several important ways.

It is, first, *elaborately developed* and more explicitly formulated in detail than a program or outlook. Typically, an ideology is elaborately derived from or built around a key concept or two; salvation might be seen as Christianity's key concept, property rights as capitalism's. Sometimes the ideology is so elaborated or developed that it can be looked to for an answer to most or all important sociopolitical questions (Marxism, say, or Islam). But such comprehensiveness probably ought not be regarded as an essential element; centrality or importance in the cultural/sociopolitical scheme of things is probably enough. As a fully-elaborated, comprehensive set of beliefs or as a less-than-comprehensive set of beliefs about central concerns or values, an ideology will set the outer limits on and shape subordinate programmatic activities.

Sometimes the ideology is expressed in a single authoritative promulgation or near-sacred text (Lenin's writings, the Koran). But not always; a looser, somewhat less coherent and somewhat less authoritative collection of sources can probably be taken as sufficient (the several key founding documents of the United States, perhaps). Some writers (e.g., Shils, 1968) contend that an ideology must be born of alienation, must entail a rejection of or reaction against established culture, orthodoxy, institutions. However, other authors (Marx, Mannheim) insist that an ideology can itself be or become the orthodoxy, affirming and defending the status quo; Western liberalism (or democracy) and Soviet Marxism-Leninism stand as examples of official ideologies.

A second feature of ideologies, as distinct from programs or outlooks, is their *closed, dogmatic* character. Whether comprehensive or "merely" central, authoritative or diffuse, deviant or orthodox, ideologies are inflexible if not rigid, ideologists are doctrinaire if not fanatical. Ideologies and ideologists are resistant to change, to innovation, to contrary evidence, to argument, to reason. Frequently they become arrogant and pretentious, perhaps in their subconscious attempts to mask insecurity with stridency. Insofar as sociopolitical knowledge is constantly changing, a closed ideology will—at least eventually—involve important distortions of truth, though it may also include accurate, valid facts, assertions, and theories.

Third, ideologies are *idealistic* in that they (and their exponents) claim to strive for some higher, transcendent aims and principles. The quest is for something noble, even sacred or at least moral. Spiritual values and symbols are frequently shrouded in mystical rituals conducted by theologians invoking prophets and priests employing scriptures. The list of aims espoused by one or another of the world's dominant ideologies would include such worthies as justice, self-government, salvation, equality, and freedom.

Fourth, ideologies entail a strong *affective* or emotive element. Ideologies involve passion, intensity. They include beliefs and convictions strongly felt, ideas emotionally embraced rather than "merely" thought. Commitment to salvation through faith or to equality or the class struggle may begin as an intellectual activity, but it becomes eventually an intensely emotional involvement as the thinker becomes the true believer. Over time these thoughts converted into beliefs become unquestioned "givens," so taken for granted that to question them at first puzzles the believer and next leads him to suspect disloyalty or at least deviance in the questioner. For together with intense belief goes a sense of urgency of application, proselytizing demands for acceptance and observance. Ideologies and ideologists are *demanding;* they demand agreement, subservience, and obedience. And, of course, as such, they carry authoritarian seeds or tendencies.

A fifth and, for our purposes, final special feature of ideologies is their tendency to generate and inspire the *ideological primary in-group* of believers, sharers, comrades. Led by the often charismatic promulgators, the insiders develop an institutionalized collective membership of the elect, the true believers, the custodians of the faith who cultivate solidarity among themselves and promote loyalty to the dogmas they protect.

II

It seems possible, without stretching things too much, to see nuclear deterrence as an ideology thus defined. Nuclear deterrence involves an elaborately developed set of convictions, quite stable over time (maybe even closed), idealistic in intent, emotionally embraced by nearly all, especially by the insiders.

"Nuclear deterrence" is a convenient shorthand label for a complex, elaborately-developed collection of facts, beliefs, assertions, theories, and aims built around the central core value of communal safety or national security (or "peace through strength"). As an ideology, it serves as the foundation of United States defense policy, supporting and limiting and shaping such dependent and resultant programmatic things as budgets and weapons systems acquisition, deployment, and tactical (usage) policies.

Though there is no single authoritative promulgation of the ideology of deterrence, the annual budget or "posture" statements of defense secretaries come close and are remarkably similar from administration to administration. Or perhaps a better candidate for sacred text of the nuclear deterrence ideology would be the Single Integrated Operational Plan (SIOP), the master list of Soviet targets and the American warheads aimed at them, the major document guiding the faithful, guarded and continuously revised by an inner circle of specially-selected technicians working deep within isolated control centers. A few dozen academic strategists (Thomas Schelling, Bernard Brodie, Albert Wohlstetter) might be viewed as subordinate scribes refining and interpreting the official orthodoxy from such satellite sanctuaries as the Rand Corporation, the Hudson Institute, and various prestigious universities.[3] The ideology of deterrence might even be seen as a reaction against and replacement for traditional military doctrines rendered obsolete by mid-twentieth century weapons and communications technology; the warriors of

the 1950s were not pleased to have to accept Bernard Brodie's dictum that henceforth their principal, new role would be to prevent, rather than to fight, wars (Brodie, 1946).

As noted, nuclear deterrence doctrines have remained stable over time, prompting Warner R. Schilling, for example, to write recently (1981:59):

> one could have gone to sleep during the strategic nuclear debate in 1970, awakened in 1980, and rejoined that debate with remarkably little sense of intellectual loss or confusion.

The basic notion—of threatening retaliation to deter attack and working to develop the capability to carry out the threat and to demonstrate the willingness to do so—have not changed since the 1940s, despite the advent of new weapons, changed political realities, differing administrations in Washington, and a rearmed Soviet Union. The exponent of nuclear deterrence would ascribe this resistance to change to the fundamental soundness of the doctrine; but it might also be a reflection of the closed nature of the doctrine and the doctrinaire, settled minds of two generations of supporters. These supporters have along the way also pretentiously cloaked nuclear deterrence in the garb of science (systems analysis, operations research, computer-assisted simulations) to impress a society inclined to be more impressed if values, beliefs, and social policies can be thus tricked up, made to look scientific, even if crude distortions result (see Green, 1968; Fallows, 1981: 139–170).

The ideology of nuclear deterrence centers, of course, on the quest for such idealistic, almost spiritual, aims as national security, liberty and other human rights, sovereign independence, peace, preserving the American Way of Life. These values are invoked in official pronouncements and symbolically employed, as with the motto of the U.S. Air Force's Strategic Air Command: Peace Is Our Profession.

Nuclear deterrence is emotionally embraced by elites and masses alike. It has become so central, so entrenched, so faithfully relied upon that it has

---

[3]James Fallows (1981) examines their views in his chapter six, entitled, significantly, "Theologians."

become one of the "given:" in American political discourse. From Barry Goldwater on the right to George McGovern and beyond on the left, regardless of race, age, religion, sex, or class, nearly all Americans—who would disagree among themselves on most other sociopolitical issues or programs—faithfully subscribe to nuclear deterrence as The Cornerstone. One has only to imagine the fate of an American politician who announced that he did not believe in nuclear deterrence and would work, if elected, to dismantle the edifice; perhaps threatening Social Security would be the only quicker path to political oblivion. The occasional critic of nuclear deterrence is regarded as naive, peculiar, possibly disloyal by the sometimes belligerently defensive enthusiast who has usually done little or no *thinking* on the matter but still is convinced, "on faith," of the virtues of nuclear deterrence. The few thoughtful critiques of nuclear deterrence (e.g., Green, 1968) appear to have shaken the conviction of very few people or resulted in any substantial doctrinal amendments. It is hard to find anyone uncertain in his faith in nuclear deterrence; excepting only a scattering of doubters, pacifists, worriers, and moralists, nearly all Americans are Believers.

Finally, of course, the ideology of nuclear deterrence has generated the primary in-group of sharers, believers, promulgators, and custodians:

- the political elite, regardless of their other differing outlooks and programs;
- uniformed military personnel, especially senior officers;
- the academic strategists and "think tank" defense analysts;
- the "lesser disseminators" in universities and the media, both general and specialized; and
- the manufacturers of the strategic arsenal and their publicists.

Sharing the assumption that nuclear deterrence is The Answer, the proper and reliable cornerstone, they debate how best to implement or strengthen or stabilize it. They attend conferences where nuclear deterrence itself is not questioned, their ar-

ticles are published in serious quarterlies edited by fellow believers. Even arms control enthusiasts mostly accept nuclear deterrence as the cornerstone, limiting their goals to implementing deterrence with fewer warheads, or at less cost, with better safeguards and controls.

So nuclear deterrence seems to fall within our definition of ideology. At the very least, it seems fair to think of nuclear deterrence as a quasi-ideological or ideology-like phenomenon.

III

Before examining nuclear deterrence, before questioning its merits, it will be well to recognize the analytical implications of concluding that nuclear deterrence can be understood as an ideology, its exponents as ideologists. Two implications seem especially pertinent.

If nuclear deterrence is an ideology (or an ideology-like phenomenon), at least some part of an assessment of its merits ought to show awareness of this special ideological character. That is, nuclear deterrence ought, at least in part, to be evaluated as an ideology. This approach would especially invite examination of the beliefs, the convictions emotionally embraced by the faithful; nuclear deterrence invites the examination of the moral philosopher with his questions. At the same time, if nuclear deterrence is an ideology like most—closed and dogmatic, resistant to evidence and reason—it naturally invites skeptical scrutiny by the social scientists able to bring to bear scientific or quasi-scientific knowledge about political behavior, the latest evidence and best reasoned interpretations about the real world that the ideology must accommodate successfully if it is to be judged meritorious.

Secondly, treating nuclear deterrence as an ideology to be evaluated puts the analyst on notice regarding the difficulties, obstacles, and resistance apt to be encountered. Critically examining an ideology, questioning matters of faith, grappling with beliefs emotionally embraced is more likely to be frustrating than critically examining a mere program or policy or outlook bearing little or no emotional baggage. The faithful can be expected to smile patronizingly, to snicker smugly, to invoke authority or special knowledge inaccessible to outsiders, to deny plain facts, to refuse serious debate on fundamentals, to ignore telling arguments, to retreat into defensiveness, or to make various accusations of naiveté, deviance, even disloyalty. Nuclear deterrence and its exponents, like any ideology and its ideologists, must be regarded as slippery subjects for examination, formidable targets for the would-be critical analyst.

But vulnerable. Vulnerable to the two kinds of examination just alluded to: that of the social scientist and that of the moral philosopher. The social scientist can raise enough troubling questions about the validity of the basic assumptions, assertions, and theories that have become the beliefs of nuclear deterrence to make us doubt its *reliability,* its practical effectiveness as the intellectual/ideological underpinnings for an array of political/military programs and activities. And the moral philosopher can raise enough troubling questions about propriety of nuclear deterrence and all that it entails and implies to make us conclude that it may be a morally bankrupt ideology, calling into question the morality of this same array of political/military programs and activities.

IV

The social sciences, as "soft" and primitive as they are, have developed a great deal of knowledge about the behavior of people, including those people who operate the world's governments and their military machines. And most of what we now know (and are daily discovering and refining) about the very human behavior of political/military decisionmakers should make us skeptical about the rosy picture the confident exponents of nuclear deterrence paint.

According to the ideology of nuclear deterrence, the government in Moscow can be counted upon to behave like a rational, or at least sensible or reasonable, individual person. It will value national survival more than any other goal. It will be well-informed. It will carefully calculate all the consequences and all the pros and cons of each option in every crisis. It will tightly control the actions of subordinates. It will cautiously adopt limited objectives in the international arena so as not to incur American wrath and revenge. It will remain a dependable custodian of nuclear weapons of awesome lethality indefinitely, or for the next few decades anyway. So deterrence—the ideology insists—is the answer, the permanently reliable response to the danger of nuclear apocalypse.

And yet. The Soviet government is run by a collection of people. The "It" of all those sentences in the preceding paragraph is a convenient writer's shorthand that may cause us to lose sight of the reality: "It" is really "They," a collection of Soviet leaders, of people.

And, as we know from history, psychology, sociology, political science, and our own common experiences, people can be counted upon to behave sensibly only part of the time, unreasonably, foolishly, even irrationally and self-destructively the rest. Frequently throughout history they have held some things more dear than "mere" individual or national survival; honor and glory come to mind as transcendent values frequently invoked. To some extent people are also usually captives of habit or ideology; we think of Moscow's leaders as at least to some extent ideologically inspired or motivated in their policymaking. An ideological component in decisionmaking, passion and fervor, generally erodes rationality.

These same rulers may be poorly informed, especially about secrecy-shrouded military capabilities and intentions. Nuclear deterrence, of course, involves deliberate ambiguities: Moscow is supposed to be kept guessing, be kept off guard and thus more fearful and cautious as Washington keeps obscure the precise circumstances that would trigger American nuclear retaliation as well as the precise form the retaliation would take. (Would the American president order retaliation if the Soviet Union invaded Norway or Saudi Arabia? If West Berlin or the Guantanamo base in Cuba was seized?

If a United States submarine near Soviet waters or a United States warship in the Mediterranean were destroyed? If some military targets in continental United States were destroyed? No one can know, perhaps least of all Soviet leaders with their inevitably sketchy understanding of America and Americans.) Though perhaps useful in promoting deterrence, these deliberate ambiguities might also understandably allow the misperceptions, misunderstandings, delusions, and miscalculations usually found too late to have led up to the major and minor wars of the twentieth century (Stoessinger, 1981).

The problem may be compounded when such decisions are made by small groups of people rather than by single individuals. What psychologist Irving Janis (1982) calls "groupthink" sets in, with all the members of the decisionmaking group so anxious to get along with each other, maintain their power positions, appease the group leader, and push the interests of their respective bureaucracies that they suspend the critical thinking required for sensible decisionmaking. Not knowing very well what goes on behind the closed doors of the Kremlin, we tend to exaggerate the unity and underestimate the diversity of the collective Soviet leadership, thus neglecting the role of those non-rational bureaucratic politics and "groupthink" factors we almost automatically look for when analyzing the somewhat more visible policymaking process of Western governments. In the very political processes of the Kremlin that we occasionally glimpse, we see at work some of those factors degrading the unitary rationality that nuclear deterrence ideology assumes.

The problem is certainly further aggravated in a crisis situation when time pressures, poorer information, fear, exhaustion, higher stakes and risks, and a tendency toward belligerent posturing for domestic consumption all cause a deterioration in the already reduced level of rationality we can expect from the nervous officials at the controls. A rich literature has demonstrated that perception, cognition, and decisionmaking are all adversely affected by the extreme stresses a crisis entails

(Holsti, 1972; Jervis, 1976). Aged and sometimes ailing men under extreme stress are more likely to make potentially catastrophic mistakes than they are to make exclusively the sensible decisions the ideology confidently insists they will always make. Concern about Richard Nixon's mental balance near the end of his days in office led his Secretary of Defense James Schlesinger to advise military commanders to double-check with him before executing any dramatic commands from their troubled Commander-in-Chief. Similar concerns were expressed about the late Soviet leader Brezhnev, obviously ill and heavily medicated in his final year in office but still possibly in control of Soviet strategic forces. It is one of the paradoxes of the nuclear era that the junior officers manning the American strategic forces (and probably the Soviet's) are screened and continuously scrutinized by psychologists to try to weed out the dangerously unstable, while no such screening is employed to be sure their civilian superiors remain as sensible (if not perfectly rational) as nuclear deterrence ideology requires and confidently asserts them to be.

Social science and common experience also cast doubt on another key assumption of nuclear deterrence: the leader's tight, near-perfect control of a large number of subordinates in a complex organization spread over a huge country and beyond at sea. For nuclear deterrence to be as dependable as its exponents suggest it is, the possibility for human error or communications breakdown or unauthorized action must be reduced to near zero; this is clearly a difficult if not impossible task, people, organizations, and machines being what they are. Mechanical errors or computer failures must also be eliminated or reduced to near zero, another formidable task, as we know from reports of problems in the American military machinery that we are told—not very reassuringly, actually—is more sophisticated and more carefully operated by more carefully screened functionaries than is the Soviet machinery. How confident can we be that the collective leadership in Moscow has such tight control over its strategic forces that a single rogue Soviet ICBM launch officer or submarine commander cannot independently send his missiles with multiple warheads towards dozens of American targets? How confident can we be that the Soviet Union's surveillance satellites, radars, sensors, and computers—all technologically primitive compared to those of the United States—will not malfunction disastrously, leading to the catastrophe?

We also know that positive inducements and rewards work better than negative sanctions and punishments. Threats are usually the least effective way of eliciting desired behavior: they arouse debilitating fears and anxieties; they stimulate defiance and counter threats; they hinder compromise and constructive problem solving. We try to apply this knowledge in child rearing, in education, in social relationships, in industry, and in commerce. Within the military itself, the effective commander knows how to manipulate inducements rather than foolishly rely on threats to assure the obedience of his troops. Yet as a people we place our principal reliance—our faith—in the basically negative approach of nuclear deterrence, despite our knowledge that such sanction-oriented methods of eliciting behavior are less than perfectly effective or reliable and are, in fact, usually counterproductive and even dangerous. Only in the terribly important superpower relationship do we assume that this primitive approach will always work, will work better than any other, may be the *only* approach that will work to influence Soviet leaders who are inconsistently characterized by the ideologists of nuclear deterrence as both sophisticated *and* beyond the reach of positive inducements, as sensible and calculating enough to be deterred by threats but *not* enough to be persuaded by rewards for cooperative behavior.

Can Americans—and others naturally enough interested in the outcomes—really trust the Soviet system always to work so well, producing wise leadership groups that will behave so sensibly and run everything so well on into the 1990s and beyond even in the gravest crises? Most of us understand psychology, politics, and technology too well to have that kind of confidence in the perfor-

mance of *any* political system, perhaps especially a highly personalistic authoritarian regime lacking institutionalized controls on executive discretion and operating very fragile machinery that must never malfunction. Paradoxically, those Americans (and Europeans and others) most critical and suspicious of the Soviet government, who ought to have the gravest doubts about Kremlin dependability are, nonetheless, the staunchest and most confident supporters of nuclear deterrence doctrines and attendant weapons systems and budgets. They profess to see Soviet leaders as too ambitious, too zealous, too ruthless, too casual about human life, too little concerned with civilized values, too different from more traditional Western leaders to be trusted . . . except with nuclear weapons.

"But," someone is sure to say, "deterrence has worked pretty well these past thirty-plus years, hasn't it?" Can we really be sure, though? Perhaps, like the fellow standing on the corner waving his arms and blowing a whistle who had managed to convince himself that he was thereby successfully keeping the elephants from attacking, we have convinced ourselves that the only reason the Russians have not conquered Europe is because we have frightened them into restraint. They, of course, have likewise managed to convince themselves that the only reason their empire has not been dismantled and their system overthrown by sanctimonious Westerners is that they have frightened us into abandoning such goals. Historians may well conclude that neither side's leaders ever had the intentions the other side's leaders feared and thought they had discouraged with threats of nuclear retaliation.

And, anyway, even if it could somehow be shown that nuclear deterrence has kept the peace for the past thirty-odd years, these same historians would be quick to point out that thirty years is not a very long time, that devices for keeping the peace in other times have worked as long only to fail later, that deterrence itself has been confidently tried countless times throughout history, failing repeatedly because the adversary did not believe the threats or miscalculated relative strengths or called the bluff or got carried away by popular or ideological passions.

It ought to be clear to all of us that deterrence—really a form of applied psychology—is historically, psychologically, and politically naive to a dangerous degree; our confidence in it is quite unwarranted. Americans (and others) are now betting their lives that the Soviet leaders will remain, in perpetuity, dependable custodians of thermonuclear weapons. It requires a great leap of faith in men and machines to remain so confident of nuclear deterrence, to believe that in this critical arena Murphy's Law and all its corollaries can be forever avoided.[4]

One of these days—if, alas, nuclear weapons are unleashed—perhaps the survivors will say: "Of course deterrence was bound to fail; how silly that we ever had any faith in it!"

V

A close examination of the *moral* implications of the ideology of nuclear deterrence likewise yields disturbing findings. Nuclear deterrence involves and implies a number of immoral actions that will here be usefully, though perhaps a little crudely, sorted into three categories:

1. Nuclear deterrence involves or contemplates, first, actions difficult if not impossible to reconcile with the moral obligations and codes supposed to govern states and statesmen in the global community.

Deterrence doctrine openly contemplates the deliberate killing of tens of millions of people, most of them innocent noncombatants. By most accounts, even a "limited" attack with accurate missiles carefully aimed only at military targets would kill millions of Soviet noncombatants, either quickly

because many military targets are located in heavily populated areas or slowly from radioactivity or the results of the serious economic dislocations sure to follow even a limited nuclear strike. In the authoritarian countries against which the United States would retaliate, the citizens have so little to say about their government's decisions that they could hardly be deemed culpable of aggression and thus "deserving" of punishment. And in neighboring countries not even parties to the quarrel, the citizens and ecological support systems would nonetheless suffer permanent radioactive poisoning. This disproportionate and indiscriminate genocidal and ecological destruction could hardly be deemed justifiable violence sanctioned by the dominant just war tradition with its central demands that violence must be proportionate and discriminating. Measured against the stricter tests of Christian (or humanist) pacifism grounded in the sanctity of the person, the death and destruction threatened would be even more unacceptable morally.

The only purpose that could be served by the retaliation, by carrying out the threat if deterrence fails, would be vengeance. It can be argued that vengeance of this magnitude could not possibly be reconciled with the Western moral tradition in any of its various versions. Indeed, in some of its versions, no vengeance of *any* sort is sanctioned.

The moral status of the deterrent *threat* can even be called into question. Even if the retaliation is never ordered, is the *threat* to do it immoral in itself? Many ethicists have answered that it is wrong to *threaten* to do something if to actually *do* it would be wrong, that *intending* and *preparing* to do evil are themselves wicked acts.

Such threats to use force and violence also appear to be prohibited by Article 2(4) of the United Nations Charter:

> All members shall refrain in their international relations from the threat or use of force against the territorial integrity or political independence of any state, or in any other manner inconsistent with the Purposes of the United Nations.

---

[4]Murphy's Law: Whatever Can Go Wrong Will. One of the better, more relevant corollaries: If there is a possibility of several things going wrong, the one that will cause the most damage will be the one to go wrong.

The Charter is a treaty that has been incorporated into the law of the land which United States officials are solemnly sworn to uphold.[5] It might also be seen as a partial codification of an emergent global consensus on some basic values and rules of conduct in international relations.

It would seem difficult, too, to justify the threat of nuclear retaliation or its execution as legitimate self defense, authorized by Article 51 of the United Nations Charter, since defense of the victims of a nuclear first strike is not possible and not promised or involved in the threat to retaliate; rather, the government threatens, on behalf of the victims, to harm the attackers' relatives. We would not call it self defense if the mugger's victim, after helplessly and passively absorbing the assault, burned down the mugger's grandmother's home late the following night. We would regard as quite improper a *threat* of this sort of revenge made ahead of time by a person understandably fearful of being mugged and eager to deter would-be muggers. Or, as Michael Walzer suggests (1977:272), we would not deem it proper public policy to try to discourage murder by threatening punishment of a murderer's children.

If the threat is a mere bluff that the leaders deep down inside have no intention of carrying out, if they say to themselves that they are not guilty because they are not *truly* intending an evil act, the ethicist can still charge them with the guilt of implicating thousands of subordinate officers on down the chain of command, people ordered to form an intention to carry out the retaliation, people wrongly ordered into an immoral posture.

Further, nuclear deterrence doctrine holds whole peoples as hostages, thus apparently violating the strictures of many moral codes against treating human life as a means, even though the Soviet "hostages" are not confined or very much inconvenienced in this particular arrangement. We generally

condemn "terrorists" who seize hostages and use them, even if the hostages are not physically harmed but "only" psychologically traumatized (as, for example, the Americans held for fifteen months in the American embassy in Teheran). Psychologists suggest that living under the mushroom cloud is psychologically harmful to those held hostage by the nuclear threat (Lifton and Falk, 1982). If the ruffians in Teheran are guilty of this charge of wrongfully using hostages and causing trauma, the senior officers of the American government might likewise be judged guilty of the same crime against innocent Russian hostages.

Successful deterrence requires vulnerable hostage peoples, but leaders who are protected so that they can remain in control. While they shelter themselves from attack, the leaders must leave their charges unprotected; this raises important moral questions about the presumably fundamentally protective obligations of government. And a shelter system for a privileged elite should make both ordinary American citizens and American officials alike morally uncomfortable.

Deterrence leads inevitably to a preoccupation, almost an obsession, with credibility since the continuous task is to persuade the opponent that one's essentially incredible threat is, in fact, credible. Each quarrel or controversial situation then becomes a test, thus stimulating overreactions, increased readiness (almost eagerness) for interventions everywhere, the search for opportunities to prove credibility, resolve, toughness. No situation anywhere can be ignored or even handled softly, lest Moscow read the results as indicating that American resolve is weakening. Proper caution and morally prudent statecraft are put at risk. Numerous illustrations could be cited, but two should suffice. In May 1975, newly-installed President Gerald Ford and his advisors, headed by Secretary of State Henry Kissinger, gave the impression that they almost welcomed the Cambodian government's seizure of the "Mayaguez" so that the amiable new president could dramatically send in the marines, thereby signaling to Moscow that he was just as tough, just

---

[5]For a recent analysis that concludes that it would be illegal to carry out the threat to devastate Soviet society but not illegal to *threaten* to do so, see Builder and Graubard (1982).

as capable of using violence, as his predecessors. In May 1983, President Ronald Reagan, urging the Congress to support his request for increased military involvement in Central America, invoked the fear that to deny him the aid would indicate to adversaries on the far side of the Atlantic that the United States had lost its will to such an extent that its deterrent threats would no longer be credible. So the requirements of effective deterrence appear to contribute to a crisis climate that results over time in a continuous supreme emergency which is then invoked to license the extreme act of genocidal slaughter promised if deterrence fails.

The deterrent threats usually leave the triggering conditions ambiguous (supposedly to stimulate uncertainty and thus caution as well as to discourage aggressive movement right up to the line drawn, arguably too precisely, in the sand). But this calculated ambiguity seems unfair in that it improperly misleads, confuses, tempts. The ambiguous threat improperly involves unnecessary risk. And the threatening leader is at least partially morally responsible for any catastrophic accidents or misjudgments by the other party. For thirty-odd years American leaders have coyly refused to say precisely which Soviet actions would trigger precisely what sorts of retaliatory responses, leaving it to the Soviet leaders to guess or imagine what was in the minds of American leaders they hardly knew and understood but poorly. One can envisage World War III beginning not like World War II (with the very clear "bolt from the blue" attacks that were perhaps almost unavoidable) but rather more like World War I (whose beginnings were much more confused and full of blunders); the leaders of such a World War III might reasonably blame each other's coyness and ambiguous signals for the catastrophe, with whatever surviving historians and ethicists nodding their assent.

Ethicists and others have suggested that it is immoral for the wealthy superpowers to devote scarce resources, talents, and energies to maintaining their nuclear deterrents in a world plagued with poverty, ecological deterioration, and resource depletion.

Churchmen, Third World writers, even bankers and such figures as former President Dwight Eisenhower have argued that nuclear deterrence and the associated arms spending constitute a form of theft from the poor as the spending for implementing deterrence prevents the rich from discharging their humanitarian obligations. As Eisenhower put it in April of 1953, early in his eight years as president:

> Every gun that is made, every warship launched, every rocket fired, signifies in the final sense a theft from those who hunger and are not fed, those who are cold and are not clothed.

And the contemporary international system presided over by the superpowers encourages and seems to license the governments of impoverished countries to take their cues from the great powers and rely on expensive military programs, even nuclear weapons, to accomplish their own domestic and international political objectives, taking scarce resources from their own needy peoples. It is illogical and hypocritical for an American president to insist in one breath that military solutions are appropriate and nuclear weapons are indispensable . . . and then in the next breath to try to discourage a Third World leader's military programs and quest for prestigious nuclear weapons. As indicated previously, too, the need to continuously demonstrate credibility that nuclear deterrence entails drives United States policy in the direction of continuous, globalist interventionism, frequently on the side of repressive (though anticommunist) regimes. So the imperatives of nuclear deterrence ideology conveniently complement other ideological inclinations and commercial motivations to result in an immoral foreign policy of support for dictatorships and hostility toward progressive, even revolutionary, movements that the United States might otherwise tolerate, even support.

2. Nuclear deterrence entails activities difficult to reconcile with the rules any responsible, professional policy architect or official functionary is supposed to follow as conscientiously as possible while

he does his work. The professional ethical norms, the principles in the code of conduct supposed to govern public policy officials, have been too much ignored, bent, and violated in this critical policy field.

The official adoption of deterrence itself has involved various improprieties. As noted above in section IV, Western nuclear deterrence rests on numerous intellectual assumptions about human behavior, the historical process and record, alternatives, risks, probabilities, and political and bureaucratic processes in the imperfectly-understood Soviet Union. The faithful, confident American believer in nuclear deterrence is convinced of such propositions and predictions as: people respond predictably and appropriately to threats; military power translates into political/diplomatic efficacy; deterrence works, cooperation is naive or doubtful, appeasement whets appetites and leads to war; Soviet leaders are expansionist for historical or ideological reasons; countervailing force is the only language dictators understand; Moscow's collective leadership will always be sensible and prudent if faced with enough Western power and resolve; the balance of terror can be stabilized and controlled indefinitely; the peace is best kept by preparations for war.

But most of these propositions are at best dubious; hardly any are axiomatic or intuitively obvious or proven; few are well supported with evidence; several are circular or untestable or unfalsifiable, thus suspect; some have been refuted or discredited. The officials who created and implemented deterrence policies built upon these shaky assumptions can fairly be faulted for having acted in intellectually irresponsible fashion: they have acted too casually, too hastily, too confidently, too pretentiously, too dogmatically, thus intellectually and (thus, again) morally irresponsibly.

Similarly, it can be plausibly argued that the deterrent strategy (or approach) has never properly been compared with available (or imaginable) alternatives to see if its intellectual assumptions, likely effectiveness, costs, risks, and moral qualities are relatively superior. Such a comparison has been improperly neglected, even foreclosed by the claims and, worse, the demands of deterrence's sponsors for acceptance of their answer. It is frequently argued by the supporters of nuclear deterrence—even as they acknowledge its imperfections—that there is no alternative to it. But, of course, there are alternatives, alternatives that the over 160 countries in the world without nuclear weapons must practice or that writers have urged:

● development and deployment of some sort of technological defense against incoming Soviet missiles;
● national self defense with conventional weaponry;
● accommodations with powerful neighbors;
● an altered national standard of living to enable greater self-sufficiency that would reduce the "need" for a quasi-empire of suppliers, customers, military allies, sea lanes, and ideological associates continuously in need of protecting;
● preparations for sophisticated civilian resistance to discourage efforts at conquest;
● positive commercial inducements to cooperate instead of threats of negative military sanctions for noncooperation;
● pacifism coupled with hope and faith;
● constructive efforts to move beyond the inadequately-organized nation state system made obsolete by twentieth century technology, i.e., world federalism of some sort.

Some of these alternatives might be impractical or otherwise objectionable; but few would argue that they had all been properly evaluated or compared with nuclear deterrence and found inferior as a cornerstone for national security.

In common with other military approaches which tend to militarize politics and skew priorities, deterrence emphasizes prevention of military attack which would endanger such *penultimate* values as political sovereignty and territorial integrity. As national security is seen almost entirely in military terms, other threats to truly *ultimate* values of human rights and interests are not seen as military threats to sovereignty or territory and are thus unfortunately and irresponsibly discounted or neglected.[6]

Also improperly neglected are possible alternatives to retaliation or military defense against attack, alternatives that might yield sovereignty or territory but protect human life and preserve human rights, such as the non-violent and occasionally violent civilian resistance traditionally employed by conquered but undefeated peoples or threatened by the weak as a means of discouraging the strong from attacking.

3. Presumably, any official, regardless of political system, would have some obligation to try to perform in compliance with the professional and intellectual norms of the previous section, norms that have not been very faithfully met over the past thirty years, norms that the ideology of nuclear deterrence makes it difficult for a conscientious official to follow today. But an official in a *democratic* polity has an additional set of important norms supposed to govern his behavior, peculiarly democratic norms that nuclear deterrence endangers. The ideology of nuclear deterrence and the practices it supports are in some crucial ways anti-democratic (see Falk, 1982).

Nuclear deterrence involves the serious possibility of at least two sorts of morally troublesome deception. First, if the thermonuclear threat is a bluff that the leadership would not actually carry out, if there is a gulf between declaratory policy and action policy, this massive public deception raises the usual moral problems that deception raises, especially deception by public officials in a democracy grounded on an informed citizenry. If the

highest officials can, for years, dissemble about this most important matter, it will become too easy for them to lie on all manner of lesser matters. Second, if the leaders know, as they must, that deterrence might fail and they nevertheless still profess such confidence in it (partly to promote credibility), their confident, soothing reassurances involve improper deception damaging to the delicate bond of trust that should exist between the leaders and the citizenry in a democracy.

If retaliation decisions must be virtually automatic and instantaneous, the decisions can hardly be based on moral choice which requires time-consuming reflection and consideration of alternatives, as well as, in the American system, at least some role for the national legislature and even for public opinion. So nuclear deterrence demands immorally casual decisions, leaving decisionmakers with no choice but to act hastily and leaving citizens and even their elected representatives with no possibility of meaningful participation. As technology continues to yield quicker and ever more accurate missiles, making a disarming Soviet first strike at least theoretically possible, pressure mounts to adopt "launch on warning" policies ("Use 'em or lose 'em") or even to turn the enterprise over completely to fully automatic computer operation, thus heightening this particular moral problem of maintaining human, moral choice.

Nor can it truly be argued that the appropriate public debate has taken place. Rather, policies not very carefully or openly entered into forty years ago during wartime were altered slightly in the 1940s (replacing Hitler with Stalin, fascism with communism), continued, and rigidified into ideological (or quasi-ideological) form. In a fascinating piece of painstaking archival research, historian David Alan Rosenberg (1983) shows that momentum, technological possibilities, corporate pressures, bureaucratic and electoral politics, interservice rivalries, and various sorts of confusion and sloppiness characterized the development of United States strategic doctrine between 1945 and 1960. Throughout at least the earliest years of this period,

---

[6]Infringement of his human rights by the citizen's own government or harm to his well-being caused by harsh economic circumstances call forth less official concern than the remote chance that another country might attack and jeopardize those same rights or interests. Or the on-going destruction of New England's forests by acid rain arouses less official concern than a Soviet seizure of Maine's beaches would arouse, though acid rain is more of a real threat to the interests of all Americans, including the citizens of Maine.

public debate was improperly stifled by excessive secrecy and pretentious claims of expertise; later, debate was chilled by demands of unqualified support for nuclear deterrence (required, again, by the need to continuously buttress credibility). And here, too, of course, the moral question arises of whether science has been misused and language debased in the process of tricking up nuclear deterrence in scientific garb to make it respectable and appealing in a technological society.

Finally, the American society's core values that nuclear deterrence is supposedly designed to protect can themselves be seen as endangered by the nuclear deterrent itself. It is problematic for a traditionally liberal, humane polity governed by elected civilians to long endure even as:

● deterrence technology costs money that might have been spent on other social needs;
● military men and military thinking gain in political influence; and
● the society and its leaders become calloused by their acceptance of nuclear war as a possible instrument of national policy.

Adopting nuclear deterrence as the cornerstone of policy risks the slide to the garrison state operated by tough guys whose commitment to protecting human rights or their society's other liberal core values will decline as they inevitably come to regard them eventually as sentimental, dangerously anachronistic luxuries. All manner of compromises with and erosion of cherished rights and values are justified by reference to the imperatives of "national security" and the importance of tough stances to enhance the credibility of the deterrent threats. Social programs to meet human needs are cut back as "unaffordable." Military spending damages the general economy in numerous demonstrable ways. Frightened children lose confidence in a future of any sort. Individuals in a society whose respectable leaders are openly and calmly ready to incinerate the globe become themselves more inclined to employ violence and threats for their own personal ends. The nuclear deterrent corrupts the society that adopts it.

And if (when?) deterrence fails, whichever Americans survive will surely not enjoy the blessings of liberty and democracy during the extended harsh recuperative period under some form of martial law (if the society survives in any form at all).

So nuclear deterrence is the sort of *means* which itself endangers or surrenders the *ends* it is supposed to serve; as such, a nuclear deterrence must be regarded as quite vulnerable to the moral philosopher's critique.

After wrestling with these thorny issues and weighing the various contending arguments for several years, America's Catholic bishops, by an overwhelmingly one-sided vote, promulgated an important pastoral letter in April 1983 on the subject of nuclear war. Among their conclusions, the bishops argued that nuclear deterrence is morally odious, that it is barely tolerable as a shabby, temporary device for war avoidance, provided that serious efforts are being made by the powers to rid the earth of nuclear weapons. The pastoral letter does not elaborate on the reasoning behind this conclusion; but the bishops were evidently persuaded by arguments similar to some of those elaborated in the previous few pages of this essay.

VI

Nuclear deterrence as the ideological foundation for United States (and Western) security policy must, thus, be regarded as doubly unacceptable. Unacceptably unreliable, almost certain to fail eventually, with catastrophic consequences; unacceptably improper, morally bankrupt.

If this critique is persuasive, it reveals the weakness of so many recent prescriptions from various governments, arms control groups, and anxious individuals who want to "stabilize" or "improve" or "strengthen" the nuclear deterrence that they ought instead to be seeking to replace. Tinkering around the edges with a scheme so fundamentally flawed must be seen as pitifully inadequate. The mistake so many make is to accept nuclear deterrence as "given" and then to work from there; if the critique sketched in these pages is persuasive, nuclear deterrence must be abandoned as dangerous and repugnant.

Five centuries ago people still looked to moats and fortresses for their personal and communal safety, clung emotionally to the ideological underpinnings of feudalism, and sought ways within this given intellectual framework to "improve" their moats and fortresses to protect themselves against threats (from gunpowder, commerce, revolutionary ideals) that they could not quite see were undermining the entire feudal sociopolitical order. That ideological outlook and the security institutions and practices built upon it were doomed, destined to be replaced by the current, 400-year-old nation state system.

Today's situation, again largely a result of technological changes, may be similar to that prevailing in the fifteenth century. We are probably now living in the transition period between the age of nation states and whatever era is around the corner.

REFERENCES

Brodie, Bernard (1946). *The Absolute Weapon*. New York: Harcourt Brace.

Builder, Carl H. and Graubard, Morlie H. (1982). *The International Law of Armed Conflict: Implications For the Concept of Assured Destruction*. Santa Monica, California: The Rand Corporation. R-2804-FF.

Falk, Richard (1982). "Nuclear weapons and the end of democracy," *Praxis International* 2 (April): 1–11.

Fallows, James (1981). *National Defense*. New York: Random House.

Green, Philip (1968). *Deadly Logic: The Theory of Nuclear Deterrence*. Columbus, Ohio: Ohio State University Press.

Holsti, Ole R. (1972). *Crisis, Escalation, War*. Montreal: McGill University Press.

Janis, Irving, L. (1982). *Groupthink*. Boston: Houghton Mifflin Co.

Jervis, Robert (1976). *Perception and Misperception in International Politics*. Princeton: Princeton University Press.

Lifton, Robert Jay and Falk, Richard (1982). *Indefensible Weapons*. New York: Basic Books.

Rosenberg, David Alan (1983). "The origins of overkill: Nuclear weapons and American strategy, 1945–1960," *International Security* 7 (4): 3–71.

Sartori, Giovanni (1969). "Politics, ideology, and belief systems," *The American Political Science Review* LXIII (2): 398–411.

Schilling, Warner R. (1981). "U.S. strategic nuclear concepts in the 1970s: The search for sufficiently equivalent countervailing parity," *International Security* 6 (2): 49–79.

Shils, Edward (1968). "Ideology," in *Encyclopedia of the Social Sciences*. New York: Macmillan Company & The Free Press, Vol. 7, pp. 66–75.

Stoessinger, John G. (1981). *Why Nations Go to War*. New York: St. Martin's Press.

Walzer, Michael (1977). *Just and Unjust Wars*. New York: Basic Books.

Statement by Secretary of Defense Caspar W. Weinberger to the Senate (Excerpts) 14 December 1982

. . . Today, deterrence remains—as it has for the past thirty-seven years—the cornerstone of our strategic nuclear policy, and indeed, of our entire national security posture. Our strategy is a defensive one, designed to prevent attack—particularly nuclear attack—against us or our allies. To deter successfully, we must be able—and must be seen to be able—to retaliate against any potential ag-

From Caspar W. Weinberger, [On Deterrence], "Statement by Secretary of Defense Caspar W. Weinberger to the Senate," (Excerpts), December 14, 1982.

gressor in such a manner that the costs we will exact will substantially exceed any gains he might hope to achieve through aggression. We, for our part, are under no illusions about the consequences of a nuclear war: we believe there would be no winners in such a war. But this recognition on *our* part is not sufficient to ensure effective deterrence or to prevent the outbreak of war: it is essential that the Soviet leadership understands this as well. We must make sure that the *Soviet* leadership, in calculating the risks of aggression, recognizes that *because of our retaliatory capability, there can be no circumstance where the initiation of a nuclear war at any level or of any duration would make sense*. If they recognize that our forces can deny them their objectives at whatever level of conflict they contemplate, and in addition that such a conflict could lead to the destruction of those political, military, and economic assets which they value most highly, then deterrence is enhanced and the risk of war diminished. It is this outcome which we seek to achieve.

THE EVOLUTION OF U.S. STRATEGIC POLICY

During the late 1940s and early 1950s, America's virtual monopoly of intercontinental nuclear systems meant that our requirements for conventional deterrence were relatively small. The Soviet Union understood that, under our policy of 'massive retaliation', we might respond to a Soviet attack, however limited, on the U.S. or our allies, with an atomic attack on the U.S.S.R. As the fifties ended and the sixties began, however, the Soviets began developing and acquiring long-range nuclear capabilities. As their capacity for nuclear and conventional aggression continued to grow, the U.S. threat to respond to a conventional or even limited nuclear attack with a massive nuclear retaliation became less and less credible. Accordingly, in the 1960s the U.S., and later the NATO Allies—adopted a policy of 'flexible response'. Under this concept, the United States and NATO planned to strengthen general purpose warfare forces in order to better equip them to deal with a Soviet conventional attack; at the same time, U.S. nuclear capabilities

were increased in order to provide the President with the option of using nuclear forces both to support our general purpose forces and to respond selectively (on less than an all-out basis) to a limited Soviet nuclear attack. The option of retaliation on a more massive scale was retained in order to deter the possibility of a major Soviet nuclear attack. This concept of flexible response remains as a central principle of our strategy today.

Of paramount importance to the flexible response strategy is the requirement for *flexibility*— for our nuclear forces and plans for their use to be designed and developed in such a way that our response is appropriate to the circumstances of the aggression against us. This means that they should be capable of being used on a very limited basis as well as more massively. This does not imply that through flexible response we seek to fight a limited nuclear war, or, for that matter, to fight a nuclear war under any conditions. Our basic strategy, in direct support of our policy of deterrence has been, and remains, the prevention of any aggression, nuclear or conventional. But it would be irresponsible—indeed immoral—to reject the possibility that the terrible consequences of a nuclear conflict might be limited if deterrence should fail. To be sure, there is no guarantee that we would be successful in creating such limits. But there is every guarantee that restrictions cannot be achieved if we do *not* attempt to do so.

While we work toward insuring deterrence, we need to think about the failures of deterrence (for whatever reason). If that were to occur we cannot predict the nature of a Soviet nuclear strike, nor assure with any certainty that what may have started out as a limited Soviet attack would remain confined at that level. Nevertheless, we must plan for flexibility in our forces and in our response options so that there is a possibility of re-establishing deterrence at the lowest possible level of violence, and avoiding further escalation. I assure you it is not pleasant to think in these terms, but it would certainly be the gravest irresponsibility for those of us who are charged with the nation's defense *not* to do so.

Of course, this concept of seeking to contain the

level of destruction by having flexible and enduring forces is not new. It has been squarely in the mainstream of American strategic thinking for over two decades. . . .

Thus, the past three and a half decades have taught us two central lessons with regard to implementing our policy . . . lessons which we must continue to take into account in the years ahead:

- first, in order for our retaliatory threat to be seen as credible, we must be able—and be seen to have the means—to respond appropriately to a wide range of aggressive actions; if our threatened response is perceived as inadequate or inappropriate, it will be seen as a bluff and ignored;
- secondly, deterrence is a dynamic effort, not a static one. In order to continue to deter successfully, our capabilities must change as the threat changes, and as our knowledge of what is necessary to deter improves.

. . . Throughout the 1960s our strategic posture presented the Soviet planner with a dilemma if he decided to pre-empt against the United States: due to the relatively small number of weapons the U.S.S.R. possessed and their ineffectiveness against any U.S. strategic forces, such an attack was impossible to execute successfully. If the Soviet planner targeted our hardened missile silos and alert bomber bases, he found that he would deplete his arsenal while not significantly reducing U.S. retaliatory forces. In other words, his ability to limit the certain massive destruction to his own forces and society was rather small. If, on the other hand, the Soviet planner targeted U.S. cities, he would feel the full brunt of a U.S. retaliatory strike against his own cities, a U.S. arsenal quite larger and much more capable than his own, by any measure. Again, he was deterred.

During the course of the 1970s the Soviet arsenal began growing both in quantity and in quality (although the U.S. qualitative edge remained). The Soviets expanded their land-based missile force and hardened their protective silos. At the same time, the U.S. made a conscious choice not to upgrade the yield/accuracy combination of its own missile forces or to build force levels of sufficient size to

threaten the Soviet Union with a sudden disarming first strike. The net result of this was to allow the Soviets a 'sanctuary' for its ICBM force, since U.S. forces could not attack it effectively. The Soviets, however, did not follow our lead and developed a new generation of ICBMS specifically designed to attack U.S. missile silos. By the late 1970s, this combination of vulnerable U.S. missiles and a Soviet sanctuary had eased the earlier dilemma of the Soviet planner. Now, he potentially could envision nuclear confrontation in which he probed U.S. resolve to retaliate by attacking a smaller and smaller subset of the U.S. military forces—while U.S. options for retaliation were limited. If the Soviet leadership came to accept this as plausible, our deterrent policy, and, as a result, global stability, would be severely threatened. As the 'imbalance of imbalances' continued to grow in the late 1970s, that is, as the Soviets began tipping the theater nuclear balance in their favor while maintaining their superiority in conventional forces, the risk became greater that this type of limited attack would appear attractive to the Soviet military.

The strategic modernization program which President Reagan set forth in October 1981 is designed to address in part this adverse and imbalanced situation. It restores the margin of safety we require in order to continue to deter successfully Soviet strategic aggression. In essence, the program is designed to accomplish two general goals: first, to improve the survivability of our present and planned forces in order that they do not serve to destabilize potential crises by offering lucrative targets for Soviet preemption; and, secondly, to sustain the credibility of our deterrent policy by developing the capability to threaten, and destroy if necessary, the full spectrum of potential Soviet targets. This combination of improved survivability and military capability is intended to assure that Soviet leadership will continue to recognize clearly and unambiguously that they can realize no conceivable benefit from initiating nuclear aggression. . . .

Perhaps the most vulnerable of our retaliatory forces are the *Minuteman* and *Titan* ICBMS which were designed and housed in the late 1950s and

1960s. Designed to deter a Soviet threat of the past, these missiles have served us well. The *Peacekeeper* is designed to meet both the current and future Soviet threat, both in capability and survivability. *Peacekeeper* in Closely Spaced Basing will, at long last, provide a feasible, affordable solution to the ICBM vulnerability problem. . . .

Let me conclude by returning to the point at which I began. There is nothing new about our policy. Since the era of nuclear weapons began, the United States has sought to prevent a nuclear war through a policy of deterrence. That policy has worked successfully for almost four decades. We are dedicated to ensuring that it continues to do so.

QUESTIONS FOR DISCUSSION

1 What are the political and military requirements for nuclear deterrence to work?
2 Are these requirements now in place?
3 Will these requirements be in place in the future?
4 What are the alternatives to deterrence?
5 Has the absence of war between the superpowers been caused by deterrence?

SUGGESTED READINGS

Cockburn, Andrew. *The Threat: Inside the Soviet Military Machine.* New York: Random House, 1983.

Correll, John T. "Deterrence Today." *Air Force Magazine* 67 (February 1984), pp. 40–45.

Draper, Theodore. "Nuclear Temptations." *The New York Review of Books* (January 19, 1984), pp. 42–50.

Garthoff, Raymond L. "Mutual Deterrence and Strategic Arms Limitation in Soviet Policy." *Strategic Review* 10 (Fall, 1982), pp. 36–51.

Gelb, Leslie H. "Is the Nuclear Threat Manageable?" *New York Times Magazine* (March 4, 1984), pp. 26, 28–32, 34–36, 65, 80, and 92.

Ground Zero. *Nuclear War: What's In It for You?* New York: Pocket Books, 1982.

Lens, Sidney. "The Deterrence Myth." *Progressive* (February 1984), pp. 16–17.

Nacht, Michael. "Nuclear Deterrence to the End of the Century." *Naval War College Review* 36 (November-December 1983), pp. 75–85.

Payne, Keith B. "Deterrence, Arms Control, and U.S. Strategic Doctrine." *Orbis* 25 (Fall 1981), pp. 747–69.

Pipes, Richard. "Soviet Strategic Doctrine: Another View." *Strategic Review* 10 (Fall 1982), pp. 52–58.

Powers, Thomas. "Nuclear Winter and Nuclear Strategy." *Atlantic Monthly* (November 1984), pp. 53–64.

Quinlan, Michael. "Thinking Deterrence Through," in R. James Woolsey (ed.). *Nuclear Arms: Ethics, Strategy, Politics.* San Francisco, California: ICS Press, 1984, pp. 53–62.

Rothschild, Emma. "The Delusions of Deterrence." *The New York Review of Books* (April 14, 1983), pp. 40–50.

Sloss, Leon and Marc Dean Millot. "U.S. Nuclear Strategy in Evolution." *Strategic Review* 12 (Winter 1984), pp. 19–28.

Stegenga, James A. "The Immorality of Nuclear Deterrence." *Arms Control* 4 (London) (May 1983), pp. 65–72.

Tucker, Robert W. "The Nuclear Debate." *Foreign Affairs* 63 (Fall 1984).

3 Is Nuclear War Likely to Occur by Accident?

YES

James E. Muller

On Accidental Nuclear War

NO

General James Hartinger

Nuclear War by Accident—Is It Impossible?

On Accidental Nuclear War
James E. Muller

When the horror of nuclear war forces its way to consciousness, many cling to the belief that it is so horrible that no rational person will ever push the button. This discounts our stated policy that we would push the button in self-defense, but it does provide comfort—until the possibility of accidental nuclear war is considered.

The military, to whom we have delegated the task of managing nuclear weapons, well understands the danger of unintentional nuclear war. A special program called the Personnel Reliability Program (PRP) exists for individuals with access to nuclear weapons. More than 100,000 are included in the program; to enter it, an individual must show evidence of emotional stability and good social adjustment and not have had a problem with alcohol or drug abuse. Physicians assist in the screening process and periodically monitor those selected.

The results of this surveillance are shocking. They should be known by everyone who believes nuclear weapons bring national security, every world leader, every arms-control negotiator—indeed, everyone living in the nuclear age—yet it seems very few are aware of the numbers buried on page 323 of the 1979 report of "Hearings Before a Subcommittee of the Committee on Appropriations of the House of Representatives." In 1975, 5,128 personnel were removed from access to nuclear weapons because of violations of the PRP; in 1976, 4,966 and in 1977, 4,973—an annual rate exceeding 4 percent. Reasons for removal in 1977 included alcohol and drug abuse; the primary drug abused was marijuana, but more than 250 were removed for abuse of drugs such as heroin and LSD. In the same year 1,289 were removed for a "significant physical, mental or character trait or aberrant behavior, substantiated by competent

medical authority," which might "prejudice reliable performance of the duties of a particular critical or controlled position."

In addition to these medical disqualifications, 828 were disqualified for negligence, 350 for court-martial or civil convictions of a serious nature and 885 for evidence "of a contemptuous attitude toward the law." Description of this misconduct should not be interpreted as a criticism of the military, for it is we who have asked them to accomplish the impossible in handling nuclear weapons safely.

Computers, which occasionally tell us we have died, or never existed, or must pay a bill a second time, are also intimately involved in the nuclear arsenals. The record of mistakes is extensive. During an eighteen-month period, the North American Air Defense Command had 151 false alarms. Four resulted in orders that increased the state of alert of B-52 bomber crews and intercontinental-ballistic-missile units. A major false alert, lasting a full six minutes, occurred when a technician mistakenly mounted on an American military computer a training tape of a Soviet attack. Mechanical malfunction and human errors have also led to a number of accidents with nuclear weapons.

The risk of an accident increases as we increase the size of our arsenal and the number of personnel involved. Our move to "counterforce" warfare, in which each side becomes concerned that it must fire its missiles before they are destroyed, decreases to less than 30 minutes the time available to evaluate the computer signals of a possible attack and decide to launch. The spread of nuclear weapons to less-developed countries with limited technical sophistication also increases the risk.

What are the implications of this understandable but somehow startling evidence of technical and human fallibility? Can a group of individuals whose judgment is impaired decide to launch a nuclear weapon without authorization or fail to respond properly to a computer error? Although the Pentagon has stated that no single person can launch a nuclear weapon, under certain conditions the crew of a submarine can fire nuclear weapons on its own. Our survival also depends on the proper conduct of Soviet personnel and computers. Alcoholism is a major health problem in the Soviet Union and is at least as likely to exist among their military as it is among ours.

An unauthorized launch would undoubtedly require a combination of failures, but the opportunities are numerous and increasing. Must we drift passively toward that moment when chance brings together the critical mass of plutonium and drugs, alcohol, psychosis or computer error that will destroy us and all we value?

We are moving inexorably and unwittingly toward a finale similar to that so powerfully described in "Hamlet." At the play's conclusion, Fortinbras enters and finds the recently slain Hamlet, Laertes and the King and Queen of Denmark, and Hamlet's friend Horatio explains how such a disaster occurred:

And let me speak to th' yet unknowing world

How these things came about. So shall you hear
Of carnal, bloody and unnatural acts,
Of accidental judgments, casual slaughters,
Of deaths put on by cunning and forced cause,
And, in this upshot, purposes mistook
Fall'n on th' inventors' heads.

We are now the "inventors." We have set the stage for "accidental judgments," "forced cause" and "purposes mistook" to lead us, not to a series of palace murders, but to an event of unimaginable horror in which millions of innocent people will die agonizing deaths. Physicians who survive will be unable to provide even minimal pain relief for most of the dying.

There is really only one cause for optimism: the phenomenal growth of the mass movement for total nuclear disarmament. Hope and a sense of common purpose have replaced despair and isolation for tens of thousands. If others with similar concerns act on their belief, the movement can become an unstoppable force. The coming spring can be a time of renewal of the belief that humanity can survive. Such progress is needed: the hour is late. We can live with the threat of accidental nuclear war for 10 or 20 or 30 years, as we have—but not forever.

Nuclear War by Accident—Is It Impossible?
General James Hartinger

Q General Hartinger, how many false warnings have you had of a possible missile attack on the U.S.?

A We've had two in the past four years or so. The first occurred on Nov. 9, 1979, when a technician inadvertently loaded an exercise-scenario tape into the operational system. So the displays at the Strategic Air Command and National Military Command Center showed possible missiles that were being tracked.

It took a few minutes to determine that this was a human error.

Q How were you able to determine that it was an error and not a real attack?

A We have an instantaneous conferencing capability with all the sensor sites—all of our tracking stations. We went to them and ascertained that none were tracking any missiles. So we knew it had to be a computer error or, in this case, a personnel error.

From General James Hartinger, "Nuclear War by Accident—Is It Impossible?" *U.S. News & World Report*, December 19, 1983, p. 27. Copyright, 1983, U.S. News & World Report, Inc.

As a result of that incident, we took steps that guarantee that it could never recur. We developed an off-site test facility in 1980 here in Colorado Springs where we test all the software and all the hardware before we install it in the computer system in our combat operations center in Cheyenne Mountain. So none of our testing is done any longer on the operational system.

Q How did the second false attack warning occur?

A It was on June 3, 1980. Again, our automatic computer-generated displays appeared to show missiles being tracked.

Our missile-warning center again conferenced all the sensor sites and determined that no missiles actually were being tracked. So it had to be a computer error. It took less than a minute and a half to determine that.

We spent many hours investigating, and, finally, after we managed to duplicate the fault, we isolated the problem to a little chip on the circuit board that had been in the system for some time.

Once we determined the cause, we went off that major computer system, and we did many things to see that an accident like that would not recur.

Q What did you do to prevent this from happening again?

A Well, one of the things we did was to increase each computer-message word length to 32 bits so there would be more redundancy in checking whether these were valid messages. About five months after that second incident, we went back on the major computer string after we had incorporated these fixes. In the three years since then, we have sent out over 175 million messages, and we have not sent one false message.

Q In those incidents involving false warnings of attack, how close was the United States to stumbling into a nuclear war by mistake?

A We didn't come close at all. By going to all the sensor sites, we determined in less than a minute and a half that there was a computer fault and no one was tracking any missiles.

Q Are you saying that it would be impossible to have a nuclear war triggered by a false attack warning—for example, a computer error in your headquarters?

A Obviously, there can be computer faults—hardware and software errors; there can be personnel errors; there can be solar activity—solar blanking that affects sensors; there can be auroral effects. Also, a decaying satellite can look like an incoming warhead to a sensor. That is the reason we have a man in the loop. On every space or missile launch, that is why I assess whether it's a threat to North America. Human judgment will always be there to insure that we provide reliable, timely, unambiguous warning.

Q How can you be sure that someone at the command headquarters in Cheyenne Mountain won't push the button and fire off missiles in response to a false alarm?

A There are no buttons to push. Our mission is to provide early warning and attack assessment to the national command authorities through the National Military Command Center in the Pentagon. So there are no buttons to push, as in the "WarGames" movie.

Q Do you think it is possible for a computer hacker to get into your system and trick your computers, as happened in "WarGames"?

A A person like a student could not gain access to the computer system in Cheyenne Mountain, because we are not on the commercial telephone network. No one can dial up our computer system.

All the data that comes from the sensor sites to Cheyenne Mountain is scrambled—that is, it's encrypted. When it arrives at Cheyenne Mountain, it is unscrambled. And then it has to face a most trying, taxing protocol interface to be able to enter the computer system. So it would be impossible for somebody to get into our computer system in Cheyenne Mountain.

Q Since all this publicity about computer hackers breaking into secure computers, have you taken any additional measures to protect the integrity of the system here?

A Well, we have looked at our system, and we feel that we were taking every precaution possible before the movie "WarGames" was made. . . .

QUESTIONS FOR DISCUSSION

1 Is war by accident more likely to occur today because of nuclear weapons than was the case in the prenuclear weapons era?

2 Do technological innovations make nuclear war by accident more or less likely?

3 If accidental nuclear war is to occur, do you think it is more likely to be initiated by one of the superpowers or by another state? Why?

4 Would the accidental launching of a nuclear weapon inevitably lead to a nuclear holocaust?

5 Is there anything that the superpowers should be doing to make accidental nuclear war less likely to occur?

SUGGESTED READINGS

Ball, Desmond. *Can Nuclear War Be Controlled?* Adelphi Paper no. 169. London: International Institute for Strategic Studies, 1981.

Beres, Louis René. *Apocalypse: Nuclear Catastrophe in World Politics.* Chicago: University of Chicago Press, 1980, pp. 34–52.

Blair, Bruce G. *Strategic Command and Control: Redefining the Nuclear Threat.* Washington, D.C.: Brookings Institution, 1985.

Bracken, Paul J. *The Command and Control of Nuclear Forces.* New Haven, Connecticut: Yale University Press, 1983.

Calder, Nigel. *Nuclear Nightmares: An Investigation into Possible Wars.* New York: Viking Press, 1980.

Ford, Daniel. *The Button: The Pentagon's Command and Control System.* New York: Simon and Schuster, 1985.

Frei, Daniel. *Risks of Unintentional Nuclear War.* Geneva, Switzerland: United Nations Institute for Disarmament Research, 1982.

Larus, Joel. *Nuclear Weapons Safety and the Common Defense.* Columbus: Ohio State University Press, 1967.

Pringle, Peter and William Arkin. *SIOP: The Secret U.S. Plan for Nuclear War.* New York: W. W. Norton, 1983.

Steinbruner, John D. "Nuclear Decapitation," *Foreign Policy* no. 45 (Winter 1981–82), pp. 16–28.

U.S. Congressional Budget Office. *Strategic Command, Control, and Communications: Alternative Approaches for Modernization.* Washington, D.C.: Government Printing Office, 1981.

U.S. Congress: Senate. *Recent False Alerts from the Nation's Missile Attack Warning System,* by Gary Hart and Barry Goldwater, Committee Print. Washington, D.C.: Government Printing Office, 1980.

"U.S. Nuclear Weapons Accidents: Danger in Our Midst," *Defense Monitor* 10, no. 5 (1981), entire issue.

4 Is It Virtually Certain That a Major Nuclear War Would
Be Followed by Such Devastating Climatic Changes As
to Constitute a Global Catastrophe?

YES

Anne Ehrlich

Nuclear Winter

NO

Caspar W. Weinberger

*The Potential Effects of Nuclear War on the Climate: A
Report to the U.S. Congress*

Nuclear Winter
Anne Ehrlich

A new understanding of the calamitous destructive power of even a "small" nuclear conflict has begun to penetrate the world's consciousness. This awareness stems in large part from the *Conference on the World After Nuclear War,* held in October 1983, at which leading atmospheric scientists and biologists presented their findings in an environmental impact statement. In a packed hotel ballroom bristling with cameras, lights and audio equipment, the scientists described the dire conclusions of their studies and deliberations conducted over the previous 18 months.

Some presentations were highly dramatic—Carl Sagan's brief but graphic "slide show," for example—but mostly they resembled standard conference fare, low-key and unemotional. Yet if anything, the matter-of-fact tone served to underscore the horrors of the picture they were painting of the world after a thermonuclear exchange.

Unlike most scientific conferences, this one offered no controversies or disagreements. Each of the 13 speakers and panelists provided details from his own area of specialization, building on and dovetailing with all the other presentations. Piece by piece, they constructed an image of an unlivable world.

Policy statements were rigorously banned, the speakers all affirming that they would reserve their opinions on policy matters for other occasions. This event was to focus on the stark facts.

Keynote speaker Donald Kennedy, president of Stanford University, described as "most disturbing" the possibility of major climatic consequences from nuclear war "so profound that they could dwarf all of the other long-range effects described so far." While there are still many uncertainties, Kennedy warned that these findings had been carefully reviewed by many respected scientists and were much too important to be ignored by policy planners.

"Our most thoughtful projections show," he said, "that a major nuclear exchange will have, among its plausible effects, the greatest biological and physical disruptions of this planet in its last 65 million years."

The possible climatic and biological effects of a nuclear war were long neglected under the assumption that they were trivial compared to the terrible immediate impacts on human populations. The World Health Organization recently estimated that a large-scale exchange might kill 1.1 billion people outright and seriously injure an equal number.[1] Nearly half of the 1984 human population thus would be immediate casualties of a nuclear war, regardless of any environmental effects. But this calamity would be only the beginning.

ATMOSPHERIC CONSEQUENCES

Carl Sagan presented the TTAPS study (named for coauthors R.P. Turco, O.B. Toon, T.P. Ackerman, J.B. Pollack and C. Sagan) on the atmospheric consequences of a nuclear war. Across a variety of scenarios . . . the TTAPS simulations produced remarkably consistent results. In a nuclear war involving both urban and military targets, thousands of detonations would inject tremendous quantities of both dust and soot into the atmosphere of the Northern Hemisphere, where the majority of likely targets are located.

The vast fires that would be ignited by attacks on cities were described by panelist Richard Turco of the TTAPS team. World War II firestorms in German cities, he warned, "presage the fierceness

---

[1] S. Borgstrom and others, "Effects of a Nuclear War on Health and Health Services," World Health Organization, *Publication A36.12* (1983).

of the nuclear fires that might occur in modern cities, except that the nuclear fires . . . would be unprecedented in scale and much more intense, dwarfing any of the World War II conflagrations."

Within one or two weeks, the individual plumes of dust and soot would coalesce in an enormous dark cloud shrouding most of the Northern Hemisphere, particularly the mid-latitude belt encompassing most of the United States, Canada, the Soviet Union, Europe, China and Japan. Beneath the spreading clouds, very little sunlight—in the worst cases, as little as a tenth of one percent of the normal light level, averaged over the hemisphere—could reach the surface. . . . Even relatively limited wars could reduce light intensities by 95 percent or more.

Clouds of dust alone would admit some light because dust particles reflect and scatter much of the light that strikes them, and some would reach the surface. Smoke clouds, by contrast, would absorb most of the solar radiation striking them, very effectively blocking out sunlight as long as they persisted.

With most of the sunlight blocked, temperatures at the surface would plummet tens of degrees, dropping far below freezing in continental interiors a week or so after the exchange, whatever the season. Extremely cold temperatures would last for many weeks, even months, returning to normal only very slowly . . . . Coastal areas and islands would be spared the extreme cold by the moderating influence of the oceans' vast thermal inertia. But the huge temperature difference between the oceans and the continental interiors would subject coastal areas to months of unremitting violent weather.

How far temperatures fell and how long they remained significantly below normal would depend on the details of the conflicts and the actual values of the uncertain physical parameters. Obviously, the largest numbers of weapons would produce the worst effects. The 10,000-megaton "severe" scenario could plunge average surface continental temperatures in the northern mid-latitudes to around minus 50 degrees centigrade and keep them below freezing for a year or longer.

Yet surprisingly harsh and lasting effects could be generated even by relatively modest exchanges. The baseline scenario (5,000 megatons) could drop average continental temperatures in the Northern Hemisphere to about minus 23 degrees centigrade. Shockingly, even 100 megatons detonated on cities alone could produce sufficient smoke to blacken skies and chill continental areas to below minus 20 degrees centigrade, with recovery taking over three months.

Sagan stressed the "robustness" of these findings: "If 0.8 percent of the global strategic arsenals were dropped—100 megatons on 1,000 cities—that would trigger an effect about as bad as the 5,000 megaton case. In other words, these climatic results are very independent of the kind of war we're talking about. And there is a rough threshold of 100 megatons, more or less . . . at which this climate effect can be triggered." He also emphasized that any attack above that "threshold" would be suicidal, regardless of retaliation.[2] As panelist Stephen Schneider noted wryly, an attacker would "win" for only about two weeks.

The extent to which these severe atmospheric effects might spread from the northern mid-latitudes to the tropics or even to the Southern Hemisphere remains uncertain, but TTAPS and other studies using different kinds of models indicate that such propagation is very possible.[3] Schneider offered preliminary results of the National Center for Atmospheric Research (NCAR) study, using a three-dimensional model, which indicated fairly rapid transport of aerosols to the Southern Hemisphere. So did the model used by the Soviet Academy of Sciences, as reported by Soviet scientist Vladimir

[2]Carl Sagan, "Nuclear War and Climatic Catastrophe: Some Implications," *Foreign Affairs 62* (Winter 1983), pp. 257–92.
[3]C. Covey, S.H. Schneider, and S.L. Thompson, "Global Atmospheric Effects of Massive Smoke Injection from a Nuclear War: Results form General Circulation Model Simulations," *Nature* (submitted); V.V. Aleksandrov and G.L. Stenchikov, "On the Modeling of the Climatic Consequences of the Nuclear War," USSR Academy of Sciences, Computing Center, The Proceedings on Applied Mathematics (Moscow: 1983); J. Knox, *Report UCRL-89907*, Lawrence Livermore Laboratory (1983).

The Scenarios*

Caseª	Total yield (megatons)	% Yield surface bursts	% Yield urban or industrial targets	Warhead yield range (megatons)	Total number of explosions
A. Baseline exchange	5,000	57	20	0.1–10	10,400
B. 3,000-MT counterforce only	3,000	50	0	1–10	2,250
C. 100-MT cities only	100	0	100	0.1	1,000
D. 10,000-MT maximum exchange	10,000	63	15	0.1–10	16,160
E. 5,000-MT severe counterforce only	5,000	100	0	5–10	700
F. 10,000-MT severe exchangeᵇ	10,000	63	15	0.1–10	16,160

*In these scenarios, attacks are concentrated in the Northern Hemisphere. The 100-megaton cities-only scenario (C) assumes about a third higher smoke emission from urban fires than the other scenarios and no wildfires. "Severe" cases assume a sixfold increase in fine dust lofted per megaton of yield and a greater fraction of soot injected into the stratosphere. (*Source:* TTAPS)

ªThe cases selected from the TTAPS study have been relabeled for this article. The original TTAPS case numbers are: case A = 1; B = 11; C = 14; D = 9; E = 16; F = 17....

ᵇCase F has the same parameters as D; more severe results are posited for F to show the range of possible effects following a maximum exchange.

In their atmospheric models, the TTAPS group analyzed the impacts of some 40 different scenarios on the course of a nuclear war: the numbers, sizes, altitudes, fission yield fractions, and locations of weapons detonated, as well as variations of uncertain physical parameters such as dust and soot particle size distributions, absorption coefficients and so on (see table).

The war scenarios ranged in scale from a relatively modest one involving "only" 1,000 weapons with fission yields totalling 100 megatons (one megaton is equivalent in explosive power to one million tons of TNT) detonated on 1,000 cities, to a very severe one of some 10,000 megatons expended on a variety of targets: cities, major industrial sites, missile silos and other important military installations.

The study also included a 25,000-megaton "future war" scenario, which exceeds in megatonnage the nuclear arsenals of today but will become possible if current plans for expansion are carried out. Two scenarios were given particular attention by TTAPS: a "baseline" case of 5,000 megatons, striking both military and civilian targets; and a 3,000-megaton preemptive strike on silos only, with no retaliation. The biologists focused on the 10,000-megaton "severe" scenario, wishing to apprise decision-makers of a plausible "worst case" outcome.

The kinds of targets and the altitudes of detonations make a difference in the atmospheric effects produced. A high-yield explosion on or near the surface (as most likely would be used against missile silos) tends to hurl vast quantities of very fine dust high into the atmosphere. . . . Because of the stability of temperature and the low water content of the stratosphere, it is subject neither to the rapid vertical mixing nor to the cleansing effects of rain found in the troposphere (lower atmosphere). Very small particles therefore may remain in the stratosphere for long periods—on the order of a year.

While it is uncertain exactly how much dust would be injected into the stratosphere by nuclear detonations, research from nuclear bomb tests indicates a range of roughly 100,000 to 600,000 tons of dust per megaton of yield. Most of the TTAPS scenarios specified production of 330,000 tons of stratosphere dust per megaton exploded in surface bursts and 100,000 tons per megaton in near-surface bursts. The "severe" scenarios were calculated with more adverse, but still plausible, parameters for dust injections.

Large numbers of lower-yield air bursts, which probably would be used to inflict maximum damage on cities, would ignite huge fires and deposit enormous quantities of smoke and soot in the troposphere, where they would linger for many weeks. Under normal conditions of air movement the soot particles would gradually settle out of the atmosphere or be removed in precipitation.

The quantities of smoke that would be produced by nuclear detonations are even more uncertain than those of dust. The baseline scenario conservatively assumed partial burning of about 240,000 square kilometers of urban area and total burning of 500,000 square kilometers of forest, brush and grassland area, producing altogether about 225 million tons of smoke particles—roughly equivalent to a year's normal worldwide smoke emissions—within a few days. Their particular composition and their persistence, however, give them a far greater capacity to perturb the atmosphere.

At the Conference, panelist John Holdren of the University of California at Berkeley confirmed the credibility of the TTAPS war scenarios, pointing out their similarity to reference scenarios in other recent studies of the consequences of nuclear war. The baseline case, he noted, "involves the use of about a third of the total [nuclear] inventories, or about a half of the strategic inventories altogether." Even the 10,000-megaton severe case was plausible under very adverse circumstances, such as a small conflict escalating from battlefield weapons to use of the full strategic arsenals.

Aleksandrov. If they are right, the atmospheric effects—the cold and the darkness—of a nuclear war would engulf the entire globe.

In most respects, both the NCAR and Soviet studies confirmed the TTAPS results. "Everything we've seen so far," Schneider said, "suggests that, although the details do vary . . . the basic picture [is] very hard to get rid of." Turco and other speakers nevertheless stressed the continued uncertainty on details of the atmospheric effects despite the general agreement.

A point emphasized in the Soviet study was that normal precipitation might be suppressed by the dust-laden, warmed atmosphere following a nuclear conflict. The Soviets also found that, as the solar-heated soot clouds cleared, surface temperatures could become much *warmer* than normal—as much as 25–35 degrees centigrade above average—in continental interiors. (But this effect may well be an artifact of the model, in which soot clouds dissipate suddenly rather than gradually over months.)

Beyond the "nuclear winter," the TTAPS study found that massive burning of synthetic materials in urban and industrial areas would release—besides smoke—a deadly mix of toxic fumes (labeled "pyrotoxins" by TTAPS) such as carbon monoxide, oxides of nitrogen, ozone, cyanides, dioxins and furans, to blanket much of the Northern Hemisphere for months.

TTAPS also confirmed earlier findings that a nuclear war could cause destruction of stratospheric ozone, allowing penetration of radiation in the ultraviolet-B range. While the smoke and dust clouds persisted, they would absorb most of the ultraviolet-B, but the ozone shield would be reestablished more slowly. Thus, clearing skies would expose Earth's surface to the damaging radiation for some years.

The baseline scenario projects a reduction of ozone concentrations of up to 30 percent, averaged over the Northern Hemisphere. This would produce ultraviolet-B exposures at the surface roughly twice the normal level after cloud dissipation. Higher megatonnage wars would produce relatively greater depletion of the ozone shield—twice as much for a 10-megaton exchange, for instance.

In addition, the TTAPS report included new predictions on the distribution and, especially, the timing of radioactive fallout. Previous studies, based on high-yield test explosions, had focused on immediate and long-term fallout. But they had neglected medium-term fallout, that occurring between a few days and a few months after a nuclear exchange. Virtually everyone exposed to immediate lethal doses of radiation from fireballs would be killed by blast and heat. Prompt fallout (within a day or two) also would be largely confined to target areas. Earlier intermediate and long-term radiation estimates rested on the generally unspoken assumption that most radioactive debris would be injected into the stratosphere where it would remain for one to two years. By then, most of the radioactive elements, which are fairly short-lived, would have decayed to relatively harmless levels.

Calculations by the TTAPS team, however, indicated that the medium-term component, mainly from rapid washout and fallout of radioactive debris deposited in the troposphere by low-altitude and ground-level bursts, might be substantial. Thus, for a conflict of any given size, the average exposure to survivors far from targets might be increased by an order of magnitude over earlier estimates. Panelist John Holdren compared these new findings to those of another recent study conducted at the Lawrence Livermore Laboratory. Both studies had revealed the likelihood of considerable intermediate-term fallout, which would, as he put it, "contribute rather nastily to the total dose."

For the baseline case, the average medium-term, whole-body, external dose of gamma emissions to unsheltered people in the Northern Hemisphere could be about 20 rad. The average dose in the northern mid-latitudes might be 50 rad, and exposure to local "hot spots" and internal doses from food could easily add another 50 rad. A great many individuals, especially downwind of major targets, would receive far greater than average doses.

Average doses of 100 rad or so imply serious problems for an exposed population, especially in the probable absence of even minimal medical care and with simultaneous exposure to numerous other severe stresses. With adequate medical care, the whole-body radiation dose that would kill half of the exposed healthy adults is thought to be about 350 to 500 rad if received in 48 hours or less. Under adverse conditions, the lethal dose might be much lower. If so, at least half of the surviving populations of combatant nations in a nuclear war of even moderate size could be exposed to life-threatening doses of radioactivity in the aftermath, and nearly everyone could suffer some resulting illness.

A nuclear conflict involving greater megatonnage would produce proportionately larger radiation doses. The 10,000-megaton severe scenario in the TTAPS study might result in exposures of about 500 rad over 30 percent of the Northern Hemisphere land areas, killing at least a half-billion people.

Questions from the audience dealt with several other points:

• Why the climatic consequences had not been discovered before was unanswerable. The basic physics and chemistry had been available for 20 years, and governments had a responsibility to study them.

• Whether massive disruption of the hydrological cycle would cause torrential rains and heavy erosion was difficult to predict. In the absence of sunlight, evaporation would be sharply reduced, thus possibly diminishing the moisture content of the atmosphere and suppressing precipitation.

• Could these discoveries be made public in the Soviet Union? Golitsyn replied that some aspects of his work had already been published in the proceedings of the Soviet Academy of Sciences.

BIOLOGICAL CONSEQUENCES

"The environment that will confront most human beings and other organisms will be so altered and so malign that extreme and widespread damage to living systems is inevitable," declared Paul Ehrlich, who presented the biologists' consensus on the biological implications of the TTAPS discoveries.

The reduction of sunlight by more than 95 percent for several weeks would represent a severe assault on green plants—the foundation of all significant ecosystems. Virtually all animals, including human beings, are directly or indirectly dependent on the energy green plants capture from sunlight in the process of photosynthesis.

Panelist Joseph Berry, a plant ecologist at the Carnegie Institute, reminded the audience that photosynthesis is the "major . . . energy input in the biosphere . . . the driving force for the operation of natural and agricultural ecosystems." In most plants, photosynthetic activity is proportional to the amount of light they receive, and 15 percent or more of the energy fixed is needed to maintain life processes. If light falls below that point, plants begin to "consume themselves," and animals also consume them. A severe loss of light thus means loss of biomass.

Under the smoke-shrouded skies of a nuclear winter, for several weeks light intensities would be too low to permit growth in most plants. The 10,000-megaton "severe" case could turn midday into the equivalent of a moonlit night for many weeks—too dark for any photosynthesis at all—and complete recovery to pre-war light levels would take more than a year.

The darkness, drastic in itself, would be accompanied by plummeting continental temperatures. Growing plants are as sensitive to temperatures as they are to light intensities; even quite small changes can make significant differences. A reduction in average temperatures of one degree centigrade at critical times can reduce corn crop yields by as much as 10 percent, for example.

Temperatures far below freezing during the growing season would annihilate annual plants, including most crops, and kill or severely damage even the hardiest perennials. Even normally cold-tolerant species, such as winter wheat and deciduous trees, need time to acclimate to winter cold. More sensitive plants, including many important crops, could be seriously harmed by low temperatures that only *approached* freezing during the growing season.

Moreover, the effects of cold and darkness would interact synergistically, each intensifying the other. Cold-damaged plants need abundant sunlight to repair the damage and the rate of photosynthesis is retarded by low temperatures. Plants in the tropics and subtropics are particularly vulnerable; if the climatic effects spread southward, both crops and natural vegetation in those regions would be devastated.

Extreme cold and darkness would also have disastrous impacts on animals. In seasons that are normally warm, animals would be especially vulnerable to sub-freezing temperatures. Hibernating animals need a full summer's buildup of fat reserves to last through a normal winter, let alone a protracted, super-cold nuclear winter. Herbivores would starve and their deaths would deprive carnivores of food. Lacking human care, domestic animals would be in similarly desperate straits; most would soon perish.

Thirst would be another problem, Panelist John Harte, of the University of California, has calculated that ice, one to two meters thick, would form on inland surface waters. If precipitation were reduced as well, people and farm animals would die of thirst—one more malign synergism. "It's interesting how synergies seem to work with you when things are going well," he remarked, "and they turn against you when you and nature are down."

Aquatic ecosystems, sometimes thought to be a potential source of food for human survivors of a nuclear war, would also suffer. Marine phytoplankton, the photosynthesizing base of marine ecosystems, are highly susceptible to prolonged darkness; their disappearance would quickly lead to starvation of animals higher in marine food chains. These systems moreover would be inundated by runoff from shore of toxic compounds released from ruptured storage and industrial facilities and of silt from denuded, burned-over lands. And the violent storms likely to prevail along coasts would make harvesting any surviving sea life difficult if not impossible.

Ionizing radiation would be an additional threat to all forms of life. Most birds and mammals are nearly as sensitive to radiation as are human beings. Sensitivity varies substantially among plants but is higher among conifers and some crops. Fallout could kill or damage millions of trees, rendering forests susceptible to wildfires, and adding to the atmospheric soot burden. Radiation also inhibits photosynthesis, an effect exacerbated by low temperatures and lack of light.

George Woodwell, moderator of the biological panel, reported that his early experiments with radiation effects on forests had indicated biotic impoverishment and quicker recovery of species with short life cycles and high reproductive potential, namely, pests. He emphasized the central importance of forests in the biosphere; their destruction would cause an enormous acceleration of extinctions. A postwar world would contain few forests; they could quickly be destroyed, but very slowly replaced.

When skies cleared, ultraviolet-B radiation, admitted at twice or more pre-war levels, could significantly affect virtually all organisms. It can reduce productivity in plants, especially under low light conditions, and might severely disrupt oceanic food webs. In mammals, ultraviolet-B can suppress immune systems, as can ionizing radiation, and cause visual damage and blindness.

Persistent darkness, below freezing temperatures, ionizing radiation, toxic air pollution, widespread fires and completely unpredictable, possibly extreme weather are each capable of causing disasters. The combined assaults of *all* of these, occurring simultaneously or in rapid succession over weeks or months, followed by more months of exposure to enhanced ultraviolet-B radiation, would have catastrophic, often synergistically amplified, effects on both natural and agricultural ecosystems. . . .

Joseph Berry noted ominously that, over geologic time, global photosynthetic productivity has been remarkably constant, varying only about 5 percent. The devastation of plant life caused by a nuclear winter could cut photosynthesis in the Northern Hemisphere by 80 to 90 percent in the first year. Because of the sharp reduction in biomass and the retarding effects of ultraviolet-B on growth, restoration of productivity to normal levels would be very slow.

Uncountable populations of plants and animals throughout the Northern Hemisphere would be obliterated; their disappearances would reverberate through ecosystems as the loss of one population led to the eradication of others dependent on it. In subtropical and tropical regions, where species diversity is far richer, but where most organisms are less able to tolerate loss of light and warmth, the cascade of extinctions could reach proportions unequalled since the dinosaurs disappeared at the end of the Cretaceous period. Even if climatic conditions returned essentially to normal within a year or two, ravaged ecosystems would require far longer to recover a semblance of their former productivity and stability—possibly millennia.

The vital services that natural ecosystems provide in support of humanity depend on their productivity and stability.[4] Those services include maintenance of the quality and composition of the atmosphere, moderation of climate and weather, regulation of the hydrological cycle, cycling of nutrients (including those needed in agriculture), disposal of wastes, replenishment of soils, pollination of crops, and a vast "genetic library" from which society has already drawn the very basis of civilization.

The loss or severe disruption of those services would inevitably follow the massive destruction of natural ecosystems by a nuclear war—just when human populations needed them most. John Harte vividly explained: "All of us on Earth are dependent on the ecosystems surrounding us as an intensive care patient is on I-V bottles and life-supporting medical equipment. Waging nuclear war would be akin to throwing a stick of dynamite into an intensive care ward, rupturing the vital links that ensure survival." Thomas Eisner of Cornell University noted the difficulty of preparing a detailed environmental impact statement for nuclear war, because biological systems are extremely complicated and still poorly understood; the impacts would be all-encompassing; and recovery from such a host of massive assaults would be slow, compounded by synergisms.

Like natural ecosystems, agricultural and other managed systems would be devastated. Any farmers still able to farm would be cut off from supplies of seeds, fertilizer, pesticides, and fuel. Starving animals, domestic or wild, might invade fields in search of food, and pests would proliferate unchecked. At least in the northern mid-latitudes, agricultural production in the first year after a nuclear war of significant size would be essentially nil, and it would be problematic for subsequent years. Modern agriculture as practiced today in developed countries would probably never be seen again. Panelist Mark Harwell of Cornell University noted that human survivors would therefore be dependent on natural ecosystems for sustenance, an additional pressure that would surely delay the recovery of those systems.

IMPACTS ON THE HUMAN POPULATION

Human survivors of a large-scale nuclear conflict would face a dark, swiftly chilling, radioactive, smoggy world in which most of the social services we take for granted—medical care, food and water distribution systems, centralized heat and power supplies, communications and so on—had completely broken down. Cities and industries would be in ruins; surface water supplies would quickly run out; and no assistance from the outside could be expected.

The few healthy survivors would be burdened by masses of corpses and seriously injured friends, neighbors and relatives needing care. In the absence of functioning sanitation systems and medical care, diseases would flourish in a population weakened by exposure, radiation and malnutrition. The psychological burdens can be only dimly imagined.

[4]P.R. and A.H. Ehrlich: *Extinction, The Causes and Consequences of the Disappearance of Species* (New York: Random House, 1981).

Apart from the difficulties of keeping warm, finding unfrozen water, and avoiding radiation exposure and the choking smog, food would be the most urgent need. The war undoubtedly would have destroyed much food in storage as well as crops in the fields. Worldwide food production rarely is abundant enough to provide carry-over stocks that would last for more than two months under normal consumption patterns.

Only grains are stored in large quantity, usually far from population centers. Thus any grain that escaped destruction would be largely inaccessible. Without agricultural production, even a heavily decimated population would face severe and continuing food shortages in a short time—although they would be alleviated somewhat in developed countries by the disappearance of livestock as competitors for grains.

Many European countries, Japan, and often the Soviet Union are deeply dependent on food imported mainly from North America, as are numerous developing nations. Shipments of food and other commodities obviously would halt immediately, throwing many regions into almost instant famine. In the sub-tropics and tropics, people might turn in desperation to the remaining forest areas, try to convert them to subsistence agriculture, and thereby greatly accelerate the already disastrous current rate of tropical deforestation, compounding the destruction caused by the atmospheric disturbances.

In the northern target regions, it is unlikely that more than a tiny fraction of the original population could survive the first few months after a nuclear war of appreciable scale. Even though atmospheric conditions might return more or less to normal in a few years, other aspects of the environment would be altered beyond recognition. Ecosystems would recover slowly, with entirely new structures, impoverished species compositions and a reduced capacity to support human life. Local climates would probably be novel and unpredictable. Pre-war cultural adaptations would be useless in such a changed, hostile, unstable world.

The familiar complex technological civilization that supports us doubtless would be shattered beyond repair. Once destroyed, that technological superstructure could not easily be rebuilt, because the resources used to build it the first time would no longer be at hand.

Ehrlich concluded: "If there is a full-scale nuclear war, odds are you can kiss the Northern Hemisphere good-bye. . . . Odds are also that the effects will be catastrophic in the Southern Hemisphere." If so, he declared, the scientists had decided for the first time that they "could not preclude the extinction of *Homo sapiens*." Small isolated human groups might persist for several generations in a strange, inhospitable environment in the Southern Hemisphere, their adaptive capacities sapped by inbreeding and a burden of genetic defects from the postwar exposure to ionizing radiation and increased ultraviolet-B—a classic recipe for extinction.

WHERE CAN WE GO FROM HERE?

Clearly, society can never again view the prospect of nuclear war as it did before. Any possibility of meaningful survival has been removed, and no place on Earth is safe from the nuclear winter. But these newly discovered consequences of nuclear war are so all-encompassing and so devastating that most people need some time to absorb the implications. The question, therefore, is how soon a realization of the significance of these findings can be translated into a concerted, worldwide effort to reduce international tensions.

Critics of the conference and its conclusions have contended that release of the findings was premature and would frighten an already frightened public. In fact, the findings were held in confidence until they had been carefully reviewed by dozens of competent specialists and even confirmed in other studies.

The public no doubt will be frightened. But in recent years the details of the *known* consequences have repeatedly been underplayed by government representatives and largely ignored by the media and educational authorities. The pervasive feeling among the American public seems to have been that it would never happen or, if it did, it would be terrible, but many would survive and civilization would soon be rebuilt.

The latter myth has now been given the lie, in no uncertain terms. Far worse than merely running the economies of the superpowers and their allies—as was the case in Europe and Japan following World War II—nuclear war could render all but uninhabitable the only known habitable planet in the universe. Nothing of value to anyone alive today is likely to survive such a catastrophe—and least of all, the ideologies that supposedly motivated it. The virtues of freedom—or communism—pale when survival is not an available option and there may be no future generations to whom it can be bequeathed.

Advocates of deterrence would have us believe that these findings confirm its value. After all, a nuclear war hasn't happened yet, and the newly perceived consequences only make it that much more unthinkable. Deterrence, therefore, will be more effective than ever.

This view, however, allows for no mistakes, no human or computer error. Yet over the past few years there have been hundreds of computer errors, telling the United States that attack was imminent; no doubt similar errors have been made by less sophisticated Soviet computers. Six months ago human military minds misjudged the intentions of a Korean Airline pilot and killed over 200 civilians—hardly enhancing the credibility of deterrence.

Can the world risk *everything* on the shaky hopes based on deterrence? Even now the Soviets may be moving toward "launch on warning," and tensions between the two superpowers have never been higher. The public—including citizens of every nation on Earth—indeed has reason to be frightened and the right to demand a complete change in policy.

The Potential Effects of Nuclear War on the Climate: A Report to the U.S. Congress
Caspar W. Weinberger

1. TECHNICAL ISSUES

The Climatic Response Phenomena The basic phenomena that could lead to climatic response may be described very simply. In a nuclear attack, fires would be started in and around many of the target areas either as a direct result of thermal radiation from the fireball or indirectly from the blast and shock damage. Examples of the latter would be fires started by sparks from electrical short circuits, broken gas lines and ruptured fuel storage tanks. Such fires could be numerous and could spread throughout the area of destruction and in some cases beyond, depending on the amount and type of fuel available and local meteorological conditions. These fires might generate large quantities of smoke which would be carried into the atmosphere to varying heights, depending on the meterological conditions and the intensity of the fire.

In addition to smoke, nuclear explosions on or very near the earth's surface can produce dust that would be carried up with the rising fireball. As in the case of volcanic eruptions such as Mt. Saint Helens, a part of the dust would probably be in the form of very small particles that do not readily settle out under gravity and thus can remain suspended in the atmosphere for long periods of time. If the yield of the nuclear explosion were large

From Caspar W. Weinberger, "The Potential Effects of Nuclear War on the Climate: A Report to the U.S. Congress," *Congressional Record*, 99th Cong., 1st Sess. (March 6, 1985), pp. S2580–S2583.

enough to carry some of the dust into the stratosphere where moisture and precipitation are not present to wash it out, it could remain for months.

Thus, smoke and dust could reach the upper atmosphere as a result of a nuclear attack. Initially, they could be injected into the atmosphere from many separate points and to varying heights. At this point, several processes would begin to occur simultaneously. Over time, circulation within the atmosphere would begin to spead the smoke and dust over wider and wider areas. The circulation of the atmosphere would itself be perturbed by absorption of solar energy by the dust and smoke clouds, so it could be rather different from normal atmospheric circulation. There may also be processes that could transport the smoke and dust from the troposphere into the stratosphere. At the same time, the normal processes that cleanse pollution from the lower- and middle-levels of the atmosphere would be at work. The most obvious of these is precipitation or washout, but there are several other mechanisms also at work. While this would be going on, the physical and chemical characteristics of the smoke and dust could change so that, even though they are still suspended in the atmosphere, their ability to absorb or scatter sunlight would be altered.

Depending upon how the atmospheric smoke and dust generated by nuclear war are ultimately characterized, the suspended particulate matter could act much like a cloud, absorbing and scattering sunlight at high altitude and reducing the amount of solar energy reaching the surface of the earth. How much and how fast the surface of the earth might cool as a result would depend on many of the yet undetermined details of the process, but if there is sufficient absorption of sunlight over a large enough area, the temperature change could be significant. If the smoke and dust clouds remained concentrated over a relatively small part of the earth's surface, they might produce sharp drops in the local temperature under them; but the effect on the hemispheric (or global) temperature would be slight since most areas would be substantially unaffected.

However, the natural tendency of the atmosphere, disturbed or not, would be to disperse the smoke and dust over wider and wider areas with time. One to several weeks would probably be required for widespread dispersal over a region thousands of kilometers wide. Naturally, a thinning process would occur as the particulate matter spread. At the end of this dispersal period, some amount of smoke and dust would remain, whose ability to attenuate and/or absorb sunlight would depend on its physical and chemical state at the time. By this time, hemispheric wide effects might occur. Temperatures generally would drop and the normal atmospheric circulation patterns (and normal weather patterns) could change. How long temperatures would continue to drop, how low they would fall, and how rapidly they would recover, all depend on many variables and the competition between a host of exacerbating and mitigating processes.

Uncertainties also pervade the question of the possible spread of such effects to the southern hemisphere. Normally, the atmospheres of the northern and southern hemispheres do not exchange very much air across the equator. Thus, the two hemispheres are normally thought of as being relatively isolated from one another. However, for high enough loading of the atmosphere of the northern hemisphere with smoke and dust, the normal atmospheric circulation patterns might be altered and mechanisms have been suggested that would cause smoke and dust from the northern hemisphere to be transported into the southern hemisphere.

There is fairly general agreement, at the present time, that for major nuclear attacks the phenomena could proceed about as we have described, although there is also realization that important processes might occur that we have not yet recognized, and these could work to make climatic alteration either more or less serious. However, the most important thing that must be realized is that even though we may have a roughly correct qualitative picture, what we do not have, as will be discussed later, is the ability to predict the corresponding climatic effect quantitatively; significant uncertainties exist about the magnitude, and persistence of these effects. At this time, for a postulated nuclear attack and for a specific point on the earth, we cannot predict quantitatively the materials which may be injected into the atmosphere, or how they will react there. Consequently, for any major nuclear war, some decrease in temperature may occur over at least the northern mid-latitudes. But what this change will be, how long it will last, what its spatial distribution will be, and, of much more importance, whether it will lead to effects of equal or more significance than the horrific destruction associated with the short-term effects of a nuclear war, and the other long-term effects such as radioactivity, currently is beyond our ability to predict, even in gross terms.

Historical Perspective   New interest in the long-term effects on the atmosphere of nuclear explosions was raised in 1980 when scientists proposed that a massive cloud of dust caused by a meteor impact could have led to the extinction of more than half of all the species on earth. The concept of meteor-impact dust affecting the global climate led to discussions at the National Academy of Sciences (NAS) in 1981. In April 1982, an ad hoc panel met at the Academy to assess the technical aspects of nuclear dust effects. At the meeting, the newly-discovered problem of smoke was brought up. The potential importance of both smoke and dust in the post-nuclear environment was recognized by the panel, who wrote a summary letter recommending that the academy proceed with an in-depth investigation. In 1983, the Defense Nuclear Agency [DNA] agreed to sponsor this investigation, on behalf of the Department of Defense. The results were published in the National Research Council report "The Effects on the Atmosphere of a Major Nuclear Exchange," released in December 1984.

Appreciation of smoke as a major factor resulted from the work of Crutzen and Birks. In 1981, Ambio, the Journal of Swedish Academy of Sciences, arranged a special issue on the physical and biological consequences of nuclear war. Crutzen was commissioned to write an article on possible strat-

ospheric ozone depletions. He and Birks extended their analysis to include nitrogen oxides (NO_2) and hydrocarbon air pollutants generated by fires. Arguing from historical forest fire data, they speculated that one million square kilometers of forests might burn in a nuclear war. They estimated very large quantities of smoke would be produced as a result. Subsequent evaluations based upon hypothetical exchanges have yielded much smaller burned areas and smoke production. Nevertheless, their work provided insight and impetus for subsequent studies.

The first rough quantitative estimates of the potential magnitude of the effects of nuclear war on the atmosphere were contained in a paper published in Science in December 1983[1] generally referred to as TTAPS, an acronym derived from the first letter of the names of the five authors. This study estimated conditions of near-darkness and subfreezing land temperatures, especially in continental interiors, for up to several months after a nuclear attack—almost independent of the level or type of nuclear exchange scenario. TTAPS suggested that the combination of all of the long-term physical, chemical, and radiobiological effects of nuclear explosions could, on a global scale, prove to be as serious or more serious than the immediate consequences of the nuclear blasts, although no specific damage or casualty assessments were carried out for either the immediate effects or the effects of the postulated climatic changes.

While the Crutzen and Birks studies stirred some interest in scientific circles, the TTAPS study, and its widespread dissemination in various popular media, brought the problem to wide attention. Because of its widespread dissemination, it is important to review this work in detail, and, because the salient feature of our current understanding is the large uncertainties, we will begin by discussing the nature of the uncertainties, using the TTAPS study as a vehicle for the discussion.

[1]Turco, R. P. et al.; *Nuclear Winter: Global Consequences of Multiple Nuclear Explosions*, Science 23 December 1983, vol. 222, number 4630.

Uncertainties   The model used in the TTAPS study was actually a series of calculations that started with assumed nuclear exchange scenarios and ended with quantitative estimate of an average hemispheric temperature decrease. Since these phenomena are exceedingly complex and outside the bounds of our normal experience, one is forced to employ many estimates, approximations, and educated guesses to arrive at quantitative results. To appreciate the significance of the predictions derived from the TTAPS model, it is necessary to understand some of its features and limitations.

Looked at most broadly, there are three phases to the modeling problem: the initial production of smoke and dust; its injection, transport, and removal within the atmosphere; and the consequent climatic effects.

In the TTAPS model, the amount of smoke initially produced for any given scenario was probably the most uncertain parameter. This is because a large number of poorly-known variables were combined to determine the amount of smoke that could be produced from any single nuclear explosion. In actuality, the same yield weapon could produce vastly different amounts of smoke over different target areas and under different meteorological conditions. Some of the factors that must be considered—although not taken into account in the TTAPS study—include: the thermal energy required for ignition of the various fuels associated with a particular target area, the sustainability of such a fire, the atmospheric transmission and the terrain features which will determine the area receiving sufficient thermal energy from the fireball to cause ignition, the type and quantity of combustible material potentially available for burning, the fraction that actually burns, and finally, the amount of smoke produced per unit mass of fuel burned. Every target is unique with respect to this set of characteristics, and a given target may change greatly depending on local weather, season, or even time of day.

The TTAPS study did not attempt to analyze the individual targets or areas used for their various scenarios; rather, it made estimates of average or plausible values for all the parameters needed to satisfy the model. This procedure is not unreasonable and is consistent with the level of detail in the analysis, but the potential for error in estimating these averages is clearly quite large. In one case, a more detailed assessment of smoke production has recently been completed as a result of the ongoing DOD research in this area. Small and Bush[2] have made an analysis of smoke produced as a result of hypothetical non-urban wildfires which one can directly compare with the corresponding modeling assumption used in this TTAPS scenario. Bush and Small studied 3,500 uniquely located, but hypothetical targets, characterizing each according to monthly average weather, ignition area, fuel loading, fire spread, and smoke production. The results showed a significantly smaller smoke production—by a factor of over 30 in July to almost 300 in January—than comparable TTAPS results. An effort is underway to resolve this great difference. It is cited here to illustrate the very large current uncertainties in only one of several critically important parameters.

In the TTAPS analysis, smoke was more important than dust in many cases, and as a result popular interest has tended to focus on fires rather than dust. This may or may not be the correct view. If smoke is systematically overestimated, especially in scenarios that should emphasize dust production over smoke (such as attacks on silos using surface bursts), analytic results will be skewed. Additionally, uncertainties associated with the lofting of dust are large because of limited data from atmospheric nuclear tests carried out prior to 1963. This is because most tests were not relevant to the question of surface or near-surface bursts over continental geology, or the relevant measurements were not made. The range of uncertainty for total injected mass of submicron size dust, that which is of greatest importance, is roughly a factor of ten, based on our current knowledge.

---

[2]Small, R. D., Bush, B. W., *Smoke Production from Multiple Nuclear Explosions in Wildlands*, Pacific Sierra Research Corporation, in publication.

After generation of smoke and dust is estimated, a model must then portray its injection into the atmosphere, the removal processes, and the transport both horizontally and vertically. The TTAPS model did not directly address these processes since it is a one-dimensional model of the atmosphere. By one-dimensional, one means that the variation of atmospheric properties and processes are treated in only the vertical direction. There is no latitudinal or longitudinal variation as in the real world. A one-dimensional model can only deal with horizontally averaged properties of the entire hemisphere. Of great significance, the land, the oceans, and the coastal interface regions cannot be treated. This is a critical deficiency because the ocean, which covers almost three-fourths of the earth's surface, has an enormous heat capacity compared to the land and will act to moderate temperature changes, especially near coastlines and large lakes. The TTAPS authors did acknowledge this limitation and pointed out that these effects would lessen their predicted temperature drops.

Because there is no horizontal (latitude and longitude) dependence in a one-dimensional model, the extent to which smoke and dust would be injected into the atmosphere over time was not estimated in a realistic way. Instead, the total smoke and dust estimated for a given scenario was placed uniformly over the hemisphere at the start of their calculation. The most certain effect of all this is that the hemisphere average temperature drops very rapidly—much faster than it would in a more realistic three-dimensional model using the same input variables.

The one-dimensional model has other shortfalls. Recovery from the minimum temperatures would largely be accomplished through the gradual removal of smoke and dust, and it was assumed that this removal rate would be the same in the perturbed atmosphere as it is in the normal atmosphere. Even in the normal atmosphere, removal of pollutants is a poorly understood process. Most pollution removal depends on atmospheric circulation and precipitation, but in an atmosphere with a very heavy burden of smoke and dust, the cir-

culation and weather processes may be greatly altered. Some potential alterations could lead to much slower removal than normal, others to more rapid removal. Currently we have little insight into this uncertainty.

This discussion of the deficiencies of the one-dimensional TTAPS model is not meant as a criticism. A one-dimensional model is a valuable research tool and can provide some preliminary insights into the physical processes at work. The three-dimensional models needed to treat the problem more realistically are exceedingly complex and will require very large computational resources. The DOD and Department of Energy, in conjunction with the National Center for Atmospheric Research (NCAR) and other agencies, are pursuing the development of three-dimensional models to treat the atmospheric effects problem. Our work is progressing, and the first results of this effort are now beginning to appear. Though very preliminary and not a complete modeling of any specific scenario, they suggest that:

Substantial scavenging of smoke injected into the lower atmosphere from the continents of the Northern Hemisphere may occur as the smoke is being more widely dispersed over the hemisphere.

Lofting of smoke through solar heating could act to increase the lifetime of the remaining smoke and may reduce the sensitivity to height of injection.

For very large smoke injections, global-scale spreading and cooling are more likely in summer than in winter.

Despite good initial progress, many basic problems remain to be solved in the areas of smoke and dust injection, transport, and removal. In order to make the results produced by these models more accurate, we must improve our understanding of the basic phenomena occurring at the micro, meso, and global scale.

One final problem should be mentioned. Dust and smoke have differing potentials to affect the climate only because of their ability to absorb and scatter sunlight. The absorption and scattering coefficients of the various forms of smoke, dust, and other potential nuclear-produced pollutants must be known before any realistic predictions can be expected. Here again there is a large uncertainty, and what we do know about pollutants in the normal atmosphere may not be correct for the conditions in a significantly altered atmosphere.

National Academy of Sciences Report, 1984 Following their preliminary review of the possible effects of nuclear-induced smoke and dust in April 1982, the NAS came to an agreement with DNA, acting on behalf of the DOD, to support a full-fledged study. The first committee meeting occurred at the NAS in March 1983. The NAS committee adopted the one-dimensional TTAPS analysis as a starting point for their investigation. During the course of the study, virtually all of the work going on pertinent to this phenomenon was reviewed.

The result of this effort was the NAS report, "The Effects on the Atmosphere of a Major Nuclear Exchange," released on December 11, 1984.

The conclusion of the report states that:

. . . a major nuclear exchange would insert significant amounts of smoke, fine dust, and undesirable species into the atmosphere. These depositions could result in dramatic perturbations of the atmosphere lasting over a period of at least a few weeks. Estimation of the amounts, the vertical distributions, and the subsequent fates of these materials involves large uncertainties. Furthermore, accurate detailed accounts of the response of the atmosphere, the redistribution and removal of the depositions, and the duration of a greatly degraded environment lie beyond the present state of knowledge.

Nevertheless, the committee finds that, unless one or more of the effects lie near the less severe end of their uncertainty ranges, or unless some mitigating effect has been overlooked, there is a clear possibility that great portions of the land areas of the northern temperate zone (and, perhaps, a large segment of the planet) could be severely affected. Possible impacts include major temperature reductions (particularly for an exchange that occurs in the summer) lasting for weeks, with subnormal temperatures persisting for months. The impact of these temperature reductions and associated meteorological changes on the surviv-

ing population, and on the biosphere that supports the survivors, could be severe, and deserves careful independent study.

. . . [A]ll calculations of the atmospheric effects of a major nuclear war require quantitative assumptions about uncertain physical parameters. In many areas, wide ranges of values are scientifically credible, and the overall results depend materially on the values chosen. Some of these uncertainties may be reduced by further empirical or theoretical research, but others will be difficult to reduce. The large uncertainties include the following: (a) the quantity and absorption properties of the smoke produced in very large fires; (b) the initial distribution in altitude of smoke produced in large fires; (c) the mechanism and rate of early scavenging of smoke from fire plumes, and aging of the smoke in the first few days; (d) the induced rate of vertical and horizontal transport of smoke and dust in the upper troposphere and atmosphere; (e) the resulting perturbations in atmospheric processes such as cloud formation, precipitation, storminess, and wind patterns, and (f) the adequacy of current and projected atmospheric response models to reliably predict changes that are caused by a massive, high altitude, and irregularly distributed injection of particulate matter. The atmospheric effects of a nuclear exchange depend on all of the foregoing physical processes, (a) through (e), and their ultimate calculation is further subject to the uncertainties inherent in (f).

The Interagency Research Program (IRP) The genesis of this program stems from ongoing DOD and DOE research efforts. In 1983, both the DOD and the DOE started research on the atmospheric response phenomena. In addition to sponsoring the NAS study just discussed, the DOD portion of the program addressed a broad range of issues associated with the long-term global climatic effects of nuclear exchange. This program ($400 K in FY83, $1100K in FY84, $1500K in FY85, $2500K in FY86 and continuing at appropriate levels into the future) supports research on several fronts—at numerous government laboratories, universities, and contractors.

The DOD portion of the IRP emphasizes research in (1) the smoke and dust source terms, including the definition of total ignition area, fuel loading and fire spreading, and particulate production, (2) large-scale fire characteristics, particulate lofting, scavenging, coagulation, rain-out, and atmospheric injection, (3) chemistry, including the chemical kinetics of fire and fireballs, the chemical consequences of mesoscale and global processes, and radiative properties (optical and infrared absorption, emission, and scattering), and (4) climatic effects, including the improvement of mesoscale and global climate models to incorporate better particulate source functions; horizontal advection processes; vertical mixing; solar radiation; particulate scavenging; inhomogeneities; particulate, radiative, and circulation feedbacks; seasonal differences; and particulate spreading.

The effort supported by the DOE is fully coordinated with that of the DOD and is currently funded at roughly $2M per year. The LLNL [Lawrence Livermore National Laboratory] program is broadbased and includes modeling of urban fire ignition, plume dynamics, climate effects, radioactive fallout, and biological impacts. The LANL [Los Alamos National Laboratory] program focuses on developing comprehensive models for global-scale climate simulations. It is coordinated with complementary efforts at NCAR and NASA [National Aeronautics and Space Administration] Ames. The IRP came into being with approval of the draft Research Plan for Assessing the Climatic Effects of Nuclear War prepared by a committee of university and government scientists. The plan was initiated by Presidential Science Advisor Dr. George Keyworth, with the National Climate Program Office of NOAA [National Oceanic and Atmospheric Administration] heading the preparation effort. This program augments and coordinates the research activities currently underway in the DOD and the DOE with other government agencies. The program focuses particularly on the problems of fire dynamics, smoke production and properties, and mesoscale processes. The proposed additional research includes increases in theoretical studies, laboratory experiments, field experiments, modeling studies, and research on historical and contemporary analogues of relevant atmospheric phenomena.

The IRP recognizes the need for expertise from a number of experts inside and outside of the Federal Government—many are already at work on the problem. Participating government agencies would include the Department of Defense (DNA), Department of Energy, NOAA, National Science Foundation (NSF), National Bureau of Standards, NASA, Federal Emergency Management Agency (FEMA), and the U.S. Forest Service. The IRP Steering Group is chaired by the President's Science Advisor and is composed of representatives from the Department of Defense, Department of Energy, Department of Commerce, and the National Science Foundation.

The major goals of the IRP are to accelerate the research to reduce the numerous uncertainties in smoke sources and to improve modeling of atmospheric effects. Although it is recognized that not all of the uncertainties could be reduced to uniform or perhaps even to acceptable levels, it is clearly possible to improve our knowledge of the climatic consequences of nuclear exchanges.

2. SUMMARY OBSERVATIONS ON THE CURRENT APPRECIATION OF THE TECHNICAL ISSUES

The Department of Defense recognizes the importance of improving our understanding of the technical underpinnings of the hypothesis which asserts, in most rudimentary form, that if sufficient material, smoke, and dust are created by nuclear explosions, lofted to sufficient altitude, and were to remain at altitude for protracted periods, deleterious effects would occur with regard to the earth's climate.

We have very little confidence in the near-term ability to predict this phenomenon quantitatively, either in terms of the amount of sunlight obscured and the related temperature changes, the period of time such consequences may persist, or of the levels of nuclear attacks which might initiate such consequences. We do not know whether the long-term consequences of a nuclear war—of whatever magnitude—would be the often postulated months of subfreezing temperatures, or a considerably less severe perturbed atmosphere. Even with widely ranging and unpredictable weather, the destructiveness for human survival of the less severe climatic effects might be of a scale similar to the other horrors associated with nuclear war. As the Defense Science Board Task Force on Atmospheric Obscuration found in their interim report:

> The uncertainties here range, in our view, all the way between the two extremes, with the possibility that there are no long-term climatic effects no more excluded by what we know now than are the scenarios that predict months of sub-freezing temperatures.

These observations are consistent with the findings in the NAS report, summarized earlier in this report. We believe the NAS report has been especially useful in highlighting the assumptions and the considerable uncertainty that dominate the calculations of atmospheric response to nuclear war. While other authors have mentioned these uncertainties, the NAS report has gone to considerable length to place them in a context which improves understanding of their impact.

We agree that considerable additional research needs to be done to understand better the effects of nuclear war on the atmosphere, and we support the IRP as a means of advancing that objective. However, we do not expect that reliable results will be rapidly forthcoming. As a consequence, we rary analogues of relevant atmospheric phenomena.

Finally, in view of the present and prospective uncertainties in these climatic predictions, we do not believe that it is possible at this time to draw competent conclusions on their biological consequences, beyond a general observation similar to that in the NAS report: if the climatic effect is severe, the impact on the surviving population and on the biosphere could be correspondingly severe.

QUESTIONS FOR DISCUSSION

1 What effect does the prospect of nuclear winter have on the likelihood of a major nuclear war?
2 Why do scientists differ in their interpretations of evidence of a nuclear winter?
3 What do you think should be the implications to strategic planners of existing scientific evidence on nuclear winter?
4 What is certain and what is uncertain about the scientific evidence concerning nuclear winter?
5 Would the certainty of nuclear winter in the event of nuclear war make it more or less likely that nuclear weapons will be used in war?

SUGGESTED READINGS

Ehrlich, Paul R., Carl Sagan, Donald Kennedy, and Walter Orr Roberts. *The Cold and the Dark: The World After Nuclear War*. New York: Norton, 1984.

Glasstone, Samuel and Philip J. Dolan (eds.). *The Effects of Nuclear Weapons*. Washington, D.C.: U.S. Department of Defense, 1977.

Katz, Arthur. "Would the Living Envy the Dead?" *The Amicus Journal* 5 (Winter 1984), pp. 31–37.

Leaning, Jennifer and Langley Keyes (eds.). *The Counterfeit Ark: Crisis Relocation for Nuclear War*. Cambridge, Massachusetts: Ballinger, 1983.

Martin, Brian. "Critique of Nuclear Extinction," *Journal of Peace Research* XIX, no. 4 (1982), pp. 287–300.

Peterson, Jeannie (ed. for Ambio Magazine). *The Aftermath: The Human and Ecological Consequences of Nuclear War*. New York: Pantheon, 1983.

Powers, Thomas. "Nuclear Winter and Nuclear Strategy," *Atlantic Monthly* (November 1984), pp. 53–60, and 63–64.

Revkin, Andrew C. "Hard Facts About Nuclear Winter," *Science Digest* (March 1985), pp. 62–68, 77, 81, and 83.

Sagan, Carl. "Nuclear War and Climatic Catastrophe: Some Policy Implications," *Foreign Affairs* 63 (Winter 1983/84), pp. 257–92.

Scheer, Robert. *With Enough Shovels: Reagan, Bush and Nuclear War*. New York: Random House, 1982.

Teller, Edward. "Widespread Aftereffects of Nuclear War," *Nature* 310 (August 23, 1984), pp. 621–24.

Turco, R. P., O. B. Toon, T. P. Ackerman, J. B. Pollack, and Carl Sagan. "Nuclear Winter: Global Consequences of Multiple Nuclear Explosions," *Science* 222 (December 23, 1983), pp. 1283–92.

———. "The Climatic Effects of Nuclear War," *Scientific American* 251 (August 1984), pp. 33–43.

U.S. Congress: House of Representatives. *The Consequences of Nuclear War on the Global Environment.* Hearing before the Subcommittee on Investigations and Oversight of the Committee on Science and Technology, 97th Cong., 2nd Sess., 1982.

Zuckerman, Edward. *The Day After World War III: The U.S. Government's Plan for Surviving a Nuclear War.* New York: Viking Press, 1984.

Chapter Two

Nuclear Arms Limitation: General Principles

Many of those seeking to end or at least to minimize the risk of nuclear war believe that the most promising course is to seek nuclear disarmament agreements. Accordingly, it is to this theme that the present section is devoted. First, it should be noted that the term "disarmament" is often used in an imprecise fashion by nonexperts. It must be kept in mind that placing limitations on nuclear arms is not at all the same thing as abolishing them altogether. Hence, we may more accurately speak of "nuclear arms control" than "nuclear disarmament" in all cases not involving the total destruction of nuclear weapons.

The quest for outright nuclear disarmament has a long but discouraging history. Indeed, the United States first advanced a proposal for achieving it as long ago as 1946 in the form of the Baruch Plan. This called for the internationalization of all nuclear energy production as the only means of ensuring that no other national government joined the United States as a possessor of atomic bombs. If this had been accepted by the Soviet Union, the United States would have been willing, or so it said, to surrender for destruction to the proposed international commission its then extremely small stock of atomic weapons. The Soviets rejected the proposal, however, objecting to the proposed control commission's composition, which, given what was then the prevailing character of the international system, would have inevitably had a majority of members with a pro-Western mindset. The Soviets countered with the suggestion, which was unacceptable to Washington, that all countries should agree to renounce nuclear weapons, but did not offer serious provisions for verification and enforcement.

In the absence of agreement, the Soviet Union duly became a nuclear-weapon state in 1949, the year it carried out a successful nuclear test. The genie was out of the bottle. Great Britain (1952), France (1960), and China (1964) joined the nuclear weapons club as well, also openly carrying out nuclear-weapon tests. Subsequently, at least three other countries may have become "undeclared" nuclear-weapon states: namely, India (which in 1974 actually conducted a nuclear test, designated as being for "peaceful purposes"), Israel, and South Africa. There are at least ten additional near-nuclear-weapon states, nations which could soon acquire nuclear arms if they devoted sufficient effort and resources to the task. These are states involved to at least some degree in the peaceful exploitation of nuclear energy, which can be fairly easily diverted to military purposes.

One of the fundamental questions regarding the survival of our species is whether the nuclear "genie" can ever be put back into the bottle, even if the states concerned really desired it and were willing to sign a nuclear disarmament agreement. Doubts on this have existed since at least 1955 when Jakob Malik, the Soviet ambassador to the United Nations, proclaimed with unusual candor that no amount of inspection could any longer be relied upon to reveal stocks of fissile material (from which nuclear weapons can be made) if governments saw fit to conceal them. Significantly, no Western government has ever contradicted Malik, although all have been reticent in spelling out the implications of his statement. Those implications are surely somber. If Malik is correct, they mean that the assured abolition of nuclear weapons by agreement among sovereign states is impossible to achieve. According to some authorities, even the abolition of sovereign states and the creation of a world government (whether in fact or in name) would not necessarily overcome the problem. For, even in that unlikely event, who could be certain that small groups of dissidents in one or more regions had not concealed stocks of fissile material with hopes of sooner or later bringing about a breakdown of that world government and forcing the re-creation of sovereign states?

TOTAL NUCLEAR DISARMAMENT

In our first encounter political scientist Hedley Bull and best-selling writer Jonathan Schell attempt to grapple with the issues involved in the quest for total nuclear disarmament. Bull is candidly skeptical about whether this can be achieved in other than in an entirely remote future—though for him this is not necessarily an unwelcome conclusion as he fears that in the absence of nuclear weapons other forms of warfare would become more common. His basic conclusion is underscored in two sentences: "In the case of the destruction of nuclear stockpiles, an evasion which left only a few nuclear explosives in the hands of the evader, would, in a world disarmed in respect of nuclear weapons, constitute great power. The techniques of inspection at present available do not promise a degree of reliability anywhere near sufficient to allay anxieties of this kind." Thus Bull expects no agreement for total nuclear disarmament to be negotiable in our time.

Jonathan Schell, for his part, questions whether the supposedly "great power" in the hands of a "successful" evader is as decisive as imagined by Bull and his followers, and hence is more hopeful that an agreement abolishing nuclear weapons could be reached. He concedes in one significant sentence that, as far as he knows, "No one has ever devised a system of verification that could, even theoretically, preclude significant cheating." But he holds that such cheating could be countered by parties to a nuclear disarmament treaty, if the parties had antinuclear defensive arrangements along the lines proposed by President Reagan in his Strategic Defense Initiative of March 1983 and if these parties maintained a high state of readiness to initiate a renewed build-up of offensive nuclear weaponry should an adversary brandish a concealed stock. Critics wonder whether Schell's plan really does amount to assured nuclear disarmament. Is he not in practice proposing a world in which nations agree merely to say such disarmament has taken place?—which is not at all the same thing. Supporters of Schell, on the other hand, hold that whether or not this would constitute nuclear disarmament such a world could be a great improvement over present conditions. But however that may be, can we not conclude that it is an experiment we are unlikely to see put into practice at an early date?

ARMS CONTROL

If total disarmament is a distant and maybe unattainable goal, should we instead concentrate on nuclear arms control as the best means of preventing a nuclear catastrophe? Most governments have proclaimed their support for just that, although the results of their endeavors have been somewhat meager. The principal achievements have been as follows:

1963—The Limited Nuclear Test Ban Treaty, involving the United States, Great Britain, and the Soviet Union, halted testing in the atmosphere, in the oceans, and in space.

1967—The Outer Space Treaty required that parties to the treaty not place in orbit around the Earth any objects carrying nuclear weapons, nor install such weapons on celestial bodies, and not station them in outer space in any manner. It also forbade military bases or installations and weapons testing on any celestial bodies.

1968—The Non-Proliferation Treaty (NPT) bound the United States, Great Britain, and the Soviet Union not to provide other countries with nuclear weapons, and to seek to limit their own nuclear inventories. It further provided for non-nuclear weapon states to renounce nuclear weapon aspirations in return for assistance from existing nuclear weapon states in the area of nuclear energy. (More than one hundred non-nuclear-weapon states have subsequently adhered to the NPT.)

1972—The Strategic Arms Limitation Talks Agreement (SALT I) limited the numbers of offensive and defensive nuclear missile systems possessed by the United States and the Soviet Union.

There have, of course, been numerous other agreements, but they have either not been ratified (as in the case of SALT II), or have been of relatively minor or at least of only regional significance (as in the case of the Tlatelolco Treaty providing for the denuclearization of Latin America).

Despite this uninspiring record, all leading governments continue to pay lip service to the desirability of nuclear arms control. However, increasing doubts have been expressed, particularly in the United States since the emergence of conservative critics, about whether the process is a waste of time, or even fundamentally harmful to Western interests. Something of the flavor of this debate is to be found in the polemical exchange between George Will and Senator William Proxmire.

Will, a noted conservative journalist, is convinced that the open nature of American society effectively prevents serious cheating on agreements, but that no such inhibitions apply in the Soviet Union. Furthermore, he holds that the Soviets do not see arms control agreements as other than a means of obtaining military advantage. The Americans, on the other hand, according to Will, are often the victims of self-inflicted wounds caused by a "foolish thirst for agreements." Will contends that, in practice, any agreements reached will not only favor Moscow but, in addition, serve to divert competition into other areas of nuclear arms improvement, quantitative or qualitative.

Proxmire directly challenged Will's arguments in the United States Senate. In this challenge, reprinted here from the *Congressional Record*, he first draws attention to some of the existing arms control agreements, which Will sees fit to ignore. For example, can Will seriously hold that the world would be any safer if the Limited Test Ban Treaty of 1963 had never come into force? Proxmire also believes that both superpowers have an interest in facing nuclear deterrents which are stable and invulnerable to disarming strikes, and he argues accordingly that this shared objective can be well served by nuclear arms control agreements.

Another issue centers on treaty verification. Proxmire concedes that some agreements may be flawed because they contain inadequate provisions for inspection and enforcement. In this category many experts place the Biological Weapons Convention of 1972, which prohibits the development, production, and stockpiling of biological and toxic weapons. He nevertheless rejects the conclusion, unlike Will, that inadequate provisions for verification suggest that *all* arms control is undesirable. Proxmire maintains instead that future treaties should be adequately verifiable as well as in the mutual interest of the signatories.

UNILATERALISM

Whatever critics may think of Will's rather sweeping judgment, few are likely to maintain that the arms control agreements reached to date have gone very far towards halting the superpowers' nuclear arms competition, let alone towards creating stable conditions in which a genuinely peaceful relationship could develop. This has led some commentators to argue that more radical actions are now appropriate. In particular, there are those who believe that unilateral moves of restraint in nuclear-systems acquisition by NATO states (as well as it is hoped, by members of the opposing East European alliance, the Warsaw Pact) could serve to help halt and even reverse the nuclear arms race.

An advocate of a "unilateralist" approach was the late Herbert Scoville, Jr., a former deputy director of the U.S. Central Intelligence Agency (CIA) and a former assistant director of the U.S. Arms Control and Disarmament Agency (ACDA). Perhaps surprisingly for someone with his background, Scoville evidently did not believe that unilateral restraint by the United States constituted a manifestation of weakness. His article, published in 1977, took full account of the SALT I agreements of 1972, but obviously could not anticipate the terms of the SALT II agreement negotiated in 1979. It seems unlikely, however, that Scoville would have wished to amend this thesis, even taking SALT II into account, particularly when it is recalled that SALT II, whatever its merits and demerits, has not been ratified by the United States—and presumably never will be.

Scoville is careful not to condemn all formal arms control agreements, but he sees definite limits to what can be achieved by this route. He is conscious that technological innovation is likely to outpace the efforts of negotiators. Hence such agreements (necessarily limited in scope) are likely to be followed by diversion of endeavor into other areas of arms competition. Again, because of technological advances, negotiators cannot always anticipate the form which loopholes in present agreements may take, resulting in the proliferation of allegations—sincere or not—of cheating or of sharp practice when advantage is taken of such loopholes. This may in turn poison the atmosphere between the superpowers, perhaps leading to consideration of the ultimate abrogation of agreements. The creation in 1972 of the Soviet-American Standing Consultative Commission, whose purpose is to review allegations of cheating, has done a little, but not enough, to overcome these problems arising from formal agreements.

Another of Scoville's concerns relates to the emphasis on the acquisition of "bargaining chips" that tends to accompany periods of intense arms control negotiations between the superpowers. Weapons which otherwise might never have been deemed appropriate are thus procured, thereby often fueling, rather than damping down, arms competition. Still another feature of arms controlling is the propensity to offer for destruction by agreement obsolete weaponry which otherwise would have been unilaterally scrapped—a tactic which rarely impresses or deceives the negotiating partner.

All of these considerations have led not only Scoville, but other distinguished Western commentators, such as Christoph Bertram, former director of the International Institute for Strategic Studies (IISS), and Thomas Schelling of Harvard University, to urge that more informal methods of promoting arms limitation between the superpowers may be more appropriate. Scoville starts from the assumption—by no means universally shared—that the balance of terror between Washington and Moscow is in no way delicate or precarious. He writes, on the contrary, of the "extraordinary stability of the strategic balance." He believes that there are fairly negligible risks involved in either superpower engaging in sincere acts of unilateral restraint. These, he trusts, will evoke reciprocal responses. If such reciprocal responses do not arise in any particular case, then a unilateral act of restraint can be unilaterally reversed with a minimum of fuss and ill feeling.

Some Western commentators, however, see great risks in this approach. Above all, most American conservative hard-liners deny that the balance of terror is in any way stable. They have warned consistently, since the mid-1970s, of a "window of vulnerability," and some of those concerned established the Committee on the Present Danger, which held that the Soviet Union was on the point of achieving a nuclear superiority that could enable it to subject the West to either irresistable blackmail or even a successful nuclear first-strike. Other observers, without going this far, held that asymmetries in the political systems operating respectively in NATO and the Warsaw Pact meant that unilateral restraint by the West was unlikely to be reciprocated and might well be read in Moscow as merely a sign of weakness and lack of resolve.

Historian Philip Towle provides an example of this line of reasoning, although he first argues in a notable spirit of fairness that "it is very difficult for the Soviet Union to make effective unilateral gestures." The secrecy which is so much a feature of the Soviet system would surely make it far from easy for the West to know whether a proclaimed act of unilateral restraint was sincere. Whereas we know of some genuine Western unilateral limitations, "that take place before production has begun," we cannot rely on having comparable, reliable information about Soviet weapons at this stage of development. Still less is it possible, in the absence of public debate in Moscow, to know which weapons projects are intended as mere "bargaining chips." Hence, according to Towle, "the Soviet leaders can only occasionally make an effective gesture of renouncing them." The reciprocity on which Scoville relies is thus, in Towle's view, unlikely to materialize.

Also striking is the extent to which Towle, writing from what is admittedly a British perspective, rests his arguments against "unilateralism" largely on British precedents from the interwar years. Critics may think that this is a misuse of history, since nuclear weapons did not exist in the 1930s and therefore nobody could plausibly have referred, as Scoville now does, to the "extraordinary stability of the strategic balance." All the same, it must be remembered that some proposed forms of "unilateralism" today *do* bear some relationship to the acts of disarmament-by-example carried out by British governments in the late 1920s and early 1930s. Yet support for such proposals today is strongest in Western Europe, where they are usually endorsed by people who are not solely or even primarily motivated, as Scoville was, by a desire to promote a more stable Soviet-American relationship. West European "unilateralists" have in fact a great variety of motivations. Some are pro-Soviet sympathizers; some are religiously inspired pacifists; some are genuine neutralists who hold that the security interests of their countries are endangered rather than served by nuclear-weapon involvement with Washington; and some, while genuine supporters of NATO, are anxious to reduce or eliminate unilaterally the alliance's reliance on nuclear weapons in the European theater. In Great Britain, and to a much lesser extent in France, there are also "unilateralists" whose primary targets are not superpower nuclear capabilities, but their own countries' independent nuclear forces, which could conceivably be used in defiance of both superpowers. Thus Towle's opposition to most of these forms of "unilateralism" should not be confused with his disagreement with Scoville's call for unilateral restraint on the part of the superpowers. And Scoville's pleas for unilateral restraint in the context of the "extraordinary stability of the strategic balance" between the superpowers does not imply that he necessarily endorses various forms of "unilateralism," sometimes chauvinistic in character, advocated in Western Europe. (It is no doubt for this reason that some Americans who share Scoville's outlook avoid the use of the word "unilateralism" and speak instead of a policy of "peace initiatives.")

In short, imprecision in the use of the term "unilateralism" is arguably not centrally addressed by either Scoville or Towle. "Unilateralism," in one form or another, has had a long history, most of it not deserving of the excoriation which has been heaped upon the variant pursued by Great Britain in the interwar period. On this point we recall the still pertinent words written by Hedley Bull in 1961:

> A nation's armaments policy is nearly always unilateral, in the sense that it is carried out in the absence of reciprocal undertakings by other nations about their armaments policies. This is as much true of policies of disarmament as of policies of rearmament. The history of disarmament is, for the most part, the history of unilateral reductions of armaments; if we except the discriminatory disarmament imposed by victors on vanquished powers, like that imposed on Germany by the Treaty of Versailles, it is doubtful whether any very substantial reduction (as distinct from limitation and regulation, of which there are examples) of armaments has been brought about by treaty in modern times. Unilateral disarmament is constantly carried out in respect of particular categories of armaments, as they become obsolete; and is carried out in respect of armaments generally, when, and to the extent that, it is believed that there exists no external occasion for their use.[1]

If Bull is correct, does it not then follow that the future nuclear deployments of the superpowers are likely, as in the past, to be determined primarily by unilateral decisions, rather than by treaty negotiations? Incidentally, will not the same predominance of unilateral decision making probably also apply for the foreseeable future to the majority of states having any serious prospect of joining the nuclear club? We shall return to this point in a later section when we give particular attention to the issue of proliferation.

---

[1]Hedley Bull, *The Control of the Arms Race*, (London: Weidenfeld and Nicholson, 1961) p. 77.

5 Is Complete Nuclear Disarmament an Unattainable
Dream?

YES

Hedley Bull

Nuclear Disarmament

NO

Jonathan Schell

A Deliberate Policy

Nuclear Disarmament
Hedley Bull

. . . Nuclear explosives, besides providing the chief present impetus behind the movement for disarmament, constitute the most powerful and militarily important weapons available to the great powers, what distinguishes them in military terms from lesser powers as well as what makes them respect each other. This is the chief obstacle to nuclear disarmament. The problem of inspection is most serious in this field, and makes the conclusion of a nuclear disarmament agreement more unlikely than it would otherwise be. But it is not the most basic obstacle, for it has risen to prominence only because nuclear explosives are so crucial to the balance of military power. Because nuclear weapons are small enough to escape detection by espionage or a rudimentary inspection system, but at the same time so militarily important that a quite minor evasion of a control agreement would bring a decisive advantage, the concern for a very reliable, a *watertight*, system of detection has attained its present intensity. Now, as in the past, nations are least willing to relinquish those weapons that are most important to them.

The abolition of nuclear explosives, promising an absolute security against nuclear war, is one of the most irresistible of political ideas. None of the major governments has felt able to omit this item from its disarmament policy, and the disarmament programmes of the two blocs as recently as the 1960 Disarmament Conference included it, though in the last phase and unaccompanied by any account of how it would be controlled. The renunciation of this objective would be disastrous for any government, party or person with the ambition to survive in political life: for it is an objective deeply rooted in the fears and hopes of masses of men.

A system of security based on the assured abolition of nuclear explosives, and their assured perpetual absence, would be generally preferred to the security provided by the nuclear balance. There is good reason to believe that the destruction of nuclear explosives, removing as it does the chief source of the fear of war, would increase the probability of war. But this is a prospect which many people would be willing to face if, in choosing the prenuclear world of inferior deterrents and more frequent wars, they were able to choose also to liberate themselves from the fear of the great catastrophe.

But no such choice exists: it is not within the competence of a disarmament agreement to restore a world that is innocent of nuclear technology. We must assume that the future, even if it were to include the destruction of existing nuclear explosives, will include the knowledge of how to make them, and the will under the stress of war to do so. The technological environment in which any future war will occur will include nuclear technology as an increasingly commonplace part of it, and many other branches of advanced technology susceptible of military utilization besides.

The abolition of existing nuclear explosives, were it now practicable, would provide only relative security against nuclear war, for it would entail risks of the resumption of the nuclear arms race in an uncertain world, and it would not preclude the continued prosecution of the qualitative arms race in other fields. It is at least open to doubt whether the security thus afforded would be greater than that provided by the known presence of a small but sufficient quantity of nuclear explosives in a stable and controlled balance. But this question can be answered only by speculations, and is not of immediate relevance, as the conditions for an agreed abolition are not present. The pressures making against the controlled abolition of existing stocks

From Hedley Bull, "Nuclear Disarmament," in *The Control of the Arms Race: Disarmament and Arms Control in the Missile Age*, 2nd ed. (New York: Praeger, 1965), pp. 97–102.

of nuclear explosives are at present overwhelming. In the first place nuclear weapons now occupy a central place in the military policies of the great nations. At one time nuclear weapons were few, their military implications had not been thought out, military planning and organization had not been built around them, and they were largely extraneous to military policy. All this was true of nuclear weapons at the time the Baruch Plan was introduced, in 1946. Now they are deeply embedded in military thinking and military arrangements: it is increasingly difficult to go into reverse.

In the second place the powers, if they do contemplate abandoning their nuclear weapons, will undertake to do so only if they can agree on a system of inspection able to give them confidence that each other's undertakings are fulfilled. Because the military consequences of the evasion of a prohibition of nuclear weapons are so serious, they require very firm assurances against such evasion. There is at present no system for the detection of secret stocks of these weapons that is effective in this sense.

In general, the effectiveness of an inspection system does not mean only technical reliability of the detection of evasions, but the degree of reliability acceptable to the negotiators in the context of the prohibition to be inspected. The degree of reliability that the negotiators will expect is perhaps in no case 100%. How reliable they will require it to be will depend on the particular prohibition: on the seriousness to them of the consequences of evasion, which is determined by the importance of the weapon prohibited, and the remedies available to them in the event of a successful evasion. In the case of the destruction of nuclear stockpiles, an evasion which left only a few nuclear explosives in the hands of the evader, would, in a world disarmed in respect of nuclear weapons, constitute great power. The techniques of inspection at present available do not promise a degree of reliability anywhere near sufficient to allay anxieties of this kind. Nuclear explosives can be very small objects, and there is no way of finding them except by looking for them everywhere. When nuclear weap-

ons were as few as they were in 1946, it might have been possible to check reliably the inventories of them and ensure that they were all destroyed: but they are now very numerous. If nuclear weapons were very large objects, and easily identifiable by photography, radar or other instruments, this problem might not be so important: the reduction and limitation of capital ships under the Washington Naval Treaty, for example, was carried out without any inspection system. If there were some limited series of places to inspect (this is what gives some promise to the idea of a cessation of further production of nuclear explosives), it would not be so serious. It is true that inspection systems do not aim to make evasion impossible, but merely to deter evasion by posing a sufficient risk. But while this risk is as slight as it now appears, the controlled abolition of nuclear weapons is not a negotiable proposition.

A judgment as serious as this should not be made without the closest scrutiny. The following qualifications should be attached to it. One is that it is a judgment made in the context of the techniques and technology of inspection available at the present time. This is subject to change, and might change considerably if resources were devoted to the study of the technology of arms control on a fraction of the scale on which they are devoted to armaments. Another qualification is that the effectiveness of any system of inspection depends on political and social factors: the willingness of populations and governments to cooperate in detection or evasion. This factor has been a decisive one in the evasion of arms control systems that have been imposed on alien populations, like the German evasion of the disarmament provisions of the Versailles Treaty. It cannot be assumed, as it sometimes is by writers on disarmament, that in the case of an agreed, universal system of arms control, 'the people' are bound to be on the side of the inspectors and of the international organization they represent. But the point should be made that the direction of public sympathies is an element of great importance in the working of any inspection system that does not depend merely on instruments, and this is a factor which is not known in advance. A third qualification is that the effectiveness of measures to detect the evasion of stockpiles, such as it is, is likely to increase to the extent to which it is combined with other kinds of control (e.g. of budgets, military manpower, systems of delivery, etc.) in a more comprehensive system of controlled disarmament.

These qualifications, however, refer to remote contingencies which do not detract from the force of the judgment that effective inspection of the abolition of nuclear explosives is not now feasible. This is, moreover, a judgment in which the Soviet Union and the Western powers have concurred since 1955.

Apart from the question of the effectiveness of inspection arrangements, there is some doubt as to the acceptability of these arrangements to the powers: as to whether the sort of inspection arrangements that would be involved in any attempt to control the destruction of stockpiles—vast numbers of men with unlimited rights of access—would be tolerated by them.

In the Soviet Union, such inspectors could scarcely fulfil their functions without undermining the whole character of Soviet society. Though the business of inspection concerns the examination of material objects, this is not possible without interference in social and political arrangements. Unlimited rights of access, the immunity of citizens volunteering information from police control, their duty not to withhold information, appear to undermine the secrecy endemic in Soviet society and to set the authority of the inspectorate above that of the government. The Western powers have been consistently the champions of thorough-going inspection arrangements. They would themselves, however, experience great difficulty in accepting arrangements which destroyed industrial secrecy and authorized general delation.

Finally, there is the question of sanctions. Evasions must not only be detected, but deterred or put right by measures of enforcement. Some kind of sanction must underlie a system of arms control: to discourage evasions by showing that their detection will be followed by corrective or punitive action; and to provide those powers which do not evade the system with some security against those which do. The primitive sanction behind a measure of arms control is the resumption of the arms race, just as the sanction behind a truce is the resumption of war. In the case of the prohibition of nuclear weapons, however, nations are not likely to regard their own resumption of the arms race in the event of an evasion as a sufficient deterrent of such an evasion, or as a sufficient protection for themselves against it. The power which covertly retained a stock of nuclear explosives, and found itself the sole possessor of such a stock in a disarmed world, would be the master of it. No sanction is an adequate deterrent to such an evasion, and none affords the disarmed, remaining powers with adequate protection against the evader, except that provided by another nuclear force. The abolition of nuclear weapons from the arsenals of sovereign powers entails a central force equipped with nuclear weapons. If by such a central force we understand simply the present nuclear powers acting in concert to preserve their monopoly, such a prospect, though it may appear remote, is within the range of contingencies we are entitled to contemplate. It is conceivable, and perhaps desirable, that the United States and the Soviet Union should combine to impose nuclear disarmament on the rest of the world, and employ their own nuclear power as the sanction behind it. But if by this central force we understand a supranational institution or government imposing its will on all the powers, this is something which belongs to a world very different from our own. . . .

The Abolition—A Deliberate Policy
Jonathan Schell

. . . The key is to enter into an agreement abolishing nuclear arms. Nations would first agree, in effect, to drop their swords from their hands and lift their shields toward one another instead. They would agree to have not world government, in which all nations are fused into one nation, but its exact opposite—a multiplicity of inviolate nations pledged to leave each other alone. For nations that now possess nuclear weapons, the agreement would be a true abolition agreement. For those that do not now possess them, it would be a strengthened nonproliferation agreement. (A hundred and nineteen nations have already signed the nonproliferation treaty of 1968.) Obviously, an agreement among the superpowers on both the nature of the status quo and the precise terms of abolition would be the most difficult part of the negotiation. The agreement would be enforced not by any world police force or other organ of a global state but by each nation's knowledge that a breakdown of the agreement would be to no one's advantage, and would only push all nations back down the path to doom. In the widest sense, the agreement would represent the institutionalization of this knowledge. But if nuclear weapons are to be abolished by agreement, one might ask, why not go all the way? Why not abolish conventional weapons and defensive weapons as well? The answer, of course, is that even in the face of the threat of annihilation nations have as yet shown no willingness to surrender their sovereignty, and conventional arms would be one support for its preservation. While the abolition of nuclear arms would increase the margin of mankind's safety against nuclear destruction and the peril of extinction, the retention of conventional arms would permit the world to hold on to the system of nation-states. Therefore, a second provision of the agreement would stipulate that the size of conventional forces be limited and balanced. In keeping with the defensive aim of the agreement as a whole, these forces would, to whatever extent this was technically possible, be deployed and armed in a defensive mode. There is also another reason for retaining defenses. One of the most commonly cited and most substantial reasons for rejecting the abolition of nuclear arms, even if the nuclear powers should develop the will to abolish them, is that the verification of a nuclear-abolition agreement could never be adequate. And, as far as I know, it is true that no one has ever devised a system of verification that could, even theoretically, preclude significant cheating. Like defense, it seems, inspection is almost inherently imperfect. When arsenals are large, the argument runs, a certain amount of cheating on arms-control agreements is unimportant, because the number of concealed weapons is likely to be small in relation to the size of the arsenals as a whole. But as the size of the arsenals shrinks, it is said, the importance of cheating grows, and finally the point is reached at which the hidden arsenals tip the strategic balance in favor of the cheater. According to this argument, the point of maximum—indeed, total—imbalance is reached when, after an abolition agreement has been signed, one side cheats while the other does not. Then the cheater, it is said, has an insuperable advantage, and holds its innocent and trusting co-signer at its mercy. But if anti-nuclear defenses are retained the advantage in cheating is sharply reduced, or actually eliminated. Arrayed against today's gigantic nuclear forces, defenses are helpless. Worse, one side's defenses serve as a goad to further offensive production by the other side, which doesn't want the offensive capacity it has decided on to be weakened. But if defenses were arrayed against the kind of force that

From Jonathan Schell, "The Abolition: II—A Deliberate Policy," *The New Yorker* (January 9, 1984): pp. 61–64.

could be put together in violation of an abolition agreement they could be crucial. On the one side would be a sharply restricted, untested, and clandestinely produced and maintained offensive force, while on the other side would be a large, fully tested, openly deployed, and technically advanced defensive force. Such a force might not completely nullify the danger of cheating (there is always the man with a suitcase), but no one can doubt that it would drastically reduce it. At the very least, it would throw the plans of an aggressor into a condition of total uncertainty. Moreover, as the years passed after the signing of the agreement the superiority of the defense would be likely to increase, because defensive weapons would continue to be openly developed, tested, and deployed, while offensive weapons could not be. Therefore—probably as a separate, third provision of the agreement—anti-nuclear defensive forces would be permitted.

President Reagan recently offered a vision of a world protected from nuclear destruction by defensive weapons, many of which would be based in space. The United States, he said, should develop these weapons and then share them with the Soviet Union. With both countries protected from nuclear attack, he went on, both would be able to scrap their now useless nuclear arsenals and achieve full nuclear disarmament. Only the order of events in his proposal was wrong. If we seek first to defend ourselves, and not to abolish nuclear weapons until after we have made that effort, we will never abolish them, because of the underlying, technically irreversible superiority of the offensive in the nuclear world. But if we abolish nuclear weapons first and then build the defenses, as a hedge against cheating, we can succeed. Abolition prepares the way for defense.

However, none of these defensive arrangements would offer much protection if the agreement failed to accompany them with one more provision. The worst case—which must be taken into account if nations are to have confidence in the military preparations for thwarting aggressors—is not mere cheating but blatant, open violation of the agree-

ment by a powerful and ruthless nation that is determined to intimidate or subjugate other nations, or the whole world, by suddenly and swiftly building up, and perhaps actually using, an overwhelming nuclear arsenal. This possibility creates the all-important limits mentioned earlier. As soon as it happened, the underlying military superiority of the offensive in the nuclear world would again hold sway, and the conventional and anti-nuclear defenses permitted under the abolition agreement would become useless. (Just how soon in this buildup the offensive weapons would eclipse the defensive ones would depend on the effectiveness of the defenses that had been built up.) The only significant military response to this threat would be a response in kind: a similar nuclear buildup by the threatened nations, returning the world to something like the balance of terror as we know it today. But in order to achieve that buildup the threatened nations would probably have to have already in existence considerable preparations for the manufacture of nuclear arms. Therefore, a fourth provision of the abolition agreement would permit nations to hold themselves in a particular, defined state of readiness for nuclear rearmament. This provision would, in fact, be the very core of the military side of the agreement. It would be the definition, in technical terms, of what "abolition" was to be. And it would be the final guarantor of the safety of nations against attack. However, this guarantor would not defend. It would deter. The most important element in this readiness would simply be the knowledge of how to make the weapons—knowledge that nations are powerless to get rid of even if they want to. This unlosable knowledge is, as we have seen, the root fact of life in the nuclear world, from which the entire predicament proceeds. But, just as the potential for nuclear aggression flows from the knowledge, menacing the stability of the agreement, so does the potential for retaliation, restoring the stability of the agreement. Its persistence is the reason that deterrence doesn't dissolve when the weapons are abolished. In other words, in the nuclear world the threat to use force is as self-cancelling at zero nuclear weapons as it is at fifty thousand nuclear weapons. Thus, both in its political ends—preservation of a stalemate—and in its means—using the threat of nuclear destruction itself to prevent the use of nuclear weapons—the abolition agreement would represent an extension of the doctrine of deterrence: an extension in which the most terrifying features of the doctrine would be greatly mitigated, although not finally removed.

The agreed-upon preparations would be based on the knowledge. In all likelihood, they would consist both of inspectable controls on nuclear reactors and on other facilities producing weapons-grade materials and of rules regarding the construction of delivery vehicles. One question that the policymakers would put to the scientists would be what precise level of technical arrangements would permit some particular, defined level of armament to be achieved in a fixed lead time to nuclear rearmament—say, six weeks. Possible lead times would be defined in such terms as the following: an eight-week lead time to the production of two hundred warheads mounted on cruise missiles, or a six-week lead time to a hundred warheads mounted in military aircraft. The lead time would have to be short enough so that the would-be aggressor, seeking to make use of the interval as a head start, would not be able to establish a decisive lead. "Decisive" in this, or any, nuclear context refers to the ability to destroy the victim's retaliatory capacity in a preëmptive first strike. Preëmption is the spectre that haunts the deterrence strategists, for if one side can destroy the retaliatory capacity of the other side in a preëmptive strike, then deterrence dissolves. This is the point at which victory looms up again as a possibility, and force stops being self-cancelling. (At least, it does in the short run. It's much more difficult to see how a nuclear aggressor could escape retaliation over a longer run.) So it is today, and so it would be in a world of zero nuclear weapons. The task for strategy in a nuclear-weapon-free world would be to design a capacity for nuclear rearmament which could not be destroyed in a first strike by a nation that took the lead in rearmament by abrogating the abolition agreement, secretly or openly. Retaliatory capacity would have to be able to keep pace with aggressive capacity—to the extent that a disarming first strike would be excluded. If that requirement was satisfied, possession in a nuclear-weapon-free world of the capacity for rebuilding nuclear weapons would deter nations from rebuilding them and then using them, just as in our present, nuclear-armed world possession of the weapons themselves deters nations from using them. Today, missile deters missile, bomber deters bomber, submarine deters submarine. Under what we might call weaponless deterrence, factory would deter factory, blueprint would deter blueprint, equation would deter equation. In today's world, when the strategists assess one another's arsenals they see that every possible escalation in attack can be matched by an escalation on the other side, until the arsenals of both sides are depleted and both nations are annihilated. So the two sides are deterred from attacking one another. With weaponless deterrence in effect, the strategists would see that any possible escalation in rearmament by one side could be matched by an escalation on the other side, until both were again fully armed and ready to embark on mutual assured destruction. So they would be deterred from rearming.

It has often been said that the impossibility of uninventing nuclear weapons makes their abolition impossible. But under the agreement described here the opposite would be the case. The knowledge of how to rebuild the weapons is just the thing that would make abolition *possible,* because it would keep deterrence in force. Indeed, the everlastingness of the knowledge is the key to the abolition of nuclear arms within the framework of deterrence. Once we accept the fact that the acquisition of the knowledge was the essential preparation for nuclear armament, and that it can never be reversed, we can see that every state of disarmament is also a state of armament. And, being a state of armament, it has deterrent value. In pointing out the deterrent value of preparations for nuclear rearmament, and even of the mere knowledge of how to rebuild the weapons, we make the reply to the present opponents of abolition which Bernard Brodie made to Robert Oppenheimer. Oppenheimer, rightly observing that nuclear weapons could not be defended against, called them inherently "aggressive" weapons and predicted that they would inevitably be used in lightning-swift aggressive war. In such a world, of course, there would have been no stability whatever. But to this Brodie responded that the would-be aggressor would not be the only one possessing nuclear weapons, and that when the aggressor saw that its foe possessed them—and was ready to retaliate with them—its aggressive fever would be cooled down. Now we are told that aggressors will take advantage of the abolition of nuclear weapons to rebuild and use nuclear weapons, and to this the answer again is that the intended victims will have the same capacities, and these will act as a deterrent, saving the world's stability.

The notion that abolition is impossible because uninvention is impossible appears to stem from a failure to distinguish clearly between these two things. The confusion is exemplified in "Living with Nuclear Weapons," a recently published book by six authors associated with Harvard University, in which, in support of their conclusion that a world without nuclear weapons is "a fictional utopia," the authors write, "The discovery of nuclear weapons, like the discovery of fire itself, lies behind us on the trajectory of history: it cannot be undone. Even if all nuclear arsenals were destroyed, the knowledge of how to reinvent them would remain and could be put to use in any of a dozen or more nations. The atomic fire cannot be extinguished." The authors fear that "the knowledge of how to reinvent" the weapons will upset any abolition agreement. But if one has "the knowledge," there is no need to "reinvent" anything, because one can go ahead and rebuild the weapons right away by using that knowledge. If, on the other hand, reinvention is really required, then one must have somehow lost the knowledge, but this is impossible. Of course, if one speaks of the knowledge of how to rebuild the weapons rather than "the knowledge of how to reinvent" them, the inconsistency disappears; but then one is speaking of rearming after abolition rather than after uninvention. By inadvertently blurring the distinction between the two, the Harvard authors, like many other propo-

nents of deterrence, make abolition appear to be, like uninvention, impossible, and confer upon the world's nuclear arsenals a durability and irremovability that in fact only the knowledge of how to make them possesses. Though uninvention is impossible, abolition is not. Or if it were true that both were impossible it would have to be for completely different reasons—in the case of uninvention because we don't know how to rid the world of basic scientific knowledge, and in the case of abolition because we lack the necessary political will. If the distinction is kept clear, then the hope opens up that the impossibility of uninvention, which is the fundamental fact of life in the nuclear world, makes abolition, which is just one of the conceivable ways of organizing that world, possible. For it was the invention, not the buildup, of nuclear arms that irreversibly placed mankind within reach of its own self-slaughtering hand, ruined war as the final arbiter in global affairs, and set mankind adrift in a new and unfamiliar political world. . . .

QUESTIONS FOR DISCUSSION

1 Can anything be done to guarantee that no state would evade a total nuclear disarmament treaty?
2 If a country were able to successfully evade a total nuclear disarmament treaty by hiding a few nuclear weapons, would this give the cheating nation a decisive edge to rule the world?
3 Would a total nuclear disarmament treaty strengthen the security of nations?
4 Would the presence on Soviet soil of an extensive inspection system composed of representatives from different nations undermine the whole character of Soviet society?
5 What kinds of sanctions would be effective if an evasion of a complete nuclear disarmament treaty were detected?

SUGGESTED READINGS

Carlton, David. "Verification and Security Guarantees in International Disarmament Negotiations: Lessons from the Past," in C. F. Barnaby (ed.), *Preventing the Spread of Nuclear Weapons*. London: Souvenir Press, 1969, pp. 127–43.

————. "International Systemic Features Inhibiting Disarmament and Arms Control," in David Carlton and Carlo Schaerf (eds.), *Reassessing Arms Control*. London: Macmillan, 1985, pp. 28–35.

Clark, Grenville and Louis Sohn. *World Peace Through World Law: Two Alternative Plans*. Cambridge, Massachusetts: Harvard University Press, 1966.

Forbes, Henry W. *The Strategy of Disarmament*. Washington, D.C.: Public Affairs Press, 1962.

Potter, William C. (ed.), *Verification and Arms Control*. Lexington, Massachusetts: Lexington Books, 1985.

Wright, Michael, *Disarm and Verify: An Explanation of the Central Difficulties and of National Policies*. New York: Frederick A. Praeger, 1964.

6 Is Nuclear Arms Control Harmful?

YES

George F. Will

Why Arms Control Is Harmful

NO

William Proxmire

Why We Need Nuclear Arms Control

Why Arms Control Is Harmful
George F. Will

Today's arms-control controversy is remarkable for the virtual absence of the most important argument. It is that the arms-control process is injurious to U.S. interests. That argument offends conventional wisdom and (what is much the same thing) wishful thinking. It has the redeeming merit of being true, as Seymour Weiss knows. In a paper presented at the Lehrman Institute, Weiss, retired ambassador and State Department director of political and military affairs from 1960–67, argues that enthusiasm for the arms-control process—a process barren of achievements—reflects misapprehensions about the usefulness of that process in slowing the arms race, saving money and taming the Soviet Union.

The idea of an arms "race"—often described as "spiraling"—is odd. The U.S. nuclear-weapons inventory has been sharply reduced. It contains 8,000 fewer warheads and 25 percent less megatonnage than in the 1960s. This is the result not of arms agreements but of modernization programs that produced safer, more effective weapons—modernizations of the sort that arms-control advocates try to block with agreements.

During the era of détente and arms control the Soviet nuclear arsenal has grown quantitatively and qualitatively. A study commissioned during the Carter administration compared 41 categories of nuclear capabilities (warheads, megatonnage, delivery systems, etc.) in the period beginning with the Cuban missile crisis. It concluded that the United States had been well ahead in every category in 1962 and was behind in all but two by the late 1970s. Since SALT II was signed in 1979 the Soviet Union has added more than 3,400 warheads. Does anyone think the world is safer than it was when the SALT process began in 1969?

The achievement most celebrated by arms-control enthusiasts is the 1972 treaty effectively banning antiballistic missiles. True, we saved the cost of ABM's. But partly as a result of that decision we will spend many more billions on MX missiles, an unsatisfactory response to the fact that our undefended land-based ICBM's are vulnerable. Because MX is unsatisfactory, billions more may be spent on smaller, mobile "midgetman" missiles. Why is MX so unsatisfactory? Because of an arms agreement.

SALT I limited the number and size of launchers—basically, holes in the ground—rather than numbers or megatonnage of warheads. Limits on those would be hard to verify, given Soviet secrecy. So SALT I drove arms planning toward big missiles packing maximum megatonnage. SALT I did what arms agreements usually do: it did not restrain competition, it turned it in a new direction. It was a direction in which the Soviet Union, with its huge SS-18s, had a lead. SALT I ratified a Soviet advantage and, by giving rise to the inherently vulnerable MX, reduced the stability of deterrence.

This republic overflows with laws, lawyers and faith that the world can be tamed by words on parchment. Americans see arms control as a way of freezing the status quo; the Soviets see it as one arena in a comprehensive, unending competition. Furthermore, Weiss says, persons who think arms control should be the "centerpiece" of U.S.-Soviet relations ignore the fundamental incompatibility of U.S. and Soviet objectives. The configuration of the Soviet buildup in the arms-control era is unambiguous. The arms are not designed for defense but for producing a world pliant to Soviet designs. Weiss says there is no reason to expect the Soviets to negotiate away advantages, and ample reason to expect the Soviets to exploit the American thirst for agreements.

In addition to selling discord among U.S. allies and paralyzing U.S. procurements, Soviet negotiators have, Weiss says, five aims. First, limit the wrong things (e.g., launchers). Second, make sure the limits on important things are ambiguous. (SALT I limited but did not define "heavy" missiles.) Third, accept specific limits only if they are unverifiable (e.g., the ban on biological weapons or the SALT II limits on cruise-missile ranges). Fourth, evade even strict, verifiable limits by claiming they do not apply to this or that program. (The Soviets claim their ABM system is just a defense against bombers.) Fifth, get the treaty to legitimize violations of the treaty. (SALT II's flimsy verification terms forbid encryption of data from missile tests—except when encryption is not intended to evade arms-control limits. But given that it is encrypted, how are we to tell?)

Because ours is an open society, our government cannot cheat on agreements, and because our society invests such hope in arms control, even an administration as starchy as Reagan's is apt to forgive Soviet cheating or mute even required reports of it. When, complying with a Senate demand, the administration submitted a list of Soviet violations, The New York Times denounced the—you guessed it—administration for "initiating this damaging laundry list."

The arms-control era has coincided with unparalleled Soviet aggression and threats, from Indochina through Afghanistan. Try to tell victims of "yellow rain" about the wonders of arms control.

Biological weapons are controlled—on paper. What has violation of the controls produced? A U.S. clamor for yet more agreements. And arms-control enthusiasts, their enthusiasm impervious to evidence, continue to use slogans that were threadbare when Dean Acheson refuted them.

Acheson demolished the bromide that "as long as the Russians are talking they are not fighting." Acheson said that Americans are so wedded to the belief that negotiations are means of ending conflicts that they are blind to the fact that negotiations are equally suited to continuing conflicts. Of the slogan "There is no alternative to negotiations with the Russians," Acheson said: "This is, of course, silly. For if there is no alternative, and if the Russians will only negotiate, as is now the case, on their own terms, then there is no alternative to surrender."

For that reason someone should tell Ronald Reagan to quit saying that nothing is more important than "development of a better working relationship with the Soviet Union." Such talk worsens the asymmetry in U.S.-Soviet negotiations by building pressure on the U.S. government for concessions to produce "movement." An immoderate and unempirical belief in arms control produces a policy of apologetic retreats.

Why We Need Nuclear Arms Control
William Proxmire

Mr. President, like millions of other Americans I enjoy reading George Will. Who would not? He is learned. He is amusing. And he angers or bullies or challenges you into thinking. He does not mind taking on motherhood, brotherhood, or Little Red Riding Hood. He is also sometimes wrong. In his column in the latest Newsweek, George Will is very wrong. This time he kicks around arms control. Believe it or not he even wades into President Reagan for being soft on arms control. Will tells Reagan to stop saying that "nothing is more important than development of a better working relationship with the Soviet Union." Such talk, says Will, builds pressure on our Government to make costly concessions to the Soviets just so that we can have an arms control agreement.

From William Proxmire, "Why We Need Nuclear Arms Control," *Congressional Record*, vol. 130, no. 80 (June 13, 1984), p. S7017.

Mr. Will says arms control has not brought us a safer world, but a more dangerous one. It has stopped us from building missiles that would defend our country (the ABM treaty) and forced us to produce hair trigger weapons like the MX. Arms control, according to Will, has also given the Soviets an immense advantage in nuclear capability. Will reasons that the Soviets will not negotiate away advantages, but oh—how they will exploit "the American thirst for agreements." For us arms control will continue to be a losing game. Why? Because the United States is an open society with a critical, inquisitive press poised to expose any departure on our part from our arms control commitment. In other words, we cannot cheat. And the Soviets? Well—the Soviet press prints precisely what the Kremlin leaders want them to print and not a word more. So, according to Will they can and do cheat to their hearts content. Will cites the yellow rain in Afghanistan as a prime example.

Does Will really mean this? Would Will abandon arms control in any form and let the nuclear arms race have its head taking us wherever it should lead? Does he really believe the world will be safer if we throw off all the arms control shackles? How about the test ban treaty that has kept both superpowers from exploding nuclear weapons in tests in the atmosphere, in outer space and underwater for the past 20 years? Would the world be safer today without the restraints of SALT I or SALT II or the Anti-Ballistic Missile Treaty or the Outer Space Treaty? Admittedly, whatever these treaties have accomplished, the world is not safer from nuclear war today than it was 25 years ago before any of the arms control agreements were signed. Yes, indeed, we do live in a more dangerous world. But is this the fault of the arms control treaties or is it the fault of the onrushing nuclear arms race which arms control is trying to restrain?

Will finds two virtues in the arms race: First, it sometimes moves the superpowers toward more stable, less vulnerable weapons systems. It moves both adversaries away from stationary, land based use 'em or lose 'em, MIRV'd missiles. The arms race pushes Russia and the United States toward

mobile air launched or sea launched missiles. Second, and I think this was what George Will was really thinking of, with the generally superior U.S. technology, the unrestrained arms race gives the United States a better chance than arms control of staying ahead of the Soviet Union. And finally Will ends his essay on the harm of arms control with a change of pace, a kind of off-speed pitch. Consider his last sentence. He writes: "An immoderate and unempirical belief in arms control produces a policy of apologetic retreats." Think about that sentence for a minute. What Will protests is: "an immoderate and unempirical belief in arms control." Well, after all, who believes in immoderate and unempirical anything? How about a moderate and empirical use of arms control? Would Will find that also harmful? Suppose we follow an arms control strategy that seeks only those agreements that benefit both? I repeat, both—both the United States and the Soviet Union. Are there such agreements? Of course, there are. Both countries suffer heavy economic burdens from an unrestrained arms race. Both countries want to preserve their nuclear deterrents. Both countries only survive by avoiding nuclear war. Both countries will benefit immensely from stopping the proliferation of nuclear weapons. No negotiations will work between adversaries unless both benefit from them. The basis of mutual benefit for the two superpowers is obvious and very big, indeed.

Finally, will the Soviet Union with its closed society abide by any arms control agreements if it is to its interest to violate it? Certainly it will not abide by an arms control agreement or any other agreement which it can violate to its advantage provided it can get away with the violation. So what does that mean? That means we tie any arms control agreement to thorough, detailed, unambiguous verification procedures. It also means that we monitor that verification constantly. And we blow the whistle loud and clear when we find a violation. The Afghanistan yellow rain violation constitutes a Soviet breach of a treaty that has no verification or compliance features. None. Let me repeat that. The Afghanistan yellow rain violation constitutes a Soviet breach of a treaty that has no verification or compliance features. Several years ago I secured a unanimous Senate approval of a resolution calling on the President to amend that treaty or call for negotiating a new agreement based on effective verification and strict compliance terms. The administration ignored that resolution.

Mr. President, I am tempted to point out that where arms control is concerned, where there is Will, there is no way. So I will not. I agree with George Will that an immoderate and unempirical belief in arms control is wrong. But let us have arms control based on moderation and experience. . . .

QUESTIONS FOR DISCUSSION

1 Why do governments support arms control negotiations?
2 Have arms control agreements curbed the arms race?
3 Will future arms control agreements curb the arms race?
4 Are arms control agreements fundamentally harmful to Western interests?
5 What kinds of arms control agreements are effective?
6 Which nuclear arms control agreements have been the most successful? Why?

SUGGESTED READINGS

Adelman, Kenneth. "Arms Control with or Without Agreements," *Foreign Affairs* 63 (Winter 1984–85), pp. 240–63.

Bulkeley, Rip. "The Trouble with Nuclear Disarmament by Negotiations," *Bulletin of Peace Proposals* 14, no. 4 (1983), pp. 313–25.

"Charges of Treaty Violations: Much Less Than Meets the Eye," *F.A.S. Public Interest Report* 37 (March 1984), pp. 1–20.

Freedman, Lawrence. "Weapons, Doctrines, and Arms Control," *Washington Quarterly* 7 (Spring 1984), pp. 8–16.

Hedlin, Myron. "Moscow's Line on Arms Control," *Problems of Communism* 33 (May–June 1984), pp. 19–36.

Kagan, Robert W. "Why Arms Control Failed," *Policy Review* no. 27 (Winter 1984), pp. 28–33.

Levinson, Macha. "Arms Control: An Essential Element of Security Policy," *International Defense Review* 17 (May 1984), pp. 541–42.

Miller, Steven E. "Politics over Promise: Domestic Impediments to Arms Control," *International Security* 8 (Spring 1984), pp. 67–90.

Øberg, Jan. "Why Disarmament and Arms Control Negotiations Will Fail—and What Can Be Done?" *Bulletin of Peace Proposals* 14, no. 3 (1983), pp. 277–82.

Stanford Arms Control Group, Coit D. Blacker and Gloria Duffy (eds.) *International Arms Control: Issues and Agreements,* 2nd ed. Stanford, California: Stanford University Press, 1984.

Union of Concerned Scientists. *Briefing Manual: A Collection of Materials on Nuclear Weapons and Arms Control.* Cambridge, Massachusetts: Union of Concerned Scientists, 1983.

Weiss, Seymour. "The Case Against Arms Control," *Commentary* (November 1984), pp. 19–30.

7 Are Unilateral Measures Likely to Promote a Slowing Down of the Nuclear Arms Race?

YES

Herbert Scoville, Jr.

A Different Approach to Arms Control—Reciprocal Unilateral Restraint

NO

Philip Towle

Unilateralism, or Disarmament by Example

A Different Approach to Arms Control—Reciprocal Unilateral Restraint

Herbert Scoville, Jr.

Formal arms control negotiations, such as the Strategic Arms Limitation Talks (SALT) and Mutual and Balanced Force Reductions (MBFR) may have outlived their usefulness. At the very least they will have to be supplemented by other approaches if reasonable progress is to be made in controlling the armaments race. Such negotiations have proved too slow: SALT officially began in 1969 after several years of preliminary discussions and produced as the conclusion to Phase I, the Anti-Ballistic Missile (ABM) Treaty and the Interim Agreement on Offensive Weapons of May 1972. SALT II was even slower: in November 1974, the Vladivostok Accords established ceilings on strategic offensive delivery vehicles, but little progress has been made in the two years since then to put these into effect with formal agreements. The MBFR negotiations have been even less productive; no concrete results have been achieved in three years, and there is no expectation of early agreement in the future.

Meanwhile, technical advances are clearly outpacing negotiations. Since SALT began the United States has completed the development of and has deployed two missile systems equipped with multiple independently targetable re-entry vehicles (MIRVs)—the Minuteman II and Poseidon. Since the 1972 Moscow Interim Agreement, the Soviet Union has begun testing and is now beginning deployment of four new inter-continental ballistic missile (ICBM) systems, three of which can deliver MIRVs and a new submarine-launched ballistic missile (SLBM). The United States, also since the Interim Agreement of 1972, has started developing and is now testing strategic cruise missiles, which can be launched from sea or air. These new strategic weapons have now become a major roadblock to the translation of the Vladivostok Accords

into treaty commitments. Similarly, NATO is reportedly deploying new types of nuclear weapons despite an offer, which has not been accepted in MBFR, to cut back on its tactical nuclear stockpiles if the Soviet Union would reduce some conventional forces.

Modern weapons technology is also becoming so complicated and also frequently has applications to so many types of weapons that it is often difficult to spell out in a formal agreement the limitations with sufficient detail to preclude evasion. In the case of SALT I Agreements, this has led to a number of accusations and counter-accusations of violations. Some of these are the inevitable result of attempts by opponents to discredit the arms control process, but others are the natural result of advancing weapons technology. The Standing Consultative Commission (SCC) established by the ABM Treaty has proved useful as a means of clarifying some of these legitimate misunderstandings. Actually the ABM Treaty is a good example of a well-drawn agreement which placed restrictions on technical advances as well as on the sizes of existing systems. However, it will be hard to duplicate this success in the offensive weapons area.

Furthermore, while the formal negotiations have been going on, they have frequently become the *raison d'être* for continuing arms development and procurement. Almost never has either nation stopped a programme in mid-stream during a negotiation because it anticipated the achievement of a future agreement. Instead, quite the contrary, continued procurement has been specifically justified to provide bargaining chips for the negotiating table. Unfortunately, these chips, once paid for, are almost never given up and only serve to force the negotiators to be satisfied with higher levels or even to

---

Herbert Scoville, Jr., "A Different Approach to Arms Control—Reciprocal Unilateral Restraint," in David Carlton and Carlo Schaerf (eds.), *Arms Control and Technological Innovation* (London: Croom Helm, 1977), pp. 170–75.

forgo any agreement altogether. For example, in 1971, when procurement of MIRVs could no longer be justified on military grounds, because it became apparent that the Soviet Union was not deploying a large ABM system, they were justified as bargaining chips for SALT. The net result was that in the Vladivostock Accords the ceiling had to be set at a level of 1,320 MIRVed delivery vehicles, a level that allows both sides to have a counter-force capability against the ICBMs of the other. Secretary of State Henry Kissinger has confessed that he wished he had understood and addressed the MIRV problem in SALT I. Similarly, he approved starting a cruise missile programme in the summer of 1972 as a bargaining chip for SALT II, and now this has been the greatest stumbling block to achieving any SALT II Agreement. Likewise, the MBFR negotiations have prevented any early reductions in American forces in Europe. The pressures in Congress led by Senator Mike Mansfield to cut these back suddenly evaporated when MBFR began.

A basic criterion for arms control agreements between the East and the West has been that the forces of the two sides must have 'essential equivalence'. However, 'bargaining chips' and 'essential equivalence' are incompatible. Each side must seek to match the bargaining chips of the other, and this stimulates the arms race to ever-higher levels.

Even after arms control treaties have been formalised, they can become the excuse for new arms programmes. If a certain type of weapon is not included in the agreement or if an agreed ceiling has not yet been reached, then the treaties can become a justification for going ahead with programmes which may not be needed for security purposes. For example, the United States had less than 2,200 strategic delivery vehicles at the time when the Vladivostok Accord set the ceiling at 2,400. Secretary of Defense James Schlesinger then used this ceiling as an excuse for procuring additional delivery vehicles which had not previously been in the approved defence programme. Likewise, the American submarine-launched cruise missile programme was supported by American naval authorities because it was the only new development alternative left open to the Navy by the Moscow Interim Agreement. The Soviet Union, in turn, proceeded to develop and then deploy new larger ICBMs to replace those then in existence because the Interim Agreement prevented it from adding to the numbers of ICBMs but placed no firm restrictions on replacing old missiles by new ones.

A new approach to arms control, or at least a supplement to present ones, might be called Reciprocal Unilateral Restraint (RUR). One nation could announce that it was not going to proceed with a new weapons development or deployment provided that future events did not indicate that such restraint would prejudice its security. It could then watch the reaction of the other side which, in turn, might exercise reciprocal restraint either in the same or a related area. Force reductions could be made in the same manner; one side discarding a given number of its delivery vehicles or withdrawing a division from a certain theatre and then await the reaction of the other.

Such unilateral restraint can be exercised today without any adverse security consequences to either the United States or the Soviet Union. The thesis that there is a delicate balance of terror is a myth which has no foundation in fact. Both the superpowers have forces far in excess of those needed to deter an attack by the other. The Americans could suspend the procurement of the B-1 or the Trident submarines or a follow-on ICBM without any security risk regardless of any Soviet action that could be taken in the next five years. The Soviet Union, in turn, could halt the replacement of its existing ICBM by the newly tested models without any danger that the United States could take military or political advantage of this restraint. Arms control policies should take advantage of the extraordinary stability of the strategic balance today.

RUR would be a far more satisfactory and cheaper way of achieving arms control than buying bargaining chips and then having to develop some formal agreement to get rid of them. It would also be much safer; mutual security would have been enhanced if MIRVs had never been deployed. Now we have to build new generations to counter the MIRV threat.

Furthermore, it is an approach which has proved successful in the past. In 1969 President Richard Nixon made the unilateral decision that henceforth the United States would cease all research, development and procurement of biological weapons and toxins. Following this initiative, the Soviet Union indicated its willingness to negotiate a formal treaty banning all such offensive biological weapons (BW) programmes and the BW Convention incorporating such provisions was signed by 112 nations in 1972. Without such a unilateral American action, it is most unlikely that this success would have been achieved. Earlier, President John F. Kennedy used similar tactics in achieving the Limited Test Ban Treaty of 1963. In June of that year he announced that the United States would halt all further nuclear testing provided that the Soviet Union exercised similar restraint, and two months later the Limited Test Ban Treaty was signed in Moscow. Such rapid progress in arms control is rare indeed.

Furthermore, RUR has the great advantage of maintaining flexibility in the light of changes in the political climate or in the technical situation. Precise details need not be spelled out and new steps could be taken to assimilate technical advances as they occur. Verification would be simpler, since every detail in a formal agreement would not have to be carefully monitored to ensure that violations were not occurring. Thus, neither the Soviet failure to finish dismantling its old ICBM silos by the time its new submarines began sea trials nor the United States temporarily covering its new ICBM silos to allow concrete to harden, both technical SALT violations, could be ignored because they have no security significance. Instead, each nation could look for major developments that could affect the military balance. This would be a reversion to the type of verification which is used continuously in the absence of any arms control agreements. Intelligence sources are continuously employed to determine whether the other side's programme presents a significant threat to security.

If some major political event occurred or if one nation appeared to be taking advantage of restraint by the other, then the action could be reversed without creating a major international incident. The abrogation of treaties can in themselves create international crises. However, this flexibility is two-edged, since it has the disadvantage of making it easier for a nation to change its mind. The formality of a treaty makes it possible for a nation's leaders to resist opposition cries for a change in policy. Therefore, the idea of formal treaties should not be discarded entirely, and it may be that only the order of the procedures should be reversed. The nations could exercise restraint on their individual programmes and then these actions could be later formalised in an agreement, as was done in the case of the BW and the Limited Test Ban Treaties.

If the United States and the Soviet Union were to adopt the strategy of Reciprocal Unilateral Restraint, what types of actions would they undertake? If this new posture is to be effective, the restraining actions must be meaningful. It would not be enough for a nation to forgo a weapons programme which it never had any intention of supporting. Thus, the removal from active forces of obsolete ineffective weapons would not serve the RUR objectives. For example, in the mid-1960s the United States offered to destroy its B-47 bomber fleet if the Soviets would reciprocate. Since it was well known that the United States could no longer afford to keep these old aeroplanes in operation anyway, this offer fell on deaf ears. Because of this offer, the B-47s were kept in the inventory at considerable expense several years longer than necessary.

In the strategic weapons area, restraint should be designed to increase stability and reduce incentives for any nation to initiate a nuclear strike. Vulnerable weapons systems could be phased out while simultaneously programmes could be carried out to enhance the invulnerability of those remaining. For example, the United States could halt its development and testing of its new ICBM (MX), maneuverable re-entry vehicles (MARVs), and the MK12A Minuteman warhead programmes, all of which are designed to improve its counter-force capabilities. The Soviet Union, in turn, might forgo further deployment of MIRVs on its heavy ICBMs which are viewed as a counter-force threat by American planners. The number of MIRVed ICBMs, which will inevitably be thought to be vulnerable in the distant future, could be cut back; thereby simultaneously reducing the number of provocative targets and the threat to destroy the other side's ICBM force.

The safety and control of nuclear weapons should, whenever possible, be enhanced so that the opportunities for launching nuclear weapons unnecessarily or by accident are circumscribed. Weapons programmes that widen the firebreak between conventional and nuclear conflicts should be supported while those that make the decision to use nuclear weapons easier, such as the tactical 'mini-nukes', should be forsworn. Precision-guided conventional munitions, which increase the effectiveness of defences and reduce the need to rely on nuclear weapons, are types whose development should be supported.

In the field of sea warfare, programmes which threaten the sea-based deterrent should be avoided, and attempts to improve tactical anti-submarine warfare should be directed towards methods which do not threaten ballistic-missile submarines. Naval mines with conventional explosives have tremendous potential in this respect. These could be used to create barriers closing off large portions of the ocean to submarines which might attack shipping. This would be a means of reducing the violence of the conflict at sea, and the need for large and expensive surface fleets without at the same time prejudicing the invulnerability of the ballistic submarine deterrent. Surface or sub-surface vessels designed for continuous long-term tracking and destroying submarines, on the other hand, are destabilising and should not be procured.

In sum, the time is now ripe to alter our approach to arms control and review the order of current procedures. There are many areas where both the United States and the Soviet Union could exercise unilateral restraint which would enhance the security of both countries, decrease the risk of nuclear war, and save vast sums of money. Once some steps have been taken in this direction, it would be easier for others to follow. Formal treaty commitments embodying the actions which had already been unilaterally taken could probably be effected more easily in such a climate than when both sides are racing to procure additional bargaining chips. RUR may be the only way to escape from the morass in which arms control negotiations are currently trapped.

Unilateralism, or Disarmament by Example
Philip Towle

Disarmament by example (as it was known in the 1930s) or unilateralism (as it is usually described today) is back in fashion after several decades when there was widespread agreement that formal arms control measures were the only way to control the arms race between the Warsaw Pact and NATO. Commentators in both the United States and Britain have suggested that the West should unilaterally renounce certain weapons in the hope that the Russians will reciprocate and that this will lead to a tacit or informal disarmament agreement.[1] In Brit-

[1]For a discussion of the advantages and disadvantages of tacit agreements see T. Schelling in David Carlton and Carlo Schaerf (Editors), *The Dynamics of the Arms Race,* Croom Helm, London, 1975. See also E. P. Thompson, 'New Thinking in the Peace Movement', *The Times,* 6 March 1981.

ain the Campaign for Nuclear Disarmament (CND) has revived, and the Labour Party has elected a unilateralist as its leader. The deteriorating international climate in the wake of Afghanistan, the NATO decision to balance the Soviet SS 20 by introducing cruise missiles and Pershing II's into Europe and the apparent deadlock in the disarmament talks in Geneva and Vienna have all contributed to the revival of interest in unilateralism.

Few subjects evoke as much passion as unilateralism and the current debate has already generated considerable venom and abuse. On the one side, those in favour of unilateralism are 'concerned with the danger of nuclear war and the threat to the survival of civilization'[2]. In particular they fear that changes in the targeting of nuclear weapons and increases in the accuracy of ballistic missiles may tempt either the United States or the Soviet Union into a preemptive nuclear attack.[3] On the other hand, those opposed to unilateralism can argue that it is difficult when you are falling behind in the arms race to indulge in the 'luxury' of unilateral reductions. In 1965 the West had an advantage over the Soviet Union in numbers of ICBMs, in surface warships, and in aviation and tank technology. Conversely the Soviets had an advantage in IRBMs, in numbers of submarines and in the scale of forces deployed in Europe. Today the West's advantages have largely disappeared. The Soviet Union now has an advantage in numbers of ICBMs (though not in warheads), it has constructed a vast surface navy, and its general level of military technology has begun to equal the West's. However in the areas where it was ahead in 1964 the Soviet Union retains a commanding lead. Thus the opponents of unilateralism suspect the CND of attempting to impose still further handicaps on the West.[4] The passions of those concerned with saving the world from nuclear destruction clash directly with the fears of those who believe that Soviet military superiority may tempt the Kremlin to attack or intimidate the West. What are the merits of the case?

Arms control theorists have always noted the fact that, in peacetime, even potential adversaries rarely arm to anything like the limits of their economic capacities despite the absence of formal restraints limiting their military activities. According to Professor Hedley Bull

> arms control expressed in a treaty we should regard as a special case, a readily perceptible and particularly prominent example of something more deep-rooted in international experience, the restraint under which two antagonists labour for fear that, if either fails to observe it, the struggle will take a form prejudicial to the interests of both.[5]

Not only do such reciprocal fears of an increase in tension sometimes inhibit the arms race but fears of an enemy attack are rarely so great that governments are prepared to put at risk all their social and economic aims by spending on armaments to the limits of their capacity. Thus, partly because of the fear of the economic effects of such actions, it was not until six months before the outbreak of the second world war that the British government ordered the maximum production of aircraft regardless of the financial consequences. Yet the international atmosphere had been darkening since 1933.[6]

It was during this period that disarmament by example, like appeasement, acquired its sinister reputation. At that time there was a wide-spread belief, particularly strongly held in England, that an arms race had caused the first world war. In his autobiography Viscount Grey wrote:

> more than one thing may be said about the causes of the war, but the statement that comprises most truth

---

[2]Dorothy Thompson and Jolyon Howorth, 'New Strategy in the Making for a Nuclear-Free Europe', The Guardian, 17 Oct. 1980.

[3]V. L. Allen, ibid.

[4]Lady Wheldon, 'One-sided Views of Nuclear Disarmament', The Times, 29 April 1981.

[5]H. Bull, The Control of the Arms Race, Disarmament and Arms Control in the Missile Age, Weidenfeld and Nicolson, London, 1961, p. xii.

[6]A. J. P. Taylor, English History 1914–1945, Clarendon Press, Oxford, 1965, p. 413.

is that militarism and the armaments inseparable from it made war inevitable.[7]

The advocates of disarmament by example suggested that, if a state could cause an arms race by increasing its armed forces, as the Germans had caused an Anglo-German naval race before 1914, so presumably it could encourage other states to reduce their forces if it reduced its own—the armaments' spiral should work in both directions. The theory had some plausibility: reductions in the armaments of any major power may improve the international atmosphere if these armaments are perceived by some as threatening. Thus such reductions could perhaps cause a general reduction of armaments. Unfortunately, however, several states may maintain a high level of armaments because of their mutual antagonisms even if one or two reduce their forces. In other cases one state may simply be searching for military superiority and reductions in the armed forces of potential opponents may only bring this superiority nearer.

British politicians occasionally suggested in the inter-war period that they were influenced by the theory of disarmament by example. In 1934 the Prime Minister, Ramsay MacDonald, claimed that Britain had

gone further in disarmament than any other country in the world. . . . No-one thinks of following our example. Disarmament by example has completely broken down and we alone are not in a position to lift effectively a little finger to protect ourselves in the event of trouble.[8]

The British armed forces had indeed been very rapidly run down after 1918. But this was largely because there were few serious enemies in sight. Despite occasional scares about French intentions, and the confrontation with Turkey at Chanak in 1922, there seemed to be no immediate threat to

the Empire. The Army was able to plan operations against a Soviet invasion of India; the Royal Air Force was able to dream of a great bomber offensive against a continental enemy; and the Royal Navy watched the activities of the United States and particularly Japan with suspicion, but there was no direct and obvious menace. As A.J.P. Taylor has written: 'British disarmament, or rather the reduction of armaments, was not initiated as an example to others . . . The great armaments of the war years were given up simply because it was held, quite correctly, that they were not required.[9] At the same time, it was widely believed that economies in military expenditure were vitally needed in order to restore the country's financial health. It was the lack of an apparent enemy and the need to economize which largely governed the reduction in British military capabilities from 1918 to 1931, although the desire to set an example was sometimes incorrectly blamed subsequently for this process.

Disarmament by example became much more important when the National Coalition government began hesitatingly to consider rearmament after Hitler had come to power in Germany. It was one of the main planks in the Labour party's opposition at the time to increases in British military expenditure. When Stafford Cripps dismissed collective security as a 'highly dangerous idea which can be seized upon to excuse the very forces it is intended to defeat';[10] when Herbert Morrison accused the government in 1935 of embarking on a 'mad and wasteful armaments race'[11] and when Clement Attlee said 'we deny the need for increased air armaments. We deny the proposition that an increased British Air Force will make for the peace of the world and we reject altogether the claim to parity'[12] (with the Luftwaffe), it was essentially

[7]Viscount Grey, *Twenty Five Years, 1892–1916*, Volume 2, Hodder and Stoughton, London, 1925, p. 52.

[8]D. Marquand, *Ramsay MacDonald*, Jonathan Cape, London, 1977, p. 757.

[9]Taylor p. 227. See also p. 184.

[10]Stafford Cripps, *The Struggle for Peace*, Victor Gollancz, London, 1936, p. 64.

[11]B. Donoughue and G. W. Jones, *Herbert Morrison, Portrait of a Politician*, Weidenfeld and Nicolson, London, 1973, p. 263.

[12]H. Montgomery Hyde, *British Air Policy Between the Wars, 1918–1939*, Heinemann. London, 1976, p. 307.

because they believed that Britain should set an example for responsible behaviour by not rearming. It was this period which discredited the idea of disarmament by example. If the policy advocated by Cripps, Attlee, Morrison and others had been followed, the country would have been in an even weaker position when it came to face the Germans in 1940. As it was, in so far as their criticisms of the government and the government's own fears of the pacifism of the electorate, combined with the government's concerns about the economic effects of rearmament, influenced policy, they helped to bring on the war, to prolong it and to increase the number of Allied casualties it produced.

It was hardly surprising therefore that, when the Cold War broke out after 1945, and Russia became the obvious potential enemy, Western governments should have sought formal reciprocal arrangements to limit the arms race. Admittedly Western forces were rapidly disbanded after the war but this was before relations with the Soviet Union reached their nadir. British forces were reduced from five million in 1945 to 787,000 in 1948, while United States forces were reduced from eleven and a half million at the end of the war to 1.34 million three years later.[13] As in the 1920s these reductions were motivated by the general desire to revert to peacetime preoccupations; by economic considerations; and, for a short time, by the lack of an apparent enemy. However Western governments—including the Attlee Labour cabinet led by the unilateralists of the 1930s—came to believe that the Soviets had not followed suit and had not disarmed to anything like the same extent. In the 1920s Soviet forces had fallen to under 600,000 men, according to Western estimates.[14] In 1951 the British Minister of Defence, Mr Shinwell, told the House of Commons

that the Russians had over four and a half million men under arms in the Soviet Union and that there were over a million in Eastern Europe. To many Western leaders this experience in the late 1940s appeared to confirm the 'lessons' they derived from the previous decade: disarmament would not come by itself, if it were to be reciprocal it would have to be laid down in formal agreements. Anthony Nutting, the Minister responsible for British disarmament policy in the early 1950s, implied that there was some truth in the suggestion 'that between the wars the approach was to unilateral disarmament, whereas since the second world war, it has been to multilateral or nothing'.[15]

There was however one important example of a tacit arms control measure in the 1950s. After the U.S. nuclear test on Bikini island in 1954 and the radioactive contamination of the Japanese fishing boat, *Lucky Dragon,* public pressure against nuclear tests steadily increased. Although East and West could not agree upon a formal measure to limit such tests, an informal moratorium began in 1958 which lasted until it was suddenly denounced by the Soviets in August 1961. As the Soviet Union immediately afterwards began a series of tests, it was clear that they had been in preparation for some time and there was a widespread feeling in the West that the Russians were trying to gain an unfair advantage in the arms race. The White House declared 'that the Soviet announcement was primarily a form of atomic blackmail, designed to substitute terror for reason in the present international scene'.[16] Similarly the U.S. representative at the disarmament negotiations in Geneva claimed that 'Soviet conduct . . . constitutes a record for the perfidy of the government of the U.S.S.R. and of its betrayal of the hopes of mankind'. President Kennedy announced some days later that the United States

---

[13]*The Disarmament Question 1945–1953,* Central Office of Information, London, 1953, p. 6.

[14]R. W. Lambert, *Soviet Disarmament Policy, 1922–1931,* U.S. Arms Control and Disarmament Agency, Washington, 1964, pp. 3–5.

[15]A. Nutting, *Disarmament—An Outline of the Negotiations,* Oxford University Press, 1959, p. 1.

[16]The statements made by the White House and by the US representative in Geneva are reproduced in *Documents on Disarmament 1961,* ACDA, Washington, 1962, pp. 350–1.

would resume underground tests, but the West had been caught off guard and preparations took some time. The whole experience deepened the West's suspicions of informal arms control measures.

On the other hand, the next decade produced one example of an apparently much more successful unilateral measure leading to a general agreement. In November 1969 President Nixon announced that the United States would destroy its stocks of biological weapons and that it would renounce all methods of biological warfare unilaterally. Subsequently the Soviets agreed to negotiate a treaty banning the production of biological weapons and a Convention to this effect came into force in 1975. Since the West had already renounced biological weapons unilaterally it did not insist that the Convention should be adequately verified. Thus it was relatively easy to negotiate, but doubts have been cast on Soviet observance of the agreement.[17]

Critics of the Biological Weapons Convention and of all other formal arms control agreements, whatever their provisions for verification, argue that they have a spurious appearance of stability. Most recent agreements give a government the right to withdraw if 'it decides that extraordinary events related to the subject matter of the Treaty, have jeopardized the supreme interests of its country'.[18] In such cases, a state should give three months' notice of its intention to withdraw to all other parties as well as to the UN Security Council. It should also explain the reasons for its withdrawal. But as the Jordanian representative at the conference held to review the Seabed Treaty pointed out in 1977, three months was a short time for other states to have warning that a major treaty was about to be denounced. Moreover it is notable that the warning period for the denunciation of the vital SALT 1

agreement was six months rather than three. No state has hitherto taken advantage of these withdrawal clauses but this is no guarantee that they will not do so in future. Nevertheless, there is a general feeling that the denunciation of a formal arms control measure would not be undertaken lightly by any of the major powers. Such a denunciation could lead to the collapse of all the East-West agreements negotiated so far and to a very drastic deterioration in relations between NATO and the Warsaw Pact.

An even more fundamental objection to formal arms control negotiations is that by concentrating attention on weaponry and therefore on deficiencies in the weaponry of one's own forces they increase international neuroses. This argument was employed extensively by Winston Churchill in the inter-war period.[19] Critics of the current MBFR negotiations argue that they have prevented or delayed reductions in the force levels of the NATO countries. In peacetime, force levels are often determined largely by domestic considerations because the size and nature of the threats posed by potential enemies are rarely spelled out. However, once thought is given to these threats, the number of potential enemies multiplies. Evan Luard, a former Minister of State in the British Foreign Office, has written:

> as soon as one power demands certain conditions to match another, third powers may require countervailing concessions to match the second. Today China may require to match the United States, or the Soviet Union or both together. India may then require a new balance to match China . . . When the various combinations and permutations, alliances and counteralliances are included as well, the complications in reaching equilibrium become almost endless.

Consequently, Mr. Luard concluded, 'the best hope of progress in disarmament is probably not through

---

[17]'A Matter of Verification', *The Times*, 22 March 1980. 'Anthrax and Arms Control', *International Herald Tribune*, 30 April 1980.

[18]This phrase is reproduced in Article X of the 1968 Nuclear Non-Proliferation Treaty, Article VIII of the 1971 Seabed Treaty and Article XIII of the 1972 Biological Weapons Convention.

[19]P. Towle, 'Winston Churchill and British Disarmament Policy', The *Journal of Strategic Studies*, Dec. 1979.

formally negotiated agreements, but through unilateral measures'.[20]

But if the disadvantages of formal arms control treaties are that they can give a spurious feeling of security and that they are excessively difficult to negotiate, there are also grave objections to unilateral measures. Unilateral gestures by the West will only encourage the Soviet Union to reduce its forces if these forces are aimed mainly at the West rather than at China; if the Soviets are not aiming for military superiority; and if they have read our intentions and capabilities correctly. Plainly the unilateral measures advocated by the Labour party in the 1930s could not have been reciprocated because Japan and Germany wanted to establish their supremacy in Asia and Europe. On the other hand, the decisions taken in the 1950s by such countries as Canada and Sweden not to develop nuclear weapons probably encouraged other countries, including Italy and the Federal Republic of Germany, to sign the nuclear Non Proliferation Treaty. Today, supporters of CND frequently argue that Britain should discourage nuclear proliferation by disbanding its own nuclear force:

> While we sit behind our nuclear smokescreen and make no effort to curb the misuse of nuclear power, then the rest of the world will ignore the Non Proliferation Treaty many of them have signed and slowly but surely follow our example and arm themselves with nuclear weapons.[21]

In fact, however, the nuclear capable countries in the developed world, such as Japan and Italy, signed the NPT not only because of the example of other countries which had renounced nuclear weapons but, even more importantly, because their security was guaranteed by the United States. They will change their minds not because Britain retains or does not retain its nuclear force, but only if the United States should allow itself to fall far behind the Soviet Union in the arms race. In the developing world the main potential nuclear powers are not considering nuclear weapons in order to match Britain; Indian nuclear weapons would be aimed at China or Pakistan; Pakistani nuclear weapons would be aimed at India or the Soviet Union; Israeli nuclear weapons would be directed towards the Arab states; whilst South African nuclear weapons would presumably be for use against any Black African state which supported a guerrilla rising in South Africa. Similarly the South Koreans and Taiwanese keep open the option of developing nuclear weapons to protect them against China, in case the United States' guarantee should be withdrawn in a fit of absence of mind or weakness. In all these cases a British decision to disband its nuclear force would have no effect whatsoever. Disarmament by example cannot work if those whom one wishes to influence have other enemies in mind. More importantly, in the case of the United States, it will, if carried to extremes, actually be self-defeating because it will weaken the US guarantee and compel states to look to their own defences.

Even more crucially disarmament by example will fail if the USSR is seeking to attain superiority over the Western alliance. Supporters of CND usually deny that 'the Soviet Union would treat unilateral disarmament by Britain or phased disarmament by the West as a sign of weakness to be exploited, but rather as a positive move to defuse a highly dangerous situation'.[22] Of course, the idea that they could present a threat to the West is vehemently denied by Soviet spokesmen who continue the traditional Soviet policy of refusing to discuss either the size of their own armed forces or the introduction into service of new Soviet weapons. According to Mr. Gromyko, the Soviet Foreign Minister, suggestions that there is a Soviet military build-up are fabricated by those who wish to use them as a

cover for their own arms race policy. What threat can stem from a country which . . . daily proposes cuts

[20]Evan Luard, *Conflict and Peace in the Modern International System,* University of London Press, 1970, p. 226.
[21]Elizabeth Butterworth, 'Implications of a Nuclear Capability', *The Times.* 6 Dec. 1980.

[22]See note 3 supra.

in arms and armed forces, a ban on nuclear weapons tests and switching over the use of nuclear energy for peaceful aims?[23]

Unfortunately words are not enough. Adolf Hitler repeatedly proclaimed his peaceful intentions and convinced many democratic statesmen that he was telling the truth.

The primary aim of the CND movement is to halt and reverse the 'race' in theatre nuclear weapons in Europe. In particular they want to dissuade NATO from introducing the cruise missile and Pershing II MRBM and to persuade the Soviet Union to dismantle its SS 20 missiles. According to Mr. E.P. Thompson,

> if European Nato states, under popular pressure, should reject cruise missiles and Pershing II's—and if the Soviet Union did not, instantly, halt and then reduce its deployment of SS-20s, we can be sure that Western unilateralist movements would at once lose their popular support.[24]

Actually we can be sure of no such thing since Western unilateralism is based on the fear of nuclear war and the more intransigently the Soviet Union behaves the greater that fear will be.

The history of medium and intermediate range missiles in Europe also makes it unlikely that the Soviets would follow suit if the West unilaterally disarmed. Indeed it seems a particularly weak area for those advocating disarmament by example to take their stand. The United States withdrew its Jupiter and Thor missiles from Europe in the early 1960s when the Polaris submarine boats (SSBN) came into service. But the Soviet Union retained its SS4 and SS5 missiles even when its equivalent to Polaris came into operation. For a time its land-based missiles were balanced by Western superiority in numbers of SSBN and long range attack aircraft such as the Vulcan or Buccaneer. Subsequently however the Russians caught up and ov-

ertook the U.S. in numbers of SSBN and this superiority of 64 to 42 was formalised in SALT 1. At the same time the Soviet Union greatly built up its long range air force with Backfire and Fencer bombers; it is building twice as many combat aircraft a year as the whole of NATO; and it has notoriously begun to replace the SS4 and SS5 with mobile SS20 missiles. It had already achieved parity before it began to deploy the SS20 and, in the absence of any Western IRBM, it had an opportunity to show forbearance and not to produce any replacement for the SS4 and SS5.[25]

Soviet reactions to other Western gestures in recent years offer little more hope. The US has deferred the replacement of its existing chemical weapons with more modern binary weapons despite the deterioration in its existing stocks. It has also deferred the production of neutron warheads and cancelled the B1 bomber. The only obvious response was Mr Brezhnev's statement that the Soviet Union would not produce neutron weapons whilst the US refrained from doing so. The problem is that the Soviets have little need for neutron warheads which are of most use for stopping a massive tank invasion and, in any case, we have no evidence whether the Soviets have really renounced neutron weapons. As far as chemical weapons are concerned, most Western military specialists believe that the Soviet Union has a large and growing stockpile although some civilian experts, such as Mr Julian Perry Robinson, disagree with this view.[26]

For a number of reasons it is very difficult for the Soviets to make effective unilateral gestures. The Western unilateral limitations listed above took place before production had begun but the West rarely has information about Soviet weapons at this stage of development and so the Soviet leaders can only occasionally make an effective gesture of ren-

[23]'Andrei Gromyko's Detailed Assessment of the Vienna Summit Meeting', *Soviet News*, 3 July 1979, p. 209.
[24]See note 1 supra.
[25]For an assessment of the theatre nuclear balance see *The Military Balance, 1980–1981*, IISS, London, pp. 116–119. This concludes, 'without the inclusion of Poseidon on the NATO side, the Warsaw Pact overall advantage in arriving warheads is about 3.1 to 1'.
[26]SIPRI, *Chemical Weapons Destruction and Conversion*, Taylor and Francis, London, 1980, p. 9 passim.

ouncing them. Secondly there is the inherent conservatism of the Soviet military establishment which makes changes of policy and the renunciation of weapons difficult.[27] Moreover, even when it does appear that the Soviets are not producing a weapon which has passed the development stage, it is hard to tell whether this was because it was a technical failure or because the Kremlin wished to placate Western critics of their arms procurement policies. A case in point was the Soviet decision to defer or to cancel the deployment of mobile SS16 missiles. Was this caused by the technical failure of the missile, by its excessive cost or by fear of Western reaction to its deployment? Secrecy may be an effective military weapon for the Soviet Union but it is one of the greatest stumbling blocks to arms control and to the improvement of East-West relations in general.

For its part, the Soviet Union may also have doubts about the balance of motives for the cancellation or removal of equipment by Western governments. For example, the Western announcement that NATO would withdraw 1000 of the 7000 U.S. nuclear warheads in Europe was no doubt dismissed by the Soviet leadership on the grounds that the warheads were superfluous or obsolete—which was in fact the case, although Western governments also hoped that the unilateral gesture would improve East-West relations. A parallel example was Mr Brezhnev's announcement that the Soviet Union would withdraw 20,000 men from the German Democratic Republic.[28] In both cases, those whom the unilateral gestures were intended to influence politically regarded them with considerable cynicism. Nor is such cynicism always unjustified: unilateral measures will very often be taken in areas of maximum military convenience.

A more important example of a unilateral gesture was President Carter's decision to cancel, at least for the time being, the production and deployment of neutron warheads. Here there was no doubting the utility of the weapons. But the Kremlin may have dismissed the gesture as motivated by fear of Western public hostility to the new weapons. Unilateralists would say that, if this were so, the Soviet Union would respond appropriately. In the event the Soviets merely said that they would not produce neutron warheads either, a predictable but not particularly appropriate response, it being as clear to them as it is to anyone else that this was not a military *quid pro quo*.

If the Soviet response to unilateral Western gestures and to the general slowdown in the US strategic nuclear armaments' programme since the onset of the Vietnam War has been discouraging, recent experience demonstrates that the Soviet leaders do respond to the opposite tactic of bargaining. It was only when the US showed clear signs of deploying its own anti-ballistic missiles that the Soviets became interested in limiting them; it was only when the US deployed its own modern cruise missiles that the Russians wanted them included in SALT; and it was only when the NATO countries made clear their intention of deploying large numbers of Pershing II MRBMs and cruise missiles that the Soviets hinted that they might be prepared to enter negotiations to limit the number of missiles they have aimed at Western Europe. Of course it is not merely the Soviet Union which acts in this way. There have been no naval arms control negotiations designed to limit the size of the US and Soviet surface fleets since 1945, because it is only recently that the Russians have had a surface navy comparable to Western ones. Sometimes however public opinion may push a democratic government into negotiations which are contrary to its strategic interests. There are no similar forces to act on the Soviet authorities.

Despite the difficulty of negotiating formal arms control agreements, therefore, they are clearly superior to tacit agreements or to unilateral measures. As the examples of chemical weapons and neutron warheads have shown, tacit agreements are frequently inherently unstable because we have no way of knowing whether the Soviets are abiding by them. Furthermore, if one state makes a uni-

[27]A. J. Alexander, *Decision Making in Soviet Weapons Procurement*, Adelphi Papers, numbers 147–148, IISS, London, 1978–9, p. 41.
[28]See *Strategic Survey, 1979*, IISS, London, p. 117 passim.

lateral gesture it is unlikely that its potential enemy will make what is generally considered an adequate response. This is particularly true in the case of dictatorial governments which have no public opinion to push them into making militarily inconvenient reductions in their forces.

Finally, the history of the last sixteen years suggests that the Soviets respond to tough minded bargaining rather than to unilateral Western reductions. Neither the Soviet Union nor the United States is arming to the limits of its capacity. They are restrained by economic and social considerations as well as by the desire not to become involved in an unlimited arms race. However, over the past sixteen years these considerations have operated more effectively to limit Western rather than Soviet armaments, hence the change in the balance of world power over this period. There seems to be no reason to believe that the Soviet leadership will respond to unilateral Western restraint in the future any more than it has in the past. On the contrary, if the Kremlin is seeking military superiority—as the change in the 'correlation of forces' since 1965 would suggest—then Western unilateralism will only make that superiority more easily attainable.

QUESTIONS FOR DISCUSSION

1 What kinds of unilateral measures could the United States or the Soviet Union take which could be expected to lead to an appropriate response by the other superpower?

2 Would unilateral restraint by the United States be viewed as a sign of weakness by the Soviet Union?

3 What benefits would the unilateral approach offer compared to negotiated agreements?

4 What weaknesses would the unilateral approach offer compared to negotiated agreements?

5 Are there some aspects of nuclear arms control which are better handled through unilateral measures than negotiated agreements?

SUGGESTED READINGS

Axelrod, Robert. *The Evolution of Cooperation.* New York: Basic Books, 1984.

Bertram, Christoph. *The Future of Arms Control: Part II: Arms Control and Technological Change: Elements of a New Approach.* Adelphi Paper no. 146. London: International Institute for Strategic Studies, 1978, pp. 15–17.

Bulkeley, Rip. "The Trouble with Nuclear Disarmament by Negotiations," *Bulletin of Peace Proposals* 14, no. 4 (1983), pp. 313–25.

Bull, Hedley. *The Control of the Arms Race: Disarmament and Arms Control in the Missile Age,* 2nd ed. New York: Frederick A. Praeger, 1965, chap. 4.

Einhorn, Martin B., Gordon L. Lane, and Miroslav Nuncil. "Strategic Arms Control Through Test Restraints," *International Security* 8 (Winter 1983–84), pp. 108–51.

Hardin, Russell. "Contracts, Promises, and Arms Control," *Bulletin of the Atomic Scientists* 40 (October 1984), pp. 14–17.

Kistiakowsky, G. B. "The Good and the Bad of Nuclear Arms Control Negotiations," *Bulletin of the Atomic Scientists* 35 (May 1979), pp. 7–9.

Long, Franklin A. "Unilateral Initiatives," *Bulletin of the Atomic Scientists* 40 (May 1984), pp. 50–56.

Luttwak, Edward N. "Why Arms Control Has Failed," *Commentary* (January 1978), pp. 19–28.

Øberg, Jan. "Why Disarmament and Arms Control Negotiations Will Fail—and What Can be Done?" *Bulletin of Peace Proposals* 14, no. 3 (1983), pp. 227–82.

Schelling, Thomas. "The Importance of Agreements," in David Carlton and Carlo Schaerf (eds.), *The Dynamics of the Arms Race.* New York: Wiley, 1975, pp. 65–77.

Seaborg, Glenn T. *Kennedy, Khrushchev, and the Test Ban.* Berkeley: University of California Press, 1981.

Wiesner, Jerome B. "Unilateral Confidence Building," *Bulletin of the Atomic Scientists* 40 (January 1984), pp. 45–50.

York, Herbert F. "Bilateral Negotiations and the Arms Race," *Scientific American* 249 (October 1983), pp. 149, 153, and 155–60.

Chapter Three

Superpower Nuclear Arms Control: Some Prescriptions

The early years after World War II saw no significant agreements on nuclear arms control between the superpowers. Instead, the Soviet Union and the United States engaged in nonstop polemics on the subject, both countries consciously putting forward proposals known in advance to be unacceptable to the other. There was one fundamental reason for the longevity of this charade: the asymmetry in nuclear capability between the superpowers. The United States had a nuclear monopoly from 1945 to 1949 and thereafter, for at least another decade, a massive nuclear advantage. The Soviets were simply not interested in any verifiable agreement which would have left them frozen in a condition of inferiority, whereas the United States was, in practice, opposed to all proposals, with the exception of the outright internationalization idea enshrined in the Baruch Plan (mentioned in Chapter 2), which would have involved establishing parity in some or all aspects of nuclear capability.

The prospects for realistic nuclear arms control negotiations began to improve only after 1957, when the Soviets launched Sputnik, the first earth-orbiting satellite. This gave clear notice that the invulnerability of the United States heartland was at an end and that in the long term Moscow had the ability to achieve an approximate nuclear parity with Washington. In the United States presidential election of 1960 there was even a debate about a supposed missile gap which might soon leave the Soviets in a position with some degree of superiority. This fear was unfounded, as President

Kennedy quickly realized, and as was demonstrated practically to the entire world in 1962, during the Cuban missile crisis, when the Soviet Union backed down from its attempt to place nuclear missiles in Cuba after being threatened with a military attack by the United States. It was nonetheless widely recognized that the two superpowers were likely to arrive eventually at approximate strategic equivalence whereby each side would have similar nuclear-weapons destructive capability. Hence both superpowers had every reason to enter seriously into nuclear arms limitation negotiations. A foretaste of what was to characterize these agreements was the Limited Nuclear Test Ban Treaty of 1963, which, while not in itself exactly a measure limiting any particular arms, did contain provisions that, it was hoped, would slow down the pace of technological innovation on both sides to some degree.

Realistic nuclear arms control negotiations between the superpowers only moved to the center of the international stage at the end of the 1960s. The catalyst would appear to have been the domestic debate in the United States about whether to deploy anti-ballistic missile (ABM) systems to shield American cities or, alternatively, to protect American land-based offensive missiles from a Soviet first-strike. After wide-ranging discussions were conducted, both public and private, any effective protection for American cities (the so-called Sentinel proposal advanced by President Lyndon B. Johnson in September 1967) was widely judged to be beyond the technological competence of the United States—at any event, if the Soviets were the adversary—and the Sentinel proposal was duly abandoned by President Richard Nixon. But opinions differed about the desirability of missile-site defense. Some authorities held that any investment would be wasted, as the Soviets would easily be able to counter such a defensive system, and at lower cost, with an increase in offensive capability. Others disagreed and favored deployment of defensive systems. A third school of thought contended that any American deployment of ABMs, effective or not, would be provocative to Moscow and might be perceived as aimed at destabilizing the balance of terror which had already been soundly established by the late 1960s on the basis of Mutual Assured Destruction (MAD), a strategic relationship of deterrence in which each side can absorb a nuclear attack but still retaliate with devastating nuclear force. In March 1969, however, Nixon decided to seek congressional approval for a ballistic missile defense (BMD) of United States offensive missile fields (a plan known as "Safeguard") and obtained a narrow victory. These various developments led the Soviets to express a keen interest in discussing in a private and nonpolemical fashion possible limitations on strategic nuclear systems, both offensive and defensive. The Strategic Arms Limitation Talks (SALT) accordingly commenced in earnest in late 1969, culminating in the SALT I accords of May 1972.

The firmest element in SALT I related to BMD systems, dealt with in the formal ABM Treaty, which was to be of indefinite duration. The treaty allowed each side to build two ABM sites, one around the nation's capital and the other around an ICBM site. (In a summit meeting in Moscow in 1974, both powers signed a protocol to the treaty limiting each side to only one area of BMD deployment—either around the national capital or around one missile field. The Soviets now have such a system around Moscow; the Americans have chosen so far not to exercise their option.) Otherwise, the deployment of ABMs is forbidden.

Accompanying the ABM Treaty was the Interim Agreement on Offensive Forces, involving a temporary limitation on offensive strategic missiles. The Soviets were to retain 1608 fixed launchers for land-based intercontinental ballistic missiles (ICBMs), whereas the Americans' total in this category was to be 1054. At sea, the Soviets were permitted 950 submarine-launched ballistic missiles (SLBMs) to be launched from a submarine fleet of 62 built for this purpose, while the Americans could have 710 SLBMs on 44 submarines.

This bargain was not as advantageous to Moscow as these figures might suggest. One important category in which the Americans had a great advantage was left unlimited, namely that of manned bombers. Nevertheless, in the past decade many doubts have been expressed in the United States about whether SALT I's centerpiece, the ABM Treaty, should have been approved by the U.S. Senate, given the relative lack of precision applied to offensive missiles. The most fundamental difficulty has arisen as a consequence of both superpowers being at liberty, under the Interim Agreement, to multiply the number of warheads on their permitted missiles. The process came to be known as MIRVing (i.e., the installation of multiple independently-targetable re-entry vehicles inside the basic ICBM). No one suggests that this was impermissible under the SALT I Accords. But, as Henry Kissinger has ruefully and candidly acknowledged, its full implications were clearly not anticipated by the Nixon administration. It is the extent and effectiveness of the MIRVing process that has greatly increased doubts about whether American ICBMs could survive a Soviet first-strike. Yet Washington's clear intention in negotiating SALT I was to shore up—and not weaken—MAD. Hence, with the passage of time, that purpose seems increasingly to many observers to have been undermined by SALT I, since it limited ABMs, but did not simultaneously tackle the problem of MIRVs.

Nobody in the West can say with certainty whether the Soviets also approached SALT I with a view to preserving rather than undermining MAD. Some Americans, who give them the benefit of the doubt in this respect, ask whether Moscow might now be interested in revising the ABM Treaty as the best practical means of reducing the allegedly destabilizing threat posed to U.S. land-based missiles (a threat which the United States could eventually duplicate vis-à-vis the Soviets). According to those supporting this view, the ABM Treaty would not have to be abandoned altogether, but merely modified to permit limited ABM deployment around certain specified missile fields. The advantage of such an arrangement over a unilateral repudiation of the 1972 treaty by the United States would of course be the averting of an uncontrolled ABM race which, in turn, if progress was uneven between the two superpowers, could itself eventually undermine MAD.

(As mentioned above, under an agreement reached in 1974, the United States retains the thus far unexercised option, under the existing ABM Treaty, to deploy a small BMD system around *one* ICBM field.)

If, however, the ABM Treaty is to be left in place, how otherwise could the problem of ICBM vulnerability be tackled? One course for the United States might be to try to solve the problem by unilateral means, such as the deployment of mobile MX or Midgetman missiles (an option we shall touch upon in our next chapter). But an alternative is to attempt to revert to the remedy favored in the 1970s. Then most United

States authorities—including successive American Administrations—believed that further bilateral negotiations should take place between the superpowers with a view to limiting offensive nuclear capabilities. Hence the Interim Agreement of 1972 was the subject of prolonged discussion in the SALT forum and by various stages a second SALT Agreement was reached by 1979. (For a summary of its provisions see Table 3-1.) The Carter Administration did not, however, feel confident that the SALT II Agreement would be approved by the Senate and accordingly saw fit to treat the matter as in effect an executive agreement which both superpowers would consent to observe on a non-binding day-to-day basis—something with which even the Reagan Administration has also in practice gone along.

SALT II

Why did Carter come to feel that SALT II would not be approved by the necessary two-thirds majority in the Senate? In part, problems arose because of Soviet conduct in other contexts, such as Cuba and Afghanistan. This constitutes the so-called linkage aspect, in which nuclear arms control agreements are tied to other international political events and trends. But it is also possible that, even if Soviet conduct had been quite different in 1979, there would have been insuperable problems in the Senate on the merits of SALT II itself. This is in contrast to the debates surrounding SALT I, which was approved by the Senate without serious difficulty.

What, then, was found to be significantly more dubious about SALT II? Several factors merit mention. First, there was a good deal more uncertainty as to whether the proposed treaty made cheating possible. What are called "national technical means" of verification (i.e., satellite surveillance) were agreed to be appropriate for covering the limitations in SALT I, but were held by many to be significantly less so for monitoring SALT II. Second, the limitations involved in SALT II did not, according to some experts, go to the heart of the problem of ICBM vulnerability. And, third, the late 1970s saw the rise to influence in the United States of a conservative movement which, right or wrong, perceived the dawn of an era of Soviet nuclear superiority. To most supporters of this third position, any binding limitations on American ability to catch up were unacceptable.

Some of these tenets were shared by Edward Rowny, whose case against SALT II forms part of our next debate. While ostensibly favoring superpower nuclear arms control agreements in principle, Rowny, who served as the Joint Chiefs of Staff representative on the U.S. SALT negotiating team, held, in his 1979 Senate testimony, that SALT II was inequitable and would have had the effect of freezing the United States in a position of inferiority in a number of important respects. An alternative view is presented in the testimony, offered to the Senate at the same time, by Paul Warnke, former director of the Arms Control and Disarmament Agency. He started with his conviction that the United States was not in a position of strategic nuclear inferiority vis-à-vis the Soviet Union. He further saw the SALT II Agreement as being in the interests of both superpowers and thus likely to enhance mutual deterrence. He rejected the idea that nuclear arms control should be "linked" to improved Soviet

Table 3-1 Salt II Agreement in Brief

Treaty

- Would remain in force until December 31, 1985
- Numerical ceilings
  - —2,250 ICBM launchers, SLBM launchers, heavy bombers, and long-range ASBMs (i.e., air-to-surface ballistic missiles with ranges greater than 600 kilometers)
  - —1,320 launchers for MIRVed ICBMs, launchers for MIRVed SLBMs, MIRVed ASBMs, and heavy bombers equipped with long-range cruise missiles
  - —1,200 launchers for MIRVed ICBMs, launchers for MIRVed SLBMs, and MIRVed ASBMs
  - —820 launchers for MIRVed ICBMs
- Prohibitions
  - —No construction of additional fixed launchers for ICBMs and no relocation of such launchers
  - —No conversion of launchers for light ICBMs to launchers for heavy ICBMs
  - —No mobile launchers for heavy ICBMs
  - —No heavy SLBMs and no heavy ASBMs
  - —No increases in the numbers of reentry vehicles on existing types of ICBMs
  - —No flight-testing or deployment of new types of ICBMs, with an exception of one new type of light ICBM with no more than ten reentry vehicles
  - —No flight-testing or deployment of SLBMs with more than fourteen reentry vehicles

Protocol

- Would have expired on December 31, 1981
- Prohibitions
  - —No flight-testing of ICBMs from mobile launchers
  - —No deployment of mobile launchers for ICBMs
  - —No flight-testing or deployment of ASBMs
  - —No deployment of long-range cruise missiles on land-based or sea-based launchers

Source: The Harvard Nuclear Study Group, *Living with Nuclear Weapons* (New York: Bantam Books, 1983), p. 97.

conduct in other respects. To this end he quoted the Soviet dissident Andrei Sakharov as stating, "I believe that the problem of lessening the danger of annihilating humanity in a nuclear war carries an absolute priority over all other considerations."

The election of Ronald Reagan in 1980 brought an end to Warnke's hopes that SALT II would ever be ratified. Most commentators agree that no alternative proposal for far-reaching arms control was ever seriously looked at during the course of Reagan's first term. True, both superpowers engaged for a brief period in the appearance of worthwhile discussions in the Strategic Arms Reduction Talks (START). But these negotiations were terminated at the end of 1983 when the Soviets walked out in protest over the deployment in Western Europe of cruise and Pershing II long-range theater nuclear forces (LRTNF), or, as they are sometimes known, intermediate range nuclear forces (INF). START was, however, unlikely in any case to have yielded significant results during Reagan's first term. (Whether Reagan's second term will reveal a different pattern remains to be seen. At the time of this writing, the two superpowers have entered into wide-ranging discussions in Geneva, although no dramatic results are expected at any early date.)

The Reagan Administration, then, has seemed, to many critics, lukewarm about the quest for bilateral strategic nuclear arms control. Reagan's attitude has not prevented these American critics, who include leading spokespersons of the Democratic party, from arguing strongly in favor of such an approach. Many proposals, ranging from the somewhat modest to the highly ambitious, were advanced during the early 1980s. Here we have space to consider only two of these prescriptions, chosen for the considerable followings they have engendered. At the modest end of the scale, we consider the case for a bilateral comprehensive test ban treaty (CTBT). At the other extreme, we examine the demand for a total freeze on the testing, production, and deployment of all nuclear systems.

COMPREHENSIVE TEST BAN TREATY

A CTBT would not in itself constitute a means of immediate nuclear arms limitation or reduction. But, as with the Limited Test Ban Treaty of 1963, it would be intended to slow down the pace of arms competition. To understand the background of this debate, it is first necessary to consider why the 1963 Treaty omitted the underground environment. The reason for this is that at the time it was widely considered highly unlikely that even quite large underground nuclear explosions could be distinguished from natural earthquakes without permission for extensive on-site inspection. The Soviets, while not absolutely opposed to such inspection, were unwilling to agree to meet minimum American requirements for the extent of inspection. The Soviet position has not significantly changed in the subsequent two decades. What has altered is the extent to which reliable evaluations of seismic events can be made outside a country's national boundaries. Hence in 1974 and 1976 the superpowers negotiated the Threshold Test Ban Treaty (TTBT) and the Peaceful Nuclear Explosion Treaty (PNET), which, although not ratified by the United States, have been held to be in force by both Moscow and Washington. They provide in effect for a ban on underground military tests above 150 kilotons (1 kiloton = 1,000 tons of TNT).

The urgent issue for the late 1980s is whether the United States should seek to negotiate a more comprehensive agreement, as some experts hold that the 150-kiloton ceiling is absurdly high in light of modern national verification techniques. Physicist Hugh DeWitt is in favor of such a course, while Robert Barker, an assistant associate director for arms control at the Lawrence Livermore National Laboratory, is opposed. Neither is able to state with certainty whether a CTBT would be acceptable to the Soviets and, if so, to what extent they would make concessions on verification. Yet United States "hawks" remain sceptical about the reliability of any assurance or undertakings the Soviets might give, in light of their alleged record of cheating under the existing treaties of 1974 and 1976. Probably most United States "doves" are more inclined to give the Soviets the benefit of the doubt; DeWitt shares this approach. He is mainly concerned, however, with showing that some American "hawks" are not particularly interested in the verification aspect, but are really intent on avoiding a CTBT on any terms. He is particularly critical of the influence of those in American weapons laboratories whom he sees as having a vested interest in promoting arms competition. To some extent Barker's approach confirms DeWitt's contentions, for Barker in no way stresses the verification problem. An employee of the Lawrence Livermore National Laboratory, Barker clearly feels that a CTBT on any terms is likely to be harmful to United States security. There is little doubt that most prominent United States opponents of a CTBT share his view, and would thus not be greatly influenced by further improvements in verification techniques nor by Soviet concessions in the matter. Such opponents were therefore no doubt gratified when the Reagan administration indefinitely suspended the CTBT negotiations with the Soviets, negotiations which in Jimmy Carter's time had shown signs of progressing towards agreement.

In summary, apparently acute disputes among American experts about verifiability of nuclear arms control agreements may sometimes be of less than central importance. Sometimes these vocalized objections serve merely as a cloak for more fundamental opposition to a particular proposal. This does not mean, however, that the problem of verification is invariably of only marginal significance. For example, when we look at the proposal for a bilateral nuclear freeze on the testing, production, and further deployment of nuclear warheads, missiles, and other delivery systems, it is essential to appreciate that verification is among the formidable central difficulties.

NUCLEAR FREEZE

The "freeze" proposal came to the fore in the United States in 1982 when Senators Mark Hatfield and Edward Kennedy promoted an unsuccessful resolution on the issue in the Senate. In congressional elections of the same year as many as a quarter of American voters had a chance to register their views in referenda. The idea was also cautiously endorsed by Walter Mondale in the presidential election of 1984. Most Americans, judging by the ballots and by opinion polls, were sympathetic to the idea. But Mondale's failure in the election suggests that support was less than fervent and that the freeze issue was not at the forefront of electors' minds. In this section we see Senator Kennedy present a case for the "freeze," and, representing an opposite point of view, David Petraeus, a captain in the U.S. Army. On the verification issue we can only observe that Kennedy has little to say about the fundamental problems involved. And Petraeus, too, rather surprisingly concentrates on other arguments. Our readers should not assume, however, that, because the issue of verification is not greatly explored in this particular debate, it would not be a dominating question in any serious negotiation on a total freeze that arose between Moscow and Washington. "National technical means" would assuredly be insufficient to ensure compliance.

Petraeus and Kennedy differ most markedly on another issue: whether the Soviets had nuclear superiority at the beginning of the 1980s. The dispute will not be new to those who have followed earlier debates in this volume, and we shall encounter it again in later chapters. What is striking in this context is Petraeus's ambiguity in his use of the term "superiority" as applied to the Soviets. At one point he discerns great

Soviet advantages in present nuclear systems, which he deems increasingly liable to be translated into political gains. He argues that the United States must take appropriate countermeasures to avoid being frozen into inferiority. Yet at the end of his article he tells us that the Soviets "are bent on achieving true strategic superiority which they can exploit to achieve their political, economic and geostrategic aims." Maybe so. But if they are bent on achieving "true superiority," it rather suggests they do not have it now. The questions we are left with, then, are whether significant nuclear arms control will ever be possible if experts in Washington and Moscow cannot even decide whether their present relationship is one of essential equivalence; and what can possibly be hoped to result from bilateral negotiations if either the United States or the Soviet Union (or both) believes that the other has "a strategic advantage" or "true strategic superiority" (whatever these terms may mean)? Are we destined to have to choose only from among various unilateral measures for the foreseeable future?

8 Should SALT II Have Been Ratified?

YES

Paul C. Warnke

[*The Case for SALT II*]

NO

Edward Rowny

[*The Case Against SALT II*]

[The Case for SALT II]
Paul C. Warnke

Mr. Chairman and members of the committee, it is a privilege to appear before this Committee. As I am sure you will appreciate, however, I regret that the SALT II Treaty has not already been ratified and this appearance made unnecessary. Prompt entry of the treaty into force will prevent a significant increase in the Soviet strategic nuclear threat. If the SALT restrictions are delayed, as some have suggested, we may find that some of the more important restrictions have been overtaken by developments to the disadvantage of our national security.

Accordingly, I believe that it is time to turn the debate back to the basics of the treaty itself and to address what I regard as some of the principal misconceptions.

One is that the SALT II Treaty is more important to the Soviets than it is to us and that it can thus be held hostage to other issues in the complex U.S./Soviet relationship. This has emerged most recently in the argument that ratification should be delayed because of the presence of 2,000–3,000 Russians with combat equipment in a brigade stationed in Cuba.

Another challenge still presented is the baseless charge that the SALT II Treaty freezes the United States into a strategic disadvantage and gives the Soviets a ready road to strategic superiority.

There are still others who maintain that SALT is not really important because without the SALT controls the Soviets wouldn't do much if anything more than they can do with SALT.

Then from the other side of the arms control spectrum, there are those who criticize SALT as not being genuine arms control but simply the joint United States/Soviet management of the arms business.

Taking up these misconceptions in order, I would like to deal first with the challenge to SALT presented by those who argue that it should be linked directly to the intermittent ups-and-downs in United States/Soviet relations. Some carry this argument about linkage to the extreme and contend that our two countries are so different in world view and internal organization as to make any useful agreements impossible. Some would use SALT as a bribe or punishment, going ahead with strategic arms limitation efforts when the Soviets behave and suspending them when they engage in activities which we find disagreeable.

This approach misses, I think, the fact that SALT is not a favor to the Soviets but a step that we are taking in our own interest to promote our own security, and to spare the world a greater risk of nuclear devastation. There are, of course, fundamental and serious differences between our two countries. We rightfully resent Soviet attempts, with the help of Cuban troops, to warp nationalist movements and advance their ideological objectives. We deplore the Soviet leadership's inability to tolerate internal differences of opinion and their disregard of human rights.

But we should not lose our perspective or our sense of priorities. Senator Robert Byrd, the Senate Majority Leader, put it vividly earlier this month: "We should not permit political myopia to obscure our wider vision of U.S. national interests in the field of central strategic nuclear systems—which is what the SALT II Treaty is all about." The Soviet Union and the United States can negotiate usefully about the control of nuclear weapons because this is an area in which there are certain clear and compelling common interests. Both countries have an interest in national survival and the leadership of each must know that this requires that nuclear war be prevented. Each country has a major stake in discouraging the proliferation of nuclear weapons. The security of each would be gravely endangered

From Paul C. Warnke, Statement to U.S. Senate, *Military Implications of the Treaty on the Limitation of Strategic Offensive Arms and Protocol Thereto,* Hearings before the Committee on Armed Services, 96th Cong., 1st Sess. (1979), part 3, pp. 1254–57.

if nuclear weapons were to come into the possession of unstable governments, of bitter rivals in regional disputes, or of subnational terrorist groups. We both need SALT. But we're kidding ourselves if we think they need it or want it more than we do.

A compelling judgment on the role of linkage was expressed by a courageous Soviet dissident, Andrei Sakharov, Mr. Sakharov has written: "I believe that the problem of lessening the danger of annihilating humanity in a nuclear war carries an absolute priority over all other considerations."

We should continue to challenge Soviet conduct that we find incompatible with any improvement of relations and with our own national interests. But we should not expect to use the SALT process for this purpose. It is too important in its own right and, moreover, we drive too hard a SALT bargain to be able to use it as a carrot in other areas of United States/Soviet relations.

The independent and overriding importance of SALT has been recognized in the past. In May of 1972, we were engaged in a bloody and divisive war in Indochina. The Soviet Union supplied the weapons that were killing American soldiers. A month earlier, President Nixon had ordered the mining of Haiphong Harbor. But nonetheless he went that May to Moscow and signed the SALT I agreements.

Obviously, the United States/Soviet arms control process would be facilitated if fewer frictions were caused by incidents of Soviet adventurism. The climate of relations inevitably influences the pace of negotiations. But if we could count on the Soviet leadership always to do what we would like it to do, then as President [Carter] pointed out in his speech on October 1st, "we would not need a treaty to reduce the possibility of nuclear war between us."

The fact that we will remain competitors, and frequently bitter competitors, for the foreseeable future makes progress in SALT all the more urgent. SALT won't guarantee détente. But a collapse of the SALT process would dim if not doom any hope for a lessening of tensions.

The second criticism I want to discuss is the contention that SALT freezes us at a strategic disadvantage. Those who make this charge are, I believe, really complaining about the consequences of military decisions made years ago, long before SALT. They refer to the Soviet advantage in land-based intercontinental ballistic missiles generally and the very heavy ICBM's in particular. They downgrade the deterrent efficacy of the submarine launched ballistic missiles where the greater part of our strategic nuclear retaliatory force is concentrated. They argue that a Soviet lead in ICBM throw weight and megatonnage will put us at risk in the near future, if we have not already reached that stage. In essence, they argue that we have made the wrong strategic decisions and the Soviets the right ones.

I believe we've made the right decision. But these critics never explain how any of their fears about the strategic balance would be alleviated if there were no SALT II Treaty. Nor do they explain how SALT would prevent any useful actions that we might take to modernize our strategic nuclear forces. The fact is that SALT will block certain additions to the Soviet strategic forces that would increase the risk to the United States. The further fact is that, as a result of hard bargaining in the SALT process, we have preserved each of the options deemed by the Pentagon to be important to upgrade each part of our nuclear deterrent triad.

Confirmation of the contribution SALT makes to the security of the United States was expressed most succinctly in the statement delivered at the SALT hearings last July on behalf of the Joint Chiefs of Staff. In the words of their spokesman, General David Jones, the Chairman of the Joint Chiefs: "[T]here are a number of important restrictions in SALT II which operate primarily to our advantage," and "the specific limits on the United States are quite nominal."

With the SALT II Treaty, with its constraints on Soviet strategic threat and with its provision for improvements in our own retaliatory capability, we add to the only security that can exist in the nuclear weapons age. This is the certainty that our potential adversary must know that, were it to launch a nuclear war, it could not hope to gain any advantage. Its nuclear aggression would only mean the devastation of its own society.

Secretary Brown in testifying before the Armed Services Committee this summer, gave a couple of figures that indicate the impact of SALT. He pointed out that without the SALT II Treaty the Soviets would increase their strategic nuclear delivery systems from the present approximately 2,500 to something like 3,000 and that in those 3,000 systems they could have as many as 18,000 separate nuclear warheads, each one of them with many times the explosive power of the primitive bomb that devastated Hiroshima. Even with SALT the numbers of Soviet missiles and Soviet warheads will increase greatly. But they will have about one-quarter [fewer] missile launchers and one-half the total warheads than if SALT were not to go into effect. And with SALT, the diversified strategic forces that make up our deterrent Triad—ICBM launchers, ballistic missile submarines and strategic bombers—can each be upgraded.

Some critics of SALT argue that its success may lull us into a false euphoria and prevent the expenditure of funds needed to improve our military posture. This fear is reflected in efforts to bind the executive branch to a higher level of defense spending. I am confident that the President and the Congress can work together to arrive at a correct judgment of our real defense needs and that these need not be inflated in an effort to buy off SALT opponents. Arms control and a strong defense are not competitors. They are both important parts of a sound national security policy.

The third misconception to which I have referred is that SALT is an unnecessary exercise because the Soviets would not really do much more without it, and the threat they pose wouldn't increase economic constraints preventing them from adding additional thousands of warheads.

Coming from some SALT critics, I find this a curious argument. They've been trumpeting about the Soviet threat for all of these years and now they tell us the Russians are paper tigers, that we've got them pushed to the wall, that they're at the end of

their economic tether and, as a consequence, we don't need SALT because they can't do much anyway. The history of the arms race, the history of the Soviet buildup, however, is such that I can't feel comfortable in thus denigrating the potential Soviet threat.

What we are dealing with is a totalitarian society. Certainly the standard of living of the Soviet worker would be much higher if the funds spent on strategic nuclear and conventional arms were less immense. But the little progress that has been made in raising that standard of living can promptly be sacrificed by a government that doesn't have to face an aggrieved electorate, and that has complete control over the media. Rejection of the SALT II Treaty could be pictured as a portent of greater threat to Soviet security, and a reason for greater sacrifice.

Finally, I would like to address myself to the challenge of those who scorn SALT as too little too late. I've discussed the views of those who criticize SALT on the ground that it does not sufficiently restrict Soviet forces. But there are strong supporters of arms control who maintain that it doesn't go far enough in restricting either side.

Obviously, as I've indicated, there will be new nuclear weapons systems developed under SALT. It doesn't stop the nuclear arms race. It does not amount to significant nuclear disarmament. But in my view, there is no way that you can in a single step get from where we are today to something like significant nuclear disarmament. Neither country could afford to risk it. Neither country would be willing to take that dramatic a step. Each country has to feel its way gradually on a step-by-step basis.

We began the process with SALT I which froze the total number of ballistic missile launchers. SALT II constitutes the second and a very sound and effective step forward. It provides the firm foundation for future efforts in strategic arms control. It's not a panacea. It's not a substitute for a strong defense but it does enable us to continue to make progress. It means that we now have the basic definitions of the weapon systems to be controlled. These can continue in effect and be supplemented.

We have ceilings and subceilings which can be further reduced. We have the precedent of qualitative controls. Even if SALT II were the final agreement it would still be worthwhile in limiting nuclear weapons and reducing the risk of war.

But it's more important than that. Because SALT II is not the end of the process. It is just one step in the gradual pulling away from the abyss of nuclear destruction. It for the first time puts us in a position in which nuclear weapons are being brought under control—not just frozen. It puts us also in a position in which for the first time we can begin to move from under the shadow of nuclear destruction that has broadened and deepened during the past three decades. I think it's about twenty-five years ago that President Eisenhower said that, if mankind is to have a future, the wisdom that invented the nuclear weapon must be matched by the wisdom to bring it under control. Our acceptance or rejection of SALT II will indicate whether we have in fact, acquired that wisdom.

[The Case Against SALT II]
Edward Rowny

Mr. Chairman, I would like to thank you and the members of the Committee for inviting me to testify before you today. I hope that this round of Senate hearings on SALT II will do what the first round to a large extent failed to do, and consider the Treaty on its own merits.

Before beginning my statement I would like to reiterate my belief in the utility of negotiating limitations on strategic offensive arms. More than twenty years ago I began to express my views on the desirability of establishing equal levels of strategic capabilities between the superpowers at the lowest possible levels. It was largely because of my belief in arms control that I was selected to be the JCS representative on the U.S. SALT negotiating team. After six and a half years at the negotiating table I have not changed my fundamental belief in arms control, providing—and only providing—that agreements reached do not undermine our national security. Unfortunately, the Treaty now before the Senate is detrimental to our national security. If ratified in its present form the Treaty will undercut our ability to deter the Soviet Union from further adventurous and aggressive acts. Rather than help restore stability in times of crisis the net result of the military imbalance established by the Treaty will cause it to detract from that goal. The Treaty will undercut or undermine solidarity and Allied cohesion.

Because we failed to negotiate an equitable and verifiable Treaty, I feel it must be amended. In our zeal to reach an agreement the U.S. made too many concessions. We permitted large inequalities favoring the U.S.S.R. to be written into the agreement. To codify and legislate into law an unequal agreement will only exacerbate our strategic inferiority. It will make it a more costly and more lengthy process for us to regain strategic parity. Agreeing to an unequal SALT II Treaty will make it impossible for there to be an equal SALT III agreement.

Amending this Treaty will not, as some claim, spell the end to arms negotiations. Rather, the U.S.S.R. can be expected to agree to a Treaty which is more equitable and more verifiable. The Soviets want and need an agreement on strategic arms for the fundamental reason that they believe an agreement on SALT is in their long-term inter-

Edward Rowny, Statement to U.S. Senate, *Military Implications of the Treaty on the Limitation of Strategic Offensive Arms and Protocol Thereto*, Hearings before the Committee on Armed Services, 96th Cong., 1st Sess. (1979), part 3, pp. 982–89.

ests. President Brezhnev has committed his prestige to getting an agreement. He and his advisors (among them undoubtedly his successor) know that the Soviet Union, with one-half the gross national product of the United States, cannot continue to spend 12 to 14 percent of the U.S.S.R.'s GNP for arms indefinitely. They realize that the United States, because of its superior economy and because it possesses by far the greater technological base— if once aroused—can easily outdistance the U.S.S.R. in any competition in strategic armament. Soviet leaders realize that an agreement best permits them to continue their ability to pursue a policy of detente which allows them to aid the spread of what they call "good socialism" at the expense of "evil capitalism." Brezhnev and his advisors know that an agreement on SALT will establish a climate of normalization which helps them to gain most favored nation status and assists them to get credits on easy terms. It will ease their ability to obtain the technology transfers they so badly need.

Mr. Chairman, I have gone into some length on the reasons why the Soviets want and need a Treaty because I feel we fail to understand Soviet objectives and their approach to arms control. Recognizing that we have made SALT the centerpiece of our foreign policy the Soviets have concealed their own desire for an agreement. Realizing that we have linked our defense planning to expectations from an arms control agreement while they have kept the two separate, the Soviets have had every reason to allow us to woo them—to be the "demandeur." Up until now they have had only to wait us out, confident in the belief that the United States will not only insist that there is an agreement but will enter into an agreement that is favorable to the U.S.S.R.

I believe that a careful study of this Treaty on its own merits, as well as an examination of the U.S. and Soviet approaches to arms control, will lead us to look at the SALT process in the proper perspective. Rather than as a means to an end the U.S. has permitted SALT to become an end in itself. Unlike us, the Soviets first establish their long term objectives, then plan and program their forces to accomplish those objectives, and finally,

and only then consider arms control agreements. They do not permit arms control to interfere with their force planning. Thus, they view SALT to be a useful tool, especially if in the process they can inhibit or unilaterally restrain the U.S. The United States, by placing an arms control agreement at the apex of its objectives, has played into the hands of the Soviet Union.

BACKGROUND TO SALT II

I believe it would be appropriate, therefore, for me to comment briefly on the U.S. approach to arms control in SALT I and how the continuation of this approach contributed to the unsatisfactory outcome of SALT II. The Soviet objective in SALT I was to put a brake on the substantial U.S. lead in ABM technology. The objective of the United States was to place substantial limitations on strategic offensive forces. We sought to do this by establishing a firm link between offensive and defensive forces. Accordingly, we granted the Soviets the concession of agreeing to an ABM treaty in the expectation that it would open the way to a balanced and verifiable agreement on strategic offensive arms. Our hope was that such an offensive agreement would redress the imbalance between our strategic missiles and theirs, since by mid-1972 the Soviet Union had built up their ICBMs and SLBMs to numerical half again as great as ours.

At the time we signed the ABM Treaty the U.S. made it a matter of record that if there were no satisfactory agreement on strategic offensive arms within five years, supreme U.S. national interests could be jeopardized. This would constitute grounds for abrogating the ABM Treaty. However, in 1977, after five years had elapsed, we compounded the original concession of agreeing to the ABM Treaty. We granted the Soviets a second concession by abandoning the notion of making a serious review of the ABM Treaty in light of not having achieved an agreement on strategic offensive arms. These two sizeable concessions were made despite testimony of General David Jones, Chairman of the Joint Chiefs of Staff and Dr. Brown,

Secretary of Defense, that Soviet offensive and defensive forces had increased substantially in their overall capabilities while SALT II was being negotiated.

One of the most serious consequences of the inability to achieve an equitable Treaty on strategic offensive arms has been its contribution to the growing vulnerability of our strategic forces, that is our non-alert bombers and submarines, and especially our ICBMs. Some have argued that this situation came about as a result of our own decisions and not as a consequence of the SALT process. I disagree. Originally, when the U.S. decided not to proceed with a heavy missile system it did so in the belief, as expressed by Secretary McNamara, that the Soviets had neither the intention nor the capability of catching up to the U.S. strategically. Subsequent Soviet deployment of large numbers of huge missiles with accuracies approaching ours proved these earlier predictions to be wrong.

In 1972, at the time the interim agreement on strategic offensive forces was being considered the Joint Chiefs of Staff expressed serious reservations concerning its approval. However, the JCS were given assurances by their civilian superiors that the U.S. would pursue a vigorous program of modernization of its strategic nuclear systems and would expand and accelerate its research and development programs. Unfortunately these assurances, which included implementing such programs as the Trident, the B-1 bomber, NCA [National Command Authority] and site defenses, and sea-launched cruise missiles, were not fulfilled.

Our negotiating approach to the development and deployment of mobile ICBMs contributed to the vulnerability of land-based ICBM forces. The negotiating record of SALT I shows that the U.S. considered the development and deployment of mobile ICBMs to be inconsistent with the spirit of SALT. We made a unilateral statement to that effect at the time we agreed to the interim agreement on strategic offensive arms. The long period of time it has taken us to design and program a successor to our fixed ICBMs reflects our long-held reluctance to develop a mobile system. Between the

exploration of alternative basing modes for the MX missile and the expected date of deployment, some 15 years will have elapsed.

Another important U.S. concession made in SALT I which was carried over into SALT II concerned the size of follow-on missile systems. In SALT I the U.S. stated that it would consider any missile with a throwweight greater than that of the SS-11 to be a "heavy" missile. After SALT I the Soviets tested and deployed their SS-17s and SS-19s, both of which have a throwweight and hence a destructive potential three times greater than that of the Soviet SS-11 and the U.S. Minuteman missiles. The U.S. subsequently agreed to define a heavy missile as one with greater throwweight than the SS-19, thus conceding to the Soviets that their SS-17s and SS-19s could be classified as "light" ICBMs.

Our treatment of the Soviet III-X silos is an example of another category of U.S. concessions. The 151-III-X silos which the Soviets state are command and control launchers are practically identical to launchers for ICBMs and could be clandestinely converted to that use while new, hidden command and control facilities are being constructed. We also agreed not to count test and training launchers in the total aggregates, even though these launchers could be used to launch missiles against the United States. The Soviets have more than 150 launchers of this type, ten times the number of similar launchers possessed by the U.S. Taken together, these more than 300 Soviet launchers which are not counted under the SALT aggregate ceilings represent a potentially significant Soviet increase, on the order of ten percent, to their total capability.

Perhaps the most significant U.S. concession in SALT II was its failure to carry out the provisions of Public Law 92-448, the Jackson Amendment. This amendment called not only for equal numbers, but for equal levels of strategic force capabilities. Both the sponsors and opponents of that legislation agreed that "equal levels" would take into account both numbers of weapons and missile throwweight. The "numbers fallacy" which considers grossly disparate weapons systems of various yields, accuracies and basing modes as if they were identical is immediately obvious if one goes beyond simply counting numbers of systems. Our concessions on this score inevitably led to serious structural flaws which occur in this Treaty. Furthermore, our failure to insist upon true equality as the fundamental basis for SALT will continue to work against us in the future.

Mr. Chairman, we need to take another hard look at some of the major inequities contained in the SALT agreement.

ICBMS

First, the provisions of SALT II will grant the Soviets a unilateral right to over 300 heavy ICBM launchers while the U.S. is permitted none. This means that the Treaty allows the USSR to deploy over 3,000 re-entry vehicles each capable of 1 MT yield. The largest yield of a MIRVed U.S. ICBM warhead will, after the MK 12A warhead is deployed, be approximately one-third as great. The 3,000 warheads on Soviet SS-18 heavy missiles will carry more destructive potential than all U.S. ICBMs and SLBMs combined. These heavy missiles account for approximately one-half of the 6,000-odd re-entry vehicles on ICBMs the USSR will be permitted under the Treaty, a figure three times as large as the number of re-entry vehicles on U.S. ICBMs.

Second, SALT effectively prohibits us from pursuing a number of remedies to the Minuteman vulnerability problem, including a multiple vertical shelter basing scheme. The vertical shelter concept, the most timely and cost-effective way to help alleviate this problem, apparently has been discarded by the Administration because the Soviets have stated that it would be inconsistent with the provisions of SALT. Therefore, not only has SALT played a part in bringing about the vulnerability of our Minuteman force, but it is also responsible for limiting our options for dealing with this problem in the most cost-effective manner.

Third, the 820 MIRVed ICBM figure is a U.S. concession to the Soviets who would not agree to sub-limits for MIRVed ICBMs equal to ours. The United States has no plans to deploy more than 550 MIRVed ICBMs. Even if the Soviets were to deploy 920 MIRVed ICBMs, as some estimates hold, the sub-limit of 820 MIRVed ICBMs will only reduce their total number of ICBM warheads by 5 percent.

Fourth, under the Treaty provisions relating to the modernization of ICBMs, the Soviets will actually be able to deploy more than one "new type" ICBM. The ambiguity in these provisions results from Soviet refusal to agree to limit those missile characteristics which would effectively restrict them to a single new type ICBM. We should not be surprised when the Soviets proceed with the deployment of several new fifth generation ICBM systems if this Treaty is ratified, as we were surprised when they deployed their SS-17s and SS-19s after the signing of SALT I.

Because of our failure to get Soviet agreement to meaningful reductions in Soviet strategic capabilities, it will be much more difficult to get the Soviets to reduce to lower numerical levels—or to agree to qualitative limitations—in follow-on negotiations. After spending billions of rubles to develop and deploy their systems the Soviets will be quite reluctant to scrap them. Thus, the United States will have to generate and spend considerable negotiating capital to persuade the Soviets to reduce in SALT III or SALT IV. We will be far better off if we insist on equality now, in SALT II, rather than hope that the "next time around" will be easier. We should keep in mind that SALT II was to have been the "next time" as a follow-on to SALT I.

BOMBERS

The United States granted the Soviet Union a major concession by agreeing at Vladivostok to include heavy bombers in the aggregate totals. The U.S. has agreed to count 573 heavy bombers (569 B-52s and 4 B-1s) even though over 200 B-52s are in mothballs and various stages of inoperability.

The Soviets, since they will not be required to count the Backfire and because a number of their "bomber variants" will not be counted, will only count 156 heavy bombers in their totals.

The United States, therefore, agreed to include a major portion of its strategic forces in the agreement at a relatively small price in terms of Soviet strategic forces. Further, the United States by agreeing not to count Backfire in the Soviet aggregate made a concession in principle because of a failure to include all intercontinental systems in a Treaty on strategic offensive arms. In terms of reality, the so-called "assurance" Brezhnev gave us that the Soviets will "not increase the radius of action of this airplane in such a way as to enable it to strike targets on the territory of the U.S." is a nonsequitur. Since 1942 the standard method of employing heavy bombers is not to program their return to home bases but to have them land in third countries. If the U.S. were to use the Soviet definition, no modern heavy bomber would be counted in the aggregate. Neither the U.S. B-52s, nor the B-1s, can strike the Soviet Union on unrefueled radius missions.

The "assurance" that the Soviet Union will not increase the production rate of the Backfire beyond 30 a year is also meaningless. The Soviets could not build more than 30 Backfires a year without considerable effort—nor do they need to do so. The 375 Backfires that the Soviets will possess by 1985 is greater than the number of B-52s the United States will possess in its active inventory at that time. Importantly, by not counting the Backfires in their inventory, the Soviets will not have to reduce their ICBM and SLBM forces by some 375 launchers.

In addition to the principle of equality, the Backfire possesses a significant potential capability to cause damage to the United States. The 375 Backfires can carry approximately 4 million pounds of payload, and thus increase by nearly one-third the current potential of 11 million pounds of missile throwweight possessed by Soviet strategic forces. The United States will need to spend some $8 to $10 billion between now and 1985 to improve its skeleton air defenses to reduce the threat caused by the Soviet Backfire force.

It is worth repeating that the Joint Chiefs of Staff have consistently maintained that the Backfire is a heavy bomber and should be counted in the Soviet aggregate. Further, that the so-called assurances provided by the Soviets on Backfire are militarily worthless.

The United States also granted the USSR a large concession by agreeing not to count in their aggregates Soviet bomber variants—that is, Soviet heavy bombers which the USSR says they would use for other than heavy-bomber missions. The Soviets have promised to convert their dual-capable Bisons to tankers, a promise whose compliance will be difficult to verify. Furthermore, we have agreed to exclude the Soviet Bears which the Soviets say are used for ASW [antisubmarine warfare] activities even though our own B-52s which are used for ASW are counted.

Agreement to count aircraft equipped for cruise missiles in the 1,320 MIRVed missile aggregate was a major concession on the part of the United States. In January 1976 Secretary Kissinger offered to count such aircraft in the MIRVed totals if the Soviets counted Backfires in their aggregate. The Soviets pocketed our offer whereas we subsequently conceded that Backfire need not count in the Soviet aggregate. As mentioned earlier the "assurances" on the Backfire are militarily meaningless. The Soviets do not need to penetrate our air defenses—the U.S. air defense system has been virtually dismantled. Therefore the USSR does not need air-launched cruise missiles whereas our B-52 force cannot be made viable unless these bombers are equipped with cruise missiles. By agreeing to count aircraft equipped for cruise missiles in the 1,320 total, the U.S. is limiting itself to 120 systems—the difference between the 1,200 MIRVed missile sublimit and the 1,320 aggregate. To deploy even 120 cruise missile carriers, the U.S. will need to forego the deployment of some 85 MIRVed ICBM or SLBM launchers, since the planned totals of such MIRVed systems by 1985 is approximately 1,285. As further reductions to the 1,200 missile sublimit occur, the U.S. will be forced to reduce its MIRVed ICBM and SLBM launchers further—on a one-for-one basis—in order to accommodate the number of aircraft programmed for carrying cruise missiles.

CRUISE MISSILES

One of the most glaring examples of our lack of negotiating ability can be seen in our concessions regarding cruise missiles. The largest concession was in agreeing to Soviet demands to include cruise missiles in the agreement at all, especially since cruise missiles were not mentioned at Vladivostok in 1974. The Protocol forbids deployment of GLCMs [ground-launched cruise missiles] and SLCMs [sea-launched cruise missiles] with ranges in excess of 600 kilometers. These are theater weapons designed for tactical missions. Agreeing to constrain these systems without getting constraints on the SS-20, or other Soviet systems with strategic capabilities, is a serious compromise of the principle of equality. It undermines NATO cohesion and Allied solidarity.

In addition, the United States agreed to count ALCMs [air-launched cruise missiles] with non-nuclear warheads as nuclear-armed ALCMs in the Treaty. This is a serious concession because it limits their use as battlefield weapons and also because the precedent is established for a Soviet claim to treat GLCMs and SLCMs in a similar manner once the Protocol expires.

Agreeing to an average deployment of 28 ALCMs per aircraft, a major U.S. concession, represents another example of how a confused U.S. negotiating stance led to an unnecessary U.S. concession. The U.S. originally offered to limit aircraft other than heavy bombers to 35 ALCMs each and heavy bombers to 20 ALCMs per bomber. The Soviets countered with an offer to limit aircraft other than heavy bombers to 25 ALCMs. We then proposed to split the difference at 30. However the Soviets then argued that the difference should be split halfway between 20 and 35, since we had offered to

limit bombers to 20 ALCMs. Our agreement to the figure of 28 is one more example of our poor negotiating record in SALT II.

VERIFICATION

One of the most complex issues relating to the SALT II Treaty has been the issue of verification. I have stated previously that this Treaty is not "adequately verifiable" and will comment on just a few of the many verification problems.

As presently constituted, the SALT II Treaty contains a major loophole which permits Soviet encryption of telemetry we need to monitor Soviet compliance. The specific provision of the Treaty dealing with telemetry states that the encryption of data which interferes with national technical means of verification of the provisions of the Treaty is prohibited. However, the Soviets will be the final arbiter as to what information would be provided and what information would be encrypted. Furthermore, we succumbed to the inclusion of a statement in the Treaty that only encryption which deliberately denies information needed to verify the provisions of the agreement is prohibited.

The United States should have insisted on a total ban on encryption, since the only purpose of encryption of telemetry is to conceal and deny information. In this connection, the United States does not encrypt data. What would happen if we find the Soviets encrypting data which we believe is necessary to verify their compliance with the provisions of the Treaty? Calling the Soviets' hand on this could compromise our intelligence capabilities which are already quite limited. If we do confront them, and they are encrypting telemetry we consider necessary for verifying SALT, what would we do? Abrogate the Treaty? The Soviets could simply say that they are not deliberately denying information—and since we would not know what was being hidden we would have no basis for challenge. This loophole will no doubt be exploited by the Soviets in the future. As Senator Sarbanes pointed out during the first round of hearings before this Committee, there is no agreed definition of National Technical Means of Verification. We can expect this situation to be exploited by the Soviets also.

A second verification issue involves the Soviet agreement to count the 120 ICBM launchers at Derazhnya and Pervomaysk (D&P) in the 1,320 MIRV aggregate. This is considered by some to be a Soviet concession. Clearly it is not a concession, since the U.S.S.R. is placing MIRVed ICBMs in these 120 launchers. Further, by insisting that it is an exception to—rather than compliance with—the launcher-type rule, the Soviets are not prevented from exploiting future situations like D&P. So long as the Soviets maintain D&P is an "exception to" and not a "compliance with" the launcher-type rule, they undermine the putative value of this counting rule.

These are but some of the examples which show the United States made concessions in its attempt to achieve some degree of verifiability of the provisions of the agreement. This simply should not be the case, since the Soviets, having a unilateral advantage by virtue of the openness of our society, should be willing to cooperate on assuring compliance. But as the history of SALT shows, the first thing to be traded away on almost any provision is our ability to verify Soviet compliance. Proponents of this SALT Treaty agree that in the absence of a Treaty the Soviets would not be constrained from deliberately concealing their strategic offensive systems. This argument fails to recognize that there is an agreement not to deliberately conceal in the interim agreement and that this agreement has been carried over and undoubtedly would continue to be carried forward in the absence of a SALT II agreement.

CONCESSIONS

Most of the concessions the Soviets allegedly made in SALT II are actually not concessions at all: for example, Soviet reductions in order to come down to the 2,400 aggregate. This should not be labeled as a concession since equality should be the foundation of any arms control agreement. To treat such a reduction as a concession is tantamount to rewarding the Soviets for having raced ahead of the United States while SALT was in progress. Another example is the agreement not to count U.S. so-called forward-based systems (FBS) in the totals. However, as I have stated in previous testimony, this agreement was certainly more in the Soviets' interest since they have three times as many theater-capable nuclear systems possessing ten times the throw-weight of all NATO theater systems—French, British, and U.S. systems in Europe combined.

The U.S.S.R. has not provided us with an agreed data base in sufficient detail to permit us to assess future modernization of their systems. They have consistently refused to give us, for example, information on throwweight, launchweight and RV [re-entry vehicle] weight. Such data are necessary if we expect to be able to enforce complete Soviet compliance with the limitations proposed by the Treaty.

In our zeal to reach an agreement on strategic offensive arms, we made offer after offer and piled concession upon concession at almost every point of the way. This has been especially true during the last eighteen months. While the concessions are too numerous to cite here, I will give a few examples:

We agreed to give the Soviets varying periods of time after the Treaty goes into effect to make the required reductions. There is no reason why they could not begin dismantling their excess systems as soon as the Treaty is ratified instead of granting them a six month period after the Treaty goes into effect. Further, we have given them as much as a year to reduce to the lower number of systems permitted after 1 January 1981.

Our agreement to a 600 kilometer cut-off range between limited and unlimited cruise missiles favors the Soviet Union. Sea-launched cruise missiles of 600 kilometer range can strike over 75 percent of the population and industry of the U.S.

from the 100 fathom depth line, whereas SLCMs of 600 kilometers can only strike 2 percent of like targets in the U.S.S.R.

The Soviets tested air-launched cruise missiles from Bear aircraft to ranges exceeding 600 kilometers. Yet the 69 Bears capable of carrying cruise missiles are not counted in the MIRVed aggregate based on the Soviet promise that they will not deploy such cruise missiles in the future.

The United States has agreed to give prior notification on all its ICBM launches. The Soviets need only to notify the U.S. of those ICBM launches planned to extend beyond their national territory unless multiple launches are involved.

The United States attempted to reach agreement limiting depressed-trajectory SLBMs. However, because the U.S.S.R. objected, the U.S. did not pursue the issue.

The Joint Statement of Principles (JSP) the U.S. originally wanted was more specific and more binding, especially with respect to further reductions. However, because of Soviet objections, the U.S. agreed to language which is both vague and general. In this connection, several points are worth noting. First, the JSP states that resolution of issues included in the Protocol will be pursued in follow-on negotiations, thus bringing into doubt the statement often made that the Protocol will not establish precedents for the future, especially insofar as GLCMs and SLCMs are concerned. Second, the wording concerning the use of cooperative measures contributing to the effectiveness of verification by national technical means is ambiguous. Third, measures to reduce and avert the risk of surprise attack mean to the Soviets that submarine deployment zones will be established—a limitation which is prejudicial to the interests of the United States.

The list of concessions made by the United States is lengthy and far outweighs in number and importance the concessions made by the USSR.

The Soviets employed negotiating tactics which proved effective against the less determined and less patient U.S. negotiators. A prime example occurred in March 1977 when the U.S. tabled its comprehensive proposal in Moscow. Simply because the Soviets quickly and vehemently said "Nyet" to our proposal—one which would bring about a real measure of arms control—the U.S. quickly abandoned it. We did not push Secretary Brown's subsequent arguments that this package would have resulted in reductions on both sides even though it still gave the net advantage to the USSR. From that time until the SALT agreement was signed in Vienna in June 1979, the U.S. continuously made new proposals and offered additional concessions.

SOVIET NEGOTIATING TECHNIQUES

One of the most successful techniques employed by the Soviets in SALT has been to capitalize on "agreements in principle." In October, 1977, following Mr. Gromyko's visit to the White House, President Carter indicated that a SALT agreement would be reached within two to three weeks time. What subsequently happened was that the Soviets pocketed those items favorable to them and entangled and ensnared us in negotiations on those items which we thought the Soviets had agreed to. The final agreement was not reached until a year and a half later.

In late December 1978, the U.S., believing that agreement on a Treaty was this time imminent, made several more concessions to the Soviets. However, the Soviets by raising new issues and reopening old ones, were able to dead-lock the negotiations until even more favorable terms were made available to them.

The mistake made in October, 1977 was again repeated by the U.S. in April of 1979. Once again, the U.S. repeated its earlier mistake by indicating that agreement had been reached "in principle." We said that only minor issues remained to be negotiated by the "technicians" in Geneva. This was not the case—more than a score of the more important issues remained to be settled. By employing the tactic of postponing decisions, in fact until the eleventh hour, the Soviets were able to extract additional concessions from the United States.

THE "BOTTOM LINE"

The five arguments most often cited by proponents of this agreement as being the "bottom line" deserve attention. First, it is argued that this Treaty does not prohibit the U.S. from doing anything it chooses to do to improve its strategic posture. I disagree. Because of the unilateral rights granted the USSR in heavy missile launchers, the United States cannot achieve equality in missile throwweight, MIRVed ICBM throwweight, or in the number of re-entry vehicles on ICBMs; in addition, the deployment of U.S. ICBMs in a protected and relatively inexpensive mode is prohibited; and deployment of GLCMs and SLCMs with ranges greater than 600 kilometers during the period of the Protocol is prohibited.

Second, it is argued that the Treaty might restrain the Soviets from a further build up. This argument is wrong because it addresses only numbers and not capabilities of strategic offensive arms. Limits on numbers are set so high and the reductions are so minimal, that the Soviets will have more than enough weapons to destroy U.S. targets. Since meaningful qualitative limitations were not achieved, the Soviets can be expected to allocate their undiminished level of resources into unconstrained qualitative fields such as accuracy of missiles, ASW, and further build-ups in theater and conventional weapons. We must not allow the so-called "numbers fallacy" to deflect us from a realization that this Treaty permits the Soviets greater levels of over-all capabilities.

Third, proponents of this Treaty argue that with a Treaty we can predict what the Soviets will do that without it we will be in the dark. The contrary argument is nearer the truth. Numbers of systems are easier to monitor than are qualitative improvements such as accuracy, command and control and communications, etc. Thus the "number fallacy" that I mentioned in the preceding argument would

be compounded by a "monitoring fallacy" which will make Soviet behavior in the strategic field less, not more predictable.

Fourth, it is argued that in the absence of a Treaty the Soviets could interfere with our intelligence gathering and would be free to deliberately conceal their systems. Both of these arguments are faulty. The ABM Treaty and other agreements we have entered into prohibit interference with national technical means of verification. The continuation in force of the interim agreement prohibits deliberate concealment. In the absence of an agreement on SALT II, it will be to the Soviets' advantage to continue the interim agreement in force if for no other reason than it protects their current ICBM asymmetries. Even with agreements in force prohibiting deliberate concealment, the record of Soviet compliance has given us little reason to be confident that the Soviets will abide by the provisions of the agreement not to engage in concealment practices.

Fifth, it is argued that the absence of an agreement of SALT will now mark a return to the cold war and kill the prospects for an agreement later. My analysis leads me to the opposite conclusions. A codification of Soviet strategic superiority will make Soviet leaders more adventuresome and more aggressive in supporting their surrogates in wars which are quite hot where they occur. Labeling our displeasure with Soviet actions as a return to the cold war plays into the hands of the Soviet Union. Finally, as I have pointed out in my introduction, the Soviets need and want a deal on limiting strategic offensive arms and therefore the Soviets will be willing, if not anxious, once they have exploited to the full their propagandistic allegations that it was the U.S. that torpedoed the Treaty, to resume arms control negotiations.

In summary, Mr. Chairman, because of the reasons I have given to this Committee and the Foreign Relations Committee previously and because of what I have outlined above, I believe the Senate should view the SALT process in a broad perspective and relegate it to a subordinate role where it can serve a useful purpose. Based on careful analysis and more than six years at the negotiating table with the Soviets, I am strongly convinced that the Treaty before the Senate is neither equitable nor adequately verifiable. Therefore, it should not be ratified in its present form. The Senate should, in my view, offer amendments which will assure that the Treaty will be an equitable and verifiable Treaty, and recommit the agreement to negotiations with these requirements in mind. I remain firmly convinced that the Soviets want and need a SALT agreement. If we stand firm and repair our strategic posture, the Soviets will agree to a balanced Treaty. Ratification of this flawed Treaty will only prolong the period of U.S. strategic inferiority, make it more costly to regain strategic parity, and make it difficult if not impossible to negotiate any equitable future SALT agreement.

QUESTIONS FOR DISCUSSION

1 Would the SALT II Agreement have been ratified had not Soviet forces moved into Afghanistan?
2 Should United States support of arms control agreements be linked to Soviet political cooperation in the global arena?
3 Is it possible to have a worthwhile strategic arms control agreement between the United States and the Soviet Union in spite of the different capabilities of comparable weapon systems?
4 To what extent does SALT II serve legitimate Soviet security interests?

5 Was it wise for President Reagan to have observed the SALT II agreement although the treaty had not been ratified by the United States?

SUGGESTED READINGS

Donley, Michael B. (ed.). *The SALT Handbook*. Washington, D.C.: The Heritage Foundation, 1979.
Foreign Policy Association. *SALT II: Toward Security or Danger? A Balanced Account of Key Issues in the Debate*. New York: Foreign Policy Association, 1979.
Johansen, Robert C. "Arms Bazaar: SALT Was Never Intended to Disarm," *Harper's Magazine* (May 1979), pp. 21, 24, and 28–29.
Labrie, Roger P. (ed.). *The SALT Handbook: Key Documents and Issues, 1972–1979*. Washington, D.C.: American Enterprise Institute for Public Policy Research, 1979.
Luttwak, Edward N. "Ten Questions About SALT II," *Commentary* (August 1979), pp. 21–32.
Payne, Samuel B. Jr. *The Soviet Union and SALT*. Cambridge, Massachusetts: MIT Press, 1980.
Sharp, Jane M. O. "Restructuring the SALT Dialogue," *International Security* 6 (Winter 1981–82), pp. 144–76.
Talbott, Strobe. *Endgame: The Inside Story of SALT II*, New York: Harper & Row, 1979.
U.S. Congress, Senate. *Military Implications of the Treaty on the Limitation of Strategic Offensive Arms and Protocol Thereto*. Hearings before the Committee on Armed Services, 96th Cong., 1st Sess., 1979.
Wolfe, Thomas W. *The SALT Experience*. Cambridge, Massachusetts: Ballinger, 1979.

9 Is a Comprehensive Test Ban Treaty Desirable?

YES

Hugh E. DeWitt

Debate on a Comprehensive Nuclear Weapons Test Ban: Pro

NO

Robert B. Barker

Debate on a Comprehensive Nuclear Weapons Test Ban: Con

Debate on a Comprehensive Nuclear Weapons Test Ban: Pro

Hugh E. DeWitt

The 1963 Limited Test Ban Treaty prohibits nuclear explosions in the atmosphere, the oceans and space. Nevertheless, nuclear tests continue at an alarming rate—almost one explosion per week somewhere in the world—although now the testing is largely underground.

In the 1963 treaty, the United States committed itself to negotiate toward a comprehensive test ban, which would end the testing of nuclear weapons altogether. Many people in this country and in other countries strongly believe that a comprehensive test-ban agreement between the major nuclear powers would put a brake on the current runaway development of new nuclear weapons, and reduce the possibility of nuclear war. As a physicist for 26 years on the staff of the Lawrence Livermore National Laboratory, I have observed the development of nuclear weapons from the inside of the weapons establishment. During this time I have reached some possibly heretical conclusions for a weapons-lab employee, and the rest of this article should be understood in their light:

- Some form of comprehensive test ban treaty that ends nuclear testing is both feasible and vital to the security of the world.
- The weapons labs themselves bear a heavy responsibility for our present situation in which the two superpowers compete to obtain an illusory nuclear superiority.

Both of these personal convictions contrast sharply with positions taken by the weapons laboratories. The labs' stance on the first point was well summarized by Livermore director Roger Batzel when he stated:[1]

---

[1]This September 1978 statement by Roger Batzel is quoted in the abstract of J. K. Landauer, *National Security and the Comprehensive Test Ban Treaty*, Lawrence Livermore National Laboratory report number UCRL-52911(SRD), 29 February 1980. The abstract has been declassified; the report is classified as Secret Restricted Data.

. . . I believe the continued credibility of the US nuclear weapon deterrent cannot be assured for long without nuclear testing.

On the second point, the weapons laboratories maintain that they do not make national policy, but carry it out, and that when they advise policymakers they simply present the scientific truth. In this article I want to take a close look at these claims as a way of addressing the question of why even now, . . . the labs feel that it is so important to continue nuclear testing.

LABS ARE AN ACTIVE LOBBY

Glenn T. Seaborg, as chairman of the Atomic Energy Commission during the Kennedy Administration, was deeply involved in the US-Soviet negotiations that culminated in the Limited Test Ban Treaty and moved nuclear testing underground. He has recently written a very significant book,[2] *Kennedy, Khrushchev and the Test Ban*, in which he describes the intricate negotiations that began in 1958 and culminated five years later in the first serious nuclear weapons treaty between the rival superpowers. At the time, Seaborg himself was strongly in favor of a treaty to end all nuclear weapons tests, and he still holds this position. Furthermore, as he explains in his book, both Kennedy and Khrushchev had a deep commitment to a total ban on nuclear testing. Indeed, both men felt that such a ban would be a major step in the direction of world peace.

With this kind of commitment, coupled with the scale of the 1962 Cuban missile crisis, one may ask why Kennedy and Khrushchev were not able

---

[2]G. T. Seaborg, *Kennedy, Khrushchev, and the Test Ban*, U. Calif. P., Berkeley (1981).

to attain their goal of a comprehensive test ban in 1963. Obviously, each man had to contend in his own country with powerful forces opposed to a nuclear test ban. Seaborg discusses some of the opposition and how it affected the treaty negotiations. A recurrent theme in his book is the role of the American nuclear weapons labs and the efforts of leading weapons scientists to block the treaty; Khrushchev evidently had similar troubles with the Soviet nuclear-weapons establishment. A few examples from the American side illustrate the influence of the U.S. weapons labs:

• In 1957, Edward Teller and Ernest Lawrence met with President Eisenhower to argue against a moratorium on testing. They told Eisenhower that the Soviets could cheat with clandestine tests, and that US testing must continue anyway, to develop "clean" bombs, which they foresaw coming within seven years. These fallout-free devices would be deployed as tactical nuclear weapons in Europe. It has now been 26 years since the meeting with Eisenhower, and we have no "clean" bombs.

• As the test-ban negotiations proceeded, verification became a major issue because of studies from the weapons labs suggesting that nuclear bombs could be exploded in large cavities deep underground and decoupled sufficiently to look like much smaller explosions. One such study suggested that a 300-kiloton bomb might look like a one-kiloton explosion. There were also arguments about testing in space, on the other side of the Sun, for example. By 1963 the weapons labs prevailed and nuclear testing was allowed to continue underground.

I don't have the space to detail the numerous later examples of the influence of the weapons labs on U.S. policy, but a recent example is important.

• President Carter began his four-year term with a determination to complete the comprehensive test-ban treaty negotiations. In the summer of 1978, Department of Energy secretary James Schlesinger took Harold Agnew, director of Los Alamos, and Batzel to see Carter to argue against United States participation in a comprehensive test-ban treaty. At that time, the Soviet Government was in favor of the treaty, and agreement seemed to be very near.[3] Yet the arguments of the weapons-labs leaders were apparently persuasive, and progress toward a comprehensive test-ban treaty stopped after that visit. Agnew later said[4] concerning that meeting,

> No question about it . . . We influenced Carter with facts so that he did not introduce the [treaty] which, we subsequently learned, he had planned to do.

At this point, one can only speculate as to what alarming facts caused Carter to change his mind on the need to complete the comprehensive test-ban treaty. The Reagan Administration is far more inclined to see things the same way as the nuclear-weapons establishment, and on 19 July 1982 Reagan announced[5] an end to negotiations toward a comprehensive test-ban treaty, and thus a change in a 20-year-old US policy.

Corporate Survival

The nuclear-weapons establishment occupies a very secure place in the American government. This is illustrated by the revealing testimony[6] of Major General William W. Hoover, director of the Department of Energy's Office of Military Application, before the Procurement and Military Nuclear Systems Subcommittee of the House Armed Services Committee. Hoover, speaking to a friendly Congressional subcommittee, indulged in a bit of humor and likened the weapons establishment to a large corporation:

> We are something unique in the U.S. Government— that is, a totally government-owned, integrated industry. A corporation, if you will, for which we are responsible.

[3]Science **201**, 1105 (22 September 1978).

[4]Interview with Harold Agnew, Los Alamos Science, volume 2, number 2 (Summer/Fall 1981).

[5]Widely reported in national newspapers of 20 July 1982. Implications of this announcement are discussed at length in The Defense Monitor, volume XI, number 8, Center for Defense Information, Washington, D.C. (1982).

[6]Excerpts from General Hoover's testimony given in Public Interest Report, Federation of American Scientists, Washington, D.C. (October 1982), page 8.

I would like the committee to consider themselves as the board of directors of that corporation. My remarks are in essence a prospectus of our corporation, and the record of this hearing will serve as our stockholders report.

Let me touch briefly on the assets of our corporation . . . The total number of employees is about 35,000. That includes production plants, test facilities, and the laboratories—those people who work for the weapons program.

. . . The results of our R&D activities lead to our product line . . . warheads supporting weapons systems of the Department of Defense.

Hoover goes on to describe the weapons laboratories' "product line," which includes nine different types of mainly strategic nuclear warheads, such as the W76 for the Trident I missile, the W87 for the MX missile, and the B83, a "modern strategic bomb" for high-speed low-altitude delivery. He also talks of the "theater nuclear product line," meaning smaller nuclear bombs for fighting tactical nuclear wars.

I must comment at this point that many Livermore staff members who are committed to their work on weapons design believe sincerely in the idea of deterrence, and they will say that their nuclear bombs are designed and made for the purpose of never being used. One can only ask: Does the General's "theater nuclear product line" really mean only deterrence? I should also mention here that the Livermore Lab, which designs and develops many of these devices, is a large establishment with over 7000 employees and a proposed FY 1984 budget of 584 million dollars. Nuclear weapons work is big business!

Later in this testimony, Hoover makes a significant statement about the weapons laboratories' stake in testing:

Like any good corporation, we have an investment strategy which we have been pursuing for the last couple of years and we intend to pursue it in the decade of the eighties . . . We think we need to increase our manpower in research, development, and technology by about 15% above what it was a couple of years

ago. We think we need to increase the level of underground testing.

This kind of direct statement to Congress from a high Department of Energy military official provides one clear answer as to why we have no comprehensive test-ban treaty now and are not likely to have one in the near future. The nuclear-weapons establishment is a very powerful "corporation," staffed with intelligent and dedicated people whose livelihoods are tied to never-ending nuclear-weapons work. This establishment will not remain neutral and quietly allow elected representatives to curtail their enjoyable and profitable weapons work through limitations such as a comprehensive test-ban treaty.

OBJECTIONS TO A TEST BAN

There are more serious reasons given for the ongoing nuclear testing. Two suggested reasons come from an unlikely source, Jack Anderson's nationally syndicated newspaper column. In a column[7] titled "Test Ban Folly," Anderson refers to classified White House documents presented at a secret Pentagon technical briefing and shown to him. From this information Anderson makes essentially two points:

• The Soviet Union is believed to have cheated extensively on the Threshold Test Ban Treaty of 1974, and is supposed to have exploded as many as 11 underground shots above the agreed-on 150-kiloton limit since 1978. (Although the United States has not ratified this treaty, the U.S. and the U.S.S.R. have said they will comply with the 150-kt limit.)

• Nuclear weapons testing must continue indefinitely because the weapons labs are not confident that new bombs manufactured from proven designs will actually explode to design specifications. In other words, without continued proof testing, America's nuclear stockpile cannot be relied on in the future.

[7]See, for example, the *San Francisco Chronicle*, 10 August 1982.

On both points it is my impression that Anderson was taken advantage of and shown the supposedly sensitive documents to spread ideas that cannot withstand scrutiny.

Let me first dispose of the question of Soviet cheating on the 150-kt limit. Reputable seismologists outside the weapons establishment have not confirmed the claim of Soviet cheating. In their recent article[8] in *Scientific American* on the verification of a comprehensive nuclear test ban, Lynn Sykes of Columbia University and Jack Evernden of the United States Geological Survey state that

> When the correct calibration is employed, it is apparent that none of the Russian weapons tests exceed 150 kilotons, although several come close to it.

From inside the weapons establishment we have a statement[9] by Michael May, associate director-at-large of Livermore, that classified documents "conclude that there was no evidence that the Soviets had cheated on the Threshold Test Ban Treaty. . . ." Gerald E. Marsh gives more details on this subject in his commentary in the March issue of the *Bulletin of the Atomic Scientists*. While people in the nuclear-weapons labs believe in their work, they are honest and don't believe in the story of Soviet cheating. That story emanates from officials in Washington, and it has the appearance of an attempt to justify American renunciation of the unratified Threshold Test Ban Treaty so that the U.S. can once again test at above 150 kilotons.

Anderson's second point is far more serious. From the documents shown to him, he states that leaders of the U.S. nuclear-weapons labs believe that they must have the ability to test up to five kilotons to guarantee the performance of weapons in the U.S. stockpile. He quotes from one of the unspecified White House documents:

> In the continued non-nuclear testing of weapons components, it turns out with some regularity that individual components fail or degrade. Even acceptable components may become unavailable as manufacturers shift product lines or go out of business.

Note that this reason for the necessity of continued testing has nothing to do with developing new designs or even modifying proven old designs. The documents that were shown to Anderson claim that even to maintain a dependable stockpile of nuclear weapons manufactured from well-tested designs, it is necessary to test the bombs occasionally. This would preclude a comprehensive test-ban treaty forever, because no U.S. president is likely to sign such a treaty knowing that the U.S. stockpile of nuclear weapons may degrade to the point of unreliability.

The suggestion that certain necessary materials might become unavailable as manufacturers change their line of products is a startling excuse for reserving the right to continue to set off nuclear bombs. Surely the Department of Energy can somehow solve this problem, given the money and resources available to it! Furthermore, if present-day proven bomb designs are that sensitive to slight changes in materials, then one must ask why the weapons labs have produced such designs. I think the answer is simply that the weapons labs have never had to contend seriously with the prospect of cessation of nuclear tests, and thus felt no need to design bombs that could be dependably manufactured in the distant future. I will come back to this problem later to argue that the weapons labs could solve it quickly if they felt the need to do so.

Exciting New Weapons

Another reason why the labs want to avoid the restrictions of a comprehensive test-ban treaty is the exciting prospect of developing a whole new class of nuclear weapons. These are described rather vaguely as directed-energy weapons or third-generation weapons, and they have been widely promoted by Edward Teller. . . . The nature of these new devices is hidden behind walls of secrecy, and I may say very little about them. Teller claims that it is imperative for the U.S. to develop these weap-

[8]L. Sykes, J. Evernden, Sci. Am., October 1982, page 47.
[9]Letter from Michael May to Gerald E. Marsh, 17 December 1982.

ons because they would be "defensive" in nature and would provide a reliable defense against a Soviet nuclear attack. One of the ideas is the bomb-pumped x-ray laser described[10] a couple of years ago in *Aviation Week and Space Technology*. This marvelous device would supposedly send a burst of x rays at a Russian missile high above the Earth's atmosphere, and destroy it long before it reached the U.S. Teller and his colleague Lowell Wood from Livermore are reported[11] to have met with President Reagan last summer to promote the new weapons ideas and to propose a major increase in funding—$200 million per year—for the x-ray laser and related systems.

These ideas for new weapons provide excitement and challenge for the weapons laboratories. Regardless of whether they will ever work as weapons systems, they have their own dangers, I think, and should be examined carefully. The promise of a new nuclear defense against Soviet missile attack, as described by Teller, is misleading and dangerous if accepted uncritically by the American public and ill-informed officials. I see a number of serious consequences:

• For the x-ray laser to be developed into a weapon, it would have to be tested in space. This would probably violate the Outer-Space Treaty of 1967, which prohibits the placement of nuclear weapons in space. A U.S. abrogation of this treaty could lead to the unraveling of all the arms-control agreements negotiated with such difficulty since 1963.
• Any complicated and expensive system, such as the x-ray laser, would be subject to a variety of countermeasures. For example, pieces of metal chaff near the target missile may give the same radar image as the missile itself.
• Reliance on new "defensive" nuclear weapons could lead to a false sense of security for the nation. Maybe these new ideas could be made to work after a few decades of expensive development, but for now they strike me as high-technology fixes that belong in "Star Wars" stories.

Finally, I want to point out that the new weapons systems give the weapons labs an additional strong argument against a test-ban treaty. If the third-generation weapons ideas are sold to the Reagan Administration and the Congress, then the weapons labs will need many years if not decades to develop them, and during that time a comprehensive test-ban treaty would obviously be impossible. This, in my opinion, is the main danger of Teller's new third-generation weapons.

DETECTABILITY

Sykes and Evernden conclude that seismological monitoring techniques have become so good in recent years that compliance with a comprehensive test-ban treaty could be effectively verified. They state that present-day seismic monitoring methods are capable of detecting and identifying underground explosions in the Soviet Union down to yields of one or two kilotons. If an array of 15 unmanned seismic monitors were placed in the Soviet Union by treaty agreement—something the Soviets have already agreed to in principle[12]—then the detectability limit would be reduced to a fraction of a kiloton. Sykes and Evernden base these estimates on explosions in rock.

Decoupling by conducting explosions in cavities complicates the issue considerably. Sykes and Evernden say that with conceivable cavities in rock or in salt domes, the largest blast that the Soviet Union could mask in the presence of 15 seismic monitors is still only two or three kilotons. As one might expect, the weapons labs are quite disturbed by Sykes and Evernden's conclusions, and they dispute them. Milo Nordyke, who is in charge of treaty verification work at Livermore, says[13] that it is possible to decouple relatively small explosions. He suggests that in a large cavity, a 10-kt explosion may give the seismic signal of a 0.2-kt explosion. Such a decoupling by a factor of 50

---

[10]*Aviation Week and Space Technology*, 23 February 1981.
[11]*Aviation Week and Space Technology*, 20 September 1982.

[12]See Herbert York's article, PHYSICS TODAY, March 1983, page 24.
[13]Quoted in *The New York Times*, 8 March 1983, page 13.

would be a serious matter for treaty verification purposes—but note that the yields being discussed in 1983 are far smaller than the 300 kilotons that Teller in 1957 told Eisenhower could be hidden. There seems to be a healthy technical debate going now among seismologists in the nuclear-weapons labs and outside, and the Defense Advanced Research Projects Agency is making every effort to dispute and discredit the Sykes and Evernden work.[14] Whatever the outcome of this debate, it now seems clear that seismologists can detect quite small nuclear explosions and that this represents a serious threat to the weapons labs. If explosions above one kiloton were prohibited by a new treaty, the labs would be effectively out of business.

Clearly, the present 150-kiloton limit of the Threshold Test Ban Treaty is unrealistically high. Some future U.S. Administration may resume test-ban negotiations with the Soviet Union. If the direction of future negotiations is simply to modify the 150-kt limit, then it will be necessary to consider a treaty based on either a yield limit or a detectability limit. A yield limit would have to be determined by what both sides agree is a yield large enough to be detected in spite of decoupling. This might be considerably more than 10 kilotons in salt-dome cavities, for example. Conversely, the negotiating countries could try for a treaty based on a seismic detectability limit that might, for example, correspond to a 0.2-kiloton explosion in rock. It is important to note that a yield limit would be much more favorable in the eyes of the weapons laboratories, because to be realistic such a limit would have to be at least 10 kt. The labs could then continue their work with explosions below that limit. A detectability limit of a fraction of a kiloton, however, would seriously restrict the weapons labs.

One problem in negotiating a limit based on seismic detectability is that it would require much discussion of the masking of larger explosions in decoupling cavities. One would expect that in such

[14]Unpublished notes from the office of Thomas C. Bache Jr., Geophysical Sciences Division, Defense Advanced Research Projects Agency, January 1983.

negotiations the American weapons labs will argue strongly that the Soviets might clandestinely cheat occasionally with explosions of a few kilotons in expensive cavities. At some point, the political leaders of the U.S. and the U.S.S.R. would have to come to some understanding as to whether there is any advantage to be gained from small-scale clandestine weapons programs that risk detection as seismological methods improve.

PROOF TESTING

As I see it, the nuclear-weapons establishment likes the protracted argument over verification of a comprehensive test ban or a low-yield threshold test ban because it focuses attention on the possible cheating capabilities of the Soviets. The seismic verification questions, as long as they sound alarming, serve the purpose of distracting attention from the really serious argument against a test ban that Anderson publicized. If the seismologists can make their case that verification of a test ban is really no longer a problem, then the labs will have to face the real question: Can dependable working bombs be manufactured in the future from today's proven designs? People at the top of the weapons-labs hierarchy say that bombs manufactured in years to come will not be dependable without continued nuclear testing. Other weapons experts deny this assertion. In August of 1978, when it seemed that negotiations with the Soviets on a comprehensive test-ban treaty were close to success, three men from Los Alamos wrote President Carter a very significant letter concerning testing and the reliability of the stockpile. They were Norris Bradbury, director of Los Alamos from 1945 to 1970, J. Carson Mark, head of the Theoretical Division of Los Alamos for 26 years, and Richard Garwin, a consultant at Los Alamos since 1950. In their letter they argue that it is possible to have a reliable stockpile even with a comprehensive test-ban treaty. They pose the question,

Can the continued operability of our stockpile of nuclear weapons be assured without future nuclear testing? That is, without attempting or allowing *improvement* in performance, reductions in maintenance cost, and the like, are there non-nuclear inspection and correction programs which will prevent the degradation of the reliability of stockpiled weapons?

Their answer is "yes," and they go on to address several problems that must be solved to maintain and manufacture reliable bombs, including the problem of materials acquisition mentioned by Anderson. They further point out that

> It has also been rare to the point of non-existence for a problem revealed by the sampling and inspection program to *require* a nuclear test for its resolution.

Livermore personnel disagree with the assessment of Bradbury, Mark and Garwin. Thus, as I quoted earlier, Livermore's director Batzel stated in September 1978 that continued nuclear testing is necessary to keep the U.S. stockpile credible.

The disagreement among weapons scientists in 1978 may have provoked some further thinking about the problems of a potential comprehensive test ban treaty. In February 1980, Joseph Landauer, then assistant associate director for arms control at Livermore, wrote a classified report[15] titled *National Security and the Comprehensive Test Ban Treaty*. Later that year he released a declassified version[16] that is fairly close in content to the classified document. This report gives reasons for and against a comprehensive test ban treaty—primarily against—and is a rare example of what amounts to a publicly available policy statement from a weapons laboratory. As one argument against a comprehensive test ban treaty, Landauer raises the question of materials replacement, saying:

> We expect that all nuclear weapons will have to be replaced or remanufactured within a few decades of their original manufacture. More and more of our

stockpiled weapons are approaching retirement age. No amount of good intentions or executive decisions will ensure the availability of exact replacement materials or prevent subtle changes in manufacturing processes.

The implication is clear that nuclear testing is required in the future to make sure that replacements or newly manufactured bombs actually work. There are also some classified aspects of current weapons designs that persuade people at Livermore that standard bombs built in the future must be tested to make sure they work. These design questions need to be examined by qualified scientists from outside the weapons laboratories.

Clearly, what has happened in the 20 years since the signing of the Limited Test Ban Treaty is that the weapons laboratories have produced sophisticated designs that are very efficient but so delicate that the labs seem to have no confidence that they can be manufactured reliably in the future. This raises two questions:

● Why have the laboratories been allowed to produce weapon designs that effectively preclude the U.S. from ever signing a comprehensive test-ban treaty? Surely this is strange considering that such a treaty has been a U.S. policy goal for 20 years.

● Can this situation be changed? That is, can the weapons laboratories quickly modify some of their designs so that bombs can be built reliably in years to come in the event of a comprehensive test-ban treaty?

Landauer makes another point that we have to consider seriously. He notes that Russian nuclear bombs are generally heavier, possibly less sophisticated, and possibly more dependable for manufacturing in the future. Thus he fears a serious degradation gap favoring the Soviets after a few years of a comprehensive test ban. He says

> We cannot assume that stockpile degradation will be symmetrical in respect to U.S. and Soviet weapons. We do not know how Soviet weapons are made, what

---

[15]J. K. Landauer, UCRL-52911(SRD), see reference 1.

[16]J. K. Landauer, *National Security and the Comprehensive Test Ban Treaty*, Lawrence Livermore National Laboratory report number UCRL-84848, August 1980 (unclassified).

their remanufacturing problems are, or by what means the Soviets can maintain the skills of their weapon scientists.

It would be ironic indeed if the cruder and more robust Soviet bomb designs allow the Soviets to be better prepared for a comprehensive test ban. I believe—for whatever it's worth—that the Livermore and Los Alamos Laboratories are full of clever weapons scientists who can in a short time meet the technical challenge posed by a test ban, and can produce bomb designs that avoid stockpile degradation problems. Certainly this should be one of the duties of the weapons laboratories.

Nominally, the University of California manages both the Livermore and Los Alamos laboratories under contract with the Department of Energy. The University of California obviously cannot interfere with the nuclear weapons design work done at the two labs, but it does have some oversight role. Part of this role is handled by a committee, the Livermore and Los Alamos Scientific and Academic Advisory Committee, which reports to the president of the university and occasionally to the university's regents.

WHAT SHOULD BE DONE?

In February 1982, Ray Kidder, one of my colleagues at Livermore, made a formal presentation to the Advisory Committee concerning the question of the necessity of continued nuclear testing to assure stockpile reliability. He asked the committee to look into this question as a technical scientific matter and to try to resolve the conflicting claims of weapons experts. In July of last year, Kidder sent a letter to David Saxon, then president of the university, stating that

> The purpose of the report [of the Advisory Committee] would be to provide government policy makers with information that is of fundamental importance in the formulation of national policy concerning nuclear

weapons, and that directly concerns the statements and activities of the two weapons laboratories under the stewardship of the University.

After some months of prodding, the answer finally came. It was *no,* the Scientific Advisory Committee would not be authorized to take up the question. Evidently this question impinges on national policy and is simply too difficult for the university to study.

To conclude, I will give my own opinions on what should be done.

- I think Congress or some part of the US Government should appoint a high-level committee of competent scientists, with members from outside the weapons establishment, to examine carefully the problem of bomb replacement and to figure out what needs to be done so that a comprehensive test-ban treaty will be possible.

- Congress, with the help of a group of qualified scientists from outside the weapons establishment, should examine carefully all the ideas for third-generation weapons, and make sure that they don't instantly become mammoth secret projects that attain their own momentum and destabilize the present precarious arms-limitation agreements.

- Technology for seismic verification of a comprehensive test-ban treaty appears to be sufficient already, and I am not convinced by the labs' arguments about the need for indefinite nuclear testing. The world needs to stop nuclear testing even more now than it did in 1963. Thus I hope that a more enlightened Administration in a few years will approach the Soviets again and complete the agreement that Kennedy and Khrushchev tried to attain, namely a comprehensive test-ban treaty. Not everybody agrees that stopping continued nuclear-bomb development will reduce the possibility of nuclear war, but I think so.

Seaborg concludes his book with a strong recommendation for a renewed effort to reach agreement on a comprehensive test-ban treaty. The final words in his book reflect the urgency of this task: "The hour is late. Let us hope not too late."

Debate on a Comprehensive Nuclear Weapons Test Ban: Con

Robert B. Barker

We are seeing today an unprecedented public interest in the control of nuclear arms. The resulting plethora of books and articles on all aspects of nuclear weapons and nuclear-weapon strategies is providing the basis for a new, informed discussion of arms-control objectives and priorities. While there may be a general desire for the elimination of all nuclear weapons, there is also an appreciation that nuclear weapons will be with us for the foreseeable future, and that we will achieve bilateral and verifiable reductions only over time. The public understands that even as we work for reductions in nuclear arms, those nuclear weapons that do exist should continue to preserve deterrence and stability between the two nuclear-weapons superpowers, the Soviet Union and the United States. Hence we should measure all proposals for arms control or arms reductions against their ability to reduce the numbers of nuclear weapons while preserving deterrence and stability.

Just as it is appropriate to assess each new arms-control proposal against this criterion, it is appropriate to use this same measure to reassess past proposals. A comprehensive test ban has been a stated goal of both the United States and the Soviet Union since 1958. (Herbert York discusses the subsequent history in his article in PHYSICS TODAY, March, page 24.) The Reagan Administration has reaffirmed that goal in the context of deep and verifiable arms reductions, expanded confidence-building measures and improved vertification capabilities. There has, however, been little recent public discussion of the significance and advisability of a comprehensive test ban. Should a comprehensive test ban be a current goal because it has been one since 1958? Should a comprehensive test ban be a current goal because, according to the

1982 edition of *Arms Control and Disarmament Agreements*,[1] the non-nuclear weapons signatories of the 1968 Non-Proliferation Treaty view it as a *sine qua non* for the prevention of nuclear proliferation?

Recognizing that this is not 1958, or 1968, or even 1978, we should reexamine and debate the desirability of a comprehensive test ban. The executive and legislative branches of the government will ultimately determine U.S. policy on this issue, assessing in the process international political as well as technical issues. This article is a personal assessment of the technical issues. I will examine the objectives of nuclear testing and ask the reader to evaluate their compatibility with nuclear-arms reduction and the maintenance of deterrence and stability.

GOALS OF TESTING

For too many people, the objectives of continued nuclear weapons tests are unnecessarily a mystery. While classification rules prevent discussion of some specifics, one can discuss the rationale for current testing.

The current U.S. nuclear testing program has several goals: ensuring the reliability of existing nuclear weapons; providing new designs for nuclear weapons intended to replace aging and ineffective weapons in the national stockpile; developing nuclear weapons; with better safety and security features; guaranteeing against technology surprise through research on new weapons con-

[1]*Arms Control and Disarmament Agreements*, 1982 edition, United States Arms Control and Disarmament Agency, Washington, D.C. (1982).

cepts; improving the fundamental understanding of nuclear-weapon performance; and maintaining the competence of nuclear-weapons scientists and engineers. All nuclear tests are carried out for the Department of Energy by this country's two nuclear-weapons laboratories, the Los Alamos National Laboratory in Los Alamos, New Mexico, and the Lawrence Livermore National Laboratory, in Livermore, California. The actual testing takes place at the Nevada test site, north of Las Vegas.

Reliability

The number of nuclear weapons in the U.S. stockpile is often cited as approximately 30,000. The weapons range from those delivered by missiles and aircraft to those carried by artillery shells. Whatever their delivery system, these weapons have no place in the stockpile if the nation does not have confidence that they are capable of fulfilling their role if called upon to do so. As we will see, the current nuclear weapons testing program plays a critical role in maintaining confidence in the country's nuclear deterrent.

Exactly how is this "confidence" established and maintained? Periodically, the Department of Energy must certify to the Department of Defense that weapons in the stockpile continue to meet the criteria established for them. While nuclear weapons are designed to last for the lifetimes of the systems that carry them—10, 20 or even 30 years—age does take its toll and not always in ways that were anticipated. Therefore DOE periodically samples non-nuclear components of nuclear weapons in the stockpile and tests those components to ensure that age has not impaired their function. Scientists and engineers of the weapons laboratory responsible for the initial design disassemble and examine the nuclear components, and make an assessment as to whether any age-related changes will degrade the performance of the weapon.

In general, the Department of Energy performance certification is based upon non-nuclear testing and the judgment of experienced personnel. However, when these inspectors find unacceptable deterioration, nuclear testing may be necessary to determine whether performance is truly unacceptably degraded. Acceptable nuclear test performance results in DOE certification; unacceptable performance requires that weapons in the stockpile be replaced through a new production of identical weapons or by weapons of a new design not subject to the same deterioration. The decision on which course to take is based on the age of the weapon. It makes little sense to rebuild if several rebuilds will be required during the life of the weapon system. If a new design is required, nuclear testing will be necessary to certify that it performs as predicted.

The weapons designers have done a good job throughout the history of the U.S. nuclear stockpile, but perfection has escaped them. Only infrequently has nuclear testing been required to verify adequate performance or to develop a new weapon to replace one that no longer works. However, in those few cases, until a solution was found and the testing was done, the weapons systems involved were suspect—confidence was lost—and the effect was the same as if they had been unilaterally removed from the stockpile.

Modernization

[Modernization] of U.S. nuclear-weapons delivery systems has been an ongoing process. Weapons systems based on newer technology replace those that have lost effectiveness because of obsolescence; for example, air-launched cruise missile carriers and B-1 bombers are to replace the B-52s. Weapons systems whose survivability may be threatened are replaced with less vulnerable systems; thus the Trident missile system is replacing the Polaris and Poseidon systems.

In every case to date, the replacement system has required a nuclear weapon different from that of the system it replaces. In some cases, physical dimensions alone preclude use of the older weapon. In other cases, existing warheads cannot survive the heat, acceleration, vibration and environmental extremes that a nuclear weapon will meet in the stockpile or during delivery. Even the yield requirement of the new system may be different from that of the system it replaces. As J. Carson Mark, retired head of the Theoretical Division of Los Alamos, noted[2] recently in the *Bulletin of the Atomic Scientists,*

> The nuclear explosive and its carrier constitute a "weapon system" of which neither part is of much use without the other . . . The weapon, tailored for . . . [its] particular delivery mode, cannot easily be used in any other way.

A substantial fraction of current nuclear testing is directed toward providing new weapons for new delivery systems. The Navy designed its C-4 missile to have a longer flight range, thereby permitting the Poseidon and Trident submarines to operate in larger ocean areas. No existing Navy reentry body could survive the harsher reentry environments associated with the greater missile range; a new reentry body with a new warhead made the C-4 system possible. The B-1 bomber will replace the B-52 in its role as a penetrating bomber. For the new bomber to fulfill its mission of deterrence, it must credibly be able to penetrate Soviet air defenses, deliver its weapons and escape. Accordingly, bombs delivered by the B-1 must be able to withstand release at greater speed, survive ground impact, and delay detonation while the aircraft flies out of range of the bomb's explosion. The criteria are very different from those for bombs designed for delivery by the B-52. The weapons labs have developed new nuclear designs to enable the B-1 to fulfill its mission.

In the area of tactical nuclear weapons, new development work has established the survivability of nuclear weapons in long-range artillery. The original nuclear artillery shells were designed to withstand the acceleration associated with the range of the 8-inch and 155-mm howitzers of the 1960s. In the following decades, U.S. and Soviet artillery

doubled in range. Without new nuclear shells, capable of withstanding the acceleration associated with the longer range, U.S. nuclear artillery would be "outranged" and therefore vulnerable to destruction by conventional weapon fire.

While concern for survivability is the primary motivation for modernizing nuclear weapons systems, there are other important reasons for doing so. The military effectiveness of established systems declines as the hardness of intended targets increases. To reestablish past destructive capability requires new nuclear weapons systems. Another motivation for modernization comes directly from developments in the area of nuclear-weapons design: In the last decade the nuclear-weapons laboratories have developed the technology to increase dramatically the safety and security of nuclear weapons.

Improved Safety and Security.

In the laboratories' work on nuclear-weapons safety, the concern is not that of an accidental nuclear explosion. As Mark has stated,[3]

> The high explosives which have been mostly used in connection with nuclear weapons . . . can reliably withstand the jolts and impacts encountered in normal handling, even if they should be dropped from modest height; but they might detonate on falling on to a hard surface from a plane, for example. The concern is not that a full-scale nuclear explosion would result, since that requires a thoroughly symmetric detonation of the explosive which could not be induced by impact at one point.

In fact, two aircraft accidents have caused the high explosives in nuclear weapons to detonate: in 1966 at Palomares, Spain, and in 1968 in Thule, Greenland. In both cases there was no nuclear chain reaction, but the explosions dispersed plutonium, requiring extensive clean-up operations to eliminate the hazard to health.

As a result of developments at the nuclear weap-

---

[2]J. C. Mark, Bulletin of the Atomic Scientists, March 1983, page 45.

[3]Ibid., p. 48.

ons laboratories, it is now possible to preclude accidents that disperse plutonium. There are some relatively insensitive high-explosive mixtures that can survive quite violent impacts. The laboratories are now in the process of incorporating such explosives in new weapons systems as they are modernized. Due to the number of different nuclear-weapons designs in the U.S. stockpile, it will be many years before all the weapons incorporate this improved safety feature. Because the weapons with insensitive explosives are based on new designs that differ substantially from those using older explosives, testing will play a critical role in the conversion to safer nuclear weapons.

Security is another area where recent developments in design are leading to dramatic improvements. Again, as weapons systems are modernized, features are being included that make it impossible for unauthorized persons to make use of a nuclear weapon. These features are an intimate part of the nuclear design and require nuclear tests to ensure that only authorized use would result in the expected performance.

Technical Surprise

One long-standing mission of the nuclear-weapons laboratories is to understand all means by which a nuclear explosion might be of military use. In part, this represents a desire to understand all the ways in which the U.S. might employ such explosives to enhance its security. It also represents a desire to avoid surprise from the advantages others might obtain from nuclear-weapons developments.

The evolution of nuclear-weapons design is not a one-dimensional process; there is no unique path that a nuclear-weapons state must follow from its first nuclear explosion to subsequent developments. One cannot be confident that findings by the United States match those of the Soviet Union. With the maturity of the U.S. nuclear program, new concepts are less frequent, but they do occur. Nuclear testing is critical to determining whether a new concept will work.

Verification that a concept is feasible does not imply that it will be incorporated into weapons in the U.S. stockpile. Far from it. But establishment of feasibility does permit the evaluation of the threat to this country should the Soviet Union have already incorporated it into their nuclear arsenal.

Fundamental Understanding

Despite the lengthy history of nuclear-weapons testing in the United States, weapons scientists do not fully understand some fundamental phenomena that bear on the performance of nuclear explosives. The nuclear-weapons laboratories possess the country's most impressive computer resources and a very impressive cadre of theoretical physicists. Yet, there are sometimes substantial discrepancies between calculation and experimental results; the mathematical models are just not yet adequate to predict reality. Economic considerations alone motivate the nuclear-weapons laboratories to maximize the role of calculations so as to husband the scarce and expensive resource of nuclear tests. Thus, the objective of some nuclear tests is to improve calculations by exploring fundamental phenomena that are not yet understood, and which may be the cause of the discrepancies between calculation and experiment.

A further very real consideration since 1958 has been the recognition that a comprehensive test ban may someday preclude testing, leaving the laboratories with calculation as the sole tool for meeting their obligation to maintain confidence in the U.S. nuclear-weapons stockpile. We are not now at the point where we can maintain current confidence requirements with calculation alone.

Experienced Judgment

Nuclear testing also plays an essential role in developing and maintaining the competence of the scientists and engineers at Livermore and Los Alamos who are responsible for the nuclear weapons' reliability. The same personnel who are charged with assessing the reliability of stockpiled nuclear weapons are involved in developing nuclear weapons. In their development work they are continuously having their judgments, based upon calculation and experience, tested against the reality of nuclear tests. Discrepancies between expectations and results are a constant reminder of the fallibility of computer calculation and "experience." Without testing, confidence in the judges of reliability will justifiably erode even in the unlikely event that the weapons laboratories can retain experienced personnel under such a circumstance.

REOPEN THE DEBATE

As we have seen, nuclear weapons testing plays a major role in maintaining confidence in the country's nuclear deterrent. Some have argued that the United States understands fundamental nuclear-weapons phenomena well enough. Some have, as an act of faith—not through hard evidence—asserted that the U.S. understanding of the application of nuclear explosions for military purposes encompasses all Soviet developments. They have said that U.S. weapons are already safe enough and secure enough. They have argued that modernization without nuclear testing can maintain the survivability of weapons systems even in the face of as-yet-unknown threats; and they assert that the United States can, without testing, maintain confidence in its stockpile, or that, in any case, for some unspecified reason, confidence in the nuclear-weapons stockpiles of the United States and the Soviet Union will erode at the same rate.

There should be a debate on the subject. The United States in 1983 should reevaluate the desirability of a comprehensive test ban as a national goal. Indeed, it should be more than a national debate, it should be an international debate, because U.S. confidence in its nuclear deterrent has international implications.

In 1983 we find nuclear weapons parity between the United States and the Soviet Union. It is a delicate balance. Will a comprehensive test ban increase chances of maintaining that stability or will it detract? Will a comprehensive test ban allow the U.S. to maintain the reliable deterrent that a majority of its citizenry wants? A real discussion is called for. An informed debate should begin.

QUESTIONS FOR DISCUSSION

1 What would have been the consequences to the arms race between the United States and the Soviet Union had the superpowers agreed to a CTBT in 1963?
2 If verification techniques improve so as to guarantee detection of low-yield underground nuclear explosions, would the United States agree to a CTBT?
3 Are the benefits of a CTBT now worth the risks of inability of detection of nuclear-weapons tests at low kiloton levels?
4 Would a CTBT serve Soviet or American interests, or would it affect each country equally?
5 What role do bureaucratic interests play in the testing controversy?

SUGGESTED READINGS

"Banning the Ban," *The New Republic* (August 16–23, 1982), pp. 7–9.

Caldwell, Dan. "CTB: An Effective SALT Substitute," *Bulletin of the Atomic Scientists* 36 (December 1980), pp. 30–33.

Firestone, Bernard J. *The Quest for Nuclear Stability: John F. Kennedy and the Soviet Union*. Westport, Connecticut: Greenwood Press, 1982.

Hannon, W. J. "Seismic Verification of a Comprehensive Test Ban," *Science* 227 (January 19, 1985), pp. 251–57.

Hughes, Peter C. and William Schneider, Jr. "Banning Nuclear Testing," in Richard Burt (ed.), *Arms Control and Defense Postures in the 1980s*. Boulder, Colorado: Westview Press, 1982, pp. 21–37.

Hussain, Farooq. *The Future of Arms Control: Part IV: The Impact of Weapons Test Restrictions*. Adelphi Paper no. 165. London: International Institute for Strategic Studies, Spring 1981.

Pavlov, A. "For a Complete Ban on Nuclear Tests," *Soviet Military Review* No. 11 (November 1983), pp. 49–50.

Seaborg, Glenn T. "Chance of U.S.-Soviet Nuclear War: 1 Percent per Year," *U.S. News & World Report* (March 29, 1982), p. 58.

———. *Kennedy, Khrushchev, and the Test Ban.* Berkeley: University of California Press, 1981.

Sykes, L. R. and J. F. Evernden. "The Verification of a Comprehensive Nuclear Test Ban," *Science* 247 (October 1982), pp. 47–55.

Wiesner, Jerome B. "What Is a Comprehensive Test Ban?" *Bulletin of the Atomic Scientists* 38 (June 1982), p. 13.

10 Is a Bilateral Nuclear Freeze Desirable?

YES

Edward Kennedy

[Freeze Now!]

NO

David H. Petraeus

What Is Wrong with a Nuclear Freeze?

[Freeze Now!]
Edward Kennedy

Mr. President, I offer this amendment on behalf of myself and the Senator from Oregon, Senator Hatfield, and 27 other cosponsors. They are Senators Baucus, Cranston, Huddleston, Leahy, Metzenbaum, Moynihan, Pell, Sarbanes, Tsongas, Glenn, Levin, Lautenberg, Biden, Hart, Dodd, Bingaman, Matsunaga, Bradley, Burdick, Eagleton, Melcher, Mitchell, Riegle, Stafford, Bumpers, Proxmire, and Inouye.

Mr. President, this afternoon, the full Senate will have its first opportunity to vote on the nuclear weapons freeze issue. The fundamental rationale for the freeze is the self-evident proposition that the best way to stop the nuclear arms race is to stop it. That is why Senator Hatfield and I and 32 other cosponsors of the nuclear freeze and reductions resolution first introduced this proposal in March 1982. That is why we have pressed it before the Foreign Relations Committee for the past 19 months, and that is why we are pressing it here on the Senate floor today.

Our nuclear freeze resolution is now on the Senate Calendar, ready for Senate action. As supporters of the freeze, we would have preferred that the resolution be brought up for full debate in its own right. But the most important thing is for the Senate to be able to vote this year on the freeze, and the present strategy seems to be the only way to achieve that goal.

Twenty years ago, at American University, President Kennedy called for a treaty to ban nuclear tests—as the first step in a strategy of peace to ban nuclear war.

The words he spoke then ring now with a timeless truth. Despite loose talk today about a nuclear warning shot and a winnable nuclear conflict, we know the abiding truth of his warning then that "total war makes no sense" in this age. And so we insist once more as clearly as we can that there is no such thing as a limited nuclear war.

In the dangerous times of the present, I believe that we must demand a national leadership which will spend less time preparing for nuclear war—and more time preventing one.

On the arms race, the essential truths of 1963 remain the same in 1983. But some things have changed—and many of them for the worse.

We found reason for hope in the Test Ban Treaty and other agreements that followed it. At least, we have not fought the third and last world war. At least, we are all still here.

But that is also far less than we could have sought—and far less than we should have achieved. For the mere absence of war has been accompanied by the increasing insecurity of a precarious nuclear peace. The knife's edge of the nuclear balance has been steadily sharpened. Arms control has often been twisted into a means for managing a faster arms race. In 1960, the combined total of deliverable nuclear explosives on station on both sides was 6,500. By 1983, that lethal number has multiplied by sevenfold to 50,000.

While the negotiators have bargained, their governments have developed and deployed new missiles with more warheads, greater accuracy, and shorter warning time. Relentlessly, we have reduced the narrow span of minutes in which the fate of humanity can be decided by human beings.

The U.S. Senate has failed to ratify SALT II and other relatively modest treaties which would widen a little the margin between our existence and extinction. In Moscow, Soviet leaders reach for potential first strike weapons. In Washington, the President claims he favors arms control and that his administration has proposed it—but, in fact, and sometimes in the strongest terms, he has opposed every single arms control agreement since he entered public life two decades ago.

So we have come to the dangerous place where we now find ourselves—in the midst of cold war

From Edward Kennedy, speech, *Congressional Record*, 98th Cong., 1st Sess. (October 31, 1983), pp. S15008–S15010.

two. We can continue to practice that brinkman-ship—and to proclaim our own toughness. And if those who advocate such mindless toughness prove to be mistaken, and their mistakes lead to the last great war, they may be safe in a protected bunker, inside a mountain and behind steel doors. But the rest of the Earth will be dying—and there will be few if any of us around to blame them for the most catastrophic error in all recorded history.

I reject that risk—and I reject the advice that we must not offer an alternative because it will un-dermine the present negotiations. That is what other administrations have said in their effort to mute dissent in other dark days on other difficult issues. And in the case of Vietnam, tens of thousands of Americans and hundreds of thousands of Vietnam-ese died before the lesson was learned that the answer to failure is not more of the same.

The greatest strength of a free society is that we can differ and speak out; we can develop and stand for different policies. On the nuclear issue, that strength may be the saving virtue of our national life and the life of all the world.

We now have the obligation and the opportunity to turn aside from another cold war—and to create instead a new strategy of peace. That strategy must be based on a realistic assessment of our relation-ship with the Soviet Union.

For too long, we have strayed between two mis-conceptions about the Russians—between over-blown illusions of cooperation and overstated no-tions of confrontation. An arms control treaty will not tame Soviet misconduct in other areas and the refusal to negotiate such an agreement, even when it is in our national interest, will not free Afghan-istan or break the repression in Poland.

In short, we cannot punish the Russians by rais-ing the risk of nuclear war. We hear about link-age—but we must not forget our fundamental com-mon link as people on this planet—that we shall all live or die together.

We shall find ourselves at odds with the Soviet Union far into the foreseeable future. We need not fear an economic competition—for our economy is rich in resources and potential and capable of performing at much higher levels than it has in recent years. The Soviet economy is inefficient, corrupt, and dependent on the catalyst of Western technology.

Nor need we fear an ideological rivalry. We believe in individual liberty and human dignity and with inspired leadership, that belief can have the most powerful appeal, as it has in the past, to the rest of the world. How many immigrants have ever moved to the Soviet Union in search of a better life? In this arena, the Soviets can gain only when we betray our own best ideals.

The one place where the Russians know they can compete is in military power—and they will pay any price to prevent us from forcing them into a position of military inferiority. We can and we should maintain strategic parity—which requires a sufficient and a secure deterrent. We can and we should strengthen our conventional forces so that we can limit our reliance on nuclear retaliation during a crisis.

But for both great powers, arms control is a far saner way to preserve strategic parity than an end-less arms race. Despite the differences which di-vide the United States and the Soviet Union today, and which will divide us for years or generations to come, what must unite us is an unflagging de-termination to avoid nuclear annihilation. We must seek to maintain our freedom and the peace at the same time, for there will be no such thing as liberty in a lifeless land.

The United States and the Soviet Union now possess the equivalent of 3 million Hiroshima bombs—a total of 4 tons of TNT for every man, woman, and child presently living on this planet. Even in the unlikely event of a successful Soviet first strike against our land-based missiles, we would still have over 3,500 warheads at sea and on bomb-ers—enough to destroy every Soviet city and town seven times over. The Secretary of Defense and the members of the Joint Chiefs of Staff have tes-tified that they would not exchange the deterrent forces of the United States for those of the Soviet Union.

Because this is so, a year ago, a number of us

in Congress took up a cause and a challenge that has already stirred at the grassroots across this country. We called for an immediate, mutual, and verifiable freeze on the testing, production, and deployment of Soviet and American nuclear weapons. That idea has enlisted the energies of ordinary citizens everywhere—and in every region of America, wherever they have had the chance, citizens have voted overwhelmingly for a freeze.

Those who oppose a nuclear weapons freeze have put forth a changing array of arguments that range from the disingenuous to the dishonest.

First, we repeatedly hear the outright falsehood that the freeze is somehow unilateral. The purveyors of that distortion either cannot read the resolution or care more about making their case than keeping to the facts. Perhaps they think that if they repeat themselves often enough, they can fool at least some of the people some of the time into believing some of their false charges.

The freeze is plainly, unequivocally, and indisputably bilateral. In supporting it, we do not and would not suggest that Americans on the other side want a nuclear war. So I wish they would stop suggesting that, in some sense, we want unilateral disarmament.

Second, the opponents of the nuclear freeze contend that we cannot halt the arms race in the face of a continuing Soviet buildup. In fact, a bilateral freeze is the best way to prevent that build-up. It would halt the entire new generation of weapons which the Soviets are now developing—including the Blackjack bomber, the Typhoon missile, and new cruise and land-based mobile missiles. The cries of alarm about Soviet advances in the future amount to a compelling reason to freeze the present balance of forces—and to stop the threatening trends now.

The administration instead prefers to respond with massive American military spending and a massive American military build-up. But the lesson of the last generation is that the Soviets will match us bomber for bomber, missile for missile, warhead for warhead.

Third, we are told that a freeze at this time would prevent us from perfecting our own deterrent—for example, by creating a new type of bomber which, for at least a while, will be less vulnerable to Soviet defenses. But at any time, there will always be some imperfections in the military forces on either side—and that reality can be used every time to justify just one more little round of the arms race. That is all they want, they say, and then we will have enough. But the Soviets have learned to make that argument too. And so we drift, as Einstein said, toward unparalleled catastrophe. We must reject policies which claim for the moment to make the world a little more secure, but in the end make the world a more unsafe and unstable place.

Fourth, our opponents say that a freeze is impossible to verify. This may be the most deceptive contention of them all, for impartial experts have testified again and again that a freeze is at least as verifiable as and probably more so than other arms control agreements, including the President's own START proposal. Moreover, we have made it clear from the beginning that anything which cannot be verified will not be frozen. The administration had better be careful—or their careless and baseless attacks on verification will become a basis and a rallying cry for extremists who will oppose any and every arms accord. We do not advocate a freeze because we trust the Russians, but we do distrust those who would continue the arms race at any and all costs.

Fifth, some opponents of the freeze argue that it is inappropriate to press the issue now, because we must not pull back from the planned deployment of the Pershing II and ground-launched cruise missiles in Europe. The Kennedy-Hatfield amendment calls for a global nuclear weapons freeze between the two superpowers. We reject a freeze in Europe alone. We must not put the nuclear weapons cart before the arms control horse. Our overriding goal should be to secure a nuclear weapons freeze that prevents any further escalation of the nuclear arms race—not only in Europe but in every other region of the world.

Finally, there are opponents of the nuclear freeze who explain that they favor reductions instead. But there is a darker side to their slogan. Reductions are not all they want. While professing limits in some areas, they want no limits on the newest and most modern weapons—which are also the costliest and the most threatening.

Indeed, the administration's own START proposal for reductions proves the point. For example, it would permit us to build the B-1 bomber—which is nothing more than a supersonic Edsel in the sky. And the administration's proposal would even permit the unrestrained pursuit of their new star wars scheme for outer space—which would open another arena for the arms race and set another trip-wire for nuclear war.

You know, this really is a very strange idea. We cannot found national policy on fond memories and radio serials, dreams of the Old West, and the thrilling days of yesteryear. We must reject the preposterous notion of a Lone Ranger in the sky, firing silver laser bullets and shooting missiles out of the hands of Soviet outlaws. The best defense against nuclear war is arms control and then disarmament.

The administration answers that we need the threat of new weapons as bargaining chips for negotiation. And they say we need the MX missile because of the window of vulnerability. Now let us all try hard to understand this. Mr. Reagan claimed we were vulnerable because the Russians could hit and destroy our existing Minuteman silos. So he appointed a Commission which reviewed every conceivable solution to the problem of Minuteman vulnerability. And do you know what they came up with, Mr. President? They want to put the new MX missile in the old, vulnerable Minuteman silos. You know what this is like? It is like having a car that is getting wet because of a leaky garage roof—and then trying to solve the problem by changing the make of the car.

The President has already declared that the MX is not on the bargaining table at the START talks—that he will never trade it away. So let us say now—it is time for Congress to take it away. It is time for the President of the United States to admit that the MX is a mistake—that it is a missile without

a mission and a weapon without a home. It is time to make it clear that, even by the administration's own logic, the MX in Minuteman silos is a sitting duck and to state clearly that, by any rational standard, the MX missile in any form should be a dead duck.

Both sides should renounce forever the pursuit of the phantom of nuclear superiority. We must free our diplomacy from the myth that more megatons mean bigger bargaining chips. We must reject the foolish theory that we can have fewer bombs tomorrow if only we have more bombs today. The administration defends this as a negotiating strategy. I call it voodoo arms control.

We must ask a simple question of them. Instead of piling overkill upon overkill, why not start now with a freeze? Why not stop where we are—so that, at last, we can begin to turn the arms race around?

We face a new and uncertain time. The continued advance of technology will move us steadily back from the possibility of peace. But a nuclear freeze can give the two great powers breathing room before they rush into a nuclear future that may threaten the future itself. It can halt new technologies that will be dangerous and destabilizing, and may be impossible to stop once they are started.

Some critics say that the freeze does not go far enough—which is what so many of them said 20 years ago, when a test ban treaty was proposed. We remember the answer that was given then: "A journey of a thousand miles begins with a single step." And so today, we reply: The long journey of survival in the nuclear age begins with the nuclear freeze.

Support for the freeze does not mean that we seek a weaker America. We have watched in recent months as ministers of the Gospel have been urged to preach in favor of an escalating arms race. But in the Scriptures I have read, nowhere does it say: "Blessed are the warmakers and the munition manufacturers." We have witnessed the revival of McCarthyite tactics which equate dissent with disloyalty and which imply that the advocates of a freeze are, somehow or other, Soviet dupes or pawns.

But someone should tell the apostles of this reincarnated Red Scare that the freeze movement began in Massachusetts and Vermont, not in Moscow and Vladivostok.

Support for the freeze does not mean opposition to a strong national defense. I favor a real growth of 5 percent in the military budget to assure that readiness and reliability of our forces. The President is demanding twice as much. We cannot afford military waste which weakens the Nation—and which has subverted the national consensus of sustained improvement in our defenses, especially our conventional capability. Instead of lavishing our treasure on first-strike weapons, let us spend it on first-class schools.

And let us never forget that national security includes the condition of our society as well as the size of our missiles. The world in an arms race is also a world impoverished. For America, running that arms race cripples our capacity to do anything else.

Today we are cutting immunization for children in order to finance the weapons that may someday kill them. Every new shelter for a missile means fewer homes for our families. Every new warhead guidance system that can read enemy defenses means more pupils who will not learn to read. Every new escalation that could mean death at an early age across the Earth also darkens the golden years of our senior citizens now.

We hear rhetoric from our highest officials about eliminating budgetary waste. If they are serious, let them enter into a nuclear freeze; let them pursue nuclear reductions; let them eliminate the expenditures that now make a desert of our dreams—and that someday could make a cold wasteland of all the Earth.

What more can we gain if we drain more of our resources into nuclear overkill? The American and Soviet arsenals are already bristling with weapons that could kill more people, burn more buildings, and sack more cities than in all the conflicts from the beginning of history until now. The greatest works of human enterprise and spirit could be vawork of human invention. Despite all our bombs and all our missiles, we stand essentially defenseless upon a stage on which the human drama could be closed in the flashing of a fireball.

As an American, I believe in a national defense second to none, sufficient to deter any attack from any adversary. But I also believe that we must preserve and protect a world which is now only a second away from nothingness.

A moment of history and a sense of hope calls all of us to a work as great as any that has gone before—indeed the greatest work of our time and of all time—the work of peace. The challenge comes especially in this decade because the danger has become so present and so clear. The difference each of us can make, if all of us will try, may make the difference between peace and war, between a just society and a garrison state.

Let us resolve that this Atomic Age will not be succeeded by a second Stone Age. Let us stop the nuclear arms race, before it stops the human race.

Mr. President, I ask unanimous consent that a fact sheet on my amendments may be printed in the RECORD.

There being no objection, the material was ordered to be printed in the RECORD, as follows:

FACTSHEET: KENNEDY-HATFIELD NUCLEAR WEAPONS FREEZE AND REDUCTIONS AMENDMENT No. 2464

Purpose and Provisions: The nuclear weapons freeze and reductions amendment is based on the self-evident proposition that the best way to stop the nuclear arms race is to stop it. The amendment calls for a mutual and verifiable nuclear weapons freeze between the United States and the Soviet Union, followed by reductions in the nuclear arsenals on both sides.

The freeze applies to the "testing, production and further deployment of nuclear warheads, missiles, and other delivery systems."

The reductions are to be achieved "through annual percentages or equally effective means."

The freeze and the reductions are to be carried out with special emphasis upon destabilizing weapons.

A freeze is workable, because both the United States and the Soviet Union are now at essential nuclear equivalence. . . . We are ahead in some areas, and they are ahead in others; but overall we are at parity. By the crucial measure of warheads, the United States is actually ahead, by 9,900 to 7,800.

The freeze by its explicit terms is bilateral; it is not unilateral disarmament; it is the only arms control proposal that will stop the nuclear arms race on both sides, and that will halt the Soviet Union's development of more powerful bombers, missiles, and warheads. . . .

The history of the nuclear arms race since 1945 proves the irrationality of pursuing the phantom of nuclear superiority. The Soviet Union will match us warhead for warhead and missile for missile as the arms race escalates to higher and higher levels of danger and uncertainty.

The freeze is also the only arms controls proposal that offers the real prospect of substantial budget savings. If a comprehensive freeze is successfully negotiated, it will save $100 billion over 5 years.

Support for the freeze: The nuclear freeze and reductions resolution has been endorsed by prominent experts such as William Colby, George Ball, Clark Clifford, Henry Cabot Lodge, Averell Harriman, George Kennan, Gerard Smith, Paul Warnke, Hans Bethe, General James Gavin, Admiral Noel Gayler and Ambassador Thomas J. Watson, Jr. It has been adopted in referenda by 9 of the 10 states that have considered it, by 370 city councils, by 71 county councils, by 46 New England town meetings, and by 15 state legislatures.

Harris and ABC News/Washington Post polls, after the Soviet destruction of the Korean jetliner, found continuing support for the freeze, with 77 percent (Harris) and 80 percent (ABC/Post) of Americans favoring such a freeze. In a July poll by the National Association of Evangelicals, 60 percent of evangelicals supported the freeze.

Verification: In fact, a freeze is probably more ver-ifiable than other arms control agreements. Intelligence experts such as former CIA Director William Colby and former CIA Deputy Director Herbert Scoville have clearly stated that a nuclear freeze is verifiable. In any event, anything that can be verified will not be frozen.

European Missile Deployment: The amendment calls for a global freeze and reductions, not a Europe-only freeze. Whatever the outcome of the current INF negotiations and the planned deployment of U.S. Pershing II and cruise missiles in Europe, a global freeze on nuclear weapons is in the highest interest of the security of the United States. A freeze would be negotiated only after full consultation with our NATO allies and Japan.

Build-down: Although the build-down proposal is better than START, it is still far from good enough. Its fatal flaw is that it is not just a build-down; it is also a build-up, because it permits the continued development and deployment of the MX missile and other dangerous and destabilizing new weapons systems. The nuclear weapons freeze is the only arms control proposal which stops MX and its Soviet counterpart (SSX), and which deals with both the quantitative and qualitative aspects of the nuclear arms race.

Newer Soviet Strategic Weapons

	Under freeze
Backfire bomber	180
Blackjack bomber	1
Under START	400
Typhoon missile	20
New solid-fuel ICBM	0
Under START	1,200
Accurate cruise missile	0
Under START	3,500

What Is Wrong with a Nuclear Freeze?
Captain David H. Petraeus, U.S. Army

With the world increasingly in a nuclear shadow and this country faced with troubling budget deficits, few ideas have proved more seductive than that of freezing the nuclear arms race. Combining widespread fear of nuclear war, concern about the high cost of nuclear weapons, anxiety over a seemingly endless arms race and frustration at the lack of progress in arms-control negotiations, the nuclear freeze movement has gained considerable support throughout the United States and Western Europe.

The freeze crusade long ago ceased being one of those movements that can be dismissed as the emanations of fringe elements. While it does have its share of activists looking for a cause, by far the largest percentage of support comes from serious-minded citizens worried about nuclear weapons and seeking ready solutions.

The widespread support for a nuclear freeze has been reflected in many different forums. In the 1982 elections, one-fourth of all U.S. voters were offered nuclear freeze resolutions.[1] Freeze referendums were approved in eight of nine states and in 32 of 35 localities. In Vermont, 178 of 246 communities adopted resolutions calling for a nuclear freeze.

A freeze resolution failed by only two votes in the 1982 House of Representatives, and a version linked to arms reductions was adopted by the 1983 House. The National Conference of State Legislators adopted a freeze resolution in 1982, and the United Nations General Assembly adopted similar resolutions by wide margins in December 1982.[2]

Even the churches have become involved, with the Catholic bishops and some Baptist, Presbyterian and Jewish officials endorsing various freeze proposals.

In the face of such considerable support, many government officials, military leaders and strategists have cautioned against the concept of a freeze. President Ronald Reagan and Secretary of Defense Caspar W. Weinberger have repeatedly warned against the adverse effects of a nuclear freeze on this country's nuclear deterrent. They have stated that a freeze would leave a significant percentage of U.S. strategic deterrent forces ineffective, eliminate incentives for the Soviets to negotiate meaningful arms reductions and prevent the United States from modernizing its aging bomber and intercontinental ballistic missile (ICBM) forces.[3]

Reagan administration officials are not alone in their unfavorable assessment of a nuclear freeze. Many strategists argue that a freeze would lock in the "window of vulnerability" of the United States' strategic triad and increase the significance of asymmetries favoring the Soviets in the areas of civil defense, air defense and even space defense. They also remind us of the serious intermediate-range nuclear force imbalances that exist in Europe which would be preserved by a freeze.

Others, who claim to be "realists," describe a freeze as a triumph of "hope over experience."[4] The realists explain that the deceptive simplicity

---

[1]Joyce E. Larson and William C. Bodie, *The Intelligent Layperson's Guide to the Nuclear Freeze and Peace Debate*, preface by Gerald L. Steibel, National Strategy Information Center Inc., N.Y., 1983, p 3.

[2]"Nuclear Freeze Plans Endorsed," *Army Times*, 15 November 1982, p 63; "Vermonters Voice Anti-Nuclear Attitudes," *The Kansas City Times*, 3 March 1983, p A-11; Michael Zie-

lenziger, "Nuclear Freeze Backers Plan Lobby Blitz," *The Kansas City Times*, 5 March 1983, p A-5, "Legislators Vote to Seek Nuclear Freeze," *The Kansas City Times*, 11 December 1982, p A-19; "UN Supports Freeze on Nuclear Arms," *The Kansas City Times*, 14 December 1982, p A-13; and "House Links Nuclear Freeze to Arms Reductions," *The Kansas City Times*, 5 May, 1983, p A-1.

[3]"Weinberger Urges Nuclear Freeze Rejection," *Army Times*, 8 November 1982, p 8.

[4]Kelly H. Burke, "Arms Control in the Real World," *Armed Forces Journal International*, November 1982, p 108.

David H. Petraeus, "What Is Wrong with a Nuclear Freeze?," *Military Review* 53 (November 1983), 49–64.

of a freeze masks many complex and crucial issues that would have to be resolved—if indeed they could be resolved. For example, agreements would have to be hammered out over verification and dual-purpose systems such as bombers which can carry conventional or nuclear weapons. Negotiations with the Soviet Union over such points have in the past proved extremely difficult.

Unfortunately, debates over the nuclear freeze issue often degenerate rapidly from substantive issues into emotional arguments. Dispassionate analyses and discussions are rare. Freeze proponents have frequently presented their case by asking questions such as: "Are you for a nuclear freeze or for nuclear war?" That is tantamount to asking "are you for peace or war?" Of course, there are other alternatives, but they are difficult to explain in the charged atmosphere of the typical freeze debate forum.

On the other side, opponents of a nuclear freeze frequently dismiss the "freezeniks" by unfairly characterizing them as pacifists and unilateralists. Such anti-freeze groups are fond of arguing that a nuclear freeze falls into that category described by H. L. Mencken who once said, "There's always an easy solution to every human problem—neat, plausible, and wrong."[5]

But what about the issues? Is the present-day window of vulnerability really crucial? Would a freeze eliminate hopes for arms reductions and undermine NATO? Or could we be in what Jerome B. Wiesner, president emeritus of the Massachusetts Institute of Technology, feels is an optimum time for a nuclear freeze—a "window of opportunity" for safer, saner alternatives to a major arms buildup?[6] Who is right?

WHAT IS A NUCLEAR FREEZE?

As illustrated by the resolution presented in 1982 by Senators Edward M. Kennedy and Mark O. Hatfield, the overall concept of a nuclear freeze is simple and easily understood. The Kennedy-Hatfield Resolution states that, as:

> . . . an immediate strategic arms control objective, [the United States and the Soviet Union should] decide when and how to achieve a *mutual* and *verifiable freeze* on the *testing, production* and further *deployment* of nuclear warheads, missiles, and other delivery systems.

They would then move on to nuclear arms reductions. As Leon V. Sigal noted in his article, "Warming to the Freeze":

> The freeze idea captures the layman's sense that both superpowers have enough nuclear weapons to destroy each other as viable societies and that further deployments would at best compound redundancy, or at worst, precipitate Armageddon.[7]

The wonderful simplicity of a freeze and its deceptively easy solution to a costly and terrifying nuclear problem have made it very appealing. But what would it take to achieve a mutual and verifiable freeze in which both sides could have confidence? And how would a freeze affect the strategic balance, NATO and hopes for arms reductions?

WOULD THE UNITED STATES BE FROZEN INTO STRATEGIC NUCLEAR INFERIORITY?

Whether the concept of nuclear superiority has any validity in these days of grotesque overkill is debatable. But we would be remiss in not at least considering if the Soviet Union has gained some strategic nuclear edge that would be preserved by a freeze and, more importantly, what a Soviet edge would mean to the United States. In assessing the strategic nuclear balance, we find that the traditional U.S. advantage in bombers and warheads is vanishing, and the balance of strategic nuclear power has shifted steadily toward the Soviets over the past two decades.

---

[5]Ibid.
[6]Jerome B. Wiesner, "Russian and American Capabilities," *Parameters*, Volume XII, Number 4, p 86.

[7]Leon V. Sigal, "Warming to the Freeze," *Foreign Policy*, Fall 1982, p 56.

The Soviet Union's advantage now is more than 600 strategic delivery vehicles—ICBMs, bombers and submarine missile launchers— and an almost 3-to-1 ratio in missile throw weight. In addition, there has been a precipitous decline in the effectiveness of U.S. systems against the increasingly large number of Soviet hardened targets such as Soviet command and control facilities as well as ICBM and antiballistic-missile silos—their *SS17, SS18* and *SS19* ICBMs are housed in the world's hardest silos.[8]

Improvements in Soviet ICBM accuracy and warhead yield now provide the Soviet Union with a first-strike capability (which the United States does not share) that threatens this country's 1,045 land-based missiles.[9] Further, besides being deployed in more survivable, hardened silos, several types of Soviet missiles have a cold-launch capability (which the United States lacks) that allows reloading (generally in not less than 24 hours) for a theoretical second strike.[10]

Still, many nuclear freeze advocates feel that such Soviet advantages are marginal, at best, or at least not militarily significant, and are offset by the greater survivability of a larger percentage of U.S. warheads—primarily those on submarine-launched ballistic missiles (despite the missiles' lack of hard target kill capability which limits targeting options). Freeze supporters also argue that the United States has greater flexibility because of a more even distribution of warheads throughout its triad and because of a larger number of weapons on manned bombers. Bombers can be called back after launching or retargeted in flight in a way that missiles cannot.

As Albert Wohlstetter explained more than 20 years ago in his classic article "The Delicate Balance of Terror," to deter an attack means being able to strike back in spite of it—in other words, a capability to strike second. This is especially true for the United States which has traditionally shunned the idea of a pre-emptive strike—no U.S. president wants to be the "American Tojo." Wohlstetter also described the many obstacles which a second-strike capability must overcome and showed that deterrence is not merely an automatic consequence of both sides having nuclear weapons.[11]

Today, certain scenarios of Soviet counterforce first strikes are very unsettling—especially those which place the U.S. forces at a day-to-day alert status. But there should be little doubt as to the effectiveness of the U.S. ability to conduct a second strike and, therefore, to deter an all-out nuclear war. Despite the current vulnerabilities of U.S. land-based ICBMs, bomber bases, submarine home ports and strategic command systems to a Soviet first strike (hence, the window of vulnerability), and despite reduced confidence in the ability of U.S. bombers and cruise missiles to penetrate the increasingly sophisticated Soviet air defenses, the relatively secure U.S. nuclear missile submarines at sea should still provide an effective deterrent.

Beyond whatever U.S. ground-based ICBMs and bombers survive an attack, each *Trident* submarine alone is capable of launching enough nuclear warheads—each approximately eight times as powerful as the bomb dropped on Hiroshima—to theoretically destroy 192 Soviet cities.[12] The Soviet leaders would have to be mad to contemplate a nuclear exchange that could produce such a result. Thus, an effective, if less than optimum, deterrent still exists at the strategic nuclear level. And it

---

[8]Sources for the figures in this paragraph are *Soviet Military Power,* 1983, US Government Printing Office, Washington, D.C., 1983, pp 18–27; Anthony H. Cordesman, "M-X and the Balance of Power: Reasserting America's Strength," *Armed Forces Journal International,* December 1982, pp 29–41; *Annual Report to Congress FY 1984,* US Government Printing Office, Washington, D.C., 1 February 1983, pp 51–55; *United States Military Posture for FY 1984,* Organization of the Joint Chiefs of Staff, US Government Printing Office, Washington, D.C., 1983, pp 13–18; and "Preparing for Nuclear War: President Reagan's Program," *Defense Monitor,* Volume X, Number 8, 1982, pp 1–16.

[9]Theodore H. White, "Weinberger on the Ramparts," *The New York Times Magazine,* 6 February 1983, p 17.

[10]Andrew C. Tuttle, "Strategic Balance in the 1980's," *National Defense,* July–August 1982, p 24.

[11]Albert Wohlstetter, "The Delicate Balance of Terror," *Foreign Affairs,* January 1959, p 213.

[12]Sigal, *op. cit.,* p 57.

should continue to exist for at least the near term barring unexpected Soviet technological breakthroughs in antisubmarine warfare or antiballistic-missile defenses.

However, we should not forget that at least one leg of the U.S. nuclear triad—the ICBM force—has become vulnerable to a Soviet first strike in a way that the massive Soviet land-based force is not. This enables the Soviets to threaten destruction of "a very large part of our strategic force in a first strike, while retaining overwhelming nuclear force to deter any retaliation we could carry out."[13] The aged *B52* and *F111* bombers, and even the air-launched cruise missiles, will have increasing difficulty in beating the rapid advances in Soviet air defenses—advances which would not be halted by a freeze.

For example, Soviet *SA10* air defense missiles now being deployed are effective even against the current generation of U.S. cruise missiles.[14] Of course, there is disagreement concerning the chances of a Soviet first strike taking out all of this country's ICBMs, and there is still little likelihood of Soviet air defenses defeating all of the U.S. bombers and cruise missiles. Besides, the United States would still have its submarines. But what if the command and control link to those submarines became vulnerable or there were an unprecedented Soviet breakthrough in antisubmarine warfare?

John D. Steinbruner argues that the U.S. strategic command system could no longer survive a deliberate attack by the Soviet Union and that as little as "50 nuclear weapons are probably sufficient to eliminate the ability to direct U.S. strategic forces to coherent purposes."[15] And what is the situation in regard to antisubmarine warfare? The United States has made great strides in that area, why should the Soviet Union not do likewise?[16]

[13]*Annual Report to Congress, FY 1984, op. cit.,* p 53.
[14]"Estimates of Missile Defense Costs Rise," *The Kansas City Times,* 18 May 1983, p A-2.
[15]John D. Steinbruner, "Nuclear Decapitation," *Foreign Policy,* Winter 1981–82, p 18.
[16]Joel S. Witt, "Advances in Antisubmarine Warfare," *Scientific American,* February 1981, pp 15–25.

The current structure of the ICBM forces of both sides, with a large percentage of the missiles mounting multiple warheads and all in fixed silos, may not be optimum in terms of crisis stability. Coupled with advances in warhead accuracy, the increased number of multiple independently targetable re-entry vehicle missiles has created a situation in which the side which strikes first can theoretically gain significant advantages.

The improvements in accuracy provide an extremely high probability of kill when two warheads are targeted against a single launch silo. If the missile in the silo is not launched in time, the missile and its warheads will be destroyed. Very favorable exchange ratios are possible if the missile knocked out happens to be carrying more than two warheads. U.S. missiles carry up to three warheads, and Soviet missiles carry up to 10 warheads. This also illustrates why the *MX* missile, with its 10 warheads has been labeled a "first-strike weapon" and why the Scowcroft Commission and others have recommended the development of a mobile, single-warhead missile.

The current ICBM structure may be destabilizing in two respects. Since the side which launches first stands to gain advantages in a strategic exchange, there are destabilizing incentives for being the first to launch. In addition, since neither side would want to be caught with its missiles still in its silos, the current structure creates pressures for the rapid launching of a retaliation strike by the side which detects an incoming strike from the other side.

Obviously, pressures for quick action are hardly desirable when such critical decisions hang in the balance. Thus, as Henry A. Kissinger has noted, the current situation has revived "the destabilizing danger of surprise attack. From this point of view, a 'freeze' would perpetuate an inherently precarious state of events."[17]

Thus, we find the United States with serious strategic vulnerabilities and both sides with ICBM structures that are potentially destabilizing. Cou-

[17]Henry A. Kissinger, "A New Approach to Arms Control," *Time,* 21 March 1983, p 25.

pled with possible Soviet technological breakthroughs in antisubmarine and antiballistic-missile warfare, and continued improvements in Soviet civil defense capabilities, neither of which would be limited by a freeze, such a situation could prove disastrous in a time of crisis. It is possible to see how Soviet leaders might perceive that they could emerge from a nuclear exchange in so much better shape than the United States that they would be tempted to push a confrontation to the brink to protect or achieve a vital national interest.

IMPLICATIONS OF THE SHIFT IN THE STRATEGIC BALANCE

While deterrence at the strategic level may be the major issue, it is far from being the only concern. Perceptions regarding the nuclear balance—and perceptions are the key—permeate world affairs today. The strategic deterrent is the fulcrum on which all military force pivots and, beyond its value as a deterrent, has tremendous political utility. As such, it seems to follow implicitly that major asymmetries in the overall strategic balance critically influence Soviet risk calculations and policies and could lead to Soviet encroachments on U.S. allies or vital interests.[18]

Recent international events appear to indicate that the Soviets' "relative strength at the strategic level emboldens [them] at lesser levels and allows them to coerce friends, foes, and neutrals alike."[19] It appears that the Soviets now feel freer in the use of force at lower levels, confident that the United States will shy away from a threat of escalation.[20]

The standoff at the strategic level, with both sides desiring to avoid an exchange that would trigger national suicide, coupled with the gradual shift in the global military balance and the unprecedented "correlation of forces" toward the Soviet Union, has been an important factor in recent increases in Soviet risk-taking at lower levels—such as in Afghanistan, Angola and Ethiopia. This ability of Soviet military power to deter a decisive U.S.-allied response to such lower level initiatives, and, therefore, to consolidate geographic expansion without a major war, is clearly desirable in the Soviet view.[21] The increasing Soviet aggressiveness would not be possible but for the *perceptions* of emerging Soviet strategic superiority. Kissinger cautioned in a speech at the Naval War College:

We like to believe that we can prevail through the superiority of our maxims and, of course, our moral convictions are of great importance. But there can be no security without equilibrium.[22]

That equilibrium could be threatened by a freeze when there are serious deficiencies in U.S. nuclear forces which lead to overreliance on one leg of the nuclear triad or at a time when Soviet nuclear and conventional advantages have undermined deterrence on a number of levels.

COULD A FREEZE BE ADEQUATELY VERIFIED?

Before his retirement, General David C. Jones, then chairman of the Joint Chiefs of Staff, warned that "it would be sheer folly for us to enter any [freeze] agreement which did not include very stringent and workable stipulations to verify compliance."[23] Understandably, most U.S. citizens feel the same way and would never support a freeze that could not be verified.

Virtually all nuclear freeze resolutions reflect such sentiments and call for the freeze on the testing, production and deployment of nuclear weapons to be mutual and verifiable. However, it would be extremely difficult to achieve the levels of verification required. There are many almost insur-

---

[18]Leon Goure, "Another Interpretation," *Bulletin of the Atomic Scientists,* April 1978, p 51.

[19]Donald Rumsfeld, in a letter to *Armed Forces Journal International,* February 1983, p 8.

[20]Larson and Bodie, *op. cit.,* p 39.

[21]Richard B. Foster, "On Prolonged Nuclear War," *International Security Review,* Winter 1981–82, p 501.

[22]Henry A.Kissinger, "The Admiral Spruance Lecture," *Naval War College Review,* Summer 1978.

[23]David C. Jones, "Can We Be Secure with a Nuclear Freeze?" *Defense/82,* July 1982, p 15.

mountable difficulties that frustrate efforts to adequately verify compliance with a freeze of nuclear weapons production, deployment and testing.

Few freeze advocates acknowledge U.S. inability to verify a freeze on the *production* of nuclear weapons. Yet, with present national technical means, it is not possible to closely monitor what is produced on assembly lines—satellites and spy planes just cannot see through roofs of manufacturing plants. In fact, as Sigal has cautioned, "even agreements providing for on-site verification could not offer firm assurance against covert production."[24]

However, many freeze supporters will argue that an inability to verify a freeze on production is unimportant because, even if unauthorized nuclear weapons were produced secretly, they could not be *deployed* in militarily significant numbers without detection. That may have been the case in the past when large, difficult-to-conceal launch silos had to be dug for each missile. Nowadays, it is becoming much more difficult to detect missile deployment due to the Soviet Union's increasing use of mobile launchers and cold-launch capability (which allows existing missile silos to be "reloaded" and used again).

Obviously, it is relatively easy to conceal mobile launchers such as the *SS20* in large garages. And, even when they are not under cover, it is difficult to follow mobile launchers around the countryside to accurately count them. Further, the Soviet ICBM reload capability negates the axiom that one silo equals one missile, especially if the extra missiles are deployed covertly and hidden from satellite observation.

Freeze supporters will correctly claim that a freeze on *testing* is relatively verifiable and that this would dissuade both sides from producing new, untested weapons. They also argue that neither side would be likely to spend the money to produce and deploy a new weapon if reliability testing had not been conducted. However, they fail to note the difficulties in verifying low-yield nuclear weapons tests and bench tests of system components and the pos-

sibility of covert Soviet production and deployment of more nuclear systems of the types already tested and fielded.

It should be noted that, as a closed society, the Soviets "enjoy" several advantages in the realm of verification relative to the United States. Soviet intelligence acquisition, and hence verification of agreements, is much easier because of the openness of this nation's democratic society and the wide publicity given defense (especially nuclear) issues. There are no Soviet counterparts to the antinuclear or "defense watchdog" organizations that exist in the United States.

For example, imagine the grateful appreciation of the Soviets to the publication of the *Defense Monitor* which in one 1982 issue provided a seven-page list detailing the locations and numbers of U.S. nuclear weapons, delivery means, Strategic Air Command and air defense bases, production facilities, ICBM fields and much more.[25] Yet none of that information came from classified sources. I am not implying criticism of such organizations or publications. I am merely illustrating the intelligence acquisition and verification advantages enjoyed by the Soviets because of this democratic society. U.S. intelligence agencies can look forward to no such Soviet assistance in attempting to verify compliance with arms agreements.

Since normal means of verifying arms agreements (national technical means) would be inadequate in monitoring compliance with some testing, production and deployment aspects of a freeze, could other methods be employed? There are other measures that could be used to construct a verification system capable of providing a high degree of confidence. Examples include provisions for frequent on-site inspections (which the Soviets have in the past "viewed as a form of espionage"[26]) and monitoring the use of special nuclear materials such as uranium and plutonium.

[25] "Preparing for Nuclear War: President Reagan's Program," *Defense Monitor, op. cit.*
[26] Amos A. Jordan and William J. Taylor Jr., *American National Security,* The Johns Hopkins University Press, Baltimore, Md., 1981, p 518.

[24] Sigal, *op. cit.*, p 55.

Even better would be for each side to allow the other free access, on very short notice, to *any* location requested—thus precluding covert production of nuclear weapons. However, such measures go far beyond those of SALT I and are almost certainly more than the Soviet Union would be willing to accept. In fact, such measures are so unrealistic that we are left with the conclusion that the United States could not confidently verify Soviet compliance with a freeze agreement given the assets realistically available.

WOULD THE SOVIETS HONOR A FREEZE AGREEMENT?

If the United States and the Soviet Union could reach an agreement on verification of a nuclear freeze, there is some doubt that the Soviets would honor the accord. There have been press accounts of deliberate Soviet interference "with the means of verifying compliance with the SALT I treaty."[27] Soviet violations have included digging unauthorized silos, scrambling *SS20* radio signals during missile tests (which complicates US efforts to determine the *SS20's* capabilities) and attempting to conceal movements of a new ICBM.[28] In addition, there is good evidence "that the USSR has stretched the meaning of the SALT provisions to stockpile far more than the permitted number of missiles."[29]

Soviet disregard for other international agreements is also illuminating. The Soviet Union was a party to the Geneva Protocol of 1925 which banned the first use of chemical agents and to the 1975 Biological Weapons Convention which renounced the use and production of biological weapons. In spite of those agreements, the United States has acquired overwhelming evidence indicating that the Soviets and their allies used chemical and biological (toxin) weapons in Laos, Kampuchea and Afghanistan.[30]

In addition, an outbreak of pulmonary anthrax in the Soviet Union at Sverdlovsk, the suspected result of an accident in a biological weapons production facility, still remains unexplained.[31] Such actions create considerable doubt about the Soviets living up to any treaty or verification measures—even in the unlikely event that they agreed to the stringent measures on which the United States would insist.

And what would the United States do if the Soviets violated a freeze agreement? What could this nation do if it discovered that some unauthorized Soviet activity had left it more vulnerable than before? A realistic appraisal reveals that it would be possible to do little more than rue the day the Soviets were allowed to mount their deception, engage in some tough talk and economic reprisals, cancel the freeze and try to catch up from an even weaker position.

WOULD STRATEGIC ARMS-REDUCTION TALKS BE FROZEN TOO?

A "satisfactory" nuclear freeze would have to contain many, if not all, of the elements we normally associate with arms-reductions talks. It would necessarily be far more complicated than the simplistic resolutions so widely supported and would have to include agreements on many items other than just nuclear arms. To prevent further deterioration of strategic stability, agreements would be required for dual-purpose weapons systems (for example, aircraft or missiles that can carry conventional as well as nuclear warheads), maintenance and safety improvements to existing systems, civil defense measures, development of antisubmarine warfare

---

[27]Robert Jastrow, "Why Strategic Superiority Matters," *Commentary*, March 1983, p 30.

[28] *Ibid*.

[29]Larson and Bodie, *op. cit.*, p 4.

[30]*Chemical Warfare in Southeast Asia and Afghanistan*, Department of State Special Report Number 98, US Government Printing Office, Washington, D.C.

[31]*Use of Chemical Weapons in Asia*, Department of State Bulletin, US Government Printing Office, Washington, D.C., January 1982, p 54.

technology, air defense systems and perhaps even space weapons.

As explained earlier, the underpinning for such an agreement would have to be provided by the negotiation of complex verification measures. Obviously, such an accord might well be more difficult to negotiate than arms reductions. However, unlike the hoped-for arms-reductions agreements, even a relatively all-inclusive freeze would leave the United States with the undesirable vulnerabilities in our nuclear deterrent that exist at the present time. Equitable arms-reduction accords, on the other hand, would leave us with increased strategic, crisis and arms-race stability.

What would happen to our hopes for an arms-reduction treaty if we indicated the willingness to settle for a freeze? Weinberger contends that the acceptance of a freeze would show a lack of resolve to strengthen U.S. nuclear defenses and would virtually destroy this country's ability to negotiate genuine arms reductions. Weinberger argues that the United States must continue to demonstrate resolve:

. . . to modernize our nuclear capability, even though we of course earnestly hope to negotiate major and effective arms reductions agreements. Only by maintaining our strength can we produce the pressure necessary to get the Soviets to agree to advantageous arms reduction agreements.[32]

The United States' efforts to obtain a verifiable ban on chemical warfare through bilateral arms-control agreements with the Soviet Union are illustrative of the impossibility of gaining an agreement when one side is asked to surrender an advantage. Because the Soviets have a significant margin of superiority in chemical warfare capabilities, they have shown little interest in seriously negotiating an agreement which includes adequate verification.

The Soviets have everything to lose and, because of lack of comparable modern weapons as a result of U.S. unilateral restraint since 1969, little to gain.[33] It is now apparent that, until the United States improves its chemical deterrent, there will be no incentive for the Soviets to negotiate a comprehensive, verifiable ban on chemical weapons.

A similar situation existed in the 1960s when the Soviets initially refused to negotiate an antiballistic-missile treaty. Initially, when only the Soviet Union had an antiballistic-missile system fielded, the Soviets showed no inclination to reach an agreement. It was not until the United States developed its own system that the Soviets changed their minds and negotiated in earnest.[34]

While the Soviets do not have superiority in strategic nuclear weapons comparable to that which they enjoy in chemical weapons, the failure to reach agreement on chemical weapons shows that the United States cannot successfully negotiate from a position of relative weakness. Therefore, if we accept the premise that the United States' nuclear deterrent has certain vulnerabilities in its ICBM and bomber forces not shared by the Soviet Union, it seems logical that the Soviets will not surrender their position unless they perceive that this nation intends to correct the existing deficiencies to ensure strategic balance.

Only then can the United States expect the Soviets to realize that it would be futile and extraordinarily expensive to continue their effort to achieve decisive strategic advantages. And only then will they recognize that arms reductions are in their best interests.

Such reasoning should also illustrate precisely why the Soviets would have no motivation to negotiate more stabilizing arms reductions if the United States settled, instead, for a mere freeze and a continuation of the status quo. Kissinger summed up the situation quite well when he wrote that:

[32]Caspar W. Weinberger, "Seeking a Consensus for the Common Defense," *Defense/82*, December 1982, p 7.

[33]*Annual Report to Congress, FY 1984, op. cit.*, p 237.
[34]Charles Doe, "Study Sees Standoff on Strategic Arms Control," *Army Times*, 9 May 1983, pp 23–24.

If the U.S., by its abdication, guarantees the invulnerability of Soviet missile forces while the Soviets keep ours exposed, any Soviet incentive for serious negotiation will vanish.[35]

WHAT ABOUT WESTERN EUROPE AND NATO?

Our focus to this point has primarily been at the strategic nuclear level. Now, we need to look at Western Europe—an area of vital interest to the United States—focusing specifically on NATO's Central Region to assess the effect of a nuclear freeze on that area. While the balance of forces between NATO and the Warsaw Pact is endlessly debated, with the numbers often manipulated to support various arguments,[36] few would disagree that the Warsaw Pact has a significant advantage in virtually every area of conventional, chemical and theater nuclear arms.

The NATO forces, by virtue of the large number of US artillery and *Lance* missile nuclear warheads, retain "approximate parity" only in short-range— less than 100-kilometer range—nuclear weapons.[37] The lack of conventional balance is especially acute in the critical Central Region where the failure of NATO conventional forces to stop a Warsaw Pact offensive could result in escalation to nuclear weapons.

A relatively best case (for NATO) estimate of the conventional balance, which includes French forces and US-based ground and air reinforcements often left out of such comparisons, indicates that the NATO forces in the Central Region would be at about a 1-to-2 disadvantage in numbers of divisions (although Warsaw Pact divisions have fewer personnel than most NATO divisions, the combat power is roughly the same), a 1-to-3 disadvantage in numbers of tanks, a 1-to-4 disadvantage in artillery and mortars, and about a 1-to-1.4 disadvantage in numbers of combat aircraft. The figures would be roughly the same even under conditions that prevented reinforcement from the United States and the Soviet Union.[38]

Despite the unfavorable statistics, the NATO forces in the Central Region should not be lightly dismissed. They pose a very significant war-fighting capability, particularly considering that they will have the advantages of being the defender. Furthermore, there are several important factors which work to NATO's advantage. Some factors are the political unreliability of several of the Warsaw Pact countries (Poland is the best example), better levels of training in the Western forces and rigid (and, therefore, predictable) Warsaw Pact operational doctrine.

On the other hand, despite all of its efforts to improve interoperability, NATO still presents a less homogeneous force both in organization and equipment. Therefore, NATO suffers more from compatibility problems. In sum, despite the imbalance in the Central Region which favors the Warsaw Pact, the NATO forces have "the conventional strength to force the Soviet Union to launch a massive attack and prevent any *easy* victory in a limited war."[39]

Should a massive Warsaw Pact attack be launched across the West German border and should NATO's conventional forces prove unable to stop it, NATO would have to resort to short-range nuclear weapons—"the capstone of NATO's deterrent and the linchpin of [the U.S.] strategy of flexible response."[40] As noted here, the NATO forces have approximate parity in this area. However, the ma-

[35]Kissinger, "A New Approach to Arms Control," *Time, op. cit.,* p 26.

[36]For an excellent discussion of the shortcomings in the numbers used for force comparisons, see Milton Leitenberg, "The Numbers Game or Who's on First?" *Bulletin of the Atomic Scientists,* June–July 1982, pp 27–32.

[37]Donald R. Cotter, James H. Hansen and Kirk McConnell, *The Nuclear 'Balance' in Europe: Status, Trends, Implications,* U.S. Strategic Institute Report Number 83-1, U.S. Strategic Institute, Washington, D.C., 1983, p 3.

[38]Anthony H. Cordesman, "NATO's Estimate of the Balance: The Meaning for Security Policy," *Armed Forces Journal International,* August 1982, pp 56–57.

[39]*Ibid.,* p 57.

[40]Richard R. Burt, *Implications of a Nuclear Freeze,* Department of State Current Policy Number 470, US Government Printing Office, Washington D.C., 9 March 1983, p 2.

jority of the NATO warheads are on relatively old artillery and *Lance* missile rounds whose use is limited due to their short range (hence, the U.S. Army's current willingness to reduce the numbers of such nuclear rounds in Europe).

This is a serious limitation as it decreases the NATO threat to the lucrative deep targets presented by the follow-on echelons of the Warsaw Pact. The Soviet counterparts to these weapons, though less plentiful, have superior range and accuracy. One step up the "ladder of escalation" are the tactical surface-to-surface missiles in which the Warsaw Pact heavily outguns the NATO Alliance by 6-to-1 in missile launchers and 5-to-1 in warheads.[41]

In addition, NATO still has not deployed any weapon comparable to the accurate and mobile Soviet *SS20* theater nuclear missile which is reloadable, has a range of 3,000 miles and has three warheads on each missile. At the present time, the Soviets have more than 243 *SS20* launchers deployed in Europe, and each *SS20* unit is assessed to be equipped with an additional refire missile per launcher.[42]

Some have argued that the absence of NATO counterparts to the *SS20* is of little consequence because U.S., British or French strategic nuclear weapons can just as adequately target a location as theater-range missiles can. The NATO Alliance has not shared their view. The allied strategic nuclear missiles are not as accurate or responsive to targeting changes as the *Pershing II* and cruise missiles promise to be. Beyond that, however, the paramount issue for the NATO countries has been ensuring deterrence born of the "coupling" or "linkage" between U.S. medium-range nuclear missiles and the U.S. strategic nuclear force.[43]

The result was the NATO decision of 12 December 1979 to deploy U.S. *Pershing II* and cruise missiles in five European countries beginning in December 1983. Not surprisingly, the Soviet Union has used every available political and psychological tool to oppose this deployment, including a massive propanganda effort and outright attempts to bully NATO.[44] Yet, despite well-organized and very vocal campaigns in Western Europe to prevent the upcoming deployment of the *Pershing II* and cruise missiles, no major allied government has given in. Were the United States to adopt a nuclear freeze—thereby precluding following through on the 1979 decision—it would cut the ground out from under the European leaders who have steadfastly held to the implementation of that decision.

Thus, it should be evident that a nuclear freeze would have a serious impact on NATO, particularly in the critical Central Region where the Warsaw Pact forces have true advantages in conventional, chemical and nuclear forces. A freeze would preserve the weakened state of deterrence that results from NATO's lack of theater nuclear forces and leave the key issue of coupling unresolved. In preventing the deployment of U.S. *Pershing II* and cruise missiles, a freeze would weaken the Atlantic Alliance and encourage perceptions of growing Soviet strength at a time of U.S. weakness and decline.

"Such perceptions have already led some Europeans to urge their governments to reduce ties with the United States and NATO,"[45] and the United States' acceptance of a nuclear freeze would seem to confirm the feelings of those Europeans urging reduced reliance on the United States. Soviet leaders would certainly promote and manipulate such European anxieties in hopes of weakening the unity and resolve of the NATO Alliance and in an effort to extend Soviet influence without risking the dan-

[41]"NATO Behind Nuclear 8-Ball, Study Says," *Army Times*, 31 January 1983, p 22, and Cotter, Hansen and McConnell, *op. cit.*, p 13.

[42]*Soviet Military Power, op. cit.*, p 37; and "New Soviet Missile Bases Reported in Asia," *The Kansas City Star*, 1 May 1983, p A-2.

[43]Richard H. Ullman, "Out of the Euromissile Mire," *Foreign Policy*, Spring 1983, p 44.

[44]Anthony H. Cordesman, "Using a Strategy of Fear to Counter a Fear of Strategy," *Armed Forces Journal International*, February 1983, p 60; "Soviets Launch Propaganda Effort Against U.S.," *The Kansas City Times*, 16 March 1983, p A-6; and "Moscow Issues Warning on Nuclear Retaliation," *The Kansas City Times*, 30 November 1982, p A-1.

[45]Larson and Bodie, *op. cit.*, p 39.

gers of a major war.[46] Thus, while a freeze would by no means be a guarantee of a Warsaw Pact invasion, the NATO nations would very likely have to pay a heavy political price somewhere down the road.

THE IMPACT OF THE SOVIET STRATEGIC ORIENTATION

Ultimate deterrence is achieved by each side holding the other side's civilian population hostage. However, this assumes that "both the U.S.S.R. and United States will freely offer up their populations for massacre."[47] Unfortunately for the United States and deterrence, the Soviet Union has seen things differently. Because of a history filled with invasions in every century, to include three in the 20th century, the Soviets have been very concerned about protecting their citizens in case of war. Consequently, the Soviets have:

> . . . implemented large programs for defending their citizens from nuclear attack, for shooting down American missiles, and for fighting and winning a nuclear war.[48]

Together with the huge buildup in their offensive nuclear capabilities, such Soviet actions are quite destabilizing, especially when they are not matched by similar U.S. efforts. The result is a belated realization by the United States that mutual assured destruction never became mutual—as Senator Daniel P. Moynihan described it, "a policy in ruins."[49]

What is usually forgotten or overlooked is that while the strategic orientation of the United States emphasizes measures for *preventing* war, Soviet deterrent thinking "concentrates largely on the requirements for responding effectively and surviving in the event deterrence fails."[50] Studies in 1977–78, directed by Secretary of Defense Harold Brown, concluded that the Soviets are serious about *winning* a global nuclear war. the Soviets believe that "victory" is an attainable goal for a nation that studies the problems of nuclear war, works out a strategy for victory and develops doctrines, forces and strategic defensive programs, together with an allocation of economic and human resources for the implementation of such a strategy.[51]

The result of these different approaches is that while the United States' civil defense program has been neglected for years, the Soviet Union has forged ahead with a huge, well-coordinated effort. Annually, the Soviets spend approximately 20 times as much as the United States on civil defense.[52]

To maximize their chances of national survival and to secure the optimal outcome, the Soviets have also been developing a massive strategic defensive force. This force includes active defenses such as modern interceptor aircraft, surface-to-air missiles (there are none defending the United States) and ballistic missile defense systems (the United States has had none since 1976). It also includes passive defenses such as surveillance and warning systems, hardened bunkers and electronic countermeasures.[53]

The late Herman Kahn, one of this country's foremost nuclear strategists, argued that the United States would be more responsible and probably enhance deterrence if, after trying to "deter the use of nuclear weapons by others," we would "then go one painful step further and envisage their use."[54] However, only the Soviet Union seems to have heeded his advice, although Presidential Directive 59, under President Jimmy Carter, and recent Reagan administration initiatives indicate gradual U.S. recognition of civil defense and command, control and communications system survivability as elements of the strategic balance.[55]

[46]*Ibid.*, p 40.
[47]Jastrow, *op. cit.*, p 27.
[48]*Ibid.*, p 28.
[49]*Ibid.*
[50]Captain John F. Troxell, "Soviet Civil Defense and the American Response," *Military Review*, January 1983, p 37.

[51]Foster, *op. cit.*, p 497.
[52]Henry Kearney, "Can We Defend Against the Bomb?" *Army Reserve*, Fall 1982, p 22.
[53]*Soviet Military Power*, *op. cit.*, pp 7, 30 and 31.
[54]Herman Kahn, "Thinking About Nuclear Morality," *The New York Times Magazine*, 13 June 1982, p 50.
[55]Troxell, *op. cit.*

While Soviet strategic defense programs are far from perfect, the distinct asymmetries that have emerged could contribute to a Soviet belief that they could survive a nuclear exchange and emerge in much better shape than the United States. Such Soviet perceptions could encourage them to take greater risks in a crisis situation and possibly lead to miscalculations concerning the limits of deterrence.

A nuclear freeze would exacerbate such destabilizing problems since the typical resolutions fail to address any of these areas which are so important in determining the success of deterrence. While a freeze would not prevent the United States from attempting to catch up with the Soviet head start in some of these areas, the resulting asymmetries would be difficult to overcome. In combination with the vulnerabilities frozen into the U.S. ICBM and bomber forces, such asymmetries could reduce the United States' confidence in its deterrent forces (and increase Soviet confidence in theirs) as well as hamper U.S. actions in the international arena.

CONCLUSION

While the United States recognizes that there could be no winner in nuclear war, to ensure effective deterrence it is paramount that the Soviet leadership understands this as well. This is especially important because the Soviet buildup in the 1970s:

> . . . has belied the action-reaction theory of the arms race which holds that the Soviet military build-up is always a response to increases in American defense spending.[56]

Unilateral U.S. restraint during the 1970s, which was tantamount to a freeze, was not met with similar Soviet restraint. On the contrary, the Soviets built far greater numbers of ICBMs than would be necessary for a deterrent capability[57] and complemented their strategic offensive capabilities with the development of massive strategic defenses.

The new generation of Soviet ICBMs was specifically designed to attack U.S. missile silos and allows Soviet planners to envision a nuclear confrontation in which they probe U.S. resolve to retaliate by attacking a smaller and smaller subset of our military forces while U.S. options for retaliation are limited.[58] In the same period, the Soviets deployed mobile *SS20* theater nuclear missiles to decouple U.S. nuclear weapons in NATO from this country's strategic ballistic missiles. The inescapable conclusion is that the Soviets are bent on achieving true strategic superiority which they can then exploit to achieve their political, economic and geostrategic aims.

A nuclear freeze would codify Soviet advantages and leave a significant number of the U.S. strategic retaliatory forces ineffective against Soviet targets or vulnerable to Soviet attack. A freeze would also eliminate Soviet incentives for meaningful arms-reduction talks and prevent the United States from modernizing its aging strategic triad.

A freeze could also leave each side with inherently destabilizing ICBM structures which, because of their large number of multiple independently targetable reentry vehicle missiles, offer tremendous theoretical advantages to the side which strikes first. In addition, the Soviets could continue to improve their sophisticated air defenses, but we could not replace our *B52* bombers which are now more than 25 years old.[59] This hardly seems like the path to increased stability, particularly considering the improbability of achieving adequate verification.

However, those are not the only shortcomings. A nuclear freeze would also have serious consequences for NATO because it would prevent the deployment of the *Pershing II* and cruise missiles called for under the 1979 NATO decision. In so doing, the United States would seriously undermine the Atlantic Alliance and undercut the European leaders who have steadfastly supported the

---

[56]Jastrow, *op. cit.*, p 30.
[57]*Annual Report to Congress, FY* 1984, *op. cit.*, p 26.

[58]*Ibid.*, p 5; and Burt, *op. cit.*
[59]"Weinberger Urges Nuclear Freeze Rejection," *Army Times, op. cit.*

deployment decision in the face of vocal opposition.

Finally, a freeze would carry with it the serious international implication that the United States lacks the resolve and national will to maintain an effective nuclear deterrent. Soviet perceptions of such a weakness could very well increase Soviet political bullying and risk-taking at all conflict levels and thereby further threaten world stability.

Though it is difficult to argue against "virtuous talk of peace, reduced defense budgets, and moral rectitude,"[60] hopefully, this article has dispelled some of the illusions regarding a nuclear freeze. It is time this nation's citizens realize that, instead of providing the answer to their fears and frustrations, a nuclear freeze leaves only the paradox that a proposal intended to prevent nuclear war would actually increase the likelihood of such conflict.

QUESTIONS FOR DISCUSSION

1 Why is the freeze such a popular idea?
2 What are the verification problems of a freeze?
3 If there is a freeze on the testing, production, and further deployment of nuclear warheads, will the superpower nuclear arms race end?
4 Since the Reagan administration was responsible for significantly increasing America's strategic nuclear forces, does a freeze now serve America's security interests?
5 What effect would a superpower nuclear freeze have on the use of force by the superpowers in world politics?

SUGGESTED READINGS

AuCoin, Les. "Freeze," *Bulletin of the Atomic Scientists* 40 (November 1984), pp. 7–9.

Dyson, Freeman. *Weapons and Hope*. New York: Harper & Row, 1984.

Edwards, Mickey. "The Case Against a Nuclear Freeze," *Washington Times* (March 18, 1983), p. 1-C.

Ford, Daniel, Henry Kendall, and Steven Nadis. *Beyond the Freeze: The Road to Nuclear Sanity*. Boston: Beacon Press (for the Union of Concerned Scientists), 1982.

Forsberg, Randall. "A Bilateral Nuclear-Weapon Freeze," *Scientific American* 247 (November 1982), pp. 52–61.

———, et al., *Seeds of Promise: The First Real Hearings on the Nuclear Arms Freeze*. Andover, Massachusetts: Brick House Publishing, 1983.

Garfinkle, Adam M. *The Politics of the Nuclear Freeze*. Philadelphia, Pennsylvania: Foreign Policy Research Institute, 1984.

Gray, Colin S. "Nuclear Freeze?" *Parameters* 13 (June 1983), pp. 74–80.

Kaplan, Fred. "Can a 'Freeze' Be Verified?" *Boston Globe* (April 23, 1984), pp. 37 and 39.

Kennedy, Edward M. and Mark O. Hatfield. *Freeze! How You Can Help Prevent Nuclear War*. New York: Bantam, 1982.

Miller, Steven E. (ed.). *The Nuclear Weapons Freeze and Arms Control*. Cambridge, Massachusetts: Ballinger, 1984.

Stoertz, Howard Jr. "Monitoring a Nuclear Freeze," *International Security* 8 (Spring 1984), pp. 91–110.

U.S. Congress: Senate. *Nuclear Arms Reduction Proposals*. Hearings before the Committee on Foreign Relations, 97th Cong., 2nd Sess., 1982.

U.S. Congress: Senate. *U.S.-Soviet Relations: Part 2*. Hearings before the Committee on Foreign Relations, 98th Cong., 1st Sess., 1983.

[60]Colin S. Gray, "Nuclear Strategy: A Regrettable Necessity." *SAIS Review*, Winter–Spring 1983, p 14.

Chapter Four

United States Nuclear Policy Options

In the previous chapter we saw that there is no consensus in the United States about whether the Soviets have achieved strategic nuclear superiority, nor how such superiority may be defined, nor to what practical use it could be put by Moscow. The Soviets, for their part, insist that they do not presently have, and do not seek, "superiority." All this makes far-reaching nuclear arms control agreements difficult to negotiate, as we have seen. The matter is further complicated by the existence of an influential American lobby which openly proclaims its desire to see the United States obtain nuclear superiority. Clearly no Soviet government would willingly consent even to negotiate with an adversary having such a proclaimed purpose. It is therefore perhaps not surprising that in 1984 President Reagan refused to state that nuclear superiority was his aim in any talks with Moscow. The suspicion must remain, however, that he and many of his principal advisers are nevertheless fundamentally sympathetic to those who wish to restore a significant degree of American nuclear advantage. Obviously, if this could be achieved—and it may be impossible—it could only be done by unilateral American measures, and not in negotiations with Moscow. Hence, the present chapter is largely devoted to a consideration of a variety of unilateral measures.

First, it is important to reiterate that "superiority" is often used imprecisely in this context. The United States had indeed unambiguous superiority over the Soviet Union between 1945 and 1949, for it had a total monopoly of possession of atomic weapons.

From 1949 until the 1960s, however, Washington had no more than a strategic advantage—admittedly, a considerable one—arising out of the relative invulnerability of the United States heartland (which gradually eroded) and a vast disparity in numbers and quality of delivery systems. And in recent years the strategic nuclear relationship has clearly been much closer to parity, with even the experts differing as to whether Moscow, Washington, or neither has the advantage or "superiority." These disputes become more difficult to evaluate when taking into account that the Soviets are generally held to be ahead in certain areas (especially in the number of launchers and throw-weight), whereas the Americans are believed ahead in others (especially in the number of warheads and accuracy). At any rate, only an astonishing technological breakthrough would allow either superpower to achieve today the absolute nuclear supremacy that the United States had between 1945 and 1949. No significant lobby in the United States, however, regards such a breakthrough as likely in the near future, and hence the quest for such a breakthrough is not at the center of any serious policy prescriptions. What some American experts do regard as possible, however, is something approaching the kind of "superiority" vis-à-vis Moscow that existed around the time of the Cuban missile crisis of 1962. If achieved, this might enable the United States to expect it could prevail in a conflict of resolve, and if not, that it could emerge from an actual nuclear encounter in better shape than the Soviet Union, although of course not undamaged.

Why should there be a significant lobby in the United States that desires "superiority" in this limited sense? In short, why cannot there be American consensus in favor of seeking approximate nuclear parity with the Soviet Union, so that a stable relationship based simply on Mutual Assured Destruction could be built? The principal explanation is to be found through an understanding of the development of post-World War II American foreign policy. In February 1945, at the Yalta Conference, President Franklin D. Roosevelt indicated to Soviet leader Joseph Stalin and British Prime Minister Winston Churchill that the United States would withdraw all its forces from Europe after the defeat of Nazi Germany. He evidently believed that the Soviet Union would not seek to dominate postwar Europe or, alternatively, was unwilling to allow the United States to be drawn into a situation in which it might feel obliged to take military steps to prevent Soviet domination. Roosevelt's successor, Harry S Truman, gradually moved away from his predecessor's optimistic or indulgent attitude towards Moscow. Outraged by evidence of the brutality employed by the Red Army and its few local supporters in the Bolshevization of various Eastern European countries during 1945 and 1946, he was converted to the idea that the United States had a duty to call a halt to the process. Accordingly, in March 1947, the Truman Doctrine was enunciated, whereby the United States in effect undertook to succor the remaining non-Communist governments in Europe, Greece and Turkey in particular. The Marshall Plan soon followed, involving the provision of massive economic and financial aid. And in 1948–49 American armed forces began to assert themselves again in Europe, particularly in the matter of the Berlin blockade. In that encounter an airlift—principally operated by the United States—broke the Soviet Union's efforts to intimidate West Berliners by closing off surface-transit routes between the western-occupied zones of Germany and West Berlin, which was located in the Soviet zone. In 1949, the

North Atlantic Treaty Organization (NATO) was established. Its original members were the United States, Great Britain, France, Italy, Canada, Norway, Belgium, Denmark, the Netherlands, Luxembourg, Portugal, and Iceland. Other countries entered the alliance later: Greece and Turkey (1952), West Germany (1955), and Spain (1982).

Within a few years after the formation of NATO, a considerable United States conventional presence was established in Western Europe, and was buttressed by an American threat to have recourse to nuclear weapons if these conventional forces were overrun by the vastly superior conventional forces at Moscow's disposal. As the United States' nuclear guarantee of Western Europe was offered at a time when the United States itself was totally invulnerable to any Soviet nuclear strike, the guarantee was relatively easy to give. In short, Washington could threaten a first use of nuclear weapons on Soviet targets with the certainty that American cities were immune. It is by no means clear, however, that any such nuclear guarantee would have been given to Western Europe, or, if given, been accepted by the American people, had the Soviets not been a vastly inferior nuclear-weapon state at the time.

Today that Soviet inferiority is no more, although the American moral obligation and commitment by treaty to defend the conventionally inferior West Europeans remains. The present U.S. administration can thus be said to have inherited from another era (in which entirely different military conditions applied) this formidable task of sustaining "extended deterrence." For a minority of Americans, on both the right and the left, the answer is simply to move away from the commitment to the West Europeans and to concentrate on defending the Western hemisphere and the Pacific basin. The majority appears, however, to wish to maintain this commitment, widely seen as a crucial symbol of the integrity of the United States as a supporter of pluralistic democracy, and of the country's prestige as a superpower. This desire is shared by the United States Catholic Bishops but, as will be seen, they have serious doubts (as do many other Americans) about whether it is ethically justified to be prepared to seek to defend allies or even Americans by threatening the use (and particularly the first use) of nuclear weapons. Moreover, even if the U.S. Government does not adhere to these moral scruples, one must wonder whether the nuclear guarantee of defense of the West Europeans remains entirely credible in an age when the Soviets have achieved strategic nuclear parity (or better). Doubts about this go far in explaining the demand, among some U.S. analysts who do not share the Bishops' outlook, that a determined effort should now be made to reestablish a degree of nuclear superiority over the Soviet Union.

A second but not unrelated major concern of many American strategists relates to the growing vulnerability of ICBMs which, as we have seen in the previous chapter, has been a significant element in the SALT controversies. For more than a decade successive U.S. administrations attempted to grapple with the problem, but were constrained by a number of factors, including the existence of the ABM Treaty of 1972, divisions in Congress, budgetary pressures, and a desire to keep open the door to Moscow in the hope of solving the problem by a bilateral arms limitation on offensive forces.

The kernel of the problem has two aspects. First, American Minutemen are now highly vulnerable to a Soviet first-strike, whereas Soviet land-based missiles may not be vulnerable to the same extent; in any case, the Americans claim to have a particular need (not shared by the Soviets) for their ICBMs to be survivable so that they can have the option under their limited nuclear war doctrine to make precision strikes on Soviet military targets. Second, the United States has a long-standing commitment to maintain, if possible, a nuclear capability vis-à-vis the Soviet Union on a "triad" basis. Fearing a possible future Soviet breakthrough in antisubmarine warfare (ASW), the Pentagon has been reluctant to rely solely or even mainly on a submarine-based deterrent, although by the 1990s the American Trident II system will be an extremely formidable threat, not only in terms of its capacity for devastation (true as well of earlier generations, namely Polaris and Poseidon), but also in terms of its accuracy.

There is, then, a strong desire in Washington to maintain simultaneously the threat traditionally constituted by manned bombers and land-based missiles. The most effective way for Washington to meet this perceived need for invulnerability of its land-based missile force, in the absence of an arms control agreement reducing the number of offensive Soviet warheads, would be a limited BMD deployment. But as we have seen in a previous chapter, there are doubts about whether the Soviets would consent to any revision of the ABM Treaty, and no administration, not even Reagan's, has been eager to repudiate it unilaterally. The result has been a decade-long American dalliance with the idea of building a large number of MX missiles. At times it has been argued that ways could be found to make at least a good proportion of such missiles invulnerable to a first strike. Carter, for example, favored building 4,000 silos, but only 200 MX missiles, with the idea of moving the latter between silos by rail in a random fashion so as to confuse the Soviets as to their location at any particular time. Reagan, on the other hand, supported the dense pack plan, which would have involved the deployment of a large number of MX missiles in one location, counting on the destruction of incoming missiles in the confined target area by one another through "fratricide," the process of rendering incoming nuclear warheads impotent through the detonation of nuclear explosives. But Congress was unimpressed by these plans, as were most experts. There was simply insufficient evidence that the vast expenditure involved would be worthwhile in terms of increased invulnerability (if any).

An alternative route was to attempt to increase the vulnerability of the Soviet Union to a first strike against *its* land-based missiles. The danger in this course was that it could create a "hair-trigger" relationship between the two land-based systems. On the other hand, it would restore equality of vulnerability, and hence might serve to persuade the Soviets to negotiate a more stable arrangement. But many in Congress disapproved of this approach also.

To try to resolve the congressional impasse, Reagan established, in 1982, a bipartisan commission, headed by General Brent Scowcroft, a former national security adviser. In April 1983 the commission came out in favor of deploying 100 MX in existing silos, and further recommended that in the long run, as a means of meeting the "triad" requirement, there be deployment of a large number of single-warhead Midgetman missiles which, because of their size, number, and mobility would be less vulnerable than Minuteman. There was, however, frank acknowledgment by Scowcroft that the first stage of his plan, the deployment of MX in existing silos, was essentially a domestic political compromise that did not resolve the vulnerability problem, but he held that it would nonetheless put pressure on Moscow to negotiate. Meanwhile, as the commission candidly recognized, the Soviets will "probably possess the necessary combination of ICBM numbers, reliability, accuracy and warhead yield to destroy almost all the 1,047 U.S. ICBM silos, using only a small portion of their own ICBM force." Reagan, however, endorsed the Scowcroft Report and recommended it to Congress.

Scowcroft's proposal was only partially embraced on Capitol Hill in 1984. Instead of agreeing to build 100 MX, Congress consented to the construction of only 21. In 1985, Congress capped the total number of MX missiles at 50. It remains to be seen whether these 50 MX missiles will have any significant influence on Soviet thinking, and hence whether historians will judge the expenditure as essentially wasteful, as many critics now argue.

THE MORAL CHALLENGE

In our first debate we consider the ethical underpinnings of American strategic policies. The most important recent intervention in this area has of course come from the National Conference of Catholic Bishops on War and Peace. This took the form of the famous Pastoral Letter of May 1983, the summary of which we reproduce here. We also append to the summary a brief extract from the body of the Letter covering specific recommendations on Counter-Population Warfare, Initiation of Nuclear War, and Limited Nuclear War.

It is important to appreciate that not all the statements made by U.S. Bishops would necessarily be endorsed by the Pope, nor by, say, a similar collection of French Bishops. For as they remind us in their summary: "At times we state universally binding moral principles found in the teaching of the Church; at other times the pastoral letter makes specific applications, observations and recommendations which allow for diversity of opinion on the part of those who assess the factual data of situations differently."

Keith Payne, whose article we reproduce to illustrate the other side of the argument, clearly holds that the most controversial of the Bishops' recommendations, among them the urging that the United States should adopt a no-first-use policy, do indeed derive in the main from an assessment of factual data that can be disputed. He indicates his own disagreement with the Bishops' assumptions, in particular that "(1) In the nuclear age defense is impossible; the offense will always get through. (2) A limited nuclear war is virtually impossible; once nuclear weapons are employed, escalation to unlimited nuclear destruction will be rapid. (3) So-called war-fighting strategic capabilities (e.g., counterforce capabilities) are destabilizing—that is, they increase the probability of war."

Readers will not need reminding that these are very contentious issues indeed. But whether the Bishops' position is really as centrally dependent on factual assessments as Payne suggests is open to doubt. For example, they state, in the context of limited nuclear war, "that the burden of proof remains on those who assert that meaningful limitation is possible." They might well question whether Payne produces the kind of proof they require.

A final point to note is that the Bishops have not only been criticized by those who, like Payne, think they go too far in criticism of U.S. government policies, but also by those who argue no less forcefully that the Bishops, given their stated premises, should have condemned *any* reliance, however temporary, on nuclear deterrence in any form—a position they declined to take. A good example of this criticism is found in the article by Susan Moller Okin listed in the bibliography to debate 11. This serves as a reminder to our readers that, as we stressed in the preface, despite the superficial impression created by this book's debate format, there can be more than two sides to a given controversy.

MX DEPLOYMENT

In our second debate we offer an extract from Scowcroft's Report providing the essence of his justification of the original proposal for a rapid deployment of 100 MX and a longer-term concentration on Midgetman. Opposing the Report is Democratic Congressman Wyche Fowler. He concentrates on the MX recommendations in the Report and argues that deployment would subtract from, rather than add to, strategic nuclear stability; he is not persuaded that the Soviets would necessarily respond with arms control proposals, as Scowcroft would hope.

CIVIL DEFENSE

Whatever the merits and demerits of the Scowcroft Report, it would be impossible to claim that anything approaching a restoration of United States nuclear superiority is envisaged therein. But as has been seen, some experts hold that nothing less will suffice if "extended deterrence" (i.e., the U.S. guarantee of the security of Western Europe) is to remain credible. One possible means to regaining such superiority might be for the United States to concentrate vast resources on civil defense. Clearly, if U.S. population centers could be made much less vulnerable to nuclear attacks than their Soviet counterparts, the possible first use by the United States of nuclear weapons in a European conflict would become more credible. But at the present time it is the Soviets, not the Americans, who have some advantage in this respect, as Moscow has invested large sums in civil defense. Furthermore, the Soviet population is less concentrated in urban centers than is that of the United States. Thus, even equality in this respect, let alone superiority, will not be easily attained by the United States.

During his term of office President Kennedy found the issue so divisive that he concluded he would do more harm than good for consensus in the national security area by emphasizing the topic. President Reagan also found little popular support for civil defense. His adminsitration introduced its own program for civil defense, the Crisis Relocation Plan, in which large-scale evacuation from American cities was proposed in case nuclear war seemed imminent. In 1985, however, the plan was quietly scuttled after it had been criticized by many communities as unworkable.

Something of this potential for divisiveness is echoed in our encounter between Jennifer Leaning, a member of the National Executive Committee, Physicians for Social Responsibility; and Leon Gouré, the director of the Center for Soviet Studies Science Applications. The former's position rests essentially on the contention that civil defense "serves to delude Federal officials and a few members of the populace into thinking that nuclear war can be waged with relative impunity." The latter argues that "worst-case scenarios are by no means the most probable ones or the only ones for assessing the utility of civil defense." He does not deny, and few experts would, that any kind of nuclear war would be a catastrophe. But is it not also realistic to recognize, as Colin S. Gray does in another context, that "catastrophe can come in different sizes"?

Gouré also addresses the question of the relevance of American civil defense to strategic stability. He holds that it is a mistake to suppose that it would "make it easier for the American government and people to resort to rash actions which could provoke a nuclear war with the Soviet Union." "No conceivable U.S. administration," he writes, "would believe that it can act more aggressively and court a nuclear war with the Soviet Union because it has some capabilities to mitigate its consequences." That judgment may beg the question of whether a U.S. administration, possessing such "mitigating" capabilities, could thus more confidently contemplate threatening first use of nuclear weapons in response to massive conventional aggression in Europe. Most arguments in this area ultimately come back to the problem of "extended deterrence."

How then does the Reagan administration intend to tackle this problem? In the longer term, there is the Strategic Defense Initiative (SDI), also dubbed "star wars". In the short run, reliance on flexible nuclear response is favored (as enunciated in Jimmy Carter's Presidential Directive 59 of July 1980, and later endorsed by Reagan). Accordingly, we have debates on both these topics.

"STAR WARS"

On Reagan's March 1983 proposal of the SDI we have physicists Sidney D. Drell and Wolfgang K. H. Panofsky pitted against Robert Jastrow, a former director of the National Aeronautics and Space Administration Institute for Space Studies. It is first essential to appreciate that the implications of the SDI have been widely misunderstood. The world's media have tended to perpetuate the impression, somewhat carelessly created by the occasional use of exaggerated and imprecise language by both Reagan and Weinberger, that the U.S. administration is confident that it can attain complete immunity to nuclear attack in the near future. The achievement of that degree of perfection is not credible until well into the next century, if indeed it ever proves possible. In the foreseeable future—and even in this case we mean decades, not years— we are actually considering only the possibility that the United States, after a long period of intensive research, might be enabled to achieve a degree of invulnerability, along the lines of that probably existing in the late 1950s or early 1960s. At the very least, the problem of vulnerability of United States land-based missiles might thereby eventually be solved, and at best the majority of Americans could hope to survive a nuclear conflict.

If we dismiss the quest for total invulnerability and the consequent obsolescence of nuclear weapons as being of no practical relevance for the foreseeable future, we are left with two serious lines of dispute about the SDI which merit our attention. Some critics argue that even the most modest hopes for ICBM vulnerability will be dashed, because United States defensive programs can always be outdistanced by less costly Soviet offensive developments. Here some see a parallel to the loss of confidence in the technological feasibilty of Sentinel that occurred in the late 1960s (which was discussed in Chapter 3). Other critics assume, at least for the sake of argument, that the SDI could eventually become operational and effective to a fair degree not only in protecting missile fields, but even in providing a limited degree of cover for the general American population. But they maintain that in the interim the Soviets would not be inactive nor concentrate solely on building up offensive forces. They might become so apprehensive or angry over the prospect of losing the strategic nuclear parity (or advantage) to which they have devoted so many resources that they could react by threatening a preventive attack. Or, more plausibly, they might engage the Americans in a "star wars" race, with highly unpredictable consequences.

Indeed, there are many American experts who claim that such a race is already taking place in that the Soviets, although they made no announcement comparable to Reagan's, have been engaged in "star wars" research for several years. Assuming that Reagan was less than serious in his offer (made in a television debate with Walter Mondale) to share SDI technology with Moscow, many American strategists would expect the United States to come out ahead in such a competition. But few would deny that tensions between Moscow and Washington would thereby be exacerbated.

In preferring to run the risks involved in such increased tension, some American strategists are influenced by the argument that the American government cannot hope in the long run to sustain the credibility of "extended deterrence" by any other means. Ironically, however, the West European leaders who have the greatest interest in strengthening "extended deterrence" have been cool to the SDI. Maybe this is because, bewitched by Reagan's rhetoric, they assume that the SDI will be so successful that in the long run both superpowers will become totally invulnerable. If that happened, of course, the United States' threat to engage in a first use of nuclear arms against the Soviet Union in the event that the latter used conventional forces to attack NATO Europe would indeed lose its effectiveness. Concomitantly, the British and French independent nuclear capabilities would also become worthless vis-à-vis the Soviet Union. Moreover, even if both superpowers achieved only a modest degree of mutual population protection, that might also significantly devalue the European independent nuclear forces. In such circumstances, however, the credibility of the American nuclear guarantee of Western Europe might be marginally enhanced. Thus for West European governments a great deal clearly depends on the precise form superpower defensive systems take, and on the superpowers' respective achievements in developing any effective defensive cover.

LIMITED NUCLEAR WARFARE: PRESIDENTIAL DIRECTIVE 59

The Reagan Administration's short-term prescription for maintaining "extended deterrence" is enshrined in Presidential Directive (PD) 59, which was inherited from Jimmy Carter. This prescription is debated by political scientist Louis René Beres and military analyst Colin S. Gray. The first point to appreciate, as both authors do, is that PD 59 was by no means a revolutionary departure in United States targeting policy, but merely a refinement of ideas that have enjoyed currency since at least the period in the 1960s when Robert McNamara was at the Pentagon. Beres's critique could thus largely be applied to the entire drift of U.S. strategic nuclear policy over the last two decades. Most of his numerous premises do not need underlining here, for they are brought out (and criticized) in Gray's direct rejoinder. But Beres's opening sentence merits close scrutiny at this point. "Since the dawn of the Atomic Age, the overriding objective of American strategic force has been to deter nuclear war." In fact, it would be more correct for Beres to say that this is what he wishes it had been, for he himself quotes Harold Brown, the secretary of defense in the Carter administration, as holding a contrary position: "And strategic forces, in conjunction with theater nuclear forces, must contribute to deterrence of conventional aggression as well."

This need to be prepared to use nuclear weapons to counterbalance Soviet conventional advantages in Europe (and elsewhere) has caused every U.S. administration, at least since that of Dwight Eisenhower, to contemplate initiating limited nuclear war. The assumption has simply had to be made that if deterrence should fail and limited nuclear war should break out, the Soviets would in practice play according to the American rules and not escalate at once to all-out nuclear war. Nobody *knows* that they would do so. But equally, nobody *knows,* despite their declaratory statements, that they would not. Hence, United States secretaries of defense have worked hard to evolve credible plans for waging such limited nuclear conflicts (notwithstanding the skepticism expressed by such analysts as Paul Bracken and Desmond Ball as to their practicability, as seen in Chapter 1). To this end, at the strategic level, counterforce options (i.e., military targets) have been given declaratory preference over countervalue (i.e., city-busting) options. This in turn has led to deep concern about the survivability of United States land-based ICBMs.

The importance of ICBMs, according to some analysts, is primarily that they are presently the most reliable and accurate means available to the United States of engaging in precision strikes on Soviet military targets; and this will remain the case until the submarine-launched Trident II system comes into full service. True, given the desirability of developing invulnerability to a disarming first strike, there is also, as we have seen, a case for maintaining, if possible, the "triad" of ICBMs and manned bombers in addition to the SLBMs, for some strategists wish to guard against a possible destabilizing breakthrough by the Soviets in antisubmarine warfare (ASW) techniques. But for the present this may be judged to be only a secondary justification for the "triad," as no decisive breakthrough is generally thought to be even on the horizon. Thus, the concerns on this score expressed, for example, in the MX debate might be largely ignored, provided the United States decided to rely on its present relatively inaccurate submarine-launched systems to support a second-strike massive retaliation doctrine. Yet today such an approach, in the opinion of many analysts, could only carry credibility as a deterrent to a Soviet nuclear attack on the United States heartland. They hold it not to be believable as a means of bolstering "extended deterrence" in Europe which, may already be too reliant on theater-based nuclear forces.

Beres obviously recognizes the force of the foregoing analysis, and responds by simply urging that the essence of "extended deterrence" be abandoned. It is thus no surprise to find that he favors an American no-first-use declaration with respect to nuclear weapons.

NO FIRST USE

This brings us to our next debate. The case for adopting such a no-first-use posture is made by four distinguished Americans, namely McGeorge Bundy, George F. Kennan, Robert S. McNamara, and Gerard Smith, all of whom have served in important posts involving national security. Their article was originally published in the Spring 1982 issue of *Foreign Affairs* and was for a time a major national and even international point for discussion. Many NATO strategists and political leaders, led by U.S. Secretary of State Alexander Haig, were outraged by the article, and attempts at refutation have been numerous. For our collection, we have selected an article by Colin S. Gray.

There are a number of background points that may help readers to follow this debate. First, a no-first-use declaration by the United States would, in present circumstances, be of a reciprocal character, for Andrei Gromyko, then the Soviet Union's foreign minister, already unilaterally made such a declaration in June 1982 at the United Nations General Assembly, although no changes in Soviet military deployments have ensued. Second, it must be appreciated that the lesson of history is that a mere declaration—whether unilateral, bilateral, or multilateral—does not in itself change any military relationship and may or may not be respected if ever an armed conflict breaks out. For example, in 1928 many nations adhered to the Kellogg-Briand Pact that bound them not to use armed force as a means of resolving international disputes, but these pledges carried absolutely no weight in the following decade. Even the more superficially successful Geneva Protocol of 1925, prohibiting the first use of chemical weapons, has had something of a charmed life and a debatable hold on its signatories. For example, we now know that Winston Churchill's war cabinet would have been willing to break the protocol if German troops had succeeded in crossing the English Channel in 1940. We are thus justified in asking whether similar pledges relating to nuclear weapons would carry significant weight if a major conventional war between the superpowers seemed about to end in the humiliation and defeat of one of them.

In the article by Bundy et al., however, more is urged than a mere no-first-use pledge, such as the one Gromyko made. It is recognized that the maintenance of the European balance might be jeopardized by such a pledge, and hence it is argued not only that United States forces should remain in Western Europe, but also that a major conventional build-up by NATO is desirable. But would such a build-up be sufficient to deter a Soviet conventional attack? And what if the Warsaw Pact decided to engage NATO in an all-out conventional arms race? Some critics, unable to find satisfactory answers to these questions, will wonder if there is any credible halfway point for the United States between, on the one hand, willingness to threaten to engage in the first use of nuclear weapons—tactical and strategic—on behalf of Western Europe and, on the other hand, reversion to the "fortress America" posture of the interwar era, which involved America's military strength being directed at protecting only the United States and its possessions.

NUCLEAR SUPERIORITY

We are thus once again face to face with the fundamental security issues for the United States in the last years of the twentieth century. These issues are centrally and lucidly addressed in the debate between Robert Jastrow and Robert Jervis. If areas outside the Western hemisphere are believed vital to United States interests, how can they be defended without willingness to engage in the first use of nuclear weapons? But if such threats are considered indispensable, as many American strategists believe, how can they be made credible to Moscow? Is it necessary, as Jastrow maintains, to strive for and achieve a measure of United States superiority (provided, of course, that we can define it and that it is attainable at all)? Or is approximate nuclear parity enough, as Jervis believes, provided the United States signals its unambiguous determination not to tolerate various clearly defined Soviet assaults on the global status quo? In short, if meaningful military superiority is not available to either superpower in the nuclear age, will the decisive factor in any major confrontation turn out quite simply to be the amount of resolve possessed by each superpower and its leaders?

11 Should the United States Act on Principles of the U.S. Catholic Bishops' Pastoral Letter on War and Peace?

YES

National Conference of Catholic Bishops on War and Peace

The Pastoral Letter on War and Peace: The Challenge of Peace: God's Promise and Our Response

NO

Keith B. Payne

The Bishops and Nuclear Weapons

The Pastoral Letter on War and Peace: The Challenge of Peace: God's Promise and Our Response

National Conference of Catholic Bishops on War and Peace

SUMMARY

The Second Vatican Council opened its evaluation of modern warfare with the statement: "The whole human race faces a moment of supreme crisis in its advance toward maturity." We agree with the council's assessment; the crisis of the moment is embodied in the threat which nuclear weapons pose for the world and much that we hold dear in the world. We have seen and felt the effects of the crisis of the nuclear age in the lives of people we serve. Nuclear weaponry has drastically changed the nature of warfare, and the arms race poses a threat to human life and human civilization which is without precedent.

We write this letter from the perspective of Catholic faith. Faith does not insulate us from the daily challenges of life but intensifies our desire to address them precisely in light of the gospel which has come to us in the person of the risen Christ. Through the resources of faith and reason we desire in this letter to provide hope for people in our day and direction toward a world freed of the nuclear threat.

As Catholic bishops we write this letter as an exercise of our teaching ministry. The Catholic tradition on war and peace is a long and complex one; it stretches from the Sermon on the Mount to the statements of Pope John Paul II. We wish to explore and explain the resources of the moral-religious teaching and to apply it to specific questions of our day. In doing this we realize, and we want readers of this letter to recognize, that not all statements in this letter have the same moral authority. At times we state universally binding moral principles found in the teaching of the Church; at other times the pastoral letter makes specific applications, observations and recommendations which allow for diversity of opinion on the part of those who assess the factual data of situations differently. However, we expect Catholics to give our moral judgments serious consideration when they are forming their own views on specific problems.

The experience of preparing this letter has manifested to us the range of strongly held opinion in the Catholic community on questions of fact and judgment concerning issues of war and peace. We urge mutual respect among individuals and groups in the Church as this letter is analyzed and discussed. Obviously, as bishops, we believe that such differences should be expressed within the framework of Catholic moral teaching. We need in the Church not only conviction and commitment but also civility and charity.

While this letter is addressed principally to the Catholic community, we want it to make a contribution to the wider public debate in our country on the dangers and dilemmas of the nuclear age. Our contribution will not be primarily technical or political, but we are convinced that there is no satisfactory answer to the human problems of the nuclear age which fails to consider the moral and religious dimensions of the questions we face.

Although we speak in our own name, as Catholic bishops of the Church in the United States, we have been conscious in the preparation of this letter of the consequences our teaching will have not only for the United States but for other nations as well. One important expression of this awareness has been the consultation we have had, by correspondence and in an important meeeting held at the Vatican (January 18–19, 1983), with representatives of European bishops' conferences. This consultation with bishops of other countries, and, of course, with the Holy See, has been very helpful to us.

Catholic teaching has always understood peace in positive terms. In the words of Pope John Paul II: "Peace is not just the absence of war. . . . Like a cathedral, peace must be constructed patiently and with unshakable faith." (Coventry, England, 1982.) Peace is the fruit of order. Order in human society must be shaped on the basis of respect for the transcendence of God and the unique dignity of each person, understood in terms of freedom, justice, truth and love. To avoid war in our day we must be intent on building peace in an increasingly interdependent world. In Part III of this letter we set forth a positive vision of peace and the demands such a vision makes on diplomacy, national policy, and personal choices.

While pursuing peace incessantly, it is also necessary to limit the use of force in a world comprised of nation states, faced with common problems but devoid of an adequate international political authority. Keeping the peace in the nuclear age is a moral and political imperative. In Parts I and II of this letter we set forth both the principles of Catholic teaching on war and a series of judgments, based on these principles, about concrete policies. In making these judgments we speak as moral teachers, not as technical experts.

I. SOME PRINCIPLES, NORMS AND PREMISES OF CATHOLIC TEACHING

A. On War

1 Catholic teaching begins in every case with a presumption against war and for peaceful settlement of disputes. In exceptional cases, determined by the moral principles of the just-war tradition, some uses of force are permitted.

2 Every nation has a right and duty to defend itself against unjust aggression.

3 Offensive war of any kind is not morally justifiable.

4 It is never permitted to direct nuclear or conventional weapons to "the indiscriminate destruction of whole cities or vast areas with their populations. . . . " (*Pastoral Constitution, #*80.) The

intentional killing of innocent civilians or non-combatants is always wrong.

5 Even defensive response to unjust attack can cause destruction which violates the principle of proportionality, going far beyond the limits of legitimate defense. This judgment is particularly important when assessing planned use of nuclear weapons. No defensive strategy, nuclear or conventional, which exceeds the limits of proportionality is morally permissible.

B. On Deterrence

1 "In current conditions 'deterrence' based on balance, certainly not as an end in itself but as a step on the way toward a progressive disarmament, may still be judged morally acceptable. Nonetheless, in order to ensure peace, it is indispensable not to be satisfied with this minimum which is always susceptible to the real danger of explosion." (Pope John Paul II, "Message to U.N. Special Session on Disarmament," #8, June 1982.)

2 No *use* of nuclear weapons which would violate the principles of discrimination of proportionality may be *intended* in a strategy of deterrence. The moral demands of Catholic teaching require resolute willingness not to intend or to do moral evil even to save our own lives or the lives of those we love.

3 Deterrence is not an adequate strategy as a long-term basis for peace; it is a transitional strategy justifiable only in conjunction with resolute determination to pursue arms control and disarmament. We are convinced that "the fundamental principle on which our present peace depends must be replaced by another, which declares that the true and solid peace of nations consists not in equality of arms but in mutual trust alone." (Pope John XXIII, *Peace on Earth, #*113.)

C. The Arms Race and Disarmament

1 The arms race is one of the greatest curses on the human race; it is to be condemned as a danger, an act of aggression against the poor, and a folly which does not provide the security it promises. (Cf: *Pastoral Constitution, #*81, *Statement of the Holy See to the United Nations,* 1976.)

2 Negotiations must be pursued in every reasonable form possible; they should be governed by the "demand that the arms race should cease; that the stockpiles which exist in various countries should be reduced equally and simultaneously by the parties concerned; that nuclear weapons should be banned; and that a general agreement should eventually be reached about progressive disarmament and an effective method of control." (Pope John XXIII, *Peace on Earth*, #112.)

D. On Personal Conscience

1 *Military Service:* "All those who enter the military service in loyalty to their country should look upon themselves as the custodians of the security and freedom of their fellow countrymen; and when they carry out their duty properly, they are contributing to the maintenance of peace." (*Pastoral Constitution*, #79.)

2 *Conscientious Objection:* "Moreover, it seems just that laws should make humane provision for the case of conscientious objectors who refuse to carry arms, provided they accept some other form of community service." (*Pastoral Constitution*, #79.)

3 *Non-violence:* "In this same spirit we cannot but express our admiration for all who forego the use of violence to vindicate their rights and resort to other means of defense which are available to weaker parties, provided it can be done without harm to the rights and duties of others and of the community." (*Pastoral Constitution*, #78.)

4 *Citizens and Conscience:* "Once again we deem it opportune to remind our children of their duty to take an active part in public life, and to contribute towards the attainment of the common good of the entire human family as well as to that of their own political community. . . . In other words, it is necessary that human beings, in the intimacy of their own consciences, should so live and act in their temporal lives as to create a synthesis between scientific, technical and professional elements on the one hand, and spiritual values on the other." (Pope John XXIII, *Peace on Earth*, #146, 150.)

II. MORAL PRINCIPLES AND POLICY CHOICES

As bishops in the United States, assessing the concrete circumstances of our society, we have made a number of observations and recommendations in the process of applying moral principles to specific policy choices.

A. On the Use of Nuclear Weapons

1 *Counter Population Use:* Under no circumstances may nuclear weapons or other instruments of mass slaughter be used for the purpose of destroying population centers or other predominantly civilian targets. Retaliatory action which would indiscriminately and disproportionately take many wholly innocent lives, lives of people who are in no way responsible for reckless actions of their government, must also be condemned.

2 *The Initiation of Nuclear War:* We do not perceive any situation in which the deliberate initiation of nuclear war, on however restricted a scale, can be morally justified. Non-nuclear attacks by another state must be resisted by other than nuclear means. Therefore, a serious moral obligation exists to develop non-nuclear defensive strategies as rapidly as possible. In this letter we urge NATO to move rapidly toward the adoption of a "no-first-use" policy, but we recognize this will take time to implement and will require the development of an adequate alternative defense posture.

3 *Limited Nuclear War:* Our examination of the various arguments on this question makes us highly skeptical about the real meaning of "limited." One of the criteria of the just-war teaching is that there must be a reasonable hope of success in bringing about justice and peace. We must ask whether such a reasonable hope can exist once nuclear weapons have been exchanged. The burden of proof remains on those who assert that meaningful limitation is possible. In our view the first imperative is to prevent any use of nuclear weapons and we hope that leaders will resist the notion that nuclear conflict can be limited, contained or won in any traditional sense.

B. On Deterrence

In concert with the evaluation provided by Pope John Paul II, we have arrived at a strictly conditional moral acceptance of deterrence. In this letter we have outlined criteria and recommendations which indicate the meaning of conditional acceptance of deterrence policy. We cannot consider such a policy adequate as a long-term basis for peace.

C. On Promoting Peace

1 We support immediate, bilateral verifiable agreements to halt the testing, production and deployment of new nuclear weapons systems. This recommendation is not to be identified with any specific political initiative.

2 We support efforts to achieve deep cuts in the arsenals of both superpowers; efforts should concentrate first on systems which threaten the retaliatory forces of either major power.

3 We support early and successful conclusion of negotiations of a comprehensive test ban treaty.

4 We urge new efforts to prevent the spread of nuclear weapons in the world, and to control the conventional arms race, particularly the conventional arms trade.

5 We support, in an increasingly interdependent world, political and economic policies designed to protect human dignity and to promote the human rights of every person, especially the least among us. In this regard, we call for the establishment of some form of global authority adequate to the needs of the international common good.

This letter includes many judgments from the perspective of ethics, politics and strategy needed to speak concretely and correctly to the "moment of supreme crisis" identified by Vatican II. We stress again that readers should be aware, as we have been, of the distinction between our statement of moral principles and of official Church teaching and our application of these to concrete issues. We urge that special care be taken not to use passages out of context; neither should brief portions of this document be cited to support positions it does not intend to convey or which are not truly in accord with the spirit of its teaching.

In concluding this summary we respond to two key questions often asked about this pastoral letter:

Why do we address these matters fraught with such complexity, controversy and passion? We speak as pastors, not politicians. We are teachers, not technicians. We cannot avoid our responsibility to lift up the moral dimensions of the choices before

our world and nation. The nuclear age is an era of moral as well as physical danger. We are the first generation since Genesis with the power to threaten the created order. We cannot remain silent in the face of such danger. Why do we address these issues? We are simply trying to live up to the call of Jesus to be peacemakers in our own time and situation.

What are we saying? Fundamentally, we are saying that the decisions about nuclear weapons are among the most pressing moral questions of our age. While these decisions have obvious military and political aspects, they involve fundamental moral choices. In simple terms, we are saying that good ends (defending one's country, protecting freedom, etc.) cannot justify immoral means (the use of weapons which kill indiscriminately and threaten whole societies). We fear that our world and nation are headed in the wrong direction. More weapons with greater destructive potential are produced every day. More and more nations are seeking to become nuclear powers. In our quest for more and more security we fear we are actually becoming less and less secure.

In the words of our Holy Father, we need a "moral about-face." The whole world must summon the moral courage and technical means to say no to nuclear conflict; no to weapons of mass destruction; no to an arms race which robs the poor and the vulnerable; and no to the moral danger of a nuclear age which places before humankind indefensible choices of constant terror or surrender. Peacemaking is not an optional commitment. It is a requirement of our faith. We are called to be peacemakers, not by some movement of the moment, but by our Lord Jesus. The content and context of our peacemaking is set not by some political agenda or ideological program, but by the teaching of his Church.

Ultimately, this letter is intended as an expression of Christian faith, affirming the confidence we have that the risen Lord remains with us precisely in moments of crisis. It is our belief in his presence and power among us which sustain us in confronting the awesome challenge of the nuclear age. We speak from faith to provide hope for all who recognize the challenge and are working to confront it with the resources of faith and reason.

To approach the nuclear issue in faith is to recognize our absolute need for prayer: we urge and invite all to unceasing prayer for peace with justice for all people. In a spirit of prayerful hope we present this message of peace.

. . .

MORAL PRINCIPLES AND POLICY CHOICES

*146.** In light of these perspectives we address three questions more explicitly: (1) counter-population warfare; (2) initiation of nuclear war; and (3) limited nuclear war.

1. Counter-Population Warfare

147. Under no circumstances may nuclear weapons or other instruments of mass slaughter be used for the purpose of destroying population centers or other predominantly civilian targets. Popes have repeatedly condemned "total war" which implies such use. For example, as early as 1954 Pope Pius XII condemned nuclear warfare "when it entirely escapes the control of man," and results in "the pure and simple annihilation of all human life within the radius of action".[1] The condemnation was repeated by the Second Vatican Council:

> Any act of war aimed indiscriminately at the destruction of entire cities or of extensive areas along with their population is a crime against God and man itself. It merits unequivocal and unhesitating condemnation.[2]

148. Retaliatory action whether nuclear or conventional which would indiscriminately take many wholly innocent lives, lives of people who are in no way responsible for reckless actions of their government, must also be condemned. This condemnation, in our judgment, applies even to the retaliatory use of weapons striking enemy cities after our own have already been struck. No Christian can rightfully carry out orders or policies deliberately aimed at killing non-combatants.[3]

149. We make this judgment at the beginning of our treatment of nuclear strategy precisely because the defense of the principle of non-combatant immunity is so important for an ethic of war and because the nuclear age has posed such extreme problems for the principle. Later in this letter we shall discuss specific aspects of U.S. policy in light of this principle and in light of recent U.S. policy statements stressing the determination not to target directly or strike directly against civilian populations. Our concern about protecting the moral value of non-combatant immunity, however, requires that we make a clear reassertion of the principle our first word on this matter.

2. The Initiation of Nuclear War

150. We do not perceive any situation in which the deliberate initiation of nuclear warfare, on however restricted a scale, can be morally justified. Non-nuclear attacks by another state must be resisted by other than nuclear means. Therefore, a serious moral obligation exists to develop non-nuclear defensive strategies as rapidly as possible.

151. A serious debate is under way on this issue.[4] It is cast in political terms, but it has a significant moral dimension. Some have argued that at the very beginning of a war nuclear weapons might be used, only against military targets, perhaps in limited numbers. Indeed it has long been American and NATO policy that nuclear weapons,

---

* Paragraph numbers have been retained as originally printed in *The Pastoral Letter on War and Peace*. Footnotes have been renumbered for easier reference.

[1]Pius XII, "Address to the VIII Congress of the World Medical Association.". . . .

[2]Vatican II, the *Pastoral Constitution on the Church in the Modern World* (hereafter cited: *Pastoral Constitution*), #80. . . .

[3]Ibid.

[4]M. Bundy, G. F. Kennan, R. S. McNamara, and Gerard Smith, "Nuclear Weapons and the Atlantic Alliance," *Foreign Affairs* 60 (Spring 1982), pp. 753–68; K. Kaiser, G. Leber, A. Mertes, F. J. Schulze, "Nuclear Weapons and the Preservation of Peace," *Foreign Affairs 60* (1982):1157–70; cf. other responses to Bundy article in the same issue of *Foreign Affairs*.

especially so-called tactical nuclear weapons, would likely be used if NATO forces in Europe seemed in danger of losing a conflict that until then had been restricted to conventional weapons. Large numbers of tactical nuclear weapons are now deployed in Europe by the NATO forces and about as many by the Soviet Union. Some are substantially smaller than the bomb used on Hiroshima, some are larger. Such weapons, if employed in great numbers, would totally devastate the densely populated countries of Western and Central Europe.

152. Whether under conditions of war in Europe, parts of Asia or the Middle East, or the exchange of strategic weapons directly between the United States and the Soviet Union, the difficulties of limiting the use of nuclear weapons are immense. A number of expert witnesses advise us that commanders operating under conditions of battle probably would not be able to exercise strict control; the number of weapons used would rapidly increase, the targets would be expanded beyond the military, and the level of civilian casualties would rise enormously.[5] No one can be certain that this escalation would not occur, even in the face of political efforts to keep such an exchange "limited." The chances of keeping use limited seem remote, and the consequences of escalation to mass destruction would be appalling. Former public officials have testified that it is improbable that any nuclear war could actually be kept limited. Their testimony and the consequences involved in this problem lead us to conclude that the danger of escalation is so great that it would be morally unjustifiable to initiate nuclear war in any form. The danger is rooted not only in the technology of our weapons systems but in the weakness and sinfulness of human communities. We find the moral responsibility of beginning nuclear war not justified by rational political objectives.

[5]Testimony given to the National Conference of Catholic Bishops Committee during preparation of this pastoral letter. . . .

153. This judgment affirms that the willingness to initiate nuclear war entails a distinct, weighty moral responsibility; it involves transgressing a fragile barrier—political, psychological, and moral—which has been constructed since 1945. We express repeatedly in this letter our extreme skepticism about the prospects for controlling a nuclear exchange, however limited the first use might be. Precisely because of this skepticism, we judge resort to nuclear weapons to counter a conventional attack to be morally unjustifiable.[6] Consequently we seek to reinforce the barrier against any use of nuclear weapons. Our support of a "no-first-use" policy must be seen in this light.

154. At the same time we recognize the responsibility the United States has had and continues to have in assisting allied nations in their defense against either a conventional or a nuclear attack. Especially in the European theater, the deterrence of a *nuclear* attack may require nuclear weapons for a time, even though their possession and deployment must be subject to rigid restrictions.

155. The need to defend against a conventional attack in Europe imposes the political and moral burden of developing adequate, alternative modes of defense to present reliance on nuclear weapons. Even with the best coordinated effort—hardly likely in view of contemporary political division on this question—development of an alternative defense position will still take time.

156. In the interim, deterrence against a conventional attack relies upon two factors: the not inconsiderable conventional forces at the disposal of NATO and the recognition by a potential attacker that the outbreak of large-scale conventional war could escalate to the nuclear level through accident or miscalculation by either side. We are aware that NATO's refusal to adopt a "no-first-

[6]Our conclusions and judgments in this area although based on careful study and reflection of the application of moral principles do not have, of course, the same force as the principles themselves and therefore allow for different opinions, as the Summary makes clear.

use" pledge is to some extent linked to the deterrent effect of this inherent ambiguity. Nonetheless, in light of the probable effects of initiating nuclear war, we urge NATO to move rapidly toward the adoption of a "no-first-use" policy, but doing so in tandem with development of an adequate alternative defense posture.

3. Limited Nuclear War

157. It would be possible to agree with our first two conclusions and still not be sure about retaliatory use of nuclear weapons in what is called a "limited exchange." The issue at stake is the *real* as opposed to the *theoretical* possibility of a "limited nuclear exchange."

158. We recognize that the policy debate on this question is inconclusive and that all participants are left with hypothetical projections about probable reactions in a nuclear exchange. While not trying to adjudicate the technical debate, we are aware of it and wish to raise a series of questions which challenge the actual meaning of "limited" in this discussion.

- Would leaders have sufficient information to know what is happening in a nuclear exchange?
- Would they be able under the conditions of stress, time pressures, and fragmentary information to make the extraordinarily precise decision needed to keep the exchange limited if this were technically possible?
- Would military commanders be able, in the midst of the destruction and confusion of a nuclear exchange, to maintain a policy of "discriminate targeting"? Can this be done in modern warfare, waged across great distances by aircraft and missiles?
- Given the accidents we know about in peacetime conditions, what assurances are there that computer errors could be avoided in the midst of a nuclear exchange?
- Would not the casualties, even in a war defined as limited by strategists, still run in the millions?
- How "limited" would be the long-term effects of radiation, famine, social fragmentation, and economic dislocation?

159. Unless these questions can be answered satisfactorily, we will continue to be highly skeptical about the real meaning of "limited." One of the criteria of the just-war tradition is a reasonable hope of success in bringing about justice and peace. We must ask whether such a reasonable hope can exist once nuclear weapons have been exchanged. The burden of proof remains on those who assert that meaningful limitation is possible.

160. A nuclear response to either conventional or nuclear attack can cause destruction which goes far beyond "legitimate defense." Such use of nuclear weapons would not be justified.

161. In the face of this frightening and highly speculative debate on a matter involving millions of human lives, we believe the most effective contribution or moral judgment is to introduce perspectives by which we can assess the empirical debate. Moral perspective should be sensitive not only to the quantitative dimensions of a question but to its psychological, human, and religious characteristics as well. The issue of limited war is not simply the size of weapons contemplated or the strategies projected. The debate should include the psychological and political significance of crossing the boundary from the conventional to the nuclear arena in any form. To cross this divide is to enter a world where we have no experience of control, much testimony against its possibility, and therefore no moral justification for submitting the human community to this risk.[7] We therefore express our view that the first imperative is to prevent any use of nuclear weapons and our hope that leaders will resist the notion that nuclear conflict can be limited, contained, or won in any traditional sense. . . .

---

[7]Undoubtedly aware of the long and detailed technical debate on limited war, Pope John Paul II highlighted the unacceptable moral risk of crossing the threshold to nuclear war in his "Angelus Message" of December 13, 1981; "I have, in fact, the deep conviction that, in the light of a nuclear war's effects, which can be scientifically forseen as certain, the only choice that is morally and humanly valid is represented by the reduction of nuclear armaments, while waiting for their future complete elimination, carried out simultaneously by all the parties, by means of explicit agreements and with the commitment of accepting effective controls.". . . .

The Bishops and Nuclear Weapons
Keith B. Payne

Any formulation of nuclear doctrine and strategy necessarily entails a consideration of the issue of morality. Nevertheless, many professionals in the fields of nuclear strategy and arms control have tended to consider moral questions side-issues and the domain of a handful of specialists.[1] This situation, however, will change now that the National Conference of Catholic Bishops has entered the U.S. strategic debate with its pastoral letter, "The Challenge of Peace: God's Promise and Our Response."[2] The letter is long and at times makes use of intentional ambiguity; but its rejection of the traditional U.S. approach to nuclear policy and deterrence is clear. This approach is predicated upon threatening nuclear retaliation to a Soviet attack against the United States or its allies. Following the lead of Pope John Paul II, the bishops indicate that nuclear deterrence is morally acceptable only under certain specific conditions. Those conditions, as presented in the letter, are, unfortunately, inconsistent with U.S. deterrence policy.[3] The bishops, for example, have clearly rejected nuclear first use, an option maintained by the United States and NATO to deter Soviet nuclear or nonnuclear attack against NATO Europe.

Unfortunately, the bishops' pastoral letter reflects a particular set of assumptions that are associated with the antinuclear movement and that are certainly not beyond dispute: (1) In the nuclear age defense is impossible; the offense will always get through. (2) A limited nuclear war is virtually impossible; once nuclear weapons are employed, escalation to unlimited nuclear destruction will be rapid. (3) So-called war-fighting strategic capabilities (e.g., counterforce capabilities) are destabilizing—that is, they increase the probability of war.

These are not moral judgments, nor are they subject to moral analysis—they are technical and political considerations. Unfortunately, the pastoral letter appears to have been informed by one particular politico-technical view of these issues; and the validity of the bishops' moral conclusions are, ultimately, dependent upon the validity of these preliminary, amoral assumptions.

Given the bishops' assumptions that defense is impossible and escalation virtually inevitable, for example, it is easy to conclude that the use of nuclear weapons cannot be in accord with just-war doctrine. St. Augustine and St. Thomas Aquinas developed the doctrine of just war to govern why and when recourse to war is permissible (*jus ad bellum*), and also to govern how war is to be conducted (*jus ad bello*). Under just-war doctrine, recourse to war is legitimate only under certain conditions. War is viewed as an unfortunate but sometimes necessary means to restrain evil and protect the innocent.

The pastoral letter argues that nuclear use (inevitably escalating to unlimited nuclear war) could virtually never be compatible with just-war criteria for resorting to or waging war. These criteria are discrimination, proportionality, and probability of success.

The principle of discrimination directly prohibits intentional attacks on noncombatants and nonmilitary targets. The pastoral letter emphasizes that the destructive potential of nuclear weapons has

---

[1] See, for example, William V. O'Brien, *The Conduct of Just and Limited War* (New York: Praeger, 1981), and "The Churches and the Bomb: After Nineteen Years, Let Us Begin," *Worldview*, December 1964, pp. 11–13.

[2] See National Conference of Catholic Bishops, "The Pastoral Letter on War and Peace, the Challenge of Peace: God's Promise and Our Response," *Origins*, May 19, 1983. (Hereafter, NCCB, *1983 Pastoral Letter*.)

[3] On June 12, 1982, Pope John Paul II addressed the UN Special Session on Disarmament, stating: "In current conditions 'deterrence' based on balance, certainly not as an end in itself but as a step on the way toward a progressive disarmament, may still be judged morally acceptable." Quoted in L. Bruce van Voorst, "The Churches and Nuclear Deterrence," *Foreign Affairs;* Spring 1983, p. 836.

Keith B. Payne, "The Bishops and Nuclear Weapons," *Orbis* 27 (Fall 1983), pp. 535–543. By permission of the publisher, Foreign Policy Research Institute.

brought about a unique challenge to the principle of discrimination. It argues that nuclear weapons and strategies for their use are inherently indiscriminate. Even "limited" strikes against military targets would inflict casualty levels that "would be almost indistinguishable from what might occur if civilian centers had been deliberately and directly struck."[4] The problem is not one of intention or strategy, but nuclear weapons' technology and geography: "This problem is unavoidable because of the way modern military facilities and production centers are so thoroughly interspersed with civilian living and working areas."[5] The U.S. policy of avoiding intentionally targeting civilian centers and noncombatants does not satisfy the principle of discrimination, according to the letter, because even the use of highly accurate, "discriminating" nuclear weapons would entail the grave threat of escalation, which could result in massive civilian casualties.

The principle of proportionality applies to both the decision to engage in warfare and the waging of war. As is the case with the principle of discrimination, the bishops maintain that the destructive potential of nuclear weapons has rendered proportionality of special significance. This is said to be the case because "today, it becomes increasingly difficult to make a decision to use any kind of armed force, however limited initially in intention and in the destructive power of the weapons employed, without facing at least the possibility of escalation to broader, or even total, war and to the use of weapons of horrendous destructive potential."[6]

In regard to *jus ad bellum,* an assessment must be made that the evil to be committed (in terms of the prospective damage inflicted and costs incurred by war) is proportional to the good to be realized by taking up arms. Proportionality is a requirement even in the decision for self-defense: "The response to aggression must not exceed the nature of the aggression."[7] The letter concludes that the possibility of unlimited escalation that could result from recourse to nuclear war renders it disproportional to the good to be achieved.

In regard to *jus ad bello,* the principle of proportionality must be applied to waging war. The military means employed must be proportional to the military objectives to be served. This principle prohibits destructive actions not justified by military necessity, and it obviously entails judgment and interpretation. The bishops emphasize, however, that even a primarily "counterforce" nuclear strike with obvious countermilitary intentions would not satisfy the principle of proportionality: "The location of industrial or militarily significant economic targets within heavily populated areas or in those areas affected by radioactive fallout could well involve such massive civilian casualties that in our judgment such a strike would be deemed morally disproportionate, even though not intentionally indiscriminate."[8]

Finally, the principle of probability of success must also be considered in a decision to resort to war. This principle is intended to guard against an irrational resort to arms when the outcome would be disproportionate or futile. The bishops believe that nuclear use would affront this principle, given the possibilitiy of escalation, the difficulties of limiting nuclear war, and the massive civilian destruction that would be likely to result from any nuclear exchange. As the letter observes: "One of the criteria of the just war tradition is a reasonable hope of success in bringing about justice and peace. We must ask whether such a reasonable hope can exist once nuclear weapons have been exchanged. The burden of proof remains on those who assert that meaningful limitation is possible."[9]

In short, the bishops conclude that the use of nuclear weapons—particularly because of their destructive potential and the possibility for escalation following even a limited use of nuclear weapons—

---

[4]NCCB, *1983 Pastoral Letter,* p.18.
[5]Ibid.
[6]Ibid., p.11.

[7]Ibid.
[8]Ibid., p. 18.
[9]Ibid., p.16.

is inconsistent with just-war principles and doctrine.

Given their view concerning the immorality of the operational use of nuclear weapons, the bishops faced a dilemma. Deterrence appears to be the only method currently available for maintaining peace in a nuclear-armed world, and Pope John Paul II has declared deterrence to be acceptable (if accompanied by the pursuit of disarmament). Yet nuclear deterrence clearly is the intended effect of a threat to *employ* nuclear weapons. The dilemma for the bishops was how a state could threaten an immoral action (i.e., employing nuclear weapons) for the morally pristine purpose of ensuring deterrence. As the bishops noted: "The political paradox of deterrence has also strained our moral conception. May a nation threaten what it may never do? May it possess what it may never use?"[10]

If the bishops placed themselves in opposition to deterrence because it is predicated upon the threat of a morally unacceptable action, they would, in effect, be rejecting the one strong foundation for avoiding war. The effect of their stand would be to increase the probability that what they oppose, nuclear war, would occur. The difficult task confronting the bishops was to determine how to maintain the stabilizing effect of nuclear deterrence without acknowledging the acceptability of a threat to employ nuclear weapons.

The solution to this dilemma involved accepting the possession of nuclear weapons but rejecting plans for using them. The pastoral letter explicitly rejects targeting civilian centers—consistent with the just-war requirement of discrimination. It also rejects targeting military assets—consistent with the bishops' acceptance of the judgment of the antinuclear movement that such a "counterforce" orientation is destabilizing, and prone to escalation beyond appreciable limitation. In short, targeting either military or civilian assets for deterrence purposes is declared off limits by the bishops. Indeed, the pastoral letter is silent concerning what type of nuclear threat would be permissible in support of

deterrence. Unfortunately, the bishops found it too "awkward" to address that question.[11] Given the adamant language against nuclear use, however, the implication of the letter is that all types of nuclear use are eschewed. As the letter states: "Our no to nuclear war must in the end be definitive and decisive . . . [and] there must be no misunderstanding of our profound skepticism about the moral acceptability of any use of nuclear weapons. It is obvious that the use of any weapons which violate the principle of discrimination merits unequivocal condemnation."[12]

The non-use of nuclear weapons is the bishops' solution to the deterrence dilemma. The deterrent effect of the possession of nuclear weapons is expected to sustain stability. Yet there would be no explicit threat to use, and indeed no plan to use, the weapons in support of deterrence. The Soviets' uncertainty about whether these weapons would be employed would, it is hoped, have a deterrent effect; yet the United States would not employ these weapons under any circumstances. Thus, according to the bishops, deterrence should stem from the Soviet leadership's uncertainty about the possibility of U.S. nuclear use rather than an immoral threat explicitly made by the United States. The solution to the deterrence dilemma suggested by the pastoral letter, then, is deterrence through a grand bluff.

The letter, again following the lead of Pope John Paul II, admonishes that the possession of nuclear weapons, and hence even deterrence by bluff, is acceptable only as an interim step toward arms control, disarmament, and an overarching international authority. The bishops endorse deep reductions in nuclear weapons; and as a first step toward disarmament, endorse a freeze ("halt") in the production, testing, and deployment of nuclear weapons.

Based upon their interpretation of just-war criteria, the bishops are in opposition to the U.S.

---

[10]Ibid., p. 14.

[11]See van Voorst, "The Churches and Nuclear Deterrence," pp. 827–52.
[12]NCCB, *1983 Pastoral Letter*, pp. 14, 19.

policy of an explicit nuclear first-use threat, planning for nuclear retaliation in the event of a Soviet first strike, planning for the limited use of nuclear weapons, counterforce targeting, attempting to "prevail" in a nuclear war should it occur, and modernizing nuclear forces (e.g., MX, Trident, B-1B, Pershing II, and GLCMs). In general, the bishops oppose the traditional U.S. position of providing an explicit nuclear threat in support of its deterrent policy.

However, the bishops are not in opposition to all aspects of U.S. policy. They do, by implication, endorse the Reagan administration's efforts to achieve deep force-level reductions in START; and the just-war doctrine's requirement for discrimination is in line with the U.S. policy of not intentionally targeting civilian population centers. Nevertheless, the bishops' concept of deterrence by bluff (as an interim step toward disarmament and a new international order) is in direct contrast with U.S. and Soviet policies and supporting those policies with credible preparations for employing nuclear weapons.

This solution to the deterrence dilemma reflects shortsighted escapism and, if actually implemented, would both increase the probability of a nuclear war and ensure the maximal level of destruction should that war occur. The "morally" acceptable approach to deterrence suggested in the pastoral letter, if adopted by the United States, would make more likely the most immoral of outcomes, a nuclear holocaust in which there would be no possibility for defense, discrimination, proportionality, or Western success (by any definition).

The effectiveness of deterrence to maintain stability is not simply a function of the capability to pose a threat, but the opponent's perception of the credibility of that threat. The effect of the pastoral letter, if endorsed officially, would be to destroy the credibility of the U.S. deterrent.

The bishops endorse the stabilizing effects of nuclear deterrence, but their admonitions would only eviscerate the threat upon which deterrence is predicated. If the United States indicated an ab-

solute refusal to employ nuclear weapons, even in retaliation, the Soviets would see little risk in pursuing highly provocative behavior. In the context of an acute U.S.-Soviet crisis, wherein the Soviet leadership would confront questions of direct military confrontation and nuclear use, what deterrent to Soviet aggression would be available to the United States if it had virtually disavowed the employment of nuclear weapons? A definitive answer to this question cannot be offered. What is clear, however, is that the United States must provide the strongest deterrent barrier to war feasible, and effectively withdrawing the threat upon which that deterrent is based would only undermine that objective. If the Soviet leadership can be relatively certain that the United States will not employ nuclear weapons in response to aggression against itself or its allies, the ultimate mainstay of the U.S. deterrent against war would be severely weakened. In short, the bishops' recommendations would serve only to increase the probability of nuclear war by degrading deterrence stability.

The bishops repeatedly observe that the barrier to nuclear war must be strengthened; one theme of the pastoral letter is that we must "say no to nuclear war . . . we must reject nuclear war."[13] That desire is not unique to the bishops; it is shared by nuclear strategists and defense professionals of all stripes. The question is not whether nuclear war should be opposed or supported—no reasonable person advocates nuclear war with the Soviet Union. The real question is how best to establish an effective barrier to nuclear war. Despite the fine intentions and the sincerity of the bishops, their recommendations would only weaken that barrier. Ironically, in their search for a morally acceptable approach to deterrence, the bishops would increase the probabilty of war.

Is there a more acceptable solution to the moral quandary of deterrence—a readiness to commit an evil in the hope of preventing an even greater evil? One potential solution to this deterrence paradox exists that is superior to the deterrence by bluff

[13]Ibid., p. 14.

suggested in the pastoral letter—an approach to deterrence that could both accommodate the principles of just war and also maintain an effective deterrent. Choosing between those two objectives clearly must be avoided if any feasible alternative exists. Unfortunately, the politico-technical assumptions regarding nuclear war (noted above) on which the bishops' subsequent moral assessment was based excluded the possibility that their analysis could have moved in a more fruitful direction. Had the bishops accepted as a politico-technical assumption the existence of a great potential for limiting damage in nuclear war through strategic defensive forces, for example, their subsequent analysis could have been strikingly different.

Offensive targeting discrimination, combined with a commitment to damage limitation, would go beyond the theory of deterrence expressed in the pastoral letter. Redirecting the U.S.-Soviet strategic relationship toward serious preparations for strategic defense could establish the conditions necessary for an approach to deterrence that would be both effective and, arguably, compatible with the principles of discrimination, proportionality, and probability of success. In addition, in contrast to the United States, the Soviet Union gives considerable attention to strategic defense. Consequently, unlike the pastoral letter's recommendations, the approach I am suggesting has some relevance to what might be endorsed by the Soviet Union.

Effective strategic defenses and discriminating offensive targeting could satisfy the bishops' primary objection to an explicit and planned nuclear threat as immoral on the ground that even the limited and discriminating use of nuclear weapons could escalate to a total conflagration that would exclude the possibility for discrimination, proportionality, or success. A commitment to targeting discrimination and a much more defensively oriented strategic relationship could give operational reality to the current U.S. policy of avoiding the intentional destruction of noncombatants and civilian centers. It would also provide the basis for complying with the principle of proportionality in both *jus ad bellum* and *jus ad bello*. Regarding the "probability

of success" principle: a defensive-countermilitary approach to strategic planning would provide a much greater chance for the successful functioning of deterrence than would the approach envisaged in the pastoral letter. In the event that deterrence fails— a possibility the bishops do not address in their suggested approach to deterrence—a defensive-countermilitary orientation would at least hold out the possibility of successfully saving scores of millions of lives and preserving U.S. allies. This, of course, would be a limited success, but it certainly would constitute a worthy, morally pristine objective. In contrast, the deterrence by bluff formula of the pastoral letter presents no option other than an indiscriminate, disproportional holocaust in the event that deterrence fails. Indeed, the bishops' recommendations, and particularly their endorsement of a comprehensive freeze, argue against a commitment to strategic defense and discriminating countermilitary capabilities.[14]

Finally, a defensive-countermilitary approach to deterrence can be viewed as part of a medium-to-long-term solution to the problem of living in a nuclear-armed world. The bishops suggest that deterrence by bluff is an interim measure to be employed only until the goal of nuclear disarmament and a reordering of international authority can be realized. If deterrence by bluff is to provide for Western security until those goals are realized, such a deterrent structure must be sufficiently sturdy to stand for decades, if not longer. The probability that either nuclear disarmament or the establishment of a centralized international authority will occur within the foreseeable future is so low as to be irrelevant. Anyone can suggest less dangerous and more peaceful world orders, and we all appreciate the vision; unfortunately, as has been repeatedly demonstrated, the problem is not imagining better worlds, but getting from here to there.[15]

In summary, the bishops suggest that the United States abandon its now-traditional approach to de-

----

[14]Ibid., pp. 16, 18.
[15]See, for example, Kenneth N. Waltz, *Man, the State, and War* (New York: Columbia University Press, 1954).

terrence and rely upon a deterrent that is highly questionable, until a new world order, which is unlikely ever to be achieved, is achieved. Fortunately, such a course of action is not the only potential means for establishing a morally acceptable deterrent. A defensive-countermilitary approach to strategic planning should provide a more effective deterrent and accommodate the principles of just war. Such a "defensive" solution to the moral dilemma of deterrence could not, of course, be achieved immediately—a defensive transition would take years to achieve. Nevertheless, it is undoubtedly more feasible and closer to realization than the disarmament and new-world-order solutions the bishops suggest. Unfortunately, it appears that the bishops' preliminary assumptions and perhaps predispositions did not permit them to explore such a solution to the moral question of deterrence.

QUESTIONS FOR DISCUSSION

1 Is nuclear deterrence morally justified?
2 How valid are the technical and political judgments made by the bishops about nuclear weapons and strategy?
3 Is the use of nuclear weapons ever morally justifiable?
4 What (if any) kind of nuclear targeting policy is justified under the just-war concept of discrimination?
5 Would the acceptance by the United States of the bishops' recommendations in the Pastoral Letter help or hurt America's security interests? Would it make nuclear war more or less likely?

SUGGESTED READINGS

Castelli, Jim. *The Bishops and the Bomb: Waging Peace in a Nuclear Age.* Garden City, New York: Doubleday, 1983.

Krauthammer, Charles. "On Nuclear Morality," *Commentary* (October 1983), pp. 48–52.

Krol, John Cardinal. "The Catholic Bishops' Concern with Nuclear Armaments," *Annals of the American Academy of Political and Social Science* 469 (September 1983), pp. 38–45.

Novak, Michael. "Moral Clarity in the Nuclear Age," *National Review* (April 1, 1983), pp. 354, 356, 358–60, 362, 364–68, 370, 380–85, 386, and 388.

Okin, Susan Moller. "Taking the Bishops Seriously," *World Politics* 36 (July 1984), pp. 527–54.

Russett, Bruce M. "Ethical Dilemmas of Nuclear Deterrence," *International Security* 8 (Spring 1984), pp. 36–54.

Steinfels, Peter. "Pastoral Preceedings," *New Republic* (May 30, 1983), pp. 15–17.

Tanter, Richard. "Breaking the Nuclear Faith," *Alternatives* 9 (Summer 1983), pp. 99–110.

van Voorst, L. Bruce. "The Churches and Nuclear Deterrence," *Foreign Affairs* 61 (Spring 1983), pp. 827–52.

Waltzer, Michael. *Just and Unjust Wars.* New York: Basic Books, 1977.

Wohlstetter, Albert. "Bishops, Statesmen, and Other Strategists on the Bombing of Innocents," *Commentary* (June 1983), pp. 15–35.

12 Should the United States Deploy the MX Missile?

YES

Brent Scowcroft

Report of the President's Commission on Strategic Forces

NO

Wyche Fowler

[The Case Against the MX]

Report of the President's Commission on Strategic Forces
Brent Scowcroft

1. ICBM LONG-TERM SURVIVABILITY: TOWARD THE SMALL, SINGLE-WARHEAD ICBM

The Commission believes that a single-warhead missile weighing about fifteen tons (rather than the nearly 100 tons of MX) may offer greater flexibility in the long-run effort to obtain an ICBM force that is highly survivable, even when viewed in isolation, and that can consequently serve as a hedge against potential threats to the submarine force.

The Commission thus recommends beginning engineering design of such an ICBM, leading to the initiation of full-scale development in 1987 and an initial operating capability in the early 1990s. The design of such a missile, hardened against nuclear effects, can be achieved with current technology. It should have sufficient accuracy and yield to put Soviet hardened military targets at risk. During that period an approach toward arms control, consistent with such deployments, should also seek to encourage the Soviets to move toward a more stable ICBM force structure at levels which would obviate the need to deploy very large numbers of such missiles. The development effort for such a missile need not and should not be burdened with the uncertainties accompanying a crash program; thus its timing can be such that competitive development is feasibile.

Decisions about such a small missile and its basing will be influenced by several potential developments: the evolution of Soviet strategic programs, the path of arms control negotiations and agreements, general trends in technology, the cost of the program, operational considerations, and the results of our own research on specific basing modes. Although the small missile program should be pursued vigorously, the way these uncertainties are resolved will inevitably influence the size and nature of the program. We should keep in mind,

however, that having several different modes of deployment may serve our objective of stability. The objective for the United States should be to have an overall program that will so confound, complicate, and frustrate the efforts of Soviet strategic war planners that, even in moments of stress, they could not believe that they could attack our ICBM forces effectively.

Different ICBM deployment modes by the U.S. would require different types of planned Soviet attacks. Deployment in hardened silos would require the Soviets to plan to use warheads that are large, accurate, or both. Moreover, for those silos or shelters holding a missile with only one warhead, each would present a far less attractive target than would be the case for a silo containing a large missile with many MIRVs. Mobile deployments of U.S. missiles would require the Soviets to try to barrage large areas using a number of warheads for each of our warheads at risk, to develop very sophisticated intelligence systems, or both. In this context, deployment of a small single-warhead ICBM in hardened mobile launchers is of particular interest because it could permit deployment in peacetime in limited areas such as military reservations. Land-mobile deployments without hard launchers could be threatened by a relatively small attack—in the absence of an appropriate arms control agreement—unless our own missiles were distributed widely across the country in peacetime. The key advantages of a small single-warhead missile are that it would reduce the value of each strategic target and that it is also compatible with either fixed or mobile deployments, or with combinations of the two.

As discussed below (Section VI), deployment of

From Brent Scowcroft, *Report of the President's Commission on Strategic Forces*, April 1983, pp. 15–18.

such small missiles would be compatible with arms control agreements reducing the number of warheads, in which case only a small number of such missiles would probably need to be deployed. If the Soviets proved unwilling to reach such agreements, however, the U.S. could deploy whatever number of small missiles were required—in whatever mix of basing modes—to maintain an adequate overall deterrent.

2. IMMEDIATE ICBM MODERNIZATION: LIMITED DEPLOYMENT OF THE MX MISSILE

a. The MX in Minuteman Silos

There are important needs on several grounds for ICBM modernization that connot be met by the small, single-warhead ICBM.

First, arms control negotiations—in particular the Soviets' willingness to enter agreements that will enhance stability—are heavily influenced by ongoing programs. The ABM Treaty of 1972, for example, came about only because the United States maintained an ongoing ABM program and indeed made a decision to make a limited deployment. It is illusory to believe that we could obtain a satisfactory agreement with the Soviets limiting ICBM deployments if we unilaterally terminated the only new U.S. ICBM program that could lead to deployment in this decade. Such a termination would effectively communicate to the Soviets that we were unable to neutralize their advantage in multiple-warhead ICBMs. Abandoning the MX at this time in search of a substitute would jeopardize, not enhance, the likelihood of reaching a stabilizing and equitable agreement. It would also undermine the incentives to the Soviets to change the nature of their own ICBM force and thus the environment most conducive to the deployment of a small missile.

Second, effective deterrence is in no small measure a question of the Soviets' perception of our national will and cohesion. Cancelling the MX, when it is ready for flight testing, when over $5 billion have already been spent on it, and when its importance has been stressed by the last four Pres-

idents, does not communicate to the Soviets that we have the will essential to effective deterrence. Quite the opposite.

Third, the serious imbalance between the Soviets' massive ability to destroy hardened land-based military targets with their ballistic missile force and our lack of such a capability must be redressed promptly. Our ability to assure our allies that we have the capability and will to stand with them, with whatever forces are necessary, if the alliance is threatened by massive conventional, chemical or biological, or limited nuclear attack is in question as long as this imbalance exists. Even before the Soviet leaders, in a grave crisis, considered using the first tank regiment or the first SS-20 missile against NATO, they must be required to face what war would mean to them. In order to augment what we would hope would be an inherent sense of conservatism and caution on their part, we must have a credible capability for controlled, prompt, limited attack on hard targets ourselves. This capability casts a shadow over the calculus of Soviet risk-taking at any level of confrontation with the West. Consequently, in the interest of the alliance as a whole, we cannot safely permit a situation to continue wherein the Soviets have the capability promptly to destroy a range of hardened military targets and we do not.

Fourth, our current ICBM force is aging significantly. The Titan II force is being retired for this reason and extensive Minuteman rehabilitation programs are planned to keep those missiles operational.

The existence of a production program for an ICBM of approximately 100 tons[1] is important for two additional reasons. As Soviet ABM modernization and modern surface-to-air missile development and deployment proceed—even within the limitations of the ABM treaty—it is important to

---

[1]MX weights 195,000 pounds. Thus it is a "light ICBM" under the terminology of SALT II, approximately the same size as the 330 newly-deployed Soviet SS-19 ICBMs. The MX is well under half the dimensions of the much larger 308 newly-deployed SS-18s; the latter are designated as "modern heavy ICBMs" under SALT II.

be able to match any possible Soviet breakout from that treaty with strategic forces that have the throw-weight to carry sufficient numbers of decoys and other penetration aids; these may be necessary in order to penetrate the Soviet defenses which such a breakout could provide before other compensating steps could be taken. Having in production a missile that could effectively counter such a Soviet step should help deter them from taking it. Moreover, in view of our coming sole reliance on space shuttle orbiters, it would be prudent to have in production a booster, such as MX, that is of sufficient size to place in orbit at least some of our most strategically important satellites.

These objectives can all be accomplished, at reasonable cost, by deploying MX missiles in current Minuteman silos.

In the judgment of the Commission, the vulnerability of such silos in the near term, viewed in isolation, is not a sufficiently dominant part of the overall problem of ICBM modernization to warrant other immediate steps being taken such as closely-spacing new silos or ABM defense of those silos. This is because of the mutual survivability shared by the ICBM force and the bomber force in view of the different types of attacks that would need to be launched at each. . . . In any circumstances other than that of a particular kind of massive surprise attack[2] on the U.S. by the Soviet Union, Soviet planners would have to account for the possibility that MX missiles in Minuteman silos would be available for use, and thus they would help deter such attacks. To deter such surprise attacks we can reasonably rely both on our other strategic forces and on the range of operational uncertainties that the Soviets would have to consider in planning such aggression—as long as we have underway a program for long-term ICBM survivability such as that for the small, single warhead ICBM to hedge against long-term vulnerability for the rest of our forces.

None of the short-term needs for ICBM force modernization set forth above would be met by deploying any missile other than the MX.

The Commission examined the concept of a common missile to serve the function of both the Trident II (D-5) missile, now under development for the Trident submarine, and of MX. At this point such a common missile would essentially be a modified Trident II. But deployment of that missile as an ICBM would not only lag several years behind the MX, its payload at the full ICBM range would be reduced. Since a larger number of Trident II missiles would need to be deployed in order to have the same number of warheads as the MX force, there would be no cost savings.

The Commission also assessed the possibility of improving the guidance on the Minuteman ICBM to the level of accuracy being developed for the MX. Such a step, however, would take some two to three years longer than production of the MX and would not redress the perceived imbalance between U.S. and Soviet capabilities. The wisdom of placing new guidance systems on the front ends of aging 1960s-era missiles is highly questionable. Moreover, shifting to such a program at this point would not provide the increased throw-weight needed to hedge either against Soviet ABM improvements or against the need to launch satellites in an emergency. Most importantly, a Minuteman modification program would not provide the incentive to the Soviets to negotiate that would be provided by production of the MX.

A program of deploying on the order of 100 MX missiles in existing Minuteman silos would, on the other hand, accomplish the objectives set forth in this section and it would do so without threatening stability. The throw-weight and megatonnage carried by the 100 MX missiles is about the same as that of the 54 large Titan missiles now being retired plus that of the 100 Minuteman III missiles that the MXs would replace. Such a deployment would thus represent a replacement and modernization of part of our ICBM force. It would provide a means of controlled limited attack on hardened targets but not a sufficient number of warheads to be able to

---

[2]An attack in which thousands of warheads were targeted at our ICBM fields but there were no early detonations on our bomber bases from attacks by Soviet submarines.

attack all hardened Soviet ICBMs, much less all of the many command posts and other hardened military targets in the Soviet Union. Thus it would not match the overall capability of the recent Soviet deployment of over 600 modern ICBMs of MX size or larger. But a large deployment of several hundred MX missiles should be unnecessary for the limited but very important purposes set forth above. Should the Soviets refuse to engage in stabilizing arms control and engage instead in major new deployments, reconsideration of this and other conclusions would be necessary. . . .

[The Case Against the MX]
Wyche Fowler

. . . . Mr. Chairman, it is with great regret that I must rise in opposition to the most recent attempt to salvage the MX missile. For though, in all honesty, I have never been an advocate of this missile, I share in the earnest desire of individuals in the executive branch, the Congress, and the private sector to develop a national consensus on the critical issue of nuclear weapons policy.

However, it is ludicrous to accept a nonsolution to our national security needs which carries a price tag of $20 billion. After many years of study, after intensive analysis of dozens of alternatives, the fact remains that no satisfactory, survivable basing system for land-based missiles has been proposed.

THE MILITARY DIMENSION

Much of the debate on the MX, in the press, in the various recommendations of the administration, and in the Halls of Congress, has been over political, or psychological, or economic issues. These are, of course, important questions. But the MX is after all a military program and in the final analysis it must be evaluated in terms of its value to our national security. As we look beyond Soviet rhetoric and Soviet intentions to consider their military capabilities when determining our own defense needs, so it is with them: we must count on the Soviets looking at the military utility of the systems we deploy, not at our expressed reasons for deploying them.

In this light, the MX is a first-strike weapon, pure and simple. Certainly, when viewed in isolation 100 MX missiles carrying 1,000 warheads would not pose a high threat to Soviet ICBM's and other hardened military and political sites. But, as the Scowcroft Commission itself pointed out in examining the question of ICBM vulnerability, we cannot consider our strategic forces in isolation, and neither can the Soviets. So to the 1,000 warhead MX must be added our existing force of 900 Minuteman III Mark 12A warheads, the current and projected air-breathing leg of the triad, the Trident II program which is now being developed, and the efforts to upgrade the war-fighting capacity of our strategic command, control, and communications systems. Taken together, these developments would pose a comparable theoretical threat to the Soviet ICBM's, which account for about 70 percent of Soviet strategic capability, faced by our ICBM's, which represent only 22 percent of our strategic arsenal.

What makes the MX a particularly threatening weapons system, to us as well as the Soviets, is its similarities to the Soviet SS-18's and SS-19's which we view as most dangerous: a large number of high-yield, high-accuracy MIRV'd warheads on each launcher deployed in a nonsurvivable basing mode. In other words, these are systems which have countersilo capacity but are vulnerable to enemy attack. Thus, they have value only as first-strike weapons.

Statement of Wyche Fowler, *Congressional Record*, July 20, 1983, pp. H5315–H5318.

As a retaliatory threat, the MX lacks credibility. According to a recent CBO [Congressional Budget Office] study, which is consistent with Defense Department estimates, the MX could contribute 3 percent in 1990 and less than 1 percent in 1996 of all surviving U.S. hard-target warheads in the event of a Soviet first strike occuring after some warning, and 5 percent in 1990 and 1 percent in 1996 of such warheads in the event of a Soviet bolt out of the blue.

And what of the retaliatory utility of those surviving warheads? Is there anyone who believes that after having launched a preemptive strike the Soviets would not place their remaining strategic forces in a launch on warning posture?

Even as a deterrent to conventional or the dubious limited nuclear warfare escalation, the MX lacks military value. A homeland-to-homeland attack on strategic missiles is not an attractive option if one wishes to control or limit hostilities.

All of this really brings us to the central issue that should surround our decision on the MX: What do we want from our strategic forces and how will this particular weapons system fit in with those objectives?

DETERRENCE

What we have demanded from our strategic nuclear bombers and missiles from the beginning is that they be able to deter Soviet attack on the United States and our allies. In this they have been successful. As Secretary Weinberger stated in his fiscal year 1984 annual report to the Congress:

> Today, deterrence remains—as it has for the past 37 years—the cornerstone of our strategic nuclear policy. To deter successfully, we must be able—and must be seen to be able—to *respond* to any potential aggression in such a manner that the costs we will exact will substantially exceed any gains the aggressor might hope to achieve. [Italics added.]

I strongly believe that these conditions for deterrence exist now, with our current forces, and will continue to exist with or without the MX.

SURVIVABILITY

For the United States, a credible deterrent requires that we be able to ride out a first strike with sufficient surviving military capability to inflict unacceptable damage on any adversary. The only major flaw that has been postulated for our current strategic force posture was the so-called window of vulnerability supposedly created by the theoretical vulnerability of our landbased ICBM's to the fourth generation of Soviet ICBM's. The Scowcroft Commission essentially dismissed this threat by pointing, correctly in my view, to the overall system survivability of our strategic Triad. Whether or not one accepts this conclusion, it is undeniable that the MX system now before the Congress does nothing to improve the survivability of our strategic arsenal.

MILITARY CAPABILITY

As to the military capability of our survivable strategic forces, they now possess, and will increasingly possess over the next several years, the ability to cover the whole range of Soviet military, political, and economic targets, with the possible exception of hardened missile silos. As I mentioned earlier, this latter set of targets is questionable at best for retaliatory, second-strike response.

While some have questioned the durability of our strategic systems because of the age of many of our launch vehicles, the previous and planned upgrades and modernizations of our existing strategic forces continue to provide for the military effectivenes of these weapons. For proof of this proposition, I would point out that even in the year 2000 the Reagan administration projects that we would still be deploying all of our current force of Minuteman II and III missiles, with the exception of 100 Minuteman III's which are to be replaced by the MX, and 96 B-52H bombers. However, regardless of how one views the current and projected retaliatory capability of our strategic forces, once again as with survivability the MX makes little or no contribution to our military posture. The aforementioned CBO study revealed that the MX will contribute at most 1 percent of survivable, hard-target-capable U.S. warheads by 1996.

STABILITY

In addition to survivability and sufficient military capability, deterrence is enhanced by weapons systems that promote crisis stability. We should deploy strategic forces that afford a maximum amount of time for reaction, on the part of both sides, to defuse or limit strategic accidents or to allow cooler heads to prevail in a period of serious tensions. But here again the MX does not contribute to deterrence. It is not a credible second-strike weapon, for reasons I mentioned earlier. Its only value from a military standpoint would come if it was governed by a first strike or launch-on-warning policy. Neither of these, quite obviously, would enhance stability.

As a military system, the MX fails on all counts in performing its essential role of deterrence. As McGeorge Bundy wrote in a recent article:

> For almost 30 years, we have made survivable second-strike strength our central strategic standard. Are we now to move, in a cloud of consensus prose and good intentions, to a non-survivable first-strike system?

THE SCOWCROFT COMMISSION

In making its case for the MX in fixed silos, the Scowcroft Commission cited four primary reasons: the MX would be an incentive for Soviet agreement to arms-control measures; it would be a clear expression of national resolve; it would redress our current disadvantage in time-urgent hard-target-kill capability; and it would address the problems caused by the aging of our strategic forces. In my opinion, none of these arguments is compelling.

THE MX AND ARMS CONTROL

Many of my friends on this side of the aisle have been persuaded to support the latest MX plan be-

cause of its supposed contribution to arms control. Under this view, the deployment of 100 MX missiles in fixed silos will cause the Soviets to see the folly of such deployments and they will negotiate away all or a substantial part of their 638 SS-18 and SS-19 ICBM's. I find this argument unconvincing for at least two reasons.

First of all, I am not at all sure that we can predict with any confidence how the Soviets will react to the proposed MX deployment. As the recent Brookings Institution study of Soviet strategic forces concluded:

> The U.S.S.R. has not attempted simply to replicate the American strategic posture, nor are its strategic responses free from its own traditions or the influences of its institutional process. Rather, such factors as the basic geographical and political situation of the U.S.S.R., its distinctive military traditions and strategic doctrine, its particular institutions and technological base are all elements in the process that shapes Soviet strategic responses.

There are a number of ways that the Soviets could react to the MX deployment besides the trade off of SS-18's and SS-19's. They could react militarily by increasing the alert rate of their strategic forces, or adopting a launch-on-warning policy, or breaking out of the SALT-imposed restraints on ICBM deployment. They could respond politically by proposing arms control agreements that would limit other areas of the strategic competition, like total numbers of warheads or missiles. If these responses sound familiar, they are among the ways that we have considered reacting to the Soviet deployment of SS-18's and SS-19's during the 1970's.

While the Soviets might react in the way we want them to, I would not assess the probability as overwhelming, certainly not enough to place a $20 billion gamble on an otherwise destabilizing weapon system.

Second, if the Soviets can be persuaded in a positive way to respond to threats to the survivability of their fourth-generation ICBM's, we already have abundant incentives in place or underway. In the words of four of my colleagues from across the aisle, Representatives Green, Leach, Schneider, and Jeffords:

> As the Scowcroft Commission pointed out, the existing U.S. deterrent is strong and credible, and the strategic modernization programs planned by the Administration—air, ground, and sea-launched cruise missiles, improvements in command and communications, the Trident II, and the "Stealth" bomber—give the Soviets ample incentive to bargain in Geneva.

To that, I would add that our existing force of Minuteman III missiles and B-52 bombers already possess the theoretical capability to destroy Soviet ICBM's. As a matter of fact, until the Trident II SLBM is deployed, it will be the bomber leg of the Triad that continues to afford by far the largest share of survivable hard-target warheads.

THE MX AND NATIONAL WILL

A second argument advanced by the Scowcroft Commission in favor of its MX recommendations is that the simple fact of MX deployment, whatever its military value, will be a necessary demonstration of national will to the Soviets and to our allies. Once again I must dissent.

In the first place, it has been my experience that the Soviet national security establishment, like our own, is more impressed with capabilities than with intentions, and more influenced by military utility than psychology. The only capability offered by the MX is that of a first-strike or launch-on-warning weapon. This is hardly the message I should think we would want to convey to the Kremlin. The military contribution of the MX, as part of the overall array of U.S. nuclear and conventional weapons, is very, very small.

In the second place, the national will argument is premised on the notion, whether expressed or not, that such a demonstration is necessary because it has been lacking. We are all abundantly familiar with this issue and we will be arguing it here in this Chamber on other issues in the near future. I believe that this claim is not only wrong but is a great insult to those Americans who have carried out and paid for many such demonstrations over the last 40 years.

Today American service men and women, diplomatic personnel, Peace Corps volunteers, and foreign aid officials are scattered around the globe demonstrating our commitment to our interests and our values, often risking their lives. From Lebanon, to South Korea, to Western Europe, to the Persian Gulf, to southern Africa, to the Caribbean Basin, to Japan: we are there. As is often pointed out when the occasion suits, we as a nation continue to shoulder more than our fair share of the defense burden for the Western Alliance, measured in total spending, or per capita spending, or men under arms, or almost any defense measure one could name.

Finally, looking exclusively at the issue of strategic nuclear forces, it is patently untrue that we have stood still over the past few years. The American people, who have financed the construction of our strategic arsenal and who have elected all of us sworn to provide for the common defense, deserve to be told the truth. For example, in the decade of the 1970's we more than doubled the number of our strategic warheads, going from 4,000 to over 9,000. We modernized each leg of the triad. Since 1980, we have already committed ourselves to an even more ambitious strategic build-up, with or without the MX, including not only new weapons systems, such as the Trident II missile and the advanced technology bomber, but also a major upgrading of our strategic command, control, and communications systems.

THE MX AND PROMPT COUNTERSILO TARGETING

The Scowcroft Commission also endorses the MX as a means for achieving time-urgent hard-target kill capability. Translated, this refers to the ability to successfully attack hardened missile silos within a matters of minutes. While our bomber force and Minuteman III missiles already possess the desired hard-target-kill capacity, the latter also representing a prompt response time, the MX is supposed to provide a unique and desirable military capability.

Yet, as we have already seen, as a retaliatory weapon the MX makes little contribution to survivable hard-target warheads. When Trident II is deployed, the MX contribution even in the more specialized category of survivable, prompt, hard-target warheads is relatively small. By 1996, the MX would furnish only between 1 and 7 percent of U.S. military capacity in this regard.

But beyond the simple question of what the proposed MX system would add to our military capability to promptly attack Soviet Union silos, the larger question is whether or not such a capability is useful to the United States.

If we consider the MX as a first-strike weapon then this missile would make a significantly larger contribution to our attack force. But I do not for a moment believe that the United States of America would ever adopt such a course as national policy. If we went to launch on warning, the MX would also become more important. But, do we really want to narrow our decisionmaking time even further when it comes down to the biggest life or death question ever faced by humanity?

Even as a retaliatory weapon, how militarily important is it to be able to promptly target missile silos? A sizable portion of such targets would have presumably been emptied in the first-strike that precipitated the response. As for the rest, it is highly unlikely that a nation which has already chosen to initiate hostilities by striking first would not place its remaining strategic forces in a launch-on-warning posture. If such is not the case and the remaining ICBM's are withheld, then the Soviet silos holding unused ICBM's would be targetable by non-prompt, hard-target warheads as well.

With the military case for the MX's time-urgent, hard-target-kill capability ambiguous at best, we are left with the psychological-military justification of mirror-imaging: that is, that we must possess this capacity because the Soviets have it.

In my view, we should not try to copy Soviet force structure. Let me say very clearly that it is

this structure, which the Soviets have constructed, that threatens nuclear stability. It is Soviet actions, particularly the deployment of their high-yield, high-accuracy, multiple-warhead fourth-generation ICBM's, that have moved us all closer to the nuclear abyss. And it is precisely because of my profound mistrust of past and future Soviet military decisions that I strongly believe we must not try to duplicate their strategic posture.

Two hands on the nuclear hair trigger are more dangerous than one, especially when we can continue to deliver a mortal blow to Soviet society in response to any first shot.

Also, we should recognize that part of the reason for Soviet concentration of more than two-thirds of their strategic striking power in land-based forces stems from their lack of confidence in the reliability and readiness of their air- and sea-based strategic systems. We should be under no similar constraint.

In summary, we should design our strategic forces to fit our own mission requirements, not those of the Soviet Union. Those requirements remain today, as they have been for almost 40 years, centered on the provision of deterrence. No other course can satisfy our national security, as well as our political and moral objectives.

THE MX AND FORCE MODERNIZATION

The last major rationale put forth by the Scowcroft Commission on behalf of its MX recommendation is that it is a necessary modernization of our aging strategic forces.

Parts of our strategic force structure are older than their Soviet counterparts, but it is military capability and not age that determines the value of a weapons system. As I pointed out earlier, even under Reagan administration modernization plans we would be retaining all of our current Minuteman missiles, except for the 100 which are to be removed in order to make room for the MX, and all of our B-52 model H's through the end of the century. And there is no technical barrier to our maintaining additional B-52's and Poseidon submarines at least until that time.

Additionally, we have been modernizing our strategic forces over the past several years to the point that our currently deployed warheads are at least as new as the Soviet arsenal of strategic warheads. At this time, I would like to insert, for the RECORD, a recent factsheet put out by the Center for Defense Information on improvements in U.S. strategic nuclear weapons from 1970 to the present.

CENTER FOR DEFENSE INFORMATION

Improvements in U.S. Strategic Nuclear Weapons from 1970 to the Present

In early October, Secretary of Defense Weinberger said, "The simple fact of the matter is that we haven't done any strengthening or any modernization of our strategic systems virtually since they were built—Minuteman in the 50's and some of the submarines in the last years."

In a press conference on 19 January, President Reagan said, "So up until now, in previous negotiations, they (the Soviets) haven't had to make any concession because we were unilaterally disarming."

The Facts:

The number of U.S. strategic nuclear weapons rose from 4,000 in 1970 to 9,200 in 1980. Today, the U.S. has approximately 9,800 strategic nuclear weapons.

1 1965–73—Replacement of Minuteman I with Minuteman II missiles.

2 1970–75—Replacement of MM I and MM II with 550 MM III missiles.

3 1970–75—MIRVing of 550 MM III ICBMs. (1650 MK12 weapons).

4 1971–76—Replacement of Polaris A-3 SLBMs with 496 Poseidon C-3 SLBMs.

5 1971–77—MIRVing of 496 SLBMs on Poseidon subs. (About 5,000 weapons).

6 1966–76—Addition of 76 FB-111 SAC bombers and 356 F-111 nuclear capable bombers to U.S. Air Forces.

7 1972–75—Addition of Short-Range Attack Missile (SRAM) to B-52, FB-111 aircraft, 1,140 now in inventory.

8 1979–83—Retrofitting of 900 MK12A weapons on 300 MM III ICBMs.

9 1978–82—Retrofitting of 192 Trident missiles on 12 Poseidon subs. (About 1,500–1,600 weapons).

10 1976–81—Construction of 8 and delivery of two Trident subs.

11 1981—Air Launched Cruise Missile operational. (At least 4,348 to go on B-52G/Hs.)

12 Throughout the 1970's—B-52 Improvements. (Some for only B-52G/H versions): Offensive Avionics, Electronic Counter Measures, Electro-optical Viewing, Terminals for AFSATCOM, Fuselage Extension, Enlarged bomb bay, EMP Hardening, New Engines, SRAM Carriage, ALCM Carriage, Wing Skin Change, Shortened Tail.

13 Throughout the 1970's—FB-111 Improvements: Larger Wings, Strengthened Landing Gear, Offensive Avionics, EMP Hardening, SRAM Carriage, New Engines, ECM, Structural Strengthening.

14 Throughout the 1970's—Other ICBM Improvements: Command Data Buffer System (MM III), Silo Hardening (MM and Titan), New Launch Control System (MM), Airborne Launch Control System (MMIII), INS-20 Guidance system (MMIII).

15 Ongoing R & D Programs throughout the 1970's—Ballistic Missile Defense (Deployed in 1976), Anti-Satellite Weapons (Testing in 1982, Operational—1985), Lasers and Particle Beam Weapons, MARV (First test in 1975), Anti-Submarine Warfare.

Finally, even without the MX, in the past 2 years the Congress has adopted a costly, multiyear commitment to further modernization of the Triad and the command, control, and communications systems.

CONCLUSION

I have tried to demonstrate that the latest MX scheme would not make a significant military contribution to our defense posture, would weaken rather than strengthen deterrence, would not improve arms-control prospects, is not necessary to demonstrate national will, is undesirable as a prompt countersilo weapon, and is not necessary for strategic force modernization.

I have not talked much about the economics of the MX, or of what else we could buy in terms of reducing the deficit or of upgrading our conventional defenses if we forego the additional $20 billion investment in the MX.

There remains the question of the Scowcroft package of MX-Midgetman arms control. Much has been said on both sides of the issue as to the necessity of linking the three elements. I suppose that the linkage rests in the eye of the beholder. For the record, as one Member of Congress, I have grave reservations about all three elements of the deal as currently understood.

The Midgetman, while clearly less destabilizing than the MX, will be laboring under the same vulnerability and verification difficulties encountered by all the other attempts to devise a new land basing mode for ICBM's, and will be facing even greater safety and security concerns.

While I applaud the general commitment to arms control negotiations, and the move toward focusing on warheads rather than launchers as the key area for control, I am troubled by the initial negotiating strategies being touted on Capitol Hill and at the White House, including the guaranteed build-down. This latter approach, as now defined, does nothing to guarantee that the force modernization it promotes will provide greater stability, and does nothing to restrain the technological competition that has done the most to destabilize the current nuclear balance.

However, the Midgetman and guaranteed build-down are new suggestions that need and deserve further study and refinement. They could yet provide useful additions to our strategic force policies. Such is not the case with the MX.

The MX is bad policy, militarily, economically, and politically. If it is the price to be paid for consensus, the Midgetman and the build-down, then it is too high a price.

We do need a national consensus to govern our national strategic policies, but such a consensus must at the very least be based on sound military and arms control strategies. I submit that the MX does not pass either test and should be rejected.

QUESTIONS FOR DISCUSSION

1 Is maintaining ICBMs essential to make the American nuclear deterrent credible?
2 What are the methods of protecting the MX against a first-strike by the Soviet Union?
3 What are the alternatives to the MX?
4 Does the deployment of the MX weaken strategic stability?
5 What effect does the deployment of the MX have on the future prospects for arms control agreements between the United States and the Soviet Union?

SUGGESTED READINGS

Canan, James W. "A Full-Bodied Triad," *Air Force Magazine* 67 (February 1984), pp. 50–54.

Edwards, John. *Superweapon: The Making of MX*. New York: Norton, 1983.

Gray, Colin S. *The MX ICBM and National Security*. New York: Praeger, 1981.

————. "Why Does the United States Need ICBMs?" *NATO's Fifteen Nations* 27 (August–September 1982), pp. 80–84.

Lawyers Alliance for Nuclear Arms Control, Inc. *The Case Against the MX Missile*. Boston, Massachusetts: Lawyers Alliance for Nuclear Arms Control, Inc., 1983.

Scoville, Herbert, Jr. *MX: Prescription for Disaster*. Cambridge, Massachusetts: MIT Press, 1981.

Stewart, Blair, "Peacekeeper: Deterrence and Crisis Stability Must Be Considered in Examining Deployment of the Strategic Weapon," *Defense Systems Review* 2 (June 1984), pp. 46–52.

U.S. Congress: House of Representatives. *Review of Arms Control Implications of the Report of the President's Commission on Strategic Forces*. Hearings before the Committee on Foreign Affairs, 98th Cong., 1st Sess., 1983.

U.S. Congress: Senate. *President's Commission on Strategic Forces*. Hearings before the Committee on Foreign Relations, 98th Cong., 1st Sess., 1983.

U.S. Congress. Senate. *U.S. Strategic Doctrine*. Hearings before the Committee on Foreign Relations, 97th Cong., 2nd Sess., 1982.

Woolsey, R. James. "The Politics of Vulnerability: 1980–83," *Foreign Affairs* 62 (Spring 1984), pp. 805–19.

13. Should the United States Make Civil Defense a High Priority?

YES

Leon Gouré

The Soviet Civil Defense Program and the Present U.S. Civil Defense Debate

NO

Jennifer Leaning

Civil Defense in the Nuclear Age: Strategic, Medical, and Demographic Aspects

The Soviet Civil Defense Program and the Present U.S. Civil Defense Debate
Leon Gouré

The ongoing debate about a civil defense program is unfortunately characterized by a great deal of misunderstandings about the role and utility as well as limitations of civil defense in a nuclear war and its implications for strategic stability and deterrence. In a large measure, proponents and opponents of civil defense talk "at" and not "to" each other, basing their arguments on different and often incompatible premises, assumptions, "scientific facts" and scenarios.

Everyone agrees on the utility of civil defense for dealing with peacetime natural or man-made disasters. Given that such disasters could be on a very large scale, involving entire states and regions and requiring massive rescue, damage-limiting and population relocation efforts, there is an obvious overlap between civil defense programs for peacetime and war threat situations. For example, civil defense is currently required to be prepared to implement large-scale evacuation of the population in the face of threats posed by hurricanes, earthquakes, accidents at nuclear power plants, in the event of nuclear terrorism, etc. Of course, civil defense measures for dealing with a nuclear war threat call for preparations and capabilities on a larger scale than those required for peacetime disasters and also for various additional measures.

In the debate on the utility of a civil defense program for a nuclear war threat situation, it is common practice to cite the cases of the nuclear strikes on Hiroshima and Nagasaki and the effects on a sheltered population of the fire raid on Dresden during World War II. In fact, however, these cases only substantiate the terrible consequences of a lack of effective civil defense rather than give evidence of its ineffectiveness. The populations of these cit-ies had not been evacuated; shelters then in use were very simple and not capable of protecting their occupants against the effects of nuclear weapons or fire storms, and they were not designed and equipped for protracted occupancy; and in the most frequently cited example of Hiroshima, most of the city's residents were not in their shelters at the time of the nuclear detonation because the attack was preceded by an all-clear signal.

Because the civil defense debate in the U.S. is still largely theoretical, it seems more useful to discuss the role and utility of civil defense in the context of an actual program such as that in the Soviet Union. The existence of a large, comprehensive, well-financed, and long-standing Soviet civil defense program has been reported on by the U.S. intelligence community and several U.S. Secretaries of Defense and is beyond question. Furthermore, the Soviet leadership and official and public media are fairly candid about Soviet views on the necessity for a civil defense program for a nuclear war situation and openly discuss its character, objectives and requirements, as well as the measures being implemented. According to U.S. intelligence assessments, only the annual costs of Soviet full time military and civilian civil defense personnel and shelter construction represent a U.S. equivalent cost of some $3 billion. The annual cost of the entire program is likely to be close to twice that amount. Despite this burden, however, the Soviet leadership obviously believes in the utility of civil defense and, as Soviet officials frequently point out, "The party and the government are paying constant attention to improving USSR Civil Defense." Indeed, according to Soviet official announcements, 1983 marks the start of a new pro-

Leon Gouré, "The Soviet Civil Defense Program and the Present U.S. Civil Defense Debate" (written statement), U.S. Cong., House of Representatives, *Defense Department Authorization and Oversight, Part 8: Civil Defense,* Hearings before the Committee on Armed Services, 98th Cong., 1st Sess., 1983, pp. 223–29.

gram to further improve Soviet civil defense capabilities and levels of readiness and to prepare "every stratum of the population" for effective and rapid implementation of civil defense measures in the event of a threat of nuclear war.

It is in the context of the Soviet civil defense program, therefore, that it may be useful to discuss some key issues pertaining to civil defense—i.e., war initiation scenarios, the role and effectiveness of civil defense in mitigating human losses and property damage, and the implications of civil defense for strategic stability and credible deterrence.

WAR INITIATION SCENARIOS

Any civil defense program, whether U.S. or Soviet, is sensitive to assumptions about the character of war initiation. The worst-case scenario which is most often cited by opponents of civil defense is based on two assumptions: 1) the enemy strikes out of the blue, i.e., he achieves total surprise, and 2) he engages in a massive counter-population attack, i.e., multi-megaton strikes against all significant cities. No one can dispute the apocalyptic consequences of such a scenario, which would be all the worse in the absence of any blast shelters for the urban population. The Soviet leadership does not discount the possibility of a surprise attack or a short warning scenario. Since the early 1970s, the stated official Soviet objective is to provide over time all residents of potentially targeted cities with protection in blast shelters. This is not, however, the preferred Soviet war initiation scenario or one which is assumed to be necessarily the most likely to happen.

The worst-case scenarios are by no means the most probable ones or the only ones for assessing the utility of civil defense. This is so for several reasons.

First, the Soviets believe in the likelihood that the start of any nuclear war will be preceded by a period of worsening political crisis or would occur as a consequence of a progressive escalation of more limited military conflicts.

Second, Soviet strategic doctrine rejects the "mutual assured destruction" concept and the strategy of targeting cities and the population per se. Soviet targeting doctrine is geared to warfighting objectives, i.e., priority is given to counterforce targets in order to destroy the opponent's warfighting capabilities, especially his nuclear delivery systems and his command and control. From a Soviet viewpoint, strikes against targets which do not directly affect U.S. retaliatory capabilities and capabilities to offer military resistance such as the general population and non-defense related elements of the economy are wasteful of valuable and limited nuclear assets.

Third, the Soviet Union as well as the U.S. has a common interest in practicing city avoidance in their targeting doctrine and strategy. Both have an advantage in holding the opponent's cities hostage rather than in initiating city attacks which will provoke retaliation in kind. This is essentially the concept of the U.S. countervailing strategy adopted by the Carter Administration and still in force.

Fourth, the Soviet military and civil defense systems still remain largely dependent on adequate pre-attack warning and a period of mobilization and preparation for nuclear war, including urban evacuation. Soviet military leaders persistently note that the preparedness for war and its effective conduct require the call up of reservists and draftees for service in the armed forces, the deployment of the Soviet Armed Forces, the repositioning of units away from probable targets of enemy strikes, the rapid conversion of the civilian industry to defense production, etc. Soviet civil defense also envisages a number of necessary preparatory measures such as: the preparation and stocking of shelters and the constructrion of additional rapidly-erectable shelters; the evacuation from the cities of leadership and elite elements, off-duty shifts of essential workers and large urban civil defense forces and their staffs *regardless* of the availability of blast shelters in urban areas; the preparation of stocks for sustaining the operations of essential industries, utilities, and services, etc.

Taken all together, it appears that while the worst-case scenario, i.e., a massive Soviet surprise attack on military as well as industrial-population targets, cannot be entirely ruled out, it is not the most likely war initiation scenario confronting the United States.

CIVIL DEFENSE AND THE MITIGATION OF LOSSES

It is possible to construct hypothetical attack scenarios which can negate the effectiveness of any civil defense program. To do so, however, one must assume that a potential enemy will have an unlimited supply of nuclear weapons and delivery systems, continuous good intelligence and a commitment to the total destruction of the opponent's country. In such a scenario, the enemy would not only target the cities and the economy, but also all identified shelters whether they are concentrated or dispersed even if the number of persons thereby killed per detonated weapon would be small, he would target the dispersed evacuated urban population in its hosting areas with the same low effectiveness per weapon, and he would maximize radioactive contamination by surface bursting all or most of his weapons. Many of the arguments of opponents of civil defense explicitly or implicitly appear to be based on such a scenario. In fact, however, it is totally unrealistic. Not only is the number of nuclear weapons in Soviet and U.S. arsenals limited and insufficient to target shelters or a dispersed population, but both countries intend to keep a significant portion of their strategic nuclear capabilities in reserve. Neither country targets the population per se. Indeed, Soviet urban evacuation plans do not anticipate any U.S. strikes against the evacuated and dispersed population and only see a need to protect it against radioactive fallout. It is also probable that a high proportion of Soviet weapons would be air rather than surface burst in order to maximize the area subjected to destructive blast overpressures.

In assessing the effectiveness of any civil defense for a nuclear war situation, it must be clearly understood that its measures can only mitigate but by no means totally negate the destructive consequences of a nuclear attack. Even under the best of circumstances these consequences would be horrendous in terms of human losses and material damage as well as long-term effects on the national economy and the population's quality of life. The utility of civil defense is primarily reflected in its ability to reduce human losses and the consequences of a nuclear attack from levels where no national survival may be possible to where prospects for such survival are at least significantly enhanced.

The mitigating effects of civil defense are often portrayed in numerical terms. According to many estimates, in the absence of any civil defense measures a massive Soviet nuclear attack against military and urban industrial targets is likely to kill 110 to 140 million American citizens and, according to former Secretary of Defense Harold Brown, possibly as many as 155 to 160 million. In other words, in the worst case, up to 70 percent of the unprotected U.S. population may die from the direct effects of a Soviet attack. If the cities had been evacuated prior to an attack and the population provided with anti-radiation shelters, it is usually estimated that U.S. population fatalities from the direct effects of Soviet strikes would be on the order of 20 to 40 million. Even a limited Soviet attack targeted only against U.S. strategic forces has been estimated to be likely to cause in excess of 10 million American fatalities if the population remains unprotected. Obviously such numbers are horrifying and in any normal sense unacceptable to Americans. The question, however, is not whether the U.S. would deliberately accept such losses, but whether—if a war is foisted on the U.S.—such losses negate the value of civil defense. In other words, the question is whether it is worthwhile and a reasonable objective to invest in measures which may save the lives of some 70 to 120 million American citizens who otherwise may die in the absence of such measures. Obviously the death of 70 percent and 17 percent of the population would have different implications for prospects of U.S. national survival.

The Soviet civil defense program and capabilities reflect a similar potential mitigation of the effects of possible U.S. retaliatory strikes. According to U.S. intelligence estimates in a worst-case scenario, i.e., with no or very short warning of an attack against Soviet military and industrial-urban targets, the Soviet Union is likely to suffer some 100 million Soviet casualties (both fatalities and injuries) or about 36 percent of the present population. With adequate warning, however, and the implementation of Soviet urban evacuation and the sheltering of the population in blast and rapidly-erected anti-radiation shelters, it is estimated that Soviet fatalities will decline to some 20–30 million or 7 to 11 percent of the present population. It is also believed that the elements of the population which the Soviet leadership especially values for system survival, sustained logistic support of the armed forces, and post-attack recovery are given the best protection and have high prospects of surviving U.S. strikes. Obviously the Soviet leadership believes the mitigating effects of civil defense to be worth large investments and efforts to achieve.

It is sometimes argued that even if civil defense measures can save a majority of the population from certain death, it is probable that large numbers will subsequently die from starvation, disease and the effects of residual radiation. Of course, the character of a post-strike environment is difficult to predict with any exactness and in any event will depend on the character of the attack itself. What can be said, however, is that many additional deaths are not inevitable. The survival of the population in the post-strike environment will largely depend not only on the nature of the attack but also on the character of the measures taken to anticipate the problems posed by the post-attack environment. For example, Soviet civil defense plans call for the stockpiling of sufficient food to sustain the population in a post-strike situation until agricultural production can be resumed, for measures to protect food and agricultural resources, and for the employment of various decontamination techniques to ensure the safety of agricultural produce. Soviet plans also very reasonably call for the evacuation

of urban public health and medical organizations and personnel prior to an attack and their compulsory integration into a civil defense medical service deployed in the exurban areas in a network of hospitals, clinics, and aid stations, as well as for the stockpiling in safe places of medical supplies. While the Soviets recognize that the population's living conditions in a post-attack environment most likely will be harsh, although not necessarily any worse than those which existed in the USSR immediately after World War II, they do not expect them to be unbearable and certainly not fraught with any high probability of resulting in the additional death of tens of millions of Soviet citizens.

CIVIL DEFENSE AND STRATEGIC STABILITY

It is often said in the U.S. that civil defense, by creating an "illusion" of nuclear war survival, would be destabilizing because it may make it easier for the American government and people to resort to rash actions which could provoke a nuclear war with the Soviet Union. People who hold this view do not believe, however, that the Soviet civil defense program, which is well advanced, would encourage the Soviet leadership to risk actions which could provoke a full-scale nuclear war. Such arguments cannot be taken seriously. They essentially imply that the U.S. government is more aggressive and war-like than the Soviet leadership, and that the U.S. government and people may deliberately disregard the risk of some 20 to 40 million American deaths and massive damage to the economy and private property. No conceivable U.S. administration would take such a frivolous view or believe that it can act more aggressively and court a nuclear war with the Soviet Union because it has some capabilities to mitigate its consequences.

There is also no basis for the argument that a U.S. civil defense program would be perceived by the Soviet Union as being destabilizing, although, no doubt, Soviet propaganda would criticize such a program. The Soviet Union has publicly rejected a strategic balance based on the concept of "mutual assured destruction." The Soviet Union openly states that civil defense is a necessary "humanitarian" measure and an essential element of a rational Soviet defense posture in the age of nuclear weapons and U.S.-Soviet rivalry. If, as Soviet spokesmen argue, Soviet civil defense is not destabilizing or provocative, surely a U.S. program will also have neither effect.

On the contrary, a strong argument can be made that a U.S. civil defense program for protecting the American people in a nuclear war situation would tend to contribute to strategic stability. At present the Soviet Union has a war survival doctrine and has developed strong active and passive strategic defense capabilities which it continues to improve. By contrast, the U.S. has neither such a doctrine nor such capabilities. There is no doubt that strategic defense constitutes the most significant area of asymmetry in the U.S.-Soviet strategic balance. Given that the Soviets regard civil defense as a "factor of strategic significance" and the sensitivity of the U.S. and Soviet Union to any significant asymmetries in the strategic balance, there is every reason to believe that Soviet perceptions of this balance are affected by the absence of a meaningful civil defense program in the U.S. If, as Soviet military leaders write, the protection of the homeland "is becoming one of the most important tasks in a war," then the lack of any such capability in the U.S. constitutes an exploitable vulnerability and, consequently, is destabilizing. Indeed, given that in the U.S. nuclear war is equated with the assured destruction of this nation and its people, this not only weakens the credibility of U.S. deterrence, but leaves the U.S. vulnerable to Soviet nuclear blackmail in crisis situations. The Soviet Union is well aware of this vulnerability.

For example, a Soviet radio broadcast in English aimed at North America, commenting on a U.S. plan to improve the survivability of the National Command Authority, asked "But what about those 140 million Americans who, according to competent experts, will die on the very first day of a nuclear war?", while *Pravda* commented that "The bosses who cooked up the nuclear mess go off to shelters while everyone else [in the U.S.] can go to hell!" One can easily envisage various crisis scenarios in which the Soviet Union could effectively resort to nuclear blackmail of the U.S. and exploit the asymmetry in the U.S.-Soviet civil defense capabilities to influence American decision-makers and public opinion. In such a situation, the existence of significant civil defense capabilities in the U.S. would at least place the two countries on an equal footing and deny the Soviet Union an obvious advantage.

Civil defense is essential in an age of increasing vulnerability of modern society to disasters of every kind, including nuclear war. It is certainly a reasonable program to adopt and support by a society such as ours which prides itself on its humanitarian values and concern for the safety of its citizens. It is neither destabilizing nor provocative nor a complication for the arms control process, but it does reflect a conscious recognition that we live in uncertain and dangerous times and that no one can guarantee that a nuclear war will never happen. Above all, civil defense offers a realistic possibility of significantly mitigating losses and suffering and enhancing the prospect of national survival in the event of such a war. The Soviet Union has long recognized this and has developed appropriate programs. Surely the U.S. cannot afford to do any less.

Civil Defense in the Nuclear Age: Strategic, Medical, and Demographic Aspects
Jennifer Leaning

Introduction

It is now becoming a matter of necessity to understand the evolution of civil defense in the last few years and its proposed function in the setting of nuclear attack and nuclear war. The civilian use of civil defense is familiar to most of us, as a series of programs designed to protect the continental U.S. non-combatant population from floods, tornados, hurricanes, earthquakes and forest fires. National disasters, often occurring without warning, have affected some of us; and we all recognize that civil defense efforts during these disasters have been important in reducing casualties and protecting property.

For a few brief years in the 1950's, during the height of the cold war, civil defense programs were introduced in a military setting as the United States became concerned about Soviet nuclear capabilities and sought measures to protect the U.S. population from nuclear attack. The efficacy of air raid drills and home bomb shelters came into question, however, as U.S. military strategists learned more about the thermal, blast, and radiation effects of these weapons from above and underground testing; as technological developments in the speed of delivery systems reduced options for population response; and as the doctrine of mutual assured destruction [MAD] became the accepted mechanism for ensuring nuclear stability. Since the weapons were so catastrophically powerful, and since both the United States and the U.S.S.R. could assure the destruction of the other were one to initiate an exchange, civil defense programs for the U.S. population in the nuclear age were allowed to dwindle into irrelevance.[1]

Now, again in response to developments in weapons systems, civil defense has re-entered the arena of national debate, promoted with a more explicit strategic rationale than ever. The weapons are more lethal, the scenarios more brazen, and the world peace more tenuous. As physicians committed to sustaining the health of our society and prepared to participate in all aspects of disaster management, the aims of civil defense in most contexts would be harmonious with our own. In the setting of nuclear war, however, a circumstance which engulfs us all in devastation of unprecedented scale, we submit that civil defense cannot ensure conditions for post-attack survival. To persist in planning as if it could divert the nation from its major task—the pursuit of a sound, comprehensive, bilateral disarmament agreement and the prevention of nuclear war.

The discussion that follows will first approach civil defense from the standpoint of the strategic uses such planning now serves and the psychological effect such planning may have. In the second section, crisis relocation, the current civil defense

---

[1]B. W. Blanchard, "American Civil Defense 1945–1975: The Evolution of Programs and Policies," University Microfilms International, Ann Arbor, Michigan, 1980, pp. 1–19. Joint Committee on Defense Production. "Civil Preparedness Review. Part I. Emergency Preparedness and Industrial Mobilization," 95th Congress, 1st session, U.S. Government Printing Office, Washington, D.C., February, 1977, pp. 3–38.

Jennifer Leaning, "Civil Defense in the Nuclear Age: Strategic, Medical, and Demographic Aspects" (prepared statement), U.S. Cong., Senate, *United States and Soviet Civil Defense Programs,* Hearings before the Subcommittee on Arms Control, Oceans, International Operations and Environment of the Committee on Foreign Relations, 97th Cong., 2nd Sess., 1982, pp. 93–111.

program, will be examined from the perspective of feasibility. The final section will analyze issues of post-attack survivability.

I. STRATEGIC AND PSYCHOLOGICAL USES OF CIVIL DEFENSE

Changes in military strategy to keep pace with technological developments in nuclear weaponry have in the last few years contributed to the replacement of the MAD concept of deterrence, based on parity, with the notion that stability can derive from superiority of arms. The United States has now openly declared its policy to be the acquisition and development of weapons systems that will produce unassailable nuclear superiority over the Soviet Union.[2] The need for superiority is based on the problems of waging war of any kind in the nuclear age. The validity of the concept is based on the notion of survivability. The civil defense is the method by which survivability is seen to be possible.

NATO doctrine calls for the first use of nuclear weapons in the European theatre if Warsaw Pact forces overwhelm allied conventional forces.[3] It is recognized among many arms control authorities that a theatre use of nuclear weapons may well not remain limited, and that the United States and the Soviet Union might well be drawn into a strategic, global exchange.[4] In a world armed with nuclear weapons, for the United States to engage in war to protect overseas interests considered vital, it ap-

pears that the United States has to be willing to use nuclear weapons, and risk global nuclear war. If the United States has achieved overwhelming superiority in nuclear weaponry, however, it is assumed that the Soviet Union will not dare escalate from a tactical to a strategic exchange, since the United States will possess a sufficient number of warheads to survive a first strike (whether it be aimed at our military-industrial targets or directly at population centers) and then demolish the Soviet Union with a counterstrike of enormous magnitude.[5]

Here we encounter the questions of "surviving" a Soviet first strike. For the United States to be in a position to retaliate with crushing effectiveness, the country must be able to withstand a 6,000 to 10,000 megaton Soviet attack. It is at this point in U.S. military strategic thought that civil defense becomes so important. The United States could not be willing to escalate to a strategic exchange if it were evident to the Soviet Union, the U.S. people, and the world in general that it had made no attempt to protect its population from Soviet attack. With such preparation, it is argued, the Soviet Union will take seriously our declared intentions; without such provision, it will be clear to all that the United States is unwilling to risk escalation from tactical to strategic warfare, and therefore probably unwilling to risk full-scale conventional confrontation (since it is probable that within days of a major conventional conflict between the interests of the United States and the U.S.S.R. the war will escalate to involve tactical nuclear weapons). In other words, without civil defense, the U.S. military cannot use its weapons. Civil defense closes the loop in U.S. offensive strategy and allows the United States to wage war.

As President Carter defined the role of civil defense in Presidential Directive 41:

> The United States civil defense program should enhance the survivability of the American people and

---

[2]R. Beres, "Nuclear Strategy and World Order: The United States Imperative," Working Paper Number 23, World Order Models Project, 1982, Institute for World Order, New York, N.Y., 1982, pp. 1–19. M. Bundy, G. F. Kennan, R. S. McNamara, and G. Smith, "Nuclear Weapons and the Atlantic Alliance," Foreign Affairs, Spring, 1982, pp. 753–768.

[3]"Nuclear Weapons," The Report of the Secretary General of the United Nations, Autumn Press, Brookline, Mass., 1981, pp. 117–122.

[4]H. Brown, Remarks delivered at the Convocation Ceremonies for the 97th Naval War College Class, Naval War College, Newport, Rhode Island, August 20, 1980. Bundy et al., op. cit. G. Kistiakowsky, "Can a Limited Nuclear War Be Won?", Defense Monitor, 1981, v. 10, No. 2, pp. 1–4.

[5]Bundy et al., op. cit.

its leadership in the event of nuclear war, thereby improving the basis for eventual recovery, as well as reducing vulnerability to a major Soviet attack;

The U.S. civil defense program should enhance deterrence and stability, and contribute to perceptions of the overall U.S./Soviet strategic balance and to crisis stability, and also reduce the possibility that the Soviets could coerce us in times of increased tension.[6]

This policy has been continued under the current administration. Among the objectives of the civil defense program as detailed in March, 1982, President Reagan sought to:

Enhance deterrence and stability in conjunction with our strategic offensive and other strategic defensive forces. Civil defense as an element of the strategic balance, should assist in maintaining perceptions that this balance is favorable to the United States;

Reduce the possibility that the United States could be coerced in time of crisis;

Provide for survival of a substantial portion of the U.S. population in the event of nuclear attack preceded by strategic warning, and for continuity of government, should deterrence and escalation control fail.[7]

It is always reassuring, when faced with an overwhelming situation, to have a plan for a way out. If confronting this overwhelming situation becomes a chronic condition, as it has for those of us in the nuclear age, having a way out becomes one of the many mechanisms we employ to avoid looking at where we are going. A civil defense plan appears to provide such an exit. The question is, for whom does civil defense planning appear to be reassuring?

There are two sectors to consider from the standpoint of Federal planning: the government bureaucracies involved in devising plans and implementing policy, and the American people, who are subjects of the plans and the recipients of the policy. What is perhaps most significant about civil defense planning, and the policy that flows from it, is that the government bureaucracies are taking these plans most seriously and seem to be using them, as we have described, as part of government military strategy. Key officials in the Federal Emergency Management Agency (FEMA) now advocate civil defense planning as a viable means of protecting the U.S. population from attack. T. K. Jones, former advisor on Soviet affairs for Boeing and now Deputy Under Secretary of Defense for Strategic and Nuclear Forces, was recently quoted as saying that the United States would recover fully from an all-out war in just 2 to 4 years, given an adequate civil defense program. "Everybody's going to make it," he observed during the interview, "if there are enough shovels to go around . . . Dig a hole, cover it with a couple of doors and then throw 3 feet of dirt on top. It's the dirt that does it."[8] George Bush pointed out in February 1980, that with a civil defense program "you have a survivability of command and control, survivability of industrial potential, protection of a percentage of your citizens and you have a capability that inflicts more damage on the opposition than it can inflict upon you."[9] Eugene Rostow, in response to a question during his Senate confirmation hearings, said that nuclear war could be considered within a strategic context and that "Japan, after all, not only survived but flourished after the nuclear attack . . . Depending upon certain assumptions, some estimates predict 10 million dead on one side and 100 million on the other but that is not the whole population."[10]

---

[6]Presidential Directive 41 (1978).

[7]Federal Emergency Management Agency, Office of Public Affairs, News Release No. 82-26, Washington, D.C., March 30, 1982, p. 2.

[8]T. K. Jones, as quoted in Los Angeles Times interview by R. Scheer, January 15, 1982, p. 22.

[9]G. Bush, as quoted in an interview with Robert Scheer of the Los Angeles Times, cited in The Washington Post, February 17, 1980, in answer to the question, "How do you win a nuclear exchange?".

[10]E. Rostow, in confirmation hearings before the U.S. Senate Committee on Foreign Relations, Government Printing Office, Washington, D.C., June 22 and 23, 1981, p. 49.

Strategic planners promote the "rational" use of nuclear war and urge that the United States achieve the "ability to wage a nuclear war at any level of violence with a reasonable prospect of defeating the Soviet Union and of recovering sufficiently to insure a satisfactory postwar world order. . . . A combination of counterforce offensive targeting, civil defense, and ballistic missile and air survival and recovery."[11] Such bureaucratic advocacy of civil defense planning suggests that the U.S. Government consider the use of nuclear weapons and the possibility of nuclear war a concrete eventuality, one to prepare to surmount with as much confidence as has previously been brought to contingency planning for other disasters.

The response of the American public to civil defense planning or nuclear war is evolving, as media discussions, educational programs, and government planning efforts become more widespread and detailed. Federal planners have found important allies in one section of public opinion, however—the survivalist movement.[12] This movement has attracted much attention and many adherents in those parts of the country most distant from target areas, most comfortable with wilderness conditions, and most individualistic in current lifestyle and political outlook. Civil defense planning falls right into behavior patterns survivalists can easily adopt: learn to travel light, live off what you carry, depend on others as little as possible, avoid crowded situations, and take care of yourself no matter what happens. The concept of fleeing to rural areas and learning to live off what the land may have holds few surprises, survivalists believe. Pamphlets, books, and journals supporting this point of view have proliferated in the past few years. Industries have developed, catering to needs for the best shelter equipment, water purifiers, masks

and decontamination kits, self-help medical supplies and instructions, home generators, and effective methods for protecting what you have from someone who may try to come take it away. Survivalism has attributes of the American individualist gone wild. In their public statements there is little recognition of the interdependence of life and their own ties to the civilization and economy they so casually write off. To quote from a prominent spokesman in their movement:

I think it is probably true that a nuclear war would severely disrupt, perhaps destroy, the economic and social structure of the United States and Western Europe. . . . It is very egotistical of us, however, to state so blatantly our belief that the destruction of America . . . would be the end of civilization . . . it will not vanish just because our cities have been badly used. Don't worry about civilization. Concentrate on staying alive to enjoy it.[13]

Nor do they appear to understand the realities of the post-attack world. They assert that although the targeted areas include two-thirds of the U.S. population they comprise only 5 percent of the U.S. land area,[14] but with this statement they do not examine the short-term radiation and long-term ecological effects on the areas not hit by blast or devastated by fire.

Civil defense planning, then, seems to be serving the psychological purpose of allowing Federal officials to think that they have taken care of things back home, and of fueling a grandiose sense of self-reliance among some members of the American public. It gives officials and some members of our society a false sense of mastery which protects them from a confrontation we are asking everyone to make, a recognition that we are dealing with a threat qualitatively different from anything we have ever been compelled to face, a threat that requires of us a qualitatively different kind of response.

---

[11]C. Gray and R. Payne, "Victory Is Possible," Foreign Policy, No. 39, Summer, 1980, p. 14, p. 19, as cited in Beres, op. cit. pp. 9–20. Issues of The Journal of Civil Defense, (The American Civil Defense Association, P. O. Box 910, Starke, Fla.), articulate this trend.

[12]See issues of The Journal of Civil Defense, (The American Civil Defense Association, P.O. Box 910, Starke, Fla., 32091).

[13]B. Clayton, "Nuclear Nonsense," Survive, Fall, 1981, p. 36.

[14]Defense Civil Preparedness Agency, "Information Bulletin, Materials for Presentation on Nuclear Protection," No. 306, Washington, D.C., April 26, 1979, p. 3.

II. CRISIS RELOCATION PLAN

In analyzing the current U.S. civil defense plan, crisis relocation, questions of feasibility require attention. The focus in this section will be as much as possible on medical issues. A full analysis of the logistics of evacuation and shelter, the transportation and administrative details, is beyond the scope of this paper. The perspective to bear in mind, however, is that even if every aspect of evacuation and shelter went according to plan, even if all systems functioned as well as anticipated by FEMA, does crisis relocation in the setting of nuclear war promote a survivable situation? A response to this question, an evaluation of demographic survival in the first 2 years after attack, is the subject of the third section.

FEMA Attack Scenario and Plan

A nuclear attack on the continental U.S. delivering 6,000 to 10,000 megatons and occurring without warning would kill 120–150 million of the U.S. population outright and millions more would die from the lethal effects of fallout, hunger, exposure, and disease. Civil defense officials have acknowledged that protection of the population in this setting, without massive commitment to in-place blast sheltering, would be unfeasible. FEMA has therefore concentrated its efforts on planning for a strike in a setting where the United States would have a 3- to 5-day period of advance notice. This setting is defined by a certain interpretation of Soviet strategy and nuclear war held by FEMA and a section of U.S. military opinion. In any attack on the United States, it is assumed that the Soviet Union would seek to destroy major military installations and industrial plants. About 250 cities with populations over 50,000 each, comprising two-thirds of the U.S. population or about 145 million people, are located directly within the blast effects of these targets. FEMA also assumes that the Soviet Union would not launch a pre-emptive strike on the United States without first protecting their own population, as much as would be possible, from the effects of a U.S. counter-attack, and would thus first execute

their own civil defense plan and begin evacuating all major cities and population centers around industrial plants.

Consequently, as FEMA foresees the course of events, in a setting of heightened world tension, such as conflict in the Persian Gulf, Eastern Europe, or the Caribbean, the Soviet Union might activate its civil defense plan. The U.S. satellite intelligence system would pick up this population movement, alert our military forces and civil defense system, and the United States would then have from 3 to 5 days (the estimated length of time for the Soviet civil defense plan to take place) in which to prepare for the anticipated Soviet pre-emptive strike. With these several days of warning, the FEMA plan calls for evacuating 145 million people from 250 cities to rural areas, where they should seek food and shelter with friends, or report to central camp areas where they would find food and supplies stockpiled and would have to build fallout shelters before the Soviet attack.[15]

Feasibility Issues

The organizational and financial commitment required to put such a plan into operation might be seen as escalatory and provocative, creating a civil defense posture that purports to prepare us to survive nuclear war. The plan is politically very cumbersome, in that the costs of estimating inaccurately are very high. If the President were to misread the Soviet Union's intentions and activate our civil defense plan unnecessarily, there would ensue at least a major erosion of public confidence with significant economic loss and social hardship. At most, this large-scale evacuation could prompt the Soviet Union to launch a pre-emptive attack out of fear that the United States was planning to launch a strike of its own.

The estimate of 250 cities is conservative, assuming the Soviet Union would not primarily target population centers or re-target once crisis relocation were put into effect. Evacuating millions of

[15]Ibid. DCPA, No. 305, op. cit. DCPA, "Information Bulletin, Research Report on Recovery from Nuclear Attack," No. 307, Washington, D.C., May 10, 1979.

people in a matter of days creates problems of social control and systems use totally without precedent. Evacuation routes are impractical; the southern half of Boston is to evacuate to Cape Cod, past the Pilgrim II nuclear plant, certain to be a target in itself, across one narrow bridge to the Cape, where sanitation facilities and water suplies can barely support the current influx of summer tourists. Destinations are casually designated, with little regard given to social reception, short-term shelter and food requirements, let alone long-term residence.

A sobering administrative problem is that completing the evacuation plans will require another 8 to 10 years, at current levels of funding; the sheltering components will take another 8 to 20 years of planning.[16] We are brought to the late 1990's, at which point American demographic patterns will have shifted sufficiently to render the evacuation plans obsolete. It is also apparent that unless arms control efforts are successful, the world will not have stood still and by the late 1990's the Soviet arsenal will be able to blanket the continental United States with blast as well as radiation effects, making population movement irrelevant.

Public Health Problems of the Evacuation and Shelter Period

It is instructive to examine some of these feasibility issues from an epidemiological perspective. FEMA proposes moving 145 million people an average of several hundred miles by air, road, rail, and water, over a 3- to 5-day period. This population constitutes a vast migrant social system, characterizable by its own epidemiology of public safety and public health. What this social system encounters, in terms of crime and disease, during its 5-day existence, will be derivable partly from what can be expected on a national or regional average for any 5-day period for that number of Americans. What variables are introduced by disruption, fear, and migration, what will be special to the refugee aspect of this social system, can only be a matter of speculation.

If we look at the evacuating population of New York City as an example, we see about 7.5 million people moving to upstate and western New York State over a 5-day period. An average 5-day period in New York City sees 404.5 deaths from heart disease, 1367.5 live births, and 944.5 total deaths.[17] It seems reasonable to estimate at least the baseline incidence of seizures, insulin reaction, strokes, respiratory arrests, and gastrointestinal hemorrhages. To what extent the stress of the evacuation would promote stress-related morbidity and mortality is unclear. A study of the incidence of depression and suicide among bombing victims in Northern Ireland from 1963 to 1977 noted that when social conditions promoted violent behavior in all sectors of the community, the incidence of severe depressive episodes and suicides declined, paralleling an increase in criminal and homicidal behavior.[18] Further data for violent crime in New York City reveals a 5-day average of 21.6 murders, 44.5 violent rapes, 520.5 aggravated assaults, and 2733.6 burglaries.[19] One factor promoting an increase in the crime rate will be the obvious extent to which surveillance must be dispersed. The usual forces for law and order will be so occupied helping the population cope with an extraordinary situation that they will have less time and attention to spend on monitoring and controlling more deviant behavior. Another factor supporting an increased crime rate is that everyone, even people not usually prone to violence, will be so stressed by the pressures of time, fear of the unknown, and anger at traffic that survival mechanisms will be at peak force and people may react more violently if frustrated. Witness vi-

---

[16]Committee on Armed Services, "Hearings on Military Posture and H.R. 2970, Part 6, Military Personnel and Civil Defense," 97th Congress, 1st session, Government Printing Office, Washington, D.C., 1981, pp. 797–798.

[17]Phone communication with Martin Seigir, Assistant to the Chief of Vital Statistics, Department of Vital Statistics, New York City, January 26, 1982, data for 1980.

[18]H. A. Lyons, "Civil Violence—The Psychological Aspects", Journal of Psychosomatic Research, v. 23, 1979, pp. 373–393.

[19]Phone communication with Simeon Wright, Staff Analyst, Crime Analysis Unit, New York City Police Department, January 19, 1982, data for 1981.

olence during the 1974 oil shortages at gas pumps across the country. The estimate of handguns held in New York City, legal and illegal, is well over a million.[20]

Deciding to what extent the medical population should be deployed to help with this volume of morbidity and mortality en route will constitute a complex administrative decision. Ascertainment of need will be haphazard: how will someone caught in traffic on the Triboro Bridge notify authorities that a passenger in his car seems to be having a heart attack? Access presents another problem: even if notification of need reaches a response station, how will the medical personnel get to the stranded victim? Given the imbalances between the resources available and the need, it might seem realistic to dispense with any attempt to affect the situation and concentrate all efforts on providing medical suport at the destination sites. A presence of medical support, such as via helicopter, even if grossly inadequate, might be essential, however, from the standpoint of maintaining public confidence.

Similar questions from an epidemiological standpoint can be directed at the shelter component of crisis relocation. The logistical problems of constructing effective shelters (with protection factors, or PF, of at least 25)[21] within the postulated time constraints invite future analysis. Here we examine some of the health considerations produced by subjecting a population such as that of New York City to a minimum 30-day stay. (This is the minimum. Data exist to suggest the stay may have to be much longer in certain areas.)[22]

The shelter situation requires that everyone remain in the shelter until ambient fallout levels have decayed to nonlethal levels. Ventures out into the environment before that time will increase risk of radiation injury, depending on the level of radioactivity and duration of exposure. Assuming that everyone stays in the shelter until an all-clear is announced, each shelter will have to be stocked with sufficient food and water for a 30-day stay by its occupants and waste material will have to be sequestered within the confines of the shelter. The problems of coping with this volume of human waste in a hastily constructed fallout shelter should not be minimized. Storage in chemically treated containers will create volume requirements that must be anticipated at time of construction. An increased risk of odor pollution and disease can be expected with some certainty.

Air ventilation will demand close attention. Radioactivity, in the form of alpha and beta particles, will be airborne and will pass through standard commercial air systems. People in shelters will therefore be at risk from inhalation of internal emitters and, depending on the density of fallout, may find that contamination from the air system deposits surface radioactivity within the shelter. Air filtration systems to remove alpha and beta contamination are not widely developed for commercial use.

Monitoring reasonable environmental temperatures within the shelters may pose significant problems if the attack scenario and crisis relocation are activated in winter. Hypothermia and morbidity from cold exposure can intervene if environmental temperatures are sustained at 40 degrees F, especially if people are undernourished, damp, and stressed. Conversely, environmental temperatures above the mid-80's will increase fluid requirements for all people, and if maintained over a period of days, can induce problems of heat stroke in the elderly or chronically ill.

The ongoing medical needs of a sheltered population will not be met in the ways in which most people have come to expect. Again, the infrastructure for the delivery of health care will have markedly changed. Those with chronic illnesses requiring daily medications must have their own 80-day

[20]Phone communication with Dr. Paul Blackman, Director of Research for the National Rifle Association, January 5, 1982. His findings show 600–800,000 handguns, owned illegally in New York City but notes that law enforcement agencies "estimate" the number to be much higher.

[21]Office of Technology Assessment, "The Effects of Nuclear War," OTA, Washington, D.C., 1979, pp. 49–50 140–145.

[22]C. M. Haaland, C. V. Chester, and E. P. Wigner, "Survival of the Relocated Population of the U.S. After a Nuclear Attack," Oak Ridge National Laboratory, Oak Ridge, Tennessee, 1976, p. 39.

supply. (Where to obtain supplies thereafter, with 80 to 90 percent of the pharmaceutical industry destroyed,[23] has not been addressed.) These people include those with diabetes, seizure disorders, cardiovascular and pulmonary disease, and steroid-dependent conditions. In a 30-day period, this shelter population, even inactive, can be expected to sustain a number of fractures and lacerations that will have to be handled on a first aid basis by other members in their household.

Gastrointestinal disease will create serious difficulties by increasing fluid requirements, thus constricting group supplies and contributing to production of waste. Risks of death from dehydration will be greater, since the option of intravenous fluid administration may well not be available. The overall incidence of gastroenteritis, as well as most infectious and communicable diseases, will probably be higher than baseline, because of the close proximity of human beings to each other, their intimate proximity to human waste, and the interacting effects of radiation exposure and malnutrition.[24]

Thromboembolic disease will also probably increase in incidence, because of the enforced sedentary posture of the sheltered population. Labor and delivery will still occur, although obstetric complications could in general not be treated and fetal and maternal morbidity and mortality could be expected to rise.

Plans for the disposal of dead bodies will need to be devised. It should be recognized that of all the pressures leading people to leave the shelters prematurely, removal of corpses might prove most powerful. Requiring people to continue to remain in the shelters with a dead body might prove impossible to enforce, medically inadvisable, and psychiatrically unwise. If people are allowed to leave the shelter to dispose of bodies, the plan

should restrict their exposure time to a minimum, perhaps by having graves, either individual or mass, dug in advance. The option of body bags is currently under investigation by FEMA authorities, who are considering furnishing each shelter with a number of bags depending on number of occupants and calculated 30-day death rate.[25]

Psychological stress in the shelters might be severe. Despite attempts to group families and friends together, undoubtedly many people of different ethnicity and class will be thrust into close quarters. Conflicts over foods, water, and space will be exacerbated by differences in life-style and coping patterns. The overall terror of impending attack and anxiety about outcome will certainly add a dimension of tension difficult to estimate. Even very stable people will find their equilibrium stressed by the tremendous social disruption, disorientation about future security, anger and grief at the turmoil and destruction, guilt about personal behavior.

III. SURVIVAL IN THE POST-ATTACK WORLD

This explication of some of the major problems and unknowns involved in crisis relocation has been marshalled to support the first proposition, that it is highly unlikely if not impossible for this process to occur as planned. Section III will examine grounds for suggesting that even if crisis relocation were to occur as planned, survival would be unattainable for a much greater fraction of the population than FEMA has estimated, and far more grim for the few who attempt it.

Survival Studies

Current civil defense planning is based on optimistic assessment of risk—i.e., that things will work well and proceed as planned. This optimism is at variance with serious planning in other realms, where, for instance, engineers plan for worst case scenarios and use materials tested to withstand con-

[23]R. L. Goen, R. B. Bothun, and F. E. Walker, Potential Vulnerabilities Affecting National Survival, Stanford Research Institute, Menlo Park, Calif., 1970, pp. 15–33.

[24]H. Abrams, "Medical Problems of Survivors of Nuclear War", New England Journal of Medicine, v. 305, No. 20, Nov. 12, 1981, pp. 1226–1232.

[25]Personal communication from Robert Carpenter, Chairman of the Emergency Preparedness and Disaster Committee, National Funeral Directors Association.

ditions more severe than expected on the basis of past experience. Official assertions that with crisis relocation 80 to 90 percent of the U.S. population will survive a full-scale nuclear war and rebuild our society in 2 to 4 years have been met with widespread public skepticism. In response, FEMA officials have claimed that their projections are based on careful evaluation of extensive research. This claim does not withstand close scrutiny.

Since the early 1970's the Defense Civil Preparedness Agency (DCPA) and then FEMA have contracted with private and government consultants from Rand, Stanford Research Institute, Systems Research Corporation, and Oak Ridge to produce background reports on issues relating to crisis relocation response to nuclear war. FEMA authorities refer to these reports, now numbering approximately 370, to support their generalizations about population movement, attack parameters, and survival fractions.[26] Analysis of some of the more frequently cited reports reveals a range of problems arising from exclusive reliance on the data and conclusions they contain. The community of authors derives from a small group of consultants and closely overlaps, so that many of the same people write several reports and cross-reference themselves and their associates in citations. Crucial generalizations about attack parameters, radiation fallout patterns, and social and economic effects derive from only a few main studies with the others drawing on these estimates to form the basis for their reports. The conclusions of the reports are often phrased more optimistically than the data within the reports would support. Much attention is devoted to transportation logistics and shelter construction, and very little to assessments of the post-attack situation beyond the first 30 days. In sum, although these studies contain interesting data, they offer less relevant, independent, or comprehensive information than one might initially expect from the list of titles. They provide insufficient grounds

for FEMA's sanguine interpretation of probable outcome after a nuclear war.

Crisis relocation, however, has no intrinsic value unless it can be shown that the reduction in immediate casualties it might afford can be sustained during the post-attack period. If crisis relocation serves merely to forestall casualties, to substitute immediate death in the cities for a more protracted but nonetheless certain death in relocated areas, then it is pointless for the United States to proceed with a plan that spells such a convulsive, cataclysmic disruption of national processes.

An estimate of survivability in the post-attack world becomes key to this policy decision. The research on this subject has only just begun. The following discussion will describe some of the pivotal factors influencing survival, summarize some of what is known, and define areas requiring further investigation. What is initiated here must be viewed as a most preliminary suggestion for a study that needs to be done.

The concept of survivability used in this discussion falls somewhere between the most sparse definition, biological persistence of the species, and the most inclusive, maintained potential to recreate modern American society. Survivability will be seen as possible if the material conditions for sustained population growth can be met. After a full-scale nuclear war on the United States, the factors affecting such sustained growth of population are:

1 *Radiation effects.*—Both immediate consequences of initially high levels of radiation exposure and the intermediate-term effects of chronic exposure to moderate levels will be considered.

2 *Food supply.*—Attention must be extended beyond the first few weeks to examine subsequent harvest potentials.

3 *Infectious diseases and epidemics.*—Discussion includes changes in the incidence of diseases known to be endemic in the population, resurgence of diseases now rare in North America, and synergism with effects of radiation exposure and malnutrition.

4 *Alterations in the ecosystem.*—Ecological consequences of weapons explosions include ef-

---

[26]Committee on Armed Services, op. cit., pp. 848–855, Massachusetts Civil Defense Agency, "Crisis Relocation Planning . . . Questions and Answers," Framingham, Ma., no date, p. 30.

fects of radiation exposure, climate change, ozone depletion, dust production, and soil erosion.

5 *Psychological will to live.*—Whether people will have the psychological strength to continue the struggle for existence and procreation may remain the most fundamentally significant factor and perhaps the one most difficult to estimate.

Suggesting a demographic perspective, the following discussion examines the effects these factors will exert on the birth and death rates in the post-attack population.

The Post-attack World

The people who remain will not recognize their world when they emerge from the shelters. Many familiar natural landmarks and most man-made ones will have been destroyed. The urban areas, home to most Americans, will be in rubble, and little will be left to draw people into the highly radioactive dust of what were once the downtown centers of life. Fires and blast effects may have destroyed or damaged much of the rural environment. Radioactive contamination of the land and water will present an incessant, uncertain hazard.

Meeting needs for shelter, food and water will be paramount. Shelters may still have to be used as home, since most of the nation's housing stock will have been destroyed. Destruction of the petroleum and much of the coal industries may force dependence on wood for fuel.[27] Building even rudimentary housing and foraging for wood takes energy. Food supplies will be very low. Food production will depend on many uncertainties, including availability of seed, extent of soil contamination, and season of the year.

Sanitary conditions will be primitive. Sewage and water systems will for the most part have been destroyed and makeshift ones may be inadequate. Millions of decomposing corpses from the attack and shelter period will require immediate burial or cremation. Insects, comparatively resistant to radiation and released from the constraints of their

pre-attack predators (all of whom share radiation sensitivities more equivalent to human thresholds) will multiply.[28]

Radiation Effects

Much is not known about the extent and intensity of fallout levels after a nuclear war on the United States. Uncertainties about attack parameters begin the list of unknowns. From the standpoint of an individual weapon release, it is estimated that a 1 megaton bomb ground burst with 50-50 fission-fusion characteristics would yield a radiation rate at 1 hour of 500 to 1,000 rads over 1,000 square miles.[29] A 1980's attack on North America on the scale of the CRP-2B model of 6,559 megatons would release lethal fallout over 5 million square miles, or approximately the area of the continental United States.[30] Targeted urban areas, if receiving several megatons at groundburst, might experience greater levels of fallout, ranging over 10,000 rads at 1 hour after explosion. It is estimated in the CRP-2B model that approximately 60,000 square miles of the United States would be so affected.[31] Whether such an attack scenario is most likely to apply, and whether the computer assumptions on which this projection of radiation release is based are valid constitute subjects for further investigation.

Survival in conditions of fallout delivering 500 to 1,000 rads per hour initially requires that the vast majority of the U.S. population be sheltered for at least 2 weeks in shelters with protection factors of at least 40.[32] Survival within the 60,000 square mile area of higher radiation will be more problematic since this area also encompasses that affected by intense blast and thermal effects. How-

---

[27]A. M. Katz, "Life After Nuclear War," Ballinger, Cambridge, Mass., 1982, pp. 161–172.

[28]V. W. Sidel, et al, "The Medical Consequences of Nuclear War", New England Journal of Medicine, v. 266, 1962, pp. 1136, 1142.

[29]B. T. Feld, "Mechanics of Fallout", in "The Final Epidemic," R. Adams and S. Cullen, eds., Educational Foundation for Nuclear Science, 1981, p. 114.

[30]Feld, op. cit., p. 115.

[31]C. M. Haaland, et al, op. cit., p. 39.

[32]Controversy over realistic protection factors is discussed in OTA, op. cit., pp. 140–145.

Penalty Table

Medical care will be needed by—	Accumulate 1 radiation exposures (R) in any period of—		
	1 week	1 mo.	4 mo.
None	150	200	300
Some (5 percent may die)	250	350	500
Most (50 percent may die)	450	600	. . .

ever, transit through or on the periphery of these or other unpredictable hot spots might well prove hazardous for several months after the attack.

Radioactive decay curves for the first 6 months after a thermonuclear weapons explosion can be approximated as a decline by a factor of 10 for every 7-fold increase in hours of elapsed time.[33] Thus, if lethal levels of 1,000 rads per hour swept across the United States, the dose in the host areas at 49 hours, or 2 days into the shelter period, would be 10 rads per hour; at 2 weeks, 1 rad per hour; and at 100 days, or about 3 months, the rate would have decayed to .1 rad per hour. It is instructive to compare this dose rate with what has been set as the reasonable level for occupational radiation exposure in peacetime U.S. industry. According to the guidelines established by the National Council on Radiation Protection [NCRP], a worker is allowed 5 rems per year, and a member of the general public 0.5 rems per year.[34] A dose rate of .1 rads per hour (for these purposes a rad is considered equivalent to a rem), will in 5 hours deliver what is considered a year's permissible exposure for a member of the general public, and in 50 hours deliver the same dose as that considered the maximum permissible annual dose for a worker. One

week at that dose rate, .1 rads per hour, experienced 3 months after the attack, delivers 16.8 rads to each individual exposed.

Very little is known about the health consequences of this level of protracted radiation exposure. Published estimates are based on data drawn from Japanese victims of the bomb, radiation accidents, clinical radiation therapy experience, and animal experiments. It is known from this data base that doses of 20 to 50 rads will produce azoospermia in men; that acute doses of 100 to 200 rads will produce fatigue, nausea, and vomiting in up to 50 percent of those exposed. An acute dose of 450 rads will kill 50 percent of the population, assuming adequate supportive medical care.[35] In the post-attack world, however, although a definite but uncertain number of people in the sheltered areas will receive significant doses of radiation within the first 2 weeks because of inadequate sheltering, the risks to the majority will be in subsequent cumulative effects of chronic exposures. It is simply not known what chronic exposure over months (to doses approximating 1,000 to 2,000 times that recommended now for the general public) means in terms of individual morbidity. The NCRP furnishes the above "Penalty Table" for estimated effects of chronic exposures on human beings.[36]

It is noteworthy that "some" and "most" are not numerically transferable to a modeling situation. Nor are morbidity questions answered by "medical

[33]J. Smith and T. Smith, "Nuclear War: the Medical Facts, Medicine and the Bomb", British Medical Journal, v. 283, Sept. 19, 1981, p. 774. National Council on Radiation Protection, "Radiological Factors Affecting Decision-Making in a Nuclear Attack," NCRP Report No. 42, pp. 12–15.

[34]K. Kahn, "Health Effects of Nuclear Power and Nuclear Weapons," Physicians for Social Responsibility, Watertown, Mass., 1980, p. 30.

[35]Ibid.
[36]Ibid., p. 38.

care will be needed by some (5 percent may die)." What kind of medical care will be needed? How sick are those who do not die? It is important to be able to estimate the proportion who will be able to work, who will suffer from nausea, vomiting, or diarrhea, who will be azoospermic or anovulatory, who will be susceptible to infection. The extent to which moderate chronic radiation exposure will decrease fertility, increase fetal wastage, and increase mortality from other causes (malnutrition, disease) are questions which require much more attention before the balance between reparative cellular mechanisms and continuous toxic effects of radiation exposure can be reliably estimated. What little is known suggests that human beings have less efficient repair mechanisms in the face of repeated doses than many species of animals.[37]

Long-term health consequences of radiation exposure are somewhat more understood and quantifiable, although much controversy still surrounds questions of linearity and threshold. New analyses of Hiroshima data suggest that induction incidence estimates should be at least doubled.[38] From what is known of the induction time and magnitude of these consequences, however, they are not relevant to the discussion of survivability in the first several years after nuclear attack. The incidence of malignancies, congenital malformations, and genetic mutations will increase significantly and will certainly alter longevity and quality of life, but will probably not have dramatic consequences for overall population growth. If the population survives, leukemia induction will begin to be expressed within 5 years after exposure, but solid tumor excess will not be seen until 10 to 40 years after the event.[39] Data that might have sobering relevance for quantifying the incidence of post-radiation cancer induction comes from a recent study of breast cancer patients, which suggests that highly fractionated

doses of low-level radiation were as effective in inducing malignancy as larger, fewer doses.[40]

This discussion so far has considered risks only from external gamma radiation. Ingestion or inhalation of radioisotopes contaminating food, water, and milk presents another source of radiation injury. Quantifying the extent of radioactive contamination of the post-attack environment and then attempting to calculate the internal radiation risk this contamination poses for human beings has not been accomplished. Isolated studies on plant and animal contamination suggest that the risk may not be insignificant.[41]

Food Supply

Whether and for how long there will be enough food to support the population remaining after a nuclear war on the United States depends in part on the estimated population size. If crisis relocation is as effective as claimed, approximately 145 million people will survive the immediate effects and they will persist into the shelter period. Food supply in the United States depends on three main factors: production, processing, and distribution. A marked imbalance between production and population characterizes U.S. agriculture. The northeast is heavily dependent on food production west of the Mississippi, in the southwest, and Middle Atlantic states. The Pacific Northwest produces five times more food than its population requirements and the northeast produces only two-thirteenths of its food needs.[42] Crisis relocation will not appreciably alter this relationship, since all people will

[37]Ibid., p. 23.

[38]E. Marshall, "New A-Bomb Studies Alter Radiation Estimates," Science, v. 212, 22 May 1981, pp. 900–903.

[39]S. Finch, "The Study of Atomic Bomb Survivors in Japan," The American Journal of Medicine, v. 66, No. 6, June, 1979, pp. 899–901.

[40]J. D. Bolce, Jr., et al, "Risk of Breast Cancer Following Low-Dose Radiation Exposure," Diagnostic Radiology, v. 131, June 1979, pp. 589–597.

[41]International Atomic Energy Agency. "Environmental Contamination by Radioactive Materials," Proceedings of a Seminar, Vienna, March, 1969, passim. D. W. Bensen and A. H. Sparrow, eds., "Survival of Food Crops and Livestock in the Event of Nuclear War." U.S. Atomic Energy Commission, National Technical Information Service, Springfield, Va., 1971, pp. 131–168, 187–190, 455.

[42]J. W. Billheimer and A. W. Simpson, "Effects of Attack on Food Distribution to the Relocated Population." v. I. Systan, Inc., Los Altos, Calif., September, 1978, p. 2-1.

move only 100 to 300 miles within their area.[43] Almost 80 percent of the food processing capacity of the country is located in high risk areas and would be destroyed in the war. Similar destruction of the distribution network (transportation systems and managerial personnel) can be anticipated.[44]

It is important to distinguish among effects on the crops growing at the time of the attack, availability of grain stores, and potential for subsequent crop production. It is estimated that approximately 43 percent of the total crop under production will survive a full-scale 6,559 megaton attack.[45] This estimate represents the average of several variables (time of year—June being the most damaging time for an attack to occur since radiation will kill germinating vegetation; kind of crop—grain, potatoes, soybeans, and rice listed in order of decreasing sensitivity to radiation). Because of destruction of distribution and processing facilities, however, it is not clear what percentage of the crop under production could be brought to the sheltered population. The breakdown of these systems, and the effects of lethal radiation, will make most of the nation's livestock supply unavailable for food.[46]

Consequently, immediate nutritional support of the post-attack population will have to be supplied by the grain stored in local warehouses and elevators near production sites and in regional wholesale centers. In general, annual grain stores in the United States since 1945 have been sufficient to meet the immediate basic needs of the population (3,000 calories per day, or 2 pounds of raw grain per person per day.) There have been several years and 6-month periods, however, when such stores have not been adequate.[47] Assuming that the attack occurs during a time when the United States has sufficient stores on hand, there are still two large problems in relying on stored grain for support of

the post-attack population. To begin with, it is not clear from the studies of food supplies in this setting what percent of the grain stores will survive a nuclear war on the United States. Grain stocks in the centrally located warehouses may well be destroyed by attacks on these risk areas.[48] Grain stored on local farms in the Midwest may be contaminated by fallout. The second problem is one of distribution. Approximately 55 million people in the post-attack population will be located in areas with zero to 10 days of food supply on hand.[49] Grain will have to be transported from remaining grain stocks in rural areas to these areas of need, within 2 to 3 weeks post-attack. No food processing will be possible and raw grain will have to be boiled to be edible. No grain is reserved for animal use.

Conditions in the post-attack world will pose tremendous obstacles to this transport task. Most railroad lines, bridges, and roads will have been destroyed. At least 60 percent of all fuel stocks will have been consumed in the attack.[50] The one government-funded study that addresses in detail the question of supplying the post-attack population with food concentrates only on the question of fuel availability, assuming that a sufficient fraction of the trucking and rail transport system will survive to carry on this transport function. The study predicts that at an estimated transport rate approaching 6 percent of pre-attack 1970 capacity, 305,000 tons of grain will have been shipped in a 6-week period several trillion miles to the areas of need. Fuel supplies, this study estimates, "would last for 236 days, which is probably adequate to carry the nation through the survival stage into the recovery stage."[51]

The problems with this analysis are numerous. Disruption of transport networks cannot be assigned fractional values because of bottleneck dysjunctions. The rate and volume of grain shipped does not match need: 150,000 tons of grain are

[43]Haaland, et al., op. cit., p. 27.

[44]Katz, op. cit., p. 157.

[45]C. M. Haaland, "Availability and Shipment of Grain for Survival of a Nuclear Attack," American Journal of Agricultural Economics, May, 1977, p. 361.

[46]Haaland, et al., op. cit., pp. 109–115.

[47]Ibid., p. 110.

[48]J. W. Billheimer and A. W. Simpson, op. cit., p. 2–3.

[49]Haaland, et al., op. cit., pp. 146–147.

[50]Haaland, op. cit., p. 364.

[51]Ibid., p. 364.

shipped in the first 2 weeks, furnishing 5.45 pounds of grain per person, assuming the population in need to be the 55 million with stocks of zero to 10 days post-attack, furnishing less than a 3-day supply for the entire 2-week period. The apparent destinations for this transported grain are listed as Boston, Hartford, New York City, Albany—all high risk areas and theoretically evacuated. Getting this grain supply to the host areas is the relevant, and more difficult task. What fuel exists in storage may not be near the trucks that may have survived the attack. Transport to the areas of need within the first two weeks may require transit through or on the periphery of intense radiation and engaging workers for this task may prove unrewarding. The study suggests that the transport effort will require an intact Federal Government and a form of Federal promissory note that local farmers will honor. Food hoarding or consumption of fuel supplies for any other task but transport of food is not considered. Finally, nothing supports the assumption that after 236 days, or 7.8 months into the post-attack period, the agricultural economy would have reached a "recovery stage." Many considerations suggest that, in fact, the food situation after the first 6 months post-attack will have become more severe.

After the first 6 months, all stored grain would have been consumed. The need to conserve seed supplies is not discussed in the government literature. Production factors in modern American agriculture include fertilizer, pesticides, heavy machinery, and irrigation. These all depend to a large extent on the existence of functioning refinery and petro-chemical industries, most of which would have been destroyed in the attack. Loss of fertilizer is estimated to result in 50 percent decrease in major crop yield. Without pesticides, production of potatoes, vegetables, and fruits would be adversely affected, especially in the setting of the post-attack world where insect vectors will have increased disproportionately because of their relative radiation resistance. Loss of fuel for farm machinery and irrigation pumps will markedly reduce agricultural yields; it is estimated that reduc-

tion of petroleum use to 20 percent of pre-attack levels would cut farm production to 30 percent of normal.[52]

Currently about 6 percent of the U.S. population is involved in agricultural production. Regardless of what extent a remnant of skilled farmers may survive the attack, the majority of the population will have had little experience with farming. People will be disoriented, hungry, perhaps ill from radiation and disease. The work required to prepare and plant fields may be beyond the capability of many.

Questions about soil and seed contamination, when people are very hungry, will most probably be dismissed, and some crops may be planted with little regard for radioactivity. Without fertilizer, pesticides, equipment, or skill, in a contaminated terrain infested by insects, planting such crops carries much risk of failure.

For all these reasons, the yield cannot be expected to compare with the pre-attack world. Estimates of production in the first several years after attack are beyond the scope of this discussion, but it is clear from the variables mentioned that problems with food production and distribution may exert significant negative constraints on population survival. In times of hunger, conserving seed from one growth's crop to use for the next season can prove socially and physically impossible. Areas that plan better and have better luck will become targets of attack from other groups in need. The situation in the course of two growing seasons could become most desperate. Living as they did on the margins of existence, two successive failures of the potato crop in 1846 and 1847 spelled death for close to 25 percent of the Irish population.[53] The starkness of this view needs no recourse to more conjectural possibilities, such as whether depletion of ozone or injection of atmospheric dust will make crop production in North America for the succeed-

[52]Katz, op. cit., p. 149.
[53]C. Woodham-Smith, "The Great Hunger," Harper, New York, 1962, pp. 411–412.

ing 5 to 20 years completely impossible. In this way, persistent famine could be seen to characterize the post-attack world.

Infectious Disease and Epidemics

The incidence and relative virulence of infectious disease will increase enormously in the years after the nuclear attack. Change in characteristics of both host and environment may lead to morbidity and mortality rates rarely before recorded. Environmental conditions post attack will create conditions for the abundant spread of disease: (1) crowding during the shelter period and thereafter because of inadequate housing stock; (2) inadequate ventilation; (3) destruction of sanitary systems with accumulation of sewage and waste; (4) absence of refrigeration leading to food spoilage; (5) the presence of millions of corpses; (6) exuberant overgrowth of insects. The population that remains will in turn be able to offer only reduced resistance to disease. The complex interactive effects of stress, malnutrition, and lingering radiation will weaken human immune systems and physiological defense mechanisms to the point where people may succumb to diseases of previously low virulence. A study of the role of communicable diseases in the post-attack environment reveals that potential pathogens include familiar respiratory and gastrointestinal diseases of high endemicity but of low mortality in the pre-attack United States, and diseases of previously low or eradicated incidence in the United States which, because of the prevailing post-attack conditions, will recrudesce and contribute significantly to increased mortality. Among the first category are the viral and bacterial diarrheas, hepatitis, pneumonia, diphtheria, whooping cough, and tuberculosis. The second category includes cholera, malaria, plague, smallpox, and typhoid fever.[54]

Throughout the history of the world, epidemic disease has struck populations with devastating mortality consequences. In some instances, as in the 19th century European cholera epidemics, the concomitant famine conditions clearly contributed to increased susceptibility of the population. In other cases, such as the annihilation of the Aztecs by smallpox or the deaths of one-third of the population of Europe during the plague, the sudden introduction of a new virulent disease to which the population had no immunity made the relative contribution of other host factors irrelevant.[55]

In the setting of the post-attack world, erosion of host defenses and environmental changes fostering the spread of endemic and epidemic disease may combine to create a potential mortality crisis of severe proportions. Public health and medical measures will be virtually non-existent. Most medical centers will have been consumed in the attack. No vaccines or antibiotics will be available beyond those stockpiled, since the pharmaceutical industry will have been destroyed. Strict rationing of antibiotics and vaccines will be necessary. In the absence of laboratory facilities, antibiotics will be prescribed at best on the basis of clinical hunch. Without supportive and intensive medical care, they can do little to combat some of the more dangerous bacterial diseases, and against most viral diseases are largely ineffective. Immunization, the only means of controlling diseases such as tetanus, measles, and poliomyelitis, may not prove effective for people whose immune systems have been weakened by radiation. Existing stocks of antibiotics and vaccines will be unable to combat whatever new pathogens or resistant strains may develop.

Under these conditions, estimates of plague incidence approach 12 percent of the population, with half of those contracting the disease dying. Within the first year after the attack, total deaths from all communicable diseases is estimated at 20 to 25

---

[54]Abrams, op. cit.

[55]W. H. McNeill, "Plagues and Peoples," Anchor, Garden City, N.Y., 1976, pp. 149, 176–185. E. A. Wrigley and R. S. Schofield, "The Population History of England 1541–1871," Harvard University Press, Cambridge, Ma., 1981, pp. 332–336. T. H. Hollingsworth, "Historical Demography," Cornell University Press, Ithaca, N.Y., 1969, p. 356.

percent of the immediate post-attack population.[56] Those at the extremes of the age spectrum, the very old and the very young, will probably succumb first to the ravages of disease.[57] Virulent diseases such as plague, however, will strike everyone, and these effects on the age structure of the population are less easy to predict.

The cumulative mortality from infectious disease in the post attack world merits further careful study. What is known from examining the historical record may have somber application to this setting: death rates among societies living at the margins of agricultural production (and such is at best a characterization of post-attack America) "show a remarkable tendency to recurrent, sudden dramatic peaks that reach levels as high as 150 or 300 or even 500,000 . . . the intensity and frequency of the peaks controlled the size of agricultural societies."[58] Furthermore, "historical experience suggests that something like 120 to 150 years are needed for human populations to stabilize their response to drastic new infections."[59]

Alterations in the Ecosystem

It is estimated that with the megatonnage exchanged in a full-force nuclear war, between 40 and 70 percent of the world's ozone layer could be destroyed.[60] This layer shields all animal and plant life from the effects of ultraviolet radiation and contributes to insulating the earth's surface from heat loss. Destruction of this amount of ozone protection will produce effects of uncertain magnitude of potentially enormous significance. Humans and animals would sustain third degree burns on ex-

posed surfaces after one hour outdoors. Sunglasses would be necessary during all daylight hours. Whether plant photosynthesis could be maintained is uncertain, raising vast related questions of carbon dioxide and oxygen supply for the earth. It is also unknown the extent to which loss of ozone would expose microscopic plankton to toxic thermal injury and thus possibly compromise an essential component of the ocean food chain. This loss of ozone might reduce the earth's temperature by one to one and a half degrees centigrade, sufficient to increase the extent of the polar ice caps, eliminate the Midwest from crop production, and constrict suitable agricultural areas in the United States to only the most southern region. It would take at least 30 years for the ozone layer to regenerate, and during this period ecological derangements could be extreme.

A full force nuclear attack would inject approximately 10^7 to 10^8 tons of dust and debris into the atmosphere, threatening in the short term to block the effects of the sun and cause measurable changes in ambient temperature. Destruction of much of the vegetation cover of North America in the initial and secondary fires of the attack would create further severe problems with dust and might markedly accelerate soil erosion.

Only an impoverished imagination would depict post-attack America as simply a frontier with fewer people in it than we have now. Eighteenth century America contained thousands of clean lakes and rivers, millions of square miles of virgin forest and rich land, and wildlife and plant forms of almost enormous abundance. The post-attack terrain may well be burnt barren of vegetation, stripped of animal life, infested by insects, and blistered by the unfiltered ultraviolet rays of the sun.

Psychological Will To Live

This discussion ventures into unexplored territory, proceeding from what is described in the disaster literature. A constant finding in retrospective studies of disasters and of people in extreme situations is that given a sufficient stress everyone will de-

[56]Abrams, op. cit., p. 1231.
[57]N. Hanunian, "Dimensions of Survival: Postattack Survival Disparities and National Viability." Rand Corporation, Santa Monica, Ca., 1966, pp. 67–69.
[58]C. M. Cinolla, "The Economic History of World Population," London, 1962, pp. 76–77. cited in E. A. Wrigley and R. S. Schofield, op. cit., p. 450.
[59]W. H. McNeill, op. cit., p. 51.
[60]National Academy of Sciences, "Long-Term Worldwide Effects of Multiple Nuclear-Weapons Detonations," NAS, Washington, D.C., 1975.

velop symptoms. The intensity of stress or the type of stress is more important in determining the nature of these symptoms than the premorbid personality of the individual.[61] Dividing the disaster experience into time stages, phases of disaster response have been described specific to each stage. The impact phase of the disaster forces people into either alert, purposeful behavior or reactions of denial and disbelief. One large study projected that 12 to 25 percent of individuals would remain effective; 75 percent would be dazed and stunned; and 12 to 25 percent would be thrown into panic or acute confusion.[62] A medical doctor witnessing the crowd fleeing Hiroshima in the first few hours after the attack wrote:

> Those who were able walked silently towards the suburbs and the distant hills, their spirits broken, their initiative gone. When asked whence they had come they pointed to the city and said, "that way"; and when asked where they were going, pointed away from the city and said, "this way." They were so broken and confused that they moved and behaved like automatons. Their reactions had astonished outsiders who reported with amazement the spectacle of long files of people holding stolidly to a narrow, rough path when close by was a smooth, easy road going in the same direction. The outsiders could not grasp the fact that they were witnessing the exodus of a people who walked in the realm of dreams.[63]

After the impact, in the inventory phase, those who have coped will have a sense of mastery, while others will continue to evince dazed apathy. In settings of massive destruction, people become so isolated that psychoses deriving from sensory deprivation may occur. An increased incidence of situational psychoses has been noted with fatigue, physical trauma, or delay in rescue. Remedy and recovery phases may never be fully achieved, even after disasters on a scale incomparably smaller than nuclear war.

From studies of natural disasters, concentration camps, Hiroshima, Nagasaki, and Vietnam, a clear picture of what has been called the "survivor syndrome" emerges.[64] In Lifton's study of the Hiroshima survivors (the hibakusha, or explosion-affected people), the survivor syndrome had the following characteristics: a pervasive guilt, feelings of having failed those who had died; a residual image of ultimate horror; primitive anxieties of separation and annihilation; continuing fear of radiation effects with psychosomatic symptoms, and a sense of grotesque contamination, applied to radiation victims and internalized by them.[65]

Generalizations from the Japanese experience and from other major disasters cannot begin to encompass the nature of psychological response after a nuclear war. Without historical precedent for an event that might destroy the totality of society, there are also no psychological precedents. The Black Death swept across Europe from 1346 to 1350, killing an estimated third of the populace, and leaving such misery in its wake that a witness, who succumbed, felt "the whole world, as it were, placed within the grasp of the Evil One."[66] According to one historian of the period:

> Emotional response, dulled by horrors, underwent a kind of atrophy epitomized by the chronicler who wrote, 'And in these days was burying without sor-

[61]F. Hocking, "Psychiatric Aspects of Extreme Environmental Stress", Diseases of the Nervous System, v. 31, 1970, pp. 542–545.

[62]D. K. Kentsmith, "Minimizing the Psychological Effects of a Wartime Disaster on an Individual," Aviation, Space, and Environmental Medicine, April, 1980, pp. 409–413.

[63]M. Hachiya, "Hiroshima Diary," University of North Carolina Press, Chapel Hill, N.C., pp. 54–55.

[64]A. H. Barton, "Communities in Disaster," Anchor, Garden City, N.Y., 1970. B. C. Chamberlain, "The Psychological Aftermath of Disaster." Journal of Clinical Psychiatry, v. 41, No. 7, July, 1980, pp. 238–244. R. E. Cohen and F. L. Ahearn, Jr., "Handbook for Mental Health Care of Disaster Victims." Johns Hopkins University Press, Baltimore, 1980. F. C. Ikle, "The Social Impact of the Bomb Destruction," University of Oklahoma Press, Norman, Oklahoma, 1958.

[65]R. J. Lifton, "Death In Life," Simon & Schuster, New York, 1967.

[66]B. W. Tuchman, "A Distant Mirror," Alfred A. Knopf, New York, 1978, p. 95.

rowe and wedding without friendschippe.' In Siena, where more than half the inhabitants died of the plague, work was abandoned on the great cathedral, planned to be the largest in the world, and never resumed, owning to loss of workers and master masons and the 'melancholy and grief' of the survivors. The cathedral's truncated transept still stands in permanent witness to the sweep of death's scythe.[67]

Yet the buildings that had been standing, remained. The infrastructure of communications, transportation, and economy persisted. The environment did not alter. When the plague had passed, the world could again become familiar.

An erosion of will to live, to struggle, to grow, to reach out to the world characterizes, for a period of time, most survivors of extreme disasters. What aborts the healing process and allows this apathy to persist in some people for the duration of their lives is not clearly understood. Enormity of loss, contributing to a sense of futility and absence of hope, may play a significant role. In the post-attack world there will be nothing, for a long time, to dilute one's encounter with death.

It might take some time before the cultural losses become real to the people who remain. Their attention, if it can be directed at anything, may be taken up with attempts to forestall hunger, cold, and disease. At some point in the months after the attack they may sink into consciousness the realization that the nation's libraries, museums, architectural treasures, and educational and scientific centers had all been destroyed. The bequests from past generations would have been consumed in a few hours.

It might also take months or years for an accurate assessment of the numbers of lives lost, assuming some people have the courage to sustain the inquiry. Initially, people in separate locales may think that they only have survived, or they may hold to the illusion that most people have lived, and the many they miss are safe in some other area. Guilt at surviving and denial of loss will most certainly be among the prevailing psychological reactions

and may contribute to a persistent, widespread depression.[68]

Summary of Demographic Effects

Questions of mortality during the first few years after a full-scale nuclear war on the United States require more comprehensive attention than they have received. The Office of Technology (OTA) analysis comparing estimates from the Department of Defense (DOD) and the Arms Control and Disarmament Agency (ACDA) provides the most extensive data available.[69] These mortality estimates are based on direct blast and thermal effects and on 30-day radiation effects. The ranges reflect varying assumptions about percent of the population evacuated and adequately sheltered. Other weapons effects, such as conflagrations and possible firestorms, have not been included in these estimates, because they are less predictable. It is assumed that only one exchange takes place, initiated by the Soviet Union. The mortality from the more realistic case, a protracted series of attacks, although considered to be much greater, has not been estimated in any published analyses. Higher order damage mechanisms, such as synergistic effects from radiation, stress, disease, and hunger during the first 30 days or into the first year, have not been quantitated.

Beginning from the preceding discussion of factors influencing prospects for survival in the post-attack period, the OTA data will be applied to a series of adjustments, in order to arrive at an assessment of cumulative mortality by the end of the first two post-attack years. These adjustments are based as much as possible on what is known about previous population encounters with radiation, hunger, infectious disease, environmental devastation, and stress. Much of what is projected has either never before occurred or never taken place on such scale, however, and the adjustments must be viewed as tentative, preliminary attempts to arrive at an appropriate order of magnitude to de-

[67]Ibid., p. 96.

[68]B. C. Chamberlain, op. cit.
[69]OTA, op. cit., pp. 140–145.

scribe the mortality that might evolve. The intention is to underscore the need to embark on a more thorough investigation of the demography of the post-attack world.

For the sake of simplicity, without sacrificing much accuracy, the discussion will begin with a range of immediate 30-day mortality taken from the OTA scenarios, representing the high figure of the low range and the low figure of the high range defined by DOD and ACDA data for an attack similar to the CRP-2B model used by FEMA. Both figures used assume 80 percent of the U.S. population has been evacuated to shelters in the host areas. The realism of that assumption can be challenged on other grounds; the discussion here focuses on survivability, granting a near-perfect performance of crisis relocation.

The mortality figures estimate only immediate direct blast and thermal effects and 30-day radiation fallout effects. Using the U.S. population base as 225 million, the low figure of 26 percent fatalities translates to 58.5 million deaths and the high figure of 32 percent to 72 million deaths. It is estimated, however, that in that attack non-fatal injuries would vary from 20 to 40 percent of total casualties.[70] Taking the mid-range, or 30 percent, the number of non-fatal casualties for the high figure would be 30.8 million.[71] Given shelter conditions, with absence of medical care, potential for disease, and synergism of radiation effects and stress, it is not unrealistic to assume that half of these non-fatal casualties would die at the end of 30 days. This number is especially conservative since some fraction of those injured would not have made it to shelters and would have died from more intense radiation levels, environmental exposure, and perhaps the effects of the fires.

With this adjustment, at the end of the 30-day shelter period, the total deaths are 71 million or 31.5 percent of the pre-attack population for the

low figure, and for the high, 87.4 million deaths, or 38.8 percent.[72]

During the remainder of the first year, some fraction of the population emerging from shelters will suffer from radiation illness, epidemics of disease, hunger or perhaps true famine, and environmental exposure. Enough is known about the effects of infectious disease during this period to suggest that first-year mortality might approach 25 percent of the remaining population. Given what is understood about levels of past mortality crises, and given the unprecedented sweep of devastation inflicted by nuclear war, it would seem plausible to suggest that the synergistic and aggregate effects of these other factors could claim the lives of another 15 percent of the population. The first-year mortality rate thus becomes 40 percent of the population surviving the shelter period. This figure is still less than that calculated for some of the worst mortality crises in past centuries, and so may, with further research, prove an underestimate.

This mortality of 40 percent of the population surviving the shelters would place the low range figure for the number of deaths at 61.6 million, and the high range figure at 55.04 million.[73] Total deaths by the end of the first year, summing deaths within the first 30 days and within the first year thereafter, become 132.6 million deaths or 58.9 percent mortality for the low figure and 142.44 million deaths or 63.3 percent mortality at the upper range.[74]

The mortality pressure will not abate, however, at the end of whatever calendar marks the year.

[70]Ibid., p. 144.

[71]Total casualties for low figure equals 83.6 million times 0.3 equals 25 million non-fatal. Total casualties for high figure equals 102.9 million times 0.3 equals 30.8 million non-fatal.

[72]Low figure: 225 million times 0.26 equals 58.5 million deaths. High figure: 225 million times 0.32 equals 72 million deaths. Total deaths at end of 30 day shelter period: Low figure: 58.5 million plus (25 million times 0.5) equals 71 million or 31.5 percent. High figure: 72 million plus (30.8 million times 0.5) equals 87.4 million or 38.8 percent.

[73]Low figure: 225 million minus 71 million equals 154 million times 0.4 equals 61.6 million deaths. High figure: 225 million minus 87.4 million equals 137.6 million times 0.4 equals 55 million deaths.

[74]Low figure: 71 million plus 61.6 million equals 132.6 million deaths or 58.9 percent first year cumulative mortality. High figure: 87.4 million plus 55 million equals 142.4 million deaths or 63.3 percent first year cumulative mortality.

Persistent inadequacy of sanitation facilities and medical care would allow continued spread of infectious disease. Epidemics have been shown to occur in waves, striking new susceptibles over several generations, and this in settings where the health of the population was not constrained by radiation effects on the immune system and severe privation.[75] Supplies of food may well be lower at the end of the year than immediately post-attack, and, as discussed, the fate of the subsequent harvest, were there to be one, would be problematic.

The second year could very arguably, then, be shown to exert the same high mortality rate, 40 percent, as the first. Such a sustained rate yields, on the low side of the estimate, a population of 55.5 million remaining, or 25 percent of the pre-attack population and on the high mortality range, 49.6 million remaining, or 22 percent of the pre-attack population.[76] By the end of the first 2 years post-attack, at least three-fourths of the pre-attack population would have died, with the cumulative deaths in those 2 years virtually equal to the numbers killed by the immediate effects of the weapons themselves.

These mortality calculations should be viewed as augmenting the baseline mortality of the U.S. population, but several factors work against a simple addition. Some of the people who would have died from cancer or stroke would die instead from burns or plague. The conditions for some causes of death, such as motor vehicle accidents, would no longer apply on a significant scale, since disruption of transportation networks and fuel shortages would eliminate most traffic. Consequently, integration of baseline mortality within the mortality of the attack and post-attack situation must await more detailed analysis.

A thorough search of the historical record and demographic literature would be necessary to define all the factors that spell extinction for one population exposed to severe mortality crises and permit re-growth for another. In general, populations who have survived these crises have done so by developing new immunities and increasing their birth rates. Both of these responses in the post-attack world may be dampened considerably because of the interactive effects of radiation and protracted malnutrition on the immune and reproductive systems.

Radiation exposure at sufficiently low levels to remain asymptomatic may still depress white blood cell counts. Lymphocytes, among the cells most essential to the immune system, are especially sensitive to radiation.[77] At a severe level of malnutrition, people become susceptible to infection, regardless of their immune status. The years it takes even basically healthy populations to develop new immunities may not be available to people in the post-attack world.

The effects of radiation exposure on the human reproductive system are complex and incompletely understood. Low radiation exposures, in the range of 20 rads, induced azoospermia among survivors of Hiroshima for several months to years after the attack. Nine months after that attack, 10 to 12 men examined were effectively azoospermic; 22 months after, another cohort of 32 men were examined, and approximately one-third had sperm counts in the range considered sterile. Menstrual disorders were common among women who had survived Hiroshima. Over 70 percent of those examined had irregular menses, with 78 percent returning to normal patterns by the end of 7 months. Fetal wastage in Hiroshima cannot be quantitated, since most pregnant women had been evacuated prior to the bombing. In Nagasaki, however, of the 177 pregnancies investigated, 18.6 percent ended in mis-

[75]W. H. McNeill, op. cit., pp. 184–186.

[76]Low figure: 225 million minus 132.6 million equals 92.4 million (times 0.4) equals 37 million deaths. 92.4 million minus 37 million equals 55.4 million remaining, or 25 percent of the pre-attack population. High figure: 225 million minus 142.4 million equals 82.6 million (times 0.4) equals 33 million deaths. 82.6 million minus 33 million equals 49.6 million remaining, or 22 percent of the pre-attack population.

[77]K. F. Hubner and S. A. Fry, eds., "The Medical Basis for Radiation Accident Preparedness." Elsevier/North-Holland, New York, 1980, p. 298.

carriage, 6.8 percent in premature delivery. The incidence of microcephaly and other congenital malformations among all births was markedly correlated with in utero radiation exposure.[78]

Conditions of the post-attack world raise doubts about the fertility potential of the remaining population, at least for the first 2 years. Infant mortality in these stark circumstances would undoubtedly exceed the high rate for the general population. Whether interest in establishing relationships and engaging in sexual activity would be sustained, and at what relative level, is no less important a question simply because it cannot be answered within the scope of this discussion. Loss of libido among Hiroshima survivors was frequently found for the first 2 to 3 months after the bombing,[79] and is a common feature of the survivor syndrome. The issue is raised, as with many others, to point out the extent to which our ignorance prevents us from quantifying very significant variables.

Drawing together this series of adjustments to the OTA estimates of initial post-attack mortality, it is seen to be very possible that the remaining population of the United States, some 50 to 55 million people at the end of the first 2 years, might continue to be reduced to a fraction of that number in the ensuing decade. To reverse the oppressive mortality rates of the first 2 years post-attack might require a regeneration of technological and economic capacity beyond the reach of those who remain. The cumulative effect of these factors sustaining high mortality rates and suppressing birth rates suggests that human population dynamics after a full-force nuclear attack on the United States might persist in a negative pattern for several years. Survivability might seem less obtainable 2 years post-attack than upon emerging from the shelters.

CONCLUSION

As an element of military offensive strategy, civil defense in the nuclear age serves to delude Federal officials and a few members of the populace into thinking that nuclear war can be waged with relative impunity. As a public health program, current civil defense plans fall short of evaluating issues of feasibility, medical care, and long-term health consequences. The demography of the post-attack world, when evaluated in light of the factors affecting survivability, does not support bright predictions of outcome.

That the problems of crisis relocation are myriad has certainly not escaped civil defense planners. They recognize some of the major drawbacks with the plan and are in the process of designing other, more extensive plans that do not rely on massive population movements and 5 days of warning. These plans, involving construction of in-place blast-resistant shelters for the entire U.S. population, have not yet been advocated as public policy. But they are suggested, in the studies under contract to FEMA, and in FEMA congressional testimony. In a few months to a year we may see such proposals, recommending expenditures of $100 billion, in fiscal year 1981 dollars.[80] So it is important for us to realize that the problem with civil defense planning in the setting of nuclear war lies not with the specific plan, but with the concept of survivability.

To evaluate that concept as applied to the post-attack world, we must stretch our understanding of what existence may or may not mean for those of us who might survive to see it. Our cities in rubble, our land burned and contaminated, our friends and relatives gone, future grimly foreshortened by prospects of famine and disease. Civil defense cannot change what the weapons can do.

If, after considered evaluation, it is seen that civil defense cannot protect the elements of our life and society we deem essential, then perhaps we

---

[78]Committee for the Compilation of Materials, "Hiroshima and Nagasaki." Basic Books, New York, 1981, pp. 152–153. J. Smith and T. Smith, "Long-Term Effects of Radiation, Medicine and the Bomb." British Medical Journal, v. 283, 3 October 1981, p. 908.

[79]Committee for the Compilation of Materials, op. cit., p. 151.

[80]L. W. Bellenson, "Selling Civil Defense," Journal of Civil Defense, December 1981, pp. 6–8. Committee on Armed Services, op. cit., pp. 816–821.

need to call for an entirely different approach to the problem of nuclear war. If we begin with the understanding that nuclear war is not in any humane or civilized sense survivable, the path becomes clear: civil defense planning for nuclear war is delusionary behavior and should not be encouraged. All our efforts must be directed at prevention.

QUESTIONS FOR DISCUSSION

1 Why does the Soviet Union spend so much money on civil defense?
2 Under what circumstances would a civil-defense program serve American security interests?
3 Would the creation of a major civil-defense program make American policy makers more likely to engage in a war against the Soviet Union?
4 What effect would a United States civil-defense program have on NATO?
5 What would be the Soviet response to an American effort to build a civil-defense program?

SUGGESTED READINGS

Dyson, Freeman. *Weapons and Hope*. New York: Harper & Row, 1984.
Gouré, Leon. "Another Interpretation," *Bulletin of the Atomic Scientists* 34 (April 1978), pp. 48–51.
Irwin, Michael H. K. *Can We Survive Nuclear War?* New York: Public Affairs Committee, 1984.
Kaplan, Fred M. "The Soviet Civil Defense Myth," *Bulletin of the Atomic Scientists* 34 (March 1978), pp. 14–20.
———. "The Soviet Civil Defense Myth: Part 2," *Bulletin of the Atomic Scientists* 34 (April 1978), pp. 41–48.
Leaning, Jennifer and Langley Keyes (eds.). *The Counterfeit Ark: Crisis Relocation for Nuclear War*. Cambridge, Massachusetts: Ballinger, 1983.
O'Heffernan, Patrick, Amory B. Lovins, and L. Hunter Lovins. *The First Nuclear World War: A Strategy for Preventing Nuclear Wars and the Spread of Nuclear Weapons*. New York: Morrow, 1983.
Perry, Ronald W. *The Social Psychology of Civil Defense*. Lexington, Massachusetts: Lexington Books, 1982.
"President Reagan's Civil Defense Program," *The Defense Monitor* 11, no. 5 (1982), pp. 1–8.
Scheer, Robert. *With Enough Shovels: Reagan, Bush and Nuclear War*. New York: Random House, 1982.
Ulsamer, Edgar. "Civil Defense in a Nuclear War," *Air Force Magazine* 65 (June 1982), pp. 70–73.
U.S. Congress: House of Representatives. *FEMA Oversight: Will U.S. Nuclear Attack Evacuation Plans Work?* Hearings before the Subcommittee on Environment, Energy and Natural Resources of the Committee on Government Operations, 97th Cong., 2nd Sess., 1982.
U.S. Congress: Office of Technology Assessment. *The Effects of Nuclear War*. Montclair, New Jersey: Allenheld, Osmun, 1980.
U.S. Congress: Senate. *U.S. and Soviet Civil Defense Programs*. Hearings before the Committee on Foreign Relations, 97th Cong., 2nd Sess., 1982.
Weinstein, John M. "Soviet Civil Defense and the U. S. Deterrent," *Parameters* 12 (March 1982), pp. 70–83.

14 Should the United States Avoid Space Weapons?

YES

Sidney D. Drell and Wolfgang K. H. Panofsky

The Case against Strategic Defense: Technical and Strategic Realities

NO

Robert Jastrow

Reagan vs. the Scientists: Why the President Is Right about Missile Defense

The Case against Strategic Defense: Technical and Strategic Realities

Sidney D. Drell and Wolfgang K. H. Panofsky

In his address to the nation on March 23, 1983, President Reagan advocated that the United States "embark on a program to counter the awesome Soviet missile threat with measures that are defensive." He called upon the American scientific community, "those who gave us nuclear weapons, to turn their great talents now to the cause of mankind and world peace, to give us the means of rendering these nuclear weapons impotent and obsolete." These words have rekindled the debate about defense against nuclear weapons—a subject that had been relatively dormant since the anti-ballistic missile (ABM) debates of 1969 and the ratification hearings for the ABM Treaty of 1972.

Throughout history, military analysts have grappled with the role of offense versus defense. Many examples can be cited in which offensive or defensive measures have proved decisive to the outcome of combat. In considering defenses against nuclear weapons, however, one must recognize that the enormous increase in the explosive power of nuclear bombs has wrought a fundamental discontinuity in the relative effectiveness of offensive and defensive measures. We must now recognize that a *single* relatively small nuclear bomb is a weapon of mass destruction. A modern nuclear warhead weighing perhaps 100 pounds can pack an explosive power equivalent to 100 kilotons or 200 million pounds of a "conventional" explosive such as TNT. This increase by a factor of 2 million stems directly from the physical fact that chemical energies are measured in electron volts while nuclear energies are measured in millions of electron volts. In nuclear explosives we are dealing with the forces that energize the sun and stars and fuel the cosmos.

Given the staggering destructive potential of nuclear bombs, effective defenses must meet a much higher standard of performance today than at any other time in the history of warfare. During World War II, air defenses were considered effective if 10 percent of the airplanes were lost in each attack: after ten such sorties only one-third of the airplanes and their crews would survive. Indeed, approximately that level of defense effectiveness brought victory to the Royal Air Force in the Battle of Britain in 1940. In the nuclear age, however, if 90 percent of the attacking aircraft or missiles are destroyed, and thus only 10 percent reach their targets, their nuclear weapons would produce a catastrophe of unimaginable proportions to the country under siege.

This example indicates the profound difficulty of using historical arguments in the discussion of offense versus defense in the nuclear age. The technical condition of the world has been so profoundly changed by the advent of nuclear weapons that simplistic historical comparisons can be, and often are, misleading.

In this article we describe the current strategic relationship of offense dominance, the potential roles for strategic defense, and the technical promise of ballistic missile defenses. We conclude by balancing the values and the risks associated with the new research and development program, the Strategic Defense Initiative.

II

The strategic relationship between the United States and the Soviet Union currently rests upon the balance of offensive forces, a situation known as "offense dominance." If either superpower launches a nuclear attack, it faces the risk of a nuclear retaliatory strike that can endanger its very existence.

Sidney D. Drell and Wolfgang K. H. Panofsky, "The Case against Strategic Defense: Technical and Strategic Realities," *Issues in Science and Technology,* Fall 1984, pp. 45–65.

While neither the United States nor the Soviet Union has made the destruction of enemy populations in response to enemy attack an explicit policy objective, both recognize that should a large fraction of the superpowers' arsenals be used—under any doctrine, any choice of pattern of attack, or for any purpose—then the threat to the survival of the two societies is very grave indeed.

Before the president's speech, it was also widely accepted that without drastic quantitative reductions and qualitative restrictions of the level of nuclear arms, it was not feasible to build a defensive shield that could effectively blunt, much less deny, a nuclear retaliatory strike.

The key element of the president's speech was a challenge to escape from this grim reliance on the threat of retaliation to deter aggression and nuclear war. "What if free people could live secure in the knowledge that their security did not rest upon the threat of instant U.S. retaliation to deter Soviet attack, that we could intercept and destroy strategic ballistic missiles before they reached our soil or that of our allies?" he asked. In expressing this hope, the president touched upon sentiments felt deeply by many citizens of the United States, the Soviet Union, and their neighboring nations, who seek a better peace than the present one in which they are mutual hostages to annihilation. Many find this situation morally repugnant; moreover, it cannot be expected to prevent nuclear war for all time. Unhappily, however, we see no technical alternative to the mutual hostage relationship—the state of Mutual Assured Destruction (MAD)—as long as nuclear armaments remain anywhere near the levels now stockpiled or continue to grow as they are today.

We are emphasizing this point here because MAD is frequently represented as a doctrine promulgated by some misguided policymakers willing to gamble with the survival of their country. Nothing could be further from the truth. The history of the nuclear weapons competition is replete with attempts by policymakers in both the United States and the Soviet Union to avoid the mutual hostage situation. Each time, however, they concluded that technol-

ogy simply does not permit such an escape unless the total level of nuclear arms in the world can be drastically lowered.

Recall President Nixon's statement[1] in 1969: "Although every instinct motivates me to provide the American people with complete protection against major nuclear attack, it is not now within our power to do so." Going back even further we find that in the early days of the Kennedy administration Secretary of Defense Robert McNamara attempted to adopt a nuclear policy of "city avoidance," in which the United States and, it was hoped, the Soviet Union would not target the opponent's cities. When combined with extensive civil defense measures, this policy would greatly reduce the risk to the people of the United States, he thought. Yet as the technical realities emerged, McNamara became persuaded that such measures would not prevent major population casualties. He concluded that a posture in which the vulnerability of population and industry did not play a dominant role was impossible.

The situation is similar on the Soviet side. In 1967 Soviet Premier Kosygin said, "I think a defensive system which prevents attack is not a cause of the arms race . . . its purpose is not to kill people but to save human lives." Yet in the subsequent years the recognition of mutual vulnerability has become central to the Soviet perception of the Soviet-American relationship. Leonid Brezhnev, for example, told the Twenty-sixth Party Congress in 1981 that "the military and strategic equilibrium between the Soviet Union and the United States . . . is objectively a safeguard of world peace." In September 1983 Marshal Ogarkov, chief of the General Staff, wrote that "with the modern development and dispersion of nuclear arms in the world, the defending side would always retain such a quantity of nuclear means as will be capable of

---

[1] For full references to these and subsequent quotations, see Sidney D. Drell, Philip J. Farley and David Holloway, *The Reagan Strategic Defense Initiative: A Technical, Political, and Arms Control Assessment* (Stanford, Calif.: Stanford Center for International Security and Arms Control, 1984).

inflicting 'unacceptable damage' . . . on the aggressor in a retaliatory strike."

Clearly, public remarks by military and civilian leaders in the United States and the Soviet Union are fallible indicators of national policy and military capability. Yet these quotations, and the changes in thought they imply, also make it clear that there is worldwide recognition that the current military balance is "offense dominated," however repugnant the notion of a mutual hostage relationship might be.

In this situation of mutual vulnerability, maintaining the stability of the military balance is the principal tool for avoiding nuclear war. The United States and the Soviet Union should do their utmost to avoid a situation in which either would be tempted in time of crisis to use nuclear weapons first on the assumption that launching a preemptive strike would be preferable to facing a likely attack by the other. In other words, "crisis stability" calls for minimizing the perceived advantage to the party attacking first.

Much has already been done in the attempt to enhance crisis stability. Essential ingredients for ensuring stability are a reliable—and survivable— command and control system, the ability of each side's retaliatory forces to survive an attack, and the demonstrable ability of retaliatory forces to reach their targets. Efforts must also be made to minimize the likelihood that unauthorized, accidental, or third party nuclear explosions might lead to all-out nuclear war.

In addition to the unilateral measures that each country can take to improve crisis stability, arms control measures can also be negotiated, based on the recognition that enhancement of stability is a matter of mutual interest to the Soviet Union and the United States. In the latter category, the ABM Treaty signed in 1972 and supplemented by a protocol in 1974 remains a key step, as we will discuss later in detail. In addition the agreement in 1963 to establish a "hot line" between Washington and Moscow, and the subsequent steps taken in 1971 and 1984 to improve that facility, is a noteworthy

attempt to avoid nuclear war through miscalculation or misinformation.

While these measures can enhance the stability of the current offensive balance, they cannot guarantee it. In the long run, the primary thrust for relieving the situation must be political; the evolution of U.S.-China relations during the past 20 years shows what can be done. The current mutual hostage relationship between the Soviet Union and the United States cannot be expected to endure forever. Insofar as technical means can contribute to relieving this relationship, we conclude that the only tool available is a *drastic* reduction of the world's nuclear arsenals. Extending the hope that, at the current levels of these arsenals, the mutual hostage relationship can be avoided through changes in doctrine or by technical measures will detract from efforts to attack the problem at its source: the existence of vastly excessive nuclear stockpiles worldwide.

III

In his speech, President Reagan proposed nothing less than a defensive system sufficiently comprehensive and impenetrable to make the American people immune to nuclear attack. His contention was that once such a shield was erected, the nuclear weapons states could be persuaded that these weapons served no useful purpose and could therefore be abolished.

Prior proponents of strategic defense have generally advocated roles short of the exceedingly ambitious goal proposed by the president. Similarly, some subsequent administration spokespersons have also stepped back from the president's "vision" and have supported considerably less ambitious missions for the administration's new research and technology effort, the Strategic Defense Initiative.

Most recent arguments in support of the Strategic Defense Initiative have emphasized the objective of "enhanced deterrence" against aggression. Indeed, this phrase was used in the Defense Department's five-year program for the new initiative submitted to Congress in March 1984. Some advocates include in this mission the protection of elements of the U.S. retaliatory forces. Other advocates have said that the Strategic Defense Initiative is intended as a useful tool in furthering the arms control process with the Soviet Union. In a different vein, Richard DeLauer, undersecretary of defense for research and engineering, has said that arms control is a necessary precondition for an effective defense. Specifically, he has said that without limits on offensive nuclear weapons "no defensive system can work." Finally, all advocates of the Strategic Defense Initiative continue to emphasize that research and technology programs on defense remain essential to keep pace with Soviet developments, thereby avoiding "technological surprise" should a Soviet system evolve on a short time scale. Let us examine in turn these potential roles of strategic defense.

Making Nuclear Weapons Obsolete A defense meeting the president's vision would require near perfection in performance. If only 1 percent of the approximately 8,000 nuclear strategic warheads in the current Soviet force penetrated a defensive shield and landed on urban targets in the United States, it would cause one of the greatest disasters in recorded history.

To attain such a level of protection, *all* means of delivery of such weapons to the United States must be interdicted with near 100 percent efficiency. This would entail not only defenses against intercontinental and submarine-launched ballistic missiles, but also against strategic aircraft and cruise missiles from air, land, or sea. Even the introduction of "suitcase bombs" would have to be prevented. Yet the Strategic Defense Initiative specifically deals with only the ballistic missile threat.

There is general consensus that U.S. air defenses, largely ignored in recent years, are incapable of dealing with any massive attack from the Soviet strategic air force. This is true even though the Soviet air force is currently much less capable than the U.S. strategic bomber force, which is now

being outfitted with long-range, nuclear-tipped cruise missiles. U.S. air defenses were downgraded in the 1960s when it became clear not only that modernization and maintenance of an effective air defense would be vastly expensive and of dubious technical success, but also that expansion of these air defenses would be a futile gesture against the delivery systems for nuclear weapons then evolving—the intercontinental and submarine-launched ballistic missiles.

By contrast, Soviet air defenses are much more extensive. Several rings of air defenses are emplaced around Moscow, and extensive networks of surface-to-air missiles are deployed throughout the Soviet Union. Soviet air defenses have gone through a number of evolutionary stages, with the new SA-12 being the most capable system. Nonetheless, the U.S. Air Force continues to believe that its manned bombers, the modernized B-52s, would be able to penetrate Soviet air defenses using such diverse penetration tactics as electronic countermeasures and a precursor ballistic missile attack to destroy Soviet surface-to-air missiles prior to the air attack. In addition, cruise missiles can be delivered in the "stand-off" mode, that is, launched from aircraft outside the range of Soviet surface-to-air missiles and beyond the range of most Soviet fighters, a tactic that appears certain to extend the bomber threat against the Soviet Union for the foreseeable future. Moreover, the "stealth" technology being pursued in the United States, which involves measures to reduce the radar cross section of penetrating bombers and of cruise missiles, makes the future air defense task exceedingly, if not prohibitively, difficult.

Conversely, it is indeed hard to imagine that, starting from the minimal system deployed to date, the United States could develop an effective air defense against an opponent determined to counter it. Nor has the administration proposed that such a program be initiated. Yet nuclear weapons could hardly be made "obsolete" unless the air strike "window of vulnerability" is closed.

Potential Soviet cruise missiles pose an even

greater threat to the United States. Following the U.S. lead, the Soviets are now acquiring long-range cruise missile technology. During the coming decades we can anticipate that cruise missiles will be deployed on aircraft, on land, and on ships and submarines, unless, of course, such deployments are ruled out by arms control treaties. The technology for defense against cruise missiles is similar in principle to that used against aircraft. However, cruise missiles have smaller radar cross sections and can follow terrain at lower altitudes, which makes them much more difficult to detect and then to destroy. In addition, there is a geographical asymmetry between the United States and the Soviet Union that heightens the danger to the United States; a much larger share of our society is built up near our coastline, within easier range of cruise missiles launched from enemy submarines and aircraft. Finally, the introduction of nuclear explosives into the United States by clandestine transport cannot be prevented by technical means, as has been demonstrated by numerous studies. Although major powers, in particular the Soviet Union, are unlikely to adopt such a tactic, it remains a potential terrorist threat.

Even ignoring these other threats, we view the possibility of erecting an impenetrable shield against ballistic missiles as very remote indeed for many decades to come. It is difficult for a responsible scientist to say flatly that a task is impossible to achieve by technical means without being accused of being a "naysayer." Indeed, many instances can be cited in which prominent scientists have concluded that a task is impossible only to be proved wrong by future discoveries. One should recognize, however, that the deployment of an impenetrable defense over the nation is not a single technical achievement but the evolution of an extensive and exceedingly complex *system* that must work reliably in a hostile environment. Furthermore, one must have continued high confidence in the defense system, although it can never be tested under realistic conditions—especially against an offense that can adopt a broad repertoire of countermeasures against it.

Protection against ballistic missiles requires many links in a defensive chain, all of which are crucial. There must be sensors to provide early warning of an attack; a command structure with authority to make decisions on committing the defensive forces on exceedingly short notice and then to implement those decisions efficiently. This raises the grave problem as to whether this chain of command, from warning to decision, must be *totally* automated or may contain human links. The defensive system must also have sensors that acquire and track the enemy missiles and then aim and fire the defensive devices, be they material interceptors, such as chemical rockets or hypervelocity guns, or directed-energy devices. Sensors must also determine which of the attacking missiles have been destroyed in order to fight secondary or tertiary engagements successfully.

Even the most optimistic protagonist for defensive systems agrees that no single layer of defense could possibly be effective. Thus the Strategic Defense Initiative describes its goal as a multilayered defense of extensive scope, capable of attacking ballistic missiles during boost phase as they are lifted into space, then during the midcourse of their flight, and finally, during their reentry over their targets.

We strongly emphasize that the issue is not whether a specific technology for the interception of incoming ballistic missiles can be demonstrated. We fully agree that a single reentry vehicle from a ballistic missile can be destroyed by nuclear explosives lofted by interceptors, as was shown to be feasible in earlier developments, or by non-nuclear, high-velocity projectiles as was demonstrated by the U.S. Air Force in June 1984. We also believe that a demonstration can be staged in which an ascending ICBM boost vehicle can be damaged by airborne or spaceborne laser beams. However, such demonstrations of the interception of cooperating targets hardly have bearing on the feasibility of the overall system or the solution of operational problems.

We will briefly discuss in the next section the technical options for a defense system. Here we simply state that the goal of a truly impenetrable shield against delivery of nuclear weapons of all kinds over the United States is, in our view, impossible to attain—to the extent that the word "impossible" can be associated with practical human undertakings. We agree with Undersecretary of Defense DeLauer that "with unconstrained proliferation, no defensive system can work."

Enhanced Deterrence   When submitting the five-year program for the Strategic Defense Initiative in March 1984, DeLauer testified before the House Committee on Armed Services that Defense Department studies have "concluded that advanced defensive technologies could offer the potential to enhance deterrence and help prevent nuclear war by reducing significantly the military utility of Soviet preemptive attacks and by undermining an aggressor's confidence of a successful attack against the United States or our allies." Program advocates claim that this mission can be met by even a less-than-perfect area defense of population and industry.

It is indeed true that if a potential attacker faces the prospect of attrition of his forces by a defense, in addition to the expected retaliatory strike, his confidence in the success of his planned attack would decrease, and the complexity of planning such a move would increase. If one could correctly anticipate that this would be the *only* Soviet reaction to an expanded Strategic Defense Initiative, one might consider this to be sufficient reason to move ahead toward deployment of a nationwide defense against ballistic missiles. However, the much more likely Soviet response would be to initiate a variety of programs to counteract the effectiveness of such defenses to retain full confidence in their deterrent. More than likely they would also move ahead with intensified defense programs of their own. The net result of these moves and countermoves would be the addition of yet another component to the arms competition between the superpowers, in both offensive and defensive forces, and the end of the ABM Treaty of 1972, which explicitly prohibits the development and deployment of nationwide

ballistic missile defenses. In consequence, the security of the United States would be diminished, not increased.

In contrast to "enhancing deterrence," the combination of our offensive strength and the damage-limiting potential of our defenses could be seen as giving us more flexibility to use nuclear weapons to punish, or threaten to punish, Soviet actions we consider unacceptable. In other words, the threshold at which we would consider the use of nuclear weapons could be lowered.

The Soviets may see our defensive programs, accompanied by our ongoing intensive effort to modernize and improve our offensive forces, as evidence of preparations for a first strike—a first strike that would leave them with a weakened retaliatory force against which our defenses, although imperfect, would be relatively more effective. Of course, the same would be true if the roles of the Soviet Union and the United States were interchanged.

The argument that is acceptable for the United States—but not the Soviet Union—to strengthen our deterrent with ballistic missile defenses while disregarding the implied first-strike threat can only be sustained by invoking an asymmetry in the moral stance of the two societies. It implies that the United States should be protected from a Soviet first strike under all circumstances, while the Soviets would not have to fear such an attack from the United States. It can be argued that during the 1950s the United States did have a first-strike potential against the Soviet Union and did not exercise it. The Soviets would find this reasoning less than persuasive, as would most other nations.

Surely, the United States would feel highly threatened if the Soviets proclaimed a policy of developing nationwide missile defenses to "enhance deterrence" and then initiated an intensified program toward that goal. In fact, Secretary of Defense Caspar Weinberger explicitly stated in December 1983 that the Soviet development of an effective missile defense "would be one of the most frightening prospects I could imagine."

We find the argument that the evolution of ballistic missile defense can serve a deterrent mission extremely difficult to support. Prima facie, it simply adds another component to the arms competition, and a relatively inefficient and potentially destabilizing component at that. It is well to keep in mind the precedent of MIRVs, or multiple independently targeted warheads. MIRV technology was originally stimulated by the initial, limited deployment—and anticipated expansion—of ballistic missile defenses around Moscow. By substantially increasing the firepower of the offense—measured in the number of warheads and damage expectancy, not megatonnage—MIRVs were designed to overpower these defenses. Yet MIRVs have not made us more secure; they themselves have become the focus of instability by their growing threat to land-based U.S. and Soviet intercontinental ballistic missiles (ICBMs).

To some extent the issue is one of relative cost. Because the purpose of an area defense is to limit damage to U.S. population and industry at a certain cost, then one must consider how much additional cost the Soviet offense would have to incur to restore the damage expectancy to the same value it had before defenses were deployed. Such a ratio of offense to defense cost, called the exchange ratio, has been calculated in the past and has always been found to be highly unfavorable to the defense. It appears unlikely that new technologies will upset this earlier economic conclusion. In addition, cost estimates for systems based on technologies in the early research stages have often proved to be notorious underestimates.

Protection of the Offensive Deterrent
Another distinct objective of ballistic missile defense, known as hardsite defense, is the protection of elements of the U.S. strategic retaliatory forces, in particular hardened missile silos and hardened command centers. Technically, this job is easier than the broader area defense of population and industry described above because only selected targets have to be protected. Moreover, hardened targets can be damaged only by a direct hit or a hit within the immediate vicinity. Consequently, there

is a narrow "threat tube," or region through which the attacking missiles must pass, to destroy a hardened target. Furthermore, protection of the retaliatory forces does not require a high standard of effectiveness: if a reasonable fraction of the retaliatory forces survive, the attacker can expect assured retaliation with an unacceptable level of damage.

The strategic mission of protecting retaliatory forces with a hardsite defense is very different from that of complete area defense for population protection envisaged by the president. The president's goal was to shift the burden for maintaining a strategic balance from offensive to defensive weapons. By contrast, protection of the retaliatory forces maintains the dominant role of offensive weapons on which the current strategic military balance is based: it enhances offense dominance by preserving the survival of offensive missiles and ensuring their capability to retaliate against the opponent.

The distinction between area and hardsite defense has played an important role in the history of U.S. missile defense efforts. During the 1960s, the United States developed a series of systems largely intended for area defense. While Secretary McNamara recognized the ineffectiveness of those ABM systems as a shield against substantial Soviet attacks, he proposed that a limited area defense, called the Sentinel system, be deployed to offer some protection against accidental or unauthorized launches and against attacks from minor nuclear powers. Subsequently, the Nixon administration recognized that even limited area defenses using then available technology were not desirable for U.S. security. These limited defenses would not effectively protect society. Moreover, because the Soviets could interpret them as the beginning of a nationwide system threatening to their retaliatory capabilities, these defenses could reduce stability. On the other hand, defense of hardened ICBM silos, if technically feasible, was judged desirable by the administration because it would provide protection from preemptive attack. As such, a hardsite defense would contribute to the stability of deterrence based on offense dominance.

This reasoning led to the proposal to deploy the Safeguard system designed to protect Minuteman sites. Unfortunately, Safeguard used the same hardware—large radars and long-range interceptor missiles—that had been developed for the earlier Sentinel area defense concept and was not technically effective as a hardsite defense. It had limited firepower, and its radars were few and vulnerable to blinding and to direct attack. In addition, its commonality of hardware with Sentinel raised the concern that it could be interpreted by the Soviets as a base for a future area defense, with its implied escalatory impact.

The stabilizing role of defenses specifically designed to defend hardened missile sites was recognized by the United States during the SALT I negotiations, but it proved impossible to formulate objective criteria to distinguish hardsite defense from area defense. Accordingly, the ABM Treaty of 1972 and its 1974 protocol allow both nations to deploy a missile defense system of no more than 100 interceptors either to protect the national capital or a single complex of ICBM silos. The Soviets opted for the former. They have deployed around Moscow the only operational, albeit limited, ballistic missile defense system today. The United States chose the latter and began building a defense of the missile fields at Grand Forks, North Dakota; the defense was soon abandoned because of its cost ineffectiveness.

In principle, hardsite defense could be made much more cost-effective than the old Safeguard system, and hardware could be designed specifically for this mission as distinct from area defense. The question of whether such a development should be pursued is raised whenever the survivability of the land-based deterrent is examined. Dedicated hardsite defense systems were extensively studied in connection with the protection of the current Minuteman fields, the MX "Racetrack" proposed in the Carter administration, and the Dense-Pack MX deployment proposed in this administration. In each case, the option was not pursued further, largely because its cost was considered excessive in relation to its projected effectiveness.

This history must be kept in mind when it is suggested that protection of the deterrent might be a useful byproduct of the Strategic Defense Initiative, whose primary stated goal is a nationwide area defense. Although such a byproduct might be of some value in stabilizing the offensive balance, it is important to remember that in the past even a fully dedicated hardsite defense has been judged of insufficient merit. Furthermore, a technology development program for hardsite defense would have major differences from one directed toward realizing the president's vision of rendering "nuclear weapons impotent and obsolete."

Keeping Pace with Soviet Technology   It has frequently been suggested that the United States should place greater emphasis on ballistic missile defense because the Soviets are undertaking an active program in this area. Yet if the United States concluded that the Soviet effort gave them a significant military edge or threatened strategic stability or U.S. security, the logical U.S. response should be to counter the Soviet threat, not to emulate it. Historically, the Soviet Union has dedicated a much larger fraction of its strategic military effort to defensive programs—motivated in part by the Russian tradition of "protecting the homeland." Yet there is little, if any, disagreement among military analysts that neither the Soviet's extensive air defense nor the Moscow missile defense offers effective protection against U.S. retaliatory forces.

The Soviets are modernizing, within the bounds imposed by the ABM Treaty, the missile defense around Moscow. Specifically, they are replacing the exoatmospheric interceptors deployed since 1970 with a combination of higher performance endoatmospheric and exoatmospheric missiles. In this respect, the Moscow system is acquiring a capability similar to the old U.S. Sentinel and Safeguard systems. One cannot, of course, dismiss the possibility that the new Moscow deployment might form the base of a future nationwide defense. The Soviets have developed modular tracking and missile guidance radars. Coupled with the Moscow system interceptors, these might result in a deployable nationwide defense system. There is no persuasive evidence, however, that the Soviets are in fact preparing for a nationwide deployment, which would constitute a "breakout" from the ABM Treaty. In any event, it would take many years before such a system could reach a level of deployment having potential for significant military effectiveness.

The Soviets have constructed large phased-array radars for early warning at three perimeter locations and have recently closed the remaining gap within this early warning coverage by a further radar of similar design at Krasnoyarsk in Siberia. This radar has probably been under construction since before 1980, but is not yet operating. It has drawn specific attention and raised serious concern because its location—away from Soviet borders, in contrast to the other early warning radars—constitutes a likely violation of the ABM Treaty. The Soviets state that this radar is designed for space tracking rather than early warning, but this is difficult to reconcile with its characteristics. Be this as it may, the military significance of this radar is minor, although its political significance is important if it does indeed constitute a violation of the treaty.

The Soviet Union has also been pursuing significant research and technology programs for ballistic missile defense, including research on the use of directed-energy weapons for this purpose. Although this Soviet effort has been proceeding steadily for well over a decade, many phases have remained essentially unchanged for some time. Soviet research differs in many details from that pursued by the United States, but its overall quality is comparable to the existing U.S. effort. One should recognize, however, that the Soviet Union lags behind the United States in many of the supporting technologies essential to a successful area defense. This is particularly true in computer hardware and software and in various sensor systems. In short, there is no need for the United States to match the Soviet ABM effort on the basis of its technical merit. Even if it were desirable for purely political reasons to keep pace with the Soviets, it would be difficult to justify an expansion of the current U.S. research and technology effort on that basis. The

possibility that the Soviet program might result in new discoveries cannot be ignored, however. Therefore, a deliberate U.S. research and technology program can be justified to allow us to interpret Soviet progress and to prevent "technological surprise."

IV

There is little controversy about whether deliberate research and technology programs on ballistic missile defense should be continued, particularly given the desire to avoid technological surprise. However, the actual magnitude of such a program—and especially public statements referring to its purpose and promise—should be tempered by balancing realistic expectations for a technically functional ballistic missile defense system against the risks of proceeding beyond the research and technology phase, should it appear feasible to do so. Above all, a realistic technical assessment of ballistic missile defense must consider operational limitations, including those stemming from countermeasures by the offense, no matter how successful the technology programs may be. The risks of going forward with deployment include intensified arms competition, a decrease in stability, and abrogation or termination of the ABM Treaty of 1972. These risks will be discussed in the next section.

For as long as there have been ballistic missiles, defenses against them have been studied. This paper can only touch upon some of the generic questions relating to the technical potential of the various defense concepts under consideration in the Strategic Defense Initiative.

Few of these technologies are genuinely new, although some have been considerably upgraded. Radars and high-performance missile interceptors, carrying both nuclear and non-nuclear warheads, high-power laser beams, particle beams—all these have been under investigation for many years. What might be considered new are the potential x-ray lasers pumped, or energized, by nuclear explosions; the use of active optics to dynamically correct the performance of mirrors used to focus beam weapons; and the great advances in the technology of handling vast amounts of information in a short time.

Ballistic missile defense systems can be deployed on the ground or in space, or both. As mentioned earlier, the Strategic Defense Initiative is considering a multitiered defense against ballistic missiles based in space and on Earth, with intercept layers proposed during the boost and post-boost (or bus) phase, during midcourse, and during warhead reentry. The purpose of such a multilayered defense is to achieve a very high level of overall system performance, beyond what is practical to achieve at each individual stage of intercept, and to attenuate the incoming force of warheads in successive steps.

Space-Based Interceptors Basing interceptors in space has advantages and disadvantages. A major advantage is that in space the atmosphere does not interfere with the propagation of the means of intercept—either such directed-energy weapons as light beams or particles, or more massive projectiles. A serious disadvantage is that space-based platforms are expensive and vulnerable—in fact, more vulnerable than ballistic missiles. Satellites in space move in precisely predictable orbits, which can be kept under observation for protracted periods. Thus an attack on space-based defenses can be executed much more deliberately than can attacks on ballistic missiles. This vulnerability is so fundamental that many have doubted the practicality of space-based battle stations for a viable ballistic missile defense.[2]

Inevitably, the basing of defensive systems in space would initiate a round of offense-defense competition in which the offense would seek to develop various options for attacking the space platforms (using a combination of antisatellite measures) while the defense would attempt to harden the space platforms and engage in evasive or oth-

erwise protective tactics. Space-basing would not offer a simple way of deploying a defensive system. More likely it would stimulate further escalation of the arms race into space. Without more study and even in-depth experimentation one cannot draw firm conclusions on the outcome of such competition—if there were a clear outcome. One can conclude, however, that escalation of such competition into space would be expensive and also dangerous to those space systems now used for surveillance, early warning, communication, navigation, and commerce.

Based on those facts now known, our judgment is that placing defensive systems on space platforms would constitute a highly undesirable escalation of the arms competition. It also appears quite unpromising on technical grounds. Under no circumstance should the remote possibility of using space for ballistic missile defense purposes be accepted as a valid argument against proceeding in serious, good-faith negotiations with the Soviet Union toward banning weapons from space.

Boost-Phase Intercept The possibility of boost-phase intercept is the principal new technical element in the ballistic missile defense picture. "Boost phase" refers to the first several minutes of powered flight before the missile releases its multiple warheads. There are several advantages to boost-phase intercept. The missile is much easier to locate and track while its engines are burning, and boosters are relatively "softer" and easier to destroy than the post-boost vehicles and reentry vehicles they carry. Destruction of a booster would eliminate its entire payload, which may contain a substantial number of warheads plus many more decoys (perhaps in the hundreds). Booster intercept would therefore reduce the difficulty of the task faced by the subsequent layers of defense.

Boost-phase intercept, however, is a formidable task. The defense has very little time to commit its resources to intercept the booster. In addition, the booster spends a fair fraction of its active burn time shielded by the atmosphere from the interceptors, be they beam weapons or homing vehicles. Fur-

[2]See Edward Teller, "Bringing Star Wars Down to Earth," *Popular Mechanics,* July 1984, 84–122.

thermore, it is possible for the offense to deploy "fast-burn" boosters, which spend essentially all of their shortened burn time in the atmosphere. Fast-burn boosters can be developed with available technology and with only a limited cost in missile efficiency as measured by its payload.

In principle, the booster can be attacked by space-based chemical lasers, space-based x-ray lasers, space-based neutral particle beams, and by massive projectiles of very high speed—the so-called "kinetic-energy weapons." In addition, the booster can be attacked by "pop-up" systems, that is, directed-energy weapons carried aboard rockets launched into space after detection of an attack. Some of the key features of the various boost-phase weapon concepts will be discussed in turn.

Let us first consider satellite-based, high-powered lasers delivering an intense beam of infrared light against an ascending booster. Aside from the general issues associated with space-basing discussed above, we face the logistical difficulties associated with effective deployment of the entire system. If the space platforms are located in lower earth orbit, then a large number must be deployed to keep within firing range all potential ICBM launch areas in the Soviet Union. The exact number required depends, of course, on the lethal range of the space-based lasers. This is also true for other intercept devices. Typical assumptions about what may be achieved technically with efficient, high-powered infrared lasers and large, high-quality optical systems for forming the laser beam lead to a requirement of several hundred laser battle stations against an ICBM threat of 1,400 boosters, the size of the current Soviet force.[3] Moreover, if this boost-

phase system is to be effective at all times, each of these battle stations must carry a power source of sufficient size so that the small fraction of lasers that are "on station" have enough fuel to be able to defend against a simultaneous attack of the entire Soviet missile force. To supply this fuel would require placing in orbit the equivalent of several hundred loads of the space shuttle.

Any specific numbers can be contested from either the optimistic or pessimistic side. On the pessimistic side, one can maintain that the boosters might be hardened beyond our assumption in the above example, or they could be rotated to spread the area over which the energy is absorbed, or their burn time could be reduced, shortening the time available for the engagement. On the optimistic side, one can project even more powerful lasers with increased range, which would reduce the number of orbiting platforms required from many hundreds to dozens. We doubt that such differences in views can be reconciled soon through additional research and development. We are dealing with a dynamic situation in which both the offense and defense participate—the issues are operational as well as technical.

A second option for boost-phase intercept is space-based neutral particle beams of high energy traveling close to half the speed of light. It has long been known that intense particle beams produced by accelerators will damage targets. The energy transfer of such a particle beam to a target is quite efficient and difficult to counteract. However, particle beam devices face formidable technical and economic obstacles. In the atmosphere, these weapons have a short effective range, owing to interactions between particle beams and the atmosphere. If used in space, the particle beams would have to be neutral rather than charged to escape deflection and dispersion by magnetic fields. Such neutral particle beams, then, would have to be formed by neutralizing beams "born charged" when produced in accelerators. The neutralizing process can be quite efficient and introduces only a small additional divergence into the beam. However, the

---

[3]If the capabilities of space-based lasers are extrapolated many orders of magnitude from present performance to a brightness of 4×10^{20} watts/steradian, corresponding, for example, to a power output of 100 MW as a feasible goal in the infrared region and to an optical system with a 4-meter diameter mirror operated at its diffraction limit, and if we assume that the fluence (i.e. energy/unit area) required to fatally damage the booster is 20 kilojoules per square centimeter, then approximately 300 laser battle stations in lower earth orbit are required. See reference 1 for more details.

logistics and power numbers that go with such devices are similar to those discussed for chemical lasers, and the costs, if anything, are even less favorable. Because of these problems and the generic issues of space-basing, we do not attribute much promise to this approach.

A third option for boost-phase intercept is x-ray lasers. It is now publicly known that nuclear explosions can be used to "pump," or supply energy to, laser devices that can generate beams in the x-ray region of the spectrum, thereby concentrating a fraction of the energy of a nuclear weapon into a narrow cone. Naturally, the narrower the cone and the higher the efficiency for converting bomb energy to laser output, the longer the intercept range. There has been some analysis of the atomic processes for making x-ray lasers in the open U.S. and Soviet literature. Intense pulses of x-ray damage the boost vehicle by "blowing off" the surface skin of the vehicle because the x-rays are absorbed in an extremely thin layer of the vehicle. This is similar to the kill mechanism of the earlier Sentinel and Safeguard systems, in which the interceptor carried nondirectional nuclear warheads to intercept reentry vehicles in space.

The use of such x-ray devices for boost-phase intercept is constrained by their very limited penetrating power, generally less than 1 millionth of the thickness of the atmosphere. Thus, if the offense chooses to shorten the burn of the booster—at some limited penalty in missile performance—so that the boost phase is completed in the atmosphere, such x-ray devices would become useless. In addition, it is clear that the source—a nuclear explosion—destroys itself once used. Although one can visualize multiple targets for a single explosion, any defense that requires a sequence of intercepts must involve separate nuclear explosions and thus separate platforms. Moreover, one has to consider offense tactics such as nuclear bursts detonated in advance of the main attack, which might interfere with the sensors that guide the x-ray laser. These advance nuclear explosions can heat the top of the atmosphere, causing it to expand and to rise,

thus shielding the booster for a longer portion of its flight.

For all of these reasons, space-basing of x-ray laser devices appears thoroughly unattractive. An alternative would be to deploy a pop-up system based on ground. In principle, an x-ray laser pumped by a nuclear explosion is sufficiently small to be launched by a missile on detection of an enemy attack. Such a system would have to be based quite near Soviet territory, offshore from the United States, in order to make it geometrically possible to achieve an intercept. Moreover, like any other system for boost-phase intercept, a pop-up system would have to operate on an automated basis, given the minimal time available between detection of booster launch and commitment of the interceptors. This raises profound policy questions about whether such nuclear devices should be prepositioned close to Soviet shores and launched without human intervention.

To avoid the problems associated with the boost-phase intercept options discussed above, various hybrid systems have been proposed. The most prominent concept calls for large mirrors placed in space to focus laser beams onto enemy targets. The laser beams would be generated by a series of ground stations, widely dispersed to hedge against adverse weather conditions, or located on mountain tops above the weather. The beams from the ground would be focused to large relay mirrors in synchronous orbit, an altitude of 36,000 kilometers. To focus the beam would require active optics systems that could compensate for the atmospheric disturbances. The relay mirrors would also have to be aimed precisely and continuously at various mission mirrors in lower earth orbit. These, in turn, would focus the beam onto the boost vehicles. In principle, this system might indeed direct damaging levels of energy at the boost vehicle, although the technical requirements are quite severe. However, relay and mission mirrors are subject to all the vulnerabilities for space-borne stations discussed previously. If some of the mission mirrors were launched into lower earth orbit on detection of an attack, there would still be the problem of the short engagement time characteristic of all pop-up systems. The economics and practicality of this system cannot really be analyzed at this stage of development.

A boost-phase defense can also be designed that relies on direct impact by small homing rockets traveling at high speeds, comparable to those of the ICBMs themselves (about 5 to 7 kilometers per second). This is a well-developed technology, which could be deployed much sooner than the more exotic directed-energy beam weapons. However, it is also a much more limited technology that could be countered by the offense with relative ease. In particular, the interceptors are much too large and heavy to "pop-up" atop a single missile and instead would have to be launched from a constellation of space-based battle stations. Such a system thus inherits the many operational problems of all space-based systems; vulnerability to direct attack; ineffectiveness against fast-burn boosters; and the large number of space platforms—and enormous tonnage—required because each is "on station" only a small percentage of time. On balance, we consider kinetic-energy systems to be of limited potential and generally ineffective for boost-phase intercept.

Midcourse Intercept Intercepting ICBMs during the midcourse of their flight has been proposed many times in the past. Midcourse lasts perhaps 20 to 25 minutes, much longer than boost phase. Although this longer engagement time is an advantage, other factors make midcourse defense exceedingly difficult and have discouraged missile defense designers in the past.

The potential targets in midcourse are both the post-boost vehicle and the individual warheads. The post-boost vehicles are, or can generally be designed to be, harder than the boosters, and their burn times can also be greatly shortened. The numerous individual warheads are even harder still. Decoys are readily deployed in midcourse because there is no atmospheric drag to affect their trajectories. In addition, the signal on which an interceptor can "home" is more difficult to generate in midcourse because there is no friction to heat up the vehicles and dissipate energy. Radar cross sections are generally small and infrared signatures weak. Background radiation can be enhanced by high-altitude nuclear explosions to confuse interceptor sensors.

The contest between midcourse intercept by any means and a coordinated attack appears quite favorable to the offense because the number of targets—real and decoy—can be proliferated almost at will at relatively low cost. Candidates for midcourse interceptors include all the devices mentioned in connection with boost-phase intercept, but in this phase the operational problems appear even more severe. To be effective, the intercept system has to operate in a hostile environment for a protracted time. Therefore, in addition to increasing the number of targets to be engaged by the defense, the offense can adopt active tactics that threaten the defense. In short, midcourse intercept remains an extremely difficult problem; the new technologies have done little to modify earlier pessimistic conclusions. In particular, even with a highly effective layer for boost-phase intercept, the overall battle management problem is severe in midcourse. Currently, there is no viable concept for a highly effective midcourse defense against a massive threat of thousands of warheads, post-boost vehicles, and perhaps many tens of thousands of decoys.

Terminal Defense Once individual reentry vehicles and decoys enter the atmosphere, lighter decoys become easily distinguishable, which greatly reduces the number of targets to be engaged by a terminal defense. Early developmental systems for terminal defense used nuclear explosives carried by high-performance ascending rockets as interceptors. Recent improvements in technology, in particular in guidance precision and in higher acceleration rockets, have made it possible to destroy an incoming warhead by non-nuclear means, as the Air Force demonstrated in June 1984.

Even with these advances, terminal defense on a nationwide basis is an enormously more difficult task than hardsite defense of selected targets. Urban industrial complexes are spread all over the nation, and they are much more vulnerable and valuable than missile emplacements. No serious claims have been made that terminal defense alone could offer significant protection of the U.S. population and industry against a massive Soviet ICBM attack. Only if boost- and midcourse-phase intercepts have eliminated all but a few percent of attacking warheads could any hope be extended for an effective terminal defense.

On the positive side, nationwide terminal defense can offer some protection against minor attacks, be they accidental or unauthorized launches or attacks by third powers using a small number of missiles. It is important to note, however, that ballistic missiles are hardly the most likely threat from minor powers, as their development and manufacture require a major technological effort. Moreover, an areawide terminal defense is exceedingly expensive, certainly amounting to tens if not hundreds of billions of dollars.

V

As noted earlier, an expanded ballistic missile defense effort poses several strategic risks, including potential conflict with arms control treaties and the risk of accelerating arms competition.

Danger of Confrontation with Arms Control Treaties The administration has been careful to describe its current program as research, and the activities it proposes for the next fiscal year appear to be in compliance with obligations under existing treaties. However, if the Strategic Defense Initiative were to expand in the future from its current research and technology focus through prototype and systems testing to actual deployment, several arms control treaties would be at risk. These are the 1972 ABM Treaty and its associated 1974 protocol, the 1963 Limited Test Ban Treaty, and the Outer Space Treaty of 1967.

The ABM Treaty explicitly prohibits regional and nationwide ballistic missile defenses, permit-

ting only a single deployment of limited firepower for the defense of the national capital or one designated ICBM complex. Although the treaty permits research and technology, it prohibits a number of new developments, including the development, testing, or deployment of mobile, land-based systems and those based in air, space, or sea. Ambassador Gerard Smith, chief U.S. negotiator of the ABM Treaty, defined the boundary between permitted and forbidden activities during the treaty ratification hearings before the Senate Armed Services Committee in 1972 as follows: "The obligation not to develop such systems, devices or warheads would be applicable only to the stage of development which follows laboratory development and testing. The prohibitions on development contained in the ABM Treaty would start at that part of the development process where field testing is initiated on either a prototype or breadboard model. It was understood by both sides that the prohibition on 'development' applies to activities involved after a component moves from the laboratory development and testing stage to the field testing stage, wherever performed." This interpretation would clearly prohibit prototype and systems testing as well as engineering development.

It has been suggested by some supporters of the Strategic Defense Initiative in and out of government that if confrontations between expanded defense activities and the ABM Treaty were to occur, then the treaty could be renegotiated to accommodate the proposed activities. The ABM Treaty is of indefinite duration and is subject to review every five years. This review, however, does not imply renegotiation, which would be a separate matter. It also contains a provision for either party to abrogate the treaty, after suitable notification, invoking jeopardy to its "supreme interests."

The Strategic Defense Initiative would also violate the Limited Nuclear Test Ban Treaty and the Outer Space Treaty if it moved ahead with tests and operational deployment in space of x-ray lasers pumped by nuclear explosions. The Outer Space Treaty prohibits the placement of weapons of mass destruction, including nuclear weapons, in space.

The 1963 Limited Test Ban Treaty prohibits nuclear explosions in the atmosphere, under water, and in outer space. Although this treaty in itself has had only minor impact on the bilateral U.S.-Soviet arms competition, it has reduced worldwide fallout by two orders of magnitude and has been a substantial moral force in the cause of nuclear nonproliferation.

Neither renegotiation nor abrogation of the three treaties mentioned above can be taken lightly for a number of reasons. First, these treaties have served U.S. national security well. Second, should outright abrogation occur the concomitant political price would be heavy. Third, should renegotiation be initiated at the request of the United States, but with the Soviet Union disclaiming interest in such a move, the United States would have to pay a price in concessions to the Soviet Union to arrive at settlement.

The ABM Treaty, in particular, has been of great value to U.S. and NATO security. The treaty has helped limit competitive and escalatory growth of the strategic arsenals, which could well have exceeded current bounds. Furthermore, as documented in the 1972 Moscow summit, the ABM Treaty was enacted by both nations in recognition that peaceful coexistence was a matter of practical necessity. In that spirit, the ABM Treaty is a key step in the political approach to preventing nuclear war. It is much more than just a symbol of arms control hopes. It is not based on idealism; instead it accepts the mutual hostage relationship between the United States and the Soviet Union as a present necessity and as an objective condition, not as an active threat. Although the Soviets have never accepted "deterrence" in precisely the same terms as those used by most U.S. analysts, they have frequently emphasized that under current conditions nuclear war would be tantamount to suicide for both sides. In this sense, deterrence is not based on mutual threats but on prudent reciprocal restraints, such as those embodied in the ABM Treaty, to avoid nuclear war.

The ABM Treaty has also helped to lift the veil of secrecy surrounding the Soviet Union by guaranteeing that satellites and other surveillance tools located outside of national boundaries—the so-called "National Technical Means" of verification—shall not be interfered with in peace time. It also established the Standing Consultative Commission, a generally effective private forum for airing queries and resolving issues of treaty compliance by the United States and the Soviet Union.

In its final 1984 report, the President's Commission on Strategic Forces (the Scowcroft Commission) observed, "Ballistic missile defense is a critical aspect of the strategic balance and therefore is central to arms control . . . no move in the direction of the deployment of active defense should be made without the most careful consideration of the possible strategic and arms control implications."

The Strategic Defense Initiative has not been greeted with expressions of support from the NATO alliance. This is not surprising, as the ABM Treaty is of great value to our nuclear-armed allies—especially the British and French—because it ensures the ability of their missiles to reach their targets. Were the treaty modified or abrogated, resulting in the expansion of Soviet missile defenses, the independent and much smaller deterrent forces of our allies would lose their effectiveness much sooner than would U.S. forces.

Clearly, careful consideration will have to be given to the future of the ABM Treaty should the activities of the Strategic Defense Initiative provide promising results.

The Risk of Escalation Whatever the long-range objective of the Strategic Defense Initiative—be it President Reagan's vision of complete protection against nuclear weapons or the more recently stated goal of enhanced deterrence—during the actual deployment of a ballistic missile defense we will face a protracted time during which the offense dominance of the strategic balance is still a reality. Even optimistic projections of the development and deployment of only a partially effective missile defense, ignoring any treaty obstacles, span a decade or more. In contemplating the wisdom of deployment, we must factor in the likely Soviet responses and their impact on stability and escalation of the arms race.

The Soviets may respond by emulating the U.S. defense initiative or by taking specific offensive countermeasures against the U.S. moves, or both. Whichever choice they make, the Soviets will react during the development time to U.S. official statements as well as to emerging technologies and their potential military effectiveness to judge whether the United States remains deterred from initiating nuclear war under all conceivable conditions. To Soviet leaders a crucial question will be, "Does the U.S. leadership still recognize that it would be suicidal to start a nuclear exchange?"

This is a troublesome issue because the president's speech and the subsequent, often inconsistent, justifications of the Strategic Defense Initiative have created a widespread impression of a drastic shift in U.S. strategic policy. In fact, little has happened yet, either in strategic posture or technical development. The program planned for the next fiscal year constitutes only a modest increase over the total ballistic missile defense activities of the Defense Department in prior years.

But what about the year after that, and beyond? The announced five-year Strategic Defense Initiative program is both ambitious and expensive, totaling $26 billion from fiscal year 1985 through 1989, as compared with a current spending rate of roughly $1 billion per year. Will this intensified program lead the Soviets to conclude, for example, that the president is really extending hope that the U.S. population can be shielded from the horrors of nuclear attack and is thereby accepting notions of limited nuclear war fighting?

Soviet leaders have continued to emphasize that they will maintain the capacity to retaliate in the face of new U.S. strategic programs. This fact, combined with a "worst case analysis" of the U.S. defense initiative, will surely lead the Soviet Union to drive for expanded offensive programs in addition to specific countermeasures to reduce the effectiveness of the emerging U.S. defenses. This risk is real, and it is futile to believe that economic pressures would coerce the Soviets to moderate their responsive deployments. Strategic nuclear forces are only a fraction, probably much less than one quarter, of the total Soviet military burden. Moreover, the Soviet Union is now spending twice the proportion of its gross national product on military programs than is the United States. The Soviet system is more capable of withstanding criticism of this economic drain than is the United States.

A further serious risk is that the effort to neutralize the effect of nuclear weapons by deploying nationwide missile defenses might make the use of such weapons appear to be more acceptable, thereby deflecting efforts to reduce through negotiations the dangers and burdens of arms competition.

On the positive side, *after* an effective arms control regime has been established through negotiated treaties and unilateral restraint, and once the level of nuclear weaponry has been reduced drastically from today's levels of more than 50,000 warheads, we can see a stabilizing role for ballistic missile defense. In particular, if the nuclear stockpiles were reduced to very low levels, a defense system would make the security of the United States and its allies less sensitive to the precise intelligence information on small numbers of weapons retained by an opponent or third parties.

In this context, the prospect of defense can add important support to negotiations leading to low levels of nuclear weaponry. However, missile defense deployments cannot *precede* such a reduction of offensive forces or be intertwined with it without incurring all the risks of instability and escalation discussed above. Therefore, we still conclude that a reversal from the current offense-dominated balance to defense-dominated stability between the United States and the Soviet Union cannot occur—"We can't get there from here"—until offensive nuclear weapons have been reduced to extremely low levels worldwide through negotiation and prudent restraint.

VI

In closing, we have grave doubts about the wisdom of expanding research and technology on ballistic missile defense as a high-priority national program with a goal of deploying a nationwide defense. We see no practical prospect whatsoever of constructing a strategic defense that can—lacking prior *drastic* arms control restraints and reductions—enhance deterrence, much less render nuclear weapons impotent and obsolete. Even if the Strategic Defense Initiative achieves all of its very ambitious technical goals, serious operational questions will still remain in view of the staggering complexity of the system and of potential offensive countermeasures. We fear that pressure for expansion of this program beyond a deliberate research and technology effort will lead to a decrease in crisis stability, to confrontation with existing treaties, and to an incentive for expanded arms competition—resulting overall in a net decrease in national security. All these warnings relate at least as much to current oratory as to actual technical programs.

We believe that the focus and size of the Strategic Defense Initiative should be restricted to research into new technologies. Such a program would also provide a hedge against Soviet technological breakthroughs or defense developments. The United States should make clear by policy declaration the limited nature of its strategic defense program and should avoid activities leading to erosion of the provisions of the ABM Treaty. It should signal its determination to comply fully with the ABM Treaty and should insist that the Soviet Union join in adhering to the treaty's strict interpretation.

The revived interest in defensive technologies should in no way deflect the nations of the world from giving highest priority to efforts to diminish the risk of nuclear war, to terminate the offensive strategic arms competition, and to reduce the world's nuclear arsenals.

Reagan vs. the Scientists: Why the President Is Right about Missile Defense
Robert Jastrow

1. THE THREAT

When President Reagan announced his proposal last spring for defending the United States against Soviet missiles, the reaction from scientists, politicans, and journalists was almost uniformly hostile. Dr. Richard Garwin, who has had a great deal of experience in defense technology, said, "It won't work." Former Defense Secretary Robert S. McNamara called the plan "pie in the sky," former National Security Adviser McGeorge Bundy described it as "astonishing," and Senator Edward Kennedy said it was "misleading" and "reckless." Anthony Lewis wrote in his column in the New York *Times* that President Reagan was indulging in "a dangerous fantasy" and James Reston entitled his *Times* column on the President's speech, "The April Fool."

This was pretty strong language. Why was everyone so irritated by President Reagan's suggestion? There were two reasons. First of all, missiles travel at very high speeds and are difficult to shoot down in full flight. As a consequence, no defense against missiles is likely to be 100-percent effective; in any full-scale attack, one or two missiles are bound to get through. Since each one carries enough nuclear explosives to destroy an entire city and kill a million people, the President's critics accused him of misleading the public when he spoke of a defense that could "intercept and destroy strategic ballistic missiles before they reach our own soil."

The other reason for opposition to the plan stemmed from the fact that many defense advisers believe the best way to defend yourself against a missile attack is to have no defense against missiles. Although this idea seems to be contrary to common sense, there is a certain logic to it. If both superpowers leave themselves entirely undefended, the Soviets will know that if they launch a missile attack against us, our own missiles will lay waste their homeland in reprisal. And, of course, we will know that if we attack the Soviet Union, our nation will be destroyed by Soviet missiles. This knowledge will deter both countries from starting a war, and will make for a very stable situation.

If, however, either side acquires an effective defense against enemy missiles, it can attack the other side with impunity, secure in the knowledge that this defense will protect it from retaliation. Therefore, runs the reasoning, the best way to avoid a war is for both sides to leave themselves entirely undefended.

In other words, a watertight defense against missiles would upset the nuclear balance between the two superpowers. In the language of the nuclear strategists, seeking to defend your country against the enemy's missiles is "destabilizing."

On the basis of this reasoning, American arms-control experts pressed the Soviets, during the SALT talks, to sign an agreement outlawing any large-scale defense against ballistic missiles. The Soviets accepted this, and the result was the ABM treaty of 1972—ABM meaning anti-ballistic missile—in which the U.S. and the USSR agreed that neither country would undertake to protect itself from a missile attack by the other. In this way, it became the official policy of the United States to keep its people undefended against nuclear attack.

Most Americans do not know that this has been our government's policy for the last twelve years. If they did, I believe they would be astounded. As Henry Kissinger has said: "It cannot often have occurred in history that it was considered an advantageous military doctrine to make your own country deliberately vulnerable."

It takes a person with an idealized view of the world to think up something like the ABM treaty. The logic of the arms-control experts was impeccable, but if you are not an arms-control expert you see the weakness in the idea right away. Suppose one side cheats on the treaty, and secretly builds up its defenses against missiles anyway. Now it can launch its own missiles without fear of retaliation. The country that continues to honor the treaty is then vulnerable to a nuclear attack. This is exactly what happened to the United States.

Starting almost immediately after the ABM treaty was signed, reports began to come in that the Soviets were testing their surface-to-air missiles at altitudes close to 100,000 feet. Some 50 to 60 tests of this kind were carried out between 1973 and 1975. Surface-to-air missiles are supposed to be used for defense against aircraft, but aircraft do not travel at an altitude of 100,000 feet. However, missiles do. The Soviets were testing their air-defense missiles in what is called an "ABM mode." Such tests are specifically outlawed by the ABM treaty.

The first Soviet ABM tests used a surface-to-air missile called the SA-5, which is not very powerful. However, the Soviets continued to work away at improving their ABM system, and a few years ago they began to test a better surface-to-air missile, the SA-12, which can accelerate to the speed of an ICBM—about 12,000 miles an hour—from a standing start in a matter of seconds. The SA-12, used as an anti-ballistic missile, is a serious threat to the security of the United States because it has the potential for shooting down our submarine missiles, which are the mainstay of the American nuclear deterrent.

All this added up to a clear Soviet violation of the ABM treaty and the SALT I agreement. Several Senators complained about this, but nothing happened.

Last summer, evidence came to light of Soviet cheating so blatant that even cautious State Department officials were ruffled. One said bluntly about the Soviets, "They've busted the SALT agreement!" The new evidence was provided by Big Bird, one of our best reconnaissance satellites. Big Bird had discovered a radar of a special type called "phased-array," deep in the interior of the Soviet Union, near the village of Abalakova in south-central Siberia.

A phased-array radar, which consists of thousands of little radars connected so that they sweep the sky electronically, is a major improvement over the rotating radars which can be seen at airports. This kind of radar is particularly useful in shooting down enemy missiles because it can create a highly detailed and accurate picture of a missile attack. One phased-array radar, backed up by a large computer, can keep track of hundreds of separate attacking missiles, figure out their paths, and assign defending missiles to intercept and destroy them.

Phased-array radars are also useful in providing warning of a missile attack. We have several of these so-called "early-warning" radars on the East and West Coasts of the United States. To be useful in giving warning of a missile attack, a radar must be located where it can pick up reflections from the attacking missile at the earliest possible moment. In other words, it has to be placed on a country's borders. The ABM treaty, recognizing this fact, says that each country is permitted to have large phased-array radars provided they are located "along the periphery of its national territory," and are therefore usable for early warning. However, the treaty forbids locating such radars in the interior of the U.S. or the USSR.

That is why everyone was upset about the phased-array radar at Abalakova. It is located smack in the middle of the Soviet Union, 1,900 miles from the Pacific, and far from the periphery of the Soviet national territory. There is no conceivable reason for placing an early-warning radar in that spot. But there is every reason for putting a missile-defense radar there, especially since Abalakova is located near a field of Soviet heavy intercontinental ballistic missiles (ICBM's), which would be one of the top priority targets of any American attack on the Soviet Union.

In fact, the radar at Abalakova has every characteristic of a radar intended for defense against enemy missiles. It is just the kind of radar that is outlawed by the ABM treaty.

Some Soviet violations of SALT have exploited loopholes in the language of the treaty, violating the spirit rather than the letter of the agreement. The radar at Abalakova rips the very heart out of the treaty. Senator James A. McClure calls it "the most flagrant Soviet SALT violation yet."

The Abalakova radar is disturbing for another reason. Radars of this kind are mammoth devices, requiring years to construct. The appearance of this radar indicates that the Soviets decided years ago to go in for a big system of missile defense, in violation of the ABM treaty. Apparently they decided to cheat on the treaty rather than withdrawing from it formally, in the hope that we would continue to honor it and thereby be placed at a disadvantage.

The Abalakova incident has discouraging implications for the future of arms-control negotiations with the Soviet Union. It is difficult to see useful results coming out of these negotiations, when, as Fred Iklé of the Department of Defense has said, "The very party with which we are currently negotiating treaties has been caught violating a treaty." The Soviet violations of the ABM treaty confirm the impression of many Americans that the arms-control process has been cynically exploited by the Soviet Union as an instrument for achieving military superiority over the United States.

Other Soviet actions reinforced the impression that arms-control discussions with the USSR were not turning out very well. Immediately after the SALT

I agreement was signed,* as the Soviets proceeded to develop their defenses against American missiles, they simultaneously began to build up their own missile forces to an awesome level. By 1980, Soviet missile strength had reached the point where a surprise attack by the USSR could cripple a large part of our missile forces and weaken our power to retaliate. That knocked the stuffing out of deterrence. The American arms-control negotiators thought they had secured a commitment from the Soviet Union that it would not menace the survivability of our retaliatory forces in this way. But almost as soon as the ink had dried on the SALT I agreement, the Soviets had begun to slide into their old silos a new generation of ICBM's—the so-called "fourth generation"—that were heavier, more destructive, and more accurate than previous models. The warheads on these missiles were accurate enough to give them a capability for destroying our missile silos and other key military sites. The result was a nightmare for American security. Our adversary had created a great force for the destruction of the military power of the United States, and we had signed away the right to defend ourselves.

One of the fourth-generation Soviet missiles, the SS-18, is twice as big as an MX missile, about as accurate, and carries 8 to 10 nuclear warheads with an aggregate explosive power of five megatons.† At last report, the USSR had 308 monster SS-18's in the field. The Soviet Union also has in the field 360 missiles of the new type known as the SS-19, each as large as an MX missile and equally accurate. The megatonnage, or power for destruction, residing in just these two types of Soviet missiles— the SS-18 and the SS-19—is far greater than the megatonnage of the entire U.S. missile and bomber force. All this has happened since the signing of SALT I and in the name of arms control.

The new Soviet missiles are a greater threat to American security than any other weapon in the Soviet arsenal. For twenty years the United States has relied on the three legs of the famous American "strategic nuclear triad" as our means of discouraging the USSR from an attack on the American homeland. The elements of the triad are Minuteman missiles on the land, B-52 bombers in the air, and Poseidon and Trident submarines in the sea. The Minuteman missiles are housed in silos—underground hollow cylinders of reinforced concrete. Most of the warheads on the Soviet SS-18 and SS-19 ICBM's are sufficiently accurate to land within 250 yards of these missile silos and the underground bunkers that house the men and equipment needed to launch the missiles. The Soviet warheads are also sufficiently powerful to cave in a missile silo at a distance of 250 yards and destroy it, even if the silo has been "hardened" by tons of concrete and steel. As a result, according to General John W. Vessey, Jr., chairman of the Joint Chiefs of Staff, the Soviet Union can now destroy 70 to 75 percent of our Minuteman missiles in a surprise attack.

Moreover, the accuracy of Soviet warheads, which is the key factor in destroying hardened targets, has improved by about a factor of two from one generation of Soviet missiles to the next.** The

---

**A twofold gain in warhead accuracy has the same effect on a hardened silo as a tenfold increase in the destructive power of the warhead. Calculations show that if the accuracy of a Soviet warhead improves from 250 yards to 125 yards, the chance of destroying a Minuteman silo jumps from 57 percent to 95 percent.[a]

[a]*Editors note:* Robert Jastrow explains in response to a criticism by Nicholas T. Sakell that he should have clarified the seeming discrepancy between his comment in the text that the Soviet Union can destroy 70 to 75 percent of the Minuteman missiles and his comment in this footnote that the figure is 57 percent. "The 57-percent figure in the footnote is the so-called Single Shot Kill Probability, i.e., the chance that one warhead will destroy the missile silo. General Vessey's estimate that 70 to 75 percent of our missiles would be destroyed in their silos is based not only on the Single Shot Kill Probability but also on information furnished by his experts as to how many warheads the Soviets would target on each silo, the likelihood of a successful launch of each Soviet ICBM, the probable strategy of their attack, and so on." *Commentary,* June 1984, p. 12.

---

*The SALT agreement and the ABM treaty are distinct documents, although Nixon and Brezhnev signed them on the same day.

†A megaton, the unit of explosive energy commonly used to describe the size of a nuclear warhead, is the energy released by the detonation of a million tons of TNT.

newest Soviet missiles of the fifth generation, currently being tested in the Pacific, may be able to eliminate 90 to 95 percent of American ICBM's outright. When to these prospects for the destruction of the missiles themselves are added the potentials for destroying, with highly accurate Soviet rockets, the launch-control centers that house the American officers who would press the buttons, and for destroying the communication links to the President that would relay the order to execute the counterattack, the chances for effective retaliation with our ICBM's dwindle to the vanishing point.

The upshot of the matter is that our Minuteman missiles—the land leg of the U.S. strategic triad—are vulnerable to a Soviet attack and becoming more so every year.

The air-based leg of the triad is even more vulnerable to a Soviet surprise attack. Seventy percent of all B-52's are normally not on the alert at any one time, and are likely to be destroyed by Soviet missiles at the outset. Of those escaping, few would get across the border of the Soviet Union. Soviet air defenses, comprising nearly 3,000 fighters, 7,000 radars, and about 12,000 surface-to-air missiles, are the most massive in the world. Our B-52's are antiquated planes, twenty-five years old on the average, and have lots of nooks and crannies in their contours that reflect radar waves strongly and cause the planes to show up clearly on Soviet radars. B-52's also fly at high altitudes, which means they can be picked up by a radar at a considerable distance.[b] Finally, they fly at the slow, subsonic speed of a commercial airliner. As a result, they are easy targets for Soviet fighter-interceptors and surface-to-air missiles. Secretary of Defense Caspar Weinberger reported a year ago, "The aging B-52 G/H bombers will not be capable of effectively penetrating the Soviet air defenses in the mid-1980's."

The air-launched cruise missile is intended to restore the usefulness of the B-52's in the triad. The cruise missile is a pilotless jet aircraft that navigates itself without human assistance, checking its radar signals against a map of the terrain stored in an onboard computer. Cruise missiles do not have an intercontinental range, but they can be carried to the borders of the USSR by B-52's and launched from the air.

Once across the border, the cruise missile is supposed to be able to penetrate Soviet air defenses more effectively than the B-52 because it flies very low, hugging the terrain and staying out of sight of Soviet radars. However, it is vulnerable to an attack from above by the new Soviet Foxhound fighter, with its look-down, shoot-down radar. The current version of the cruise missile is also as slow as a B-52, and can be shot down by the Soviet SA-10, a relatively new surface-to-air missile. Some years ago the Department of Defense said the Soviets would need up to 1,000 SA-10's to have an effective defense against our cruise missiles, and predicted that the USSR would not have that number until the 1990's. However, as of 1982, the Soviet Union already had 1,200 SA-10's in the field. The implications for the effectiveness of the air-launched cruise missile are not encouraging.

Improved cruise missiles—supersonic, and with a "stealth" design making them nearly invisible to Soviet radar—are under development, but will not be available in large numbers before the end of the decade. Until then, the air-launched cruise missile is not likely to make a major contribution to the viability of the U.S. strategic triad.

The new B-1 bombers, just going into production, will go far toward restoring the effectiveness of the air leg of the triad. The B-1 had been cancelled by President Carter on the ground that the cruise missile made it unnecessary, but the Reagan administration brought it back to life. The B-1 is designed to be considerably less visible to Soviet radar than the B-52. It also flies lower than the B-52, and is considerably faster. But Congress has only approved funding for 100 B-1's, and because of the cancellation of the B-1 program in the previous administration, even this reduced force will

[b]Editors note: In response to a letter by scientist Richard Garwin, Robert Jastrow indicates that the B-52 and the B-1 fly at a low altitude as they penetrate Soviet airspace. *Commentary*, June 1984, p. 11.

not be fully available until 1987. In the interim, the bomber leg of the triad will be severely compromised by Soviet air defenses.

So, of the three legs of the U.S. triad, two—the land leg and the air leg—are weak, and will remain weak until later in the decade. That leaves the sea leg—the nuclear-missile submarine—as the only fully effective deterrent remaining. For the present, the triad had been reduced to a monad.

That does not seem like a bad idea. The newest submarines have extraordinarily quiet engines, and therefore are very hard to pick up on sonar. They also have a long range that gives them an enormous volume of ocean to hide in; a Trident missile can reach Moscow from anywhere within 40 million square miles of ocean. As a result, submarines on station are essentially undetectable, and can be counted on to survive a Soviet attack. Of course, all American submarines in port, about half the current fleet of 33 boats, will always be an easy mark for Soviet missiles; but the remaining 15 or 20 submarines can safely hide at sea, at least for the present.*

The survivability of the Trident submarine makes it an excellent deterrent to a Soviet attack, especially since the warheads carried on a single Trident can destroy every major city in the USSR. Yet even the Trident has problems as a deterrent. One weakness is its limited ability, when submerged, to communicate with the world above. A submerged submarine is very hard to reach by radio because radio waves do not penetrate sea water. To receive a message, the submarine must rise up to or just under the surface of the ocean. But near the surface it leaves a wake, increasing the risk of

detection.† If the submarine actually rises to the surface, it becomes visible to Soviet satellites and can be picked off at will. For this reason, American submarines loaded with nuclear missiles must spend much of their time at sea incommunicado, cruising at depth. Radio contacts with the world above are sporadic, and may be separated by long intervals. This means that if a Soviet attack occurs, some submarines may not receive the message authorizing launch of their deadly cargoes until a considerable time has passed.

Perhaps a suspicious captain, observing that his radio links are dead, will take a chance on surfacing to catch a news broadcast or sample the air for radioactivity, but with Soviet planes and radar satellites reconnoitering the oceans continuously, that will be risky. And suppose the submarine captain decides he has reason to fire off his missiles. That will bring a fearsome retaliation from the Soviet Union. Do we want to entrust the fate of the American people to a naval officer out of touch with civilian authorities? Is it our intent to delegate authority for starting World War III that far down the chain of command? The problem is a serious one.

Our submarines have another weakness as a deterrent to a Soviet attack. A missile launched from a submarine is relatively inaccurate, and is not likely to land close enough to a "hardened" or protected target to do it any serious damage. That means that submarine-launched missiles cannot be used against missile silos, command bunkers, or other military installations, which are always "hardened." They are mainly useful for destroying "soft" targets, like

---

*Some experts are concerned about a possible Soviet breakthrough in anti-submarine warfare that would reveal the location of submerged submarines by means other than the underwater sounds they make—for example, a change in water temperature in the wake of the sub, or a trail of plankton churned up by its motion. If that breakthrough occurs, it is more likely to be on the American side than the Soviet; but on the other hand, what we discover, the Soviets soon steal. However, the consensus among Navy experts is that none of this will happen in the next few years.

†The Navy tries to overcome this handicap in several ways. In one procedure an airplane flies low over the water, trailing a wire several miles long, while the submerged submarine reels out a buoy that rides just under the surface of the ocean and picks up the message. Another technique broadcasts messages to the submarine on extremely low radio frequencies, which can penetrate water to a considerable depth. In time of war, all these methods would be more vulnerable to Soviet disruption than communications on the land. The recent report by the Scowcroft commission on strategic forces concludes that "communication links with submarines, while likely to improve, will still offer problems not present for land-based systems."

cities and people.* But suppose the Soviet Union were to launch an attack against our military sites while avoiding our cities. We would be deterred from launching our submarine missiles against Soviet cities in reprisal, because the USSR would then surely respond by attacking American cities with the full power of its huge arsenal. The result would be a devastating loss of perhaps 100 million American lives, far greater than if we had withheld retaliation. That millions of Soviet civilians also lay dead or dying would not be a gain to the United States. These circumstances severely limit the value of our submarine deterrent.

Many people mistrust this analysis because they feel that a Soviet nuclear attack on military targets will produce nearly as many casualties as an attack on cities. But the facts say otherwise. Suppose the Soviet Union were to direct its highly accurate SS-18 and SS-19 rockets against the American forces capable of nuclear retaliation—missile silos, B-52 airfields, submarine bases, nuclear-weapon storage depots, and military-command posts—while attempting to spare American cities. Since most of those military sites are in sparsely populated areas, civilian casualties in the U.S. would result mainly from radioactive fallout on cities lying downwind. Calculations on the effects of nuclear explosions indicate that casualties in such a Soviet attack on military sites would be very great, between 2 and 14 million according to estimates by the Department of Defense. However, they would be far fewer than the 80 to 170 million deaths that would result from a deliberate Soviet attack on our cities in response to an American attack on Soviet cities. In spite of the enormity of the two disasters, a real distinction exists between them. One case means the possibility of a recovery for the U.S., and the other case means the annihilation of the American people.

How would an American President respond to

*This situation will change when an advanced submarine missile called the Trident 2 comes into use. The new missile has an improved guidance system with the accuracy necessary to destroy hardened targets in the U.S.S.R. But that will not happen until late 1989 or 1990.

such a limited attack by the Soviets, with American military power crippled but the cities largely intact? With only our surviving submarines available for retaliation, he would be limited to two options, and both would be painful. In Henry Kissinger's words, "A President could initiate the extermination of tens of millions of people—first Soviet citizens and then our own—or he could give in." The choices, Kissinger concludes, are "suicide or surrender."

It is sometimes said that a "surgical" nuclear attack on our military sites is impossible, because some Soviet warheads are bound to miss their targets by wide margins. In the words of one critic, Soviet missiles "would be falling all over the country." This is not correct. If the accuracy of a warhead is, say, 250 yards, that means that half the warheads will land within a circle of 250 yards, and half will land outside the circle. But the warheads that land outside will still be clustered in the neighborhood of the aiming point. In fact, in the case above, 99.9 percent will land within a mile from the target.

So urban areas will not be destroyed accidentally in a Soviet attack against our military sites. But is it possible that the Soviet Union, in planning an attack on the United States, will decide, nonetheless, that its interest is served—for the purpose of intimidating the remnant of the American population, or whatever reason—by the greatest possible devastation? Will the Soviet Union elect, as part of a calculated plan of attack, to explode megaton warheads over American cities? It seems clear that this can never happen. The leaders of the USSR must know that the one action certain to provoke an attack on their cities would be a Soviet attack on American cities. They must know that some elements of our submarine force are bound to survive their surprise attack, and are sure to visit fearful retribution on Soviet civilians for an attack on American civilians.

And such an attack on American cities will be counterproductive for the USSR in other ways as well. At the least, it will reduce Soviet prospects for extracting food, technology, and industrial loot from a subdued America. At worst, it will damage the atmosphere's fragile ozone layer, cool the climate of the globe, and visit ruin upon the agricultural lands and people of the Soviet Union. The USSR has everything to lose by an attack on American cities, and little to gain.

The essence of the matter is that American submarines are an effective deterrent to a Soviet attack on our cities, but are not a deterrent to an attack on U.S. armed forces. It is a sobering fact that if the USSR should launch a massive strike against our military installations, we could do little about it, short of a suicidal strike against Soviet cities, in the current state of disrepair of our strategic triad.

Experts count and recount missile silos, bombers, submarines, warheads, and megatonnage. They argue over whether we still have a kind of parity with the Soviet Union, in spite of the vulnerability of our ICBM's and B-52's. But there can be no argument about one basic fact: Soviet missile power has been growing faster than ours, and has succeeded in placing a large part of the American strategic deterrent at risk. The trend is frightening. If continued, it will lead to the possibility, a few years hence, of a preemptive Soviet attack aimed at the total destruction of American military power.

2. THE RESPONSE

How is the United States to respond to this threat? One way would be by a massive build-up of our own missile forces, sufficient to match the threat of the Soviet ICBM's on equal terms. The result would be a nuclear stand-off between two adversaries, each armed to the teeth, and each capable of delivering a knock-out blow if it can get in the first punch. That would be a balance of sorts, but the balance would be unstable. There is a better way, and that is the way President Reagan chose in his speech on missile defense.

Suppose a brilliant inventor could devise a method to defend the United States against Soviet ICBM's. Then our own ICBM's—Minutemen and MX's—would no longer be vulnerable to a surprise attack. These ICBM's are accurate enough to destroy many hardened targets in the USSR, including the 700 hardened leadership centers sheltering the Soviet elite. If our missile silos were defended, Soviet leaders could not eliminate this threat to their existence by knocking out American ICBM's in a preemptive first strike. If nothing else deterred the Soviet leadership from an attack on the United States, that circumstance would certainly do so.

Where can we find this invention? The answer is that we already have it. Critics of President Reagan's plan spoke as if he were proposing a defense of entire cities and their populations, but he made no suggestions of that kind in his speech; and, in fact, such an "area" defense, while very comforting, would not be necessary at the start. For the protection of our Minuteman missiles, it is only necessary to establish a "point" defense—i.e., a defense of the few square yards surrounding each missile silo, and the small areas surrounding a limited number of communication centers, command posts, and other military installations. The means for such a point defense of critical military sites are in hand today. The basic technologies have been proven, they are inexpensive, and they can be put into use with relative rapidity.

The key to these techniques is the miniaturized computer. Extraordinary developments in the miniaturization of computer circuits enable millions of transistors and other electronic components to be packed into a space the size of a thumbnail. As a result, defense technicians now have the means for building elaborate computer brains into a very small missile—a mini-missile—so that it can steer itself toward its target. Sensing the target either by its delicate emanation of heat waves, or by its radar reflections, the mini-missile analyzes the product of its senses within its highly capable computer brain, and directs a succession of messages to small rockets arranged around its circumference. Delicate thrusts of these rockets steer the defending missile into the path of the oncoming ICBM warhead. The result is either destruction of the warhead by a direct impact, or an explosion of the mini-missile in the vicinity, releasing a cloud of flying metal fragments. The warhead, moving ten times faster than a bullet, tears into the cloud of fragments; the skin of the warhead is punctured in many places; its electronics are disabled; and the nuclear bomb inside it is disarmed.

In essence, the defense consists of tossing into the path of the speeding warhead some TNT and a keg of nails. What makes this simple defense work is its computer brain.

The amount of TNT need not be very large. One mini-missile of the kind described, currently being tested by the Army, contains less than 100 pounds of explosive. The reason is that the defending missile does not have to destroy the warhead to be effective; it only has to prevent the nuclear bomb inside the warhead from exploding. That happens to be fairly easy, because nuclear bombs do not go off very readily; elaborate arrangements and a great deal of fragile electronics are needed to make one explode. Accordingly, a small charge of TNT, or a cluster of high-speed metal pellets, will usually be sufficient to disarm the bomb's mechanism.

In fact, it is not even necessary to keep the bomb from going off. Suppose, for example, Soviet technicians devise a countermeasure to the American defense by wiring the warhead so that the nuclear bomb inside it explodes automatically whenever a defending missile approaches. As long as that happens at a high altitude, far above the atmosphere, the effects of the explosion will not be very damaging at ground level, either in radioactive fallout or in blast damage. An altitude above 100,000 feet is sufficient to achieve this. Progress in developing the smart little missile indicates that making the kill at altitudes above 100,000 feet is not an especially difficult task.

Thanks to the newest ultra-miniaturized computers, the defending missile can exercise a formidable amount of brain power. Suppose the Soviet technician tries to confuse our defense by arranging to throw off decoy warheads—lightweight imitations of the real thing. The decoys, necessarily thin and flimsy in their construction (if the decoy weighs as much as a real warhead, you might as well put a bomb inside), will tend to lose their heat more quickly than the real warheads as they fly through the cold of space. By the time the

cluster of Soviet warheads reenters the atmosphere, the decoys will be appreciably colder than the real warhead. The brain of the mini-missile, analyzing these differences in temperature from one "warhead" to another, will have no trouble in telling the decoy from the real McCoy. And once the real warheads have been identified, the computers can even sense which warheads are headed for empty silos, and instruct their defending missiles to ignore these and concentrate on the warheads headed for silos still loaded with ICBM's.

This kind of technology is not visionary. Its important features are already in operational use in the Pershing-2 missiles being deployed in Europe. The warhead of the Pershing 2 contains a radar "camera" that looks at the terrain beneath it, compares what it sees with an image of the target stored in the warhead's computer brain, and, guided by this comparison, changes its course and steers straight toward the target in the final moments of its flight. On the average, Pershing-2 warheads hit the ground within 30 yards of their targets, compared to an average error of 250 yards for the best missile with old-fashioned dumb warheads. When the same kind of computer technology is used in mini-missiles for defense against ICBM warheads, the error comes down to a few yards, or even feet, or even inches.

Incidentally, the clever warheads on the Pershing 2's explain the intensity of Soviet anger at the deployment of these missiles by NATO. Warheads of this kind, which can figuratively drop down the air vent of a Soviet command bunker, place at risk the military and political leadership of the Soviet Union—and they are the only weapons in the NATO arsenal with the accuracy and range required to do that. And being mobile, the Pershing 2 is also survivable; it cannot be entirely eliminated in a preemptive attack. These properties make the Pershing 2's a very effective deterrent to a Soviet attack on Western Europe.

Getting back to President Reagan's speech, one of the main criticisms of his plan was that a defense against ICBM's can never be 100-percent effective. This criticism also applies to the smart mini-missiles. If these missiles were intended for the direct defense of American cities, they might not be of much value, because even a few ICBM warheads leaking through such a defense would kill millions of Americans. However, the situation is very different when a defending missile is intended only for the protection of missile sites. Suppose, for example, that the defense of the silos is only 50-percent effective—a conservative estimate for the technologies described above. This means that roughly half the attacking warheads will accomplish their purpose. Therefore, the USSR will be required to make its ICBM arsenal twice as big as it is today, to regain the level of threat it possessed before the defense was put in place. In other words, it will have to buy another ICBM for every one it already has.

The Soviet Union has spent about $500 billion on the build-up of its ICBM arsenal over twenty years and might be hard-pressed to spend another $500 billion in a short time. Even if the USSR does increase its missile forces in an effort to overwhelm our defense, we can increase the number of defending missiles around each silo and once again reduce to an acceptable level the number of Soviet warheads that would reach their targets. This response is practical because each defending little missile costs considerably less than the warhead it is aimed at. Estimates by a team of scientists at Los Alamos indicate that if the Soviet Union tries to overcome an American missile defense by building more rockets and warheads, its costs will increase at least twice as fast as ours. In this situation, in which the ratio of costs heavily favors the defense over the offense, the Soviet Union may be led to rethink its whole strategy of striving for military dominance with weapons of mass destruction.

With the feasibility and cost-effectiveness of a "point" defense so promising, there is still the troubling possibility that a defense of our missile silos will be "destabilizing" and will undermine the policy of deterrence. According to this theory, which is held by a number of American scientists and arms-control specialists, the Soviets will perceive the defense of American silos as a signal that the

United States is preparing to attack them, and is therefore protecting its military sites against the inevitable Soviet retaliation. Feeling nervous about that possibility, the Soviet Union will move quickly to attack us before our missile defenses can be completed. In other words, so the reasoning of the arms-control experts goes, a defense of American missiles brings the United States closer to war.

It seems to me that nothing could be farther from the truth. As usual, facts determine the situation, and the main facts here are first, that the Soviets have many more ICBM warheads than we do, and second, that ICBM's are the most valuable kind of missile from a military point of view, because of their great accuracy and ability to destroy hardened targets.* We have 1,650 accurate Minuteman warheads, too few in number to do much damage to the several-thousand important Soviet military targets, but the Soviets have at least 4,560 equally accurate and far more powerful ICBM warheads that can do a great deal of damage to our military targets. If we lived in another world, in which the Soviet Union had not constructed all these late-model ICBM's and many thousands of accurate and powerful warheads, an American system for defending our missile silos might be perceived as destabilizing and a weakening of deterrence. But in the real world, in which the Soviet missiles and warheads exist, an American missile defense restores our retaliatory force, and thus strengthens deterrence.

It is not clear why the Soviets have built up this mammoth ICBM force, because the build-up has been very costly—to repeat, about $500 billion over the years—and goes far beyond any reasonable level of military power they would need as a deterrent to an American attack. Whatever the reason, the fact is that they have done it. As a result, the Soviet Union is in a position to launch an attack

*It is often mentioned that we have the same number of warheads, about 4,600, on our submarines as the Soviets have on their ICBM's. However, the submarine-based warheads are inaccurate and have relatively low explosive power, about one-sixteenth that of Soviet ICBM warheads. Consequently, they are completely ineffective against Soviet missile silos, which are even more hardened than our silos.

on the United States aimed at destroying our means of nuclear retaliation—missile silos, B-52 airfields, submarine bases, and military command posts. In other words, those 4,560 accurate ICBM warheads look like the beginning of a Soviet drive to acquire a nuclear war-winning capability. We may not understand how the Soviets think they can possibly emerge victorious in a larger sense from a nuclear war in which they suffer "only" a few million to 10 million casualties, but apparently they do think that.

In any case, the USSR has built a large number of missiles and undermined our capability for retaliation and therefore our deterrent. Protecting our forces against the Soviet missiles will not give us a nuclear war-winning capability—the nuclear warheads of the Soviet Union are too numerous and powerful for that—but it will give us a continuing capability for retaliation against Soviet attack, which is the very basis of deterrence.

There are other gains for deterrence in a point defense against Soviet ICBM's, in addition to the protection of our missile silos. The dish in California that receives the signal from our early-warning satellites can be protected. The communication lines that connect the President and top military commanders to the Minuteman launch-control centers can be protected. Our bomber airfields and submarine bases can be protected. Just two bases—one in Kings Bay, Georgia, and the other in Bangor, Washington—will support our entire fleet of Trident submarines. If these bases are undefended, half the Trident fleet—the part in port when a Soviet surprise attack occurs—must be written off at the outset. A point defense of the Trident bases against Soviet missiles will double the effective strength of the American submarine deterrent.* All

these measures improve our chance of being able to retaliate against a Soviet attack, and therefore make an attack less likely.

A point defense decreases the vulnerability of our missiles, and is good. An area defense, directly shielding our cities and their populations, would be better. Can inventive genius find still another device to accomplish this task as well? Once again, the answer is that we already have the invention. It is called the laser. Unlike the smart mini-missile, the laser defense is not inexpensive; it is not yet a proven technology; but it has the promise of protecting our cities against destruction.

A laser is like a searchlight; it produces a beam of light. This beam of light, focused on the metal skin of an ICBM, can burn right through it, just as the light of the sun, focused to a narrow spot by a magnifying glass, can burn through a piece of wood or paper. The difference between a laser beam and an ordinary beam of light is that the ordinary beam spreads out as it leaves its source, so that by the time it has traveled several thousand miles—for example, from the United States to the Soviet Union—the beam is dispersed over an area several miles in diameter. As a result, the intensity of light in any one part of the beam is too weak to hurt anything.

A laser beam, on the other hand, has the remarkable property that all parts of the beam travel in the same direction, so that the beam doesn't spread apart as it travels through space.† If the energy in the laser beam is intense enough at its source to burn through the metal skin of a Soviet ICBM, it will still be that intense, and still able to burn through metal, after it has traveled thousands of miles.

Laser beams have the advantage that they travel at the speed of light, which is 670 million miles

*When there are only a few targets, and the destruction of each one is very important to the Soviet Union, it can always try to overwhelm our defenses by allotting a large number of warheads to each target. However, by the same token, a few sites, each of enormous value to the United States, can be ringed by exceptionally strong defenses comprised of not one or two but perhaps dozens of mini-missiles or more; and this can be done at acceptable cost to the U.S., because only a few such highly valuable sites exist.

†Even in a laser beam, the light waves spill out over the edge of the beam to a limited degree and blur it somewhat, but the spreading effect is quite small. In the laser beams being designed for use against Soviet rockets, the spreading effect will be no more than a few feet over a distance of a thousand miles.

an hour, and can cross a continent in a hundredth of a second. Compared to the speed of laser beams, even an ICBM is slow, and the laser beam has no difficulty in catching up to one and intercepting it. One of the disadvantages of a laser beam is that, being a beam of light, it is blocked by clouds and haze. For that reason, laser guns work best if placed in a space station or satellite, far above the atmosphere. But putting a laser gun in a space station means that a large amount of equipment and fuel for the laser must be ferried into orbit at great cost. Another disadvantage is that the laser beam must track the moving ICBM with great precision, equivalent to hitting a dime at a distance of 100 miles, so that the beam will stay on the target long enough to melt it.

Because of these and other difficulties, a team of MIT scientists led by Kosta Tsipis concluded a few years ago that "lasers have little or no chance of succeeding as practical, cost-effective weapons." When President Reagan announced that he was proposing to set the country on this course anyway, Professor Tsipis denounced the President's plan as "a cruel hoax." Many other prominent scientists also jumped on the President for his suggestion.

But scientists do not have a very good track record when it comes to making predictions about the feasibility of bold new ideas. In fact, they seem to have a talent for rejecting proposals that later turn out to be of great practical value. Examples abound. In 1903, just before the first flight of the Wright brothers, an American astronomer named Simon Newcomb announced that the laws of physics proved man could never fly. A little later, after airplanes were flying, another American astronomer ridiculed the notion that some day there might be "giant flying machines speeding across the Atlantic . . . and carrying innumerable passengers." In 1926, A. W. Bickerton, a British scientist, said that it was scientifically impossible to send a rocket to the moon. Just before the Soviet Union put the first Sputnik into orbit, the Astronomer Royal of Great Britain announced that the idea of launching artificial satellites into space was "utter bilge." In

the weapons field, Admiral Leahy—not a scientist, but a qualified technician—said to President Truman, just before the first successful test of an atom bomb, "That bomb will never go off, and I speak as an expert on explosives." And Vannevar Bush, who directed the government's science effort during World War II, offered the following wisdom after the war:

> The people who have been writing these things that annoy me—have been talking about a 3,000-mile rocket shot from one continent to another carrying an atom bomb. . . . I think we can leave that out of our thinking. . . . I wish the American people would leave that out of their thinking.

Among the experts actually working on laser defense or advising the government on it, the consensus is that no basic scientific obstacles stand in the way of success. George Keyworth, Science Adviser to the President, said recently, "The major fundamental problems in every area [of laser defense] have been removed." Two committees, set up to advise the President on the matter after his speech, have reported that the feasibility of several kinds of laser defense against missiles can be tested in the next three or four years, and if all goes well, a complete defense can be in operation ten years after that. According to Dr. Keyworth, there has been "tremendously broad technical progress" in this area.

When the final system is constructed, it will probably be a so-called layered defense, with the first or outermost layer consisting of laser beams aimed from space at enemy ICBM's in the first minutes of flight, shortly after blast-off. A second layer of defense, either a laser or a smart mini-missile, will hit the ICBM's that have gotten through the first layer, as they fly across the void en route to their targets. A third layer of mini-missiles, with the "keg of nails" or similar technology, comes into play in the final minutes or seconds of flight as the Soviet warheads reenter the atmosphere, to destroy the intruders that have penetrated the second layer. If the "leakage-rate" in each of the three layers is 10 percent, only one warhead in a thousand will reach its target.

If the Soviets acquire an effective defense against American missiles, so much the better. They will not even have to steal it. The President has suggested that his successor can give the new technology to the Soviet Union, just to prove that there is no point in both sides keeping bulging warehouses of these deadly weapons any longer. Then, the President added, his successor can say to the Soviets, "I am willing to do away with all my missiles. You do away with all yours."

These are encouraging possibilities for the long run. The problem facing us in the short run, between now and the end of the 1980's, is the vulnerability of American ICBM's and other military installations to a Soviet surprise attack. The smart mini-missile, with its TNT and keg-of-nails technology, is less exotic than a laser defense, but it is already state-of-the-art, and can be available on relatively short notice for the protection of our missile silos, submarine and bomber bases, and command posts. In doing that, the mini-missile will strengthen and preserve the American deterrent to a Soviet attack. By strengthening our deterrent, this simple defense will also protect our cities.

For nearly forty years, since the first atomic explosion at Alamogordo, the nuclear bomb has dominated strategic weaponry. But technicians make new facts, and new facts make a new strategic calculus. We are on the threshold of revolutionary gains in the accuracy of intercontinental ballistic missiles, created by the incorporation of computer brains into missile warheads. In the future, the smart ICBM warhead, equipped with electronic brains and infrared or radar "eyes," will hitch a ride to the general vicinity of the target on its ICBM bus; then, disembarking, it will steer itself into a particular spot on the target within a yard or two to accomplish its task with nice precision. Consider the possibilities opened for the military planner by this development. A Soviet charge of TNT, carried across the ocean by an ICBM, guides itself down

the smokestack of the Consolidated Edison plant in New York; an American warhead of TNT, carried 5,000 miles in the nose of an ICBM, drops down onto a critical transformer in the Moscow power grid; a bridge is destroyed by a small explosive charge ferried across oceans and continents on an ICBM, and carefully placed at the foot of a pier. A small, artfully shaped charge of TNT is delivered to the door of a Minuteman or SS-19 silo; exploding, it pierces a hole in the silo door, spraying the interior with shrapnel and destroying the missile. It is not necessary to crush the entire silo with the violence of a nuclear warhead; missiles are fragile, and gentler means suffice to disable them.

Command posts, ammunition dumps, highways, and airport runways—all are vulnerable to conventional explosives skillfully targeted. Nearly every task allotted to nuclear weapons today can be accomplished in the future by missiles armed with non-nuclear, smart warheads.

And when nuclear weapons are not needed, they will not be used. That may seem unlikely, but consider the following facts. A nuclear weapon has many defects from a military point of view. Because of its destructive power and radioactivity, it tends to kill innocent civilians, even if used sparingly in a surgically clean strike at military targets. If used in great numbers, nuclear weapons stir up clouds of radioactive material that roll back with the prevailing pattern of the winds, carrying their poisons with them into the land of the attacker. Finally, these weapons generate emotional reactions of such intensity that the military planner can only hold them in reserve to use as a last resort; he cannot release his nuclear arsenal in gradual increments, adjusted to the military needs of each situation.

In other words, nuclear weapons are messy, and, other things being equal, the military planner will avoid them. They will never disappear entirely; some blockbusters will always be stockpiled by the superpowers as a deterrent to a genocidal attack on their cities and civilians. But as the accuracy of smart warheads increases, and more military tasks can be accomplished by non-nuclear explosives, the tasks assigned to nuclear warheads will diminish, and the size of the world's nuclear arsenals will decrease.

The shrinkage has already been observed in the armaments of the U.S. and the USSR. Nuclear weapons in the American arsenal are now one-seventh their size twenty-five years ago, and the total megatonnage of our arsenal is one-quarter what it was then.* Figures available to me on Soviet nuclear weapons go back only ten years, but in that short interval, while the number of Soviet warheads increased enormously, the average size of an individual warhead decreased by a factor of three.

These changes in the sizes of the world's nuclear arsenals have resulted from rather modest improvements in the accuracy of missiles, but the technology of the smart warhead is still in its infancy. When it reaches its maturity, and the precision of delivery of explosives across continents can be measured in feet rather than in hundreds of yards, the military uses of the nuclear bomb will dwindle into nothingness. And so it may come to pass, as President Reagan suggested, that the scientists who gave us nuclear weapons will also give us "the means of rendering these weapons impotent and obsolete."

QUESTIONS FOR DISCUSSION

1 Should space weapons be banned by international agreements?
2 Is it possible to ban space weapons effectively without the possibility that one side could cheat significantly, thus endangering the security of the other side?
3 Does the "star wars" program strengthen or weaken strategic stability?
4 What response can the Soviet Union make to meet an American active "star wars" program?

*Nuclear weapons were mated to ICBM's originally because the early models of the ICBM's wandered all over, and generally landed a mile or so from their targets. Only a nuclear warhead—with its enormous radius of destruction—could make such blunderbusses militarily effective.

5 Do space weapons strengthen or weaken the NATO alliance?
6 Should the United States share its space weapons technology with the Soviet Union?

SUGGESTED READINGS

Burrows, William E. "Ballistic Missile Defense: The Illusion of Security," *Foreign Affairs* 62 (Spring 1984), pp. 843–56.
Codevilla, Angelo. "Defense from Space," *Policy Review* no. 25 (Summer 1983), pp. 67–69.
Drell, Sidney D., Philip J. Farley, and David Holloway. *The Reagan Strategic Defense Initiative: A Technical, Political, and Arms Control Assessment.* Stanford, California: Center for International Security and Arms Control, 1984.
Fletcher, James C. "The Technologies for Ballistic Missile Defense," *Issues in Science and Technology* 1 (Fall 1984), pp. 15–29.
Glaser, Charles L. "Why Even Good Defenses May Be Bad," *International Security* 9 (Fall 1984), pp. 92–123.
Jastrow, Robert. "The War Against 'Star Wars.'" *Commentary* (December 1984), pp. 19–25.
Keyworth, George A. II. "The Case for Strategic Defense: An Option for a World Disarmed," *Issues in Science and Technology* 1 (Fall 1984), pp. 30–44.
Lupton, David. "Space Doctrines," *Strategic Review* 11 (Fall 1983), pp. 36–47.
"Militarizing the Last Frontier: The Space Weapons Race," *Defense Monitor* 12, no. 5 (1983), entire issue.
Payne, Keith and Colin Gray. "Nuclear Policy and the Defensive Transition," *Foreign Affairs* 62 (Spring 1984), pp. 820–42.
"Space Weapons Policy," *Congressional Digest* (March 1984), pp. 67–96.
Talbott, Strobe. "The Case Against Star Wars Weapons," *Time* (May 7, 1984), pp. 81–82.
Ulsamer, Edgar. "The Battle for SDI," *Air Force Magazine* (February 1983), pp. 44–53.
Union of Concerned Scientists. *The Fallacy of Star Wars: Why Space Weapons Can't Protect Us.* New York: Random House, 1984.
"Upward and Onward with Space Defense," *Bulletin of the Atomic Scientists* 39 (June/July 1983), pp. 4–8.
U.S. Congress: House of Representatives. *Hearing on H. R. 3073, People Protection Act.* Hearing before

the Subcommittee on Investigations of the Armed Services Committee, 98th Cong., 1st Sess., 1983.

U.S. Congress: Senate. *Arms Control and the Militarization of Space*. Hearings before the Committee on Foreign Relations, 97th Cong., 2nd Sess., 1982.

U.S. Congress: Senate. *Controlling Space Weapons*. Hearings before the Committee on Foreign Relations, 98th Cong., 1st Sess., 1983.

"Weapons in Space," *New York Times,* a six-part series: March 3, 1985, pp. 1 and 10; March 4, 1985, pp. A1 and A8; March 5, 1985, pp. A1 and A16; March 6, 1985, pp. A1 and B8; March 7, 1985, pp. A1 and A24; and March 8, 1985, pp. A1 and A14.

Weinberg, Alvin M. and Jack N. Barkenbus. "Stabilizing Star Wars," *Foreign Policy* no. 54 (Spring 1984), pp. 164–70.

15 Should the United States Abandon Plans for Engaging in Limited Nuclear Warfare As Embodied in Presidential Directive 59?

YES

Louis René Beres

Presidential Directive 59: A Critical Assessment

NO

Colin S. Gray

Presidential Directive 59: Flawed but Useful

Presidential Directive 59: A Critical Assessment
Louis René Beres

Since the dawn of the Atomic Age, the overriding objective of American strategic forces has been to deter nuclear war. Over the years, however, the policies designed to implement that objective have changed considerably. Today there is cause for concern that current strategic nuclear policy as embodied in Presidential Directive 59 may in fact be counterproductive to this country's security, and that such policy may even hasten the arrival of nuclear war. Reflecting such concern, this article will examine the essential elements, assumptions, and historical roots of the recently announced policy with a view to assessing whether our security has been enhanced or degraded.

DISQUIETING BACKGROUND OF THE 'NEW' POLICY

While PD 59 codifies the latest refinements in American strategic planning, its essential emphasis on counterforce targeting is hardly new.[1] Signed by former President Carter on 25 July 1980, clarified by former Secretary of Defense Brown in a

---

[1]A *counterforce* strategy emphasizes the targeting of an adversary's military capability, especially its strategic military capability and the military command and control system. A *countervalue* strategy emphasizes the targeting of an adversary's cities, industries, and population centers. *Mutual Assured Destruction* is a condition in which each adversary possesses the ability to inflict an unacceptable degree of damage upon the other after absorbing a first strike. In the current public dialogue, the strategy embodied in PD 59 is sometimes referred to as a "countervailing strategy" (see, for example, Richard Burt, "Muskie Rebuffs Soviet on Nuclear Strategy Criticism," *The New York Times,* 17 September 1980, p. A3), but in this paper we will use the more restrictive term, "counterforce strategy." For a good brief primer on the PD 59 controversy, consult the pro (Leon Sloss) and con (Paul C. Warnke) feature "Carter's Nuclear Policy: Going from 'MAD' to Worse?" *Los Angeles Times,* 4 September 1980, p. 3. For a more formal treatment, see Jeffrey T. Richelson, "The Dilemmas of Counterpower Targeting," *Comparative Strategy,* 2 (1980), 223–37.

speech at the Naval War College on 20 August 1980, and endorsed in principle by President Reagan during his campaign, this policy evolved from a war plan known as National Security Decision Memorandum 242, formulated in the closing months of the Nixon Administration. PD 59 visualizes a counterforce targeting policy, along with the forces and weapons necessary to give the policy effect, allowing the president to order discrete nuclear attacks against the enemy's missile silos, military bases, military forces, and command and control centers as alternatives to massive city-busting attacks. By providing him this flexibility, it is argued, he can, if war deterrence fails, conduct nuclear warfighting below the all-out threshold, thus avoiding the Hobson's choice of capitulation or Armageddon. In his Naval War College speech, Secretary Brown took pains to stress the essential historical continuity of PD 59:

> The US has never had a doctrine based simply and solely on reflexive, massive attacks on Soviet cities. Instead, we have always planned both more selectively (options limiting urban-industrial damage) and more comprehensively (a range of military targets). Previous Administrations, going back well into the 1960's, recognized the inadequacy of a strategic doctrine that would give us too narrow a range of options.[2]

Such a policy, it will be seen, represents the latest retreat from the doctrine of "massive retaliation" first promulgated by John Foster Dulles in January 1954. This doctrine, it will be recalled, expressed America's intention to base its security "primarily upon a great capacity to retaliate instantly by means and at places of our own

---

[2]Harold Brown, remarks delivered at the Convocation Ceremonies for the 97th Naval War College Class, Newport, R.I., 20 August 1980, p. 7.

Louis René Beres, "Presidential Directive 59: A Critical Assessment," *Parameters—The Journal of the US Army War College* 11 (March 1981), pp. 19–28.

choosing. . . . [thereby gaining] more security at less cost."[3]

Of course, the logical fallacies of the doctrine of massive retaliation became glaringly apparent as the Soviets developed their own retaliatory capacity, and a number of informed critics began the search for a more credible strategy of nuclear deterrence, one that would preserve a broader array of retaliatory options. Since an alternative strategy was founded on the notion of a spectrum of deterrence, these critics soon advanced tentative formulations of the idea of "limited nuclear war." Ultimately, many of these formulations found their way into the policies of the "McNamara Strategy" of the 1960's and the successor strategies of James Schlesinger, Donald Rumsfeld, and Harold Brown.

A full 18 years before the announcement of PD 59, Secretary McNamara, in a speech at the University of Michigan, proposed a strategy going beyond the requirements of assured destruction, one that included both counterforce and countervalue retaliatory options. Then as now, the argument was advanced that credible nuclear deterrence mandates a strategy that allows for intermediate levels of military response, including a second-strike counterforce strategy. Many elements of this strategy had been articulated several years earlier, in 1957, by Henry Kissinger. Confronting what he called "the basic challenge to United States strategy," Kissinger wrote:

> We cannot base all our plans on the assumption that war, if it comes, will inevitably be all-out. We must strive for a strategic doctrine which gives our diplomacy the greatest freedom of action and which addresses itself to the question of whether the nuclear age presents only risks or whether it does not also offer opportunities.[4]

The precise nature of Kissinger's preferred "strategic doctrine" here is preparation for limited nuclear war. While recognizing that the arguments against limited nuclear war are "persuasive," he insisted—in what must now be seen as the precursor of current strategic assumptions—that nuclear war need not be apocalyptic. Consequently, said the future Secretary of State, "Limited nuclear war represents our most effective strategy against nuclear powers or against a major power which is capable of substituting manpower for technology."[5]

These ideas of a limited nuclear war—of a strategy of controlled nuclear warfighting—were also widely accepted by James Schlesinger during his tenure as Secretary of Defense. On 4 March 1974, Schlesinger testified before Congress in support of an American capability of reacting to a limited nuclear attack with selected counterforce strikes. According to his testimony, such strikes could greatly reduce the chances for escalation into all-out strategic exchanges, thereby producing fewer civilian casualties.

In his 1974 Annual Report as Secretary of Defense, Schlesinger remarked that nuclear attacks solely against American military installations might result in "relatively few civilian casualties." Subsequently, on 11 September, the Subcommittee on Arms Control of the Senate Committee on Foreign Relations met with Schlesinger in executive session to consider the probable consequences of nuclear attacks against military installations in this country. During what transpired, the Secretary took a remarkably sanguine view, claiming that as few as 800,000 casualties could result from an attack on US ICBM silos. This view assumed (1) a Soviet attack on all American Minuteman and Titan ICBMs, with a one-megaton warhead targeted on each silo, and (2) extensive civil defense protection.

Since Schlesinger's conclusions generated a good deal of skepticism among several senators, the Office of Technology Assessment of the Congress was asked to evaluate the Department of Defense calculations. In response to the invitation, this office convened an ad hoc panel of experts, chaired

[3]See "Text of Dulles' Statement on Foreign Policy of Eisenhower Administration," *The New York Times*, 13 January 1954, p. 2.

[4]Henry Kissinger, *Nuclear Weapons and Foreign Policy* (Garden City, N.Y.: Doubleday, 1957), p. 15.

[5]Ibid., p. 166.

by Dr. Jerome Wiesner, which returned with the following summary of conclusions:

> The panel members examined the results of the analyses of nuclear attacks which were given the Senate Foreign Relations Committee by the Department of Defense, and the assumptions which went into these analyses, in some detail. They concluded that the casualties calculated were substantially too low for the attacks in question as a result of a lack of attention to intermediate and long-term effects. They also concluded that the studies did not adequately reflect the large uncertainties inherent in any attempt to determine the civilian damage which might result from a nuclear attack.[6]

Even more significantly, perhaps, the panel could not determine from DOD testimony any consistent set of hypothetical Soviet objectives in the assumed nuclear strikes. While the panel acknowledged that the Soviets could detonate a small number of nuclear weapons over isolated areas in the United States without producing significant civilian damage, it could not understand how they might possibly benefit from such an attack. The panel's assessment, therefore, was explicitly detached from any presumption that its members felt the analyzed scenarios to be sensible or realistic.

Indeed, the panel insisted that any analysis of proposed changes in American target strategy be conducted within a larger set of considerations affecting policy in this area. Such considerations, it felt, must include the extent to which new strategies could be executed without escalation to general nuclear war; the degree to which such policy increases or decreases our reliance on nuclear weapons; the extent to which it raises or lowers the threshold of nuclear first use; and the effect on our allies' perceptions of the credibility of the American commitment to their security. The panel recommended, therefore, "that the Foreign Relations

Committee ask for the additional analysis of casualties outlined in the following section only if it intends to engage in a discussion of these other issues."[7]

Ultimately, DOD completed new calculations which showed that under certain conditions an attack upon US ICBM silos could result in casualties of between 3 and 22 million, as opposed to the 800,000 to 6.7 million previously cited by Schlesinger.[8] Regrettably, however, the discussion of "other issues" called for by the panel has yet to take place. As in the case of its doctrinal antecedents, current US strategic policy is premised on the assumption that the Soviets might view a limited nuclear attack against the United States as rational.

Even if such attacks might hold out the promise of *relatively* low casualty levels, there is little reason to believe that anything short of an all-out nuclear assault would make military sense to the Soviets. According to Dr. Sidney Drell's testimony before the Senate Subcommittee on Arms Control, in order to carry out a militarily effective attack against America's 1054 ICBMs, one that would destroy about 800 of them, or 80 percent, the Soviets would have to unleash an attack which would engender approximately 18.3 million American fatalities. Thus, the attack would hardly be "limited" as far as the American population is concerned. But even so extensive a counterforce assault would not be militarily disabling, not entirely, since the remaining American ICBMs would still constitute a "healthy, robust retaliatory force."[9]

What has been developing over a period of many years in American strategic planning circles, therefore, is a counterforce doctrine that both understates the effects of so-called limited nuclear war and ignores the primary fact that such a war makes

---

[6]US Congress, Senate, Committee on Foreign Relations, Subcommittee on Arms Control, International Organizations, and Security Agreements, *Analyses of Effects of Limited Nuclear Warfare*, 94th Cong., 1st Sess., September 1975, p. 4.

[7]Ibid., p. 5.

[8]US Congress, Senate, Committee on Foreign Relations, Subcommittee on Arms Control, International Organizations, and Security Agreements, *Hearings, Possible Effects on US Society of Nuclear Attacks Against US Military Installations*, Opening Statement by Senator Clifford P. Case, 94th Cong., 1st Sess., 18 September 1975, p. 3.

[9]Ibid., testimony of Dr. Sidney Drell, p. 21.

no military sense. There is, in fact, no clear picture of what the Soviet Union might hope to gain from the kinds of limited counterforce attacks that determine the direction of current American strategic policy. Indeed, everything we know about Soviet military strategy indicates that it fails to entertain the notion of limited nuclear war. If we can believe what the Soviets say, all nuclear conflict would necessarily be total.[10]

Once the nuclear firebreak has been crossed, it is most unlikely that conflict could remain limited. Ironically, this point was hinted at by Henry Kissinger in 1965: "No one knows how governments or people will react to a nuclear explosion under conditions where both sides possess vast arsenals."[11] And it was understood by Robert Mc-

Namara, who claimed that once even tactical nuclear weapons were employed, "You can't keep them limited; you'll destroy everything."[12] While the prudent course would appear to assume that any nuclear exchange must be avoided lest it become total, current American strategic policy underscores counterforce targeting and its corollary recognition of limited nuclear warfighting. Although it is clear that once a nuclear exchange begins it will become impossible to verify yields, sizes, numbers, and types of nuclear weapons employed,[13] current policy reaffirms the notion of limited exchanges conducted in deliberate, measured, controlled fashion.

RATIONALE OF CURRENT STRATEGIC NUCLEAR POLICY

The essential rationale of the recently announced strategic nuclear policy is that it strengthens deterrence. Faced with the relentless buildup and refinement of Soviet strategic forces, and with a Soviet strategic doctrine that emphasizes nuclear warfighting, American planners are no longer comfortable with the doctrine of mutual assured destruction. Rather than being forced to choose between all-out nuclear reprisal, on the one hand, and capitulation, on the other, the United States, it is argued, requires a set of intermediate retaliatory options that include particularly the capability to strike at the Soviet military apparatus itself. Only with such options, we are told, can this country maintain the elements of a credible deterrent posture. In the words of Secretary Brown:

> Deterrence remains, as it has been historically, our fundamental strategic objective. But deterrence must restrain a far wider range of threats than just massive

[10]This view emerges repeatedly in Soviet literature on military doctrine and strategy. See, for example, an early article by Colonel V. Mochalov and Major V. Dashichev, "The Smoke Screen of the American Imperialists," *Red Star,* 17 December 1957. Two years later, Bernard Brodie, in his classic study, *Strategy in the Missile Age* (Princeton: Princeton Univ. Press, 1959), made the following observations: "Soviet commentary on the limited-war thinking emanating from the West has thus far been uniformly hostile and derisive. Especially derided has been the thought that wars might remain limited while being fought with atomic weapons" (p. 322n). More recently, Professor Richard Pipes, the Harvard Sovietologist, crystallized the Soviet stance: "In the Soviet view, a nuclear war would be total. . . . Limited nuclear war, flexible response, escalation, damage limiting, and all the other numerous refinements of US strategic doctrine find no place in its Soviet counterpart. . . ." ("Why the Soviet Union Thinks It Could Fight and Win a Nuclear War." *Commentary,* 64 [July 1977], 30). Any remaining doubts about Soviet rejection of the doctrine of limited nuclear war can be dispelled by considering recent writings of Soviet generals which appear regularly in *Strategic Review.* For example, according to General-Major R. Simonyan, a major Soviet strategic planner, "The experience of numerous wars attests most clearly to the fact that military conflagrations have hardly ever been successfully kept within their original bounds" (5 [Spring 1977], 100). And also: "The assertion made by supporters of 'limited' nuclear war that it could be kept within preplanned limits and made 'controllable' is altogether false. Every clear-headed person knows that any war unleashed by an aggressor and involving the use of strategic nuclear weapons— even if those weapons were used in limited numbers and against 'selected targets'—is fraught with the genuine threat of escalation and development into a strategic (universal) nuclear war with all its fatal consequences" (p. 107).

[11]Henry Kissinger, "Introduction," in *Problems of National Strategy* (New York: Praeger, 1965), p. 6.

[12]*Possible Effects on US Society of Nuclear Attacks Against US Military Installations,* quoted in Drell testimony, p. 19.

[13]For support of this position, see "Tactical Nuclear Weapons in Search of a Doctrine," *The Defense Monitor,* 4 (February 1975), especially p. 3: and the special report on "The First Nuclear War Conference." in *The Bulletin of the Atomic Scientists,* 35 (April 1979), 20, especially the remarks by General A. S. Collins Jr. (USA, Ret.).

attacks on US cities. We seek to deter any adversary from any course of action that could lead to general nuclear war. Our strategic forces must also deter nuclear attacks on smaller sets of targets in the US or on US military forces, and be a wall against nuclear coercion of, or attack on, our friends and allies. And strategic forces, in conjunction with theater nuclear forces, must contribute to deterrence of conventional aggression as well. . . . In our analysis and planning, we are necessarily giving greater attention to how a nuclear war would actually be fought by both sides if deterrence fails. There is no contradiction between this focus on how a war would be fought and what its results would be, *and* our purpose of insuring continued peace through mutual deterrence. Indeed, this focus helps us achieve deterrence and peace, by ensuring that our ability to retaliate is fully credible.[14]

In essence, this posture, which is the outcome of a fundamental review of American targeting policy ordered by President Carter in the summer of 1977, stresses the capacity to employ strategic nuclear forces "selectively." Anticipating the prospect of intermediate levels of Soviet aggression, it moves to impress Soviet leaders that the United States has both the will and the means to make such aggression more costly than gainful. It does this by implementing a policy of graduated strategic response calculated to make Soviet leaders more cautious. "This is," says Lieutenant General Edward Rowny (USA, Ret.), who for six years represented the Joint Chiefs of Staff at the SALT II negotiations, "a more realistic and effective way to deter the Soviet Union, which has been inexorably building its military capabilities for the last 15 years."[15] Secretary of Defense Brown, faced with what he saw as a need for deterring Soviet attacks of "less than all-out scale," proposed options to attack Soviet military and political targets while holding back a significant reserve. Such a strategy, he argued, could preclude a stark and intolerable choice between no effective military re-

sponse and spasm nuclear war. Instead, we could attack "in a selective and measured way a range of military, industrial, and political control targets, while retaining an assured destruction capacity in reserve."[16]

At first glance, such a strategy may appear eminently reasonable. After all, doesn't the prudential path to safety lie in leaving open the possibility of ending a strategic exchange before the worst escalation and damage have occurred? Mustn't it be a cornerstone of American strategic policy to inflict costs on a Soviet adversary equal to or higher than the value the Soviets might expect to gain from partial attacks on the United States or its allies? Doesn't the policy of flexibly calibrating US retaliation to the particular provocation further the overall objective of strategic deterrence?

Regrettably, the answer to each of the foregoing questions is NO, and the strategy of nuclear deterrence at issue is not as promising as it may first appear. Indeed, careful examination of its underlying principles will reveal that it contributes to, rather than constrains, the prospect of nuclear war. This is the case because it is founded upon an incomplete, erroneous, and sometimes contradictory set of assumptions, and upon a serious misunderstanding of vital interactive effects.

PROBLEMATIC ASSUMPTIONS AND OVERLOOKED EFFECTS

Current strategic nuclear policy rests on the assumption that the Soviets might have something to gain by launching a limited first-strike attack on the United States or its allies. Yet, as we have already noted, this assumption overlooks the possibility that the Soviets may not share our view of controlled nuclear conflict and that they are apt to doubt our declared commitment to proportionate retaliation. Faced with grave uncertainty about the nature of an American strategic response, Soviet leaders considering the costs and benefits of strik-

---

[14]Brown, remarks, p. 6.

[15]Edward Rowny, "That 'New' Nuclear Strategy," *The Washington Post,* 25 August 1980, p. 19.

[16]Harold Brown, *Department of Defense Annual Report for FY 1981* (Washington: GPO, 1980), p. 66.

ing first would likely have serious reservations about settling rationally for strategic self-limitation.

The current strategic nuclear policy also appears to be founded on the assumption that the Soviets are more likely to be deterred by the threat of limited American counterforce reprisals than by the threat of overwhelming, total retaliation. What this notion overlooks, however, is the oft-declared Soviet unwillingness to play by American rules. Since the Soviet Union continues to threaten the United States with all-out nuclear war once the nuclear firebreak is crossed, the credibility of the American commitment to selective counterforce strikes must be dubious. Once again, the differing viewpoints on limited nuclear war held by the superpowers impair the reasonableness of America's deterrent strategy.

The American strategy is undermined further by this country's own published doubts concerning controlled nuclear conflict. In the words of Secretary Brown:

> In adopting and implementing this policy, we have no more illusions than our predecessors that a nuclear war could be closely and surgically controlled. There are, of course, great uncertainties about what would happen if nuclear weapons were ever again used. These uncertainties, combined with the catastrophic results sure to follow from a maximum escalation of the exchange, are an essential element of deterrence.[17]

I believe he is mistaken. Rather than functioning as "an essential element of deterrence," the uncertainties to which he refers may seriously weaken the credibility of an American threat to employ a measured strategy of annihilation. And the effect of our uncertainties is made all the more worrisome by virtue of their open expression. After all, Soviet perceptions of American strategic doubts can only reinforce their rejection of graduated nuclear conflict.

Also troubling is the thought that the new strategy of deterrence is based upon a confusion of the requirement for survivable nuclear forces with the

dividends of counterforce targeting doctrine. These are discrete, logically unrelated concepts. While it is clear that a survivable and enduring strategic retaliatory capability is essential to stable deterrence, a provocative targeting doctrine is not only unessential, it is counterproductive. Perhaps the greatest confusion of the two issues can be seen in the debate concerning the deployment of the mobile, land-based MX missile. As currently conceived, the MX is designed not only with a view to maintaining the survivability of the ICBM leg of the Triad, but also with a corresponding concern for a high single-shot kill probability against hard pinpoint targets (silos, submarine pens, nuclear storage sites, and command bunkers).

Of course, the Department of Defense and other supporters of the MX argue that there can be no reason for making such Soviet targets safe from US ICBMs when comparable targets in this country are at risk from the increasingly accurate Soviet ICBMs. Colin S. Gray, for example, says:

> From the Western side, PD 59 has attracted the now-traditional charges of instability promotion. (Somehow, it is acceptable for the USSR to threaten . . . US strategic forces and the survivability of the US national chain of command [after all, that is just 'the Soviet way']—but not for the United States to reciprocate!)[18]

But such insistence upon tit-for-tat contributes to a protracted arms race that is inherently unstable. While the apparent Soviet drive to acquire a pinpoint first-strike capability against American land-based missiles must be countered by steps to ensure the continuation of our Mutual Assured Destruction capacity, it does not follow that this country must also prepare to fight a so-called limited nuclear war. Contrary to the central thesis of PD 59, the United States is not obliged to match Moscow's moves in order to preserve deterrence. Indeed, Mr. Carter's

---

[17]Ibid., p. 67.

[18]Colin S. Gray, "Debate & Discussion: New U.S. Nuclear Strategy," *The Baltimore Sun,* 20 September 1980, p. 14. A companion article by Jeremy J. Stone presents a case against PD 59.

initial wariness over counterforce doctrine was well-founded. The enlargement of selective strategic options for attacking the Soviet Union does nothing to enhance the credibility of the American deterrent, but it does enhance the Soviet inclination to preempt against the United States, and here is where the real danger lies.

In fact, the Soviets have been most explicit in characterizing the codified shift in American nuclear targeting policy as a move toward a first-strike capability. During August 1980, commentators for Tass, the Soviet press agency, and the Communist Party newspaper *Pravda* contended on several occasions that the new declarations on American strategy were linked with Washington's intentions to deploy advanced medium-range missiles in Western Europe. The link, they alleged, is based on a plan to confine Soviet retaliation to Western Europe, the anticipated launching site for the American first strike. As reported by Vladimir Goncharov, a political news analyst for Tass, there could be no doubt that this indeed was the American intention.[19]

In assessing the Soviet charges, one cannot ignore the suspicion that a retaliatory counterforce strategy is somewhat a contradiction in terms. After all, this suspicion lies at the heart of American skepticism concerning Soviet claims that their own counterforce targeting is for retaliatory purposes only. Unless the nation that strikes first were to do so on a limited basis, holding considerable follow-on nuclear strategic weapons in reserve, a counterforce capability would be useful only to the nation that strikes first. Otherwise, a counterforce attack would fall on empty missile silos. As we have already seen, however, from the Soviet view a limited nuclear first strike would be illogical. And while it is conceivable that in certain contingencies the United States might consider a limited nuclear first strike, such an act would entail a substantial risk of nuclear retaliation and subsequent escalation. In this connection, we might profitably consider the recent reply of Lieutenant General Mikhail A. Milshtein, a Soviet authority on military doctrine, when asked by a *New York Times* interviewer whether he considered it possible for the United States to deliver pinpoint strikes at Soviet military targets with only limited effect on the civilian population, General Milshtein answered:

> Absolute fantasy. There will be plenty of what those exponents of 'limited' nuclear war called 'collateral casualties.' The missile silos, the airfields, the naval bases are not located in space. There are people around.[20]

The unsuitability of counterforce doctrines of retaliation is reinforced by serious technological difficulties. In a letter written in April 1979 to Defense Secretary Brown, General Richard H. Ellis, Commander-in-Chief of the Strategic Air Command, indicated that United States strategic nuclear forces were incapable of carrying out a selective counterforce targeting strategy and would not be in a position to do so until 1986. As reported recently by Drew Middleton, little has happened in 18 months to change General Ellis's estimate. According to Middleton:

> Surveying the Strategic Air Command's prospects of launching a [counterforce] attack after an initial Soviet strike, [General Ellis] estimated that the B-52s and ICBMs in his force would be left with fewer than 1500 warheads. He conceded that the American fleet of ballistic missile submarines would probably escape crippling damage during a surprise attack. But he stressed that there would not be sufficient surviving forces to launch an effective operation against Soviet missile silos and to fulfill other tasks 'at a level much above the assured destruction of Soviet urban/industrial targets.'[21]

---

[19]"Soviet Charges Reiterated," *The New York Times*, 21 August 1980, p. A8; and Genrikh A. Trofimenko, "Moscow Isn't Worried," *The New York Times*, 22 September 1980, p. 27.

[20]Anthony Austin, "Moscow Expert Says U.S. Errs on Soviet War," *The New York Times*, 25 August 1980, p. A2.

[21]Drew Middleton, "SAC Chief is Critical of Carter's New Nuclear Plan," *The New York Times*, 7 September 1980, p. 19.

And what is the intention of this country's plan to place Soviet civilian and military leaders at hostage, as is implicit in PD 59's provisions for targeting Soviet military command posts and government control centers? Clearly, the essential rationale of limited, controlled nuclear conflict requires the *preservation* of leaders once a war has begun. To base a nuclear strategy on destroying the adversary's ruling elite at the outset is to heighten the probability of loss of rational control of nuclear war. Ironically, an understanding of this point is embedded in Presidential Directive 58 (complementing PD 59), which orders more effective procedures for protecting American leaders in the event of nuclear war. While it is assumed that Soviet leaders are less likely to strike first if they know that they are personally targeted, this assumption is at variance with General Ellis's assessment of our retaliatory potential. It follows that Soviet leaders may actually feel *less jeopardized* by striking first and that they may be tempted to do so before 1986 or whenever the United States acquires the advanced weapon systems to fully implement a counterforce strategy.

Taken together, the elements of America's counterforce nuclear strategy provide genuine incentives to Soviet leaders to strike first. These incentives would naturally be even greater during times of intense political crisis. Moreover, since apparent Soviet fears of American first-strike intentions may occasion their ultimate resort to a launch-on-warning policy or hair-trigger instrumentation for retaliation, the American nuclear strategy greatly increases the likelihood of accidental nuclear war. In the words of Gerard Smith, former Director of the US Arms Control and Disarmament Agency, if both sides feared the other would strike first, "the pernicious concept of 'launch-on-warning' will probably again become a matter of interest."[22] This might tempt the United States or the Soviets to launch retaliatory ICBMs solely on the basis of radar warnings; peace would then be hostage to the wisdom and mercy of radars and computers.[23] Indeed, should launch-on-warning policy be adopted by the Soviets, renewed American fears could lead to this country's fulfillment of the adversary's prophecy—an American first strike.

Finally, it should be observed that the strategy of deterrence based on nuclear warfighting below the all-out threshold contributes to the dangerous notion that nuclear war might somehow be endured or even "won," this in the face of an enormous body of scientific and medical evidence indicating that a large-scale nuclear exchange by the superpowers would be an unparalleled disaster for the human race. Such evidence has been well summed up by Rear Admiral Gene R. LaRoque (USN, Ret.):

> There is no nuclear war strategy that can have any outcome other than mass devastation and catastrophic annihilation of life in both this country and the Soviet Union. The conclusion ought to be obvious to both sides: the best substitute for nuclear 'victory' is a mutual agreement that none is possible, and to quit the most expensive and foolish arms race in history.[24]

---

[22]Gerard Smith, quoted in "The Nuclear Strategy: Battle of the Dead?" *The Defense Monitor,* 5 (July 1976), 8.

[23]Ibid.

[24]Gene R. LaRoque, quoted in *The Defense Monitor,* 5 (July 1976), 7. For the literature on the consequences of such a disaster, see Tom Stonier, *Nuclear Disaster* (New York: Meridian, 1964); *Long-Term Worldwide Effects of Multiple Nuclear Weapons Detonations* (National Academy of Sciences report, Washington, 12 August 1975); Bernard Feld, "The Consequences of Nuclear War," *The Bulletin of the Atomic Scientists,* 32 (June 1976), 10–13; US Arms Control and Disarmament Agency, *Worldwide Effects of Nuclear War . . . Some Perspectives* (Washington: GPO, n.d. but produced after the 1975 National Academy of Sciences report); Office of Technology Assessment, *The Effects of Nuclear War* (Washington: GPO, May 1979); Physicians for Social Responsibility, "An Open Letter to President Carter and Chairman Brezhnev," *Newsletter,* 1 (April 1980), 1; US Congress, Joint Committee on Defense Production, *Economic and Social Consequences of Nuclear Attacks on the United States,* 94th Cong., 1st Sess., March 1979; Kevin N. Lewis, "The Prompt and Delayed Effects of Nuclear War," *Scientific American,* 240 (July 1979), 35–47; Louis René Beres, *Apocalypse: Nuclear Catastrophe in World Politics* (Chicago: Univ. of Chicago Press, 1980); and Franklyn Griffiths and John C. Polanyi, eds., *The Dangers of Nuclear War* (Toronto: Toronto Univ. Press, 1979), especially J. Carson Mark's opening essay, "The Consequences of Nuclear War."

ALTERNATIVES TO PD 59

If nations continue to base their hopes for peace and security on the ability to visit nuclear destruction upon an aggressor, they will surely have nuclear war. The road to a durable peace lies not through the implementation of progressively more provocative and problematic counterforce doctrines, but rather through the incremental disengagement of states from a condition of widening nuclear terror. For the time being, the United States should hew to a strategy of Mutual Assured Destruction based upon a reasonable countervalue strategic posture. Thoughts of a counterforce strategy should be forsaken. Meanwhile, we should take three basic steps:

• First, we should reemphasize and publicize to the world the intolerability of nuclear war. The Soviet Union is not entirely immune to world public opinion, so we should undertake a long-term campaign to mobilize that opinion effectively.

• Second, a comprehensive agenda for long-term international security must be created. Such an agenda must aim at removing incentives to states to acquire, enlarge, or "refine" nuclear forces. How might this agenda be implemented? The answer lies in several, interrelated initiatives. Most obvious, perhaps, is the need for a renewed effort on our part to secure the cooperation of Western Europe and Soviet Russia in enforcing a genuine nuclear weapons nonproliferation policy. On a bilateral level, the United States should take the lead in establishing a more harmonious style of interaction with the Soviet Union. Afghanistan and Poland notwithstanding, we cannot allow our relations with the Soviets to deteriorate to a state of incendiary hostility. Needed, at a minimum, is prompt Senate ratification of SALT II; a reversal of current trends toward increased US military spending on nuclear weapons; and a serious US commitment to the principles of arms control and (ultimately) to the staged destruction of existing stockpiles of strategic nuclear weapons.

The move toward minimum deterrence must be augmented by a new American initiative toward a long-sought comprehensive test ban and by an American renunciation of the right to first use of all nuclear weapons. From the point of view of the Soviet Union, the American policy of responding with tactical nuclear weapons to a Warsaw Pact conventional attack against NATO must appear decidedly unsettling, since such a policy (1) permits rapid escalation to strategic nuclear conflict; (2) permits the initiation of general nuclear war masquerading as a circumscribed first use (either by deliberately creating conditions which lead to acts of so-called aggression or by falsely alleging that such acts have actually taken place); and (3) can be employed as a complement to counterforce targeting doctrine. Obviously, it takes two to tango, and no American initiatives will be successful lacking reciprocity on the part of the Soviet Union. But since the fate of the human race hangs in the balance, we should allow neither our pride nor our timidity to forestall the essential initiatives.

Of course, current Soviet policy is disturbing to this country. But the abandonment of the right to first use presently seems more difficult for the United States than for the Soviet Union. This greater commitment to first use stems from fears of American conventional force inferiority in the vital theaters of Western Europe, Southwest Asia, the Middle East, and the Persian Gulf.

• Third, it follows that to allow for a credible renunciation of the first-use option, this country must undertake significant efforts to strengthen its conventional forces and thus eventually to obviate all theater nuclear forces. However expensive such efforts might be (and they would be enormously expensive), their long-term security benefits would surely be "cost effective."

EPILOGUE

At this juncture in its history, the human race can choose enduring peace or global destruction. As one of the two nuclear superpowers inhabiting the globe, the United States will have a decisive voice in which course is chosen. The continuance in force of Presidential Directive 59 makes it less likely that America's voice will speak in behalf of enduring peace.

Presidential Directive 59: Flawed but Useful
Colin S. Gray

Nuclear weapons are a permanent element in international politics. Moreover, the United States, as leader of a maritime alliance of Eurasian-peripheral states, is compelled for geopolitical reasons to place greater emphasis upon nuclear threat than does the Soviet Union.[1] In discussing the particular instrumentalities through which the United States manifests that threat, I shall assume that all Western commentators on the subjects are morally equal: proponents and critics of PD 59 are united in a shared horror of the prospect of nuclear war.[2]

This article does not constitute a wholesale defense of PD 59. It is intended, rather, to defend PD 59 against ill informed and poorly conceived criticism. It is contended here that PD 59 may be thought of as a major step forward in the US quest for a prudent strategic targeting policy. However, the document as presently constituted both contains dubious elements and reflects some of the more general weaknesses of US strategic thought. What then are the pertinent facts about PD 59?

PRESIDENTIAL DIRECTIVE 59

There are more, and less, intelligent rationales for most strategic doctrines. Critics of the trend of recent years in official US strategic nuclear thinking may, if they wish, seize upon the weaker presentations of that thinking for the purpose of supporting their cases. This possibility is particularly strong with respect to PD 59 because only a handful of people have actually read the document. Secondary sources on PD 59 (such as articles in *The New York Times*) are not totally to be trusted because reporters often have an interest in presenting a particular view of an issue, and the language of presidential directives tends to the general rather than the specific. In addition, responsible officials often have quite a different understanding of what a policy document *really* says or implies. This is the case with PD 59. In short, even the document itself and primary sources such as explanations by the authors or direct contributors may be less than completely enlightening.

Today, while one can with some confidence outline what the authors of PD 59 intended, it is well worth remembering that *policy documents* do not, in and of themselves, constitute policy (particularly when an administration changes). Policy comprises capabilities, declarations, and actions. For PD 59 to merit the appellation of a new US strategy, it would have to be translated, successively, into a Nuclear Weapon Employment Policy (NUWEP) guidance document, and then into actual targeting plans by the Joint Strategic Target Planning Staff in Omaha. Neither of these essential steps toward policy, properly so-called, has yet been taken.

With particular reference to some of the claims advanced by Professor Beres, it will be useful to itemize briefly some of the beliefs that are *not* held by proponents—even somewhat critical proponents, such as myself—of PD 59. Contrary to Professor Beres' statements or obvious implications, proponents of PD 59—

---

[1]A point made strongly in Henry Kissinger, "The Future of NATO," *The Washington Quarterly*, 2 (Autumn 1979), 6.

[2]PD 59, as of 25 June 1980, presented the outline of a revised (or new, depending upon interpretation) nuclear targeting doctrine. For the original (planned) leak to the press, see Richard Burt, "Carter Said to Back a Plan for Limiting Any Nuclear War." *The New York Times*, 6 August 1980, p. A6. Also see Richard Burt, "The New Strategy for Nuclear War: How It Evolved," *The New York Times*, 13 August 1980, p. A3.

Colin S. Gray, "Presidential Directive 59: Flawed but Useful," *Parameters—The Journal of the US Army War College* 11 (March 1981), pp. 29–37.

- Do not believe that central nuclear war *will* be limited,[3] only that it *might* be limited. PD 59 offers some possibility of limitation—the Mutual Assured Destruction theme favored by Beres offers no such possibility.
- Do not assume that the Soviet Union *will* cooperate in observing targeting restraints,[4] only that the United States should endeavor to maximize Soviet incentives to be restrained and, if need be, seek to enforce restraints physically.
- Do not make "the assumption that the Soviets might have something to gain by launching a limited first-strike attack on the United States or its allies."[5]
- Do not make "the assumption that the Soviets are more likely to be deterred by the threat of limited American counterforce reprisals than by the threat of overwhelming, total retaliation."[6]

Harold Brown chose to characterize PD 59 as constituting an evolution in US strategic thinking.[7] That is a defensible position; however, the immediate authors of the document had some distinctly nonevolutionary ideas in mind. First, they had a vision of a general war which might be protracted—requiring forces as well as command, control, communications and intelligence assets (C^3I) which could survive and function for perhaps as long as six months. Notwithstanding the official endorsements in the early 1960's, renewed more vigorously in the early 1970's, of flexibility in the application of force through the Single Integrated Operations Plan (SIOP) and various sub-SIOPs, the fact is that to this day US strategic forces lack endurance, lack essential, survivable C^3I, and lack serious support and plans for post-strike reconstitution.[8] PD 59 does not say that general war *will*

be protracted, only that it may be. Soviet doctrine, sensibly, also is indefinite on this question.[9]

Second, the endurance of forces with varied characteristics married to survivable C^3I should enable the US National Command Authority to wage the war in a genuinely flexible manner. Survivable C^3I should permit genuine political direction of the war on an hour-by-hour and day-by-day basis. In practice "the fog of battle" may not permit this, but the goal is a sound one.

Third, officials have decided to downgrade in priority those kinds of targets (primarily of an "economic recovery" kind) the destruction of which would not contribute to an immediately successful outcome of a war.[10] The United States has always targeted Soviet nuclear forces, and has targeted specific political-control nodes for many years.[11] PD 59 licenses the placing of greater emphasis on Soviet military targets of all kinds, as well as on political-control nodes and directly war-supporting industry.

Fourth, although PD 59 constitutes an incomplete revolution in strategic thought, as explained below, Harold Brown, probably unwittingly, advertised the possibility of a more fundamental shift:

> In our analysis and planning we are necessarily giving greater attention to how a nuclear war would actually be fought by both sides if deterrence fails. *There is no contradiction between this focus on how a war would be fought and what its results would be, and our purpose of insuring continued peace through mutual deterrence.* [italics supplied][12]

If taken at face value, which it should not be, this statement marks a complete doctrinal conver-

---

[3]Louis R. Beres, "Presidential Directive 59: A Critical Assessment," *Parameters,* 11 (March 1981), 23 (see pp. 262–263 in this chapter).

[5]Ibid.

[6]Ibid.

[7]Harold Brown, Speech at Newport, R.I., 20 August 1980, p. 5.

[8]The appalling fragility of US C^3I has been recognized officially for several years. However, for so long as the US government anticipated a general nuclear war to be a very short-lived event, it was less than obvious why a great deal of money should be spent on the endurance of forces and C^3I.

[9]See Joseph D. Douglass Jr. and Amoretta M. Hoeber, *Soviet Strategy for Nuclear War* (Stanford, Calif.: Hoover Institution Press, 1979), pp. 12–13.

[10]See Colin S. Gray, "Nuclear Strategy: The Case for a Theory of Victory," *International Security,* 4 (Summer 1979), particularly pp. 65–67.

[11]See Walter S. Mossberg, "Fighting a Nuclear War," *The Wall Street Journal,* 27 August 1980, p. 14.

[12]Speech at Newport, R.I., 20 August 1980, p. 6.

gence of US strategic thought with Soviet strategic thought. Without apparent qualification, Harold Brown here is equating deterrence with defense. In practice, no group of senior US defense policymakers, to date, has shown sustained interest in strategic operational issues. Robert McNamara in 1962 expounded publicly on the merits of a no-cities targeting doctrine and appeared to be seriously interested in flexibility in SIOP planning,[13] but his interest soon waned. He was advised that damage limitation would be increasingly difficult to effect as the Soviet Union modernized and augmented its strategic forces, and that a damage-limiting or, in popular parlance, war-fighting posture would require the United States to "spend much more money on strategic forces, money that would have to come out of conventional force budgets."[14]

McNamara and his aides feared that a pronounced damage-limiting focus would be taken by the armed services as a license to bid and lobby for any and every new weapon system they fancied. Whatever his precise calculations may have been, there is no disputing that, although he supervised a vast improvement over the single-variant "Optimum Mix"[15] war plan of the late 1950's, he did not ensure any genuine flexibility in the SIOP. In Henry Rowen's words,

> The implementation of Secretary McNamara's flexible options initiative in the early 1960's was aborted in large measure by the withdrawal of his interest and support.[16]

The renewal of official interest in SIOP and sub-SIOP targeting flexibility under President Nixon was in good part a logical reaction to a deteriorating strategic balance.[17] Both James Schlesinger and, later, Harold Brown were seeking "strategy offsets" for a growing deficiency in relative strategic muscle. Many of the ideas for improved targeting options that are explicit or implicit in PD 59 were developed in the study process that led to the promulgation of National Security Decision Memorandum 242 in the spring of 1974,[18] and were even present in the studies conducted by Rand alumni for McNamara in 1961–62.[19] PD 59 *may* be translated into operational planning, but—since functionally similar exercises in 1961–62 and 1971–74 found only pale reflection in NUWEP guidance and the SIOP—there are good historical grounds for skepticism over the eventual fate of PD 59, indeed, of its status as supposed "policy."

On a positive note, there is good reason to believe that PD 59, although a Carter initiative, will not suffer a prompt demise under the Reagan Administration. PD 59, although quite hotly debated by the extended defense community, may fairly be characterized as reflecting a consensus of informed opinion among defense professionals. PD 59, endorsed on 25 July 1980 by former President Carter, expressed much of the sense of the "Sloss Report" of December 1978. This report by Leon Sloss[20] was compiled on the basis of the most persuasive arguments developed over the course of nearly two years of study effort. Much if not most of that study effort was conducted by people inside and out of government who were strongly critical

---

[13]For an excellent discussion see Desmond J. Ball, *The Strategic Missile Programme of the Kennedy Administration, 1961–1963*, unpublished Ph.D. dissertation (Canberra: Australian National Univ., 1972), pp. 46–50, 273–300.

[14]Henry S. Rowen, "Formulating Strategic Doctrine." in *Commission on the Organization of the Government for the Conduct of Foreign Policy*, 4, Appendix K (Washington: GPO, June 1975), 231.

[15]Ibid., p. 225.

[16]Ibid., p. 232.

[17]A useful account of the evolution of official thinking is Henry S. Rowen, "The Evolution of Strategic Nuclear Doctrine," in *Strategic Thought in the Nuclear Age*, ed. Laurence Martin (Baltimore: Johns Hopkins Univ. Press, 1979), pp. 131–56.

[18]See Lynn E. Davis, *Limited Nuclear Options: Deterrence and the New American Doctrine*, Adelphi Paper No. 121 (London: International Institute for Strategic Studies, Winter 1975–76).

[19]See Desmond Ball, *Déjà Vu: The Return to Counterforce in the Nixon Administration* (Los Angeles: California Seminar on Arms Control and Foreign Policy, December 1974), pp. 10–14.

[20]Leon Sloss headed a small office in the Office of the Secretary of Defense in 1977–79 charged with leading the strategic nuclear targeting review.

of both many details and the general framework of Carter's defense policy. In a very real sense, therefore, PD 59 belongs to the relatively small professional defense policy analysis community and has few, if any, noteworthy Carterite features. PD 59, after all, succeeded the "Sloss Report" by all of 18 months—a clear demonstration of the tepid enthusiasm for the propagation of its ideas felt by many senior policymakers in the Carter Administration.

TARGETING STRATEGY

The SIOP, based on the Nuclear Weapon Employment Policy, expresses a strategy which should be guided by a theory of deterrence. A prudent, responsible US government should develop nuclear war plans which—

● Have the desired restraining effect upon Soviet policy impulses. In other words, the United States should promise, and be able, to take military action of a kind known to be most unwelcome in Moscow.

● Are responsive to the need to support unique American foreign policy interests. As noted already, for geopolitical reasons the United States and its allies around the periphery of Eurasia are likely to continue in local conditions of conventional and theater-nuclear inferiority. This means that, as envisaged in the current NATO strategic concept of flexible response (NATO Military Committee, no. 14/3, 1967), the United States requires the capability to strike first with strategic forces and dominate any subsequent process of escalation. The Soviet Union does not have such a requirement. The Soviet need is for a strategic counter-deterrent able to checkmate the possibility of US strategic nuclear initiatives.[21]

● Would be of wartime, as well as prewar, deterrent value, and which the United States would

have an interest in implementing in the undesired event.[22]

● Have integrity, as a potential unity, from the moment of employment to war termination. This entails the clear articulation of war aims. Although war plan design should have many branches, lower-level strike options should complement higher-level options—and the whole horrific enterprise should be informed by a determination to enforce as favorable (for US interests) a postwar international order as the circumstances of nuclear war permit.

● Take full account of the possibility that a condition may arise wherein the Soviet Union would be beyond deterrence. War plans, and their associated defense capabilities, have to be judged inadequate if they assume for their success cooperative behavior by the enemy, and if they cannot be implemented in toto in reasonable expectation that the essential United States would survive.[23]

● Lack, in and of themselves, a "provocative" character such that—whatever their military rationality—they diminish US security.

WAR PLANNING: SOME CURRENT PROBLEMS

Major problems persist with reference to both the integrity of PD 59 and its associated process of targeting review. So far as physical assets are concerned, PD 59 cannot be implemented with current forces and C^3I capabilities. Even if there were no reason to question the merit of the strategic vision in PD 59, the fact remains that the United States is the better part of a decade away from a matching force posture. Paradoxically, in the very same speech in which he sought to explain PD 59, Harold Brown announced the contemporary non-survivability of America's silo-housed ICBM force.[24] In the absence of a large fraction of such a force, PD 59 could not be executed.

[21]Which is not to say that the Soviet Union does not welcome the measure of strategic advantage that relative US inactivity in the 1970's has accorded her. See Seweryn Bialer, *Stalin's Successors: Leadership Stability and Change in the Soviet Union* (Cambridge, England: Cambridge Univ. Press, 1980), ch. 12.

[22]This argument is developed in Gray, "Nuclear Strategy: The Case for a Theory of Victory."

[23]See Colin S. Gray and Keith B. Payne, "Victory Is Possible," *Foreign Policy*, 39 (Summer 1980), 14–27.

[24]Speech at Newport, R.I., 20 August, 1980, p. 2.

Conceptually, PD 59 reflects all too faithfully the poverty of US strategic thinking over the past 20 years in that it addresses only the issue of US *offensive* strategy. However, given the estimated character of Soviet targeting strategy,[25] the near-certain impact on the fog of battle, and the very human nature of American presidents, US strategic employment initiatives could not, or should not, be ordered in the absence of some tolerably robust theory of domestic damage limitation. Faith, let alone trust, cannot be reposed in a hypothesized willingness on the Soviet part to play the nuclear game according to American rules. In short, if an American president ever feels moved, in desperation, to begin what he hopes will be only a small, very limited nuclear war, he had better have at hand plans and capabilities which indicate how the United States can survive a very large nuclear war.

As readers may discern, some elements in the analysis in this article are congruent with those presented by Professor Beres. We agree that the Soviet Union may well not "play" in ways compatible with American interests and expectations, and that a small nuclear war could all too easily become a large nuclear war. Where we part company is in our respective diagnoses of the US security condition and in our identification of feasible and prudent alternatives. Beres contemplates the possibility of nuclear war—which he views as a certainty "if nations continue to base their hopes for peace and security on the ability to visit nuclear destruction upon an aggressor"[26]—and recommends that the United States "hew to a strategy of Mutual Assured Destruction based upon a reasonable countervalue strategic posture."[27] In addition, he urges the United States to "take the lead in establishing a more harmonious style of interaction with the Soviet Union,"[28] to renounce "the right to

first use of all nuclear weapons,"[29] and to strengthen its conventional forces so as "eventually to obviate all theater nuclear forces."[30]

These recommendations are simply unworldly—a fact which vitiates whatever merit they might have. A massive buildup of Western conventional forces is not feasible politically or economically, and is flawed in terms of strategic logic. There is an essential unity to military posture. If we choose to emphasize one element of the posture, particularly at the lower level of potential conflict, we virtually invite adversary escalation to a level where *he* has an advantage.[31] Moreover, if the United States could not sell a conventionally oriented defense to its European NATO allies in the early and mid-1960's, why does Professor Beres believe success in such an enterprise would be probable in the 1980's and 1990's? Given the uncomfortable but enduring facts of Western conventional inferiority in vital regions, Beres' recommendations for an American no-first-nuclear-use declaration would promote panic in Western Europe, the Middle East, and Japan, and would vastly encourage nuclear proliferation. The path to hell is paved with good intentions.

While I share with Professor Beres a wish for Western (and Japanese) conventional forces to be greatly strengthened, and a desire to inhibit nuclear proliferation insofar as that is possible, I believe that the United States has no choice but to continue to rely upon strategic nuclear threats as an important backstop to foreign policy. Such threats can be credible, and can be invoked prudently, only if their contemplation does not paralyze a US president into indecision. The first duty of the US government is to avoid defeat, not to enforce defeat upon the enemy. We should take small consolation from the knowledge that the United States could defeat the Soviet Union, in Soviet terms, if the

[25]See Douglass and Hoeber, *Soviet Strategy for Nuclear War.* I am also indebted to William T. Lee for the work he has conducted on this subject for many years.
[26]Beres, "Presidential Directive 59," p. 26 (see p. 266 in this chapter).
[27]Ibid.
[28]Ibid.

[29]Ibid.
[30]Ibid., p. 27.
[31]See Richard Burt, "Reassessing the Strategic Balance," *International Security,* 5 (Summer 1980), 49–50.

price tag for that accomplishment is known to lie close to 100 million prompt American deaths.

Many in the US defense community today do not appear to recognize that the offense cannot be executed if the country cannot be defended. Domestic damage limitation is not an optional extra— it is a vital necessity if the SIOP is to have any operational value. Damage limitation, no matter how assiduously pursued, must always be imperfect. This author agrees with those critics who argue that nuclear war would be a catastrophe unprecedented for the United States.[32] Anyone who asserted that a nuclear war against a first-class enemy would be cheap to conduct would have to be judged a dangerous charlatan. The important point to recognize, however, is that the United States *may have no practical alternative* to waging a nuclear war.

Professor Beres asserts that "the prudent course would appear to assume that any nuclear exchange must be avoided lest it become total."[33] Such avoidance will be impossible if the Soviet Union decides to begin such a war, or if, in defense of vulnerable friends and allies, the United States decides that, *in extremis,* nuclear war is preferable to capitulation. So long as the United States needs a nuclear strategy, which is prospectively forever, it should—from choice—select a strategy which (a) has maximum deterrent impact on enemy minds; (b) poses measured destructive effects against the enemy for calculated political purposes rather than a gross destructive effect for its own sake (which is the case with Professor Beres' preferred strategy of assured destruction);[34] and (c) would not, if executed in full, guarantee the near-total destruction of the United States by way of enemy retaliation.

A damage-limitation capability comprising counterforce strikes, multilayer ballistic missile defense, air defense, and civil defense—though not perfect or "leakproof"—should make the difference between a United States which could, and a United States which could not, survive a nuclear war. By extension, such damage-limitation provisions would restore meaning to the concept of *strategy* so far as US nuclear forces are concerned.[35] Military power and political purpose would be reunified, and the American president would have regained a useful measure of freedom of foreign policy action. The prospect of nuclear war would still be daunting: given what we think we know about probable Soviet strategic targeting "style," American casualties could still easily reach into the low tens of millions.[36] So long as the world is locked into a threat system that includes nuclear weapons, there is no practical alternative to preparing to wage nuclear war as effectively as possible. Fortunately, there is every reason to believe that probably high proficiency in war-waging yields optimum deterrent effect.

With further respect to the integrity of PD 59, and indeed of the whole trend in targeting and deterrence thought in the late 1970's,[37] it is difficult to quarrel with the proposition that the United States should place at risk those assets of highest value to the Soviet state. Preeminently that translates into the requirement to threaten the coercive instruments of Soviet state power, and the political control apparatus of that power. More generally, the external defeat of some elements of the Soviet armed forces should shake the awe in which the power of their state is held by the Soviet citizens, and should, in Moscow's war deliberations, promote

---

[32]In human and economic terms, The Great Patriotic War was a catastrophe for the USSR, thereby demonstrating that some catastrophes are survivable. Even if one could guarantee to effect catastrophe, deterrence would not, *ipso facto,* be assured under all possible circumstances.

[33]Beres, "Presidential Directive 59," p. 22 (see p. 261 in this chapter).

[34]Probably the best defense of an indefensible position (i.e. mutual assured destruction as preferred policy guidance) in this regard is that of Robert Jervis, "Why Nuclear Superiority Doesn't Matter," *Political Science Quarterly,* 94 (Winter 1979–80), 617–33.

[35]For a brilliant brief essay on strategy, see Edward N. Luttwak, "On the Meaning of Strategy . . . for the United States in the 1980s," in *National Security in the 1980s: From Weakness to Strength,* ed. W. Scott Thompson (San Francisco: Institute for Contemporary Studies, 1980), pp. 259–73.

[36]See US Congress, Office of Technology Assessment, *The Effects of Nuclear War* (Washington: GPO, May 1979).

[37]See Desmond Ball, *Developments in U.S. Strategic Nuclear Policy Under the Carter Administration,* ACIS Working Paper No. 21 (Los Angeles: Center for International and Strategic Affairs, UCLA, February 1980).

an acute anxiety over the prospects for military success and fear of military failure.

In addition, quite aside from the deterrent value of threatening Soviet military, paramilitary, and policy assets, such targets (together with political control nodes and war-supporting industry) should be accorded the highest priority for potential elimination because, by and large, they constitute the direct threat to the United States. I have no interest in effecting the *ex post facto* punishment of collective Soviet crimes; I am simply interested in degrading the physical ability of the Soviet state to do us harm.

PD 59 endorses the idea of holding the Soviet political control structure at risk, but such a threat may be conceived in two very different perspectives.[38] First, a large counter-control strike could be attempted, very early in a war, as an essential component of the damage-limitation endeavor. If Soviet forces cannot be commanded centrally, perhaps they cannot be employed. Or, to take a second perspective, one could conceive of the large counter-control strike as constituting the functional equivalent of the old urban-industrial assured-destruction strike. Such a strike could be withheld as the United States' ultimate threat to the Soviet Union. To date, the US strategy and targeting community has not thought through just what the proper role of counter-control threats should be, just as the technical feasibility of such a strike remains yet to be demonstrated convincingly.[39] Nonetheless, its deterrent potency as a threat in Soviet minds cannot seriously be doubted.

PD 59 envisages the possibility of protracted war, but the plausibility of this idea remains weak.

It is no exaggeration to say that the official US defense community has accepted the necessity for endurance in strategic forces and C^3I, but it has not thought through how or why such a war would unfold. Indeed, given Soviet targeting style, the idea of, say, a six-month central war requires considerably more persuasive arguments in its support than have been adduced thus far. Overall, the defense community appears to have endorsed the words "protracted war," and has been fascinated by the technical issues associated with survivability and endurance of military assets, but has yet to conduct the careful battle analysis which might support the new intellectual fashion.[40]

Contrary to appearances, perhaps, I am friendly to the idea both of counter-control targeting and of preparation for the possibility of protracted war. However, these ideas are approaching a fashionable status that neither reveals their thin analytical base nor much encourages critical and imaginative inquiry.

As Winston Churchill once said, "It is sometimes necessary to take the enemy into consideration." Soviet targeting intentions are, of necessity, a mystery. American defense analysts do not know for certain just how inventive and pragmatic Soviet leaders would be in practice. We do not know whether Soviet leaders would execute a somewhat inflexible war plan in a rigid way, or whether they would insist upon flexibility and instant responsiveness as invited by unique and possibly unforeseen circumstances.[41] Nonetheless, study of Soviet strategic "style" and inferences from Soviet programs, behavior, and writings do provide a dominant model of Soviet targeting practice. On the evidence, which admittedly is quite incomplete, the United States should anticipate a Soviet central war

[38]On counter-control targeting, see Jeffrey T. Richelson, "The Dilemmas of Counterpower Targeting," *Comparative Strategy*, 2 (1980), 226–27, 229–33; and Colin S. Gray, "Targeting Problems for Central War," *Naval War College Review*, 33 (January–February 1980), 12–15; and George H. Quester, *New Alternatives for Targeting the Soviet Union*, DNA 5047T (Washington: Defense Nuclear Agency, 31 July 1979), passim.

[39]Research is well launched on the issue of just what the Soviet control structure consists of as a potential target. A useful introduction to this topic is William and Harriet Scott, *The Soviet Control Structure*, Final Report, SPC 575 (Arlington, Va.: System Planning Corporation, April 1980).

[40]One can trace fashions in targeting and conduct-of-war ideas over the past 20 years.

[41]On balance, I am inclined to agree with Jack Snyder's judgment that "based on what is visible to the outside observer, Soviet crisis decisionmakers would appear intellectually unprepared for real-time improvisation of a doctrine of intra-war restraint" (*The Soviet Strategic Culture: Implications for Limited Nuclear Operations*, R-2154-AF [Santa Monica, Calif.: Rand, September 1977], pp. 39–40).

campaign that accords closely with traditional military criteria, as opposed to a campaign dominated by "bargaining" steps during an escalation process.[42] We should expect the Soviet Union to seek to neutralize American military power "in being," political and military control of that power, and military mobilization potential. While Soviet targeteers are supposed to be sensitive to the issue of unwanted collateral damage to their enemies, there is no good reason to believe that any significant short-term military price would be paid in an effort to keep such collateral damage to a low level. In short, the dominant Soviet concern would be to win the war.

While the US government, through its targeting design, threat, and execution sequencing, might be able to influence Soviet war-fighting behavior, it is no less plausible to argue that the Soviet Union would fight a nuclear war in its traditional, military-goal-directed way. US defense planners must endeavor to provide incentives for Soviet war-fighting restraint, but plan upon the distinct possibility that, in the event, they may have no choices other than surrendering or fighting a war through to a military conclusion.

CONCLUDING CONSIDERATIONS

Contrary to Professor Beres' assertion,[43] there is nothing "provocative" about the targeting doctrine outlined, *and* implicit, in PD 59. To target the forces of the other side that can hurt you is simply common sense. Moreover, on the evidence available, counterforce targeting has long been a high priority in Soviet war planning. Beres' highly challengeable assertions concerning crisis and arms race stability[44] would translate, if ever the US government were sufficiently foolish to adopt them as policy guidance, into Soviet political leverage on

a heroic scale.[45] His preference for a "reasonable countervalue strategic posture"[46] (undefined) would constitute a bluff, pure and simple, of no supportive merit for foreign policy. The United States could never, responsibly, execute such a threat (we would know it, and the Soviet Union would know we knew it!). At the technical level, it is highly unlikely that the "reasonable countervalue" threat, even if credible (which it would not be), would suffice to deter a truly desperate Soviet leadership.

The crisis instability charge against PD 59 fails for several reasons. First, as Richard Burt has argued, it is reasonably clear, on the historical evidence, that acute concerns about essentially "mechanistic [or technical] instabilities" are profoundly apolitical and are distinctively American.[47] However World War III may happen, one of the least likely outbreak scenarios is the one involving "the reciprocal fear of surprise attack."[48] Nuclear war is too serious a business for the most important political decision in Soviet history to be taken on the basis of general staff technical assessments. Second, even if Beres' instability logic be granted for the sake of argument, how could it be provocative to threaten Soviet ICBMs with *survivably based* American ICBMs? If American ICBMs could not be neutralized in a Soviet first strike, the Soviet silo-housed ICBMs would have no promising targets on American soil.

US targeting strategy continues as undeserving of the label of true *strategy* because what passes for strategy is developed quite apart from serious consideration of damage-limitation issues. Furthermore, strategy, as reflected ultimately in force allocation and targeting design, continues to be developed in unhealthy isolation from the weapon development and acquisition process and from arms

---

[42]Many, and probably most, Western defense commentators have chosen to model hypothetical nuclear wars as processes of "violent bargaining" rather than as wars. I do not believe this approach is at all congruent with Soviet style.

[43]Beres, "Presidential Directive 59," p. 24 (see p. 263 in this chapter).

[44]Ibid., pp. 24–25 (see pp. 263–264 in this chapter).

[45]I have criticized still orthodox, and I believe fallacious, stability theories in my article, "Strategic Stability Reconsidered," *Daedalus,* 109 (Fall 1980), 135–54.

[46]Beres, "Presidential Directive 59," p. 26 (see p. 266 in this chapter).

[47]"Arms Control and Soviet Strategic Forces: The Risks of Asking SALT to Do Too Much," *The Washington Review of Strategic and International Studies,* 1 (January 1978), 22.

[48]Thomas C. Schelling, *The Strategy of Conflict* (Cambridge, Mass.: Harvard Univ. Press, 1960), the title of ch. 9.

control policy. Major issues of technical feasibility lie in PD 59's emphasis upon counter-military and counter-political targeting, though the proper role of counter-political targeting is still stuck on the nursery slopes of understanding. For all that, PD 59 marks a useful step toward an intelligent US war-fighting targeting strategy *for deterrence.*

QUESTIONS FOR DISCUSSION

1 Do the premises underlying PD 59 make the use of nuclear weapons in war more or less likely?
2 What role do ICBMs play in PD 59?
3 Can nuclear war be controlled?
4 Does PD 59 strengthen "extended deterrence" in Europe?
5 Does PD 59 strengthen or weaken strategic stability?

SUGGESTED READINGS

Aldridge, Robert C. *First Strike: The Pentagon's Strategy for Nuclear War.* Boston, Massachusetts: South End Press, 1983.

Ball, Desmond. *Can Nuclear War Be Controlled?* Adelphi Paper no. 169. London: International Institute for Strategic Studies, 1981.

Black, Edwin F. "Presidential Directive 59: The Beginning of a New Nuclear Strategy," *U. S. Naval Institute Proceedings* 107 (January 1981), pp. 93–94.

Bracken, Paul J. *The Command and Control of Nuclear Forces.* New Haven, Connecticut: Yale University Press, 1983.

Clark, Ian. *Limited Nuclear War: Political Theory and War Conventions.* Oxford: Martin Robertson, 1982.

Gray, Colin S. "Nuclear Strategy: The Case for a Theory of Victory," *International Security* 4 (Summer 1979), pp. 54–87.

Jervis, Robert. *The Illogic of American Nuclear Strategy.* Ithaca, New York: Cornell University Press, 1984.

Kistiakowsky, George B. "Can a Limited Nuclear War Be Won?" *Defense Monitor* 10, no. 2 (1981), pp. 1–4.

Muskie, Edmund S. "U.S. Nuclear Strategy," *Department of State Bulletin* 80 (October 1980), p. 33.

"P. D. 59," *The Nation* (September 13, 1980), pp. 33–34.

Powers, Thomas. "Choosing a Strategy for World War III," *Atlantic Monthly* (November 1982), pp. 82–86, 91–96, 98–106, and 108–110.

Stone, I. F. "Human Costs of Limited War," *Technology Review* 83 (October 1980), p. 33.

Subrahmanyam, K. "New Nuclear Strategy," *World Press Review* 27 (November 1980), p. 53.

Thaxton, Richard. "Directive Fifty-Nine," *Progressive* (October 1980), pp. 36–37.

16 Should the United States Make a Nuclear
No-First-Use Declaration?

YES

McGeorge Bundy, George F. Kennan,
Robert F. McNamara, and Gerard Smith

Nuclear Weapons and the Atlantic Alliance

NO

Colin S. Gray

NATO's Nuclear Dilemma

Nuclear Weapons and the Atlantic Alliance

McGeorge Bundy,
George F. Kennan,
Robert S. McNamara,
Gerard Smith

We are four Americans who have been concerned over many years with the relation between nuclear weapons and the peace and freedom of the members of the Atlantic Alliance. Having learned that each of us separately has been coming to hold new views on this hard but vital question, we decided to see how far our thoughts, and the lessons of our varied experiences, could be put together; the essay that follows is the result. It argues that a new policy can bring great benefits, but it aims to start a discussion, not to end it.

For 33 years now, the Atlantic Alliance has relied on the asserted readiness of the United States to use nuclear weapons if necessary to repel aggression from the East. Initially, indeed, it was widely thought (notably by such great and different men as Winston Churchill and Niels Bohr) that the basic military balance in Europe was between American atomic bombs and the massive conventional forces of the Soviet Union. But the first Soviet explosion, in August 1949, ended the American monopoly only one month after the Senate approved the North Atlantic Treaty, and in 1950 communist aggression in Korea produced new Allied attention to the defense of Europe.

The "crude" atomic bombs of the 1940s have been followed in both countries by a fantastic proliferation of weapons and delivery systems, so that today the two parts of a still-divided Europe are targeted by many thousands of warheads both in the area and outside it. Within the Alliance, France and Britain have developed thermonuclear forces which are enormous compared to what the United States had at the beginning, although small by comparison with the present deployments of the su-

perpowers. Doctrine has succeeded doctrine, from "balanced collective forces" to "massive retaliation" to "mutual assured destruction" to "flexible response" and the "seamless web." Throughout these transformations, most of them occasioned at least in part by changes in the Western view of Soviet capabilities, both deployments and doctrines have been intended to deter Soviet aggression and keep the peace by maintaining a credible connection between any large-scale assault, whether conventional or nuclear, and the engagement of the strategic nuclear forces of the United States.

A major element in every doctrine has been that the United States has asserted its willingness to be the first—has indeed made plans to be the first if necessary—to use nuclear weapons to defend against aggression in Europe. It is this element that needs re-examination now. Both its cost to the coherence of the Alliance and its threat to the safety of the world are rising while its deterrent credibility declines.

This policy was first established when the American nuclear advantage was overwhelming, but that advantage has long since gone and cannot be recaptured. As early as the 1950s it was recognized by both Prime Minister Churchill and President Eisenhower that the nuclear strength of both sides was becoming so great that a nuclear war would be a ghastly catastrophe for all concerned. The following decades have only confirmed and intensified that reality. The time has come for careful study of the ways and means of moving to a new Alliance policy and doctrine: that nuclear weapons will not be used unless an aggressor should use them first.

II

The disarray that currently besets the nuclear policy and practices of the Alliance is obvious. Governments and their representatives have maintained an appearance of unity as they persist in their support of the two-track decision of December 1979, under which 572 new American missiles of intermediate range are to be placed in Europe unless a satisfactory agreement on the limitation of such weapons can be reached in the negotiations between the United States and the Soviet Union that began last November. But behind this united front there are divisive debates, especially in countries where the new weapons are to be deployed.

The arguments put forward by advocates of these deployments contain troubling variations. The simplest and intuitively the most persuasive claim is that these new weapons are needed as a counter to the new Soviet SS-20 missiles; it may be a recognition of the surface attractiveness of this position that underlies President Reagan's striking—but probably not negotiable—proposal that if all the SS-20s are dismantled the planned deployments will be cancelled. Other officials have a quite different argument, that without new and survivable American weapons which can reach Russia from Western Europe there can be no confidence that the strategic forces of the United States will remain committed to the defense of Western Europe; on this argument the new missiles are needed to make it more likely that any war in Europe would bring nuclear warheads on the Soviet Union and thus deter the aggressor in the first place. This argument is logically distinct from any concern about the Soviet SS-20s, and it probably explains the ill-concealed hope of some planners that the Reagan proposal will be rejected. Such varied justifications cast considerable doubt on the real purpose of the proposed deployment.

An equally disturbing phenomenon is the gradual shift in the balance of argument that has occurred since the need to address the problem was first asserted in 1977. Then the expression of need was European, and in the first instance German; the emerging parity of long-range strategic systems was asserted to create a need for a balance at less than intercontinental levels. The American interest developed relatively slowly, but because these were to be American missiles, American planners took the lead as the proposal was worked out. It has also served Soviet purposes to concentrate on the American role. A similar focus has been chosen by many leaders of the new movement for nuclear disarmament in Europe. And now there are American voices, some in the executive branch, talking as if European acceptance of these new missiles were some sort of test of European loyalty to the Alliance. Meanwhile some of those in Europe who remain publicly committed to both tracks of the 1979 agreement are clearly hoping that the day of deployment will never arrive. When the very origins of a new proposal become the source of irritated argument among allies—"You started it!"—something is badly wrong in our common understanding.

A still more severe instance of disarray, one which has occurred under both President Carter and President Reagan, relates to the so-called neutron bomb, a weapon designed to meet the threat of Soviet tanks. American military planners, authorized by doctrine to think in terms of early battlefield use of nuclear weapons, naturally want more "up-to-date" weapons than those they have now; it is known that thousands of the aging short-range nuclear weapons now in Europe are hard to use effectively. Yet to a great many Europeans the neutron bomb suggests, however unfairly, that the Americans are preparing to fight a "limited" nuclear war on their soil. Moreover neither weapons designers nor the Pentagon officials they have persuaded seem to have understood the intense and special revulsion that is associated with killing by "enhanced radiation."

All these recent distempers have a deeper cause. They are rooted in the fact that the evolution of essentially equivalent and enormously excessive nuclear weapons systems both in the Soviet Union and in the Atlantic Alliance has aroused new concern about the dangers of all forms of nuclear war. The profusion of these systems, on both sides, has made it more difficult than ever to construct rational plans for any first use of these weapons by anyone.

This problem is more acute than before, but it is not new. Even in the 1950s, a time that is often mistakenly perceived as one of effortless American superiority, the prospect of any actual use of tactical weapons was properly terrifying to Europeans and to more than a few Americans. Military plans for such use remained both deeply secret and highly hypothetical; the coherence of the Alliance was maintained by general neglect of such scenarios, not by sedulous public discussion. In the 1960s there was a prolonged and stressful effort to address the problem of theater-range weapons, but agreement on new forces and plans for their use proved elusive. Eventually the proposal for a multilateral force (MLF) was replaced by the assignment of American Polaris submarines to NATO, and by the creation in Brussels of an inter-allied Nuclear Planning Group. Little else was accomplished. In both decades the Alliance kept itself together more by mutual political confidence than by plausible nuclear war-fighting plans.

Although the first years of the 1970s produced a welcome if oversold détente, complacency soon began to fade. The Nixon Administration, rather quietly, raised the question about the long-run credibility of the American nuclear deterrent that was to be elaborated by Henry Kissinger in 1979 at a meeting in Brussels. Further impetus to both new doctrine and new deployments came during the Ford and Carter Administrations, but each public statement, however careful and qualified, only increased European apprehensions. The purpose of both Administrations was to reinforce deterrence, but the result has been to increase fear of nuclear war, and even of Americans as its possible initiators. Intended as contributions to both rationality and credibility, these excursions into the theory of limited nuclear war have been counterproductive in Europe.

Yet it was not wrong to raise these matters.

Questions that were answered largely by silence in the 1950s and 1960s cannot be so handled in the 1980s. The problem was not in the fact that the questions were raised, but in the way they seemed to be answered.

It is time to recognize that no one has ever succeeded in advancing any persuasive reason to believe that any use of nuclear weapons, even on the smallest scale, could reliably be expected to remain limited. Every serious analysis and every military exercise, for over 25 years, has demonstrated that even the most restrained battlefield use would be enormously destructive to civilian life and property. There is no way for anyone to have any confidence that such a nuclear action will not lead to further and more devastating exchanges. Any use of nuclear weapons in Europe, by the Alliance or against it, carries with it a high and inescapable risk of escalation into the general nuclear war which would bring ruin to all and victory to none.

The one clearly definable firebreak against the worldwide disaster of general nuclear war is the one that stands between all other kinds of conflict and any use whatsoever of nuclear weapons. To keep that firebreak wide and strong is in the deepest interest of all mankind. In retrospect, indeed, it is remarkable that this country has not responded to this reality more quickly. Given the appalling consequences of even the most limited use of nuclear weapons and the total impossibility for both sides of any guarantee against unlimited escalation, there must be the gravest doubt about the wisdom of a policy which asserts the effectiveness of any first use of nuclear weapons by either side. So it seems timely to consider the possibilities, the requirements, the difficulties, and the advantages of a policy of no-first-use.

III

The largest question presented by any proposal for an Allied policy of no-first-use is that of its impact on the effectiveness of NATO's deterrent posture on the central front. In spite of the doubts that are created by any honest look at the probable consequences of resort to a first nuclear strike of any kind, it should be remembered that there were strong reasons for the creation of the American nuclear umbrella over NATO. The original American pledge, expressed in Article 5 of the Treaty, was understood to be a nuclear guarantee. It was extended at a time when only a conventional Soviet threat existed, so a readiness for first use was plainly implied from the beginning. To modify that guarantee now, even in the light of all that has happened since, would be a major change in the assumptions of the Alliance, and no such change should be made without the most careful exploration of its implications.

In such an exploration the role of the Federal Republic of Germany must be central. Americans too easily forget what the people of the Federal Republic never can: that their position is triply exposed in a fashion unique among the large industrial democracies. They do not have nuclear weapons; they share a long common boundary with the Soviet empire; in any conflict on the central front their land would be the first battleground. None of these conditions can be changed, and together they present a formidable challenge.

Having decisively rejected a policy of neutrality, the Federal Republic has necessarily relied on the nuclear protection of the United States, and we Americans should recognize that this relationship is not a favor we are doing our German friends, but the best available solution of a common problem. Both nations believe that the Federal Republic must be defended; both believe that the Federal Republic must not have nuclear weapons of its own; both believe that nuclear guarantees *of some sort* are essential; and both believe that only the United States can provide those guarantees in persuasively deterrent peacekeeping form.

The uniqueness of the West German position can be readily demonstrated by comparing it with those of France and the United Kingdom. These two nations have distance, and in one case water, between them and the armies of the Soviet Union; they also have nuclear weapons. While those weapons may contribute something to the common strength of the Alliance, their main role is to underpin a residual national self-reliance, expressed in different ways at different times by different governments, which sets both Britain and France apart from the Federal Republic. They are set apart from the United States too, in that no other nation depends on them to use their nuclear weapons otherwise than in their own ultimate self-defense.

The quite special character of the nuclear relationship between the Federal Republic and the United States is a most powerful reason for defining that relationship with great care. It is rare for one major nation to depend entirely on another for a form of strength that is vital to its survival. It is unprecedented for any nation, however powerful, to pledge itself to a course of action, in defense of another, that might entail its own nuclear devastation. A policy of no-first-use would not and should not imply an abandonment of this extraordinary guarantee—only its redefinition. It would still be necessary to be ready to reply with American nuclear weapons to any nuclear attack on the Federal Republic, and this commitment would in itself be sufficiently demanding to constitute a powerful demonstration that a policy of no-first-use would represent no abandonment of our German ally.

The German right to a voice in this question is not merely a matter of location, or even of dependence on an American nuclear guarantee. The people of the Federal Republic have demonstrated a steadfast dedication to peace, to collective defense, and to domestic political decency. The study here proposed should be responsive to their basic desires. It seems probable that they are like the rest of us in wishing most of all to have no war of any kind, but also to be able to defend the peace by forces that do not require the dreadful choice of nuclear escalation.

IV

While we believe that careful study will lead to a firm conclusion that it is time to move decisively toward a policy of no-first-use, it is obvious that any such policy would require a strengthened confidence in the adequacy of the conventional forces of the Alliance, above all the forces in place on the central front and those available for prompt reinforcement. It seems clear that the nations of the Alliance together can provide whatever forces are needed, and within realistic budgetary constraints, but it is a quite different question whether they can summon the necessary political will. Evidence from the history of the Alliance is mixed. There has been great progress in the conventional defenses of NATO in the 30 years since the 1952 Lisbon communiqué, but there have also been failures to meet force goals all along the way.

In each of the four nations which account for more than 90 percent of NATO's collective defense and a still higher proportion of its strength on the central front, there remain major unresolved political issues that critically affect contributions to conventional deterrence: for example, it can be asked what priority the United Kingdom gives to the British Army of the Rhine, what level of NATO-connected deployment can be accepted by France, what degree of German relative strength is acceptable to the Allies and fair to the Federal Republic itself, and whether we Americans have a durable and effective answer to our military manpower needs in the present all-volunteer active and reserve forces. These are the kinds of questions—and there are many more—that would require review and resolution in the course of reaching any final decision to move to a responsible policy of no-first-use.

There should also be an examination of the ways in which the concept of early use of nuclear weapons may have been built into existing forces, tactics, and general military expectations. To the degree that this has happened, there could be a dangerous gap right now between real capabilities and those which political leaders might wish to have in a time of crisis. Conversely there should be careful study of what a policy of no-first-use would require in those same terms. It seems more than likely that once the military leaders of the Alliance have learned to think and act steadily on this "conventional" assumption, their forces will be better instruments for stability in crises and for general deterrence, as well as for the maintenance of the nuclear firebreak so vital to us all.

No one should underestimate either the difficulty or the importance of the shift in military attitudes implied by a no-first-use policy. Although military commanders are well aware of the terrible dangers in any exchange of nuclear weapons, it is a strong military tradition to maintain that aggressive war, not the use of any one weapon, is the central evil. Many officers will be initially unenthusiastic about any formal policy that puts limits on their recourse to a weapon of apparently decisive power. Yet the basic argument for a no-first-use policy can be stated in strictly military terms: that any other course involves unacceptable risks to the national life that military forces exist to defend. The military officers of the Alliance can be expected to understand the force of this proposition, even if many of them do not initially agree with it. Moreover, there is every reason for confidence that they will loyally accept any policy that has the support of their governments and the peoples behind them, just as they have fully accepted the present arrangements under which the use of nuclear weapons, even in retaliation for a nuclear attack, requires advance and specific approval by the head of government.

An Allied posture of no-first-use would have one special effect that can be set forth in advance: it would draw new attention to the importance of maintaining and improving the specifically American conventional forces in Europe. The principal political difficulty in a policy of no-first-use is that it may be taken in Europe, and especially in the Federal Republic, as evidence of a reduced American interest in the Alliance and in effective overall deterrence. The argument here is exactly the opposite: that such a policy is the best one available for keeping the Alliance united and effective. Nonetheless the psychological realities of the relation between the Federal Republic and the United States are such that the only way to prevent corrosive German suspicion of American intentions, under a no-first-use regime, will be for Americans to accept for themselves an appropriate share in any new level of conventional effort that the policy may require.

Yet it would be wrong to make any hasty judgment that those new levels of effort must be excessively high. The subject is complex, and the more so because both technology and politics are changing. Precision-guided munitions, in technology, and the visible weakening of the military solidity of the Warsaw Pact, in politics, are only two examples of changes working to the advantage of the Alliance. Moreover there has been some tendency over many years to exaggerate the relative conventional strength of the U.S.S.R. and to underestimate Soviet awareness of the enormous costs and risks of any form of aggression against NATO.

Today there is literally no one who really knows what would be needed. Most of the measures routinely used in both official and private analyses are static and fragmentary. An especially arbitrary, if obviously convenient, measure of progress is that of spending levels. But it is political will, not budgetary pressure, that will be decisive. The value of greater safety from both nuclear and conventional danger is so great that even if careful analysis showed that the necessary conventional posture would require funding larger than the three-percent real increase that has been the common target of recent years, it would be the best bargain ever offered to the members of the Alliance.

Yet there is no need for crash programs, which always bring extra costs. The direction of the Allied effort will be more important than its velocity. The final establishment of a firm policy of no-first-use, in any case, will obviously require time. What is important today is to begin to move in this direction.

V

The concept of renouncing any first use of nuclear weapons should also be tested by careful review of the value of existing NATO plans for selective and limited use of nuclear weapons. While many scenarios for nuclear war-fighting are nonsensical, it must be recognized that cautious and sober senior officers have found it prudent to ask themselves what alternatives to defeat they could propose to their civilian superiors if a massive conventional Soviet attack seemed about to make a decisive breakthrough. This question has generated contingency plans for battlefield uses of small numbers of nuclear weapons which might prevent that particular disaster. It is hard to see how any such action could be taken without the most enormous risk of rapid and catastrophic escalation, but it is a fair challenge to a policy of no-first-use that it should be accompanied by a level of conventional strength that would make such plans unnecessary.

In the light of this difficulty it would be prudent to consider whether there is any acceptable policy short of no-first-use. One possible example is what might be called "no-*early*-first-use;" such a policy might leave open the option of some limited nuclear action to fend off a final large-scale conventional defeat, and by renunciation of any immediate first use and increased emphasis on conventional capabilities it might be thought to help somewhat in reducing current fears.

But the value of a clear and simple position would be great, especially in its effect on ourselves and our Allies. One trouble with exceptions is that they easily become rules. It seems much better that even the most responsible choice of even the most limited nuclear actions to prevent even the most imminent conventional disaster should be left out of authorized policy. What the Alliance needs most today is not the refinement of its nuclear options, but a clear-cut decision to avoid them as long as others do.

VI

Who should make the examination here proposed? The present American Administration has so far shown little interest in questions of this sort, and indeed a seeming callousness in some quarters in Washington toward nuclear dangers may be partly responsible for some of the recent unrest in Europe. But each of the four of us has served in Administrations which revised their early thoughts on nuclear weapons policy. James Byrnes learned the need to seek international control; John Foster Dulles stepped back somewhat from his early belief in massive retaliation; Dwight Eisenhower came to believe in the effort to ban nuclear tests which he at first thought dangerous; the Administration of John F. Kennedy (in which we all served) modified its early views on targeting doctrine; Lyndon Johnson shelved the proposed MLF when he decided it was causing more trouble than it was worth; and Richard Nixon agreed to narrow limits on antiballistic missiles whose large-scale deployment he had once thought indispensable. There were changes also in the Ford and Carter Administrations, and President Reagan has already adjusted his views on the usefulness of early arms control negotiations, even though we remain in a time of general stress between Washington and Moscow. No Administration should be held, and none should hold itself, to inflexible first positions on these extraordinarily difficult matters.

Nor does this question need to wait upon governments for study. The day is long past when public awe and governmental secrecy made nuclear policy a matter for only the most private executive determination. The questions presented by a policy of no-first-use must indeed be decided by governments, but they can and should be considered by citizens. In recent months strong private voices have been raised on both sides of the Atlantic on behalf of strengthened conventional forces. When this cause is argued by such men as Christoph Bertram, Field Marshal Lord Carver, Admiral Noel Gayler, Professor Michael Howard, Henry Kissinger, François de Rose, Theo Sommer, and General Maxwell Taylor, to name only a few, it is fair to conclude that at least in its general direction the present argument is not outside the mainstream of thinking within the Alliance. Indeed there is evidence of renewed concern for conventional forces in governments too.

What should be added, in both public and private sectors, is a fresh, sustained, and careful consideration of the requirements and the benefits of deciding that the policy of the Atlantic Alliance should be to keep its nuclear weapons unused as long as others do the same. Our own belief, though we do not here assert it as proven, is that when this possibility is fully explored it will be evident that the advantages of the policy far outweigh its costs, and that this demonstration will help the peoples and governments of the Alliance to find the political will to move in this direction. In this spirit we go on to sketch the benefits that could come from such a change.

VII

The first possible advantage of a policy of no-first-use is in the management of the nuclear deterrent forces that would still be necessary. Once we escape from the need to plan for a first use that is credible, we can escape also from many of the complex arguments that have led to assertions that all sorts of new nuclear capabilities are necessary to create or restore a capability for something called "escalation dominance"—a capability to fight and "win" a nuclear war at any level. What would be needed, under no-first-use, is a set of capabilities we already have in overflowing measure—capabilities for appropriate retaliation to any kind of Soviet nuclear attack which would leave the Soviet Union in no doubt that it too should adhere to a policy of no-first-use. The Soviet government is already aware of the awful risk inherent in any use of these weapons, and there is no current or prospective Soviet "superiority" that would tempt anyone in Moscow toward nuclear adventurism. (All four of us are wholly unpersuaded by the argument advanced in recent years that the Soviet Union could ever rationally expect to gain from such a wild effort as a massive first strike on land-based American strategic missiles.)

Once it is clear that the only nuclear need of the

Alliance is for adequately survivable and varied *second strike* forces, requirements for the modernization of major nuclear systems will become more modest than has been assumed. In particular we can escape from the notion that we must somehow match everything the rocket commanders in the Soviet Union extract from their government. It seems doubtful, also, that under such a policy it would be necessary or desirable to deploy neutron bombs. The savings permitted by more modest programs could go toward meeting the financial costs of our contribution to conventional forces.

It is important to avoid misunderstanding here. In the conditions of the 1980s, and in the absence of agreement on both sides to proceed to very large-scale reductions in nuclear forces, it is clear that large, varied, and survivable nuclear forces will still be necessary for nuclear deterrence. The point is not that we Americans should move unilaterally to some "minimum" force of a few tens or even hundreds of missiles, but rather that once we escape from the pressure to seem willing and able to use these weapons first, we shall find that our requirements are much less massive than is now widely supposed.

A posture of no-first-use should also go far to meet the understandable anxieties that underlie much of the new interest in nuclear disarmament, both in Europe and in our own country. Some of the proposals generated by this new interest may lack practicability for the present. For example, proposals to make "all" of Europe—from Portugal to Poland—a nuclear-free zone do not seem to take full account of the reality that thousands of long-range weapons deep in the Soviet Union will still be able to target Western Europe. But a policy of no-first-use, with its accompaniment of a reduced requirement for new Allied nuclear systems, should allow a considerable reduction in fears of all sorts. Certainly such a new policy would neutralize the highly disruptive argument currently put about in Europe: that plans for theater nuclear modernization reflect an American hope to fight a nuclear war limited to Europe. Such modernization might

or might not be needed under a policy of no-first-use; that question, given the size and versatility of other existing and prospective American forces, would be a matter primarily for European decision (as it is today).

An effective policy of no-first-use will also reduce the risk of conventional aggression in Europe. That risk has never been as great as prophets of doom have claimed and has always lain primarily in the possibility that Soviet leaders might think they could achieve some quick and limited gain that would be accepted because no defense or reply could be concerted. That temptation has been much reduced by the Allied conventional deployments achieved in the last 20 years, and it would be reduced still further by the additional shift in the balance of Allied effort that a no-first-use policy would both permit and require. The risk that an adventurist Soviet leader might take the terrible gamble of conventional aggression was greater in the past than it is today, and is greater today than it would be under no-first-use, backed up by an effective conventional defense.

VIII

We have been discussing a problem of military policy, but our interest is also political. The principal immediate danger in the current military posture of the Alliance is not that it will lead to large-scale war, conventional or nuclear. The balance of terror, and the caution of both sides, appear strong enough today to prevent such a catastrophe, at least in the absence of some deeply destabilizing political change which might lead to panic or adventurism on either side. But the present unbalanced reliance on nuclear weapons, if long continued, might produce exactly such political change. The events of the last year have shown that differing perceptions of the role of nuclear weapons can lead to destructive recriminations, and when these differences are compounded by understandable disagreements on other matters such as Poland and the Middle East, the possibilities for trouble among Allies are evident.

The political coherence of the Alliance, especially in times of stress, is at least as important as the military strength required to maintain credible deterrence. Indeed the political requirement has, if anything, an even higher priority. Soviet leaders would be most pleased to help the Alliance fall into total disarray, and would much prefer such a development to the inescapable uncertainties of open conflict. Conversely, if consensus is re-established on a military policy that the peoples and governments of the Alliance can believe in, both political will and deterrent credibility will be reinforced. Plenty of hard questions will remain, but both fear and mistrust will be reduced, and they are the most immediate enemies.

There remains one underlying reality which could not be removed by even the most explicit declaratory policy of no-first-use. Even if the nuclear powers of the Alliance should join, with the support of other Allies, in a policy of no-first-use, and even if that decision should lead to a common declaration of such policy by these powers and the Soviet Union, no one on either side could guarantee beyond all possible doubt that if conventional warfare broke out on a large scale there would in fact be no use of nuclear weapons. We could not make that assumption about the Soviet Union, and we must recognize that Soviet leaders could not make it about us. As long as the weapons themselves exist, the possibility of their use will remain.

But this inescapable reality does not undercut the value of a no-first-use policy. That value is first of all for the internal health of the Western Alliance itself. A posture of effective conventional balance and survivable second-strike nuclear strength is vastly better for our own peoples and governments, in a deep sense more civilized, than one that forces the serious contemplation of "limited" nuclear scenarios that are at once terrifying and implausible.

There is strong reason to believe that no-first-use can also help in our relations with the Soviet Union. The Soviet government has repeatedly offered to join the West in declaring such a policy, and while such declarations may have only limited reliability, it would be wrong to disregard the real value to both sides of a jointly declared adherence to this policy. To renounce the first use of nuclear weapons is to accept an enormous burden of responsibility for any later violation. The existence of such a clearly declared common pledge would increase the cost and risk of any sudden use of nuclear weapons by either side and correspondingly reduce the political force of spoken or unspoken threats of such use.

A posture and policy of no-first-use also could help to open the path toward serious reduction of nuclear armaments on both sides. The nuclear decades have shown how hard it is to get agreements that really do constrain these weapons, and no one can say with assurance that any one step can make a decisive difference. But just as a policy of no-first-use should reduce the pressures on our side for massive new nuclear forces, it should help to increase the international incentives for the Soviet Union to show some restraint of its own. It is important not to exaggerate here, and certainly Soviet policies on procurement are not merely delayed mirror-images of ours. Nonetheless there are connections between what is said and what is done even in the Soviet Union, and there are incentives for moderation, even there, that could be strengthened by a jointly declared policy of renouncing first use. At a minimum such a declaration would give both sides additional reason to seek for agreements that would prevent a vastly expensive and potentially destabilizing contest for some kind of strategic advantage in outer space.

Finally, and in sum, we think a policy of no-first-use, especially if shared with the Soviet Union, would bring new hope to everyone in every country whose life is shadowed by the hideous possibility of a third great twentieth-century conflict in Europe—conventional or nuclear. It seems timely and even urgent to begin the careful study of a policy that could help to sweep this threat clean off the board of international affairs.

IX

We recognize that we have only opened this large question, that we have exhausted no aspect of it, and that we may have omitted important elements. We know that NATO is much more than its four strongest military members; we know that a policy of no-first-use in the Alliance would at once raise questions about America's stance in Korea and indeed other parts of Asia. We have chosen deliberately to focus on the central front of our central alliance, believing that a right choice there can only help toward right choices elsewhere.

What we dare to hope for is the kind of new and widespread consideration of the policy we have outlined that helped us 15 years ago toward SALT I, 25 years ago toward the Limited Test Ban, and 35 years ago toward the Alliance itself. Such consideration can be made all the more earnest and hopeful by keeping in mind one simple and frequently neglected reality: there has been no first use of nuclear weapons since 1945, and no one in any country regrets that fact. The right way to maintain this record is to recognize that in the age of massive thermonuclear overkill it no longer makes sense—if it ever did—to hold these weapons for any other purpose than the prevention of their use.

NATO's Nuclear Dilemma
Colin S. Gray

Speaking on June 15, 1982 on behalf of his absent and ailing chief, Soviet Foreign Minister Andrei Gromyko informed the U.N. General Assembly's special session on disarmament that "The Union of Soviet Socialist Republics assumes an obligation not to be the first to use nuclear weapons."[1]

This declaratory policy, of course, cost nothing and had a solely propaganda import, and was appropriately derided by U.S. and U.S.-allied official spokesmen. Nonetheless, it provided another example wherein the Reagan administration was placed on the defensive, seeking to explain why superficially attractive sounding ideas with an apparent disarmament connection were nothing more than a snare and a delusion. In part for reason of ill chance, but also because of political insensitivity, muddled thinking and declaratory indiscipline, the Reagan administration has suffered a veritable "time of troubles" with respect to the role of nuclear weapons in U.S. military policy. "No first use" of nuclear weapons, as a possible policy position, is a small though symbolically significant element in the current debate over the nuclear question.

Sadly for balance in defense debate, "no first use" has long been tainted fatally by its clear association with Soviet propaganda. Even had NATO been toying seriously with the idea of a "no first use" declaration in the summer of 1982, which was not the case, President Brezhnev's statement before the U.N. General Assembly special session would have served to inter it indefinitely. Somewhat uncharacteristically, the Reagan administration has betrayed an undue sensitivity to potential political peril with regard to the idea of "no first use." That undue sensitivity was shown in the ill-judged preemptive assault that former Secretary of State Alexander Haig launched against the idea in a speech

[1]John M. Goshkko, "Soviet Chief Renounced First Use of A-Weapons," *The Washington Post*, June 16, 1982, p. 1.

Colin S. Gray, "NATO's Nuclear Dilemma," *Policy Review*, no. 22 (Fall 1982), pp. 97–116.

delivered on April 6, 1982.[2] Mr. Haig was en-
deavoring to discredit in advance an article that
was about to appear in *Foreign Affairs* written by
four former government officials: McGeorge Bundy,
George F. Kennan, Robert S. McNamara, and Gerard Smith.[3] Those four authors urged a "new and
widespread consideration of the policy" of no first
use of nuclear weapons.[4]

The timing of the *Foreign Affairs* article could
hardly have been less fortunate. The administration
had been chivvied by pressure from some of its
NATO-European allies into entering the political
theater of negotiations over intermediate-range nuclear forces (INF) in Europe late in 1981, and had
seized the suitably high ground of the "zero option"
as a basis for laying claim to arms control virtue.
However, by early April 1982, nuclear protest had
ceased to be exclusively a political embarrassment
in only Western Europe; it appeared in a very well
organized way in the United States also. The
administration feared for the fate of its military
modernization program and for the strength of its
arms control bargaining hand as Soviet officials
observed and encouraged round one of the "Ground
Zero" consciousness raising (concerning the dangers of nuclear war) campaign,[5] and as political
opportunists as well as sincere, if misguided, citizens propagandized energetically for a nuclear
freeze.[6]

The Reagan administration was struggling to hold
its NATO partners to their contingent commitment,
as a NATO-wide endeavor, to permit deployment
of ground-launched cruise missiles (GLCMs) and
Pershing II ballistic missiles in Western Europe,

an important aspect of that struggle being the U.S.
high ground arms control position of the "zero option."[7] The last thing that NATO needed in the
spring of 1982 was fundamental questioning of the
wisdom in NATO's strategy by four senior public
figures who could command international attention. An administration battered by charges that it
was unduly casual about the dangers of nuclear
war; by claims from the left and center of the political spectrum that it was not really serious about
arms control (the president did not announce his
readiness to reopen strategic arms negotiations until
May 9, 1982); and by criticism from all sides to
the effect that a coherent strategic policy story was
not being advanced in support of the weapons program, was not an administration likely to respond
coolly to assault from a new direction.[8]

What Mr. Haig did on April 6, 1982, was, inadvertently, to advertise and dignify a poor idea
that in reality lacked a political constituency of any
importance either in Europe or in the United States.
In this article it will be argued that NATO should
not adopt a nuclear policy of "no first use." "No
first use" is not an idea that is bereft of all merit,
political or military. Indeed, the ill-advisability of
a NATO declaratory stance of "no first use" can
only be presented judiciously if the more persuasive of the arguments in its favor are considered
fairly. The potential for political damage to the
alliance that lurks in the wings of "no first use"
discussion is so considerable that it is vital that the
full panoply of considerations be weighed by all
sides of the debate.

[2]"Haig's Speech on American Nuclear Strategy and the Role
of Arms Control," *The New York Times*, April 7, 1982, p. A-
8.

[3]"Nuclear Weapons and the Atlantic Alliance," *Foreign Affairs*, Vol. 60, No. 4 (Spring 1982), pp. 753–768.

[4]*Ibid.*, p. 767.

[5]See "Ground Zero," *Nuclear War: What's In It For You?*
(New York: Pocket Books, 1982).

[6]See Edward M. Kennedy and Mark O. Hatfield, *Freeze!
How You Can Help Prevent Nuclear War* (New York: Bantam,
1982).

[7]In December 1979 NATO, ill advisedly, adopted the so-
called "dual track" policy of preparing to deploy new long-
range theater nuclear forces, while, at the same time, pursuing
negotiations with the Soviet Union to constrain deployment of
this class of weapons. This had the effect of inviting the Soviet
government to participate very actively in the intra-alliance
politics of nuclear modernization.

[8]On the nuclear policy troubles of the Reagan administration,
see Colin S. Gray, " 'Dangerous to Your Health': The Debate
Over Nuclear Strategy and War," *Orbis*, Vol. 26, No. 3 (Fall
1982), pp. 327–349.

NATO'S NUCLEAR STRATEGY

As a former U.S. ambassador to NATO, Harlan Cleveland, wrote many years ago, a trans-Atlantic bargain defines the outer boundary of what is politically permissible by way of adjusting NATO's defense posture and strategy.[9] That bargain has the following terms: In return for the nuclear guarantee extended by the United States, NATO-European countries will contribute enough to the common defense so as to assuage American domestic suspicions to the effect that the allies are enjoying if not a free, at least a relatively cheap ride for their security. Much of the current debate over NATO strategy, nuclear and conventional, appears to be unhealthily innocent of appreciation of the bargain to which Harlan Cleveland referred.

Some of the reasoning advanced in support of NATO adopting a declaratory policy of "no first use" of nuclear weapons has indeed pointed to real dilemmas, illogicalities, and weaknesses in current NATO policy. That much should be conceded. However, real though the problems are for NATO, it is suggested here that "no first use" is not the answer.

It is worth recalling the fact that the use of nuclear weapons in Europe has been studied and debated for more than thirty years. While one should retain an open mind as to desirable changes in policy as military technology and political and economic conditions change, the enduring character of the nuclear weapons debate suggests the strong probability that NATO's policy dilemmas and difficulties stem rather more from the structural realm of lasting geopolitical factors, than they do from folly in high places.

The authoritative concept pervading NATO's defense posture remains that of flexible response. Flexible response was adopted officially by the alliance in 1967 in the document MC-14/3. That document envisages a seamless web of deterrent effect influencing the mind of a potential aggressor. It encompasses the idea that strong conventional forces should guarantee to the Soviet Union that a *coup de main* with more than the most modest of objectives in central or northern Europe is not feasible. Moreover, the strong conventional defenses guarantee a very large war, with unpredictable consequences. The large conventional war should increase the expectation that first battlefield, and then theater, nuclear weapons would be employed, which, in their turn, particularly if they engage targets within the boundary of the European U.S.S.R., should greatly increase the prospects that the war would come to embrace the homelands of both superpowers.[10]

This grand design, of a powder trail deliberately laid from the inter-German border to the high plains of the United States, offers full doctrinal satisfaction to none. Its fragilities are more pronounced today, as the central strategic nuclear balance has shifted from a condition of marginal, or essential (to have resort to a useful, if vague, term), U.S. superiority in the mid to late 1960s, to essential Soviet superiority in the early 1980s. Nonetheless, with its problems admitted, flexible response does meet the most vital political tests imposed by a multinational alliance comprising a wide range of actual, or potential, conflicting interests. The central truth which narrowly militarily focused policy advocates tend to ignore, or fail to understand, is that NATO's European-deployed forces have never been intended physically to defend Europe. Hence, much of the recurring debate concerning whether this class of technology or that strategy would serve to deny Soviet forces a plausible plan for intervention or conquest is really beside the point. Politicians cannot admit to this in public, but NATO-Europeans do not want to see local defenses deployed that would stand a reasonable prospect of

[9]Harlan Cleveland, *NATO: The Trans-Atlantic Bargain* (New York: Harper and Row, 1970).

[10]The "spirit" of NATO's defense concept of flexible response is admirably conveyed in Kenneth Hunt, *The Alliance and Europe*, Part 2: *Defense With Fewer Men*, Adelphi Paper No. 98 (London: International Institute for Strategic Studies, Summer 1973).

containing and repelling a Soviet invasion. Whether or not that view is sensible is a valid question to pose, but it does remain a reality today. NATO-Europe wants to prevent war in Europe, of any character, and it believes that its security would suffer a net diminution were a far more robust local (conventional or nuclear) war-fighting capability to be deployed.

A truly robust-seeming non-nuclear defense for Western Europe would, in European perspective, threaten the vital alliance principle of equality of risk. In the same perspective it probably would harm the stability of deterrence by holding out to Soviet political leaders a marginally more plausible prospect of the possibility of a campaign that would not engage the superpower homelands. American critics of NATO strategy have long noticed the extreme reluctance of NATO-European governments to consider nuclear weapon employment options other than in the context of a managed process of escalation for the restoration of deterrence. What those critics have missed is a scarcely smaller NATO-European reluctance to pursue defense schemes that might markedly improve the prospects of NATO effecting a successful non-nuclear defense. As West German politicians and generals will say privately, though not publicly, a credible conventional capability for NATO-Europe (in the first instance, of West Germany) is really no more acceptable than is a credible nuclear defense.

The present situation is not a happy one. The security of Western Europe rests, ultimately, upon the willingness of an American president to risk the American homeland in order to seek to restore deterrence and reverse a rapidly unfolding local military disaster. In support of this premise, which is implicit in MC-14/3, is the deployment of some 300,000 military personnel (plus dependents) in Europe; the objectively vital nature of the U.S. interest in denying Western Europe to the Soviet *imperium;* and considerations of U.S. honor and reputation. Contrary to the argument that NATO and U.S. policy with respect to the defense of Europe is a bluff, this author believes that neither the alliance as a whole, nor the United States, is bluff-

ing in the public architecture of its deterrent strategy. But critics of many doctrinal persuasions are correct in pointing to the possibility, even probability, that current policy, if ever tested under fire, would lead to a disaster of limitless proportions. The prospect that this disaster would be of a bilateral character is, of course, the basis of the deterrence thinking of the alliance.

THE BAD NEWS

The bad news is that critics are correct in saying that NATO does not have a credible conventional capability; does not have a theory of how it would employ battlefield and theater nuclear weapons in a way that would make net military sense (and would be politically acceptable to the West German government); and does not have on hand, to redress the theater imbalance, an American strategic nuclear capability for extended deterrence which enjoys unambiguous credibility. All of this must be conceded. This author believes, with many critics of NATO defense policy, that across-the-board improvements in military capability are highly desirable. However, current problems, which to a noteworthy degree are endemic in the geopolitics of the Western Alliance, are not so severe as to require a radical shift of defense policy course, either in a declaratory sense, or by way of operational planning.

The somewhat less bad news is that NATO's conventional defenses, while far short of immaculate, are certainly adequate for their basic mission, which, to repeat, is to guarantee a very large war in the event of a Soviet assault westward, and hence to raise very substantial Soviet fears of escalation. Also, although NATO does not have an agreed doctrine for the employment of theater nuclear forces, given the role of those forces as a bridge linking the European battlefield and the superpower homelands, it is not self-evident that the absence of a doctrine should be seen as a fatal weakness. It is worth mentioning that the more strident critics of NATO's current defense plans, and particularly those who urge upon NATO the necessity or feasibility of a non-nuclear defense, essentially "solve" tactical nuclear dilemmas by ignoring them. This author has long believed that from a military, and hence deterrent, point of view, NATO should plan to employ nuclear weapons very early and in sufficient numbers so as to promote fatal disruption of a Warsaw Pact attack before it could properly roll much beyond its starting lines.[11] However, that argument is politically untenable within the alliance, regardless of its military merits. Given that NATO cannot reconcile the national interest of its members in a detailed doctrine for operational nuclear employment, the current compromise and ambiguity simply reflect the political facts of life. NATO should not be criticized for not effecting the impossible.

Finally, the credibility of extended deterrence is not a matter of all or nothing. Objectively speaking, the United States should not be able credibly to threaten to intervene with her strategic nuclear forces to turn the tide of a theater conflict in the 1980s. Today, the United States cannot escalate from a theater war to a higher level of violence in expectation, or even reasonable hope, of securing an improved outcome to a war. But the Soviet Union would have some good reasons to suspect that an American president threatening such an expansion of a conflict might not be bluffing. Hundreds of thousands of Americans would be engaged in a full-scale war in Europe, and, as careful students of power politics, Soviet leaders would know, and would expect an American president to know, that the stakes of a conflict in Europe really would amount to global hegemony. If the United States lost in Western Europe, then the Middle East, Africa, and the Gulf region, and all of East Asia inevitably would fall within a newly expanded Soviet empire. The United States would remain sufficiently powerful to defend herself, but she would be denied access to Europe, Asia, and Africa. This, of course, presumes that the Soviet Union permits the United States the luxury of deciding whether or not to attempt to extend a European conflict. It is as likely as not that during the course of a very large war in the European theater, the Soviet Union, confounding the escalation sequence and reasoning most familiar in the West, would strike a massive preventive or preemptive blow against American strategic nuclear forces and their command, control, and communications.

Nothing could be further from the truth than to suggest, as Lawrence Freedman does, that "Improved conventional forces could compensate for weakness in the nuclear component of flexible response, but the reverse is not true."[12]

As competent campaign-minded defense planners whose eyes always are focused upon the problems and requirements of general war, Soviet military leaders are most unlikely ever to recommend massive military action against NATO in the European theater unless they have a noteworthy measure of "splendid superiority" with respect to central strategic forces.[13] They would lack adequate "top cover" otherwise and would be recommending action in the absence of a comprehensive theory of victory. Mr. Freedman's belief in the efficacy of conventional substitution for erstwhile nuclear missions is wrong in logical and practical terms in several major respects. First, it ignores the Soviet incentive to engage in nuclear escalation to resolve problems at the conventional level of combat. A Soviet Union willing to invade Western Europe would not be a Soviet Union likely to hesitate to have resort to nuclear weapons to maintain the planned timetable of its advance. Second, the stronger NATO's conventional defenses, the stronger the Soviet incentive is to initiate nuclear employment early in the conflict. Third, only within narrow limits could nuclear forces compensate for conventional deficiencies, but there is no way in

[11]See Colin S. Gray, *Defending NATO-Europe: Forward Defense and Nuclear Strategy*, DNA 4567F (Washington, D.C.: Defense Nuclear Agency, November 1977).

[12]"NATO Myths," *Foreign Policy,* No. 45 (Winter 1981–82), p. 53.

[13]I have derived considerable benefit from reading a recent short paper by Fritz Ermath, "Soviet Assessment of the Strategic Nuclear Balance: The Overall Strategic and Political Context," unpublished, July 1982.

which conventional forces can compensate for nuclear deficiencies. If the Soviet Union could secure useful or decisive net advantage through nuclear escalation, the war would be lost for the West.

THE FLEXIBLE RESPONSE

It is easy to be misunderstood. This author is not arguing for the starvation of NATO's conventional, relative to its nuclear, capability. It so happens that largely for nonstrategic political reasons for intra-alliance peacetime accord (or tolerable discord), NATO has chosen an overarching defense concept that does make deterrent and military sense. Proponents of a heavy conventional emphasis in NATO's defense posture should be reminded that the alliance has twice rejected such an orientation already: in the early 1950s, in the effective repudiation of the "Lisbon Goals" for conventional rearmament and mobilization readiness, and again in the early 1960s. Two of the authors of the *Foreign Affairs* article that urges reconsideration of a declaratory stance of "no-first use," McGeorge Bundy and Robert McNamara, appear to have learned relatively little from their experience as very senior members of the Kennedy and Johnson administrations. Robert McNamara's Pentagon sought to persuade its NATO allies in the early and mid-1960s to adopt a policy of flexible response, which translated as a requirement that NATO should never be in a condition where it was unable to cope with conventional aggression by conventional means alone. This definition of "flexible response" was unacceptable to NATO-Europe in the 1960s (indeed, French displeasure with the character and stridency of American ideas was expressed by her leaving the military organization of NATO in 1966), and there is no reason to believe it will prove any more acceptable in the 1980s. By way of summary, NATO-Europe, while willing, and indeed compelled, to humor many American military doctrinal preferences, is not prepared to endorse a NATO defense concept that requires the alliance to be able to fight and win a conflict confined to Western Europe, whether that conflict be nuclear or nonnuclear.

There is a conflict of national interest between the United States and her allies in Europe which no designer of alliance defense doctrine can afford to ignore.[14] The United States, while endorsing the idea of the deterrent value of there being close linkage between NATO's Central Front and ICBMs on the high plains of the American homeland, wishes to develop and sustain at least the possibility that a war which begins in Europe would remain confined to Europe. By way of contrast, NATO-European countries appreciate that sufficient local denial capability must be maintained so as to render escalation credible (or not incredible), and so as to satisfy American domestic political requirements, but they want a relatively short fuse to connect the local battle with U.S. central strategic forces. In other words, NATO-Europe favors a planned deficiency in locally deployed forces such that the transatlantic linkage, for the sharing of risks, is clear and unmistakable.

European politicians, like prudent people everywhere, know that war is a very uncertain enterprise. Every few years the intellectually turbulent American defense community produces a new or refurbished theory for the improved defense of Europe. Too often, American defense intellectuals and policy-makers alike fail to realize not only that their NATO-European audience is skeptical of the promised benefits of, say, mobile defense (to cite but the latest doctrinal panacea), but that it would not endorse the new concept even if it believed it to hold great military promise. In European perspective, rightly or wrongly, the best guarantee of peace and stability is a highly visible American presence in and commitment to the defense of Europe. Schemes intended to improve dramatically NATO's in-theater ability to repel invasion, are perceived as being potentially harmfully erosive of the transatlantic nexus.

[14]See Colin S. Gray, "Theater Nuclear Weapons: Doctrines and Postures," *World Politics*, Vol. XXVIII, No. 2 (January 1976), pp. 300–314.

'NO FIRST USE'?

Virtually the entire community of NATO-oriented defense analysts and commentators, European and American, appears to be agreed that it would be desirable were NATO to be able to deemphasize the role of nuclear weapons in its defense planning. Notwithstanding the recurring popularity of nuclear deemphasis, it is rare for public figures, or even for scholars, to go so far as to suggest an explicit NATO declaratory stance of "no first use." Many people otherwise tempted to advocate "no first use" have recognized the political damage that such a proposal could wreak if advanced formally as a U.S. preference. "No first use," if it is anything more than a declaratory flourish intended to appease popular antinuclear sentiment, cannot help meaning that the United States would prefer, *in extremis,* that its European allies be overrun by Soviet armies rather than that the risks attendant upon firing even a single nuclear weapon should be run. In the event, though not as declared policy in peacetime (when it would weaken deterrence by reducing Soviet uncertainties), NATO-Europe might well prefer conventional defeat to being defended by battlefield and theater nuclear weapons.[15] In terms of intra-alliance politics, it clearly would be less divisive if pressure for a "no first use" stance were to emanate from Bonn than from Washington. In that case however, many voices would be raised in Congress saying that a NATO-Europe so unwilling to run nuclear risks even on its own behalf is a NATO-Europe so greatly susceptible to nuclear intimidation that it must be viewed as a very unreliable group of partners in the event of a future military crisis.

Critics of NATO's flexible response policy, with its first use connotations, have noted with much good reason that flexible response *à la* MC-14/3, to be credible, let alone operationally interesting

to a NATO alliance in military distress, requires a measure of theater and strategic nuclear superiority that has long since vanished.[16] In short, NATO is clinging to the policy idea that nuclear threat and execution can substitute for conventional weakness, even though the material basis for Western escalation dominance no longer obtains. In addition, it is argued, the prominent role of nuclear threat in NATO's deterrence theory is probably more frightening to NATO-Europe than it is to the Soviet Union. The necessity for nuclear threat and use in NATO's defense planning may well promote uncertainties in Soviet minds that are healthy for the stability of deterrence, but also they carry promise of promoting policies of accommodation among NATO-Europeans. In the words of Fred Iklé:

> The more firmly NATO leaders have expected that a conventional war in Europe would develop into a nuclear war, the more anxious they would be to terminate the fighting if a conventional war actually broke out. Every day, every hour during which the conventional campaigns were being fought would seem to prolong the risk of imminent nuclear war.[17]

Mr. Iklé is correct. Unfortunately Mr. Iklé and others are not correct when they suggest that NATO can and should look to a very considerable strengthening of its conventional forces in order noticeably to alleviate its nuclear dilemma. The dilemma lies in the fact that the alliance depends critically for its security upon a weapon that it does not know how to employ in a controlled manner at bearable cost, given the unfortunate, though now longstanding, complication that nuclear conflict would be bilateral. NATO-Europe prefers to rely upon a deterrence system that does not downgrade the uncertainties and risks of nuclear threat, even though it cannot face, let alone talk very honestly in public

---

[15]For a grim prediction of the character of a nuclear battlefield, see Arthur S. Collins, Jr., "Tactical Nuclear Warfare and NATO: Viable Strategy or Dead End?" *NATO's Fifteen Nations,* Vol. 22, No. 3 (June–July 1976), pp. 71–87.

[16]This point is forcefully argued in Fred Charles Iklé, "NATO's 'First Nuclear Use': A Deepening Trap?" *Strategic Review,* Vol. IX, No. 1 (Winter 1980), pp.18–23
[17]*Ibid.,* p. 20.

about, the military implications of the structure of the threat that it has chosen.

Critics of NATO's nuclear "first use" doctrine are correct in noting that the doctrine has tended to function as a crutch for conventional weakness, as a generally inexplicit alibi for an absence of determination to build robust non-nuclear forces, and as a serious inhibitor even of rational planning for nuclear forces themselves. If conventional defenses can be trumped, and perhaps trumped easily, by nuclear use, why waste resources on conventional forces that cannot affect a campaign outcome beyond their initial roles of denying easy access to territory, and of compelling force concentrations (necessary to attempt breakthroughs) which provide appropriate targets for nuclear weapons? Also, if there is to be early resort to nuclear weapons in the theater by NATO, with a central exchange following rapidly thereafter, there is little point in devoting time, energy, and resources to ensuring the survivability of local nuclear forces.

This author is strongly critical of NATO's current and planned nuclear force posture. In addition, he believes that NATO's non-nuclear forces can and should be strengthened. However, he does not believe that NATO's "forward defense" strategy is mistaken. The promise of a maneuver strategy, or mobile defense, as offered by such analysts as Steven Canby, Edward Luttwak, and William Lind, almost certainly is illusory.[18] NATO forces lack the territorial depth for maneuver, they lack the integrity and cohesion of command needed, and, as a general rule, they lack the necessary skills.

Unexciting though it is to record this verdict, NATO has a defense concept in flexible response which can be rescued from dangerous obsolescence by the appropriate modernization of forces at all levels. It is militarily unsound and politically not viable for the alliance to pursue seriously the prospect of changing radically the structure of its deterrence posture. NATO can, and should, redeploy and reequip its forces so as to offer Soviet planners a tougher defense crust through which they would have to gnaw. But, it is chimerical to aspire to achieve a successful all-conventional defense of Western Europe. Soviet mobilization potential for land combat is such that they will always be able to win a conventional war in Europe, if not in days or weeks, then in months or years.[19] The Soviet empire may betray internal fissures under the pressure of a long campaign, but NATO cannot assume that these fissures would have a decisive effect upon Soviet ability or willingness to prolong the struggle.[20]

Conflict in Europe must always be conducted in the shadow of nuclear weapons, no matter what NATO's declaratory policy may be. As Bernard Brodie and Thomas Schelling argued in the early and mid-1960s,[21] in fashionable opposition to the conventional deemphasis orthodoxy of that time, the Soviet Union cannot possibly believe that it would be permitted to crash from the inter-German boundary through to the Channel Coast, against a very heavily nuclear-armed enemy, without triggering nuclear employment by NATO (or the U.S., or France, or Great Britain, acting independently). Such a prospect is so unreasonable that almost certainly it is dismissed by Soviet planners. This is not to deny that the Soviet Union may well hope

[18]A useful review of the maneuver, or mobile defense, school of thinking is John J. Mearsheimer, "Maneuver, Mobile Defense, and the NATO Central Front," *International Security,* Vol. 6, No. 3 (Winter 1981–82). pp. 104–122. However, *en passant,* the critics of forward defense do offer many telling criticisms of current NATO military practices.

[19]Assessment of the military balance in Europe has become a minor industry. Particularly useful are James Blaker and Andrew Hamilton, "Assessing Military Balances: The NATO Example," in John F. Reichart and Steven R. Stern, eds., *American Defense Policy,* fifth edition (Baltimore: Johns Hopkins University Press, 1982), pp. 333–350; and Robert Lucas Fischer, *Defending the Central Front: The Balance of Forces,* Adelphi Paper No. 127 (London: International Institute for Strategic Studies, Autumn 1976). For a recent "bean count," see NATO, *NATO and the Warsaw Pact: Force Comparisons,* 1982.

[20]See Steven F. Kime, "Warsaw Pact: Juggernaut or Paper Tiger?" *Air Force Magazine,* Vol. 65, No. 6 (June 1982), pp. 67–69.

[21]Bernard Brodie, *Escalation and the Nuclear Option* (Princeton: Princeton University Press, 1966); and Thomas C. Schelling, "Nuclears, NATO and the 'New Strategy,' " in Henry Kissinger, ed., *Problems of National Strategy: A Book of Readings* (New York: Praeger, 1965), pp. 175–177.

to profit from a delay in the onset of a nuclear phase to hostilities,[22] but that is quite another matter. Brodie suggested that since nuclear threat is ineradicable from the East-West military confrontation in Europe, it would be foolish for NATO to seek to minimize whatever deterrent benefit flows from that fact.

THE CASE IN FAVOR

In their recent *Foreign Affairs* article, McGeorge Bundy and his three collaborators specified six arguments which, they claim, support the case for deliberate movement by NATO towards a "no first use" stance. In fairly summary fashion these are discussed below: much of the pertinent argument has been advanced already.

1 The first possible advantage of a policy of no-first-use is in the management of the nuclear deterrent forces that would still be necessary. Once we escape from the need to plan for a first use that is credible, we can escape also from many of the complex arguments that have led to assertions that all kinds of new nuclear capabilities are necessary to create or restore a capability for something called 'escalation dominance'—a capability to fight and 'win' a nuclear war at any level.[23]

Comment: NATO's nuclear "doctrine" today, to stretch terminology, merely accommodates the possibility, and asserts the legitimacy, of first use of nuclear weapons. That doctrine does not require or even on balance anticipate first use by NATO. Prominent among the many functions of NATO's nuclear posture today is the duty to help dissuade nuclear use by the Soviet Union. Hence, there is nowhere near a direct and absolute doctrinal opposition between "no first use" and flexible response. Given that NATO does place a heavy burden of possible second (and beyond) strike duties upon its nuclear forces, the strategic case for an

assured second strike capability should be in no need of the additional ammunition that might be provided by a "no first use" declaration.[24] McGeorge Bundy and his friends would have been closer to the mark had they argued that the absence of an agreed employment doctrine for tactical nuclear forces means an absence of doctrinal guidance—really of agreed and militarily justifiable requirements—for the modernization of NATO's nuclear arsenal. "No first use," far from encouraging serious renewed endeavor to provide enduring survivability for NATO's nuclear forces, would more likely lead to those forces languishing in decreasing official interest.

2 A posture of no-first-use should also go far to meet the understandable anxieties that underlie much of the new interest in nuclear disarmament, both in Europe and in our own country.[25]

Comment: A "no first use" declaration by NATO likely would have negligible public relations value, because that particular piece of the high ground of nuclear disarmament rhetoric already has been occupied by the Soviet Union. Moreover, contrary to the expectations of Mr. Bundy and others, the political damage that "no first use" potentially could wreak in Western Europe—as a declaration lending itself to the interpretation that it expressed a U.S. determination to decouple—would have to be offset by a very considerable refurbishment of NATO's nuclear arsenal. That, at least, is what should occur. Rather more likely is the eventuality specified in the comment on the first argument above: namely, that the nuclear force posture would languish as it was devalued doctrinally, and that the postural assurances West German and other European audiences would need to sustain their confidence in the alliance to offset the clear negative implications of "no first use" would not be forthcoming. Finally,

---

[22]See Joseph D. Douglass, *Soviet Military Strategy in Europe* (New York: Pergamon, 1982).

[23]Bundy *et al.,* "Nuclear Weapons and the Atlantic Alliance," pp. 763–764.

[24]A particularly informative discussion of the state of NATO's theater nuclear forces is Robert A. Moore, "Theater Nuclear Forces: Thinking the Unthinkable," *International Defense Review,* Vol. 14 (1981), pp. 401–408.

[25]Bundy *et al.,* "Nuclear Weapons . . . ," p. 764.

Mr. Bundy and other sophisticates may understand that a "no first use" declaration could not be effected until NATO's non-nuclear defenses had been rendered far more robust than they are today, but that opinion at home and abroad to which reference was made has shown no enthusiasm for a notable measure of conventional rearmament. In the appropriate words of the title of a recent article in *The Economist,* "Do you sincerely want to be non-nuclear?"[26] Adequate sincerity, by *The Economist's* calculations, would cost NATO countries a further 1 percent real increase per annum in defense expenditure over and above the 3 percent agreed to in 1978 (and widely honored in the breach thereafter). Much of the more strident antinuclear sentiment in NATO-Europe is not only antinuclear, it is generically antidefense. It is not sensible to adopt a militarily foolish, and really operationally meaningless, declaratory policy such as "no first use" in expectation of appeasing a body of opinion that is either ignorant of, or indifferent to, considerations of military balance.

3 An effective policy of no-first-use will also reduce the risk of conventional aggression of Europe.[27]

Comment: Given that the authors sensibly acknowledge that "no one on either side could guarantee beyond all possible doubt that if conventional warfare broke out on a large scale there would in fact be no use of nuclear weapons,"[28] it is difficult to understand what meaning should be ascribed to the important term "effective." NATO-Europeans may appear to be more resolute in their determination to resist aggression were nuclear use truly impossible. However, strategy and tactics serve national interests, not such as abstract "rule of the road" as "no first use" of nuclear weapons. No matter what NATO's public stance on nuclear use might be, NATO-Europe would fear nuclear employment. It must be admitted that Soviet leaders

and planners may confidently be expected to save us from our own folly—a NATO declaratory stance of "no first use" would influence Soviet intentions *vis à vis* nuclear use not at all. The Soviet Union knows that states behave as they believe best suits their interests at the time—regardless of peacetime declarations. In 1939 did anybody recall the Kellogg-Briand Pact of 1928, which had outlawed war? This third argument is wrong on all counts. NATO is most unlikely to augment its conventional forces notably, either prior to or succeeding a declaration of "no first use." NATO governments, like the Soviet government, would view such a declaration with total cynicism. The Soviet Union would not have to overcome much larger or more capable NATO conventional forces as a consequence of a "no first use" declaration. No NATO-European government capable of rational policy-making would choose to exchange the admittedly fragile and tenuous credibility of the flexible response concept—with which at least all parties, East and West, are long familiar (no small matter in the field of international stability)—for the vacuousness of a "no first use" declaration. First use of nuclear weapons may be incredible to many Western critics of NATO doctrine, but we do not know how Soviet leaders would assay that credibility were they approaching a decision to fight or not to fight in Europe. Since such a NATO declaration would have to weigh in the scales, if it did at all, on the side of lower risks and a greater freedom for Soviet military initiatives, it must be either neutral or of negative value for the stability of deterrence.

4 There is strong reason to believe that no-first-use can also help in our relations with the Soviet Union.[29]

Comment: Signing a mildly updated SALT II and permitting the sale of American made or licensed compressors for the Siberian gas pipeline also would "help in our relations with the Soviet

---

[26]July 31, 1982, pp. 30–32.
[27]Bundy *et al.,* "Nuclear Weapons . . . ," p. 765.
[28]*Ibid.,* p. 766.

[29]*Ibid.,* p. 766.

Union." Even if they find it impolitic to say so in public, very often, NATO politicians know that the alliance must retain the contingent operational intention to use nuclear weapons first, for reason of the fundamental geopolitical asymmetries that divide the potentially hostile parties. NATO can resist a non-nuclear assault more or less effectively, with the trading of more or less space for time, but—notwithstanding Western mobilization potential—there is no way in which NATO could defeat, or even impose an indefinite stalemate upon, the Soviet Union in a conventional war in Europe. "No first use" thinking encourages the public to neglect the facts of geopolitics. It is very difficult to understand why a NATO declaration of "no first use," which logically should be preceded by a large measure of conventional rearmament and a degree of strengthening of nuclear forces (for possible second use), should "help in our relations with the Soviet Union."

Mr. Bundy and his colleagues claim that "the existence of such a clearly declared common pledge would increase the cost and risk of any sudden use of nuclear weapons by either side and correspondingly reduce the political force of spoken or unspoken threats of such use."[30] This reasoning might be excused, perhaps even found to be admirable, in an undergraduate student, but it is sobering to find it advanced by four very experienced former officials. What the authors are saying is that a Soviet leadership would (not should, or might) deem the cost and risk (of what?) of first nuclear use, intended either to avert defeat or promote the prospect of military victory, increased by the very fact of the bilateral pledge. Given the stakes of such a conflict, and the prior fact of massive cross-border aggression, can these authors seriously suggest that the fact of a declaration of intent would have any operational significance whatsoever? Whether Soviet arms were successful or were defeated, the breaking of a "no first use" pledge would be a matter of supreme indifference in Moscow.

[30]*Ibid.*, pp. 766–767.

5 A posture and policy of no-first-use could help to open the path toward serious reduction of nuclear armaments on both sides.[31]

Comment: There are several reasons why both sides, one day, might wish to reduce nuclear armaments in, and bearing upon, Europe. However, declarations—and even genuinely operational policies—of "no first use" are not among those reasons. A robust second-use policy by NATO requires an impressive scale and diversity of theater-nuclear assets. Moreover, as noted already, the political concomitant of a "no first use" pledge by NATO should be a strengthening of the nuclear arsenal, including those elements of the arsenal which are most visible and least survivable. Notwithstanding the contemporary difficulties attending the planned deployment of GLCM and *Pershing II* in Western Europe, traditionally it has been the case that NATO-Europeans like to be able to "kick the tires" of U.S. nuclear weapon delivery systems in order to reassure themselves that the U.S. nuclear guarantee is a reality. Promises in the form of submarines, for example, can sail away all too easily.

6 Finally and in sum, we think a policy of no-first-use, especially if shared with the Soviet Union, would bring new hope to everyone in every country whose life is shadowed by the hideous possibility of a third great twentieth-century conflict in Europe—conventional or nuclear. It seems timely and even urgent to begin the careful study of a policy that could help to sweep this threat clear off the board of international affairs.[32]

Comment: Unfortunately, a "no first use" declaration would have authority only until a superpower judged it to be strongly in its interest to break it. "No first use," as a policy idea, helps not "to sweep this threat clean off the board of international affairs," but rather to foster the illusion that there is some escape from the central dilemma of nuclear deterrence—that dilemma being that the

[31]*Ibid.*, p. 767.
[32]*Ibid.*, p. 767.

ultimate guarantee of Western security is the threat of a nuclear employment that Western governments are motivated extremely highly never to exercise. As Theodore Draper has remarked: "The only cure-all for nuclear war is the complete and absolute abolition of nuclear weapons everywhere and for all time."[33]

"No first use" will not blind the hard-nosed men in the Kremlin to the realities of power politics, but such a pledge has no little capacity to encourage mischievous illusions in Western democracies. Great powers will use nuclear weapons if the anticipated net advantage is judged to be sufficiently great. Well designed, complementary NATO forces, conventional and nuclear, backstopped by invulnerable U.S. strategic forces that can threaten convincingly the more important coercive instruments of the Soviet state, should offer strong encouragement for Soviet leaders never to judge that the first use of nuclear weapons would be in their interest. Above all else, to point to a familiar European theme, NATO's overriding duty to its citizens is not to prevent nuclear war, it is to prevent war *per se* in Europe. If major conflict ever is joined in Europe, the fine edifice of Western strategic theory, with its distinctions between levels of conflict and its focus upon risk manipulation and escalation control and the like, very probably will fall early victim to the dynamic and inherent logic of military events.

THE FALLACY OF THE CONVENTIONAL SOLUTION

Nuclear weapons are an inconvenience for the planner of land, tactical air, and sea forces. Given the total absence of historical data on bilateral nuclear use, the nuclear factor tends to loom almost as a wild card, threatening to upset the analysis of the kinds of combat engagement that the planner thinks he understands. Of course, nuclear weapons are by no means the only wild card that may upset calculations—one also has to consider such variables

as weather, quality of leadership, morale and steadiness of soldiers, and the stability of the home front. In addition, it can be easy to forget that the high-technology armies of NATO and the Warsaw Pact, in their non-nuclear aspects, are near totally untested instruments. Their technology has not been field-tested realistically over terrain or in the weather conditions prevalent in Central and Western Europe, and very few of their soldiers have heard shots fired in anger. Indeed, so many are the factors that should be considered in any attempt to answer the deceptively simple question, "How well would NATO fare in the event of a Pact invasion?," that no authoritative answer is possible.

Proponents of a nuclear deemphasis for NATO tend to argue that Soviet military strength is exaggerated, and they then proceed to offer their preferred prescription that will enable NATO to hold the foe without having recourse to nuclear weapons. Not only is the Soviet Union, typically, judged conveniently to be deterred from initiating nuclear employment, but the Soviet threat is fashioned, somewhat roughly, in a form that renders it susceptible to the preferred attributes of NATO's non-nuclear defenses.

The absence of persuasive-looking historical data directly applicable to the conflict in question,[34] the horrific novelty of the nuclear shadow over the prospective battlefield, and the awesome complexity of the subject mean that there are no true experts on future military conflict in Europe. That fact admitted, policy-makers, unlike scholars and editorial writers, are required to make guesses—their ignorance notwithstanding. It is the view of this author that although NATO's military preparations are deficient in many details, the basic architecture of policy is sound. Forward defense to contest nearly every foot of West German territory is a condition

---

[33]"How Not to Think About Nuclear War," *The New York Review of Books,* July 15, 1982, p. 42.

[34]John Keegan is probably correct, and he is in a company of growing size, in maintaining that the closest historical parallel available to the task faced by NATO on the Central Front is the evidence of the performance of Army Group B of the *Wehrmacht* in its endeavors to contain the Normandy beachhead in June, July, and August 1944. See John Keegan, *Six Armies in Normandy* (New York: Viking, 1982), particularly the Epilogue.

for West German loyalty to the alliance. But, forward defense happens also to offer the best prospect for deterrence and denial, notwithstanding the denunciations offered by recent advocates of strategic maneuver.

NATO does not have a first strike strategy for nuclear employment, but it does insist prudently upon the necessity for retaining the option of having first resort to nuclear weapons in case of dire need. This author wishes that NATO as a whole had the political will and courage to declare a willingness to have relatively early resort to nuclear use for the purpose of fatally disrupting a Pact attack. He suspects that escalation to central strategic employment is virtually guaranteed, because NATO would use nuclear weapons in the theater too late and too lightly for them to have a truly decisive shock effect upon an enemy that, by that time, would likely be very deep into West Germany. Nonetheless, to cite the problems in the Western defenses at all levels suggests, to this author, the need for the alliance to perform better within the political framework of the compromise strategy of flexible response.

Improvements in the tactics and weapons of conventional warfare are greatly to be desired. But, if NATO permits itself to be outthought with respect to planning for conventional combat in a "nuclear scared" context, to planning for the transition from non-nuclear (and chemical) to nuclear combat, and to planning for the conduct simultaneously of conventional and nuclear combat, then it invites the prospect of being outfought. NATO politicians and planners should never forget that a Soviet Union sufficiently desperate or bold as to launch a massive invasion of Western Europe, prudently has to be assumed to be a Soviet Union that already has crossed the Rubicon with respect to its willingness to use nuclear weapons if need be.

QUESTIONS FOR DISCUSSION

1 Would a nuclear no-first-use pledge by the United States make a Soviet attack in Western Europe more likely?

2 What effect would a no-first-use pledge by the United States have on the need to build larger conventional forces in NATO?

3 What effect would a no-first-use pledge have on the peace movement?

4 Would a no-first-use pledge slow down the arms race?

5 Would a no-first-use pledge lead to an American withdrawal from NATO?

6 Would a nuclear no-first-use pledge be likely to be honored in the event of a major conventional war between the superpowers?

SUGGESTED READINGS

Blechman, Barry M. and Mark R. Moore. "A Nuclear-Weapon-Free Zone in Europe," *Scientific American* 248 (April 1983), pp. 37–43.

Critchley, Julian. Should the First Use of Nuclear Arms Be Renounced?" *RUSI, Journal of the Royal United Services Institute for Defence Studies* (London) 127 (December 1982), pp. 32–34.

Douglass, Joseph D. and Amoretta M. Hoeber. *Conventional War and Escalation: The Soviet View.* New York: Crane, Russak, 1981.

Holm, Hans-Henrik and Nikolaj Peterson (eds.). *The European Missile Crisis: Nuclear Weapons and Security Policy.* New York: St. Martin's Press, 1984.

Iklé, Fred Charles. "NATO's 'First Nuclear Use': A Deepening Trap," *Strategic Review* 8 (Winter 1980), pp. 18–23.

Kaiser, Karl. "NATO Strategy Toward the End of the Century," *Naval War College Review* 37 (January-February 1984), pp. 69–82.

Kaiser, Karl, Georg Leber, Alois Mertes, and Franz-Josef Schulze. "Nuclear Weapons and the Preservation of Peace," *Foreign Affairs* 60 (Summer 1982), pp. 1157–1170.

McKitrick, Myra Struck. "A Conventional Deterrent for NATO; An Alternative to the Nuclear Balance of Terror," *Parameters* 13 (March 1983), pp. 51–58.

Mearsheimer, John J. "Nuclear Weapons and Deterrence in Europe," *International Security* 9 (Winter 1984–85), pp. 19–46.

Meyer, Stephen M. *Soviet Theatre Nuclear Forces.* Adelphi Paper no. 187. London: International Institute for Strategic Studies, Winter 1983–84.

Rogers, General Bernard W. "The Atlantic Alliance: Prescriptions for a Difficult Decade," *Foreign Affairs* 60 (Summer 1982), pp. 1145–1156.

Smoke, Richard. "Extended Deterrence: Some Observations," *Naval War College Review* 36 (September–October 1983), pp. 37–48.

Steinbruner, John D. and Leon Sigal (eds.). *Alliance
Security: NATO and the No-First-Use Question.*
Washington, D.C.: Brookings Institution, 1983.

Tornetta, Vincenzo. "The Nuclear Strategy of the Atlantic Alliance and the 'No-first-use' Debate," *NATO
Review* 30, no. 5 (1982), pp. 1–7.

Treverton, Gregory F. *Nuclear Weapons in Europe.*
Adelphi Paper no. 168. London: International Institute
for Strategic Studies, 1981.

Union of Concerned Scientists. *No-First-Use: A Report
by the Union of Concerned Scientists.* Cambridge,
Massachusetts: Union of Concerned Scientists, 1983.

U.S. Congress: Senate. *NATO Troop Withdrawals.*
Hearings before the Committee on Foreign Relations.
97th Cong., 2nd Sess., 1982.

17 Should the United States Aim for Nuclear Superiority?

YES

Robert Jastrow

Why Strategic Superiority Matters

NO

Robert Jervis

Why Nuclear Superiority Doesn't Matter

Why Strategic Superiority Matters
Robert Jastrow

When I was a young physicist I spent a year work-ing on nuclear-physics problems with Robert Op-penheimer at Princeton. I then went out to the Law-rence Radiation Laboratory in Berkeley, where I shared an apartment for a time with Harold Brown, who later became Secretary of Defense in the Carter administration. My friendship with Dr. Brown brought me into contact with Herbert York and the weapons physicists in Berkeley, and that led to a job on the Greenhouse project.

The Greenhouse experiment, which took place in 1951 on Eniwetok atoll in the Pacific, was sup-posed to create the first man-made thermonuclear reaction, using the energy of a 500-kiloton atomic bomb to ignite a fraction of an ounce of deuterium and tritium placed in a small adjoining chamber. The project was more of a public-relations stunt than a genuine experiment, because everyone knew beforehand that it was pretty certain to work; using a huge atomic bomb to ignite the little vial of deu-terium and tritium was like using a blast furnace to light a match. According to my understanding at the time, Edward Teller was trying to get support for the H-bomb project, and since he could not figure out how to build an H-bomb, he thought up the Greenhouse project instead, as a demonstration piece for the people back in Washington.

In any case, my job on Greenhouse was to cal-culate the temperature of the reacting mixture of deuterium and tritium. As I recall, it was supposed to hit a million degrees or so, which is beyond the range of an ordinary thermometer. As the house theorist, I applied the methods of the branch of physics known as radiative transfer theory to com-pute the temperature inside the vessel of deuterium and tritium, using measurements on the amount of radiation coming from the outside. It was the kind of calculation astronomers do routinely for the hot gases in stars, and later on I was to do it quite

often in NASA, as a part of my work in astro-physics and planetary science.

The Greenhouse assignment led to a trip to the Pacific and a close look at a 500-kiloton atomic explosion. I also had a chance to work with some very bright people, such as Drs. Teller, York, and Brown, and later on, at Los Alamos, with Stanley Ulam, George Gamow, and others. And, of course, there was a great deal of government and Atomic Energy Commission politics swirling around the figures of Oppenheimer, Teller, and Lawrence, of which I had an intimate and revealing worm's-eye view. But that is another story.

I left nuclear research in 1958 when I joined NASA. I did not think much about it, or about nuclear bombs, for the next twenty years until, three years ago, I happened to come across a *New Yorker* article on nuclear weapons and SALT by Daniel Patrick Moynihan (November 19, 1979). In reading Senator Moynihan's article, I became aware for the first time that the policies of the United States for protecting its citizens from destruction are based on a flawed premise.

The premise is that the Soviet Union will be deterred from a surprise nuclear attack on the United States by the knowledge that such an attack would trigger a devastating American counterattack. And, of course, *we* are deterred from an attack on the USSR by the knowledge that the Soviets maintain a similar arsenal. The result is a nuclear standoff, and world peace.

In other words, each side holds the other side's civilian population as hostages. Holding hostages, and threatening their massacre, are time-honored methods for achieving one's objectives in war, but they have never been suggested before as a means of keeping the peace. The proposal for mass ex-change of hostages is a simple but brilliant strategy conceived by American intellectuals who were trying to figure out a solution to a terrible problem: how does the U.S. protect itself from nuclear destruction in an age in which missiles vault the oceans and the concept of Fortress America no longer has meaning?

The academicians who thought up this idea called it Mutual Assured Destruction, or sometimes simply MAD. It makes very good sense, as you would expect, since the policy was formulated by some of the most brilliant scientists and academicians who have ever served in an advisory capacity to our government. The trouble is that MAD is a theory, and like all theories, it depends on an assumption. This assumption has turned out to be false.

The assumption behind the theory of Mutual Assured Destruction is that both the United States and the USSR will freely offer up their populations for massacre. But this requires that each country give up all attempts to defend its own people. In other words, the two countries must agree that neither will have a civil-defense program, and neither side will try to shoot down the other side's missiles.

On the face of it, this proposal sounds peculiar. What does it mean, as Senator Moynihan wrote, to say "we must not defend ourselves because if we do the enemy will attack"? As a physicist once remarked of Einstein's theory of relativity, when you first hear this line of reasoning you think you must have misunderstood it, and when you understand it you think you must have misheard it.

Actually, MAD is a logical response to the problem of nuclear war, and it could have worked, *if* the Russians had been reasonable and seen matters our way—if they had been willing to offer up their people as hostages, just as we have done. But the Soviet Union saw things differently.

It is now clear—in fact it has been clear for a decade—that while for many years the American government adopted the strategy of Mutual Assured Destruction proposed by our scientists and academicians, the Soviet government rejected it. The USSR undertook to do exactly what our strategists say it is supposed not to do: it implemented large programs for defending its citizens from nu-

clear attack, for shooting down American missiles, and for fighting and winning a nuclear war. The result, as Senator Moynihan has said, is "a policy in ruins," and the greatest peril our nation has faced in its 200-year history.

Why did the Russians reject the American plan for avoiding nuclear war? Perhaps the reason is that the strategy of Mutual Assured Destruction is very logical, and therefore appealing to a scientist; it is what a physicist might call a "sweet" solution to a difficult problem. Now scientists have an important voice in formulating American defense policy; after all, a physicist became Secretary of Defense in the Carter administration. But in the Soviet Union scientists carry little or no weight in defense matters. Andrei Sakharov—the great colossus of Soviet atomic weaponry, with the stature of Oppenheimer and Teller rolled up in one—tells the story of a banquet attended by Soviet generals and scientists following the first test of a Russian H-bomb in 1955. Sakharov, who had designed the bomb and was responsible for its success, toasted the achievement with a wish that the Russian bomb would never be exploded over cities. The general in charge of the tests replied to the effect that the job of a scientist was to make the bombs, and how they were used was none of his business.

In any case, the Russians have made it clear that they think the theories of the American scientist-advisers are crazy, and they want no part of them. Their rejection goes beyond the concept of Mutual Assured Destruction itself; they reject the view, so widely held in America, that the mass detonation of nuclear weapons would mean the end of civilization, and, therefore, that these weapons are not useful tools of military policy.

At one time, Soviet thinking on nuclear war did echo American ideas on the impossibility of a nuclear victory. That was in the 1950's, soon after Stalin's death, when Malenkov, who was the Soviet premier, announced that nuclear war could lead to the "destruction of world civilization." But Malenkov was severely criticized by Khrushchev, who said he had it wrong; only capitalism would perish in a nuclear war. By the mid-1960's the debate was over, and the elements of Soviet nuclear policy were set in concrete. In 1979, Secretary of Defense Brown confirmed that since 1963, "The Soviets have had a policy of building forces for a preemptive attack on United States ICBM's."

And in fact Soviet military writings make it plain that the entire warfighting posture of the Soviet General Staff rests on the mass use of nuclear missiles:

The most important task of the General Staff in preparing for a modern war is the detailed planning of employment of nuclear weapons by all services of the armed forces.*

The armed forces of the Soviet Union . . . must be prepared above all to wage war under conditions of the mass use of nuclear weapons.†

The basic method of waging war will be massed nuclear rocket attack. . . . **

Nuclear missile strikes . . . and the ability to use them before the opponent does, are the key to victory.††

It is recommended that the nuclear strike be launched . . . unexpectedly for the enemy. Preemption in launching a nuclear strike is expected to be the decisive condition for the attainment of superiority.***

---

*Voyennaya mysl' ("Military Thought"), October 1964, p. 23; quoted in Soviet Strategy for Nuclear War, edited by J.D. Douglass, Jr. and A.M. Hoeber (Hoover Institution Press, 1979). According to Douglass and Hoeber, Voyennaya mysl' is a confidential journal designed for internal use by the Soviet General Staff and officers of the Soviet armed forces.
†V.D. Sokolovskiy, Voyennaya strategiys ("Military Strategy"), p. 193, edited by H.F. Scott (Crane, Russak, 1975).
**Ibid., p. 210.
††Byely et al., Marxism-Leninism on War and Army (A Soviet View), trans. U.S. Air Force, Soviet Military Thought Series No. 2 (Government Printing Office), p. 217; quoted in Douglass and Hoeber, p. 38.
***A.A. Sidorenko. The Offensive (A Soviet View) (Moscow: Voyenizdat, 1970), trans. U.S. Air Force, Soviet Military Thought Series (Government Printing Office, 1974), p. 115; quoted in The Future of Soviet Military Power, edited by L.L. Whetten (Crane, Russak, 1976).

Some American scientists and arms-control experts find it hard to believe that the Russians can actually hold these views on the massive use of nuclear weapons. They feel that if the Russian generals think they can fight and win a nuclear war, the reason must be that the generals have not thought the question through carefully. "I don't think we should substitute their judgment for our common sense," said Paul Warnke about the matter. Warnke, who was President Carter's chief arms-control negotiator, thought Russian thinking about emerging victorious from a nuclear war was "primitive," and the United States "ought to educate them into the real world of strategic nuclear weapons."

But the Russians have refused to be educated. Around 1963, in pursuit of their objective of winning a nuclear war if it should break out, they began a massive program for building nuclear bombs, missiles, and submarines. In the next few years, American satellites photographed new missile silos sprouting all over the Soviet Union. In 1967, the Russians built 160 new silos; in 1968, they added 340 more; in 1969, they drew abreast of the United States. By then each side had about 1,000 silos and a like number of missiles.

None of this bothered American strategists because their policy of Mutual Assured Destruction required that each country must have enough nuclear destructive power to kill a lot of the other fellows. Secretary of Defense Robert McNamara had figured out that we had enough bombs to kill at least 50 million Russians directly in a mass nuclear attack, in addition to millions who would die later from radiation poisoning. He stated that he thought this was sufficient to deter the Russians from starting anything. Therefore, in 1967, he froze the United States force of ICBM's at 1,000 Minutemen plus 54 of the older Titans. He also froze the number of missiles carried by our nuclear submarines at 656. Secretary McNamara had said a few years earlier: "There is no indication that the Soviets are seeking to develop a strategic nuclear force as large as our own." The Secretary was relaxed about the Soviet build-up; his feeling was that if the Soviets improved their capabilities for blowing us up, they could be more equal partners in the strategy of Mutual Assured Destruction, and the peace of the world would be more secure.

So, while the Russians were working away at increasing the size of their nuclear arsenal, the United States made no attempt to stay ahead of them, and the number of American missiles and nuclear submarines remained fixed at their 1967 levels. Meanwhile the Soviet military budget continued to climb. It went up steadily, 4 percent a year, year after year. At the same time, the American defense budget, exclusive of Vietnam, began to decline. In 1970, the two budgets crossed—one going up, and the other going down. Still the Soviet budget continued to increase, especially in the area of strategic forces—nuclear bombs, missiles, and submarines—where the Soviets spent about $40 billion a year, while American expenditures in this critical area of defense averaged about $12 billion a year.

By 1969 or 1970, the effects of the massive Soviet build-up were becoming apparent. In round numbers, the Soviet Union now had 1,400 ICBM's plus another 300 nuclear missiles in submarines. Meanwhile, the U.S. strategic forces remained frozen at their 1967 levels of 1,054 ICBM's and 656 nuclear-submarine missiles. Soviet superiority in ICBM's was roughly balanced by our edge in submarine-launched missiles. (We still had a fleet of aging B-52 bombers, but their usefulness against the massive Soviet air defenses was open to question.) Overall the Russians were about equal to us in nuclear destructive power.

Now both sides met the requirements for Mutual Assured Destruction. Each possessed enough weapons to inflict serious damage on the other fellow, and to American strategists, any further build-up by either nation would have been pointless. All that remained was to sit down with the Russians and formalize the arrangement with an arms-control treaty. SALT—the Strategic Arms Limitation Talks—was the result.

SALT, ratified in 1972, did not actually limit the number of nuclear bombs in the American and Russian arsenals. What it limited was objects that carry bombs, such as missile silos and nuclear submarines. A missile silo, as Senator Moynihan has pointed out, is a hole in the ground, and it can hurt you if you fall into it, but otherwise it is harmless. A true arms-control treaty should have limited the number and size of the nuclear weapons in the arsenals of the two countries. But the United States was never able to get the Soviet Union to agree to anything like that; the Russians would only accept a limit on items such as the number of holes in the ground.

Even so, the Russians found it difficult to live by the terms of the treaty after they signed it. Some years ago, for example, our satellites caught them in the act of digging 150 extra missile silos that were not permitted by the SALT treaty. When the United States brought this matter to the attention of the Russians, they explained that the new holes were launch-control silos, intended to house the crews and equipment which launched the missiles. But the extra silos had special doors of the kind that pop open to permit a missile's quick escape. A silo with a pop-up door is essential for launching missiles, but highly undesirable for housing the launch-control crew, which usually is housed in an underground bunker to protect it from radiation and other effects of nuclear attack. Whatever use the additional silos might be put to initially, it was obvious that they were meant to be convertible to missile silos at a moment's notice.

Specialists monitoring Soviet compliance with the SALT treaty have reported many other violations. Some are ominous because they indicate a serious intent to deceive the United States. For example, former Secretary of Defense Melvin Laird reported in 1977 that the Soviets had gone to great lengths to conceal from our satellite cameras their operations with the SS-16, a new Soviet ICBM.

Unlike our strategic missiles, the SS-16 is mobile. American satellites discovered signs that SS-16's were being moved about under cover of darkness, concealed in wooded areas, and tested on ranges partly covered with camouflage netting. As a result, Secretary Laird said, we could not be sure whether the Russians were producing SS-16's merely in numbers sufficient to replace older missiles, as the 1972 SALT treaty allows, or enlarging their missile force illicitly beyond the number permitted by SALT. All we knew was that by "elaborate concealment" the Soviet Union had deliberately interfered with the means of verifying compliance with the SALT treaty, which was itself a flagrant violation of the treaty.

Secretary Laird also reported that when the Soviets were testing their SS-20 missile—the medium-range missile that has been deployed in large numbers in Russia and aimed against targets in Western Europe—they scrambled or coded the radio signals which are normally transmitted from the missile to the ground during a test flight so that missile experts can monitor the missile's performance. Because the signals were coded, United States experts could not decipher them to determine the characteristics of the SS-20's.

When the experts finally were able to break the code, they concluded that the SS-20 missiles had been tested with a ton of ballast aboard. This ballast, replaced by fuel, would increase the range of the SS-20 and enable it to attack targets in the United States. In effect the Soviet Union has constructed a dual-use missile that can be aimed either at Western Europe or the U.S., yet its numbers are not counted in the limit on Soviet ICBM's set by the SALT treaty.

The scrambling of the SS-20 radio signals was a particularly cynical violation of SALT on the part of the Soviet Union, because it struck at the very heart of the treaty—the promise by each side that it would not interfere with the other side's "national means of verification."

How did our government handle Soviet violations of the SALT treaty? Senator Edward Zorinsky brought that point up during Senate hearings on SALT II in 1979 when he asked Paul Nitze: "Do you know of any SALT violations that were not resolved . . . ?" Nitze replied: "No; but how were they resolved? They were resolved by [our side's] accepting what had been done in violation."

SALT treaty or no, the Soviet Union continued to outspend the United States by a wide margin on bombs and missiles throughout the 1970's. The United States budget for strategic forces—bombs, missiles, bombers, and submarines—went down under the Nixon, Ford, and Carter administrations, and reached a low point of about $9 billion in 1979, at which time it was three-tenths of 1 percent of our Gross National Product. Meanwhile, Russian spending on missiles and bombs continued at a level of about $40 billion a year. By that time, the Soviet Union had spent about $1 trillion on nuclear weapons.

These numbers belie the "action-reaction" theory of the arms race, which holds that the Soviet military build-up is always a response to increases in American defense spending. As Defense Secretary Brown said: "As our defense budgets have risen, the Soviets' have risen. As our defense budgets have gone down, the Soviets' have risen."

Now the time is 1983. The Russians have been outspending us on nuclear weapons since the 1960's. In President Reagan's administration the budget for strategic forces has risen, but not enough to make up for two decades of massive Soviet weapons construction. The Soviet Union is building 150 to 200 ICBM's a year, and we are building none. They are constructing several nuclear-missile submarines a year, and we have retired old submarines faster than we have added new ones, so that the number of submarine-launched missiles in the U.S. arsenal has actually declined.

The result is that the destructive power of the Soviet nuclear arsenal is now more than twice as great as that of the United States. The missile forces of the Soviet Union also have a combination of accuracy, destructive power, and numbers that will enable them to destroy most of our Minuteman missiles in their silos in a preemptive first strike. We lack any such capability. In other words, the Soviet Union has strategic superiority.

But does it matter? As Secretary of State Henry Kissinger once asked: "What in the name of God is strategic superiority? . . . What do you do with it?" The American strategic-nuclear arsenal, divided into the population of the world, is equivalent to a half ton of TNT per person. The Soviet strategic-nuclear arsenal is equivalent to two tons of TNT per person. Nothing seems to demonstrate the folly of building additional bombs and missiles more clearly than these numbers. By any reasonable criterion, both the United States and the Soviet Union have acquired "overkill."

But the reasoning that leads to the idea of overkill, like the reasoning that leads to Mutual Assured Destruction, is based on an assumption. This assumption, again, has turned out to be false. The assumption is that the bombs of the Russians and of the Americans will be exploded over cities. This is what is meant by holding the civilian population hostage. The Russians, however, have made it plain that they find no merit in this idea. In their planning, the top-priority targets are not our cities but our missile silos, bombers, and submarines—and the communication links which would carry the orders for attack to their commanders. In other words, the Soviets aim to prevent us—in the event war should break out—from inflicting damage on their country.

How would the Soviet Union accomplish that objective? Civilian defense, air defense, and missile defense are part of the answer, and the Soviets have large programs in each of those areas. Civil defense is a fifth arm of the Soviet military, with status equal to that of the Soviet Strategic Rocket Forces, Air Force, Army, and Navy.

Another part of the answer is the 5,000 warheads on Soviet ICBM's. It is true that a small fraction of that huge arsenal could destroy every major city in the United States, but the warheads are not intended for that purpose; they are targeted against our 1,054 missile silos, probably two to a silo. This redundancy will insure nearly complete destruction of the American missile force, even when allowance is made for the fact that some Soviet missiles will not get off the ground, others will wander off course, and some will fail to explode.

Thus, the targeted American missile force accounts for approximately 2,000 of the 5,000 Soviet ICBM warheads. Another 500 warheads could be targeted on military airfields and whatever nuclear-

missile submarines are in port or can be located. An additional 500 warheads could be allotted to the destruction of our military command-and-control centers and our military-communication links, with the aim of compromising the system by which instructions flow from the President and senior officials to military commanders in the field for the launch of a retaliatory strike on the Soviet Union.

This would leave a force of 2,000 ICBM warheads still available to the Soviet Union for use in deterring the United States from launching a retaliatory second strike with the ICBM's, bombers, or submarine missiles that had survived the first strike. If our government failed to see the wisdom of submission at this stage, and launched a retaliatory strike against Soviet cities, Russian reprisal would be swift and devastating, and the life of our nation would be ended.

What about our nuclear submarines? A great many Americans feel that submarines will be the ultimate deterrent to Soviet attack, regardless of the number of ICBM's in the Soviet arsenal. American Trident submarines are nearly invulnerable to detection when at sea, and, as President Carter once pointed out, the nuclear warheads carried on a single one of these would be sufficient to destroy all the largest cities in the Soviet Union.

The difficulty with this line of thinking is that missiles launched from submarines can only be used to attack cities and similar "soft" targets. The reason is that a submarine never knows precisely where it is in the ocean. Although the path of the submarine-launched missile may be very accurately guided during its flight, if the starting point of the missile's trajectory is uncertain, the place where it lands must be equally uncertain. As a consequence, the accuracy of submarine-launched missiles is relatively poor.

American submarines and their missiles therefore cannot be used to eliminate the missile force of the Soviet Union, or its command-and-control centers, because those targets, hardened with reinforced concrete and underground construction, can be destroyed only by the pinpoint accuracy of a direct hit. (An attack on cities does not require great accuracy, since the power of the nuclear weapon will destroy a city if the bomb explodes anywhere in the vicinity.)

These considerations indicate why American submarines cannot substitute for our force of Minutemen, as a deterrent to Soviet attack. From the limited accuracy of submarine-launched missiles it follows that these missiles can only be used against cities. Therefore they cannot be used at all, because our government will know that if used in this way, they will trigger a punishing Soviet counterattack on our own cities. What President would decide to launch our submarine missiles in an attack on Leningrad and Moscow, knowing that New York and Washington would be destroyed in return? Faced with this option, any government would prefer to live and fight another day.

In the course of time, technology will improve the accuracy of our submarine-launched nuclear missiles to the point where they will have a hard-target "kill" capability, and the American deterrent will be restored. According to present estimates, that should happen by the end of the 1980's. The intervening four to five years will be, as Dr. Kissinger has said, "a period of vulnerability such as we have not experienced since the early days of the Republic."

If the nuclear-freeze movement is successful, the period of vulnerability will be extended into the 1990's. Assuming that does not happen, how will the Russians make use of the four to five years of nuclear superiority they will still enjoy?

The Persian Gulf is the most likely target of a Soviet move. Imagine a Soviet-instigated outbreak of violence in Saudi Arabia, with American businessmen taken hostage, and a pro-Soviet regime installed, backed by Russian guns and Cuban mercenaries. With a substantial part of the oil flow to Western Europe under Soviet control, and the Middle East in upheaval, the United States will be tempted to intervene with conventional forces. If the Soviets respond by sending in their own troops, and conventional war breaks out, we cannot prevail. The USSR has constructed five airfields in

southern Afghanistan, bringing the Persian Gulf within range of its fighter aircraft. The Soviet navy heavily outnumbers the American navy in surface ships and attack submarines. As a consequence, we will probably not be able to maintain our supply lines to the Gulf and the Mediterranean and simultaneously protect our sea lanes in Atlantic and Asian waters. Defeat will be almost certain.

Could we threaten to escalate to the nuclear level? Only this threat could hope to save us from defeat in the Persian Gulf. But now the Soviet superiority in nuclear weapons becomes the decisive factor. The United States has gone on a nuclear alert three times in the past—in 1948 in the Berlin crisis, in 1962 in the Cuban missile crisis, and in 1973 when the Russians threatened to intervene in the war between Egypt and Israel. We prevailed in each confrontation. In the first two cases we had strategic superiority, and in the third a rough parity. Today, this is no longer true. We would not dare to threaten the use of our nuclear weapons, because of the circumstances I have described.

What about a Soviet move into Western Europe? In Europe, the superiority of conventional Soviet forces would be overwhelming: approximately 45,000 tanks on the Soviet side against 17,000 in NATO; a Soviet superiority of 2 to 1 in aircraft, 2 to 1 in artillery, and 3 to 1 in missile launchers. NATO forces would not be able to withstand a massive Soviet thrust into Western Europe.

But a direct attack would not be necessary. Threats, accompanied by a general escalation of tension, would probably suffice to bring all of Western Europe under Soviet hegemony. Aleksandr Solzhenitsyn has described how it would happen:

At one time there was no comparison between the strength of the USSR and yours. Then it became equal. . . . Perhaps today it is just greater than balance, but soon it will be two to one. Then three to one. Finally it will be five to one. . . . With such a nuclear superiority it will be possible to block the use of your weapons, and on some unlucky morning they will declare: "Attention. We're marching our troops to Europe, and if you make a move, we will annihilate you." And this ratio of three to one, of five to one, will have its effect: you will not make a move.

Twenty years ago, or even ten years ago, the American nuclear arsenal would have been sufficient to deter a Soviet attack on Western Europe, but that is no longer the case.

When will the Russians make their move? Leonid Brezhnev supplied the timetable a few years ago, in a speech to Communist leaders in Prague:

We are achieving with détente what our predecessors have been unable to achieve using the fist. . . . By 1985, . . . we will have achieved most of our objectives in Western Europe. . . . Come 1985, we will be able to extend our will wherever we need to. . . .

And so we finally see why strategic superiority matters. We see how it is that, as Senator Moynihan has said, he who can blow the world up three times has more power than he who can blow it up only twice.

Why Nuclear Superiority Doesn't Matter
Robert Jervis

Recent debates on the role of nuclear weapons in American defense policy have not clarified the important issues or dealt with the underlying assumptions that are involved. While some of the specifics of the arguments are new, the basic questions are as old as the nuclear era and can be referred to as the dispute between those who advocate a policy of Assured Destruction (AD) and those who call for Flexible Response (FR). Proponents of AD believe that any nuclear war will be all-out war and therefore that the United States need only have an assured capacity to destroy an enemy's cities even if forced to absorb a first strike. Proponents of FR hold that there is a range of military contingencies for which the United States must be prepared and that nuclear weapons can be used in a variety of such contingencies in a more flexible, limited way. The main arguments against AD, now as in the past, are that it is not credible and would lead to disaster if deterrence failed; the central argument against FR is that it is costly, ineffective, and dangerous. This article generally defends the AD position and argues that FR misunderstands the nature of nuclear deterrence.

ASSURED DESTRUCTION AND FLEXIBLE RESPONSE

Proponents of AD argue that the vulnerability of population centers in both the United States and the Soviet Union that comes with mutual second-strike capability has transformed strategy. Because a military advantage no longer assures a decisive victory, old ways of thinking are no longer appropriate. The healthy fear of devastation, which cannot be exorcised short of the attainment of a first-strike capability, makes deterrence relatively easy. Furthermore, because cities cannot be taken out of hostage, the perceived danger of total destruction is crucial at all points in the threat, display, or use of force.

Four implications follow. First, because gaining the upper hand in purely military terms cannot protect one's country, various moves in a limited war—such as using large armies, employing tactical nuclear weapons, or even engaging in limited strategic strikes—are less important for influencing the course of the battle than for showing the other side that a continuation of the conflict raises an unac-

Robert Jervis, "Why Nuclear Superiority Doesn't Matter," *Political Science Quarterly*, Vol. 94, No. 4 (Winter 1979–80), pp. 617–33.

ceptable danger that things will get out of hand. New weapons are introduced not to gain a few miles of territory, but to engage in what Schelling has called competition in risk taking.[1] Escalation dominance—the ability to prevail at every level of military conflict below that of all-out war—is thus neither necessary nor sufficient to reach one's goals, be they to preserve the status quo or to change it. Being able to win on the battlefield does not guarantee winning one's objectives, since the risk of escalation may be too great to justify the expected benefits.

Second, it does not matter which side has more nuclear weapons. In the past, having a larger army than one's neighbor allowed one to conquer it and protect one's own population. Having a larger nuclear stockpile yields no such gains. Deterrence comes from having enough weapons to destroy the other's cities; this capability is an absolute, not a relative one.[2]

Third, if national security is provided by one's capability to destroy the opponent, not by the possession of a more effective military machine than the other side, then the force that drives the security dilemma is sapped. The security dilemma is created by the fact that in the prenuclear era weapons and policies that made one country secure made others insecure. An army large enough to protect the state was usually large enough to threaten a neighbor with invasion, even if the state did not intend such a threat. But when security comes from the absolute capability to annihilate one's enemy, then each side can gain it simultaneously. Neither side need acquire more than a second-strike capability and, if either does, the other need not respond since its security is not threatened.[3]

A fourth aspect of the AD position is that nuclear war is very unlikely because to initiate it a statesman would have to be willing to run the risk that his country's population centers would be destroyed. Not only is "the balance of terror . . . decidedly not delicate,"[4] but, because statesmen know that imprudent action could lead to all-out war, the resulting deterrence covers a lot more than attacks on one's homeland. To take any major offensive action is to run an intolerably high risk of escalation. The United States and the Soviet Union may engage in fierce rhetorical battles and even use force in such peripheral areas as Africa and Asia, but there are sharp limits to how far they can push each other. The chance that such attempts would lead to total destruction is simply too great. (And it can be too great even though it is very low. That is, even a very small probability of escalation is sufficient to deter serious encroachments.)

The Flexible Response position is different on all counts. Its logic is best seen in terms of what Glenn Snyder has called the stability-instability paradox.[5] Because the balance is so stable at the level of all-out nuclear war, each side is relatively free to engage in provocations and military actions at lower levels of violence. The most obvious application of this argument is that if NATO lacks the ability to defend Europe with conventional weapons, it faces the danger of having to fight such a war: thus the Soviet second-strike capability would "deter our deterrent" (to paraphrase the title from an article by Paul Nitze).[6] The same argument can be applied to more bizarre situations. To secure some highly valued goal the Russians might destroy most of the American Minuteman force. Since its cities were still in hostage, the United States

[1]The phrase is attributed to Thomas Schelling in Herman Kahn, *On Escalation* (Baltimore, MD.: Penguin, 1968), p. 3. The topic is discussed in Schelling, *Arms and Influence* (New Haven, Conn.: Yale University Press, 1966), pp. 92–125.

[2]Thus there is a second meaning in the title of the book of brilliant essays written in 1946 by Bernard Brodie, Arnold Wolfers et al., *The Absolute Weapon* (New York: Harcourt, Brace, 1946).

[3]Many proponents of AD also argue that the Soviet Union would feel threatened by increases in American strategic forces, however, and this fear is in some tension with the belief described here.

[4]Bernard Brodie, *War and Politics* (New York: Macmillan, 1973), p. 380.

[5]Glenn Snyder, "The Balance of Power and the Balance of Terror," in *The Balance of Power*, ed. Paul Seabury (San Francisco, Calif.: Chandler, 1965). This paradox was seen by Snyder as explaining why mutual second-strike capability could lead to conventional wars; the proponents of FR take this one step further by arguing that the overall strategic stability also allows for limited nuclear wars.

[6]Paul Nitze, "Deterring Our Deterrent," *Foreign Policy* 25 (Winter 1976–77): 195–210.

would be deterred from striking back at Soviet cities.

For the advocates of FR, the United States must be prepared to fight a war—or rather a variety of wars—in order to gain a better chance of deterring the Soviets from making any military moves, to deter them from escalating if they do move, and to secure as favorable an outcome as possible at any level of violence. In contrast to the AD view, FR argues that in the nuclear era, as in earlier times, the absolute amount of armaments on each side is less important than the relative amounts because each nation's military forces as well as its population centers are potential targets. As decision makers stop thinking that any war must be total and realize that the stability-instability paradox allows a wider range of contingencies of controlled and less self-defeating strikes, the importance of the details of the strategic balance becomes clear.[7]

Proponents of FR thus disagree with the AD position that the inherent riskiness of any major provocation in the nuclear era means that a second-strike capability protects against much more than an unrestrained assault on the country's homeland. Secretary of Defense Brown argues that "we now recognize that the strategic nuclear forces can deter only a relatively narrow range of contingencies, much smaller in range than was foreseen only 20 or 30 years ago."[8] Similarly, Brown, like Schlesinger before him, claims that "only if we have the capability to respond realistically and effectively to an attack at a variety of levels can we . . . have the confidence necessary to a credible deterrent."[9] But, the proponents of AD would reply, this argument advocating something approximating escalation dominance misses the point. No state can respond "effectively" in the sense of being able to

take its population centers out of hostage; thus, it is the willingness to run risks and the perceptions of this willingness that will determine whether a response is "realistic" and a threat is credible.

Stability, Predictability, and Soviet Intentions

Much of the difference between the two schools of thought turns on differing ideas about stability. Both groups agree on the overwhelming importance of preserving one's cities. But for the proponents of FR, the common interest in avoiding a mutually disastrous outcome can be used as a lever to extract competitive concessions. Either side can take provocative actions because the other cannot credibly threaten to respond by all-out war. Proponents of AD, on the other hand, see stability as broader, and deterrence as covering a wider set of interests, since it follows from the reasonable fear that any challenge to an opponent's vital interest could escalate. Paradoxically, stability is in part the product of the belief that the world is not entirely stable, that things could somehow get out of control.

There are two elements that influence beliefs about the extent to which the risks of escalation could be kept limited and controlled, and it is not surprising that advocates of AD and FR disagree about both. The first element is the American reaction and the Soviet anticipation of it. Advocates of FR fear that the Russians might be certain enough that the United States would not use nuclear weapons in response to a major provocation to make such a provocation worth taking. Those who support a policy of AD deny this, noting that the United States has behaved too unpredictably for any state to be sure what it will do. Part of the reason for the disagreement on this point is that proponents of both AD and FR project their views onto the governments of the United States and the Soviet Union. The latter believe, and the former deny, that a large Russian arms build-up would intimidate the United States.

The other element in the belief about whether the risks would seem controllable is a judgment about the inherent limits of manipulation and prediction in human affairs. While these factors are

[7]U.S., Congress, Senate, Committee on Armed Services, *Hearings on Fiscal Year 1975 Authorization*, 93rd Cong., 2d sess., 1974, p. 51.

[8]Department of Defense, *Annual Report, F.Y. 1980* (Washington, D.C.: Government Printing Office, 1979), p. 76. Brown's posture statement is a combination of FR and AD and so is more honest, but less coherent, than many of the previous statements.

[9]Department of Defense, *Annual Report, F.Y. 1979* (Washington, D.C.: Government Printing Office, 1978), p. 54.

rarely discussed explicitly, the tone of much of the FR writings implies that men can make fine, complex, and accurate calculations. Friction, uncertainty, failures of implementation, and the fog of battle do not play a major role. Men see clearly, their subordinates are able to carry out intricate instructions, and the other side gets the desired message. Thus, Secretary Brown recently argued that "if we try bluffing [the Russians with a threat of massive retaliation], ways can be found by others to test our bluffs without undue risk to them"[10] Such attempts would involve reasonable risks only if the situation were under complete control and seen by the Soviets as relatively safe, and then only if they believed this to be the case. (But many proponents of FR also believe that the United States cannot rely on tactical nuclear weapons to defend Europe because their use could too easily lead to all-out war. This fits oddly with the belief that the superpowers could fight a limited strategic war.)

For the advocates of AD, this is a dream world. War plans can be drawn up on this basis, but reality will not conform. Furthermore, decision makers, having experienced the multiple ways in which predictions prove incorrect and situations get out of control, do not commit the fallacy of believing that escalation could be carefully manipulated and thus would not place any faith in the precise options of limited nuclear warfare. FR advocates see the need for a policy they consider to be prudential in the sense of being able to cope with unlikely but dangerous contingencies because they do not think decision makers can be counted on to avoid terrible risks; proponents of AD do not think American policy has to cover such remote possibilities because they are confident that statesmen are at least minimally prudent.

This difference in beliefs—or perhaps I should say in intuitions—goes far to explain why some of the proponents of FR see a much greater danger of a Russian first strike than do advocates of AD. One would not expect any difference of opinion here since the question seems entirely technical.

[10]Department of Defense, *Annual Report, F. Y. 1980*, p. 75.

But it is not. To launch a first strike in the belief that one could destroy most of an opponent's strategic forces is to accept a set of complex and uncertain calculations: the weapons have never been tested under fully operational conditions; accuracies are estimated from performances over test ranges, which may be different when the missiles are fired over different parts of the earth; the vulnerability of the other side's silos (and one's own) can never be known with certainty before the war; and the effects on the environment of huge nuclear explosions can only be guessed at. The same orientation that leads one to believe that statesmen could be sufficiently confident of their ability to prevent escalation to allow them to engage in major provocations also fits with the conclusion that statesmen might place sufficient confidence in their estimates to launch a disarming strike.

If differences in beliefs about the risks inherent in major provocations are one source of the dispute between AD and FR, another is a difference in perceptions of the risks that the Russians are willing to run. Most proponents of AD argue that while the desire to expand is not completely absent, the Russians are not so strongly motivated in this regard as to be willing to endanger what they have already gained. Proponents of FR argue not that the Russians want war, but that they care enough about increasing their influence to run significant risks to reach that goal. And by acquiring massive military might, the Russians could hope to be better able to expand without courting dangerous confrontations. The proponents of AD would reply that almost no decision maker in the world's history would embark on a course of expansion while his cities were held hostage. The sort of leaders the proponents of FR posit are very rare—even Hitler probably was not an example, since he knew that if he could militarily defeat the Allies he could protect his own country.

Because the advocates of AD believe the Russians to be less strongly motivated than do those who call for FR, they believe that much less deterrence, both in terms of the damage that the United States needs to inflict and the probability that it will be inflicted, will be sufficient. Thus there is a disagreement over "how much credibility is enough": two policy analysts therefore might agree on how likely the Russians thought it was that a limited war would escalate and disagree over whether they would be deterred.[11]

SITUATIONS CALLING FOR FLEXIBLE RESPONSE

The basic concern of the proponents of FR is that the threat to attack Soviet population centers is not credible when the Russians can respond in kind. In a crisis the United States must "have a wider choice than humiliation or all-out nuclear action," to use President Kennedy's terms.[12] The danger that the proponents of FR see was expressed well by Secretary of Defense Schlesinger in 1975: "If one side should remove the other's capability for flexible and controlled responses, he might find ways of exercising coercion and extracting concessions without triggering the final holocaust. . . . No opponent should think that he could fire at some of our Minuteman or SAC [Strategic Air Command] bases without being subjected to, at the very least, a response in kind. No opponent should believe that he could attack other U.S. targets of military or economic value without finding similar or other appropriate targets in his own homeland under attack. . . . Above all, no opponent should entertain the thought that we will permit him to remove our capability for flexible strategic responses."[13]

We can examine the problem more clearly by

seeing that Schlesinger and other proponents of FR blur the distinction between two kinds of wars. The first involves demonstration attacks. Since they do not require large numbers of missiles, neither the size of each side's force nor its vulnerability is important. The second is a counterforce war of attrition in which the Russians would launch the first nuclear strike, trying to destroy as much of the American strategic force as possible, either in one blow or by moving more slowly and taking out the opposing forces in a series of strikes. Although the United States would still be able to attack the Soviet Union's cities, the only result of such a strike would be to have U.S. cities blown up thirty minutes later. If the U.S. strategic force is vulnerable, the Russians can destroy much of it without using a similar proportion of their force; if the U.S. force cannot hit protected targets, it will not be able to reduce the Russian force. But, and this is crucial, it is only in counterforce wars of attrition that the comparison of each side's counterforce capabilities matters.

Examining a number of contexts in which defense problems arise, one can see that the distinction between attacks that have an effect by demonstrating resolve and those that aim at reducing an opponent's capability recurs and is closely tied to the basic difference between the AD and FR positions. If the AD position is correct and counterforce wars of attrition are not a real possibility in the nuclear era, then the United States does not have to worry that its Minuteman force is vulnerable or that the Russians have a greater ability to destroy hard targets than the United States does. To evaluate the arguments, it is useful to examine the potentially critical situations.

Protecting Europe

One major fear is that the Soviets could launch a large-scale conventional attack that would conquer Europe unless the United States escalated. If the United States tried to stave off defeat by employing tactical nuclear weapons, the Soviets could reply in kind, nullifying any advantage the West may have gained. One FR remedy would be to develop

[11]This also partially explains why many of the proponents of FR think that the threat to destroy Russian cities would be an insufficient deterrent and that the United States should develop a targeting policy aimed at convincing the Soviet leaders that their regime would not be able to maintain control of the country after a war.

[12]"Radio and Television Report to the American People on the Berlin Crisis, July 25, 1961," in *Public Papers of the Presidents of the United States: John F. Kennedy, 1961* (Washington, D.C.: Government Printing Office, 1962), p. 535.

[13]Department of Defense, *Annual Report, F.Y. 1976 and F.Y. 1977* (Washington, D.C.: Government Printing Office, 1975), pp. II-4–II-5.

the means to defend against an attack at any level of violence. Thus the West would deploy conventional forces to contain a conventional attack and tactical nuclear weapons to cope with a like attack. This alluring argument is not correct. An aggressor could attack in the face of escalation dominance if he believed that the defender would not pay the price of resisting, a price that includes a probability that the fighting will spread to each side's population centers. The other side of this coin is that a state that could be confident of winning a military victory in Europe could be deterred from attacking or deterred from defending against an attack by the fear that the war might spread to its homeland. Only if the risk of such escalation could be reduced to zero would this element disappear and purely military considerations be determinative. The advocates of FR thus overstate the efficacy of their policy.

Of course if the United States lacks escalation dominance it would have to take the initiative of increasing the level of violence and risk in the event of a Soviet attack on Europe. But the onus of undertaking the original move would still remain with the aggressor. And since the level of risk is shared equally by both sides, what is likely to be more important than the inhibition against having to take the initiative is the willingness or unwillingness to approach the brink rather than concede defeat, a factor not linked to escalation dominance. Furthermore, some practical considerations reinforce this conclusion. As Bernard Brodie argued, it is hard to imagine that the Soviets would launch a conventional attack in the face of NATO's tactical nuclear weapons. Such an attack would require massed troops that would be an inviting target for NATO's tactical nuclear weapons. The Soviets could not be sufficiently confident that their strategic or tactical nuclear forces would deter such a NATO response to leave their armies so vulnerable.[14] And for the Russians to initiate a tactical nuclear war would raise two difficulties. First, the uncertainties about how such a war would be fought are so great that it would be hard for any country to be confident that it would win. Second, a war of this level of violence would be especially likely to trigger the American strategic force.

An alternative FR policy is for the United States to develop large enough strategic forces to threaten, and carry out if need be, a counterforce strike with some of its forces, even though doing so would not leave the Soviet Union totally disarmed. While the Soviet Union could retaliate against American population centers, it would not do so because its own cities were still in hostage. Thus the United States could launch its strike "secure in the knowledge that the United States had a residual ICBM force that could deter attack upon itself."[15] This notion of security is an odd one, resting as it does on the confident prediction that the Russians would calmly absorb a counterforce first strike. This is especially odd because while the proponents of FR tell us that we should pay close attention to Soviet military doctrine, on this point they blithely disregard these texts which stress preemption and deny that limited nuclear wars are possible.

A similar error is embodied in Secretary of Defense Schlesinger's defense of limited nuclear options on the grounds that because the United States has commitments to allies, "we require a nuclear capability that has an implementable threat and which is perceived to have an implementable threat. Unless, in the event of certain hostile acts, we have a threat that we can implement, the existence of the American force structure does not contribute logically to deterrence." If, on the other hand, the United States has the ability to launch limited nuclear strikes, he continues, it "will not be self-deterred from responding to . . . an act of aggression."[16] But the concept of "self-deterrence" is not useful and the argument cannot be sustained. The

[14]Bernard Brodie, *Escalation and the Nuclear Option* (Princeton, N.J.: Princeton University Press, 1966).

[15]Colin Gray, "The Scope and Limits of SALT," *Foreign Affairs 56* (July 1978): 788.

[16]U.S. Congress, House, Committee on Armed services, *Hearings on Military Posture and H.R. 12564. Department of Defense Authorization for Appropriations for Fiscal Year 1975,* 93rd Cong., 2d sess., 1974, part 1, pp. 47, 49.

United States is being deterred by the fear of Soviet retaliation. This danger is present as long as the Soviets have second-strike capability; thus, it is a consequence not of Soviet "superiority" but of parity. Even if the United States reached Schlesinger's goal of preserving "an essential strategic equilibrium with the USSR both in capabilities and in targeting options,"[17] the costs and risks of employing the options would remain.

The argument that the side that had better counterforce capability could safely launch such an attack even though the other side would not be disarmed pertains only in wars of attrition in which each side tries to reduce the other's strategic capability and spares the other's cities. The claim that the United States can employ this option to protect Europe is the opposite side of the coin of the claim that if the Soviet Union had a large margin of counterforce superiority, it could use it to coerce the West. The validity of this claim turns on whether a war of attrition is a serious possibility or whether the danger that such a conflict would escalate to attacks on population centers would dominate decision makers' calculations.

Preemption

Some proponents of FR think it most unlikely that the Russians would launch an attack on Europe, but fear that if the Soviet strategic force was much more effective than the American one and if a significant proportion of the American strategic force were vulnerable, the Russians might make a preemptive strike in a grave crisis, perhaps one they had not sought, if they thought that war was very likely. The ability to hit missile silos and command and control facilities that the proponents of FR call for, however, increases this danger, since it enables the United States to destroy a large proportion of USSR's land-based missiles (and most of the Soviet strategic force is land based) if the United States were to strike first. It is a bit disingenuous to argue that the United States needs a new type of missile to decrease the chance that the

Soviet Union would attack without also acknowledging that some of the incentive the Russians would have to attack those missiles comes from the very accuracy that is supposedly needed in order to fight a counterforce war.[18]

More importantly, preemption makes sense only if being struck first is much worse than getting the first blow in. A state whose leaders believe that war will lead to total devastation will have no incentive to preempt even if many of their missiles are vulnerable. Here, as at other points, the proponents of FR make the crucial mistake of concentrating on purely military factors—the numbers and characteristics of weapons on both sides—and ignoring the role of military moves as generators of risk. The FR argument is that deterrence requires a sufficient number and kind of forces so that if the other side struck first, it would be militarily worse off than if it had not. Thus it would be dangerous if the Russians were able to use, for example, 200 missiles with 2,000 warheads and knock out most of the American ICBMs. As Secretary of Defense Brown has put it: "we must ensure that no adversary could see himself better off after a limited exchange than before it. We cannot permit an enemy to believe that he could create any kind of military or psychological asymmetry that he could then exploit to his advantage."[19] But the fact that the Russians would have gained a more favorable ratio of missiles does not mean that they would be closer to any meaningful goal or even that they would be closer to it than they would have been if the United States struck first and the ratio of missiles available was less favorable to them. The only meaningful goals would be to preserve their cities and, if possible, prevail in the dispute. But gains in purely military terms do not accomplish these objectives in wartime any more than

---

[17]Ibid., p. 29.

[18]The United States might get around this dilemma by building missiles that were invulnerable, but that lacked accurate MIRVs. It is interesting to note that the U.S. Air Force has done a much better job of developing a powerful and accurate missile than it has in making that missile able to survive a Russian attack.

[19]Department of Defense, *Annual Report, F.Y. 1979*, p. 56.

they do in peacetime. As long as each side retains the ability to destroy the other's society, having more warheads than an opponent is an advantage only if it makes the opponent back down, and the proponents of FR have not shown how it will make such a contribution. The military advantages of striking first can only be translated into political gains if the war remains counterforce and the state with the most missiles left after a series of exchanges prevails without losing its population centers.[20] The FR fallacy here is parallel to that involved in the claim that escalation dominance is necessary or sufficient for deterring or prevailing in a conflict in Europe. Competition in risk taking, rather than competition in military capability, dominates.

Counterforce Wars of Attrition and the Balance of Resolve

In a counterforce war of attrition the numbers and characteristics of the weapons would matter a great deal. As in the prenuclear era, what would be crucial would not be absolute capability, but the relative strengths of the opponents. The basic argument of the AD school is undercut because the primary targets of the warheads are not population centers but other weapons. Is the likelihood of counterforce wars of attrition sufficient to warrant the necessary preparations? Could there be a nuclear war in which population centers were spared and the outcome determined by which state is able to do the better job of reducing the other's military forces? Even if the Russians had the ability to win such a war, they would have to be desperate or willing to run terribly high risks to place sufficient faith in American self-restraint to order an attack. Even if the United States could win such a war, its threat to initiate it would not be credible (for example, in response to a Soviet attack on Europe) unless the Russians believed that the United States thought that control would be maintained throughout its course.

This control would have to be maintained, furthermore, although unprecedented numbers of civilians would be killed; a large Russian counterforce strike could not be limited to destroying only military targets. Although it would be obvious to the president that most American population centers were still held hostage, sufficient damage would have been done to raise sharply the danger of an all-out response. The chance of such a reaction—which would be present even if the United States said it would not react in this way—would have to weigh very heavily on the Soviet decision makers.

But the existence of tight control would not ensure the success of a strategy of attrition. If the Russians launched a counterforce strike and the United States did not retaliate against Soviet cities, it might nullify a Russian war-fighting strategy by not responding at all. This may seem as bizarre as a counterattack on population centers, but on closer examination it makes some sense. Why should the United States retaliate? What would the Russians have gained by destroying a significant portion of the U.S. strategic force? Why would they be in a better position to work their will after a strike than before it? If the United States acts as though it is weakened, it will be in a worse bargaining position, but this is within American control. To withhold a response, while maintaining the ability to destroy Russian cities later, could as easily be taken as a sign of high resolve as of low. The United States would forego hitting many Russian military targets, but this would not sacrifice much of value since attacking them would not limit the Soviet ability to destroy the United States. Only if a war in Europe were being fought at the same time, and thus a failure to respond created or magnified an imbalance of land forces, would withholding a return counterforce strike give up something of value. But for the Soviets to attack American strategic forces (and NATO tactical nuclear forces) in conjunction with fighting a war in Europe would be to run a very high risk of an American counterattack on Soviet population centers.

The possibility of not responding to a Soviet counterforce strike points to the odd nature of a nuclear war of attrition. The benefit of the efforts

[20]This point is overlooked by Paul Nitze in "Assuring Strategic Stability in an Era of Detente," *Foreign Affairs* 54 (January 1976): 226–30, and in "Deterring our Deterrent," p. 210.

to reduce an opponent's strategic forces comes only near the end, when the state is able to take its society out of hostage. Unless and until that point is reached, the side that is "losing" the counterforce war of attrition can do nearly as much damage to the side that is "winning" as it could before the war started. Military efforts can succeed only if the "loser" allows them to by sparing the "winner's" cities. Of course it will be costly for the "loser" to initiate counterstrikes against population centers, since the "winner" will presumably retaliate. But this is true regardless of the details of the strategic balance.

If the ultimate threat, even during a war of attrition, is that of destroying cities, it is clear that such wars are more competition in risk taking than they are attempts to gain an advantage on the battlefield. To concentrate on the military advantages that accrue to one side or the other by counterforce attacks is to ignore the fact that in any nuclear war the element of threat of escalation will loom very large.[21] This general point is missed by Secretary of Defense Brown when he says that the ability to hit a wide range of military targets "permits us to respond credibly to threats or actions by a nuclear opponent."[22] But what is crucial is less the capability than the willingness to use it. Even if the United States had the ability to match the Soviets round for round, target for target, it might not do so—and the Russians might move in the belief that the United States would not respond—because the costs and risks were felt to be too great. And even if the United States lacked such a capability, the Soviet fear of an all-out response could lead it to expect that any provocation would be prohibitively costly. Since what matters in limited strategic wars, even if they involve targets that are predominantly military, is each side's willingness to run high risks, it is the "balance of resolve" rather than the "balance of military power" that will most strongly in-

fluence their outcomes.[23] Extra ammunition cannot compensate for weakness in will or a refusal—perhaps a sensible refusal—to run the risk of destruction.

The importance of competition in risk taking implies that demonstration attacks would be more useful than attempts to reduce an opponent's military capabilities. Such attacks could be aimed at a military installation, an isolated element of an opponent's strategic forces, a command and control facility, or a city. The purpose of such an action would be to inflict pain, show resolve, and raise the risks of all-out war to a level that an opponent would find intolerable. Such risks, of course, weigh on both sides, but only by willingly accepting high risks can a state prevail. In addition to high resolve, in order to engage in nuclear demonstrations a state needs to be able to carry out a certain number of limited options. But the ammunition requirements are nowhere near as high as they are for a counterforce war of attrition (and both sides can simultaneously have the capability for demonstrations).

Demonstration strikes would exert pressure in three ways. First, they would exact some degree of punishment on the other side. But the immediate pain inflicted would probably be less important than the underlying motivation of these strikes—the implied threat to do more harm unless the opponent complies with the attacking state's demands. This threat gains credibility because the attacking state has shown that it is willing to engage in very risky actions that have increased the chance that targets in its own country would be struck. When both sides have second-strike capability, one side prevails in a crisis, not by showing that it can inflict pain on the other (for this is obvious and true for the both sides), but by demonstrating that it feels so strongly about the issue at stake that it is willing to be hurt in return rather than suffer a defeat. Third, any nuclear attack increases the chance that uncontrolled escalation will occur. It is this specter

---

[21]Indeed the incentives for the state that is behind in a counterforce war to escalate increase as its military situation worsens. If it fears it may soon lose its second-strike capability, the losing state may feel greater pressure to up the ante while it still can.
[22]Department of Defense, *Annual Report, F.Y. 1980*, p. 78.

[23]For further discussion of this point see Robert Jervis, "Deterrence Theory Revisited," *World Politics* 31 (January 1979): 314–22. The Soviet stress on the importance of the "correlation of forces" is not inconsistent with this notion.

that exerts so much pressure on statesmen not to use nuclear weapons in the first place or to make concession in any conflict in which they are used. Even if one side launched a counterforce strike, the war would almost surely end before either had run out of ammunition. Resolve, not capability, would be the limiting factor. When Secretary Brown claims that "fully effective deterrence requires forces of sufficient size and flexibility to attack selectively a range of military and other targets"[24] and argues that to do this the United States needs an invulnerable ICBM, he is either thinking in terms of a war of attrition or overstating the number of warheads the United States needs.

POSSIBLE OBJECTIONS

Before drawing the conclusions that are implicit in the previous analysis, I should note three obvious objections. First, it can be argued that if I am right, and the strategic balance is quite stable, an increase in American arms will not have dire consequences.[25] Since all the United States can lose by additional deployment is money, argue the critics, it is better to play it safe and buy the extra systems. Moreover, how can anyone be sure that a war of attrition will not occur? But surely there must be some judgments about plausibility, some concern for costs, and some consideration of the chance that the United States might teach others lessons that are both incorrect and dangerous. The new weapons cost a lot of money and avoiding waste is not a goal to be scorned lightly.[26] Furthermore,

although there are no strong and direct links between the adversaries' defense budgets or between the budgets and the degree of superpower conflict, it is hard to keep the military and political tracks entirely separate. A final line of rebuttal is the most important: to develop a posture based on the assumption that limited nuclear wars are possible is to increase the chance that they will occur. If the Russians already believe in the possibility that such wars could be kept limited, U.S. acceptance of this position would increase the likelihood of their occurrence. On the other hand, if the Russians now find these kinds of war incomprehensible, they might learn to accept them if the United States talked about them long and persuasively enough. This could decrease the chance that a nuclear war would immediately involve the mass destruction of population centers, but at a cost of increasing the chance of more limited nuclear wars—which then could escalate. Such a trade-off is highly likely, and even Schlesinger acknowledged that adoption of his doctrine might increase the chance of limited nuclear strikes.[27]

The second objection is that my analysis ignores the fact that the Russians do not accept the notion that mutual assured destruction creates stability. Soviet military doctrine is an arcane field that cannot be treated in detail here, although the bulk of the evidence indicates that the Soviet view of strategy is very different from the American.[28] They appear to take war more seriously. Indeed, much of Soviet military doctrine is pure military doctrine—that is, the ideas are not particularly Russian or particularly Marxist but simply those one would expect from people charged with protecting society and winning wars. Many statements by Soviet generals are similar to statements by American generals when the latter are not influenced by the ideas or constrained by the power of the civilian leadership; many American military officials seek the

[24]Speech before the Council on Foreign Relations and the Foreign Policy Association, New York, 5 April 1979, p. 3. Also see Department of Defense, *Annual Report, F.Y. 1980*, pp. 77–78.

[25]There is a similar contradiction in McGeorge Bundy's claim that although nuclear superiority is meaningless, we need arms control agreements. "To Cap the Volcano" (*Foreign Affairs* 48 [October 1969]: 1–20).

[26]Bernard Brodie argues that the strategic balance is so stable that saving money should be the main goal of arms control ("On the Objectives of Nuclear Arms Control," *International Security* 1 [Summer 1976]: 17–36). His position is further developed in "The Development of Nuclear Strategy," ibid. 2 (Spring 1978): 65–83. I am greatly indebted to these articles.

[27]House Armed Services Committee, *Hearings on Military Posture*, p. 50.

[28]For a dissenting view, see Raymond Garthoff, "Mutual Deterrence and Strategic Arms Limitation in Soviet Policy," *International Security* 3 (Summer 1978): 112–47.

same program that the Russians are following. Thus one cannot draw from the fact that Russians probably buy more than is needed for deterrence the inference that they are willing to run high risks to try to expand. The American generals who call for higher spending are not necessarily more bellicose than those who disagree with them.[29] Both the Russian and the U.S. generals may want to prepare for the worst and get ready to fight if a war is forced on them. The Russians may be buying what they think is insurance, and we do not ordinarily think that someone who buys a lot of insurance for his car is planning to drive recklessly.

While there is considerable evidence that the Russians want military forces that would provide as good an outcome as possible should war be forced on them, there is very little evidence that they think that such forces could be used to coerce the West. It has yet to be shown that they think that a superior ability to destroy military targets provides a shield behind which they can make political advances or that Soviet military doctrine measures American deterrence in terms of the United States' ability to match their posture. The Russians may not accept the idea that mutual vulnerability is a desirable state of affairs, but they seem to understand very well the potency of the American threat to destroy their society. Indeed their outlook is uncongenial to a counterforce war of attrition. While the Russians probably would attack U.S. strategic forces in the event of war, they have not talked about sparing the opponent's cities. Instead, they seem to be planning to hit as many targets as they can if war breaks out.

Even if the Russians were to say that they believed a war of attrition was possible, the United States would not have to adopt such a view. While it takes the agreement of both sides to fight a counterforce war, this is not true for AD. If one side denies that counterforce wars could be kept limited and convinces the other side that it believes this,

the other side cannot safely act on its doctrine. The Russians understood this in the periods when McNamara and Schlesinger were enunciating their doctrines, and American statesmen took their professions of disbelief seriously. Even if the Russians were to reverse their position, they would have to take American denials seriously also.

A third objection is that although the Soviet superior ability to destroy strategic forces and the related existence of Minuteman vulnerability is not a strategic problem, it is a political problem. Accordingly, because other nations are influenced by indicators of nuclear superiority, the United States must engage in this competition. (This argument loses some credibility since most people who make it also claim that superiority is meaningful apart from these perceptions.) There are several lines of rebuttal. First, there is little evidence that European or Third World leaders pay much attention to the details of the strategic balance. Second, the United States provides most of the information and conceptual framework that underpins third-party discussions of the balance. The United States might be able to persuade others that it would behave differently because the Russians could wipe out much of the American capability to destroy Soviet missiles. But it would probably be easier to convince them that this was not true. Few world leaders expect the United States and the Soviet Union to fight a war of attrition. Moreover, if the Russians believe that superiority matters and thus may be somewhat emboldened, the bargaining advantages they will gain will be slight if the United States holds to the position that this is nonsense. If the United States convinces the Soviet Union that it does not see a meaningful difference in strength, the USSR cannot safely stand firm in crisis bargaining because it will not have any reason to think that the United States is more likely to retreat.

CONCLUSIONS

We can draw several conclusions. The question of which side has greater ability to destroy the other's strategic forces matters only in a war of attrition.

---

[29]A study of postwar situations reveals that the U.S. military often advised against foreign military adventures. See Richard Betts, *Soldiers, Statesmen, and Cold War Crises* (Cambridge: Harvard University Press, 1977).

Such a war seems unlikely enough so that it is not worth spending large sums and running considerable dangers to prepare for it. Because either side can use its nuclear weapons to destroy its opponent's population centers, the danger of escalation would play a very large role in any war and could not be controlled by having more missiles, more accurate missiles, and more invulnerable missiles than the other side. The nuclear revolution cannot be undone. As we have seen, many of the arguments about the supposed dangers following from Soviet superiority in fact are consequences of parity. The American deterrent is deterred by the fact that its cities are vulnerable, not by the fact that the Russians have some supposed military advantage. Since neither the United States nor the Soviet Union can take its cities out of hostage, the state that is willing to run the greatest risks will prevail. Many of those who call for the United States to match or surpass the Soviet's nuclear arsenal are trying to have the United States compensate for what they feel is a weakness of resolve by an excess in weaponry. But such a deficiency, if it exists, cannot be compensated. A wider range of options will merely give the Russians more ways, and safer ways of coercing the West.

If the balance of resolve is so important, is the United States at a disadvantage compared to the Soviet Union? Some would argue that the United States has shown in Vietnam that it will not fight to defend its interests and those of its allies. But few dominoes fell after April 1975; other states may have been less impressed by the final American withdrawal than they were by its willingness to spend so much blood and treasure on an unimportant country. Furthermore, resolve is not so much an overall characteristic of an actor as it is a factor that varies with the situation because it reflects the strength of the state's motivation to prevail on a given issue. The state defending the status quo has the advantage in most conflicts in which the balance of resolve is crucial because it usually values the issue or territory at stake more than its opponent does.[30] It is easier for a state to

convince the other side that it will fight to hold what it has than it is to make a credible threat to fight rather than forego expansion. A world in which resolve matters so much may not be so bad for the United States.

Even if both sides recognize the greater determination of the side defending the status quo, accidents and miscalculations are still possible, especially in situations growing out of a crisis in a third area. To rely solely on AD may be too dangerous. Some degree of insurance can be purchased by a continuation of the present American posture, which includes the availability of limited nuclear options. But these should be demonstrations, keyed to competition in risk taking, not attempts to wage a war of attrition; thus, the United States would not have to match the Soviets on any of the standard measures of nuclear power. It does not take a superior or even an equal military force to show by limited use that one is willing to take extreme measures rather than suffer a defeat. Such costs and risks are the trading chips of bargaining in the nuclear era; even if the United States had the weapons and doctrine for an FR policy, it could not avoid relying on them.

Although the United States should be able to conduct limited nuclear demonstrations, it should not stress this part of its policy. At this point there is no reason to think that such fantastic measures will ever be necessary, and they should be looked on as something to be done only in the most dire emergency, not as a tool of statecraft. Too much discussion of the possibility of such strikes might lead either or both sides to believe that the risks of a limited exchange were manageable, that escalation would remain under tight control. At best, the United States would therefore create a world in which limited nuclear wars were more likely to occur. At worst, these beliefs would be tested and proven to be incorrect.

Of course a policy of AD supplemented by the ability to conduct demonstration attacks may not succeed. The specter of all-out war is probably compelling enough to make both sides so cautious as to render forcible changes of the status quo on important issues too dangerous to be attempted.

[30]Jervis, "Deterrence Theory Revisited," p. 318.

But miscalculations are possible, even in situations that seem very clear in retrospect, and states are sometimes willing to take what others think are exorbitant risks to try to reach highly valued goals. Both a cautionary tale and reminder that superior military capability does not guarantee deterrence is provided by the Japanese decision to go to war in 1941. Japan struck because her leaders saw the alternative not as the foregoing of gains, but as losing "her very existence."[31] They were thus very highly motivated—much more so than American decision makers thought. Furthermore, they knew perfectly well that they could not win an all-out war. But they were not expecting to have to fight such a war; they thought that the war would be limited as the United States would prefer to concede dominance in East Asia rather than engage in a long and costly struggle. It is always possible that the Russians might similarly believe that a nuclear war could be kept limited because the United States would rather concede than move closer to the abyss. The penalty for miscalculation would be much greater for Russia than it was for Japan, and so their caution should be much greater. The danger remains, however, and it cannot be met by building more weapons.*

QUESTIONS FOR DISCUSSION

1 Should the United States attempt to regain strategic superiority in nuclear weapons?
2 Can the United States obtain strategic superiority in nuclear weapons?
3 How did the United States use its strategic superiority after 1945?
4 How would the United States use its strategic superiority if it were to achieve it in the near future?

5 How would either the United States or the Soviet Union know that it had achieved nuclear superiority?

SUGGESTED READINGS

Freedman, Lawrence. *The Evolution of Nuclear Strategy*. New York: St. Martin's Press, 1981.

Gray, Colin S. "The Idea of Strategic Superiority," *Air Force Magazine* 65 (March 1982), pp. 62–63.

Holloway, David. *The Soviet Union and the Arms Race*. New Haven, Connecticut: Yale University Press, 1983.

Kahan, Jerome H. *Security in the Nuclear Age: Developing U.S. Strategic Arms Policy*. Washington, D.C.: Brookings Institution, 1975.

Kennan, George. *The Nuclear Delusion: Soviet-American Relations in the Atomic Age*. New York: Pantheon Books, 1983.

Leebaert, Derek (ed.). *Soviet Military Thinking*. London: Allen & Unwin, 1981.

Luttwak, Edward N. *The Grand Strategy of the Soviet Union*. New York: St. Martin's Press, 1983.

Mandelbaum, Michael. *The Nuclear Future*. Ithaca, New York: Cornell University Press, 1983.

Pipes, Richard. *Survival Is Not Enough*. New York: Simon and Schuster, 1984.

Russett, Bruce. *The Prisoners of Insecurity: Nuclear Deterrence, the Arms Race, and Arms Control*. San Francisco, California: W. H. Freeman & Co., 1983.

Sivard, Ruth Leger. *World Military and Social Expenditures: An Annual Report on World Priorities*. Washington, D.C.: World Priorities, 1985.

Smoke, Richard. *National Security and the Nuclear Dilemma: An Introduction to the American Experience*. Reading, Massachusetts: Addison-Wesley Pub. Co., 1984.

Woolsey, R. James. "The Politics of Vulnerability: 1980–83," *Foreign Affairs* 62 (Spring 1984), pp. 805–19.

[31]Robert Butow, *Tojo and the Coming of the War* (Princeton, N.J.: Princeton University Press, 1961), p. 203.

*I would like to thank Desmond Ball, Richard Betts, Thomas Brown, James Digby, James King, George Quester, Michael Mandelbaum, Stanley Sierkiewicz, Dennis Ross, and Glenn Snyder for comments, and the Solomon Guggenheim Fund for financial support.

Chapter Five

The Wider Proliferation
of Nuclear Weapons

In the first chapter we listed, among various apocalyptic expectations, the possibility that nuclear weapons might rapidly be acquired by a large number of states, and the related belief that this, in turn, would make an early nuclear war more likely, or even inevitable. We quoted C. P. Snow as stating in 1960 that "within, at most, six years China and six other states" would have a stock of nuclear bombs, and as predicting as "a certainty" that "within, at the most, ten years, some of these bombs are going to go off . . . ." Clearly he was in error on both counts as far as the timing was concerned. Whether his fundamental assumptions are mistaken is less clear.

Within a quarter of a century, rather than a decade, Snow's prediction of there being seven nuclear-weapon states (NWSs) had become a reality (or, rather, nearly so), with five declared NWSs and two or three (almost certainly India, probably Israel, and maybe South Africa) in a position to brandish nuclear weapons, if not instantly, then within a very short time after a decision to do so. As for his other prediction, this, happily, has not yet occurred, although nobody can be sure for how long this will be the case.

Certainly a further spread of nuclear weapons seems inevitable. What is less certain is whether this will significantly increase the risk of actual use of nuclear weapons. Also unclear is whether the rate of proliferation will speed up or slow down, compared with the experience of the last quarter century, during which at most four new NWSs (declared and undeclared) have emerged—a smaller number than most authorities in, say, 1960 would have expected. What factors are likely to be most important in regulating the pace of such proliferation? There are a number of possibilities. First, there are experts who hold that proliferation is actually good for global stability. If in the future their view receives wider endorsement than it has in the first four decades of the nuclear age, we may expect that the demand for nuclear acquisitions by the non-nuclear-weapon states (NNWSs) will increase, and that the NWSs' desire and motive to deny assistance and obstruct development will diminish. Second, the amount of internecine conflict among NWSs, and even more so, among NNWSs, may be of great importance. If we enter an era, as some authorities predict, where pressures of population growth and world food shortages increase dramatically, regional contests for raw materials and foodstuffs are likely to become even more frenzied than in the past. This may serve to reduce inhibitions about nuclear weapon acquisition, and even use. Much of the third world, in particular, as the Brandt Report suggested, may be on the verge of becoming a Hobbesian jungle as a consequence of the evaporation of hopes for steadily rising standards of living and for a narrowing of the gap between the northern and southern hemispheres.[1] The world debt crisis and the unprecedentedly high real interest rates, both of which emerged in the early 1980s, suggest that the industrialized world is unlikely to be able in practice to create better conditions in the third world for several years (whether by vast increases in direct aid or by leading the world economy out of its prolonged recession). Third, there are experts who hold that the superpowers, by continuing their own nuclear arms competition ("vertical proliferation"), are setting a much-noticed example by emphasizing the importance of nuclear weapons in international politics and, that unless they cease to do so, they cannot expect other states to listen to sermons on the undesirability of nuclear spread ("horizontal proliferation"). Fourth, emphasis is sometimes put on the link between the spread of nuclear reactors for peaceful purposes (i.e., energy) and the temptation to obtain nuclear weapons. Our debates in this section are primarily addressed to these issues.

HORIZONTAL PROLIFERATION

In our first debate we consider whether "horizontal proliferation" is necessarily unhelpful in terms of world stability. Lewis A. Dunn holds that it is, whereas K. Subrahmanyam, an Indian strategic analyst, challenges the assumptions normally accepted in the West. Western governments naturally have to tread carefully when addressing this issue. They find it prudent to avoid arguments which could conceivably seem patronizing and thus offend the third-world majority in the United Nations General Assembly, whose conduct the West presumably desires to influence. Many members of the nonaligned movement are extremely sensitive to suggestions that they may be less "responsible" or less "stable" than the present NWSs. Dunn, on the other hand, evidently feels none of these inhibitions and candidly expresses his doubts about the suitability of most potential third-world aspirants for membership in the "nuclear club."

---

[1]*North-South: A Program for Survival.* Cambridge, Mass.: MIT Press, 1980.

Subrahmanyam presents an alternative view, in which he spiritedly maintains that "those who try to frighten the world with the idea of nuclear bombs in the hands of irresponsible third world rulers should ponder the equal risks of these weapons in the control of the developed nations." He adds that "within the next 10 or 15 years the high probability of nuclear weapons use in the developing world arises only with respect to intervention operations by established nuclear powers against developing countries, and by South Africa against black African states." (Incidentally, readers will notice that Subrahmanyam considers that South Africa, like Israel, is a "clandestine nuclear power," whereas he places India, alongside Brazil and Argentina, in the more transitory category of "near-nuclear weapon powers".)

It may be of value to recall here something of the history of the third world's attitude to proliferation and, in particular, to the Non-Proliferation Treaty (NPT) of 1968 (which Subrahmanyam describes as "pernicious"). The suggestion that a "non-nuclear club" should be created had originated in the previous decade, and was first brought before the U.N. General Assembly by Ireland, in 1958. In December 1961 the Assembly called upon all states, and particularly the NWSs, to use their best endeavors to secure the conclusion of an international agreement containing provisions under which the NWSs would undertake to refrain from relinquishing control of nuclear weapons and from transmitting the information necessary for their manufacture to states not possessing such weapons, and provisions under which states not possessing nuclear weapons would undertake not to manufacture or otherwise acquire control of such weapons. A further seven years elapsed before the NPT was finally negotiated. It represented a careful balance of obligations between the participating NWSs (the superpowers and Great Britain) on the one hand, and the bulk of NNWSs on the other. The critical elements in the bargain were as follows: (1) the NWSs agreed not to proliferate nuclear arms; (2) participating NNWSs agreed not to accept or seek to acquire nuclear weapons, and undertook to submit their peaceful nuclear-energy plants to inspection by the Vienna-based International Atomic Energy Agency (IAEA); (3) the NWSs agreed to assist the NNWSs with peaceful nuclear-energy development; and (4) in the famous Article VI, the NWSs undertook "to pursue negotiations in good faith on effective measures relating to cessation of the nuclear arms race at an early date and to nuclear disarmament, and on a Treaty on general and complete disarmament under strict and effective international control." This clearly placed the onus on the superpowers to halt "vertical proliferation."

Even in the world climate existing in 1968, when the third world was less alienated from the superpowers than is now the case, the NPT was by no means unanimously welcomed. Four states in the General Assembly opposed the planned Treaty in a vote on June 12, 1968, namely, Albania, Cuba, Tanzania, and Zambia, and they would no doubt also have had the support of one NWS, had China then been a UN member. Twenty-one states abstained. These included one NWS, France, as well as several NNWSs in the so-called threshold category, including Argentina, Brazil, and India.

Over the next 15 years many third-world countries became increasingly dissatisfied with the NPT. At NPT Review Conferences stress was laid on the failures of the superpowers to halt the "vertical nuclear arms race." But it is far from clear that even a full nuclear freeze between Washington and Moscow would have sufficed to halt the criticism, as more and more Third World states have come to feel that the NPT is irredeemably "discriminatory" in character. India and Cuba have held this position from the outset and have steadily gained support. It is thus uncertain whether the NPT, as a worthwhile constraint on proliferation, will survive much longer. Moreover, the abstention of most of the "threshold" states from the vote on ratification of the NPT has thrown doubt on its value. The so-called peaceful nuclear explosion carried out by India in 1974 has also done much to erode support for the Treaty. Few of India's critics or admirers doubt that the test was actually military in its implications, rather than peaceful. If India, of all countries, the land of the pacifist Mahatma Gandhi and the antinuclear Pandit Nehru, can in effect join the nuclear-weapons club, how much remains of the moral underpinning which caused the early nonaligned movement's hostility to nuclear weaponry and contributed to the framing of the NPT?

For the superpowers, too, the NPT has been something of a disappointment. They have been repeatedly pilloried for their failure to honor their obligations under Article VI. For Moscow, in particular, this is embarrassing, because on the whole the Soviets do not relish being seen by the world community as an associate of Washington, rather than as part of the world's antiestablishment forces. Yet Soviet efforts to persuade the nonaligned states that the Americans are solely responsible for the impasse in nuclear disarmament negotiations seem to fall largely on deaf ears, as more and more world figures are accepting the proposition, originally formulated by Beijing, that the two superpowers are "hegemonialists" intent on preserving their nuclear advantage over the rest of humankind. The superpowers, for their part, are becoming increasingly alarmed at the way in which the IAEA safeguards linked to the spread of nuclear energy have proved rather vulnerable to evasion. In short, both in Moscow and Washington experts are now asking whether the NPT really serves to prevent the spread of nuclear weapons to any sizeable states really desirous of obtaining them, irrespective of whether such states have ratified the NPT or been subjected to IAEA safeguards.

NUCLEAR POWER AND NUCLEAR WEAPONS

The ironic truth may be that some signatories to the NPT have received aid under the Peaceful Nuclear Energy assistance provisions of the NPT and as a result are actually nearer to becoming nuclear-weapon states than if the NPT had never been drafted. This leads into our next debate, in which Victor Gilinsky, for many years a U.S. Nuclear Regulatory Commissioner, sees acute danger of nuclear proliferation arising from an unrestrained pursuit of civilian nuclear activities. On the other hand, Sir John Hill, formerly at the British Atomic Energy Authority, claims that those states seeking nuclear weapons are unlikely to be deterred or deflected by a denial of assistance in the energy field.

SUPERPOWER RESTRAINT AND HORIZONTAL PROLIFERATION

Such diverging views as to the principal incentives and disincentives for nuclear-weapons acquisition have been commonly heard for at least two decades. Indeed, the next debate was first published in 1967, before the NPT was launched. It was a highly sophisticated encounter between two distinguished academics, the late Hedley Bull and James R. Schlesinger. (The latter later became President Nixon's secretary of defense.) It is of course bound to appear dated in certain respects—for example, it preceded the Indian nuclear explosion—but the really striking aspect is how well many of the main arguments have endured to the present. Nevertheless, it could be said that, in at least one crucial respect, both writers accepted an assumption which is now widely questioned. As Bull puts it, "it is widely recognized that the process of nuclear proliferation will be greatly influenced by the military policies that are adopted by the present nuclear powers." Bull sees a relatively "low posture" by the NWSs as, on balance, wiser; Schlesinger makes a case for a "high posture," with particular emphasis on superpower nuclear guarantees of NNWSs. Today, however, it may be doubted whether many states, particularly in the third world, would be much influenced either way, although admittedly their rhetoric does not suggest that. In particular, the United States' nuclear guarantees in Asia, to which Bull refers, may be seen as carrying no significant weight since the American failure in Vietnam and the enunciation of the so-called Nixon Doctrine, which effectively halted any extension of United States obligations in the region. Thus, if as many experts expect, Pakistan and India both become declared NWSs before the end of the century, will this not be due to their inability to resolve their mutual differences and suspicions? Is it really plausible that such a development could be averted by a superpower offer of "guarantees" or, alternatively, by an agreement between the superpowers to limit their own nuclear arms? The same arguments do not yet apply in Western Europe, where the United States' "extended deterrent," although considered frail by some, as we have seen, is nevertheless not so completely discounted as to have led West Germany, for instance, to clamor for nuclear weapons of its own. But might not such a development occur before the end of the century, with or without the Non-Proliferation Treaty?

NUCLEAR TERRORISM

Another point to which Bull and Schlesinger gave little serious attention back in 1967 was the possibility of terrorists' acquiring nuclear arms. For, until the 1970s, the phenomenon of worldwide terrorist violence was largely absent, although there had been significant guerrilla struggles in particular regions. But, appropriately or not, guerrilla warfare is not usually equated with the spate of global "international terrorist" incidents that began with a wave of aircraft hijackings, proceeded through the Munich Olympics massacre, and is now marked by the willingness of suicide squads to drive explosive-laden trucks at buildings such as embassies. Today there is a considerable number of well-established and well-financed terrorist groups, and they have many contacts with each another. It is therefore not beyond the bounds of possibility that one or more of these groups may seek to acquire a weapon of mass destruction. The next debate between Louis René Beres and political scientist Ted Greenwood addresses this issue. The argument has two essential parts: (1) could a terrorist group (with or without the assistance of a sympathetic sovereign state) take practical control of a nuclear weapon? and (2) if it could do so, what practical use could it be expected to try to make of the weapon? The second question, in particular, raises the vital issue of the real nature of terrorist groups. Contrary to popular myth, most of the well-established groups (and they are probably the only ones even remotely in a position to hope to acquire nuclear weapons through their own endeavors) are *not* run by demented psychopaths. Indeed, leaders of the larger terrorist groups see themselves as potential world leaders, and, looking at the heads of government throughout the world, one can see examples of those who have already successfully undergone such a metamorphosis. Thus, the reckless and unthinking use of nuclear weapons by such potential world leaders is scarcely to be expected in the foreseeable future. This does not guarantee that calculated threats to use nuclear weapons might not be made. Here, the critical point is to decide whether one can easily construct realistic scenarios in which such threats might be made with a fair hope of yielding practical dividends to a rational substate cause.

A somewhat more credible possibility may be that a small group, essentially loyal to a "crazy" state, could be provided by its patrons with nuclear arms for a "kamikaze" strike. This would not really constitute an independent terrorist use of nuclear weapons, however; it would rather be an act of war by a sovereign state.

18 Would the Spread of Nuclear Weapons to Developing
Countries Greatly Increase the Risk of Their Use?

YES

Lewis A. Dunn

What Difference Will It Make?

NO

K. Subrahmanyam

Regional Conflicts and Nuclear Fears

What Difference Will It Make?
Lewis A. Dunn

THE BREAKDOWN OF NUCLEAR PEACE

A number of analysts and observers, noting that predictions at the dawn of the nuclear age of a nuclear apocalypse have proved exaggerated, argue that there is little reason to fear the consequences of the further spread of nuclear weapons.[1] Frequently at the core of such optimistic assessments is the belief that the very destructiveness of those weapons will both instill prudence in their new owners, making them less willing to use even minimal conventional force out of fear that conflict will escalate to use of nuclear weapons, and lead to stable deterrent relationships between previously hostile countries.[2] But such a fear of nuclear war was only one of the underpinnings of the first decades' nuclear peace. Other equally significant geopolitical and technical supports may be absent in the conflict-prone regions to which nuclear weapons are now likely to spread.

[1]For optimistic assessments of the consequences of proliferation, often extrapolated from the experience of the first decades of the nuclear age, see K. Subrahmanyam, "India: Keeping the Option Open," in *Nuclear Proliferation Phase II*, ed. Robert M. Lawrence and Joel Larus (Lawrence: University Press of Kansas, 1974); Steven J. Rosen, "A Stable System of Mutual Nuclear Deterrence in the Arab-Israeli Conflict," *The American Political Science Review* 71, no. 4 (December 1977), pp. 1367–1383; Paul Jabber, "A Nuclear Middle East: Infrastructure, Likely Military Postures and Prospects for Strategic Stability," ACIS working paper no. 6 (Center for Arms Control and International Security, University of California, Los Angeles, September 1977), pp. 37–39; R. Robert Sandoval, "Consider the Porcupine: Another View of Nuclear Proliferation," *Bulletin of the Atomic Scientists*, May 1976, pp. 17–19; Kenneth N. Waltz, "What Will the Spread of Nuclear Weapons Do to the World?" in *International Political Effects of the Spread of Nuclear Weapons*, ed. John Kerry King (Washington, D.C.: U.S. Government Printing Office, 1979), pp. 165–196; Shai Feldman, "A Nuclear Middle East," *Survival* 23 (May–June 1981), pp. 111–115.

[2]Waltz, "What Will the Spread of Nuclear Weapons Do to the World?" pp. 184–190, 194.

Higher Stakes, Shorter Distances, and Failures of Leadership

The stakes of the long-standing rivalries and conflicts in the Middle East, South Asia, the Persian Gulf, and the Korean peninsula—contrasted to those of the superpower confrontation—are very high. Territorial integrity, political independence, and, in some instances, even national survival itself frequently are at issue. Consistent with the magnitude of the stakes, leaders of countries in these regions have proved willing in the past to use military force against their regional opponents—whether, for example, in an attempt to push Israel into the sea or to unify Korea, to dismember Pakistan and create Bangladesh, to topple a rival leader in a neighboring country, or to seize new or regain lost territory. And because they perceive the stakes to be so high, some of these countries' leaders may be ready to risk nuclear confrontation, if not even to accept a surprisingly high level of nuclear damage, in pursuit of their objectives. Thus, it would be erroneous to assume that these new nuclear powers will necessarily subscribe to the Western "minimum deterrence" point of view—that the threat of one or two atomic bombs dropped in retaliation on an opponent's capital city will suffice to deter the use of force and prevent lesser clashes.[3]

Regardless of these leaders' intentions, flash points for conflict among these new nuclear powers abound. The festering civil war in Lebanon involving Christians, Palestinians, Syrians, and Israelis; border clashes between Libya and Egypt; a renewal of the Iraq-Iran war; a new incident between the Koreas; and unrest in Baluchistan or Kashmir are all potential tripwires. And the risk of unintended es-

[3]Ibid., p. 187. For a more general critique of such ethnocentrism, also see Ken Booth, *Strategy and Ethnocentrism* (New York: Holmes and Meier, 1979).

Lewis A. Dunn, "What Difference Will It Make?" *Controlling the Bomb: Nuclear Proliferation in the 1980s* (New Haven, Connecticut: Yale University Press), 1982, pp. 69–94.

calation will be considerable. For unlike the Soviet Union and the United States, many of the next countries that may "go nuclear" share common borders or are separated only by narrow or unstable buffer zones. Once under way, limited confrontations or low-level clashes could spill over quickly into vital national territory and threaten critical national interests, perhaps even survival. Further, again in contrast to the superpowers, little if any time may be available for learning to live with nuclear weapons before the first such nuclear confrontation occurs.

Moreover, the legacy of conflict among these countries, as well as their domestic political weaknesses, could make it all the more difficult to check such a slide to all-out war.[4] In a climate of deeply rooted hostility and distrust, the leaders of, say, Israel and Iraq may refuse to make concessions during a crisis, fearing that they will be considered weak and thus subjected to further demands. Or, fearful of being thrown out of power, a weak leader could be reluctant to take the first step to defuse a crisis until it was too late. For example, the weakened Pakistani government of Yahya Khan in 1971 could not bring itself to meet East Pakistani demands for greater autonomy, resulting in the third Indo-Pakistani war and Pakistan's dismemberment. And even leaders made considerably more prudent by the threat of nuclear war can miscalculate how far they can push in a crisis, just as Nasser did when his rhetorical posturing and decision to move troops into the Sinai helped trigger the 1967 Middle East war. Similarly, although offered neutrality by Israel, King Hussein decided to enter the same war—at the cost of Israeli occupation of the West Bank.[5]

Besides, judging from recent history, it is highly unlikely that coldly calculating, cautious, and fully rational leaders—at least in the Western sense— will always be in authority in the next countries to acquire nuclear weapons. In many of these countries, the volatility of domestic politics, the psychological and personal strains caused by vast economic and social changes, and the weakness of political institutions will result in the periodic seizure of power by extremist military cliques, messianic leaders, and fundamentalist religious and ideological movements. Leaders such as the Ayatollah Khomeini, Colonel Qaddafi, and Pol Pot, committed to the pursuit of transcendental goals and societal redemption, exemplify what can be expected. Motivated by an obligation to their higher mission and destiny, these leaders are less likely to weigh carefully the costs and gains of military action and are more likely to take high-risk gambles to serve their causes.

Technical Deficiencies of New Nuclear Forces

Considerable time, money, and scientific and engineering talent have been spent by the United States since the 1950s to design, develop, and implement accident-proofing for operational nuclear weapons.[6] Efforts to insure that these weapons could, for example, withstand the heat and impact of air crashes and be dropped accidentally without producing a nuclear explosion paid off in the 1950s and 1960s, when nearly two dozen American aircraft crashed while carrying nuclear weapons.[7]

Some of those countries that may soon acquire nuclear weapons, however, probably do not have the scientific and engineering manpower or the financial resources to design and fabricate reliable, advanced accident-proofing systems integral to the

---

[4]See Fred Charles Iklé, "Can Nuclear Deterrence Last Out the Century?" *Foreign Affairs* 51, no. 2 (January 1973), pp. 269–271.

[5]Both Shai Feldman and Kenneth Waltz, for example, not only assume that new nuclear powers will accept the logic of minimum deterrence, but they greatly underestimate the dangers of escalation.

[6]The initial American mode of accident-proofing employed for the atomic strike against Hiroshima was to assemble the final components of the bomb only after the aircraft was airborne. But in the 1950s, after the United States began to deploy large numbers of nuclear weapons in a nuclear deterrent force, more sophisticated measures integral to the warhead design itself also were developed.

[7]See Stockholm International Peace Research Institute, *World Armaments and Disarmament SIPRI Yearbook 1977* (Cambridge: The MIT Press, 1977), pp. 65–67; Joel Larus, *Nuclear Weapons Safety and the Common Defense* (Columbus: Ohio State University Press, 1967), passim.

nuclear weapon itself. Their limited resources will be expended in their struggle simply to join the nuclear club. Fearful of being caught unprepared, however, these countries may be unwilling to use such a simple, if less sophisticated, accident-proofing measure as not fully assembling their nuclear weapons until they are needed. And even stock-piling disassembled weapons would not reduce the risk of an accident once those weapons have to be assembled. In fact, hasty assembly of crude weapons would augment the chances of just such an accidental detonation in the most dangerous political context—a continuing crisis or even a low-level conflict.[8]

Some of the next countries to "go nuclear," unable, say, to build invulnerable missiles, also will be forced to rely on a hair-trigger, launch-on-warning operating procedure in attempting to protect their nuclear force from surprise attack. This will heighten the risk of an accidental nuclear exchange triggered by mechanical failure or human error.[9] There will be virtually no time to verify the initial warning of attack because of the short distances separating most of these new nuclear powers; but where the stakes are high, pressure to act on such a warning lest a surprise attack succeeds will be intense.

Even with reliance on launch-on-warning, it is highly probable that at least a few of these new nuclear forces will remain vulnerable to surprise

attack, decreasing significantly an opponent's aversion to nuclear escalation. For example, in a confrontation between India and Pakistan in the late 1980s, in which Pakistan relies on aircraft for the delivery of a handful of nuclear weapons while India has available nuclear-armed missiles, an Indian nuclear first strike might virtually destroy Pakistan's nuclear force, thereby greatly reducing the threat of nuclear retaliation. Or, Israel probably would have a similar advantage in a confrontation with Iraq, Libya, or Egypt. For while these countries have unsophisticated surface-to-surface rockets, technical constraints will probably impede their development of small nuclear warheads for them. Thus, unless widely dispersed and concealed,[10] Iraqi, Libyan, or Egyptian bombers would be highly vulnerable to attack by Israeli nuclear-armed missiles.[11] In still other regional nuclear confrontations, say between Libya and Egypt or Iran and Iraq, both sides might be vulnerable to surprise attack.

Inadequate controls against the unauthorized use of nuclear weapons by disaffected military men—or against the theft of those weapons by dissidents and terrorists—is likely to be a further technical weakness of some newly deployed nuclear forces even though measures to reduce that threat are in theory available. One such control measure accessible to countries with a certain amount of technical

[8]Some proponents of the benign consequences of nuclearization of regional conflict, such as Paul Jabber and Steven Rosen, assume that this problem of accident-proofing would be solved by the enlightened transfer of technical assistance from the superpowers. That begs the question. For political and technical reasons, the superpowers might decide not to provide such assistance. Nor is it clear that "assistance" that would require access to a new nuclear power's weapon design would be accepted by those countries themselves. Other optimistic assessments, including Shai Feldman's, simply neglect this problem.

[9]Both mechanical and human error, for example, occurred in the course of breaking in both the Distant Early Warning (DEW) Line and the American Ballistic Missile Early Warning System (BMEWS) in the 1950s. However, other technical and geopolitical characteristics did not reinforce that error as might happen for new nuclear powers. See Joel Larus, *Nuclear Weapons Safety and the Common Defense* (Columbus: Ohio State University Press, 1967), pp. 37–38.

[10]Command and control problems might make widespread dispersal of nuclear-armed aircraft unattractive to an Iraqi or Egyptian government unsure of its own military; if pursued anyway, such dispersal might solve the first strike problem but exacerbate that of unauthorized access. And even if nuclear-armed aircraft were dispersed, Israel could use its nuclear weapons to blanket large areas with sufficient over-pressures from the nuclear blast to destroy above-ground missiles. Predictions of stable deterrence as the probable outcome of Middle East nuclearization skip over such difficulties.

[11]Steven Rosen, Paul Jabber, and Shai Feldman, for example, apparently rest their expectation of stable deterrence in a nuclearized Middle East on the prospect that at least one or two warheads would survive an Israeli surprise attack and that this minimum threat would suffice to deter an Israeli first strike. But that depends on the stakes involved as well as on perceptions of the risk that events would get out of hand. And, in a low-level Arab-Israeli conflict, striking first and accepting the risk of such retaliation might come to be viewed by Israel as its least undesirable course of action.

sophistication is placing an electronic permissive action link (PAL) on each nuclear weapon, thereby requiring a particular code to "unlock" and use that weapon. In less technically advanced countries, special civilian forces could guard disassembled nuclear weapons stored at some distance from their delivery vehicles. Still another possibility would be centralized storage of all nuclear warheads at one or two sites, again removed from delivery vehicles and guarded by elite military units. But in addition to a heightened vulnerability to surprise attack, the penalty for reliance on such less technically sophisticated measures is significantly decreased operational readiness and effectiveness, as it would take considerable time to remove the nuclear warheads from storage, ship them to forward bases, and "mate" them to their delivery vehicles.

In practice, some of the new nuclear powers that are unable to develop electronic control measures most likely will find the penalties of relying on less sophisticated measures unacceptable. More fearful of surprise attack, they may choose to accept the risks of unauthorized use inherent in the decentralized storage of nuclear warheads in close proximity to their delivery vehicles or in the advanced mating of warheads and delivery vehicles.[12] Consequently, for these countries—a group that could soon include Pakistan, Iraq, and Libya—maintaining control over nuclear weapons will depend heavily on the effectiveness of physical security procedures. A special "civilianized" military guard might complicate efforts by a few military men or a subnational group to seize one or more nuclear weapons but could be readily overwhelmed in a military coup d'etat. Besides, members of that guard might be bribed, coerced, or persuaded to cooperate.

The significance of these command-and-control deficiencies is magnified by the domestic political instability of most of the countries that may acquire nuclear weapons by the early 1990s. Nearly all—including Argentina, Brazil, Egypt, Iran, Iraq, Libya, Nigeria, Pakistan, and South Korea—are developing countries, while many either have experienced a successful or aborted military coup d'etat within the past decade or could in the future.[13] This lack of military subordination to higher authority would increase the importance of rigorous command-and-control measures. But for some of these countries' leaders a recognition of the need for such measures in all probability still will be outweighed by the perceived security need of an operationally ready—even if less than tightly controlled—nuclear force.

A Spiraling Threat to Peace

With the spread of nuclear weapons to conflict-prone regions, the chances that those weapons will be used again increase greatly. The heightened stakes and lessened room for maneuver in conflict-prone regions, the volatile leadership and political instability of many of the next nuclear powers, and the technical deficiencies of many new nuclear forces all threaten the first decades' nuclear peace.

Not least to be feared is nuclear war caused by accident or miscalculation. During an intense crisis or the first stages of a conventional military clash, for example, an accidental detonation of a nuclear weapon—even within the country of origin—or an accidental missile launch easily might be misinterpreted as the first shot of a surprise attack. Pressures to escalate in a last-ditch attempt to disarm the opponent before he completes that attack will be intense. Similarly, a technical malfunction of a radar warning system or a human error in interpreting an ambiguous warning might trigger a nuclear clash. Or fear that escalation to nuclear conflict no longer could be avoided might lead a country to get in the first blow, so as partly to disarm the opponent and to minimize damage.[14]

---

[12]Recent more optimistic evaluations of the consequences of proliferation, including those of Kenneth Waltz, Steven Rosen, Paul Jabber, and Shai Feldman, either neglect the command-and-control problem or simply assume that it will be solved.

[13]Gavin Kennedy, *The Military in the Third World* (New York: Scribner, 1974), pp. 337–344.

[14]The classic study of such strategic interaction is Thomas C. Schelling's "The Reciprocal Fear of Surprise Attack." See Thomas C. Schelling, *The Strategy of Conflict* (New York: Oxford University Press, 1963), pp. 4–22.

Unauthorized use of nuclear weapons by the military also is a possibility. For example, faced with imminent conventional military defeat and believing there is little left to lose anyway, a few members of Pakistan's military could launch a nuclear strike against India to damage that country as much as possible. Or a few hard-line, fanatic Iraqi, Libyan, or even Egyptian officers might use their countries' newly acquired nuclear weapons in an attempt to "solve" the Israeli problem once and for all. These officers' emotional commitment to a self-ordained higher mission would overwhelm any fear of the adverse personal or national consequences. Aside from the initial destruction, such unauthorized use could provoke a full-scale nuclear conflict between the hostile countries.

But the first use of nuclear weapons since Nagasaki may be a carefully calculated policy decision. The bomb might be used intentionally on the battlefield to defend against invasion. For example, faced with oncoming North Korean troops, a nuclear-armed South Korea would be under great pressure to use nuclear weapons as atomic demolition land mines to close critical invasion corridors running the thirty miles from the border to Seoul. Similar military logic could lead to Israeli use of enhanced radiation weapons—so-called neutron bombs—in the next Arab-Israeli war.

A calculated disarming nuclear surprise attack to seize the military advantage also is possible in these high-stakes, escalation-prone regional conflicts, particularly when one side has a decided strategic advantage. For example, in the 1980s, internal political instability in Pakistan and simmering unrest in Kashmir could erupt into a conventional military clash between India and Pakistan. A nuclear-armed India then would be under intense pressure to attack the more rudimentary Pakistani nuclear force to prevent its use—whether by accident or intention—against India. In a nuclear Middle East, as well, fear of events getting out of hand would fuel arguments in favor of an Israeli first strike once a conflict had begun.

Aside from the increased threat of actual use of nuclear weapons, the nuclearization of conflict-prone regions may have other costly or dangerous

consequences. Given the stakes, some new nuclear powers will think seriously about a preventive strike with conventional weapons to preserve their regional nuclear monopoly. Israel already has taken such military action against Iraq's nuclear weapons program and has stated its readiness to take further action as needed. And notwithstanding the limited Iraqi reaction to Israel's preventive strike—in large part due to Iraq's being tied down in its war with Iran—it might not be possible to prevent escalation after similar or larger future attacks. (Though less likely, a sufficiently desperate country might even use nuclear weapons in such a preventive strike. There is evidence that in the late 1960s the Soviet Union seriously considered a preemptive nuclear strike against the nascent nuclear force of the People's Republic of China.)[15]

Possession of nuclear weapons also may be used as an instrument of blackmail or coercion. A country with a nuclear edge may implicitly or explicitly threaten the use of nuclear weapons to enforce its demands in regional crises or low-level confrontations. Just as U.S. strategic superiority contributed to the Soviet Union's decision to back down in the 1962 Cuban Missile Crisis,[16] so might possession of nuclear weapons by Iraq, Israel, India, or South Korea affect the resolution of crises with weaker opponents.

In addition, tensions among the countries of newly nuclearized regions are likely to be exacerbated. Pakistan's nuclear weapons activities, for example, already have heightened India's suspicion and have slowed efforts to improve relations between the two countries.[17] Pakistani testing and deployment of nuclear weapons would further worsen relations between India and Pakistan, not least because such

[15]H. R. Haldeman with Joseph Di Mona, *The Ends of Power* (New York: New York Times Books, 1978), pp. 90–94; Harry G. Gelber, "Nuclear Weapons and Chinese Policy," in *The Superpowers in a Multinuclear World,* ed. Geoffrey Kemp et al. (Lexington, Mass.: Lexington Books, 1974), p. 66.

[16]See among many others, Robert E. Osgood and Robert W. Tucker, *Force, Order, and Justice* (Baltimore: The Johns Hopkins University Press, 1967), pp. 155–156.

[17]"India Gives Warning of Atom-Arms Race," *New York Times,* August 16, 1979; and "India, Pakistan Fail to Resolve Key Differences," *Washington Post,* July 17, 1980.

activity would affront India's claim to regional preeminence. Should India step up its nuclear weapons activities in response and achieve clear-cut nuclear superiority, Pakistan's fears of Indian nuclear blackmail would be increased as well. Even the anticipation of a country's "going nuclear" can have adverse political effects. For example, Iraq's efforts to acquire nuclear weapons have heightened Israel's siege mentality and stimulated efforts by Syria, Saudia Arabia, and even Kuwait at least to master basic nuclear theory and know-how.

The greater the scope, the quicker the pace, and the higher the level of proliferation, the more severe will be the threat of nuclear conflict. As more countries acquire the bomb, the number of situations in which a political miscalculation, leadership failure, geographical propinquity, or technical mishap could lead to a nuclear clash will increase. As the pace of proliferation accelerates, the time available for countries to adjust to living with nuclear weapons will grow shorter. As countries move to the more advanced levels of proliferation—from untested bombs to full-fledged military deployment, there is more chance that some of these new nuclear forces will be technically deficient. Further, nuclear weapons will cease to be isolated symbols and will become an integral part of international relations within these volatile regions.

There will be occasional exceptions where the spread of nuclear weapons does not have as adverse an impact as feared. For example, if Taiwan's acquisition of nuclear weapons does not provoke an immediate preventive strike by China, it might go far toward eliminating a military solution to the conflict between them. Or a Yugoslav nuclear force capable of surviving a Soviet disarming attack and destroying several Soviet cities in retaliation could offer needed deterrence against a Soviet military incursion. And even though acquisition of nuclear weapons by Argentina and Brazil probably would heighten mutual suspicion and political tensions between them, the risk of actual nuclear conflict is likely to be less than in other regions because of the more modest stakes of their traditional rivalry.

The initial outcroppings of more widespread proliferation in and of themselves also will call forth efforts to reduce the resultant threat of nuclear conflict. But few of the possible measures for mitigating the consequences of proliferation offer a high promise of success, while domestic and international constraints may hinder implementation of even these more limited measures. And the greater the scope, pace, and level of proliferation, the more difficult and complex management efforts will become. Thus, the spiraling risk of regional nuclear conflict will not be entirely offset by these management efforts.

THE GLOBAL SPILLOVERS

While more widespread proliferation most likely will not overturn the existing structure of world politics, it will adversely affect the superpowers, and their relationship, as well as the great powers. The optimism among some analysts about the benign consequences of further proliferation again is likely to be proved wrong.

Limits to Structural Change

The Soviet Union and the United States are involved in nearly all of the regions to which nuclear weapons may spread in the 1980s, frequently supporting opposite sides in long-standing disputes. Neither is likely to sever alliance ties, drop clients and allies, or phase out economic and military involvement after nuclear weapons spread to these regions. In all probability, the leaders of both countries will continue to believe that compelling national interests—whether, for example, Western access to Middle East oil, expansion of Soviet power toward the Persian Gulf or its containment, the protection of traditional allies, and maintenance of the military balance in East Asia—outweigh any new or enhanced risks of continuing involvement. Besides, because of the competitive nature of the superpower relationship, officials in each country may be reluctant to disengage from these regions in the absence of reciprocal action by the other country lest the opponent be given a "free hand." And an unwillingness to sacrifice past investments made in pursuit of regional influence and military-political advantage is likely to buttress these arguments against disengagement.

It is equally doubtful that more widespread proliferation will lead to a Soviet-U.S. condominium to prevent the further spread of nuclear weapons, ban their use by new nuclear powers, and restore the superpowers' absolute domination of world politics. The competing political, economic, and military interests of the Soviet Union and the United States in regions such as South Asia and the Middle East are likely to take precedence over joint efforts to reduce the risk of local nuclear conflict. The superpowers' reliance on the nuclear threat in their own defense postures also may constrain joint action, particularly since the threat of escalation to nuclear conflict is critical to NATO's defense posture. The international costs—political, military, and economic—of an attempt to restore superpower domination of regional politics also would be high, and quite possibly thought by U.S. and Soviet leaders to be excessive. For many countries, including U.S. allies in Western Europe, a superpower condominium for nuclear peace would be a grave threat to their current freedom of action. It is also doubtful that the military problems of reasserting control would be manageable at an acceptable cost in light of increased local capabilities for resistance, as exemplified by the Soviet experience in Afghanistan. Moreover, in the Middle East, the economic penalties of intervention, at least for the United States, could be great. And while the domestic political constraints on active interventionism abroad may be less for the Soviet leadership than for U.S. policymakers, in neither country can they be overlooked.

The restoration of a more multipolar global political structure is even less likely to result from the further spread of nuclear weapons. The net impact on superpower strategic dominance of the emergence of a group of lesser nuclear powers will be quite limited. Even the deployment of nuclear forces by Japan and West Germany need not fundamentally upset the existing structure: should the nuclear forces of Japan and West Germany be equivalent to those of France and the United Kingdom, there still would be a considerable gap between the threat they could pose to the superpowers and the threat the superpowers would pose in re-

turn. The United States and the Soviet Union also could raise the threshold nuclear capability necessary for Japan or West Germany to mount a serious threat to either of their homelands by renegotiating the 1972 Treaty between the United States of America and the Union of Soviet Socialist Republics on the Limitation of Anti-Ballistic Missile Systems (ABM) to permit Soviet and U.S. deployment of defenses against Japanese or West German ballistic missiles. Besides, it is quite unlikely in any case that these countries will decide to acquire nuclear weapons.

This conclusion that widespread proliferation will not overturn the existing structure of world politics rests most of all on the assumption that even in that changed environment the leaders of the United States and the Soviet Union will continue to pursue their distinct national interests and objectives, utilizing force or the threat of force and relying on prudence, crisis management, and marginal adjustment to deal with the new risks. However, it is possible that following the use of nuclear weapons by a new nuclear power—especially if that use almost produces a nuclear confrontation between them—the United States and the Soviet Union may be far more ready to negotiate about joint disengagement and other steps to isolate newly nuclear regions. Alternatively, leaders in the Soviet Union and the United States could seek to reassert their countries' capability to dictate the rules of the regional nuclear game. The likelihood of such major adjustments clearly will depend on whether the superpowers' assessment of the direct risks to themselves and of the adequacy of traditional crisis management changes markedly. But particularly in light of the limited success of recent U.S. and Soviet efforts to reach agreement on reciprocal strategic restraints as well as their conflicting global interests, ideologies, and national styles,[18] even after one or more small-power nuclear exchanges, the

[18]Soviet stress on unilateral steps rather than mutual restraint to reduce the risk of nuclear war is a specific manifestation of those stylistic differences. See John Erickson, "The Soviet Military System: Doctrine, Technology and 'Style'," in *Soviet Military Power and Performance,* eds. John Erickson and E. J. Feuchtwanger (Great Britain: Archon Books, 1979), pp. 24–29.

two superpowers probably will continue to pursue only prudent ameliorative measures to reduce the risks of competitive involvement in newly nuclearized regions.

Reduced Superpower Freedom of Action

Periodically during the past decades, the United States has intervened militarily in regional confrontations, disputes, and limited conflicts outside of the European arena. The decision in 1980 to create the Rapid Deployment Joint Task Force for Middle East and Persian Gulf contingencies reflects a continued willingness to project U.S. power into conflict-prone regions in order to protect U.S. interests, allies, and friends.[19] But the presence of nuclear weapons in some future contingencies will increase the military and political risks of intervention, reducing U.S. freedom of action.

Notwithstanding the threat of U.S. retaliation, nuclear weapons might be used against U.S. intervention forces. A desperate leader, thinking there was nothing left to lose, might launch a nuclear strike against landing troops or close-in off-shore naval operations, both of which would be vulnerable to even a few rudimentary nuclear weapons. Or, in the heat of battle, a breakdown of communications could result in the use of nuclear weapons by a lesser nuclear power. Also possible is an unauthorized attack on U.S. forces by the military of a new nuclear power. If needed adaptations of the tactics, training, and structure of these U.S. intervention forces are not made, U.S. intervention could prove very costly, and U.S. forces might even suffer stunning reversals.

Admittedly, U.S. policymakers could launch a limited nuclear strike to disarm the hostile new nuclear power rather than seek to "work around" this regional nuclear threat and risk valuable military assets. But the regional and global political costs to the United States of such a strike are likely to be so high as to make policymakers very hesitant to authorize it.

[19]Harold Brown, Secretary of Defense, Department of Defense, *Annual Report of Fiscal Year 1981*, pp. 114–117. The discussion here draws on discussions with my colleague George Wittman.

These heightened risks also are likely to reinforce the lingering, although somewhat muted, national presumption against intervention derived from the Vietnam experience. Consequently, the stakes needed to justify involvement in a newly nuclearized region probably will be greater than in the past. U.S. policymakers may choose not to intervene militarily in some situations where they previously would have acted.

The risks and complexities of military intervention will increase for the Soviet Union as well. In the eyes of a Soviet leadership that has intervened militarily only when the balance of forces appeared clearly favorable, the possible use of nuclear weapons against Soviet troops in a newly nuclearized region could be an excessive risk. To illustrate, Yugoslav deployment of battlefield nuclear weapons might discourage Soviet military action in a future domestic political struggle in Yugoslavia. Similarly, even a slight possibility that Israel or South Africa would use nuclear weapons against Soviet ground or naval forces might help deter Soviet military entanglement in those regions. And the political costs of a nuclear disarming attack on a new nuclear power are likely to appear nearly as excessive to the Soviet Union as to the United States.

The eventual development by a few new nuclear powers of even a limited last-resort capability to threaten the homeland of one or the other superpower with nuclear attack or retaliation also would reduce both Soviet and American freedom of action. For example, should Israel acquire the capability to strike Odessa, Kiev, and Baku, the Soviet leaders might not be as willing to risk direct military involvement in the Middle East to support their Arab clients. Such a capability in Yugoslav or South African hands might have a comparable restraining effect on the Soviets. Or, though less likely, a radical Arab government might threaten to destroy one or more American cities in an attempt to blackmail the United States into not resupplying Israel in the midst of the next Middle East war. Of course, the risk of carrying out such a threat to a superpower would be extraordinary. But neither superpower could ignore the possibility that a leader who thought he had nothing left to lose might do so.

However, this threat of direct attack by a new nuclear power is likely to be greater for the Soviet Union than for the United States. Hardly any of the next countries likely to acquire the bomb will seek to target the U.S. homeland. Moreover, the geographical remoteness of the United States from potentially hostile new nuclear powers in the Middle East and Persian Gulf, combined with the technological backwardness of these countries, makes American cities somewhat less vulnerable than Soviet cities to such a nuclear strike. At least in the 1980s, to attack a U.S. city, Iraq or Libya—the most plausible opponents—probably would either have to smuggle a weapon into the United States by plane or boat[20] or use a converted Boeing 707 or 747 registered as a private or corporate jet to deliver a bomb, counting on subterfuge and the steady decline of U.S. air defenses[21] to penetrate U.S. airspace. Though possibly feasible, such unconventional modes of attack would be less technically reliable, limited in magnitude, and subject to interception by intelligence agencies.

In contrast, Israel, Yugoslavia, and South Korea already possess long-range nuclear-capable aircraft that can reach the Soviet Union and may well be able to slip through Soviet air defenses. South Africa and Israel also are said to be developing a crude cruise missile that could increase their capability to hit Soviet cities. Should Japan or West Germany acquire nuclear weapons, they would have little trouble targeting Soviet cities. Barring unexpectedly rapid technological progress, the breakdown of current restraints on the sale of cruise missiles and advanced missile guidance systems, or widespread traffic in space-booster technology and boosters themselves, the United States will continue to be less vulnerable to nuclear attack by

a new nuclear power than will the Soviet Union— at least into the 1990s.

The constraining effect of more widespread possession of nuclear weapons on the superpowers should not be exaggerated.[22] The superpowers' readiness and capability to control events abroad have already been lessened by the decreased legitimacy of using force, rising nationalism, the difficulties of bringing applicable force to bear in limited disputes, the availability of advanced weapons systems to regional powers, and the strengthening of countervailing economic instruments of power.[23] So viewed, the further spread of nuclear weapons only contributes to a continuing, longer-term relative decline of superpower freedom of action. Moreover, as long as the two superpowers are ready to pay the necessary price, they could preserve a significant gap between their military capabilities and those of any new medium and lesser nuclear powers, including even Japan and West Germany. Further, in those situations where U.S. or Soviet interests are seen to justify either the military costs of working around lesser nuclear forces or the political costs of suppressing them, the superpowers most probably will be impeded but not prevented from realizing their objectives.

Increased Risk of Superpower Confrontation

Continued U.S. and Soviet pursuit of their respective interests in these newly nuclear conflict-prone regions also will entail acceptance of a higher risk of a U.S.-Soviet political-military confrontation. With the acquisition of nuclear weapons by long-standing regional enemies, there will be many more flashpoints for such a superpower clash. For instance, a preventive attack with conventional weapons, a surprise disarming strike, use of nuclear weapons on the battlefield, nuclear blackmail, a conventional attack backed by the threat of recourse to nuclear weapons, in each case by one superpower's ally against an ally of the other, all

---

[20]Ton loads of contraband drugs are smuggled routinely into this country by boat and small plane, and a variety of means of disguising a nuclear weapon to permit its being included within a larger, more innocent shipment of goods exists. These, however, are best not disclosed, for obvious reasons.

[21]Francis P. Hoeber, David B. Kassing, William Schneider, Jr., *Arms, Men, and Military Budgets: Issues for Fiscal Year 1979* (New York: Crane, Russak, 1978), pp. 36–38.

[22]For an exaggerated estimate of nuclear weapons' equalizing effect, see Pierre M. Gallois, *The Balance of Terror* (Boston: Houghton Mifflin, 1961).

[23]See Klaus Knorr, *On the Uses of Military Power in the Nuclear Age* (Princeton, N.J.: Princeton University Press, 1966).

could trigger superpower involvement and confrontation. Both the Soviet Union and the United States would be under great pressure to "do something" to help their allies. While aware of the risks, Soviet and U.S. leaders might nonetheless be drawn into the conflict for fear that otherwise their past political, military, and economic investments in the regions would be wasted, their interests sacrificed, and their "reputations for action" ruined. But by responding, the superpower could set in motion an upward spiral of response and counterresponse, of initial entanglement and increased commitment, that may result in a direct confrontation between them.[24]

Though present already, the risk of miscalculation on the part of the two superpowers also may be higher in situations involving newly nuclearized regions—again enhancing the chances of unwanted confrontation. In this new environment, either superpower may modify in unexpected ways its traditional assessment of the stakes, its preferred responses, or its readiness to run risks. Thus, whatever lessons about the other superpower's thinking and responses have been learned from prior regional crises may no longer be fully applicable. And this uncertainty could be most pronounced and most dangerous in the uncharted territory after the next use of nuclear weapons.

Nuclear weapons are likely to increase the tempo of events in regional crises and conflicts, thereby exacerbating further the potential for superpower entanglement and confrontation. For instance, because of the technical deficiencies of their nuclear forces—especially their vulnerability to surprise attack—some, if not many, new nuclear powers will be under considerable pressure to act quickly before their nuclear forces are put out of action. Or, with limited command and control of those nuclear forces if nuclear weapons are used, the pace of the ensuing conflict may be very rapid, with few opportunities to call a halt until the nuclear arsenals of regional opponents are depleted. Finally, because of the destructiveness of nuclear weapons,

the threats to the very survival of allies may arise far sooner than when conflicts involved only conventional weapons. Consequently, the superpowers may have to choose quite soon—and probably with even less information than usual—whether to act, and how, or whether to stand aside. And once involved to protect an ally or friend, the superpowers may be overtaken by the heightened tempo of events and pulled into confrontation.

The United States and the Soviet Union undoubtedly will be aware of the risk of confrontation arising out of continued competitive involvement in newly nuclearized regions. Nonetheless, they probably will refuse to sacrifice perceived regional interests, assuming instead that, if needed, they will be able to disengage from a regional conflict before events get out of control. But uncertainty about when to cut losses and disengage as well as the superpowers' declining capability to influence, let alone control, regional events threaten to falsify that assumption. To an unprecedented degree, the actions of regional nuclear powers may force the hand of the superpowers and set in motion a chain of events culminating in a military confrontation that neither the United States nor the Soviet Union wanted but that both are unable to prevent.

Fallout in Western Europe

More widespread proliferation also will reduce the freedom of action of the countries of Western Europe, many of which are involved diplomatically, politically, and in a few instances, militarily in regions to which nuclear weapons may spread. To illustrate, French advisers are stationed throughout Africa in countries ranging from Gabon to the Ivory Coast, while French troops intervened in Zaire and Chad in the 1970s. There is also a sizable French naval force in the Indian Ocean, and France has strengthened its ties to Saudi Arabia since it assisted the Saudi government in putting down the aborted seizure of the Grand Mosque in Mecca by a fanatical Moslem sect in 1979. Both French and British naval forces have been tacitly cooperating with those of the United States to buttress the Western presence in the Indian Ocean. And, although it has been reluctant to meet U.S. requests for sup-

[24] A classic discussion of these risks and uncertainties is Stanley Hoffman, "Nuclear Proliferation and World Politics," in *A World of Nuclear Powers?*, ed. Alastair Buchan (Englewood Cliffs, N.J.: Prentice-Hall, 1966), pp. 96–109.

port in the Persian Gulf, West Germany has in the past few years begun to play a more active diplomatic role in the Middle East.

But concern about even indirect entanglement in crises or confrontations that could involve the use of nuclear weapons may make policymakers in these countries more cautious in extending existing political, economic, or military ties. Domestic pressures against heightened involvement could grow as well. Moreover, because of this fear, these policymakers might be even more reluctant to support U.S. military initiatives and may not permit use of facilities and bases on their territories, or agree to reallocate or transship material and supplies, or provide military forces.

As well, these Western European countries might be the targets of nuclear blackmail intended to make them stand aside in such clashes or withdraw previously offered assistance. For example, in the midst of an Arab-Israeli conflict in the late 1980s, Egypt, Iraq, or Libya could anonymously threaten to detonate a nuclear weapon previously smuggled into Portugal unless that country rescinded landing rights at air bases in the Azores for U.S. planes on their way to Israel with needed military equipment. Or West Germany might be the target of such an anonymous nuclear threat in an indirect effort to prevent the United States from shipping military equipment from NATO stocks to the Middle East. Besides, once nuclear weapons are more widely available, it could be quite difficult to distinguish a hoax from a serious threat, and, thus, even a hoax might suffice to disrupt such U.S. operations for a time.

Under certain conditions further proliferation also would increase considerably the cost and difficulty for France and Britain of maintaining a credible nuclear deterrent against the Soviet Union,[25] Confronted by a growing threat to their homelands from

new nuclear powers, or believing that such a threat was likely to emerge by the 1990s, the superpowers might renegotiate the 1972 ABM Treaty and deploy ballistic missile defenses.[26] But to counter that change, these medium nuclear powers would have to develop and deploy costly and technically demanding systems able to penetrate those more extensive Soviet missile defenses. Failure to do so would lead to the increasing obsolescence of the French and British nuclear forces.[27]

DOMESTIC POLITICAL REPERCUSSIONS

Nuclear-Armed Terrorists, Irredentists, and Separatists

A considerably greater risk that terrorist and dissident groups will gain access to nuclear weapons will be another adverse consequence of the further spread of nuclear weapons.[28] As more countries seek to acquire a nuclear weapons option by initiating sensitive reprocessing or enrichment activities, or set up actual weapons programs, the number of sites from which these groups could steal nuclear weapons material for a bomb will increase.[29] The ensuing transportation of such material between a growing number of sites will further increase the risk of theft. Once a group possesses nuclear weapons material, the technical hurdles of processing that material and fabricating a nuclear weapon still would have to be overcome, but at least for some groups these difficulties would not be insurmountable. More important, a subnational group might opt for stealing the bomb itself, taking advantage of the probably less-than-adequate physical security measures of some new nuclear forces.

[25]For a generic discussion of the problem see Geoffrey Kemp, *Nuclear Forces for Medium Powers, Part I: Targets and Weapons Systems, Parts II and III: Strategic Requirements and Options,* Adelphi Papers nos. 106 and 107 (London: The International Institute for Strategic Studies, 1974); see also Peter Nailor and Jonathan Alford, *The Future of Britain's Deterrent Force,* Adelphi Paper no. 156 (London: The International Institute for Strategic Studies, 1980).

[26]On the significance of this restriction, see Nailor and Alford, *The Future of Britain's Deterrent Force,* pp. 10, 22–23.
[27]China's nuclear force would be similarly threatened with obsolescence by a Soviet missile defense capability.
[28]The most thorough discussion of these issues remains Theodore B. Taylor and Mason Willrich, *Nuclear Theft: Risks and Safeguards* (Cambridge, Mass.: Ballinger, 1974).
[29]The widespread civilian reprocessing, transportation, and commercial use of plutonium poses a comparable, if not greater, risk. See ibid.; R. Jeffrey Smith, "Reprocessing May Pose Weapons Threat," *Science* 209, July 11, 1980.

Hit-and-run clandestine terrorist groups, such as the Japanese Red Army, extreme left-wing Palestinian factions, the Italian Red Brigade, the Irish Republican Army (IRA), or successors to the Baader-Meinhof gang, may well regard a nuclear weapon as a means of extorting money or political concessions from a government, much as taking hostages is now.[30] The countries of Western Europe, Japan, and the United States will be especially vulnerable to terrorist threats or attack because of their open societies. A group such as the IRA, claiming to represent a legitimate alternative government and dependent on popular support, might stop short of carrying out a nuclear threat even if its demands were not met. But members of the more radical and nihilistic fringe movements, such as the successors to the Baader-Meinhof gang and the Japanese Red Army, might think otherwise. To them, carrying out the threat might appear justified as a means of bringing down corrupt bourgeois society in a spasm of violence. Or, in the eyes of the most extreme Palestinian groups, use of a nuclear weapon might be thought justified as a way of mortally wounding Israel. Yet again, with the police closing in on them, these more radical, isolated terrorists could conclude that, since all was lost, it would be preferable to fall in a nuclear *Götterdämmerung*. Such a decision would be consistent with the near-suicide mentality shown in some past terrorist actions.[31]

In contrast, the theft and threatened use of nuclear weapons may not appear a worthwhile tactic to a group such as the Palestinian Liberation Organization (PLO). Even though the PLO's freedom of action has been reduced by the Lebanese civil war, it still controls territory, administers to its refugee population, has a military force, and has been recognized by international bodies and foreign governments. Rather than enhancing the PLO's claim that it is a legitimate government in exile, possession of a few stolen nuclear weapons could have the opposite effect. Theft of nuclear weapons would reinforce the PLO's reputation for extremism and unwillingness to accept minimal norms of international behavior and would make it harder for those Western European governments moving closer to the PLO's position on the Middle East to sustain that shift. Besides, should Israeli intelligence manage to locate these nuclear weapons, pressures to carry out a preventive strike, disregarding the risk of Soviet counteraction, would be intense. If Israel could not locate the nuclear weapons but knew that the PLO had them, the result is not likely to be Israeli acceptance of the need for a Palestinian state but Israeli unwillingness to compromise on that PLO demand. On balance, therefore, the costs to the PLO of stealing nuclear weapons appear to outweigh the benefits. Still, that conclusion reflects a Western weighing of costs and gains, which may prove as unfounded in this instance of Middle East maneuverings as it has on earlier occasions.

Separatist movements such as the Kurds or Arabs in Iran, the Baluchis in Pakistan, the Bengalis in India, the Moslems in the Philippines, or even the Basques in Spain might be more inclined to steal and threaten to use a nuclear weapon. For example, a separatist Baluchi movement might threaten to use stolen Pakistani nuclear weapons if the Pakistani central government mounted a new military campaign to restore its authority. Though extreme, such a threat would not be out of line with the bitter fighting so characteristic of these struggles for greater autonomy. Fearful of the consequences of cracking down on the separatists and under international and domestic pressure to find a "reasonable" settlement, the central government might come to terms with that group. Conversely,

[30]Among recent writings on this issue of subnational groups' access to nuclear weapons, see Roberta Wohlstetter, "Terror on a Grand Scale," *Survival* (May–June 1976); Brian Jenkins, "Will Terrorists Go Nuclear?" California Seminar on Arms Control and Foreign Policy, October 1975; David M. Rosenbaum, "Nuclear Terror," *International Security* 1, no. 3 (Winter 1977). For an earlier but very suggestive analysis, also see George H. Quester, "The Politics of Twenty Nuclear Powers," in *The Future of the International Strategic System*, ed. Richard Rosecrance (San Francisco: Chandler, 1972), pp. 66–73.

[31]Many of these actions in the Middle East are reviewed in Edward Weisband and Damir Roguly, "Palestinian Terrorism: Violence, Verbal Strategy, and Legitimacy," in *International Terrorism: National, Regional and Global Perspectives*, ed. Yonah Alexander (New York: Praeger, 1976), pp. 258–310.

the central government could conclude that the costs of yielding to the separatists' demands were so great that it had no choice but to strike back, even using its own nuclear weapons against those of the separatists. But with little to lose, the Baluchis—and other separatist groups in other countries—might be ready to take that chance.[32]

The Nuclear Coup d'Etat

In the 1980s and early 1990s, politically unstable new nuclear powers—such as Argentina, Brazil, Chile, Egypt, Iran, Iraq, Libya, Nigeria, Pakistan, South Korea, and Syria—might be vulnerable to nuclear coups d'etat.[33] Particularly if the balance of political and military power between the rebels and the government were unclear, control of nuclear weapons—as compelling a symbol and instrument of national power as control of the airport, capital city, or radio and television stations—could greatly enhance the rebels' bargaining position. Control of nuclear weapons would change the psychological climate and afford rebel groups a means not only of demoralizing opponents but also of rallying supporters. The specter of nuclear destruction—should the situation get out of hand—quite possibly might lead civilian and military fence-sitters to come out in favor of a coup and even change the minds of some anti-coup forces. Moreover, just a few nuclear weapons in rebel hands could suffice to deter attack against them, assuming that the government was both unwilling to overwhelm the rebels with conventional force lest they retaliate with nuclear weapons and reluctant to use nuclear weapons first on its own territory in a surprise disarming attack. Consequently, more so than

in past coups, efforts to dislodge such rebels would remain a test of wills and bargaining strategy. Nevertheless, nuclear weapons might be employed, either intentionally, by accident, or out of contempt and hatred.

Already on at least one occasion during the first decades of the nuclear age, access to nuclear weapons has figured in a domestic political upheaval. In April 1961, French army forces stationed in Algiers rebelled, demanding that the government in Paris reverse its decision to grant independence to Algeria. At the time, French scientists were preparing to test a nuclear weapon at the French Saharan test site at Reganne, Algeria, not too far from Algiers. Noting the proximity of the rebellion, the scientists called on the general in charge at Reganne to authorize an immediate test and thus avoid the possibility that the nuclear device would be seized by the rebel troops and used for bargaining leverage.[34] Three days after the outbreak of the revolt, the order to detonate the device came directly from French President de Gaulle; there was no attempt to undertake precise experiments, only to use up all the available fissionable material.

Further, the prospect that a country's nuclear weapons might fall into the "wrong hands" could even provoke outside military intervention. A neighboring country, for example, might launch a disarming attack or, if time and the situation permitted, try to transport the entire nuclear arsenal out of the country.[35] Direct military support for a government confronted by a coup, or support for a countercoup to evict the radicals after a coup occurred, also might be offered. Thus, the nuclear coup d'etat is yet another flash point for regional conflict and possible nuclear escalation.

[32]George Quester first pointed to this aspect of the impact of nuclear weapon proliferation on domestic political life. See Quester, "The Politics of Twenty Nuclear Powers," pp. 66–70.

[33]For a more detailed discussion of how nuclear weapons could come to play a role in military coups, with descriptions of past coups, see Lewis A. Dunn, "Military Politics, Nuclear Proliferation, and the 'Nuclear Coup d'Etat,' " *The Journal of Strategic Studies* 1, no. 1 (May 1978), pp. 41–46. See also Edward Luttwak, *Coup d'Etat* (New York: Knopf, 1969); Kennedy, *The Military in the Third World,* passim.

[34]D. G. Brennan, "The Risks of Spreading Weapons: A Historical Case," *Arms Control and Disarmament,* vol. 1 (n.p., 1968), pp. 59–60.

[35]In a somewhat comparable situation, just before the fall of South Vietnam in 1975, the United States removed and flew out of the country the nuclear materials in South Vietnam's one operating research reactor to prevent their seizure by North Vietnam.

The Corrosion of Liberal Democracies?

At least some of the measures required to deal with the threats of clandestine nuclear attack—whether from a terrorist group or a new nuclear power—and of nuclear black marketing will be in tension with or in outright violation of the civil liberties procedures and underlying values of Western liberal democracies.[36] For example, to hinder clandestine efforts by a subnational group or a new nuclear power to introduce, move, or make ready a preplaced nuclear device, strong restrictions on movements into, out of, and within the United States and other open societies are likely to be adopted. An intelligence warning of an attempt to smuggle a bomb into the southwestern United States might be followed by a temporary ban on private flying in that region. New laws might be enacted as well to control more tightly the registration of aliens currently in the United States with ties to other countries, to facilitate the expulsion of both legal and illegal aliens with possible connections to terrorist or black market organizations, and to regulate more stringently the movements of aliens within this country.

Because of the stakes, there will be strong pressures to circumvent or set aside—in the United States and elsewhere—various constitutional and legal restrictions on invasions of privacy or other traditional civil liberties.[37] Unauthorized, warrantless emergency searches based on skimpy evidence or tips might be made. Or broad neighborhood—even city-wide— searches may become legitimate in these instances, although existing laws in many countries, particularly the Fourth and Fourteenth Amendments in the United States, prohibit searches without specific definition of the site and evidence sought. The use of informants, warrantless or illegal wiretaps, and the secret detention and questioning of suspects for days or even weeks might follow, all motivated by the need to acquire information as fast as possible. Highly coercive interrogation methods, ranging from painless but effective truth serum drugs to more extreme forms of physical deprivation and psychological disorientation, even to more brutal forms of torture, are not precluded. Further, limited press censorship to avert public panic and resultant pressures to make concessions, or simply to avoid tipping one's hand to the opponent, might be instituted.

Some countries acknowledged to be liberal democracies already have adopted some of these measures to deal with conventional terrorist threats. The British Parliament's Northern Ireland Act of 1973, for example, allows for detention without warrant, while in West Germany there are restrictions on the right to counsel for members of terrorist groups.[38] Even in the United States there have been past abridgments of civil liberties reluctantly justified as necessary to preserve the overall fabric and underlying democratic values. Thus, faced with an extreme nuclear threat, a future U.S. president may argue successfully, as did Lincoln during the Civil War when he suspended the writ of habeas corpus, "Are all the laws, but one, to go unexecuted, and the government itself to go to pieces, lest that one be violated?"[39]

However, it may prove possible to contain this challenge to liberal democratic procedures and values. Within the United States, both rigorous administrative supervision of any emergency measures and strict judicial review after the fact would help prevent those measures from spilling over their

---

[36]See Russell W. Ayres, "Policing Plutonium: The Civil Liberties Fallout," *Harvard Civil Rights–Civil Liberties Review* 10 (1975); Alan F. Westin, "Civil Liberties Implications of U.S. Domestic Safeguards," in Office of Technology Assessment, *Nuclear Proliferation and Safeguards*, app. 3–C, pp. 127–181; Paul Wilkinson, "Terrorism versus Liberal Democracy—The Problems of Response," *Conflict Studies*, no. 67, January 1976; Joseph W. Bishop, "Can Democracy Defend Itself against Terrorism?" *Commentary* 65, no. 5 (May 1978).

[37]See especially Ayres, "Policing Plutonium," pp. 413–424.

[38]Bishop, "Can Democracy Defend Itself against Terrorism?" p. 58; Irene Dische, "West Germany's War on Terrorism," *Inquiry* 1, no. 16, June 26, 1978, p. 17.

[39]Abraham Lincoln, "Special Message to Congress, 1861," in *Abraham Lincoln: Selected Speeches, Messages, and Letters,* ed. T. Harry Williams (New York: Holt Rinehart, 1957), p. 156.

boundaries and corrupting procedures in other areas of law enforcement. Authorizing legislation and official policy statements also could stress the extraordinary character of those restrictions as a response to an exceptional threat while reemphasizing the more basic American belief in the worth, dignity, and sanctity of the individual that underlies respect for particular civil liberties.

But if the frequency of proliferation-related threats grows, and if violations of traditional civil liberties cease to be isolated occurrences, it will become more difficult to check this corrosion of liberal democracy here and elsewhere. For that reason, as well, concern about the many adverse consequences of increasingly widespread nuclear weapons proliferation is well founded.

Regional Conflicts and Nuclear Fears
K. Subrahmanyam

In the current international environment it is difficult to define a local conflict. From the end of World War II until the end of the Falklands confrontation there have been 148 conflicts and barring perhaps ten all have taken place in the developing world. In 64 of the wars that took place up to the end of 1976 there were interventions by capitalist countries, in six by socialist countries and in 17 by other Third World countries.[1] Similarly, the Brookings Institution has calculated that there were 215 instances of use of force without war by the United States between 1946 and 1975,[2] and 195 instances by the Soviet Union.[3]

The Stockholm International Peace Research Institute (SIPRI) has calculated that between 1978 and 1982 only 3.6 percent of the Third World's arms supplies originated in those countries; the rest came from the industrialized nations.[4] Obviously, most of the conflicts in the Third World can be

sustained over a period of time only through overt or covert support from the developed countries. It is therefore difficult to define a strictly local conflict in the poorer countries. Most Third World conflicts are linked with superpower confrontation or with some regional hegemonic power which in turn leans on a superpower for supply of weapons and equipment.

Nuclear weapons can play a part in Third World conflicts in two ways: a recognized nuclear weapon power can threaten to use the weapon in the conflict situation; a clandestine nuclear power such as Israel or South Africa may do so. The U.S. declaration in regard to the use of nuclear weapons highlights this possibility. The declaration guarantees:

not to use nuclear weapons against any nonnuclear weapon state party to the Nonproliferation Treaty or any comparable international binding commitment not to acquire nuclear explosive devices, except in the case of an attack on the United States, its territories or armed forces or its allies by such a state allied to a nuclear weapon state or associated with a nuclear weapon state in carrying out or sustaining the attack.[5]

[1]Istvan Kende, "Wars of Ten Years," *Journal of Peace Research*, 15, no. 3 (1978).

[2]Barry M. Blechman and Stephen S. Kaplan, *Force without War* (Washington, D.C.: The Brookings Institution, 1978).

[3]Stephen S. Kaplan, *Diplomacy of Power: Soviet Armed Forces as a Political Instrument* (Washington, D.C.: The Brookings Institution, 1981).

[4]Stockholm International Peace Research Institute, *SIPRI Yearbook 1983* (London: Taylor & Francis, 1983), p. 272.

[5]CD/139 quoted in the U.N. "Report on Nuclear Weapons" (1980).

The phrase "associated with a nuclear weapon state" can be interpreted according to one's convenience and inclination. The attack by an adversary state need not be a nuclear attack to justify a U.S. resort to nuclear weapons. Also, the declaration leaves it vague whether an attack on U.S. armed forces would also include a counterattack by a country if the United States had launched the first attack.

The United States considered the possible use of nuclear weapons in Vietnam, after the fall of Dien Bien Phu and in the Quemoy-Matsu crisis, which was a local clash between China and Taiwan; and there was a nuclear alert during the Arab-Israeli war.[6] Use of nuclear weapons was also contemplated during the Korean and Vietnam wars.[7] In all these cases the adversary had no nuclear weapons. The interventionism of the industrialized nations—most especially the superpowers—and their tendency to resort to nuclear threats are the primary causes underlying Third World nuclear insecurity. Apologists for intervention often seek to obfuscate this issue by suggesting that prestige is the most important factor in proliferation.

The other source of nuclear threats in the Third World lies in the clandestine nuclear arsenals in the hands of nations like Israel. Pakistan is attempting to reach nuclear weapons capability. As Stephen Cohen of the University of Illinois writes:

> Pakistan belongs to that class of states whose very survival is uncertain, whose legitimacy is doubted and whose security related resources are inadequate. Yet these states will not go away, nor can they be ignored. Pakistan (like Taiwan, South Korea, Israel and South Africa) has the capacity to fight, to go nuclear, to influence the global strategic balance (if only by collapsing).[8]

The states mentioned above have close links with the United States, and their military establishments are to a considerable extent influenced by U.S. military doctrines. The only other developing nations that fall into the category of near-nuclear weapon powers are India, Argentina and Brazil.

It has been fashionable among certain Western writers to stress the possible dangers of developing nations acquiring nuclear weapons, while they maintain that such weapons in the hands of five recognized nuclear-weapon powers are quite safe. But historical evidence does not support this view. Indians and Pakistanis, Arabs and Israelis, have fought a number of wars. Deplorable as they are, relatively speaking they were fought with a great degree of restraint, unlike the war in Vietnam where more explosives—the equivalent of many megatons—were used than in all history up to that time. Genocidal bombing was part of the Western conventional military doctrine, including the destruction of cities through thousand-bomber raids, a doctrine that led logically to Nagasaki and Hiroshima. Seymour Hersh in his book *The Price of Power* recorded a drunken President talking of "nuking" the Vietnamese.[9]

Those who try to frighten the world with the idea of nuclear bombs in the hands of irresponsible Third World rulers should ponder the equal risks of these weapons in the control of the developed nations. Daniel Ellsberg has written about the authority to use nuclear weapons having been delegated since the days of President Eisenhower.[10] There has been talk of "prior release" orders in regard to tactical nuclear weapons if the threat of use of nuclear weapons in a tactical scenario is to be credible at all.[11] There is no reason to believe that the leadership of any developing country is likely to be more rash in resorting to the weapons than the leadership in the industrialized countries.

[6]The threats, other than that of 1973, are listed with original citations in K. Subrahmanyam, "The Role of Nuclear Weapons in International Relations," *The Institute for Defense Studies and Analyses Journal* 3, no. 1 (July 1970).

[7]*Ibid.*

[8]Stephen P. Cohen, "Pakistan," in *Security Policies of Developing Countries*, Edward A. Kolodziej and Robert Harkavy, eds. (Lexington, Massachusetts: Lexington Books, 1982), p. 94.

[9]Seymour Hersh, *The Price of Power* (New York: Summit Books, 1983), p. 396.

[10]Daniel Ellsberg, interview in *Nuclear Armaments* (Berkeley, California: The Conservation Press, 1980).

[11]Lord [Solly] Zuckerman in *Dangers of Nuclear War*, Franklyn Griffiths and John C. Polanyi, eds. (Toronto: University of Toronto Press, 1979), pp. 164–65.

Kenneth Waltz, in "The Spread of Nuclear Weapons: More May be Better," writes:

New nuclear states will confront the possibilities and feel the constraints that present nuclear states have experienced. New nuclear states will be more concerned for their safety and more mindful of dangers than some of the old ones have been. . . . While nuclear weapon powers have spread, conventional weapons have proliferated. Under these circumstances wars have been fought not at the centre but at the periphery of international politics. The likelihood of war decreases as deterrent and defensive capabilities increase. Nuclear weapons, responsibly used, make wars hard to start. Nations that have nuclear weapons have strong incentives to use them responsibly. These statements hold for small as for big nuclear powers. Because they do, the measured spread of nuclear weapons is more to be welcomed than feared.[12]

As pointed out earlier, the risks of the recognized nuclear weapon nations using the weapons in intervention operations in the developing world remain significant. China and the Soviet Union have offered a no-first-use pledge while the Western powers maintain their first-use doctrine, not necessarily restricted to the European context or even to nuclear adversaries. The use of nuclear weapons in certain contingencies in the Korean Peninsula and in the Persian Gulf region has been discussed in various examples of strategic literature.[13] Analysts estimate that Israel has perhaps 200 nuclear warheads.[14] Given Israel's superiority in sophisticated conventional weapons and the U.S. commitment to Israel, the probability of that state being compelled to resort to nuclear weapons against its Arab neighbors appears to be low. South Korea currently has no access to weapons-grade plutonium and may not be able to produce nuclear weapons of its own in the near future. Taiwan can, but since its adversary is China, with enormous nuclear capability, it would appear that Taiwanese weapons if they are produced at all will be used only as a deterrent to resist forcible annexation by China.

Even if Brazil or Argentina should acquire nuclear weapons it is difficult to envisage contingencies in which they will find it necessary or advantageous to use them. The British deployment of nuclear submarines and the torpedoing of the *General Belgrano* may persuade the Argentinians of the advantages of nuclear-propelled submarines but their use of nuclear weapons does not appear to be a rational possibility.

Again in the Indo-Pakistani context, if both countries were to develop nuclear weapons, probability favors an evolving situation of stable mutual deterrence. India is a *status quo* power which does not favor any alteration of existing boundaries by use of force. Within Pakistan the view that the problem of Kashmir should be left for a future generation to settle is gaining ground. There is clear realization in Pakistan that if it were to go nuclear India would overtake it both in size and sophistication of arsenals.

The history of the last four wars shows that neither side is inclined to resort to indiscriminate and excessive use of force even under war conditions. Millions of divided families live on both sides of the border and this will be one of the major restraining factors.

There has been concern in Israel about the development of a Pakistani nuclear arsenal and its being made available to an Arab country. This appears to be an exaggerated fear for two reasons. One is that the Arabs are aware of the size and capability of Israel's nuclear arsenal, and many Arab capitals are within striking distance of Israel. The other is that Pakistan knows full well that if a nuclear weapon was used against Israel the source of the weapon would be attributed to Pakistan, which might then face retaliation from the United States, whose nuclear forces are deployed in the Indian Ocean area. One may therefore rule out this eventuality also.

[12]Kenneth Waltz, "The Spread of Nuclear Weapons: More May Be Better," *Adelphi Paper* 171 (London: The International Institute for Strategic Studies, Autumn 1981).

[13]The Union of Concerned Scientists, *No First Use* (Feb. 1, 1983), Cambridge, Massachusetts.

[14]*Bangkok Post* (May 14, 1982).

That leaves the possibility of South Africa's use of nuclear weapons against the frontline black African states. This is the most credible among the scenarios in the developing world; racism and genocide go together. As the pressure on the South African white minority increases through armed struggle, the racist regime may attempt to blackmail neighboring states to prevent them from extending support to the freedom fighters within South Africa. Thus, the possibility of a nuclear "demonstration" cannot be ruled out.

Within the next 10 or 15 years the high probability of nuclear weapons use in the developing world arises only with respect to intervention operations by established nuclear powers against developing countries, and by South Africa against black African states. In the former case the neutron bomb, which produces high casualties with little collateral damage, may be a preferred weapon.

The Nuclear Non-Proliferation Treaty legitimizes the possession and use of nuclear weapons and unlimited vertical proliferation by the recognized nuclear weapon powers. It is highly probable that there has also been clandestine weapons production by Israel and South Africa. Seventeen nations have affirmed their right to resort to nuclear weapons, in defiance of the international community's demand that the use and threat of use of nuclear weapons be declared a crime against humanity.[15]

The vast literature on the so-called proliferation problem in the 1960s and 1970s has served to draw attention away from the galloping vertical proliferation in recognized nuclear arsenals and the existence of two clandestine nuclear arsenals. Most of the discussion about the use of nuclear weapons by countries which are not yet able to produce even a field gun—about their fabricating nuclear weapons with reactor-grade plutonium, which no nation in the world has ever done—appears to be an extension of the obfuscation exercise that started over 20 years ago.

There is an unconscious racial bias involved in the nuclear proliferation issue. The industrialized nations rely on nuclear war doctrines for their security but deny that right to other nations. The two clandestine nuclear powers who have gotten away with it are European-settled nations—Israel and South Africa. Many of the wars and major instances of inter- and intra-state violence in the developing world are attributed in part to the interventionism of the industrial powers, but a majority of those instances do not receive much attention in the literature. Of late, there is also a trend to focus excessive attention on the growth of defense industries in the developing world, even as the industrialized nations move into sophisticated technologies which are likely to make interventionist wars cheaper.

Nuclear weapons are unjustifiable in anyone's hands. The countries that occupied vast areas of the world during the colonial period and exploited the majority of humanity may be planning to use them in defiance of overwhelming international opinion. Their attempt at domination and perpetuation of the weapons culture must therefore be opposed with various measures, including development of deterrent nuclear weapons by nations which are victims of such domination.

Those who support the legitimacy of nuclear weapons in the hands of a few nations by supporting the Non-Proliferation Treaty cannot logically and credibly preach that other nations cannot have them. The argument that the Treaty constituted a step-by-step approach to a disarmed world is patently fallacious, as witnessed by the galloping vertical proliferation since it went into effect.[16] The fact that it has been accepted by a large number of nations does not make it any more legitimate than imperialism, which was also accepted by a world majority in its day.

The Non-Proliferation Treaty is pernicious because it legitimizes the use of nuclear weapons by

[15]U.N. General Assembly, Resolution 36/92, Dec. 9, 1981.

[16]Between 1968, when the Non-Proliferation Treaty was signed, and 1982 the number of nuclear weapons (warheads) in the hands of the United States and the Soviet Union rose from 5,350 to 19,000. Ground Zero, *Nuclear War: What's in It for You?* (New York: Pocket Books, 1982), Table C-1.

a few weapon powers. Unless it is resisted, more and more nations will be compelled to accept the legitimacy of nuclear weapons use. It will be argued that there is a rising trend of opinion in favor of "no first use." But even as this trend has developed there are discussions on the use of nuclear weapons in areas where nations—Iran and South Korea, for example—have acceded to the Treaty. Armed forces are being increasingly nuclearized and nuclear war-fighting doctrines are being advanced. The anti-nuclear feeling in Western Europe and North America, which is as yet not potent enough to have an impact on government policies, is welcome, but it is not a sufficient assurance to the developing world that nuclear weapons will not be used. It was when anti-imperialist feeling was widespread and imperialism was retreating that the bloodiest colonial wars—in Algeria, Vietnam, Southern Africa—occurred.

While murder is recognized as a crime, killing in self-defense is considered to be legitimate. If it is lawful for a few nations, which have a record of imperialist behavior and which continue their hegemonism, to have nuclear weapons so should it be for others—especially in self-defense against interventionism.

Those interested in reducing the danger of nuclear weapons use by interventionist powers and the two clandestine nuclear powers should mobilize collectively to make nuclear weapons illegal. Such a move would be mostly directed against the existing arsenals because, with a few exceptions, the developing nations are in no position to develop nuclear weapons. A delegitimization campaign needs two essential steps:

● There must be pressure on the NATO nations and their allies to join the rest of the international community in declaring in the U.N. General Assembly that threat of use, and the actual use, of nuclear weapons are crimes against humanity. These states should accede to the proposed convention to ban the use of nuclear weapons along the lines of the Geneva Convention on chemical weapons.

● If the NATO nations and their allies do not take this step, the developing nations which are

signatories to the Non-Proliferation Treaty should serve notice that they will withdraw from the Treaty.

The Treaty can be deemed legitimate only if it is universally accepted that use and threat of use of nuclear weapons are illegal and there is a time-bound program on the part of the nuclear weapon powers to reduce their arsenals. Otherwise the Treaty will continue to be an instrument to legalize nuclear arsenals and unlimited proliferation.

Since most of the signatories to the Treaty are not in a position to acquire nuclear weapons, their accession to the treaty has only served to legitimize nuclear arsenals and their vertical proliferation. The withdrawal of these countries from the Treaty will not add to proliferation risks. Rather, it will constitute a political protest against the continuing proliferation of nuclear weapons and attempts to legitimize them. In this way, the weakness of the non-nuclear nations can be converted into strength. The threat to withdraw should reinforce the peace movements in those nations whose governments continue to assert the legitimacy of use and threat of use of nuclear weapons.

The Secretary General of the Organization of African Unity has urged that African nations develop nuclear weapons as a deterrent against South Africa,[17] but that is not feasible. The collective threat by the African states to withdraw from the Treaty would be a more credible way to work toward making nuclear weapons illegal.

QUESTIONS FOR DISCUSSION

1. Is the NPT discriminatory?
2. Would third-world leaders be more or less responsible than the leaders of the superpowers in not using nuclear weapons in war?
3. What would be the effect of horizontal proliferation on the chances of nuclear war's occurring between the superpowers?

---

[17]*Hindu* (Madras, June 11, 1983), quotes from Edem Kodjo, outgoing Secretary-General of the Organization of African Unity, speaking at Addis Ababa.

4. What effect would the possession of nuclear weapons by third-world nations have on the political and military behavior of the superpowers?
5. What would be the effect of horizontal proliferation on the possibilities of an accidental nuclear war?

SUGGESTED READINGS

Beres, Louis René (ed.). *Security or Armageddon: Israel's Nuclear Strategy*. Lexington, Massachusetts: Lexington Books, 1985.

Brito, Dagobert, Michael D. Intriligator, and Adele E. Wick (eds.). *Strategies for Managing Nuclear Proliferation*. Lexington, Massachusetts: Lexington Books, 1983.

Clausen, Peter A. "Nonproliferation Illusions: Tarapur in Retrospect," *Orbis* 27 (Fall 1983), pp. 741–59.

Day, Samuel H. Jr. "The Afrikaner Bomb," *The Progressive* (September 1982), pp. 22–31.

Dorian, Thomas F. "Covert Nuclear Trade and the International Nonproliferation Regime," *Journal of International Affairs* 35 (Spring-Summer 1981), pp. 29–68.

Dunn, Lewis A. *Controlling the Bomb: Nuclear Proliferation in the 1980s*. New Haven, Connecticut: Yale University Press, 1982.

Feldman, Shai. "The Bombing of Osiraq--Revisited," *International Security* 7 (Fall 1982), pp. 114–42.

Finkelstein, Amy. "Brazil, the United States and Nuclear Nonproliferation: American Foreign Policy at the Crossroads," *The Fletcher Forum* (Summer 1983), pp. 277–311.

Jones, Rodney W. (ed.). *Small Nuclear Forces and U. S. Security Policy: Threats and Potential Conflict in the Middle East and South Asia*. Lexington, Massachusetts: Lexington Books, 1984.

Kimura, Hiroshi. "Arms Control in East Asia," in Adam M. Garfinkle (ed.), *Global Perspectives on Arms Control*. New York: Praeger, 1984, pp. 113–32.

Miller, Judith. "Trying Harder to Stop the Bomb," *The New York Times Magazine* (September 12, 1982), pp. 108–10 and 112–17.

Quester, George H. "Nuclear Proliferation," in Bernard Brodie, Michael D. Intriligator, and Roman Kolkowicz (eds.). *National Security and International Stability*. Cambridge, Massachusetts: Oelgeschlager, Gunn & Hain, 1983, pp. 227–55.

———. "Nuclear Proliferation in Latin America," *Current History* 81 (February 1982), pp. 52–55.

Spector, Leonard S. *Nuclear Proliferation Today: The Spread of Nuclear Weapons Today*. New York: Vintage, 1984.

U.S. Congress: House. *Legislation to Amend the Nuclear Non-Proliferation Act of 1978*. Hearings before the Subcommittee on International Security and Scientific Affairs and the Subcommittee of International Economic Policy and Trade of the Committee on Foreign Affairs, 97th Cong., 2nd Sess., 1982.

U.S. Congress: House. *Nuclear Proliferation: Dealing with Problem Countries*. Hearings before the Subcommittee on International Security and Scientific Affairs and the Subcommittee on International Economic Policy and Trade of the Committee on Foreign Affairs, 97th Cong., 1st Sess., 1981.

U.S. Congress: Senate. *U.S. Nuclear Nonproliferation Policy*. Hearings before the Committee on Foreign Relations, 97th Cong., 2nd Sess., 1982.

Waltz, Kenneth N. *The Spread of Nuclear Weapons: More May Be Better*. Adelphi Paper no. 171. London: International Institute for Strategic Studies, 1981.

Weltman, John J. "Managing Nuclear Multipolarity," *International Security* 6 (Winter 1981–82), pp. 182–94.

Willis, David K. "Nuclear Proliferation: Who's Next to Get the Bomb?" *Christian Science Monitor* (February 25, 1983), pp. 12–13.

19 Is the Quest for Nuclear Energy a Principal Dynamic in
the Spread of Nuclear Weapons?

YES

Victor Gilinsky

Nuclear Reactors and Nuclear Bombs

NO

Sir John Hill

The Driving Forces of Proliferation

Nuclear Reactors and Nuclear Bombs
Victor Gilinsky

For twenty-five years the conventional wisdom has been that the connection between civilian nuclear activities and the spread of nuclear weapons is at most a tenuous one and, in any event, is kept safely under control.

The fact is the link is a close one, an inconvenient reality that frequently intrudes on those who would deny it. The latest intrusion was the apparently unsuccessful bombing, at the onset of the Iran-Iraq war, of a French-built research reactor near Baghdad.[1] The objective of the air attack would appear to have been the French-supplied reactor fuel, 26 pounds of highly-enriched uranium suitable for use in nuclear weapons. Since then, the secret whereabouts and custody of the uranium has become a source of concern to governments throughout the world. The International Atomic Energy Agency [IAEA] inspectors who are supposed to keep track of the fuel, especially at critical times, were barred from entry into Iraq because of the fighting. Everyone involved was embarrassed. The IAEA, which had earlier stressed the peaceful character of the reactor and its openness to inspection, has set up a committee to study the problem of inspection in wartime.

ATOMS-FOR-PEACE

We were not always so naive about the dangers of nuclear energy. When we first began to think about nuclear energy for the generation of electricity, no one questioned that such a development had its dangerous side—that certain fuels and equipment could also be used to make bombs. That fact lay at the heart of our 1946 proposal to the United Nations for international control of nuclear energy.

It emphasized the need for international *ownership* of the dangerous activities—those most directly related to bombmaking—and stressed that mere international inspection could not cope with the dangers. For eight years following the failure of this proposal, the United States refused to share the details of nuclear technology even with allies who had participated in the wartime bomb project. Meanwhile, we pursued the possibilities of nuclear power in a leisurely fashion, as cheap fossil fuel made the new energy source only moderately interesting.

Then several events in 1953 caused us to lower our technical barriers dramatically. The British announced plans to build the world's first nuclear power station. Several countries, including India, announced intentions to follow suit. The Joint Committee on Atomic Energy held hearings on private nuclear power development and later that year, the Atomic Energy Commission received reports on the subject from four American industrial groups. Then, in August 1953, the Russians exploded a hydrogen bomb.

Soon thereafter, President Eisenhower announced the Atoms-for-Peace Program. He proposed a transfer of nuclear materials from the U.S. and Soviet military stockpiles to the United Nations for "peaceful uses." The President's primary objective was to introduce the idea of mutual reductions in U.S. and Soviet nuclear arsenals. But he was also influenced by the scientific and industrial ferment over the possibilities of civilian nuclear power.

The stockpile reduction proposal was rejected by the Soviet Union, but the rest of the program, which had raised expectations throughout the world, caught on and acquired a life of its own. Substantial U.S. assistance provided a vehicle for bilateral nuclear arrangements whose principal purpose was to serve

---

[1]This was written before the subsequent successful Israeli attack on this reactor.

Victor Gilinsky, "Nuclear Reactors and Nuclear Bombs," Remarks before the League of Women Voters Education Fund, Silver Spring, Maryland, Nov. 17, 1980, (Washington, D.C.: U.S. Nuclear Regulatory Commission, Office of Public Affairs).

political ends—moves on the American-Soviet chessboard. Under a particularly liberal agreement signed in 1958 with Euratom [European Atomic Energy Community], the U.S., anxious to encourage the European community, relinquished vital control over separation of plutonium from U.S.-supplied fuel.

Over thirty other agreements were signed and, before long, the world was dotted with American research reactors. Thousands of foreign engineers and scientists were trained at American laboratories and given free access to hitherto restricted nuclear technology; U.S. nuclear bureaucrats traveled the world, and reveled in their new importance; scientists were at last allowed to share information with their colleagues abroad; industrialists started dreaming of large U.S. exports; and the State Department enjoyed the expansion of American influence at the expense of the Soviets. There was little worry about the dangers, since all transactions were covered by "peaceful use" promises and were open to inspection by Euratom or the new IAEA.

All this astonished the Russians. Some months after President Eisenhower's U.N. speech, John Foster Dulles asked an aide about a remark by Molotov that the U.S. was making bomb material widely available. To the Secretary's surprise, the aide confirmed that Molotov was right.

But apparently it was too late for second thoughts about Atoms-for-Peace. From that time on, what had been characterized in the U.S. control proposals of 1946 as the "dangerous" aspects of nuclear power became merely "sensitive," requiring a little more attention, perhaps, but no longer regarded as inherently unprotectable by inspection alone. It was not a change in the technical facts that brought about this subtle shift. What had changed was the political and commercial climate, which left little room for any suggestion that nuclear power might threaten international security.

"DANGEROUS" ACTIVITIES IN THE NUCLEAR FUEL CYCLE

The technical facts, of course, remain unchanged to this day: nuclear power reactors and their fuel plants can be copious sources of nuclear explosives, both highly-enriched uranium and plutonium. The same techniques—and in some cases the same plants—used to produce slightly-enriched uranium fuel for power reactors can also be used to produce highly-enriched uranium for bombs. Even more significant in practical terms, the power reactors themselves produce plutonium as a by-product. For example, a standard power reactor produces about a kilogram of plutonium a day. That's about a bomb's worth a week.

The significance of this, as the former director of the Livermore weapons laboratory has pointed out, is that "the only difficult part of making a fission bomb of some sort is the preparation of a supply of fissionable material of adequate purity; the design of the bomb itself is relatively easy."

The plutonium is relatively inaccessible so long as it is locked within the radioactive spent fuel. The key for those wanting to make nuclear weapons lies, therefore, in separating the plutonium from the spent fuel in reprocessing plants. Once separated, the plutonium could be put to weapons use quickly, very likely before international inspectors could raise the alarm, and almost certainly before preventive action could be taken. Unlike power reactors, reprocessing plants, along with uranium enrichment plants, are therefore potential bomb factories, depending only on the intentions of their owners.

CONTROLS DETERIORATE

It is here that controls are sagging most seriously, particularly in the case of plutonium reprocessing. Even though these plants provide easy access to nuclear explosive materials, we are under increasing pressure to permit reprocessing in conjunction with commercial nuclear power operation, so long as the activity is covered by IAEA inspection. Incidentally, the reason we have any say in the matter at all is that most of the nuclear fuel in use today was supplied by the United States, which, except in the case of Euratom, reserves control over its disposition.

The Acheson-Lilienthal group, which drafted the original U.S. proposals for international control in 1946, was convinced that inspection alone could not prevent reprocessing plants from being used for military purposes. Their report stated that certain well-defined activities which were intrinsically dangerous should be prohibited to individual nations. Reprocessing was one of the activities on the "dangerous" list.

The Atoms-for-Peace program permanently altered that distinction between "safe" and "dangerous." Some U.S. officials were aware of the consequences of allowing "dangerous" nuclear technology to be included under the "peaceful" rubric, and tried to restrict the scope of allowed activities in drawing up the IAEA charter. But they ran into strong resistance, and the United States was reluctant to push too hard for fear the Atoms-for-Peace initiative would collapse. As a result, the requirement that nuclear activities under national control be "safe"—that is, technologically remote from nuclear bombs—was negotiated out of the IAEA Charter. It was replaced by the requirement that they be "peaceful," a label which does not explicitly rule out anything short of a bomb.

The idea of international safeguards as a means to prevent ready access to dangerous materials thus deteriorated into a system of inspection and measurement with no clear rationale, except perhaps to drop the cloak of legitimacy over nuclear commerce. In any case, the IAEA today is applying itself earnestly, where not excluded by wars, to the business of inspecting dangerous activities, the very arrangement the Acheson group characterized as unworkable.

THE PLUTONIUM BREEDER

A large share of the blame for this state of affairs has to land on our own doorstep. In the late 1950's we made plutonium separation technology widely available. Why we thought this was a safe proposition is still something of a mystery. At about the same time, interest intensified in the plutonium-fueled breeder reactor, and the idea of plutonium as the fuel of the future was passionately embraced throughout the world.

The breeder reactor is attractive because it uses much less uranium than present-day reactors do. Because the system depends on recycling plutonium extracted by reprocessing spent breeder fuel, the breeder can be a paying proposition when uranium is expensive and reprocessing is cheap. At the present time, however, the price of uranium is falling and reprocessing is expensive. But this has done little to loosen the grip of the plutonium breeder idea on the world's nuclear imagination. Any suggestion of more rigorous controls over plutonium is regarded as an assault on all that is beautiful, true and commercially promising, and is resisted accordingly. This explains the heavy bargaining that went on during the 1960's in the negotiation of the Non-Proliferation Treaty. West Germany, in particular, haggled for a year over the Treaty's safeguards in the hope of protecting commercial advantages in plutonium fuel manufacture.

The plutonium breeder was thought to be the key to energy problems even in some poor countries. Nowhere was this more true than in India, which fought the Non-Proliferation Treaty and refused to sign when it was completed in 1968. In 1974 it became clear why.

THE INDIAN BOMB AND ITS EFFECT ON U.S. POLICY

The NPT requires signatories other than the weapon states to give up the right to manufacture nuclear explosives. This would have been inconvenient for India, which was planning to divert plutonium from a research facility for use in a nuclear explosion. The plutonium was produced in a Canadian-built reactor, moderated with heavy water supplied by the United States. The use of these materials and facilities in the 1974 explosion was in direct violation of the pledges on peaceful use given Canada and the United States. After the explosion, Canada severed its nuclear relationship with India; the United

States remained silent. The use of U.S. heavy water was not revealed for two years, and then only at Congressional insistence.

The Indian bomb served as a disturbing reminder that separated plutonium is easily exploded and that reprocessing plants, which were then being ordered by a number of developing countries, provide easy access to a weapons option. The explosion also cast a new light on the news that France was contracting to sell a reprocessing plant to Pakistan, and that West Germany was selling reprocessing and enrichment technology to Brazil, another non-signatory to the NPT. These revelations triggered strong bipartisan pressure in Congress for a change in U.S. export policies.

This pressure was felt in the White House, and in October 1976, President Ford—in an important departure from past policy—announced that the United States would no longer regard the future use of plutonium as inevitable. He ordered a deferral of commercial reprocessing in the United States and urged other countries to pause in their own reprocessing activities until "the world community can effectively overcome the associated risks of proliferation." In April 1977, newly-elected President Carter promptly endorsed this position. The new Ford-Carter policy was in many ways a return to the common sense view of the Acheson-Lilienthal Report that the safe aspects of nuclear energy, such as uranium-fueled power reactors, needed to be separated from the dangerous ones.

OPPOSITION TO NEW POLICY

The Ford-Carter decision to defer reprocessing inevitably produced a storm of protest at home and abroad. It was resisted vehemently because it threatened ambitious American and European plans for large-scale commercial reprocessing and, therefore, future reliance on plutonium-fueled breeders. It also challenged the repeated insistence of the nuclear power community that nuclear weapons and commercial nuclear power had no relation to one another.

The decision on reprocessing never had much support in the nuclear bureaucracy. Our foreign affairs establishment was intimidated by the howls of pain and criticism from our allies and trading partners. Implementation of the new policy was diffident, inconsistent, and ultimately unpersuasive, succeeding mainly in convincing others we didn't know what we were doing. An indication of this was the reaction of the British and French, who were poised at the edge of heavy commercial commitments economically dependent on future U.S. reprocessing approvals. These two countries watched our performance, decided we were not serious, and proceeded with their billion dollar undertakings.

INTERNATIONAL NUCLEAR FUEL CYCLE EVALUATION

The situation was not helped by what was at best a political miscalculation. In an effort to soften the anticipated complaints and to persuade other nations to join in a deferral of reprocessing, President Carter launched an International Nuclear Fuel Cycle Evaluation [INFCE], inviting over 40 nations to join in a two-year study of the technical alternatives to plutonium. The result was hardly surprising: INFCE participants decided to stay on the course they had followed all along and, as predicted, "vindicated plutonium." Their report, which contained no serious discussion of safeguards, concluded that safeguarding of plutonium "can be readily carried out." As to the dangers of spreading nuclear explosives around the world, INFCE's view can only be characterized as mealymouthed: "The extent," the report states, "to which the possibilities of misuse vary as between fuel cycles is not easy to judge."

INFCE's economic conclusions were based on a preposterous set of projections which favored the economics of plutonium by putting the availability of uranium low and the future use of nuclear power high. INFCE's *low* projection for the next twenty years thus counted 23 nuclear plants planned by the Shah, 43 plants for Italy (a 30-fold increase in nuclear capacity), and some 60 plants for Brazil (a

100-fold increase in nuclear capacity). It also in-cluded about 100 more U.S. plants for the year 2000 than our own low projection.

Despite this dubious juggling of numbers, the commercial nuclear community obviously hopes that the credentials of the INFCE report will be sufficiently impressive, and its conclusions suffi-ciently persuasive, to force a final retreat from the U.S. decision to hold back on plutonium repro-cessing. The report may also prove a useful vehicle for an attack on the unpopular Nuclear Non-Pro-liferation Act of 1978.

NUCLEAR NON-PROLIFERATION ACT

In that Act, Congress tightened up on U.S. nuclear export controls, partly in response to the revela-tions of the Indian bomb. In a replay of the reaction to the Ford and Carter decisions to defer repro-cessing, there was strong resistance to the legis-lation from the outset. Its restrictions on trade were considered severe and unreasonable by our own nuclear industry and by many of our trading part-ners.

The Act for the first time forbids nuclear trade with any country not accepting international in-spection of all its nuclear facilities. Because such comprehensive inspection is the prerequisite for an effective international system of control, this pro-vision is universally regarded as a cornerstone of the new law.

In an historic irony, the first real test of the law's effectiveness came two years after its passage and involved an application for export of nuclear fuel from the Indian government. The application was denied unanimously by the Nuclear Regulatory Commission on grounds that India did not fulfill the legal requirement for comprehensive safe-guards, but President Carter exercised his prerog-ative to grant an exception authorizing the fuel shipment and sent his decision to Congress for re-view. There was high public interest in the ensuing battle in September 1980: almost 200 editorials appeared opposing the shipment. Although the House voted overwhelmingly against the export, the Sen-ate upheld the President by two votes and India got its fuel. The vote, in this "worst case" situation, did not augur well for the future of strict export controls. The Senate debate made clear that it was the law itself as much as the Indian question which was at issue.

Indeed, things are beginning to look bleak for such controls. The recent body blow to the new export law will soon be followed by an attempt to knock it out altogether. Hearings in the Congress have been scheduled for next spring on a Govern-ment Accounting Office report reviewing imple-mentation of the Act. Opponents of the law are seeking changes eliminating its so-called "retro-active provisions," thus preserving the trading *sta-tus quo* at the time of its enactment.

There is also talk of removing export licensing responsibility from what are regarded as the trou-blemakers at the Nuclear Regulatory Commission. This has been a long-time objective of the State Department, which has more than once encoun-tered opposition from NRC when it treated nuclear commerce as a diplomatic bargaining chip.

We will soon be confronted with requests from countries reprocessing U.S.-supplied fuel in France and Britain for permission to retrieve their sepa-rated plutonium. Such traffic in plutonium is the very thing we have been trying to prevent. And if more countries acquire reprocessing plants despite our efforts at discouragement, permission for in-digenous reprocessing of U.S.-supplied spent fuel will also be sought. In some cases, political exi-gencies will exert strong pressures for watering down the strict standards of the NNPA for such approvals. Once we go down that road, the concept of "safe" and "dangerous" activities cannot be re-tained—or rather reinstated—in any realistic at-tempt to prevent the further spread of nuclear weap-ons.

WHY IS THIS HAPPENING?

The problem is that attempts to control reprocess-ing run head-on into ambitious nuclear power plans and heavy investment worldwide. The seemingly-abstract concern about nuclear weapons spread is no match for the reality of the price rise of fossil fuels or the billion dollar stakes in commercial reprocessing facilities. Nuclear controls have never had any constituency but the old-fashioned, commonsense fear of blowing up the world.

The nuclear industry at home and abroad is worried by increased controls for a variety of reasons. Reduction in the growth rate of electrical use has slowed down nuclear orders in the United States and forced many cancellations. Even before the accident at Three Mile Island, no new plant had been ordered for years. Our domestic nuclear power industry is stuck with a terrific overcapacity and is desperate for orders. British industry, experiencing a similar slowdown, has turned to commercial reprocessing in competition with France. Several countries in western Europe are scrambling for nuclear equipment sales. The general view, particularly in Switzerland and West Germany, is that U.S. non-proliferation controls are no more than a thinly-disguised attempt to hobble foreign competition. The fact that U.S. industry is complaining about the same controls seems to make no impression.

WHAT CAN BE DONE?

But we are not talking about who beats out whom in the marketplace. We are talking about bombs, nuclear bombs with which India and Pakistan can incinerate South Asia; bombs with which Iraq or Libya can subjugate Saudi Arabia or set the whole Middle East aflame and shut off *everybody's* oil. The threat of nuclear weapons in the Middle East, or Pakistan, or South Africa does not mean we should back off our non-proliferation policies. It means just the opposite.

I know this subject is all too prone to the-sky-is-falling syndrome. But in fact the barriers to proliferation are not very formidable. We have to watch

for moves to weaken the export law and its network of political controls. We have to understand that the State Department is always, always going to think first about its constituencies among our friends and allies and about the geopolitics of international commerce. That's what our diplomats are there for, but their actions need to be weighed against that understanding. We also have to face the fact that the IAEA is too frail to cope with widespread commercial availability of nuclear explosive material.

We have to get our greed and our competitive commercial instincts under control. If, in the future, we are willing to trade some of our commercial freedom for international security, we might find a way to proceed with plutonium in relative safety. But I am convinced that we do not have to make such a choice now, since the present generation of uranium fueled power reactors can continue to satisfy the needs of electric power for many years to come.

In any case, whatever we do, let us heed some advice from George Orwell having to do with cant and hypocrisy and the effect of euphemistic and slovenly language on political thought.

Let us not say "sensitive" when we mean "dangerous"; or "strategic quantity" when we mean bomb quantity; let us not talk of "safeguards" when we mean occasional inspection of bomb material; let us not talk of becoming a "reliable supplier" again when we mean a willingness to sell dangerous material and equipment to any nation to whom it was offered in a more innocent time. Let us not talk of "potential explosives" when we mean "explosives." (Plutonium is no more a potential nuclear explosive than TNT is a potential chemical explosive.) Above all, let us not designate as "peaceful"—a term that appears in the IAEA Charter, our bilateral agreements, and the NPT—any activity that allows direct access to nuclear explosives. "Peaceful" is not peaceful unless we can protect it from use in bombs, unless it is safe.

The Driving Forces of Proliferation
Sir John Hill

Non-Proliferation, it has been said, is like motherhood. Everybody is for it. But, unlike motherhood, not everybody agrees on how to achieve it. In this paper, I hope to explore in some detail the nature and causes of the phenomenon of nuclear weapons proliferation: in particular I shall consider the question of what role, if any, nuclear power development could have in stimulating or abetting the spread of nuclear weapons. This will lead me on to the main theme of this paper: the balance between technical and political factors in the fight against proliferation.

The birth of nuclear energy can be said to have occurred in the closing years of the 1930s at which time the possibility of nuclear reactions, though known for some time by a small elite of theoretical physicists, first came under the active scrutiny of the scientific community at large. From that time on, the theoretical possibility existed for any nation desirous of so doing to harness the energy of the atomic nucleus either for controlled use in power production or for purposes of destruction. What has been termed the greatest atomic secret, the question of whether a weapon based on a nuclear reaction could be made to detonate with a significant yield, was revealed to the world at large in August 1945 with the use of the atomic bomb on Hiroshima and on Nagasaki. As from this time, the existence of a nuclear weapons technology has been an incontrovertible and irreversible fact. Any nation henceforth, if firstly it had access to the technology of nuclear weapons fabrication (by no means an easy matter), and secondly to an adequate supply of one of the fissile materials U-235, Pu-239 or U-233, to a sufficient degree of purity, was now in a position to join the nuclear arms race if it so desired. My subject here is not the question of access to weapons fabrication technology, important though this is; I wish rather to consider the routes available to a nation seeking to secure a supply of fissile material sufficient for a weapons programme, that is to say a quantity of some tens of kilograms a year or more (a smaller quantity than this would be of negligible significance). In particular, I wish to consider the extent to which a nuclear power programme could or could not facilitate this task.

In public discussions of the proliferation problem, the attention of the world has largely been focussed on just one of the fissile materials I have mentioned, namely plutonium. There are indeed undeniable hazards associated with the unsafeguarded production of plutonium and it is right that all due weight should be given to these. At the same time this should not serve to blind us to the equal or even greater importance in this respect of isotopic enrichment methods, as a means for the production of U-235: this route to the production of fissile material might, in my view, in some cases offer a potential advantage to the would-be proliferator, simply in view of the smaller scale of operations involved.

With regard to plutonium production methods, it is clear that a considerable range of techniques is available to the state seeking a supply of Pu-239. High on the list would of course be dedicated production reactors: so also would be certain types of research reactor. Lower on the list, in my view, would come accelerators and power reactors. Accelerators, because no such machine has yet been built of sufficient power to be able to produce fissile material in the kind of annual quantities we are discussing. Power reactors, simply because this is a disproportionately expensive way of obtaining the quantities of fissile material one would need. I shall attempt below to enlarge on the difficulties associated with this latter route.

The point that cannot be let slip in all of this is

Sir John Hill, "The Driving Forces of Proliferation," *Arms Control* (London) 1 (May 1980), pp. 53–63. Reprinted from the 1980 issue of *Arms Control,* published by Frank Cass and Company Limited, 11 Gainsborough Road, London Ell, England. Copyright Frank Cass & Co. Ltd.

that the possibility of producing nuclear materials of this kind does not of itself act as one of the driving forces of proliferation. The theoretical possibility of any number of nations attempting to construct nuclear weapons has, as I pointed out above, been with us for the last thirty years or more. During this time fissile materials have been isolated and processed in abundance, without more than a handful of nations having gone down the road towards a nuclear weapons capability. The Non-Proliferation Treaty of 1968 has provided over a hundred states around the globe with the means of registering in a clear and unambiguous manner their intention to abstain from nuclear weapons development. One area of the world, South America, is well on the way to the establishment of the militarily denuclearised zone, provided for by the Treaty of Tlatelolco. There are further treaties setting constraints on the deployment of nuclear weapons in outer space and the emplacement of nuclear missiles on the sea-bed. It is thus clear that the mere existence of a technology of this potential has not of itself been sufficient to drive the greater part of the world into the arms of the nuclear deterrent. The element of political will, witnessed by this reluctance by most countries to encourage the spread of nuclear weapons is, I submit, of the first importance in assessing the causes of and remedies for proliferation.

What then is the position of civil nuclear technology in the proliferation mechanism? That nuclear power is a sufficient condition of proliferation, unfailingly resulting in a spreading of the bomb, as has been alleged by some, is, I think, clearly a suggestion lacking plausibility. That nuclear power is not furthermore a necessary condition of nuclear weapons fabrication by a nation so minded to do is clear if we consider the many alternative routes to fissile material that I have outlined. But, though neither a sufficient nor a necessary condition of nuclear weapons, is nuclear power at the least one possible method of access to the fissile material needed for a bomb? The answer to this question is of course yes. The potential of nuclear materials in civil use, if diverted to military applications, has been recognised by the civil nuclear industry from its inception—hence, in large measure, the cover of secrecy under which some of the early development of the civil technology had to be carried out. What has also been known is that technical means could be devised to render the diversion of nuclear material from civil to military use extremely difficult, indeed effectively impossible without alerting the attention of the world at large. It is my belief that this technology, coupled with the inherent unsuitability of the civil nuclear fuel cycle for military use, will conspire to make this perceptibly a far less suitable route for the would-be proliferator than any dedicated facility.

Can reactor-grade plutonium be used to form the fissile core of a nuclear weapon? That some kind of explosive assembly can be put together in this way has been confirmed by the release of a report from the United States Energy Research and Development Administration (ERDA) on 5th September 1977: this announced the successful detonation, in the course of experiments understood to have been carried out in the late 1940s or early 1950s, of a nuclear explosive made with the use of plutonium of relatively low Pu-239 content, recovered by the reprocessing of nuclear fuel. But what does this really prove? That reactor-grade plutonium can be used without further purification to make an explosive of some kind? So indeed it would appear. That this is the most efficient route for constructing a nuclear weapon? Almost certainly not. That it is a course easily available to most Non-Nuclear-Weapons-States in the world today, if possessed of a civil nuclear fuel cycle? Most emphatically not. The conditions under which the ERDA explosive was assembled, in particular the cloak of secrecy which could legitimately be thrown around the proceedings, made this a situation in no way resembling that which obtains in a country whose nuclear facilities are under international safeguards.

International safeguards are the cornerstone of measures to demonstrate that civil facilities are not being used for weapons purposes. We can and should seek to ensure the enforcement in nations whose facilities are under safeguards of measures which would make it as difficult and as time-consuming to divert fissile material from its legitimate use to weapons production as to build a completely separate weapons capability.

What would this involve? The criteria one could sensibly adopt in evaluating the proliferation-resistance of fuel cycles have been looked at in the context of the NASAP programme in the United States and are currently being examined as part of the International Nuclear Fuel Cycle Evaluation programme (INFCE). On the basis of studies of this kind, it is possible to identify a number of criteria of relevance to the comparative evaluation of fuel cycles in this respect. Among these one might single out the following as being of undisputed importance:

● Quantities and distribution of Special Nuclear Material: one would need to consider the number of sites over which SNM was distributed and the transport requirements which this entailed
● Form of material: the accessibility of the material, its chemical forms, its isotopic composition
● The nature of the nuclear facilities: in particular, the time and the resources needed to divert SNM to use in a weapons programme
● Protectability: the safeguardability of the material, and the time in which and ease with which diversion and misuse can be detected.

The last two criteria are to my mind of particular importance and the elements of delay and timely warning must rank high among the objectives of the technical means adopted for non-proliferation purposes. These can broadly be divided into those which can be described as safeguards tasks proper and those, in a sense, more intrusive measures aimed at affecting not only the operation but the very nature of the nuclear fuel cycle.

With regard to the former, the IAEA was charged under its Statute with the safeguarding of nuclear materials in civil use, and the Non-Proliferation Treaty and the Treaty of Tlatelolco later referred to this function. The principles of materials ac-

countancy, containment and surveillance employed by the Agency in discharging its functions are generally familiar. The United Kingdom has also been active in seeking ways in which the concept of full fuel-cycle safeguards administered by the IAEA could be made acceptable even to countries who do not feel able to accede to the NPT.

The British Government has always given maximum support to the IAEA and to safeguards arrangements concluded under the NPT. In particular, in common with the United States, the UK has made a Voluntary Offer to the IAEA whereby all of our civil nuclear facilities are open to scrutiny by the Agency's Inspectors. We are aware that the world at large welcomes this action by the United States and Britain and indeed I feel it right that the Nuclear-Weapons-States should be seen to enjoy no special privileges in respect of their civil activities.

Nobody could say that safeguards arrangements, whether they are administered by the IAEA or whether by EURATOM, admit of no further improvements. Beyond question there is scope for improvement in the technical means adopted for the verification of nuclear materials. There will almost certainly be scope in the design of industrial-scale fuel plants for the incorporation of new design concepts aimed at facilitating the application of safeguards. And there is an unquestionable case for an increase in the number of the Agency's Inspectors.

But while there is room for improvement here, as in all other walks of human endeavour, I feel nevertheless no hesitation in asserting that the safeguards task with which the Agency is charged is, and will continue to be, carried out to a very high degree of effectiveness.

The second main sub-division of technical non-proliferation matters concerns the technical choices to be made between alternative fuel cycles. Here a great deal of work is of course in progress around the globe in the context of the INFCE programme launched by President Carter in 1977. There is of course a staggeringly large range of choices that could be made with respect to the nuclear fuel cycle, any of which might appear to bear in some degree on the question of non-proliferation. The subject is an enormous one and I seek here simply to identify some of the areas for consideration. In the first place one needs to look at the various fuel cycles currently under discussion as alternatives to the uranium/plutonium cycle: the once-through fuel cycle, the various types of thorium fuel cycle and others. All of these are rightly receiving careful scrutiny within INFCE and elsewhere; it seems however likely to me that on detailed consideration there will appear to be little to choose between these and the more conventional plutonium-based cycles, given an equivalent system of safeguards. Of course on this last point it will be important to ensure that future nuclear installations are designed so as to make the application of safeguards as easy as possible. Secondly, within the context of the uranium/plutonium cycle, one needs to consider the extent to which the separation of pure fissile material is necessary at the reprocessing stage, and whether some system of co-conversion or, perhaps at a later stage, co-processing would not be equally feasible. Increased automation and physical isolation in reprocessing and fuel fabrication plants also lead to more substantial physical barriers.

Those technical steps which tend to increase proliferation resistance also seem to be the steps which are likely to evolve naturally. Again, though here more in the context of the fight against terrorism than under the heading of non-proliferation proper, one needs to look at the whole question of transport, and the ways in which the transport of fuels of a high fissile content can be made a safe and secure operation—whether this can best be achieved by the use of special vehicles, and if necessary of armed guards, or whether it would be preferable to reduce this potential hazard by some degree of co-location. One needs to look at ways in which the improved physical protection of sites could be of value in facilitating the safeguards task. And finally, and perhaps most importantly of all, the various enrichment technologies and their relative degrees of proliferation-resistance require examination.

All of these technical choices are of great importance. But equally such technical questions cannot be considered in isolation from the institutional features that are assumed to obtain. In the last analysis, I believe, it is these institutional features that will come to be seen as the main determinants of the proliferation resistance of fuel cycles. To take one familiar example, it is often asked whether a fuel cycle involving reprocessing is a better or a worse thing from the proliferation standpoint than one simply involving the storage of spent fuel. This, I submit, is the wrong way to ask the question. For there is in my view nothing in the nature either of reprocessing or of spent fuel storage that is of itself conducive to weapons proliferation. The situation that we find in the world at present is a growing number of countries who each have at present only a small nuclear component in their generating systems. For countries in this category there is little or no attraction economically speaking in installing their own highly capital-intensive reprocessing capacity. The natural and most attractive solution for countries in this position is to purchase reprocessing services from an existing plant such as Windscale. As an alternative, such countries could participate, perhaps together with suppliers, in the establishment of some kind of multinational institution which would provide fuel-cycle services on a non-discriminatory basis to countries with a legitimate end-use for the fissile materials. The development of an internationally acceptable framework for fuel-cycle centres of this kind is likely to take some years. In addition, there is a strong case for seeking international agreement on a regime for handling separated plutonium. A system for the international storage of plutonium is already under discussion within the IAEA. Where countries have a requirement to separate plutonium for energy or research purposes, a system of this kind could make a valuable contribution to providing increased confidence that the movement and use of plutonium are internationally known and carefully monitored. An 'international plutonium storage' regime could moreover be applicable not only to material separated in the future, but also to stocks of plutonium already separated. Alternatively, where a country had no use for plutonium, complementary multi-national or international arrangements could exist for the storage of spent fuel, which would again prove economically more attractive to such countries than a national storage facility. There is no doubt in my mind that arrangements of this kind, where plutonium would be returned to customer states only under safeguards, would minimise any proliferation risk from spent fuel storage or reprocessing.

Were on the other hand arrangements of this kind not to be available for one reason or another, then countries in this position would be obliged in the short term to extend their spent fuel storage capacity: in the longer term, they might, for reasons of security of energy supply, find it increasingly attractive to provide themselves with an indigenous reprocessing capability, even despite the economic drawbacks of this course of action. Such developments, while they would of course by no means necessarily lead to the decision to separate fissile materials for military purposes, nevertheless put fewer barriers in the way of weapons proliferation than the kinds of multilateral arrangement I have just referred to.

What all of this shows is that what appear to be purely technical questions turn out on closer analysis to have a large political dimension, and while we can and should submit these technical issues to searching scrutiny, we should not forget that this is only half the story. Indeed at the end of the day it is the political measures which will in my view turn out to be the really important issue.

On the basis of what we have said so far, what should then be our strategy with respect to the future of nuclear power? Should we in fact be permitting further civil nuclear developments at all, or should we follow the advice of those who tell us that any civil nuclear activity is a potential proliferation risk and that the world should cut loose totally from the nuclear option? From what I have said, it is, I hope, clear that I do not believe that the limitation of nuclear weapons in any way calls for the curtailment of nuclear power programmes.

Stopping nuclear power programmes will not make the proliferation problem go away: the problem is primarily a political one, and the least that could be said of the proposed strategy of cutting back on nuclear power is that it would prove totally irrelevant to the task at hand. Indeed I might go further, and say that such a cut-back would if anything jeopardise our non-proliferation objectives, for the simple reason that it would prove unacceptable to those nations on whose co-operation we rely in our attempt to ensure that non-proliferation remains possible.

For the remainder of this century, there is no doubt that the world's nuclear power capacity will continue to be made up in the main of thermal reactors operating on a once-through cycle, and that the extensive commercial use of plutonium as a nuclear fuel in any part of the world is still some ten to twenty years off. This provides us with a breathing-space, which we should use to explore ways in which we can help to maximise the proliferation-resistance of plutonium-based fuel cycles, in preparation for the time when their commercial development becomes desirable. It is, I think, now generally accepted that the reprocessing of nuclear fuel and the use of plutonium will, in the fullness of time, become a necessity for many of the countries who have a nuclear power programme. How soon this necessity will arise will depend on features which will vary considerably from country to country, such as the availability and cost of indigenous uranium resources and the size of the expected nuclear power installation programme, which may in its turn depend on the availability and cost of other fuels. It may depend on other non-economic criteria also. One important objective of the INFCE will be to set out criteria for the introduction of plutonium-fuelled thermal reactors and fast reactors, which will enable countries to identify their optimal course of action given their own position in respect of energy supply and demand and other factors. Eventually however the need for the use of plutonium as a nuclear fuel will come even to those countries at present best endowed with indigenous resources. Thermal recycle will probably be seen by only a small minority of countries as a transitional stage which cushions them to some extent against high uranium prices over the next few decades until the fast reactor comes along, and for most countries the economic case for this fuel cycle will at most be marginal. The fast reactor fuel cycle by contrast will, I feel certain, come eventually to be seen by all countries with a major nuclear component in their generating systems as offering a significant economic advantage over the uranium-based once-through cycle, and will eventually supersede the thermal reactor cycle as the mainstay of the world's nuclear generating capacity. And so long as we have the right institutional features, there is in my opinion no reason why the use of plutonium as a fuel should render impracticable the task of protecting fissile materials.

Again it might be asked, would our best strategy be to retain all of our civil nuclear technology including fast reactors, but do all we can to limit the access of any further nations to this technology? Would this help to reduce the risk of the technology being put to military use? My conviction is that this would be a profound mistake. It was clear to the nations which negotiated the Non-Proliferation Treaty that if the vast majority of the countries of the world were to be persuaded to give up a defence option of great significance, then this could not be done without at the very least an adequate *quid pro quo* being offered. The incentive that was offered to the Non-Nuclear-Weapons-States in the NPT, and it was in my opinion the correct incentive, was assistance from the nations with the greatest nuclear expertise to the non-nuclear weapons states in developing all those applications of nuclear energy which could be developed without the risk of nuclear weapons proliferation. Important elements in the NPT are of course Articles I and II which outlaw the transfer of nuclear weapons technology: but an equally important article in my view is Article IV.2 whereby parties to the Treaty 'undertake to facilitate, and have the right to participate in, the fullest possible exchange of equipment and materials and scientific and technological information for the peaceful uses of nuclear energy'. The idea

that the safeguarding of the nuclear fuel cycle should go hand in hand with the promotion of the peaceful uses of atomic energy was already implicit in the Statute of the IAEA, which from its inception was given the dual task of promoting civil nuclear power and of setting up and administering the safeguards regime.

What I have said should not be taken as endorsing the unrestricted spread of nuclear facilities to countries that can make no real use of them. This would clearly be foolish. What I do however most strongly believe is that where nations are in a position to benefit from nuclear power, then the world is not only entitled but even in a sense duty-bound to assist them in the development of the peaceful uses of nuclear energy, always provided that adequate safeguards arrangements can be agreed. If the developed world is not prepared to share its use of nuclear technology in this way, this can have only one consequence. Almost inevitably, if a country is refused access to the use of this technology on reasonable terms, then it will feel itself impelled to obtain what has been refused by means of indigenous development. We have seen this after the war, where the exclusion of Canada from the UK/US accords on the protection of nuclear information led to the decision by the Canadians to develop their own reactor system, the reactor which we now know as Candu. We have seen this in other fields as well. As I have said, I feel certain that if the Western world were to persist in a refusal to provide reprocessing services to the less developed countries, then this could have only one effect: that these countries would perforce attempt to develop their own reprocessing technology. The international community would hardly then be in as good a position to regulate the uses to which reprocessing technology was put as it would have been if it had been provided adequate services in the first place.

To what extent then is non-proliferation a technical question? And how far is it a problem which can be addressed purely by political means? In a sense of course these two aspects of non-proliferation cannot really be separated. However, to the extent that we can answer this question at all, our conclusion must I believe be that it is political factors to which we must primarily look in seeking the remedies for proliferation. More than anything else, what guides the choices of nations faced with the question of whether or not to develop nuclear weapons, is their perception of their national security and of the extent to which they can rely upon the international community to protect them in the event of a nuclear attack, without the need for their own nuclear weapons arsenal. The British Foreign Secretary gave a penetrating account of this matter when, speaking in May 1977, he said: 'There is a direct link between removing the incentive to acquire nuclear weapons and the creation of conditions of stability and security. The reverse of the case is a recipe for nuclear conflict. The quantitative threat of proliferating nuclear weapons can only be contained by a qualitative improvement in the management of international relations'. In illustration of this, one finds in the statements made by a number of nations at the time that they signed the NPT in 1968 references to the importance that these nations attach to the promise of intervention by the United Nations Security Council in the event of their being threatened with nuclear attack. If we are to be successful in the struggle against nuclear weapons proliferation, one important objective must be to ensure that the non-nuclear weapons states do not regard their military security as being endangered by the non-proliferation regime. This may involve the international community in concerted political action if the occasion so demands. It also involves the protection of other vital interests including, I believe, assurance of adequate energy supplies to all nations around the world, and it is from this point of view that the development of civil nuclear technology may be of especial importance in assisting us to fight against proliferation.

Again, while technical choices in the nuclear fuel cycle are important, they are important only in the context of institutional safeguards arrangements. Political choices of this kind are an indispensable correlate of the various technical choices that I have earlier outlined. Such an exercise as INFCE will succeed in its objectives only if it manages to keep in view these aspects of the proliferation problem.

The possibility of nuclear power and the possibility of nuclear weapons have both been with us now for many years. To a very considerable extent the development of these two technologies has been separate. But in the last analysis there is no such thing as the civil atom or the military atom. An atom is a neutral thing and technology is a neutral thing. It belongs to the most important moral and political duties incumbent upon mankind as custodians of this earth to ensure that the technology of nuclear energy is one that is turned not to evil but to good.

QUESTIONS FOR DISCUSSION

1 What are the incentives for states to build nuclear weapons?
2 To what extent does the possession of nuclear reactors make NNWSs more likely to become NWSs?
3 How effective are IAEA inspection techniques in preventing the diversion of weapons-grade fissile material for military purposes?
4 Was it a mistake for the advanced industrial nations to encourage the development and production of nuclear reactors?
5 What policy should the United States pursue regarding the export of nuclear reactors?

SUGGESTED READINGS

Gyorgy, Anna. "Plutonium Politics 38 Years After Hiroshima," *Critical Mass* 8 (August 1983), pp. 3 and 7.

Holdren, John P. "Nuclear Power and Nuclear Weapons: The Connection Is Dangerous," *Bulletin of the Atomic Scientists* 39 (January 1983), pp. 40–45.

Khan, Munir Ahmad. "Nuclear Power and International Cooperation—Perceptions of the Third World," *Nuclear News* 26 (December 1983), pp. 95–102.

Lovins, Amory B., L. Hunter Lovins, and Leonard Ross. "Nuclear Power and Nuclear Bombs," *Foreign Affairs* 58 (Summer 1980), pp. 1137–1177.

Marsh, George E. "If Atoms for Peace Are Used for War," *Bulletin of the Atomic Scientists* 38 (February 1982), p. 42.

Miller, James Nathan. "The Peaceful Atom Bares Its Teeth," *Reader's Digest* (June 1983), pp. 93–98.

Spinrad, Bernard. "Nuclear Power and Nuclear Weapons: The Connection Is Tenuous," *Bulletin of the Atomic Scientists* (February 1983), pp. 42–47.

U.S. Congress: House. *Technical Aspects of Nuclear Nonproliferation Safeguards*. Hearings before the Subcommittee on Energy Research and Production of the Committee on Science and Technology, 97th Cong., 2nd Sess., 1982.

U.S. Congress: Senate. *Plutonium Use Policy*. Hearings before the Subcommittee on Energy, Nuclear Proliferation, and Government Processes of the Committee on Governmental Affairs, 97th Cong., 2nd Sess., 1982.

U.S. Congress: Senate. *U.S. Policy on Export of Helium-3 and Other Nuclear Materials and Technology*. Hearings before the Subcommittee on Energy, Nuclear Proliferation, and Government Processes of the Committee on Governmental Affairs, 97th Cong., 2nd Sess., 1982.

Walker, William and Måns Lönnroth. "Proliferation and Nuclear Trade: A Look Ahead," *Bulletin of the Atomic Scientists* 40 (April 1984), pp. 29–33.

20 Is Superpower Restraint in Nuclear-Weapons
Acquisition Likely To Help Discourage Proliferation?

YES

Hedley Bull

*The Role of the Nuclear Powers in the Management of
Nuclear Proliferation*

NO

James R. Schlesinger

The Strategic Consequences of Nuclear Proliferation

The Role of the Nuclear Powers in the Management of Nuclear Proliferation
Hedley Bull

It is widely recognized that the process of nuclear proliferation will be greatly influenced by the military policies that are adopted by the present nuclear powers. There are, however, two conflicting doctrines as to what military policies on their part would best affect it.

According to the first doctrine, which I shall call that of Low Posture, the nuclear countries can best contribute to the management of proliferation by attempting to minimise the gap that separates them from the non-nuclear. If the United States and the Soviet Union (and perhaps the lesser nuclear powers) are able to reduce the level of their nuclear armaments, to restrict their qualitative development and to diminish reliance upon them in their foreign policies and strategies, then to that extent the world will be made safer for non-nuclear powers. Countries that are at present considering whether or not to acquire nuclear weapons will be the more easily persuaded that these weapons do not bring great advantages; while if some of them nevertheless go ahead and acquire these weapons, then at least precedents will have been established that will make a world of more nuclear powers less dangerous than it might otherwise be.

These are the sorts of policies for which India, Sweden and other representative non-nuclear countries have been calling at the Eighteen Nation Disarmament Conference, and which they declare to be at once the key to the problem of non-proliferation and the condition of their adhesion to a non-proliferation treaty. If the nuclear powers were to be swayed by this line of argument they would give urgent priority to the reaching of agreements such as those proposed for a freeze and reduction of nuclear warheads and delivery vehicles, a comprehensive test ban treaty, a moratorium on the deployment of ballistic missile defence systems, and a restriction on the use of nuclear weapons against non-nuclear powers. In the absence of such agreements, they might attempt to give partial effect to some of these proposals by unilateral actions. They might, for example, seek to equip themselves and their allies with conventional forces powerful enough to be independent of the use of nuclear weapons; they might commit themselves not to be the first to use nuclear weapons, or not to use them against non-nuclear powers; they might desist from underground nuclear testing, from the deployment of ballistic missile defences and from further augmenting their strategic missile forces; and they might seek to reverse the trend towards "nuclearisation" of conventional military equipment and training, and conspicuously relegate the nuclear element in their arsenals to the role of weapons of last resort.

According to the second doctrine, which I shall call that of High Posture, the two major nuclear powers should on the contrary seek to preserve and indeed to widen the gap that divides them from the rest. By maintaining and increasing the high levels of their nuclear forces, by pressing on with their further improvement and by fully exploiting nuclear potential in their diplomacy and strategy, they will effectively preserve the bipolar structure of world power against the threat that proliferation poses to it; and potential nuclear powers can be effectively discouraged from entering the nuclear club or kept in their place if they do so.

This doctrine of High Posture has a number of advocates in the United States. It would seem to imply that any arms control agreement which bound the hands of the great nuclear powers, while leaving the aspirant nuclear states free to catch up—

From *Arms Control for the Late Sixties* by James E. Dougherty and J. F. Lehman, Jr. (eds.). © 1967 by D. Van Nostrand. Reprinted by permission of Wadsworth, Inc. Belmont, CA 94002.

even more, one which actually diminished their present lead—would only encourage the forces of proliferation, or maximise the dangers that it will bring. Continued underground testing, the deployment of ballistic missile defences and penetration aids, willingness to rely on the use of nuclear weapons in diplomacy and war, are the policies to which this doctrine seems to point.

There are perhaps three arguments that support the idea of Low Posture. The first is that by adopting some of the measures that this doctrine calls for, the nuclear powers will satisfy the conditions that the spokesmen of the non-nuclear powers have laid down for their adhesion to a non-proliferation treaty, and pave the way for their agreement to it.

It is, of course, by no means clear how far the nuclear powers would have to go along the road of Low Posture in order to satisfy these conditions. Different countries have specified different sets of conditions: Swedish representatives have spoken simply of a cessation of further production of fissile material and a comprehensive test ban, while Indian spokesmen have called in addition for actual measures of disarmament. Moreover, it may be argued that the more conditions the nuclear powers are able to satisfy, the more further conditions are likely to be introduced by India and other potential nuclear powers, whose present declarations are a political manoeuvre rather than a position seriously intended.

There is no way of proving or disproving the seriousness of India's position except by putting it to the test. Although a desire to avoid entering into commitments is one element in the debate about nuclear weapons in India, there are others operating in a contrary direction. It would therefore seem reasonable that the nuclear powers should direct their policy towards influencing the course of this debate, rather than allow it to be determined in advance by some presentiment as to what the outcome of the debate will be.

India's conditions, moreover (to take the most radical that have so far been stated at Geneva), are by no means utopian. They do not specify that China is to be among the nuclear powers taking steps toward dismantling their armaments. They invoke general and complete disarmament only as a distant goal. And they do not require that the measures of nuclear disarmament to be carried out should be completed before the non-proliferation treaty is signed. It is true that India can have little actual strategic interest in reductions of nuclear delivery vehicles by the United States and the Soviet Union; and that if these reductions were very drastic, India would actually suffer from the augmentation of China's position relative to that of India's American and Soviet protectors. Nevertheless, it is clearly of great political importance to an Indian government willing to sign a non-proliferation treaty that it should be able to present to its parliament and people some tangible *quid pro quo*.

The second argument for the adoption of a Low Posture is that by reducing the military and political incentives that non-nuclear states have for going nuclear it would make a contribution in its own right to preventing, limiting or slowing down the spread of nuclear weapons, irrespective of its effect on the negotiation of a treaty.

Proliferation is stimulated by acceptance on the one hand of the assumption that nuclear weapons are a normal and necessary ingredient in the arsenal of any militarily powerful state, and on the other hand of the assumption that they are essential to the prestige and standing of a major power. Unfortunately both these assumptions are to a large extent founded upon fact; if they were illusions it would be easier to dispel them than it is. Moreover, while the nuclear powers continue to cling to their nuclear weapons, as they show every sign of doing, there are limits to the success they can have in convincing others of their inutility.

Nevertheless, within these limitations a policy of diminishing the importance of nuclear weapons may have a great deal of scope. If, during the years since 1945, nuclear weapons had been resorted to in war, or if some attempt had been made to institutionalise the equation of possession of nuclear weapons with great powerhood, the pressures now making for proliferation would be very much stronger than in fact they are. Measures have thus been taken in the past which, though they were not consciously formulated as part of an anti-proliferation strategy, have already had an element of success in advancing its purpose. There is little doubt that a more deliberate and systematic attempt on the part of the nuclear powers to relegate nuclear weapons to the background of their foreign policies, their strategic doctrines and the training and equipment of their armed forces would serve to arrest at least some of the forces making for proliferation, especially if it were undertaken in unison and enshrined in international agreements.

The third argument for the doctrine of Low Posture is that it will minimise the dangers that further proliferation will bring in its train, should it take place. The policies and agreements that are indicated by the Low Posture idea are desirable in themselves as measures of arms control among the present nuclear powers, and have for the most part been on the agenda of arms control conferences since well before the proliferation question came to assume the prominence it now has. The character of a world of many nuclear powers will be very much shaped by the military policies and arms control arrangements that are elaborated by the five existing nuclear states now; alarming though the prospect of further proliferation may be, it will be less so to the extent that the countries now wrestling with the problems of a world of five nuclear states have developed a body of arms control practice that may be transmitted to future generations.

Persuasive though these arguments are, there are elements of the proliferation problem of which they do not take account. Some potential nuclear countries are driven to contemplate acquiring nuclear weapons much less because of any assumption that they are necessary to a modern state's equipment or a great state's standing than because they have a pressing problem of security to which a nuclear force of their own provides a possible solution. Either like America's NATO allies in relation to the Soviet Union, or like India in relation to China, they feel themselves to be threatened by a nuclear power; or, like Israel in relation to the United Arab

Republic or like Australia in relation to Indonesia, or South Africa in relation to her African neighbours, they feel that they are threatened, or might come to be threatened, by an enemy with so decisive a preponderance of conventional military strength that only nuclear weapons would provide an effective counter to it.

For many countries placed in this sort of situation the only alternative solution to nuclear weapons of their own is the protection, if it is available, of one of the existing nuclear powers. Such important potential nuclear powers as Canada, West Germany, Italy, Japan and Australia do in fact have firmly non-nuclear policies, the basis of which is their present confidence in the assurances provided by the American alliance system of which they are part. Other potential nuclear powers such as India and Sweden are outside this system, but nevertheless the belief that their security is underwritten by the United States is an unstated premise of their policies.

Part of the contribution that the United States and the Soviet Union (and possibly the United Kingdom) can make to the management of proliferation, then, is the extension of assurances or guarantees of support to non-nuclear states. In the first instance, this is a matter of preserving the assurances, or making certain existing assurances to non-aligned countries more explicit and categorical than they are at present. It may or may not prove desirable and feasible that the United States and the Soviet Union, and perhaps other nuclear powers, should join together in collective assurances of support to non-nuclear states, but whether such a development should come about or not, many states will continue to rely on the unilateral assurances emanating from the two major states that lie at the heart of the present political structure of the world.

The question is how far the adoption of Low Posture by the nuclear powers, and especially by the United States and the Soviet Union, is consistent with their fulfilling this role of guarantors. Some forms of the Low Posture doctrine require the nuclear powers not merely to desist from further building up their nuclear force, but actually to begin dismantling it; moreover, the suggestion appears to be that this process of dismantling, having begun, should go on, the initial measures of reduction of nuclear delivery vehicles being a token or down payment for further instalments to come.

It is clear that if the United States and the Soviet Union were to progress indefinitely down this road, a point would be reached at which their nuclear superiority, in relation both to China, Britain and France and to the leading non-nuclear states, would diminish. This ability to protect states which felt threatened by one of the lesser nuclear states or by a non-nuclear state would then come to be called in question. Moreover, as their ability to exploit nuclear force in relation to one another became subject to restriction and reservations, the confidence that their NATO and Warsaw Pact allies now place in them would be undermined.

The five nuclear powers do not of course constitute the close political combination or concert that their term "nuclear club" suggests; on the contrary, they are aligned on different sides of the most profound political divisions of our time. But even if the formula of a Soviet-American or a five power concert for the joint management of international affairs were solidly based in reality, it would still imply a strategic superiority on the part of states that were members of the concert over those that were not, and it would be threatened by a process of disarmament whose end product was a merging of their status with that of the rest.

Even some of the more modest steps called for by the doctrine of Low Posture might be held to call in question the efficacy of existing guarantees and to provide some of the countries that now enjoy them with a stimulus to proliferation. The adoption by the United States and the United Kingdom of a commitment not to use nuclear weapons first, for example, although it might have the beneficial effects mentioned above, would also have the effect of undermining the present strategy of NATO and of alienating West Germany and other European NATO countries from their present attachment to the alliance.

There are also uncertainties as to the extent to which the restriction envisaged would impair the ability of the United States (and possibly the United Kingdom) to preserve the guarantees which they now extend, explicitly or implicitly, to China's neighbours. At the present time the United States enjoys unquestioned strategic nuclear superiority in relation to China, and while this remains the position, as it may well do for a decade or more, such potential nuclear countries as India, Japan and Australia have no cause to doubt the credibility to China of an American threat to attack her in response to an attack on themselves. If, however, China should in the course of time develop a nuclear force that is both invulnerable to destruction and capable of attacking targets in the United States, the same sort of doubts that have been expressed about the validity of the American guarantee in NATO might come to preoccupy America's Far Eastern allies and dependents.

In this event it is very likely that the search for an acceptable alternative to national nuclear forces will tend to focus in Asia as it has in Europe upon devices for shoring up the American guarantee. This is not the place to examine the range of possible devices or to consider the applicability to the Far Eastern alliance system of the solutions to this problem that have been propounded in NATO. It is clear, however, that one of the most prominent ideas in this debate is likely to be that the United States can best maintain its position as the guarantor of China's neighbors by a deployment of ballistic missile defences that will in effect preserve its present position of strategic nuclear superiority. Such an idea, if it were accepted, would imply that a moratorium on ballistic missile deployment would have unfavourable consequences for nuclear proliferation; and that underground nuclear testing, because of its connection with ballistic missile defence, should be continued.

A policy of Low Posture, then, may weaken certain of the incentives making for proliferation but it may strengthen others. Indeed in its more radical form it is open to the objection not merely that it provides an inadequate formula for the management of proliferation but that it fails to recognise the fundamentally hierarchical basis of the present world order. In the Indian demand that "vertical proliferation" must be dealt with along with the "horizontal proliferation," and that there must be an end to all talk of a "select club" of four or five states "to work out the salvation of the world" there is an implicit claim to equality among states which could be taken up by states much less significant than India and which if seriously pressed would lead to the undoing of the whole structure of power on which, unrecognised though it is in law and diplomacy, the everyday expectations of all present international life are based.

There is a certain justice in the note of grievance which is sometimes struck by countries which see themselves as the nuclear Have-Nots or proletarians. It is true that in an international order in which the many do not have nuclear weapons, the few that retain them will enjoy privileges, however effectively they are able to disguise them. But the alternative to an international order in which certain states have a larger stake than others is probably no international order at all. The problem is not to find an international order in which no one state or group of states has a special interest, but rather to ensure that those who do have special interests recognise the special responsibilities that go with them, and conduct themselves in such a way as to engage general support for the system whose custodians and guarantors they are. It is in this latter sense that the doctrine of Low Posture is most defensible.

If the doctrine of Low Posture does not in itself provide an adequate guide to the nuclear powers, the same is true of the contrary position. The idea that the United States and the Soviet Union should adopt a High Posture (no one appears to entertain the idea that all five nuclear powers should do so) has two supporting arguments.

The first is that by doing so the two leading states will deter or discourage potential nuclear countries from acquiring nuclear weapons. By demonstrating the superior size and sophistication of their missile forces, their ability to provide for ballistic missile defence and the prominence of the qualitative arms race, they will emphasize the great distances that divide a country which has merely tested a nuclear device from one which has a replete modern weapons system, and so discredit the idea that doing so provides an easy entrée into the ranks of the great. Moreover, by maintaining the ability to disarm the nuclear forces of lesser powers or to effectively defend their cities against them, they may in fact nullify the strategic effectiveness of lesser nuclear states: the British and French nuclear deterrents, as Soviet ballistic missile defences grow, and the Chinese one, as American defences do, may come to seem without value; and potential imitators of these lesser nuclear states may be expected to draw the lesson.

A weakness of this argument is that much of the present impetus towards proliferation is among countries which do not see the United States or the Soviet Union as their antagonist, but China or some non-nuclear state. Even where it is for confrontation with one of the two great nuclear powers that a nuclear force is being sought, the validity of the argument is uncertain. The present overwhelming superiority of Soviet and American nuclear resources has not had the effect of discouraging China and France from their nuclear programmes; and indeed there is a case to be made out for the strategic logic that sustains them. They may well calculate that the effectiveness of their deterrent forces has to be judged in relation to a whole spectrum of contingencies, and that even if over a wide range of this spectrum they cannot expect to have a meaningful deterrent, there will nevertheless be some area of it for which they can purchase one even with a force whose chance of creating inacceptable damage to a great power is only slight.

The second argument is that a High Posture will enable the United States and the Soviet Union to preserve the bipolar character of international politics against the proliferation that seems to threaten it, both that which has already taken place and that which might take place in the future; and that to this extent it provides a sound formula for the maintenance of order in a world of many nuclear states.

The "bipolarity" which is assumed in this argument is one that implies cooperation between the United States and the Soviet Union in the joint management of international politics. It may be that some element of tacit cooperation between the two leading states is now perceived by their leaders at least as a possible direction in which their foreign policies might move. But the sort of bipolarity which has actually characterised international politics in recent years is of course competitive rather than cooperative; and it is the perpetuation of this competitive bipolarity that would be the more likely result of some of the policies for which the advocates of High Posture are calling. The continuation of underground testing and the deployment of ballistic missile defences, for example, have a vital bearing on the relations between the two great nuclear powers themselves, whatever their implications for relations between these two countries and lesser states. Indeed the negotiation of arms control arrangements would seem to be one of the most likely routes towards the replacement of a primarily competitive by a primarily cooperative bipolar order.

The doctrine of High Posture, moreover, does not allow for the need of the two predominant states to conciliate powers that are in the ascendant and to engage their support in the system. It may well be that the growth of new centres of power in Europe and Asia does not for the foreseeable future spell the end of Soviet-American predominance and that the changes in the structure of the international system which we are now witnessing imply no more than a qualification or loosening of the bipolar situation. This being so, it would be quite premature to treat China and France as if they were the equals of the United States and the Soviet Union, and to recast our thinking about arms control accordingly. Nevertheless, these countries have independent policies and nuclear forces of their own; and no arms control policy can be satisfactory which treats them as pariahs and does not seek to draw them into international negotiations and discussions.

The High Posture doctrine appears either to be opposed to arms control agreements as such, or at best to sanction only those sorts of agreements which preserve and solidify the Soviet and American preponderance. If, however, progress is to be made in making China above all, but also France, more arms control-minded, and in imparting to these and perhaps to future nuclear powers the restraints and disciplines which every nuclear power must practise if we are to survive, then arms control agreements must be negotiated in which these countries have a stake. To the extent that we are already living in a world in which the problems of arms control are multilateral, the search for purely bilateral solutions is unproductive.

It does not seem that we need accept as the soundest formula for managing the problems of a world of many nuclear powers this picture of struggle by the United States and the Soviet Union to overcome other contenders. It may well be that Soviet and American preponderance will continue for a long time to be a necessary presupposition of all strategic and political arrangements; but the dangers of proliferation also require that the two great powers maintain and develop the momentum of arms control, so as to strengthen traditions and precedents on which further nuclear powers can draw; and also that they put forward schemes that are consistent enough with the strategic interests of new nuclear powers as to draw them into the international arms control conversation.

Neither of the two doctrines I have been discussing would appear by itself to provide an adequate guide to the nuclear powers; and there is little doubt that a concerted effort on their part to shape their military policies so as best to affect the spread of nuclear weapons would require them to strike some balance between the two. The question of nuclear proliferation is of course unlikely to be the decisive consideration in determining whether the United States and the Soviet Union adopt a High or a Low Posture. What prospect there is that the United States and the Soviet Union will concert themselves to follow a common policy of any sort in these matters, and what success they would have in managing the problem of proliferation if they did, it is beyond my present purpose to discuss.

The Strategic Consequences of Nuclear Proliferation
James R. Schlesinger[1]

The responsibility assigned to me is to examine the strategic consequences of nuclear proliferation. If we limit ourselves strictly to the strategic area—to the possible employment of additional nuclear capabilities against military or urban targets—one cannot avoid the conclusion that considerable exaggeration has crept into public discussion of proliferation's consequences. This observation rests, in part, upon a distinction between strategic and socio-political consequences, which some will regard as arbitrary and which in any event cannot be made precise. If we isolate the strategic from the socio-political consequences, it is plain that the latter could be quite serious. The very countermeasures through which harmful strategic consequences can be avoided are likely to be viewed as undesirable on social or political grounds. At the very least, the spread of nuclear weapons generates fear. When publics or governments become fearful, they can act in ways which seriously reduce the amenities of living in society. For example, one possible result of the spread would be for societies partially to close their borders and to police incoming goods and people more carefully than at present. This might easily be associated with the decline in the tolerance of dissent within the society. In the specific case of the United States, it is sometimes felt that the idealistic flavor characterizing much of its foreign policy would tend to disap-

pear—to the disadvantage particularly of those who live in the underdeveloped world. These are consequences which few would view without some trepidation. But these are *political* consequences. They do not imply a major alteration of the military balance or for that matter the physical security of most of the world's population.

For these reasons, most public discussion of proliferation's *strategic* consequences must be judged to be seriously defective. However, nothing said here regarding the exaggerations of these strategic consequences should be construed as a criticism of the basic objectives of U.S. policy or of the desirability of preventing further nuclear spread. It is dubious, however, whether any such policies can be completely successful. There is a danger in expecting too much as well as in being too fearful. Moreover, since the writer believes that the effects of proliferation would be less severe than currently anticipated, he would be inclined to set a lower price on what the United States should be willing to pay to prevent proliferation than would some other analysts . . ., and would be particularly reluctant to pay a very high price in terms of offending friendly nations merely to get paper acquiescence to a non-proliferation treaty.

Nevertheless, despite the exaggerations of public discussion, it is plain that we should bend our efforts to avoid or to limit the spread of weapons. Proliferation adds to the problem of managing the world. It increases the number of uncertainties and the number of variables that must be watched. One can put the menace of proliferation in another way,

[1]Any views expressed in this paper are those of the author. They should not be interpreted as reflecting the views of The RAND Corporation or the official opinion or policy of any of its governmental or private research sponsors.

From *Arms Control for the Late Sixties* by James E. Dougherty and J. F. Lehman, Jr. (eds.). © 1967 by D. Van Nostrand. Reprinted by permission of Wadsworth, Inc. Belmont, CA 94002.

as has William C. Foster, the Director of the United States Arms Control and Disarmament Agency: further nuclear spread would lead to a reduction of the relative influence of the United States on the world scene. This appears like a self-serving plea, and for this reason, the argument may have less initial appeal to outsiders than to Americans. Nonetheless, the argument contains a surprisingly large element of altruism. A decline in the relative influence of the United States on the world scene may be more closely associated with increased difficulty in keeping the world relatively stable and peaceful than many non-Americans might be willing to concede at first blush. In a world in which nuclear weapons were more widely held and in which the United States sought to avoid "entanglements," the gravest misfortunes would be reserved for the populations in the unstable portions of the world rather than for the favorably-situated publics of the nuclear superpowers.

1. SOME EXPRESSIONS OF CONCERN

If, then, we acknowledge that there are weighty reasons for opposing the spread, how much despair should we be prepared to feel, if our efforts at control turn out to be unsuccessful? It is on this point that prophecies of disaster appear to dominate public discussions and that public statements diverge most sharply from a sober assessment of the risks. The view that nuclear spread poses a single, overwhelming threat to the continued existence of mankind strikes many responsible analysts as a distortion of reality which, if taken seriously, could lead to a misallocation of our national efforts. The noticeable discrepancy between the paramountcy nominally attributed to the problem and the policies we stand ready to adopt indicates that the more extreme expressions of alarm are not, in fact, taken too seriously. Among leading public figures Senator Robert F. Kennedy has most vividly dramatized the disastrous consequences to be expected from proliferation. In a recent statement he asserted that alongside proliferation control "nothing else means anything." This is a bit of political hyperbole, the force of which would appear to be weakened by the Senator's allocation of his own energies. He himself devotes intense effort to numerous other issues, but aside from public statements has given relatively little attention to the problems of proliferation.

To move from the survival of mankind to the survival of the United States, we have heard on even higher authority that the survival of the United States is at stake—if we fail to prevent the spread of nuclear weapons. Once again, for reasons that will be extensively developed below, this statement is simply misleading. The risks to the American society—and in this respect we must distinguish sharply between the American society and societies in the third world—are very much exaggerated. The United States is in a position to reduce the risks to itself to very low levels. The United States can both adjust its policies and adopt countermeasures which reduce the damage that limited nuclear capabilities could inflict. Such countermeasures would maintain or increase the already enormous gap between U.S. military capabilities and those possessed by non-superpowers. A package of such countermeasures could sharply reduce the risks of proliferation in several respects: 1) the ability to inflict damage on the United States would be kept low, 2) the United States, if it so desired, would remain in a position to deter attack by lesser nuclear powers against third countries, and 3) the incentives to acquire capabilities would consequently be altered—and possibly reduce toward the vanishing point. Countermeasures taken by the Soviet Union would, of course, reinforce the process.

One can make a cogent argument that the ability to implement such countermeasures—to make crystal clear to all nuclear aspirants that acquisition of nuclear weapons cannot significantly alter the strategic balance—provides the best hope over time of controlling proliferation and its consequences. Hedley Bull has characterized this position as one of "high posture." He has—on this occasion as on prior ones—expressed misgivings regarding its suitability. There is no need at this point to argue whether the psychological repercussions of augmenting the gap between the superpowers and other states will be of the sort that Mr. Bull foresees. My purpose at this juncture is merely to indicate a) that such countermeasures are well within the capacity of the United States, and b) that the survival of the United States is scarcely brought into question by the further spread of limited nuclear capabilities. This last specter is one we had best put to rest.

It is scarcely imaginable that any American president will fail to accept at least some of these countermeasures. However, let us place such issues to one side. Whatever their resolution, it is plain that, if proliferation to additional countries takes place, we shall go right on living with it. We may continue to complain about it, but we shall live with it—while continuing to enjoy the benefits—if that is the appropriate term—of a rising standard of living. The very leaders who now assert that non-proliferation is indispensable to our security will then find other subjects to dramatize.

The attempt to allay some of the anxieties regarding proliferation would seem to be necessary not simply because we should recognize that existence will continue to be quite tolerable, even if proliferation takes place. What is perhaps more important, an attitude of desperation regarding the spread of nuclear weapons is not merely inaccurate, but may also be counterproductive in our efforts to achieve control. By understating the difficulties of acquiring a serious nuclear capability and by exaggerating what a nuclear aspirant power may obtain through acquisition of a capability, we may actually strengthen the incentives for acquisition. The danger inherent in exaggerated chatter regarding the damage that additional capabilities can foster is that it revivifies the false notion of nuclear weapons as "the greater equalizer" in international conflict. Hopefully, most nations will penetrate the smokescreen and perceive the difficulties. However, some may be lured into believing that nuclear weapons do provide an answer to their security problems. Others may be encouraged in the notion that acquisition will provide an instrument of threat,

or blackmail which can be directed toward the rest of the world.[2]

To illustrate the way in which such illusions can be fostered, Senator [Robert] Kennedy has misappropriated some words of his brother, the late President, to the effect that "every man, woman, and child, lives under a nuclear sword of Damocles hanging by the slenderest of threads, capable of being cut at any moment by accident or miscalculation or by madness."[3] The Senator's point is that each additional nuclear capability, no matter how limited, automatically creates an additional Damoclean sword. But this suggestion is simply not true. In relation to the indicated levels of destruction, the damage potential of small nuclear forces is too limited. In assessing the damage that might result from nuclear spread, it is essential to recognize that the acquisition of a significant nuclear weapons and delivery capability, although it depends heavily on the quality of a nation's technology, has become even more a quantitative problem than a qualitative one; the superpowers number their nuclear weapons in the thousands or tens of thousands. The quantitative aspects are subject to calculation, but in the public excitement over the threat of proliferation these calculations are normally ignored. Such oversight seems indispensable in generating both needless anxiety and the nuclear-weapons-as-equalizers illusion.

2. DIMENSIONS AND MEASUREMENT

Any serious attempt to assess the dimensions of the proliferation threat should begin with some calculations regarding the spectrum of strategic ca-

---

[2]Fortunately, a number of those nations to which such a motive might reasonably be attributed appear to have such weak technical and industrial bases that it is doubtful whether they could develop a capability, even if so moved.

[3]The nuclear sword of Damocles in President Kennedy's United Nations address quite obviously referred to American and Soviet capabilities. While some poetic license seems understandable in relation to such vast destructive power, it does not seem particularly relevant in relation to the extremely modest forces that other powers would develop.

pabilities given varying levels of investment. Further development of the point that proliferation in certain essential respects is a quantitative problem is basic to our understanding. Proliferation is really quite unlike pregnancy, though in the intuition of many something akin to pregnancy is used as a rough analogue. It is frequently observed—usually by way of admonition—that there is no such thing as being a little bit pregnant. But this is because the results and the time involved in the process are pretty well defined. In size and weight full-term babies tend towards a normal distribution; the variance is not a matter of great moment. But suppose that in pregnancy there were no tendency toward a unimodal distribution of the results and that the time involved in gestation were subject to enormous variation. Suppose again that the ultimate progeny could be Lilliputians or Brobdingnagians—or, for that matter, a varied assortment of misshapen dwarfs, possibly lacking essential organs, limbs, or faculties—and that the specific result depended upon not only the intake of the mother but her intelligence. This is really a more revealing analogy. It explains why being a *little bit proliferated* may be a meaningful concept, while being a little bit pregnant is not. In this area controlling the ultimate dimensions may be even more important than preventing conception or birth.

The range of possible nuclear capabilities is simply enormous. One must be aware of the importance of the distinctions to be drawn among capabilities—and how these distinctions relate to size and vulnerability. Consider the existing array of nuclear capabilities. The United States, which has invested most heavily, possesses a capability which is not only a solid deterrent, but which is not incredible in terms of a carefully controlled, countermilitary initial strike. The Soviet Union, which has invested less, has an impressive second-strike force, which is an effective deterrent. Britain possesses a much more limited capability, presently dependent for delivery on obsolescent aircraft; both the influence and the credibility of the British "independent contribution to the deterrent" are stead-

ily on the wane. The French capability is even more limited in respect to its potential for inflicting damage upon the Soviet Union, though it promises to exploit more advanced delivery systems indigenously-produced. Finally, the Chinese capability—presently drawing the lion's share of attention—is barely past the embryonic stage. There is some question whether it should even be referred to as a *capability*.

The degree to which a nuclear capability is strategically exploitable—and this is substantially dependent on the credibility of the threat to employ—is determined by its size and sophistication and by the vulnerability of the society it is designed to protect. Strategic posture ultimately depends upon the ability to inflict and to limit damage. All these are roughly correlated with the volume of resources the society has invested or is able to invest in its capability. Happily for the wealthy and powerful, this ability is subject to considerable variance. As someone has astutely observed, there is no cheap substitute for money. It is doubtful whether the inexorable requirement for money is anywhere more decisive than in relation to the development of a nuclear capability. Sophisticated nuclear weapons and sophisticated delivery systems are terribly expensive. The cost of developing a capability which could seriously disturb the superpowers (as opposed to one's unarmed neighbor) is staggering.[4]

Let me indicate roughly what kind of sums are involved. In order to develop a convincing second-strike capability against one of the superpowers, a nation must be prepared to spend billions of dollars annually—and these expenditures would continue for a decade and longer. Estimates differ; five billion dollars a year may be too high and three billion dollars a year might be adequate. These sums, however, run well beyond what most nations have been prepared to spend—including some that are present members of the nuclear club. Resources will be

---

[4]The potential of small nuclear capabilities for precipitating regional confrontations or regional destruction would remain as a major source of trouble. Its attenuation—in the case of continued great power involvement—will be treated below.

required not only for delivery systems and compatible weapons, but also for certain supplementary capabilities whose costs are rarely reckoned. How often do we remember to include such indispensable items as reconnaisance and intelligence in the list of required outlays? But any nation contemplating a confrontation with a superpower had better learn something about the location of targets and about the location and capabilities of its opponent's air defense and missile defense systems. The upshot is that only through very heavy outlays can a nation develop more than a very minimal threat against a superpower.

To illustrate the problem, let us consider some historic cost figures. Take the matter of weapons development and stockpiling. Down to early 1966, the United States had invested on the order of eight billion dollars in the development of nuclear weapons. For AEC operations generally, it has now appropriated close to $40 billion. These are substantial amounts. How many nations are in a position to spend even 20 percent or 25 percent of these amounts? Yet, for the creation of a serious capability, requiring deliverable weapons in the megaton range, heavy investment in weapons development is unavoidable.

Though the spread of *missile* capabilities is now a matter of increasing concern, the problem of compatibility implies that development of advanced weapons is preliminary to deployment of an effective missile force. To develop a warhead for an early-generation missile with limited thrust and size (the goal of a development program or the initial goal of a program for an aspiring nuclear power), there must be heavy investment in weapons testing in order to get yield-to-weight ratios to a point where a weapon adequate for target destruction can successfully be delivered in the vehicle. Moreover, there will have to be major investment in guidance technology simply to insure that missiles will be accurate enough to place weapons near the point targeted—whether military bases or cities. In this respect, it is vital to recognize the tradeoff between weapon size and weapon accuracy. With very large yields, considerable inaccuracy may be tolerated.

However, with the very low-yield weapons of the sort that can be developed with small amounts of money, yet which must be delivered with limited-payload vehicles, the accuracy requirements become very severe. But missile accuracy is neither cheap nor easy to obtain.

The implication is that no nation is going to be in a position to develop a strategic capability that is both sophisticated and cheap. In the absence of major investments or extraordinary outside assistance the only option open to most nuclear aspirants is the aerial delivery of rather crude nuclear weapons. Though such capabilities can, of course, dramatically transform a regional balance of power (provided that the superpowers remain aloof), the superpowers themselves will remain more or less immune to nuclear threats emanating from countries other than the principal opponent. For the foreseeable future, only the Soviet Union will be able to deliver the requisite megatonnage to threaten major devastation in the United States. Threats from other quarters may be faced down.

The superpowers therefore will remain in a position in which they can dominate any nuclear confrontation. Only a superpower—and in this connection the term applies particularly to the United States—will be able to intervene in such confrontations in third areas. If it desires to pay the costs and is willing to run the risks, other nations, including the present three minor members of the nuclear club, will continually be deterred. Not only will they be precluded from implementing nuclear thrusts, but in the relevant cases, their capabilities will remain vulnerable to a disarming first strike unless they are given protection by an associated superpower. In any showdown with a superpower, a minor nuclear power relying on its own resources will simultaneously be deterred and be subject to disarming.

This asymmetrical relationship between major and lesser nuclear powers brings us back to a point raised earlier: why it may be counter-productive to talk in a panicky way about proliferation's threat to mankind-as-a-whole. If we are to dissuade others from aspiring to nuclear capabilities, what we should stress is that, if weapons spread, they are not likely to be employed against the superpowers. The penalties for proliferation would be paid, not by the United States, or the Soviet Union, but by third countries.

The likelihood that the first nuclear war, if it comes, will originate in and be confined to the underdeveloped world should play a prominent role in any assessment of proliferation's consequences. The tenor of the existing discussion of proliferation has led some people in the underdeveloped countries to conclude that the major powers would be the chief beneficiaries of curtailing the spread. If nuclear spread is to be effectively opposed, it should be made crystal clear just whose security is placed at risk and whose is not.

3. COUNTERMEASURES

The problem of nuclear spread is not exhausted by the attempt at prevention. The effort to dissuade additional states from acquiring nuclear capabilities, while good in itself, is not likely to be wholly successful. Control includes much more than simply preventing nuclear dispersion. Influencing the character and consequences of whatever nuclear spread does take place should not be neglected out of disappointment with the "failure" to prevent proliferation entirely.

We should recognize that the long-run problem is how to live with the spread at minimum risk. This implies a form of control which will require continuing effort over time; it is not an all-or-none problem to be settled in some particular time period. If we adopt the position that the issue is simply one of *counting* those nations claiming nuclear weapons status and setting this number as a ceiling on the assumption that *if this number increases* we are undone, then we will fail to examine the second-stage opportunities for control. Given our policy of trying to minimize the number of nuclear powers, there should be additional strings to the non-proliferation bow, to be employed as the number of nuclear weapons states increases. What are these additional strings? First, if new weapons programs are launched, we may hope to keep the re-

sulting capabilities as limited as possible. (This would reduce the damage potential of any nuclear wars taking place in third areas.) Second, we can take steps to reduce the likelihood that these capabilities, whatever their size, will or could actually be employed by rational political leaders, especially against the United States. Moreover, any actions which sharply reduce the size or the likelihood of employment of additional capabilities may also serve to weaken the motives for acquisition.

Under the heading of limiting the size of additional capabilities, the methods at our disposal are indirect ones. Recognizing the ordinary tradeoff between cost and quantity, our actions should be designed to keep the cost of strategic capabilities at a high level, thereby weakening the temptation to acquire larger capabilities. This implies a policy of withholding direct assistance from the strategic nuclear programs of other nations, save in rare and unusual circumstances. Through rigorous strategic trade controls we may also hope to limit indirect assistance. Above all, we should make every effort to see that international assistance intended for the support of peaceful nuclear programs is not diverted to support of military programs. These are not easily achievable goals, and we ought not pitch our definition of success at too high a level. The instruments for control are imperfect. Moreover, costs of themselves cannot exclude other nations from seeking nuclear capabilities. Given the existing system of national sovereignties, the ability to influence the decisions of other states is quite limited. Nonetheless, something can be achieved. To whatever extent we can prevent the deflation of costs, we can limit the size and the potential destructiveness of budding nuclear capabilities.

The second heading—reducing the likelihood that new capabilities will be actually employed or, if employed, limiting the potential damage—represents that aspect of living-with-proliferation-at-minimum-risk over which we ourselves have most control. There are certain hardware possibilities and other physical arrangements that can limit the potential for damage. One obvious possibility may be to buttress the air defense capabilities of threatened states. A more controversial possibility is the deployment of new systems that will sharply reduce the damage that Nth countries could inflict on the major nuclear powers. The most dramatic current illustration of this type of possibility [is] the development of an ABM system. . . .My remarks should not be taken as an endorsement of the ABM system, for that decision involves complex arms control, strategic, and cost-effectiveness calculations, which are beyond the scope of this paper. But one factor that is relevant to the final decision deserves stressing here: deployment of an ABM system or other systems that substantially reduce the damage that can be inflicted on the United States may serve to curtail the harmful consequences which might otherwise flow from proliferation. Through such damage-limiting measures, the willingness and ability of the United States to intervene in third areas when the use of nuclear weapons is threatened is enhanced. Consequently the U.S. ability to prevent the misuse of nuclear capabilities will be strengthened. The strongest deterrent to a lesser power's employing its capability is the possibility that a major nuclear power will enter the lists against it.

Given the existing preponderance of U.S. power, the deployment of major new systems may not be essential to achieve this result. Certain types of developments do appear desirable, however, in order to exploit the discrepancy between major and lesser nuclear powers for the purpose of driving home to lesser powers how ill-advised they would be to initiate the use of nuclear weapons. For example, in a world of many nuclear powers in which anonymity is at least a hypothetical possibility, we should invest considerable effort in developing methods for "finger-printing" nuclear weapons and parallel systems through which we may in a crisis quickly ascribe responsibility for any detonation that occurs. Then, if we wish to offer protection to threatened nations, we could see to it that punishment for any irresponsible nuclear act would be swift and condign.

An approach of this sort, which relies on superpower preponderance to withstand the potentially baleful effects of proliferation, is not one that is universally and automatically appealing. Hedley Bull has characterized this approach as "high posture" and has contrasted it with one that he prefers: the "low posture" in which the differences between the greater and lesser powers are muted. Let me therefore say a few words in defense of the so-called "high posture."

First, phrases like "high posture" and "low posture" have a certain allure, but the question must be raised whether they accurately describe the underlying realities or the true alternatives. The gap in military nuclear power between the superpowers and other nations is enormous and will continue to be so. In fact, it is more likely to increase than diminish.[5] If we accept that the strategic gap will continue to be enormous, what seems desirable is that the character and width of the gap be sufficient to permit the superpowers to exert a stabilizing influence on the restless third areas of the world. Moreover, this stabilizing function needs to be perceived by those who may come to possess a minor nuclear capability. This potential stabilizing function should not lightly be discarded in the quest for a somewhat mythical "low posture."

Second, the spread of nuclear capabilities into third areas will very much intensify the existing elements of instability and magnify the danger of instability beyond what it is today. The new nuclear capabilities will be unsophisticated and vulnerable. Given the existence of vulnerabilities and the temp-

---

[5]Pious comments regarding diminution of the strategic-military gap separating the superpowers from other nations, nuclear and non-nuclear alike, is reminiscent of some high-flown discussions regarding the "income gap" which were particularly popular in the 50s. It was frequently stated at that time that it was essential to diminish the gap between the affluence of the developed nations and the poverty of the underdeveloped nations. In the intervening period per capita GNP in the United States has risen by more than $1,000, while there remains some question whether per capita income in the underdeveloped countries has risen at all. Diminution of the income gap was simply not a feasible objective. Similarly, in the strategic area we are not going to have any diminution of the gap between the superpowers and the rest for the foreseeable future. It is never sensible to base one's policies on hopes for the unobtainable. Therefore, let us avoid repetition of this particular class of past errors. Whatever else our policy is based on, it should not be on an expected diminution of the strategic gap.

tation to exploit a temporary strategic edge, the likelihood of nuclear initiation through a hair-trigger response seems obvious. Most persons who seek a more peaceful world would find beneficial the ability of the superpowers to forestall the initial use of such capabilities. In seeking arms control arrangements, we must keep in mind the bilateral U.S.-Soviet relationship, but we should also remember that increases in our capabilities, when matched by the Soviet Union, may serve to diminish the risks of dangerous outbreaks in third areas of the world.

Third, most nations, even when they strongly disapprove of specific aspects of U.S. policy, desire that the United States stand ready to counter nuclear threats against nations lacking in the means of self-protection. The United States, in particular, is being called upon to perform functions that other nations are not called upon to perform. If the United States is expected to play the role of a nuclear Galahad, risking nuclear retaliation and loss of population in behalf of others, it does not seem unreasonable for the United States to possess protective measures of a type not universally available. Nor does it seem wholly consistent for those who rely on U.S. protection simultaneously to urge the United States to accept a low posture *and* to stand ready to intervene in the defense of nuclear "abstainers." If a nation is expected to accept losses on behalf of others, it seems reasonable that plans should be laid to hold the potential losses to a minimum. That those on whom the role of nuclear Galahad is thrust should desire thicker armor seems quite understandable.

4. CONCLUSION

There has been a tendency to exaggerate the strategic importance of proliferation because the problem has been viewed qualitatively in respect to enumerating those nations that might acquire a small capability rather than quantitatively in respect to the destructive potential of the capability that might be achieved. As far as we can see into the future, the strategic environment will continue to be dominated by the preponderant military power of the United States and the Soviet Union. It is possible that the spread of weapons will increasingly inhibit the use of power by the United States or the Soviet Union in regions of less than vital concern. The degree of inhibition will depend upon the risks that we (or the Soviets) are willing to run. However, if we desire to accept the risks, we could, because of our preponderant power, continue to intervene in unsettled areas to diminish the risk of small-scale nuclear war.

With the spread of weapons there would be a greater likelihood of use or misuse, but the risk of use or misuse will be concentrated primarily in the third areas of the world. Given the current and prospective stable military balance between the United States and the Soviet Union, it is difficult to envisage conflicts in third areas escalating into exchanges between the homelands of the two major powers. This implies, of course, that proliferation would impose enlarged risks primarily on other nations. The superpowers will continue to be relatively immune to strikes from the parvenus; the threat of them will continue to come primarily from each other. In all analyses of proliferation this asymmetrical distribution of the risks should be stressed because of its possible impact on the incentives of aspiring nuclear powers.

A substantial diminution of the strategic gap between the superpowers and others is simply not in the offing. The only way in which reduction of the gap could be influential is if it undermines the credibility of intervention by a superpower to stabilize conditions in third areas being subjected to nuclear threat. This is not necessarily beneficial, and it is doubtful whether those in threatened areas would desire such an outcome, if they were to think seriously about the problem. What may be desirable is to make crystal clear that despite nuclear spread the major powers will retain the ability to intervene to deter nuclear threats or to punish nuclear irresponsibility without risking substantial damage to themselves. This does not necessarily mean that the major powers will be forced to deploy all those systems, like ABM, which hold some promise in this regard; it does mean that they shall be forced to work diligently so as continually to upgrade their ability to detect, deter, disarm, or punish the national source of nuclear irresponsibility.

While nuclear spread is basically destabilizing, its strategic consequences need not be too severe. Simple nuclear capabilities cannot play the role of "equalizers" in international conflict. The strategic position that the United States and the Soviet Union currently enjoy is so unassailable that even continuing action by third parties is unlikely to upset the central strategic balance for the next twenty years. Properly exploited, this central strategic balance could continue to provide some stability in regional conflicts—even in the face of nuclear proliferation.

QUESTIONS FOR DISCUSSION

1 How credible in the context of nonproliferation are NWS security guarantees to NNWSs?
2 Is there a difference in the credibility of an American security guarantee to Western Europe than to America's other allies?
3 To what extent have developments since the late 1960s proven Schlesinger right or wrong about security guarantees?
4 Is the gap between military nuclear forces of the superpowers, on the one hand, and those of other NWSs, on the other, still as significant as Schlesinger judged it to be in the late 1960s?

SUGGESTED READINGS

Brito, Dagobert, Michael D. Intriligator, and Adele E. Wick (eds.). *Strategies for Managing Nuclear Proliferation.* Lexington, Massachusetts: Lexington Books, 1983.

Carlton, David. "The Anglo-American Nuclear Relationship: Proliferatory or Anti-Proliferatory?" in David Carlton and Carlo Schaerf (eds.), *Arms Control and Technological Innovation.* London: Croom Helm, 1977, pp. 132–45.

Dunn, Lewis A. *Controlling the Bomb: Nuclear Proliferation in the 1980s.* New Haven, Connecticut: Yale University Press, 1982.

Goheen, Robert F. "Problems of Proliferation: U.S. Policy and the Third World," *World Politics* 35 (January 1983), pp. 194–215.

Harkavy, Robert E. "Pariah States and Nuclear Proliferation," *International Organization* 35 (Winter 1981), pp. 135–63.

Jones, Rodney W. (ed.). *Small Nuclear Forces and U.S. Security Policy: Threats and Potential Conflict in the Middle East and South Asia.* Lexington, Massachusetts: Lexington Books, 1984.

Kemp, Geoffrey, Robert L. Pfaltzgraff, Jr., and Uri Ra'anan (eds.). *The Superpowers in a Multinuclear World.* Lexington, Massachusetts: Lexington Books, 1974.

Kolodziej, Edward A. and Robert E. Harkavy (eds.). *Security Policies of Developing Countries.* Lexington, Massachusetts: Lexington Books, 1982.

Schoettle, Enid C. B. "Arms Limitation and Security Policies Required to Minimize the Proliferation of Nuclear Weapons," in David Carlton and Carlo Schaerf (eds.), *Arms Control and Technological Innovation.* London: Croom Helm, 1977, pp. 102–131.

———. *Postures for Non-proliferation: Arms Limitation and Security Policies to Minimize Nuclear Proliferation.* London: Taylor & Francis, 1979.

21 Are Terrorists Likely to Get Nuclear Weapons?

YES

Louis René Beres

Hic Sunt Dracones: *The Nuclear Threat of International Terrorism*

NO

Ted Greenwood

Non-State Entities

Hic Sunt Dracones: The Nuclear Threat of International Terrorism

Louis René Beres

From the end of the 11th century, when a Muslim sect known as the Assassins (a translation from *Hashishaya*) willingly sacrificed their own lives in pursuit of what they termed righteousness and salvation, special difficulties have been involved in dealing with terrorists. Not until very recently, however, have these difficulties entailed the prospect of large-scale nuclear catastrophe. Today, the failure of counterterrorist strategies can give rise not only to locally destructive acts of rage and violence, but to genuinely apocalyptic events triggered by nuclear weapons. The nightmare that began with the Manhattan Project may end with megadeath, and the primary actors may not be governments, but terrorists.

How can this be possible? The answer lies largely in the fact that the ability to acquire and use nuclear weapons has now passed into the hands of private individuals and groups. Coupled with the orientation to violence of terrorists, their relative insensitivity to orthodox threats of deterrence, and the growth of interterrorist cooperation, this ability signals an inexorable drift toward nuclear destruction. This paper will explore the different components of the hazard of nuclear terrorism and will offer certain recommendations for understanding how to keep the problem within manageable limits.[1]

THE TERRORISTS

Who, exactly, are today's terrorists? Recognizing the extraordinary heterogeneity of purpose, power, and popular support which distinguish one group from another, they include such far-flung organizations as Japan's Red Army (*Sekigun*), which has mounted operations in Malaysia, Lebanon, Israel, Mexico, Cuba, West Germany, and Libya; West Germany's Baader-Meinhof Group, sometimes known as the Red Army Faction; Northern Ireland's Provisional Irish Republican Army; Italy's Red Brigades; and the various organizations that coexist uneasily under the loose umbrella of the Palestine Liberation Organization: Al Fatah, the Popular Front for the Liberation of Palestine (PFLP), the Popular Front for the Liberation of Palestine–General Command (PFLP–GC), and the Popular Democratic Front for the Liberation of Palestine (PDFLP).[2]

Ideologically, these groups are a tangled skein of variegated purpose and composition. Their intellectual and spiritual mentors include Bakunin, Marx, Lenin, Sorel, Marighella, Mao, Giap, Fanon, Marcuse, Guevara, Debray, Trotsky, and Guillen. And, insofar as all modern revolutionary

---

[1]The notions of hazards and limits suggest the appropriateness of the phrase *Hic sunt dracones* in the title. *Hic sunt dracones,* meaning "Here are dragons," was the phrase which medieval cartographers used to mark uncharted areas on their maps. Also by way of definition, terrorism, as used in this article, refers to the violent activity of insurgents who wish to challenge existing centers of power rather than to the violent activity of incumbents seeking to maintain power. In the language adopted by Thomas Perry Thornton, we are concerned with "agitational terror" rather than with "enforcement terror." [See Thornton's "Terror as a Weapon of Political Agitation," in *Internal War*, ed. Harry Eckstein (New York: The Free Press,

1964), pp. 71–99.] This is not to suggest that terrorism practiced by governments against their own people is less reprehensible than "agitational terror" (it may, in fact, be much more reprehensible), but only that the threatened use of nuclear explosives or radioactivity is intrinsically unsuited to the tactics of "enforcement terror."

[2]This paper makes no attempt to draw distinctions between different terrorist groups in terms of the legitimacy or reasonableness of their claims. Rather, it rests upon the assumptions that every terrorist group, however reasonable or unreasonable its rationale, has the potential to precipitate extraordinary levels of global instability and is acting wrongly and illegally when it engages in random killing and destruction.

Louis René Beres, *"Hic Sunt Dracones:* The Nuclear Threat of International Terrorism," *Parameters—Journal of the US Army War College* 9 (June 1979), pp. 11–19.

terror has certain roots in the French Reign of Terror (1793–94), the names of Robespierre, Marat, Saint-Just, and Fouché must also be counted as fountainheads of current terrorist dogma.

With respect to the kinds of individuals who become engaged in terrorist activities, the literature is replete with motives and explanations. Some scholars distinguish between genuine political actors and those persons who feign political concerns for purely private ends.[3] Others focus on the psychological dimension of involvement, emphasizing such dynamics as frustration-aggression theory[4] or psychoanalytic theory with special reference to psychopathology and madness.[5] Whatever the motives that give rise to terrorist activity, be they a deeply rooted commitment to specific political objectives or the need to escape from one form or another of private anguish,[6] virtually all of today's terrorist actors would offer obeisance to Clausewitz' remark: "The political object . . . will be the standard for determining both the aim of military force and the amount of effort to be made."[7]

TERRORIST ACCESS TO NUCLEAR WEAPONS

Terrorists can now gain access to nuclear weapons either by theft of assembled systems from military stockpiles and production facilities or by self-development from pilfered nuclear materials. To acquire an assembled weapon, terrorist operatives might direct their attention to any of the tens of thousands of nuclear weapons now deployed across the world in national arsenals. In the future, such terrorists are likely to have a significantly enlarged range of possibilities for stealing nuclear weapons. This is the case because the number of national members in the so-called "Nuclear Club" is growing steadily.

To fashion their own weapons from basic nuclear materials, terrorist groups would require both the materials and the expertise to create an explosive device or radiation dispersal implement. How difficult would it be for them to fulfill these requirements? Not very! As increasingly large amounts of fissionable materials are produced by the nuclear power industry in the years ahead, the opportunities for terrorists to exploit the manifestly catastrophic possibilities that lie dormant in nuclear fuel will skyrocket.

How difficult would it be for terrorists to actually get their hands on fissionable materials?[8] According to Mason Willrich and Theodore Taylor, coauthors of a special report to the Energy Policy Project of the Ford Foundation, the extant system of safeguards in this country is so inadequate that it is only a matter of time before terrorists are able to surreptitiously remove the essential fissionable materials from nuclear power plants.[9] Although significant improvements in American safeguards have taken place since this appraisal was offered, parallel improvements have not always been implemented abroad. This situation has portentous overtones, since American safeguards do not secure us against nuclear weapons fashioned from materials

---

[3]Stephen Schafer, for example, distinguishes between the "convictional criminal," who has an altruistic-communal motivation, and the "pseudoconvictional criminal," whose motivation is egoistic. See Stephen Schafer, *The Political Criminal: The Problem of Morality and Crime* (New York: The Free Press, 1974), p. 147.

[4]This theory is founded on Dollard's principle that "the occurrence of aggressive behavior always presupposes the existence of frustration and, contrariwise, that the existence of frustration always leads to some form of aggression." See John Dollard, et al., *Frustration and Aggression* (New Haven: Yale University Press, 1939), p.1.

[5]Psychoanalytic explanations draw sustenance from Harold Lasswell's *Psychopathology and Politics* (Chicago: University of Chicago, 1930) and Eric Hoffer's *The True Believer* (New York: Harper and Brothers, 1951).

[6]This need is perhaps best described by André Malraux in his characterization of the terrorist Ch'en in *La Condition humaine* (New York: French & European Publications, 1933).

[7] Karl von Clausewitz, *On War*, ed. and trans. E. M. Collins (Chicago: Henry Regnery Co., 1962), p. 71.

[8]While an enormous amount of plutonium is apt to be produced by the nuclear power industry in the years ahead, only some 11 to 20 pounds are needed to construct a crude explosive device. Moreover, only $3\frac{1}{2}$ ounces are needed to make a radiation dispersal device capable of killing thousands.

[9]See Mason Willrich and Theodore Taylor, *Nuclear Theft: Risks and Safeguards* (Cambridge, Mass.: Ballinger, 1974), p. 115.

stolen elsewhere. To be genuinely worthwhile, the protection of nuclear materials from terrorist groups must be global in scope.

Regrettably, the amount of fissionable materials present in other countries which might become the target of terrorists is likely to expand at an almost unbelievable rate. India's manufacture of a nuclear device with technology supplied by Canada, the West German–Brazilian and French–Pakistani deals involving pilot reprocessing plants to extract weapons-grade plutonium from spent reactor fuel rods, and the continuing development of fast-breeder reactor plants by Japan, the Soviet Union, France, and West Germany signal very dangerous conditions. Unless immediate and effective steps are taken to inhibit the spread of plutonium reprocessing and uranium enrichment facilities to other countries, terrorist opportunities to acquire fissionable materials for nuclear weapons will reach intolerable limits.

To fabricate its own nuclear weapons, a terrorist group would also require expertise. According to Willrich and Taylor:

> The design and manufacture of a crude nuclear explosive is no longer a difficult task technically, and a plutonium dispersal device which can cause widespread radioactive contamination is much simpler to make than an explosive.[10]

Since as early as 1954, declassification and public dissemination of information about the design of fission weapons have been extensive. As a result, such widely publicized cases as the one involving the 20-year-old MIT undergraduate who put together a devastatingly accurate technical design for a nuclear explosive—a case documented in the NOVA science series on public television,

9 March 1975—assume a high degree of credibility.[11]

The fact is that such cases are not really all that remarkable. According to Willrich and Taylor:

> Under conceivable circumstances, a few persons, possibly even one person working alone, who possessed about ten kilograms of plutonium oxide and a substantial amount of chemical high explosive could, within several weeks, design and build a crude fission bomb. By a 'crude fission bomb' we mean one that would have an excellent chance of exploding, and would probably explode with the power of at least 100 tons of chemical high explosive. This could be done using materials and equipment that could be purchased at a hardware store and from commercial suppliers of scientific equipment for student laboratories.[12]

What would happen if such a bomb were made and exploded? Since a nuclear explosion yields deadly penetrating radiations (gamma rays and neutrons) as well as blast wave and heat, even a "small" nuclear weapon could generate terrible destruction. Consider the following examples provided by Willrich and Taylor:

> A nuclear explosion with a yield of ten tons in the central courtyard of a large office building might expose to lethal radiation as many as 1000 people in the building. A comparable explosion in the center of a football stadium during a major game could lethally irradiate as many as 10,000 spectators. A nuclear explosion with a 100-ton yield in a typical suburban residential area might kill perhaps as many as 2000 people, primarily by exposure to fallout. The same explosion in a parking lot beneath a very large sky-

---

[10]Willrich and Taylor, p. 1. A crude nuclear explosive made from pilfered plutonium would probably have a yield in the range between several hundred and several thousand tons of high explosive. If such an explosive were detonated in a crowded metropolitan area, as many as 10,000 people might be killed directly while tens of thousands of others might suffer severe fallout problems.

[11]More recently, there is the case of a 21-year-old undergraduate physics major at Princeton, John A. Phillips, who designed an atomic bomb in four months with information obtained entirely from public documents. The point of his design, said Phillips, "was to show that any undergraduate with a physics background can do it, and therefore that it is reasonable to assume that terrorists could do it, too." See *The Princeton Alumni Weekly*, 25 October 1976, p. 6. Most recently, of course, is the controversy over the article written by Howard Morland which was published in the November 1979 issue of *The Progressive*.

[12]Willrich and Taylor, pp. 20–21.

scraper might kill as many as 50,000 people and destroy the entire building.[13]

A terrorist group might also choose to use its plutonium in the form of a radiation dispersal device. In this case, the plutonium would be transformed into an aerosol of finely divided particles that could be distributed uniformly into the intake of a large office building's air conditioning system. According to Willrich and Taylor, only $3\frac{1}{2}$ ounces of this extraordinarily toxic substance (its toxicity is at least 20,000 times that of cobra venom or potassium cyanide[14]) would pose a lethal hazard to everyone in such a building.[15]

How would such a weapon work? Consider the following scenario:

The plutonium aerosol is distributed into the intake of a large downtown office building's air conditioning system by a criminal or terrorist group. Only three and one half ounces could prove a deadly risk for all of the occupants. Death by lung cancer would probably come to anyone inhaling between ten and one hundred *millionths* of a gram. Death due to fibrosis of the lung would be the probable fate of those who retain a dose of about a dozen *thousandths* of a gram. [Emphasis added.][16]

---

[13]*Ibid.*, p. 22.

[14]It should be pointed out that despite its extraordinary toxicity, a prospective plutonium thief would be safe as long as the metal did not come into contact with an open wound or reach his lungs.

[15]Willrich and Taylor, p. 25. It is interesting to point out that the companies involved in the nuclear energy industry take issue with this conclusion. In a "position paper" advertisement appearing in *Fortune* magazine, John W. Simpson, Director-Officer of the Westinghouse Electric Corporation and Chairman of the Energy Committee, states the following:

The release of plutonium in an enclosed area—as say in a building's ventilating system—would have a limited effect from a terrorist point of view. The filters and ducts would prevent a substantial amount from being circulated in the system. Hence use of plutonium as a radiological weapon would be effective only in the immediate vicinity of the point of release and that area can be decontaminated.

See the advertisement "Nuclear Energy and the Future, Position Paper #5, Managing and Safeguarding Wastes and Fissionable Material," *Fortune,* 91 (May 1975), 138.

[16]Willrich and Taylor, pp. 24–25.

What makes this scenario particularly macabre is that the building occupants who absorb lethal but not massive doses of plutonium might not know of their poisoning for weeks, or months, or perhaps even years. One can only imagine the reaction of thousands of office workers to the disclosure that they have been lethally irradiated. The concrete human implications, the social and economic dislocations, and—last but certainly not least—the political implications are staggering.

Plutonium might be dispersed in still other ways. One scenario that has been considered at the Nuclear Regulatory Commission Office in Washington, D.C., is described as follows:

During what appears to be a normal day at the Pacific Coast Stock Exchange a large beaker filled with boiling liquid is noticed in the window of a nearby hotel. Police investigate, but it is too late. The boiling acid in the beaker has been dissolving and dispersing half a pound of plutonium, enough to expose everyone within several city blocks to a high risk of lung cancer.[17]

Rather than use plutonium for nuclear explosives or radiation dispersal, terrorists might also find it agreeable to sabotage nuclear plant facilities. Such sabotage could yield extensive death and property damage via radiation release. Although the chances of accidental reactor meltdown are generally believed to be extremely small (a belief, however, that has been tempered somewhat by the recent events at Three Mile Island in Pennsylvania), the case is quite different with respect to deliberate reactor meltdown. Consider the following scenario, another in the collection of the Nuclear Regulatory Commission's Office of Nuclear Material Safety and Safeguards:

Under the cover of night, a dozen men storm the gates of a nuclear power plant, killing the two guards and taking the operating staff hostage. After placing charges of high explosives next to the plant's critical cooling

---

[17]See Robert R. Jones, "Nuclear Reactor Risks—Some Frightening Scenarios," *Chicago Sun-Times,* 30 April 1976, p. 12.

systems, they phone the mayor of a nearby large city. Send $5 million, they demand, or we will blow the plant, sending radioactive particles drifting over the city's neighborhoods.[18]

Such acts could pose monumental problems for the appropriate authorities. Although a great many steps have already been taken to diminish the vulnerability of nuclear power plants in this country, successful sabotage is certainly not out of the question. By penetrating the physical barriers between themselves and the fission material in the reactor, and by disabling the cooling systems to the reactor core, saboteurs could cause the reactor to melt through its protective shielding and release deadly radioactivity into the atmosphere. Alternatively, since today's nuclear plants are unable to withstand the impact of large aircraft, a kamikaze-type plane crash into a nuclear plant could create a calamitous reactor core meltdown. Comparatively speaking, however, it would be more difficult for terrorists to "pulse" a nuclear reactor core to destruction than to make a radiological weapon or a crude fission bomb.

TERRORIST ORIENTATIONS TO VIOLENCE

Today's terrorist groups typically share an orientation to violence that has been shaped largely by the preachings of Bakunin, Fanon, and Sorel.[19] All too frequently, these groups operate without a code of honor that distinguishes between combatants and noncombatants. As a result, the imperative to create limits to violence is ignored, and terrorist anger is vented almost randomly.[20] At the same time, the level of adopted violence is constrained only by the limits of available weaponry. These facts imply an unacceptably high probability of nuclear terror-

ism should access to weapons or power plants be realized.

To a certain extent, this orientation to violence stems from the conviction that the absence of inhibitions to apply maximum force to virtually any segment of human population is expedient. Since war is still the *ultima ratio* between states, it is argued, so must internal war be the final arbiter within states. Such "gun-barrel" thinking is often taken as an adaptation from the aphoristic philosophy of Mao Tse-tung.

To another extent, this orientation derives from the romanticization of violent actions exemplified by Bakunin's dictum that "the passion for destruction is a constructive passion." Fused with the categories of Sorel and Fanon, and the existential idea of Sartre that "irrepressible violence . . . is man recreating himself," such romanticization breeds a cathartic view of violence.

Finally, today's terrorist orientations to violence stem, in part, from the presence of psychopaths and sociopaths who enjoy carnage for its own sake. Here, the complete inversion of Judaeo-Christian notions of conscience and compassion flows not from any means-end calculation or from devotion to the "creativity" of violence, but from purely psychotic motive. Where such motive is present among terrorists who are suicidal schizophrenics, the problems of effective counterterrorist action are greatly exacerbated. This is the case because such terrorists—whose incentive is to use violence nihilistically rather than politically—are apt to regard the threat of death as a stimulus rather than as a deterrent.[21]

TERRORIST INSENSITIVITY TO THREATS OF DETERRENCE

As we have just seen, the viability of deterrent threats against terrorist actors may be undermined

[18]*Ibid.*

[19]Sorel, in turn, speaks of his own *Reflections on Violence* (1914; rpt. New York: AMS Press, 1975) as "Proudhonian in inspiration."

[20]This imperative to create limits to violence is discussed by Camus in his work, *Les Justes* (New York: French & European Publications, 1950).

[21]One is reminded, in this case, of Sergei Nechayev, portrayed by Dostoyevsky as "possessed," who states in *Revolutionary Catechism:* "Our task is terrible, total, universal, and merciless destruction." Quoted in Walter Laqueur, ed., *The Terrorism Reader: A Historical Anthology* (New York: New American Library, 1978), p. 69.

when these actors are impelled by psychotic motive. It must now be pointed out that the ability to deter violent behavior by terrorists is in doubt with *all* categories of terrorist, including those whose actions spring from purely political concerns. Since a great many modern terrorists place a higher value on the achievement of certain political and social objectives than they do upon their own lives, these groups are essentially insensitive to orthodox threats of retaliation. Faced with an international actor for whom the "deadly logic" of deterrence is immobilized, states bent upon an effective counterterrorist strategy are at a significant disadvantage.

Consider the following examples of terrorist "rationality":

- Arab terrorists, in April 1974, seized an apartment building in Northern Israel, and ultimately accepted death rather than capture.
- SLA members, during the widely publicized California shootout in May 1974, preferred death to incarceration.
- Two Red Army terrorists, during their attack on Israel's Lod International Airport in May 1972, killed themselves.
- Holger Meins, of the Baader-Meinhof group, succumbed to self-inflicted starvation in 1974.

What are the implications of this particular behavioral characteristic of terrorist actors for the threat of nuclear terrorism? Quite plainly, the most significant implication is that should terrorists obtain access to nuclear explosives or radioactivity and calculate the prospective costs and benefits of use, the fear of retaliatory destruction might not figure importantly in this calculation. In effect, this means that traditional threats of deterrence might have little or no bearing on the terrorist decision concerning the use of nuclear force.

It follows that unless diplomatic or other forms of persuasion can prove successful, the only means left to prevent the threatened nuclear act would be a "surgical" or preemptive strike. In certain instances, of course, even this option might prove inappropriate or ineffectual.

COOPERATION AMONG TERRORIST GROUPS

Consider the following:

- Venezuelan terrorist Illich Remirzed Sanchez receives weapons training from the PFLP in Lebanon.
- Members of the Japanese Red Amy terrorist group receive weapons training in Lebanon.
- Joint training programs and arms transfers take place between the Turkish People's Army and Black September.
- Members of the American Weathermen, Northern Ireland's IRA, and Nicaragua's *Sandinista* movement are trained in Palestinian camps.
- Black September operatives demand the release of German insurgents who had been involved in the killing of German policemen.
- Liaison between PFLP and Japanese Red Army agents produces the Lydda Airport massacre; an attack on the American Embassy in Kuala Lumpur, Malaysia; the hijacking of a JAL flight; an assault on the Japanese Embassy in Kuwait; and a takeover of the French Embassy at The Hague.[22]

These are only a few of the most glaring examples of a new phenomenon in world politics—systematic cooperation and collaboration between terrorist groups. Terrorists have always formed alignments with sympathetic state actors, but they are now also beginning to cement patterns of alliance and partnership with each other.[23] The net effect of such behavior patterns is a mirror image of Trotsky's theory of "permanent revolution."

From the standpoint of nuclear terrorism, cooperation between terrorist groups is particularly ominous. Such cooperation greatly facilitates terrorist acquisition of nuclear weapons and their exchange between different groups. It also increases

[22]See Robert Fisk, "The World's Terrorists Sometimes Are United," *The New York Times,* 17 August 1975, Section 4, p. 3; Yonah Alexander, "Some Perspectives on International Terrorism," *International Problems,* 14 (Fall 1975), 27; and John B. Wolf, "Black September: Militant Palestinianism," *Current History,* 64 (January 1973), 37.

[23]With regard to sympathetic states, today's most obvious "sponsors" are Libya, Uganda, Algeria, Syria, Vietnam, Iraq, Somalia, and the People's Democratic Republic of Yemen.

the prospect of shared expertise in the technology of nuclear destruction and enlarges the opportunity for reciprocal privileges which might be crucial to successful operations.

IN CONCLUSION

The subject of terrorism resembles the writing of Franz Kafka: It is easy to appreciate, but difficult to understand. A potpourri of actors, motives, and methods, terrorism presents a complex admixture of sources and styles that overshadows the great simplicity of its effects. This admixture is a phantasmagoria rather than a fixed pattern, a succession of shifting images of purpose and prospect that defies "capture" by even the most skillful social scientists. Complicated by the developing possibility of nuclear terrorism, these characteristics bode an inconceivably mad ending to the absurd drama of international political life.

What is to be done? What palliatives, if any, can be applied to alter the trajectory of our collective descent toward nuclear terrorism? What evidence, if any, exists to counter the impression that the long litany of increasingly destructive terrorist incidents will be interrupted before even greater (i.e., nuclear) violence is unleashed?

To answer these questions, our attention must be focused on two basic options: technological and behavioral. In an effort to halt the spread of nuclear technology and nuclear materials throughout the world, steps can be taken to discourage the theft of assembled weapons or fissionable materials and the sabotage of nuclear reactors. In fact, such steps—in the form of vaults, barriers, locks, alarms, remote surveillance, and armed guards—are already underway, spurred on by the awareness that calamitous possibilities exist and must be removed. Additionally, there is growing international concern for President Carter's aim to prevent nuclear exports to states which do not submit to International Atomic Energy Agency (IAEA) safeguards and control.

All such steps, however, are bound to be inadequate when the underlying problem is one of "safeguarding nuclear materials in a world of malfunctioning people."[24] The prospect of nuclear terrorism will not be impaired by the application of a technological "fix."[25] Rather, what is required is a thoughtful behavioral strategy, one that is directed toward producing certain changes in the behavior of both terrorist and state actors.

The "core" of such a strategy must necessarily be based upon a sound understanding of the risk calculations of terrorists. Until we understand the unique terrorist stance (vis-à-vis that of states) on the balance of risks that can be taken in world politics, we will not be able to identify an appropriate system of sanctions. Faced with actors whose preference orderings often run counter to those of states, we must explore their decisional calculi before we can know what threats to apply or rewards to promise.

Although terrorist actors are typically apt to tolerate substantially higher levels of death and injury than states, there *is* a threshold beyond which certain costs become intolerable. No less than states, terrorists choose between alternative courses of action by assessing the perceived consequences of each course in cost-benefit terms. While such assessments are bound to be rough and imprecise, their use suggests that counter-nuclear-terrorism measures can succeed once the threshold of unacceptable costs is understood.[26]

---

[24]See Mason Willrich, "Terrorists Keep Out: The Problem of Safeguarding Nuclear Materials in a World of Malfunctioning People," *The Bulletin of the Atomic Scientists,* 31(May 1975), 12.

[25]Quite simply, a technological "fix" will not work. Even if the United States succeeds in developing new and elaborate protection systems for nuclear weapons, special nuclear materials, and nuclear reactors, such systems would have to be replicated internationally. And, even if this highly improbable replication were to take place, techniques could always be figured out to circumvent vaults, locks, armed guards, etc. Moreover, at the time of this writing there is no evidence that major national suppliers of nuclear technology will agree to a general moratorium on sales of plants or materials, or that the major national developers of plutonium-fueled reactors will drop plans for fast-breeder plants.

[26]Of course, as in the case of states, terrorists are subject to acting irrationally. Here, the problem of preventing nuclear violence is especially severe, since it is impossible to know in advance what contingencies of reinforcement are appropriate.

To understand this threshold, scholars must begin to address themselves to the following ten principal questions:

• Is there a particular ordering of preferences that is common to many or all terrorist groups, or is there significant variation from one group to another? If it can be determined that many or all terrorist groups actually share a basic hierarchy of wants, a general strategy of counter-nuclear-terrorist operations can begin to be shaped. Alternatively, if significant variation in preference orderings can be detected between terrorist groups, myriad strategies of an individually "tailored" nature will have to be identified.

• Are there particular preferences which tend to occupy the highest positions in the preference hierarchies of terrorist groups, and how might these preferences be effectively obstructed? In this connection, it is especially important to examine the widely held assumption that terrorists, like states, are most anxious to avoid negative physical sanctions. In fact, a great deal of sophisticated conceptual analysis and experimental evidence appears to indicate that such sanctions are apt to be ineffective in limiting aggression and may actually prove counterproductive.[27]

• To what extent, if any, would the obstruction of terrorist preferences prove offensive to some of the principal values of states? In this case, we must be concerned about the very real possibility that effective counter-nuclear-terrorist measures might be injurious to such values as social justice and human rights within particular states. Here, states must first decide whether the prospective benefits of proposed antiterrorist activity are great enough to outweigh the prospective costs to major segments of their own populations.

• To what extent, if any, are the risk calculations of terrorist actors affected by geographic dispersion and intermingling with state actors? Since terrorists do not occupy a piece of territory in the manner of states, they are not susceptible to orthodox threats of deterrence. How, then, might effective counter-nuclear-terrorist efforts be reconciled with the reality of geographic dispersion?

• To what extent, if any, might the decisional calculi of terrorist actors be receptive to positive cues or sanctions as opposed to negative ones, and exactly what rewards seem to warrant consideration? In this connection, special attention might be directed to studies of child rearing, which indicate with overwhelming regularity that positive sanctions (rewards) are generally far more effective than negative ones (punishment).

• To what extent would the implementation of effective counter-nuclear-terrorist measures require special patterns of international cooperation, and how might such patterns be created? In principle, the surest path to success in averting nuclear terrorism lies in a unified opposition to terrorist activity by states; yet, at least in the immediate future, this kind of opposition is assuredly not forthcoming. We must, therefore, ask ourselves what cooperative patterns between *particular* states can cope with the problem under discussion.

• To what extent, if any, are the risk calculations of terrorists affected by their relations with "host" states? Since terrorist actors necessarily operate within the framework of individual states, the character of the relationship between "visitor" and "host" may affect the viability of counter-nuclear-terrorist measures. How, therefore, might we exploit what is known about such relationships in curbing the threat of nuclear terrorism?

• To what extent, if any, are the risk calculations of terrorist actors affected by alignments with state actors or with other terrorist groups? And how, therefore, can we use what we know about such effects to devise an effective counter-nuclear-terrorist strategy?

• To what extent, if any, are the risk calculations of terrorist actors affected by the terrorist pattern of random and uninhibited violence? In asking this particular question, we treat terrorist orientation to violence as an independent variable in order to treat it more effectively as a dependent variable later on.

• To what extent, if any, are the risk calculations of terrorist actors affected by the degree to which their policies evoke sympathy and support

---

[27]See, for example, Ted Robert Gurr, *Why Men Rebel* (Princeton: Princeton University Press, 1970), especially pp. 241–42, 259, and 274; Arnold H. Buss, *The Psychology of Aggression* (New York: Wiley, 1961), p. 58; and Leonard Berkowitz, *Aggression: A Social Psychological Analysis* (New York: McGraw-Hill, 1962), p. 96.

from others? Since almost all acts of terror are essentially propagandistic, it is important to understand their desired effects on selected publics in order to prevent escalation to a nuclear option.

By considering these basic questions, students of nuclear terrorism can progress from their presently misconceived emphasis on a technological "fix" to a genuinely auspicious behavioral strategy. With such a strategy in hand, steps can be taken to create inhibitions in the use of violence by terrorists and to impede the growing cooperation of terrorist groups. In the absence of such a strategy, the threat of nuclear terrorism remains fraught with almost unimaginable peril.

In Skinnerian terms, we are describing the search for a "behavioral technology" that can reduce the probability of terrorist nuclear violence.[28] As with all other groups of human beings, terrorists acquire a repertoire of behavior under the particular contingencies of reinforcement to which they are exposed. The "trick" is to understand this repertoire and to use it to inform the differential reinforcement of alternative courses of action. Once this is done, the specter of nuclear terrorism can be confronted with countermeasures that are grounded in a systematic body of theory, and we can dispense with the notion that we are navigating in uncharted areas. No longer will the motto of medieval cartographers, *Hic sunt dracones,* serve any meaningful purpose.

[28]See B. F. Skinner, *Beyond Freedom and Dignity* (New York: Knopf, 1971).

Non-State Entities
Ted Greenwood

Non-state entities acting independently, be they individuals or large, organized revolutionary organizations, and whatever their motivations, lack the legitimacy (both in the possession and use of force and in the control of territory) that international law and tradition afford to sovereign states. Thus they form a special category in the analysis of nonproliferation. Nuclear tests by a country on territory it controls, whatever the political implications, are not considered acts of belligerency. However, a detonation by a non-state entity anywhere except on the high seas would necessarily be on territory claimed by a sovereign state and would necessarily elicit severe retaliation and reprisals.

Just as states employ force or the threat of force for political purposes, so do organized groups of revolutionaries, guerrillas, and terrorists. Thus they can be distinguished, at least for analytical pur-poses, from criminals motivated by profit and from psychopaths who derive psychic gratification from violence. In fact, however, this distinction is not clear-cut. Small terrorist groups, such as the Japanese Red Army, the Symbionese Liberation Army, and the Baader-Meinhof Gang, act largely out of frustration and alienation. While being motivated by a diffuse political ideology, but lacking nationalistic orientation, they may actually have more in common with criminals and psychopaths than with large, nationally oriented groups such as the Palestinian Liberation Organization, the Irish Republican Army, the Tupamaros, or the Eritrean Liberation Front. All of these groups and individuals are of concern in thinking about non-state use of nuclear weapons. However, since the problems relevant to criminals, psychopaths, and small terrorist groups are quite different from those raised by large

Ted Greenwood, "Non-State Entities," in Ted Greenwood, Harold A. Feiveson, and Theodore B. Taylor, *Nuclear Proliferation: Motivations, Capabilities, and Strategies for Control.* 1980s Project/Council on Foreign Relations. (New York: McGraw-Hill Book Co., 1977), pp. 99–107.

revolutionary organizations, they will be considered separately.

There is no need here to open the controversial issue of how various non-state entities might go about fabricating a nuclear explosive or precisely how difficult it would be to do so. Our concern here is more with motivation than with feasibility. Suffice it to say that obtaining weapons-grade material and fabricating even a crude nuclear explosive are reasonably difficult. They require substantial financial and technical resources, a capability for planning and coordinating complex activities, and sufficient cohesiveness and motivation to assure continuity of effort over an extended period of time. Assuming equal incentive, a sizable, organized group is much more likely to succeed than an individual or any small group except in the unlikely event that its members have extensive training in relevant technical areas.

Revolutionaries strive actively to destroy or topple an established political authority or to seek major political or territorial concessions. In doing so they might consider using nuclear weapons in conjunction with guerrilla, terrorist, or traditional military tactics.[1] Nuclear explosions might be used to disable or impede the operation of the government's deployed forces or to destroy important economic values or symbolic targets. They could also be used to intimidate; to attract attention to a cause; to undermine the legitimacy and authority of a government; to deter the carrying out of targeted activities; or to induce terror, fear, or alarm. They seem particularly attractive for the latter purpose because of the sheer extent of their concentrated power and the strong taboo against their use. The psychological impact of a nuclear explosion would be enormous and global no matter how few actual casualties were caused. There is probably no more dramatic or horrifying weapon of terror or more effective means of instilling fear of the perpetrating

organization than a nuclear explosion. It would guarantee immediate, extensive, and continuing world attention.

Yet the power, destructiveness, and radioactive nature of nuclear explosives are potential disadvantages as well. An explosion in a populated area would result in large-scale and wanton killing. Even in their terrorist activities, revolutionary groups do not see killing as useful in and of itself. While people are frequently killed during terrorist attacks, the killing is usually limited, controlled, and calculated to serve one or more specific purposes. Mass killing would have no additional function beyond those served by conventional explosives. The immediate aims of terrorist acts (as opposed to the ultimate objectives of terrorists) have been quite limited. Grand objectives simply cannot be achieved within the time scale of a single act of terror and may simply be unattainable. Governments will not destroy themselves or radically alter the societies they govern in direct response to threat or coercion, no matter how serious. To date, revolutionary terrorists have refrained from many very destructive acts they could accomplish without nuclear weapons. Presumably there has been no particular need or reason to do them.

Despite their revolutionary program and ideology, nationally oriented revolutionary groups have their own extensive stakes in the status quo which they would be loath to jeopardize by resorting to nuclear explosives. For instance, they seek international respectability as a means to legitimize their requests for political support and other aid. Groups engaged in protracted struggle include this endeavor as part of their revolutionary activities. Others may have time to establish respectability only after gaining power. In either case, any use of nuclear weapons that caused widespread destruction would seriously undermine claims to respectability and thus discourage states from granting recognition and support.

More important, any revolutionary group needs a base of support for sanctuary, supplies, and weapons. For groups operating within the territory controlled or claimed by the target government and

---

[1]They might also consider seizing or damaging nuclear facilities or stealing nuclear material for reasons other than to manufacture weapons. While of great concern, such activities are not considered here.

relying on the support of the general population, a use of nuclear weapons that killed large numbers of people or destroyed important national values or symbols would risk alienating that support and inducing severe repression. The target government would surely gain significant popular support and possibly external aid for its efforts to suppress the perpetrating organization or retaliate against its supporters. Extreme tactics of torture and the unbridled use of military power would be condoned and assisted by the population as never before. Indeed, the likelihood of a popularly based revolutionary group surviving long after its first destructive use of nuclear weapons within the state it was seeking to control seems small. Even revolutionaries that do not rely on popular support (such as military dissidents) are not likely to use nuclear weapons against significant military or symbolic targets. No individual or group wants to achieve control of a nation in which the population and politically significant elites are so alienated that it is unable to govern.

Revolutionary or terrorist groups that receive sanctuary, protection, or significant resources from governments other than the one under attack would risk losing that support as well if they used nuclear weapons. All states have an interest in maintaining a taboo against non-state possession of nuclear weapons and in punishing and suppressing its violators. Sanctuary states in particular would view a nuclear revolutionary group within their borders as a threat to their own security. They would be similarly reluctant to assist the rise to power in a neighboring state of a group whose nuclear capability would make it that much more difficult to control or restrain. As the collapse of the Kurdish rebellion following Iran's withdrawal of support, the rapid decline in airline hijacking after the U.S.–Cuban extradition agreement in 1973, and the history of piracy have demonstrated, the loss of sanctuary and foreign support is fatal to terrorist or revolutionary organizations.

The one way that a revolutionary group might be able to use a nuclear explosive destructively to further its cause, yet not elicit overwhelming opposition from those it was seeking to govern, would be to direct it against an external power, perhaps the United States or Soviet Union, that was supporting the opposed government. The purpose would be to persuade the external power to cease its support. A crude weapon delivered in a boat to a harbor or coastal area would serve the purpose. Although such an operation might be conducted covertly, the revolutionary group could not expect to derive any coercive value from its action if it remained anonymous. Significant costs would therefore be incurred. First, the group's claim to international legitimacy would be jeopardized. Second, its own protectors might reduce or remove their support because of their reluctance to assist a group having nuclear weapons to become a sovereign entity. Third, the target state, particularly if it possessed a large military establishment, would probably redouble its efforts—whether or not supported by states in the geographical region in which the group operated—to eradicate the perpetrating organization. Nuclear use against either the Soviet Union or the United States could be expected to result in immediate and ruthless retaliation.

There are nondestructive ways in which a revolutionary group could use a nuclear weapon. These include detonations deep underground, deep in the ocean, in a remote and unpopulated area, and at high altitudes. Deep underground implacement is very difficult if even reasonable confidence is required that extensive venting will not occur. A deep ocean explosion would not vent but, like one deep underground, might not become publicized in the unlikely event that governments with appropriate detection equipment chose to suppress their intelligence information and succeeded in doing so. A remote land area that was accessible and was governed by a sovereignty that the revolutionary group was willing to affront could provide a relatively costless opportunity to demonstrate nuclear capability. Still, the explosion's long-range, long-term, unpredictable, and uncontrollable radiological effects could be expected to act as an enduring goad for revenge against the perpetrators. Perhaps the best way that a revolutionary group could demonstrate its nuclear capacity would be a high-altitude explosion. If sufficiently high, it would cause minimal fallout and no damage beyond retinal burns to those who looked directly at the fireball. With a careful choice of location, it could be very dramatic. There is ample evidence to suggest that obtaining an appropriate airplane would not be very difficult.

A revolutionary group that employed nuclear explosives in any of these nondestructive ways might avoid loss of legitimacy, loss of support, and severe retaliation; at least it might suffer them to a lesser degree. While nondestructive use might be linked to short-term objectives such as inducing terror or gaining publicity, it would be more fruitful as a component of a long-term political strategy. A revolutionary group with demonstrated nuclear capability could exploit nuclear threats against military or urban-industrial targets for coercive purposes. It might thereby be able to achieve political objectives short of overthrow of the opposed government or to exert significant influence on political events. Nondestructive use therefore seems to be the most serious threat from revolutionary groups in possession of nuclear weapons.

Nuclear incentives might be stronger and disincentives weaker for smaller, less capable terrorist organizations that are neither nationally oriented nor in any sense embodiments of the political aspirations of a religious, cultural, or linguistic group. Since they are neither motivated by a well-articulated political program nor tied to a geographical area, these groups (such as the Japanese Red Army or the Baader-Meinhof Gang) have much to gain and little to lose from publicity and the creation of panic. Almost all governments already are actively seeking their destruction. With less stake in the status quo than revolutionary groups with national aims, they might be more likely to use nuclear weapons destructively. Like either individual criminals or psychopaths or small groups of them, however, small terrorist groups generally would not have the resources or support—as nationally oriented revolutionary movements more often would—necessary either to obtain weapons material or, having accomplished that task, to fabricate an explosive. More important, the historical record suggests that even small groups of political extremists, criminals, and psychopaths do not generally perceive mass murder and widespread devastation as useful. Even though non-nuclear means to these ends have long existed, their use has rarely been contemplated seriously.

This discussion suggests that non-state entities are likely to use a nuclear weapon in inverse proportion to their ability to obtain one and that those most able to acquire nuclear weapons would probably use them, if at all, in a manner calculated to minimize destruction. When this analysis is considered with the foregoing observations about the degree of difficulty of making nuclear explosives and the extent of the incentives and disincentives to use them, it leads to the conclusion that the likelihood of nuclear destruction by non-state entities is quite small and that of any use only slightly greater. Nonetheless, this optimistic assessment does not mean that the likelihood is zero even for a very destructive explosion or that there is no cause for concern and appropriate caution. Indeed, while these conclusions seem to be reasonable extrapolations from the past, the future is as unpredictable in this respect as in any other.

There are several ways to keep the likelihood of nuclear use by non-state entities small or even to reduce it. Most important is to make stealing or otherwise obtaining a weapon or weapons material exceedingly difficult by adequately protecting all fissile material and particularly all weapons stockpiles. Guarding against large armed attacks would be very expensive, perhaps prohibitively so, but protection against the small groups and individuals that pose the greatest threat is less difficult. Nations in which there is a history of violent and socially disruptive struggles for power or in which terrorist groups have been able to operate with relative impunity pose the greatest risks. If they acquire civilian power facilities, stringent measures should be taken to reduce the chances that nuclear material can be seized under any conditions ranging from tranquility to extreme disintegration. Similar security measures will also be necessary if such states actually acquire nuclear weapons. Unfortunately, such requirements are easier to enunciate than to implement.

Governments could also try to anticipate which non-state groups are most likely to seek a nuclear capability and to suppress or dissuade them. For criminals, psychopaths, and small terrorist groups, suppression would be appropriate but has its limitations. Even an extensive intelligence capability may be unable to identify high-risk individuals or groups until they have acted. Some observers argue that the level of government surveillance or other sorts of intrusions into citizens' lives which would be necessary for potential nuclear terrorists to be recognized and suppressed would significantly undermine the foundations of democratic societies. Their claim is based upon assumptions and conclusions—about the ease of fabricating or stealing nuclear explosives and about the likelihood that someone will try to obtain weapons and will use them if successful—that are quite different from those reached in this analysis. There is indeed a limit to the degree of suppression possible and desirable in democratic societies and a limit to its effectiveness anywhere. However, these limits seem far beyond what is necessary to render the likelihood of nuclear terrorism very small. Indeed, the primary focus should be on protection of materials, not surveillance and suppression of potential terrorists.

The matter of identification and dissuasion is more complex for nationally oriented revolutionary groups. States are likely to support or oppose such groups for political reasons unconnected to nuclear potential. Changing a policy of opposition to one of support of a group because it seems about to launch a nuclear program would provide a major incentive for others to follow suit and would thereby expose states to easy manipulation and blackmail. It is not, therefore, either a useful or a likely method

of dissuasion. Instead, states backing revolutionary groups would be well advised to make their support conditional on nuclear abstinence. While this position cannot be made formal by treaty or public statement, it nonetheless should and probably will be adopted and implemented subtly as a matter of pure self-interest.

Nuclear threats by non-state entities are a matter quite different from nuclear use. For nationally oriented revolutionary groups, the incentives and disincentives for employing nuclear threats would not be very different from those already discussed for nuclear use, although perhaps not as strong. The primary incentive would be the desire to coerce, extort, or terrorize. The primary disincentives would be the loss of legitimacy and support and the possibility of increased active repression.

But nuclear threats can be made by anyone (including criminals, psychopaths, and pranksters), for any purpose, with only a phone call or a letter. However, making the threat believable, whether to government officials or to the general public, is another matter. Under some circumstances, proof of possession of nuclear material or perhaps publication of a weapons design might be necessary. Yet even a totally unsupported threat that is well publicized might be all that is required to cause public alarm. The requirement would surely depend on the particular circumstances, including how the threat is made and how responsible officials and the media react. Although nuclear threats have been made in the United States and the Middle East and may very well be made again, none so far has been credible.

There seems to be little that can be done to prevent such threats except to minimize the expectation that they will result in benefit or personal gratification. For that purpose, the less discussion of threats the better, except when discussion focuses on states' determination to resist decisively. Since fashions seem to develop in the activities of criminals, psychopaths, and pranksters and since an important objective of terrorist threats, no less than of attacks, is publicity, governments at all levels should attempt to conceal the existence of a nuclear threat except, of course, if there is good reason to believe it is real. In this effort they should seek the understanding and cooperation of the media.

Reactions of resistance and minimal publicity may seem a lame prescription for deterring nuclear threats, but short of pervasive state surveillance of citizens' activities, there appear to be no alternatives. The reactions to and outcomes of the first few threats will strongly influence the frequency of subsequent ones. Protection and monitoring of fissile material is again critical; if sufficient confidence exists that no fissile material has been lost, nuclear threats will not be credible and cannot be real.

An international convention for the suppression of nuclear terrorism has been proposed, modeled after the Convention for the Suppression of Unlawful Seizure of Aircraft of 1971. It would be useful to the extent that it fostered the adoption of stringent physical security measures by all states, assured the denial of sanctuary to nuclear terrorists, and established a useful norm of national behavior. But its usefulness for deterrence would be limited. Those groups or individuals most likely to engage in nuclear terror or threat either are actively pursued anyway by national and international security organizations or would operate solely within the national borders of a single state.

More important are the encouragement of national governments' efforts to develop and employ very strict physical protection measures and the strengthening of the IAEA's role in assisting them. Adequate physical protection standards, no less than adequate safeguards, should be and are increasingly becoming a prerequisite to the sale of nuclear reactors or fuel-cycle equipment and technology. The recent nuclear suppliers' agreement included a provision requiring states purchasing nuclear facilities and materials to furnish rather stringent physical protection. Industrialized states with already large nuclear programs should lead the way by sharing technology and experience and, where necessary, by offering subsidies. Finally, the likelihood of social and political disorder that might so erode normal physical protection arrangements

as to make access to weapons-grade material relatively easy for non-state entities should be seriously considered in decisions about which countries pose too high a risk for the transfer of reactors and other fuel-cycle facilities.

QUESTIONS FOR DISCUSSION

1 Of what use can nuclear weapons be to terrorists?
2 Is it likely that terrorists will get nuclear weapons with the support of a NWS?
3 If terrorists obtained nuclear weapons, how and where would they be likely to use them?
4 Are terrorists rational?
5 Why have terrorists been unable to obtain nuclear weapons thus far?

SUGGESTED READINGS

Blair, Bruce G. and Garry D. Brewer. "The Terrorist Threat to World Nuclear Programs," *Journal of Conflict Resolution* 21 (September 1977), pp. 379–403.

Carlton, David. "The Future of Political Substate Violence," in Yonah Alexander, David Carlton, and Paul Wilkinson (eds.), *Terrorism: Theory and Practice.* Boulder, Colorado: Westview Press, 1979, pp. 201–30.

Feld, Bernard T. "Nuclear Violence at the Non-Governmental Level," in David Carlton and Carlo Schaerf (eds.), *Contemporary Terror: Studies in Sub-State Violence.* New York: St. Martin's Press, 1981, pp. 37–49.

Hutchinson, Martha Crenshaw. "Defining Future Threats: Terrorists and Nuclear Proliferation," in Yonah Alexander and Maxwell Finger (eds.), *Terrorism: Interdisciplinary Perspectives.* New York: John Jay Press, 1977, pp. 298–316.

Jenkins, Brian M. "Nuclear Terrorism and Its Consequences," *Society* 17 (July-August 1980), pp. 5–15.

Luchaire, Fabienne. "Subnational Proliferation, Technology Transfers, and Terrorism," in Adam M. Garfinkle (ed.), *Global Perspectives on Arms Control.* New York: Praeger, 1984, pp. 113–32.

Mullen, Robert K. "Mass Destruction and Terrorism," *Journal of International Affairs* 32 (Spring-Summer 1978), pp. 63–89.

Norton, Augustus. "Terrorists, Atoms, and the Future: Understanding the Threat," *Naval War College Review* 32 (May-June 1979), pp. 30–50.

Norton, Augustus R. and Martin H. Greenberg (eds.). *Studies in Nuclear Terrorism*. Boston: G. K. Hall, 1979.

Orr, Kelly. "How U.S. Would Deal with Nuclear Terrorists," *U.S. News & World Report* (February 7, 1983), pp. 49–50.

Schelling, Thomas. "The Terrorist Use of Nuclear Weapons," in Bernard Brodie, Michael D. Intriligator, and Roman Kolkowicz (eds.), *National Security and International Stability*. Cambridge, Massachusetts: Oelgeschlager, Gunn & Hain, 1983, pp. 209–25.

————. "Thinking About Nuclear Terrorism," *International Security* 6 (Spring 1982), pp. 61–77.

Stohl, Michael (ed.). *The Politics of Terrorism*. New York; Marcel Dekker, 1983.

Taylor, Theodore B. and Mason Willrich. *Nuclear Theft: Risks and Safeguards*. Cambridge, Massachusetts: Ballinger, 1974.

U.S. Congress: Senate. *IAEA Programs of Safeguards*. Hearings before the Committee on Foreign Relations, 97th Cong., 1st Sess., 1981.